The
Dark Corners
of the Lindbergh Kidnapping

The Dark Corners

of the Lindbergh Kidnapping

Volume II

Michael Melsky

THE DARK CORNERS OF THE LINDBERGH KIDNAPPING VOLUME II

iUniverse books may be ordered through booksellers or by contacting:

iUniverse
1663 Liberty Drive
Bloomington, IN 47403
www.iuniverse.com
1-800-Authors (1-800-288-4677)

ISBN: 978-1-5320-5100-5 (sc)
ISBN: 978-1-5320-5099-2 (e)

Library of Congress Control Number: 2018906377

Print information available on the last page.

iUniverse rev. date: 06/12/2018

Contents

Acknowledgments

With over seventeen years of research, I've had so many people assist me in some way that there is no way to thank them all. This page will identify people who I believe have helped me the most concerning this specific volume. I apologize in advance for anyone I may have missed.

Once again, I must say that first and foremost without Mark Falzini my books could never be written. Mark is super intelligent, well-rounded, and a selfless individual I am proud to call my friend. For anyone who is interested in this crime, I highly recommend his two books: *Their Fifteen Minutes, Biographical Sketches of the Lindbergh Case* (iUniverse, 2010), and *New Jersey's Lindbergh Kidnapping and Trial* (Arcadia, 2012), which he coauthored with James Davidson.

Another friend, Dr. Lloyd Gardner, is someone else I cannot say enough about. He has both inspired and assisted me over the years at levels that are immeasurable. He is one of my many "go-to" people when I need to bounce an idea or am in need of a different perspective. Both he and his wife Nancy aren't only smart, but they are both great people. Lloyd's book, *The Case That Never Dies* (Rutgers, 2004) provides all the vital information and background on this event and is another book that should be read before picking up either of my books.

My other two partners in crime include Siglinde Rach, and Dolores Raisch. I rely constantly on Siglinde for her steel-trap memory since she is able to see connections that no one else ever would, and she also shares freely any of her research findings that she has assembled over the years. I depend on Dolores for her rational, grounded, and common-sense approach where she looks at things that can sometimes be missed by the rest of us who at times cannot see the forest through the trees. Without them this book simply would not exist.

Margaret Sudhakar has made a major impact on my study of the case since my first volume, and has been extremely helpful through our communications, and by developing material unique to our discussions. Kurt Tolksdorf, Kevin Kline, and Rab Purdy have always helped me tremendously over the years with their thoughts, ideas, insights, and skills – and still continue to. Also, any and all New Jersey State Troopers who worked the desk at the Museum & Recruiting Unit from 2000 thru 2018. They always treated me well and exemplify why the New Jersey State Police is the very best and most professional police force in the country.

Special thanks to Andy Sahol who has unselfishly shared many of Ellis H. Parker's unique materials with me, as well as the family recollections concerning him. I have worked with him over the years to assist with his attempts to get his Grandfather the posthumous pardon he deserves. Andy has done everything in his power to see this happen and has vowed to never stop until it does.

Furthermore, I must acknowledge the following for their assistance. Remove one of these people below and, without their interaction, I might never have been able to get to the point where I felt "ready" to write this second volume:

Michael Keaten, Lydia Keaten Bowen, David Holwerda, Susan Candy, Irvin Moran, Michael Beggs, Sam Bornstein, Ronelle Delmont, Joe Czulinski, Steve Romeo, Wayne McDaniel, Frederick "Rick" Green III, Richard Sloan, Larry Kline, Nathan Weinberger, John Douglas, John Reisinger, Dr. Robert Knapp, Justin Berns, Rob O'Keefe, David Sims, Dick Anderson, John Sasser, and George Joynson.

Last but not least, I would also like to acknowledge all contributors to my Proboards Venue: *Lindbergh Discussion Board* (lindberghkidnap. proboards.com), especially "Amy35." Amy has not only assisted with her ideas both on and off the board but has kindly provided me with source documentation that I had never seen before. Without her, and the members of this board, I would never have been challenged and/ or my ideas properly tested.

Introduction

This book will follow the same path as Volume One by continuing to explore the dark corners of the Lindbergh kidnapping. All of the topics throughout this volume will be ones that were never properly examined or evaluated anytime in the past, and the facts revealed cause the historical account to become very unlikely—if not impossible—as a result. As with the first, it is an unorthodox style, a book that may not transition from one chapter to the next as is typical. There may be places where I repeat certain information, and/or mention different versions which may not always match up. I do this intentionally, so the reader will have all of the information necessary to draw a personal conclusion.

I have been very fortunate to be able to access a number of sources that are either not well-known or privately held. Each of these has enhanced my knowledge of the case, and I have tried very hard to communicate the essential findings of each of these to you in this book. In this regard my book is unique and should offer new information to anyone who reads it, including the most seasoned researchers.

A substantial portion of the first five chapters is devoted to the illumination of John F. Condon, surely one of the strangest characters in the cast. No researcher to date has "figured him out" because of his peculiar actions and prolific and inconsistent statements. It's frustrating to even make an attempt; one usually just gives up, declaring him a demented old man—or simply insane. I do not. This volume strives to lay all of Condon's cards on the table in such a way as to make sense of him by employing a thorough and organized scrutiny. As a result, I believe I have (at least in part) cracked the nut, so to speak.

The subsequent chapters are tightly intertwined with the findings on Condon and the ransom money (while simultaneously shedding new light on Hauptmann) and should be considered in relation to the discoveries in the earlier chapters. Hence, the intentionally large book, for which I offer only a mild apology. A unified and overarching view should be sought when considering these people and topics.

As any casual enthusiast of the Lindbergh Kidnapping Case would tell you, there are fundamentally two camps of thought in the debate—the Lone Wolf theorists and the Hauptmann Was Innocent theorists. But serious students/scholars know that neither of these positions is viable. The tendencies of the extremists go something like this, depending on the extreme: A Lone Wolfer can't come to grips with the possibility that more than one person was involved because that might be exploited and end up pointing somehow to Hauptmann's innocence, and an Innocence proclaimer can't consider any involvement of Hauptmann at all for fear that that admission would be enough to end the search for the real solution once and for all. More than ever I am convinced, as I feel certain most other scholars are, that Hauptmann was somehow involved but did not act alone. Unfortunately, I sometimes see well-intentioned researchers slipping into the strategies one extreme side or the other might employ—to the detriment of finding a solution to the case. For instance, I've seen many deny some of the most basic facts as they pertain to Hauptmann, such as the beating he took at the Greenwich Police Station the day after his arrest. When it comes to investigating and understanding what actually happened, the real facts should never be lost—whether by oversight or by intent. The reality of the Hauptmann beating is made clear in police reports—as long as one reads all of the reports and understands the circumstances under which the examinations were made and the reports written. Whatever the facts, they must all be considered and embraced and synthesized. Besides, I've found that researching some of the most basic facts leads to other unknown or long-hidden facts, so shrugging anything off is a huge mistake.

Nevertheless, these kinds of denials are a form of protecting one's position. It's easy to become dogmatic about this case: everyone who researches it arrives at a personal conclusion and is happy to defend it, whether sensible or not. We've all thought hard about the case and want others to know. Perhaps the worst offense among LKC researchers, though, is the nasty habit of pontificating. We need to abandon this poor practice as it serves no one and no purpose. It certainly doesn't advance our knowledge of the case or put us any closer to the solution. We who truly want the case solved cannot afford pontification without thorough investigation. Similarly, a position cannot be justified via pontification. What we like or do not like to espouse is immaterial IF the truth is what we actually seek.

1

Additions & Errata

I wanted to start off by writing a chapter not unlike Governor Hoffman's *Liberty Magazine* article, "More Things I Forgot to Tell."[1] Here is where I'd like to correct any mistakes or misunderstandings while also adding to, complementing, or supplementing other facts in the chapters of Volume I with even more new material.

Footnotes

*The cited documents will usually be written as in their sources. I've noticed that most can quite often include mis-spellings or typographical errors. Others use the language of the day, for example, "clew" for "clue," "machine" for "car," or words like "forenoon" which no one uses anymore. Whenever possible I will always cite it as written.

*The Federal Bureau of Investigation changed its name several times over the course of this matter. They were known as the "Bureau of Investigation" until June 30, 1932, the "United States Bureau of

---

[1]   Hoffman, Harold. "More things I forgot to tell." *Liberty Magazine.* July 9, 1938. New Jersey State Police Museum and Learning Center Archives.

Investigation" from July 1, 1932 thru June 30, 1933, the "Division of Investigation" from July 1, 1933 thru 1935, and finally the "Federal Bureau of Investigation" from sometime in 1935 to present. With this in mind, they would continue to use their pre-printed blank reports, memos, and letter-head which contained their *previous* name after the switch until those supplies were exhausted which was done as a way to save money. This creates a nightmare for anyone trying to accurately document their research, and I do my best to exemplify this situation within the footnotes. Next, throughout this volume I have decided to use "FBI" as a way to remain consistent throughout instead of the confusing back & forth which would exist by referring to a different name depending upon the date.

Chapter 1 – "Strange Vehicles"

*In this chapter I brought up the account of Roscoe LaRue. There's been a lot of interest concerning the plate LaRue saw on that car and who it belonged to. A researcher on the Message Board may have solved this mystery... According to "Amy35" a man by the name of George Foley was the Morrow's first secretary, and he at one time lived on Jay Avenue in Englewood. His employment as such gave way to Arthur Springer in 1915.[2]

Chapter 2 – "NYU Dinner"

* In this chapter I believe it to be an important fact that Lindbergh calling at 7:00 PM proves he was closer to Highfields than his testimony suggested. More to this point, I think it's necessary to add that he made a similar call the day before (Monday the 29th):

---

[2] "Amy35". Private Message. February 6, 2017. lindberghkidnap. proboards.com.

"About 7 P.M. Colonel Lindbergh called up and said he would be late and thought it would be too late to be out here at all that night."[3]

This fact alone seems to prove the situation the following night. If he's too far away calling at 7 PM on Monday, then certainly he'd be too far away calling on Tuesday at the exact same time unless he's actually closer and calling from somewhere else.

Chapter 4 – "The Warped Shutters"

*One of the important points to come out of this chapter was Betty Gow's assertion that the shutters were closed and locked to prevent them from blowing in the wind.[4] Forgetting for a moment this position completely contradicts Anne Lindbergh's statements to police, Gow also made the statement that:

"We didn't lock the shutters as a precautionary measure, only to keep them closed."[5]

So while the shutters on the French window and those on the window to the left of the fireplace were locked, all windows were found to be

---

[3] Whateley, Mrs. Elsie Mary. Statement. March 10, 1932. Made to Lieutenant John J. Sweeney and Detective Hugh Strong, Newark Police Department. New Jersey State Police Museum and Learning Center Archives.

[4] See *TDC Volume I*, page 35.

[5] Gow, Betty Mowat. Statement. March 3, 1932. Made to Commissioner Edward A. Reilly, Chief of Police, and James A. McRell, Deputy Chief, and Frank E. Brex, Newark Police Department. New Jersey State Police Museum and Learning Center Archives.

closed but unlocked by Police.[6] This could be viewed as being in line with Betty's rationale above, that is, there were no "precautionary measures" employed by the family to guard against intruders. While testifying in Flemington, once Lindbergh was asked if anyone had ever indicated to him they had ever locked that window Lindbergh replied that it *"wasn't the custom to lock windows."*[7] He would later testify:

> *"We did not make a practice of locking windows, and I don't believe that had ever been locked, as far as I know."*[8]

Eliminating common sense, the next problem about the fact the windows were not locked that night concerns the purposes of the locks on these types of windows. One function would be security, but the primary function would be to seal the windows. This would be especially important on the cold, and windy night of March 1st. Kevin Kline, a Master Carpenter, recently wrote me this fact:

> *"If the wind was blowing that night, then the unlocked shutters and windows would certainly have moved and made some noise."*[9]

And so even if the routine wasn't to lock these windows, certainly the weather would have created a reason to deviate from the norm that

---

[6]   Bornmann, Lewis J. Testimony. The State of New Jersey vs. Bruno Richard Hauptmann, <u>Hunterdon County Court of Oyer and Terminer</u>, page 378, 1935. New Jersey State Law Library.

[7]   Lindbergh, Charles. Testimony. The State of New Jersey vs. Bruno Richard Hauptmann, <u>Hunterdon County Court of Oyer and Terminer</u>, page 144, 1935. New Jersey State Law Library.

[8]   Ibid. pages 155-6.

[9]   Kline, Kevin. E-mail to Author. March 27, 2017 (Note: Kevin Kline is a Master Carpenter and Lindbergh Kidnapping Expert who focuses on that aspect of the crime).

night despite the French window being opened for a time. When Gow offered up the explanation that the shutters were closed to keep them from banging, the fact that there was no deviation with the window locks when the exact same reason existed there as well makes little sense. How could it not cross her mind in doing it for one set of circumstances but not for the other? Finally, what made these Kidnappers so sure <u>nothing</u> would be locked at the particular location they selected? How could they possibly believe the shutters would not be bolted, and the window unlocked – most especially on a night like this?

Chapter 6 – "Strange Noises the Lindberghs Heard (And Did Not Hear)"

*To further emphasize that the wind was blowing on this night I wanted to introduce more information coming from Alfred Hammond who was mentioned in Chapter 1 of Volume I. Ordinarily, while working the gates at the Rail Road Crossing, Hammond kept the gates down and would lift them for oncoming traffic.[10] Hammond also stated that this post was vacated at 7:15 PM every night and that the gates would be locked in the up position at that time.[11] However, he also said that on March 1st "*it was so windy*" that they could not use the gates and instead had to use a lantern.[12]

---

[10] Hammond, Alfred. Statement. March 2, 1936. Philadelphia and Reading Railroad West Trenton Station. Stenographer's Notes. New Jersey State Police Museum and Learning Center Archives.

[11] Ibid.

[12] Ibid.

Chapter 7 – "A Tale of Two Dogs"

*The man history accepts as Hauptmann's "first" attorney, James M. Fawcett, hired multiple Private Investigators who quickly pounded the pavement in search of any facts to help his client. Among them was James Walsh, a PI out of Brooklyn.[13] Like so many in his field, once his employer (Fawcett) was fired, he faded into the background of this case. In fact, he's another person completely forgotten by history and for most (if not all) who claim expertise concerning this crime, and if they haven't read Volume I yet, this is probably the first time they've ever heard about him.[14] He would explain that he completely lost interest in the case and *"got really disgusted when I followed Reilly's practices in court"* but that he had renewed interest once he was contacted by Ellis Parker inquiring about his investigations.[15] Walsh would inform Parker that it was an indisputable fact that Col. Lindbergh had two dogs, one being a "Scottish Terrier" that *"usually slept in the nursery nearby."*[16] He confirmed the dog was left behind and asks:

> *Who brought the best dog of the two away that day so he could not interrupt this kidnapping?*[17]

[13] Parker, Ellis H. Burlington County Chief of Detectives. Letter from Ellis H. Parker to His Excellency, Harold G. Hoffman. January 2, 1936. New Jersey State Police Museum and Learning Center Archives.
[14] Walsh is first mentioned in *TDC Volume I*, page 317 at footnote 933.
[15] Walsh, James. Private Investigator. Letter from James Walsh to Ellis H. Parker. January 8, 1936. Author's Possession.
[16] Walsh, James. Private Investigator. Report. Report to Mr. Ellis H. Parker from James Walsh. Undated. (January 8, 1936). Author's Possession.
[17] Ibid.

He asks this question sincerely because he does not know – but while we may not know who took him "away" we certainly know who left him behind.[18]

Chapter 8 – "Murray Garsson ("G" Man)"

*Garsson's small army of investigators did quite a bit of investigating in the relatively short period of time they were there. For example, while the State Police had created and attempted to cover all homes in the Hopewell area in a grid type search, the Special Investigators of the Department of Labor did something similar. They retraced the State Police efforts, and in some cases, were able to find and interview persons the NJSP seemed to have missed. While reviewing their house to house summary report, I discovered something on the page which included their Wertsville Road investigations mentioned at "564":

> *Hoffman with daughter and brother, saw New Jersey car License No. P25-524 in Wertsville Road with two young fellows around for two days straight on the 2nd and 3rd of March. They came out of the Lindbergh Road. One had brown hair and the other had a dark complexion. Acted suspicious.*[19]

Upon seeing this eyewitness account had occurred AFTER the kidnapping it seemed odd they had even bothered to mention it. After all, the area was completely swarmed with Cops, Reporters, and Sightseers by then. However, I later stumbled upon the actual

---

[18] See *TDC Volume I*, page 58.

[19] Department of Labor. <u>Report of Investigations</u>. Summary. Page 6. Unsigned & Undated (March 1932). New Jersey State Police Museum and Learning Center Archives

report of this investigation. On March 29, 1932, Special Investigator Ewer reported the following:

> *Daughter and son of native by the name of Hoffman stated that at about dusk, each alone, two nights before the kidnapping, saw a New Jersey auto, (Plates No. P-25524) with two male occupants emerge from on the Lindbergh road onto the Wertsville road. Both men in the auto looked and acted suspicious, one man had dark hair, the other was dark complected. Daughter saw car one evening, the son saw same car next night, both daughter and son agree it was the same car, as one of the front fenders was knocked off.*[20]

Because of the fact I have never seen any other "strange" automobile accounts which match this car, I consider these sightings to be unique. And since these men are leaving via Lindbergh's private lane onto Wertsville road on two nights in succession PRIOR to the night of the kidnapping – then it is worthy to note. Who were these men? Had they been actual visitors to the Estate, or was their presence there at these times supposedly unknown to the family and/or their staff?

*In this chapter I use a letter written by Morris Bealle to prove Garsson was pulled off the Lindbergh Case by President Hoover.[21] Bealle repeatedly made this claim, and would write to Governor Hoffman over a year later continuing to emphasize this fact believing

---

[20]   Brown, E. F. Special Investigator US Department of Labor. United State Department of Labor Report. March 29, 1932. New Jersey State Police Museum and Learning Center Archives.

[21]   See *TDC Volume I*, page 74.

it was one of the *"best looking clues"* concerning this crime.[22] Bealle
was the publisher of *Plain Talk Magazine*, and the reason why he is
such a good source about it is because this information came directly
from Garsson, who he had spoken with earlier in preparation for an
upcoming article.[23]

Chapter 9 – The Whateleys

*One of the hardest things I've faced is that I have so much
information there are times I am not sure what to use and what not
to. In one regard, I feel like I am cheating readers by picking and
choosing certain items, while at the same time I don't want to dilute
the topic by adding in trivial or worthless facts. Since I've received so
much communication about the Whateley confession I've decided to
add here a couple of things that I previously left out of Volume I. The
question that Governor Hoffman asks is, in essence, "What caused
Lindbergh to drop everything and take up the Curtis matter?"[24] I
think it's important to understand that a main part of Curtis's story
was that someone from the inside was involved and he specifically
told Lindbergh it was Olly Whateley.[25] It was this information, in
addition to the fact that the pantry door had been locked, which

[22] Bealle, Morris A. Letter from Morris A. Bealle to Hon. Harold G.
Hoffman. January 14, 1937. New Jersey State Police Museum and
Learning Center Archives.

[23] Bealle, Morris A. Letter from Morris A. Bealle to Hon. Harold Hoffman.
December 28, 1935. New Jersey State Police Museum and Learning
Center Archives.

[24] See *TDC Volume I*, page 312.

[25] Gardner, Lloyd C. (2004). *The Case That Never Dies*. Rutgers University
Press. Page 89. (**Note:** First read about it in this book but later read the
document at the NJSP Archives myself.)

convinced Lindbergh he was in touch with the Kidnappers.[26] How can this be if what he told both Rosner and Thayer was what he truly believed?[27] Also, to further support Curtis's naming of Whateley, on December 31, 1935 Lt. Robert Hicks claimed that:

> *"Curtis told me in detail that Ollie Whateley the butler, who was familiar with the household routine, assisted the kidnapers by locking a certain door to block the passage of the other members present in the house, while the baby was being carried out of the house down the back stairs."*[28]

Beyond all else, what's important about the Curtis angle was his ability to convince Lindbergh previously that he was in touch with the Kidnappers with this information. Now the fact he was a confessed "hoaxer" must be taken into consideration when looking at specifics such as this whether one believes his confession was coerced or not. Could it be that he had an inside source which provided him with this piece of information right from the start? Regardless of Curtis being a dubious source, the fact he actually named someone, and that it was accepted by Lindbergh contrary to his previous (and later) rock solid position against it, is information that I believe should be considered.

*Another incident which relates to Whateley comes from Charles Ellerson. He would claim that while out with Olly driving one day before the baby had been found dead, Olly asked him to stop the

---

[26]   Lindbergh, Charles A. Testimony. The State of New Jersey vs. John Hughes Curtis, <u>Quarters Session</u>, page 74, June 28, 1932. Excerpts found at New Jersey State Police Museum and Learning Center Archives.

[27]   See *TDC Volume I*, page 85.

[28]   Hicks, Robt. W., Criminologist. <u>Letter from Lt. Robert Hicks to Honorable Harold G. Hoffman</u>. January 2, 1936. New Jersey State Police Museum and Learning Center Archives.

car so that he could answer the call of nature.[29] Sometime later, once the child had been discovered, Ellerson learned this stop was *"within fifty feet of where"* the body had been found.[30]

*A different source of information comes from the Hoffman Collection in the form of a document which looks more like a partial "to do list" for the Governor in preparation for Court of Pardons. Included on this list is the following (typed):

> *Check hospital record of death of Wakely* [sic] *in Princeton Hospital. Find out name of doctor and nurse. Nurse still living around Princeton.*[31]

And handwritten in Governor Hoffman's handwriting below that:

> *Subpoena Records*[32]

*Another intriguing "tidbit" comes from Lindbergh Kidnapping Expert David Holwerda. His research predates mine by 20 years, and during that time he interviewed all of the well-known characters of this case. Back then, without the internet, Dave either used the telephone or hopped onto a plane to attempt an interview. Quite often he became very friendly with people through his research and there's probably no one left alive who is more familiar with them (collectively) now. Unknown to me before writing Volume I, Dave was aware of Whateley's "confession" during the years he was

---

29   Unsigned. Memo. Undated. *"H-File Ellerson."* New Jersey State Police Museum and Learning Center Archives. (Note: Hoffman Collection Memo found in Governor's "Ellerson" file.)
30   Ibid.
31   Unsigned. List. Undated (1936?). Hoffman Collection. New Jersey State Police Museum and Learning Center Archives.
32   Ibid.

actively conducting his research.[33] He also unselfishly shared with me a conversation he had with Betty Gow back in 1983. Dave had several phone conversations with her, and it was during one that she told him *"she didn't care for Olly"* and that he *"even said I was involved."*[34]

Chapter 10 – "The Nursemaids"

*One of my main goals in this chapter was to answer the question as to *when* certain things took place. The rotation of the Nursemaids was one I never believed was properly explained partly due to the fact that Annette Copin's employment was at first denied then later lied about. In putting together this information, I consulted Marie Cummings's official statement (something certain people who boast knowledge about this case have never laid eyes on). It's in this statement that she claims Miss Copin started work on *"July 15, 1932."*[35] This was clearly a mistake in the statement either by Miss Cummings, by one of the Officers taking it, or by the person typing it up. I quickly noticed this during one of my many reviews and made the correction based upon another part of the statement. Unfortunately, this correction never made it into the book, and thinking it had, I never revisited it. Fact is when Miss Copin quit, Cummings returned to the Lindbergh family as nursemaid again on October 16, 1930.[36] So exactly when Copin started her employment there depends upon which source one finds more credible. The FBI

---

[33] Holwerda, David. Message Board Post. November 15, 2016. lindberghkidnap.proboards.com

[34] Holwerda, David. Telephone Interview with author. December 6, 2016.

[35] Cummings, Marie, alias, Ella May Cummings. Statement. March 20, 1932. Made to Sergeant Carl Stein and Detective Hugh Strong, Newark Police Department. New Jersey State Police Museum and Learning Center Archives.

[36] Ibid.

Summary report claims that an *"unknown"* second nurse worked for *"three months."*[37] The source for their information came from a Private Investigator named T. J. Cooney, who worked for The Thiel Service Company.[38] Another source was Mrs. Jung who told Special Agent Seykora that Miss Copin worked as nursemaid *"four weeks"* before resigning.[39]

*On page 116, I wrote that Betty left Englewood at 11:45 PM with Ellerson. This is obviously a mistake. They left at 11:45 AM.

*As seen in Volume I, it's well documented that Red and Betty had run into trouble with the Palisades Park Police by being there after hours on several occasions.[40] However, it's clear that Betty wasn't being truthful during cross examination concerning her several interactions with police by claiming she believed she had been to Palisades Park "once" with Red, but that she did not "recall" any difficulty.[41] She also didn't remember ever going to a Roadhouse but when asked for third time finally did admit to going to one on New Year's Eve. When asked point blank if she could recall any conversation with Police when she was at Palisades when she was

[37] Sisk, T. H. DOI (FBI) et. al., DOI Report. <u>Summary</u>. NY File No. 62-3057, p. 74. February 16, 1934. National Archives at College Park Maryland.

[38] Cooney, T. H., Assistant General Manager of the Thiel Service Company. Notes. Untitled Notes for Report to Special Agent Sisk, (FBI). (circa 1934). New Jersey State Police Museum and Learning Center Archives. (**Note**: this company was a private investigation/detective agency used by various law enforcement agencies, including the FBI.)

[39] Seykora, J. E. Special Agent, DOI. DOI (FBI) Report. Unknown Subjects. <u>Kidnapping and Murder of Charles A. Lindbergh, Jr.</u> May 18, 1934. New Jersey State Police Museum and Learning Center Archives.

[40] See *TDC Volume I*, pages 113-4.

[41] Gow, Bessie Mowat. Testimony. The State of New Jersey vs. Bruno Richard Hauptmann, <u>Hunterdon County Court of Oyer and Terminer</u>, page 285, 1935. New Jersey State Law Library.

with Red, she slipped in a question about the amusement park that suggested she was unfamiliar with it, then said "*no*."[42]

*To further support Salvy Spitale's position that the Kidnapping was an "*inside job*" a recent book written by his niece, Catherine Spitale, revealed that he believed the child had "*issues*" and that:

> "*Lindbergh did not want his wife or himself to raise a child with afflictions*."[43]

Chapter 12 – "The Crime Scene"

*To clear up any possible confusion, Hopewell Police Chief (Marshal) was Harry H. Wolfe. In some instances within the source material his name is misspelled "Wolf." There were times within this chapter where I followed that pattern by dropping the "e." The first State Police Officer to arrive at the scene, Corporal Joseph Wolf, was always spelled "Wolf" in both the documentation and in Volume I.

*Sometimes one has to "get lucky" to find a source which reveals the unofficial beliefs of certain key figures related to this case. Just such an occasion occurred for me when Chief Harry Wolfe's nephew, Irvin Moran, began communicating his thoughts on the case via the Message Board, and private email. Sometime in the mid-1980s Irvin read Kennedy's *The Airman and the Carpenter*. Since his uncle Harry had died in 1959, knowing that his mother, Emily Moran, had been extremely close to her brother, he asked her about his uncle's position on the case. She was able to tell him some of what Harry had related to her concerning his observations. Here is one of them:

---

[42]   Ibid.
[43]   Spitale, Catherine. 2015. *Mumza*. BYCT Publishing, page 86. (Thanks to Michael Beggs for directing me to this source).

> *"From the moment Uncle Harry entered the Lindbergh house that night of the kidnapping, he had a strong gut reaction that there was an 'inside' aspect to this case. He apparently had strong suspicions in regards to Betty Gow and Violet Sharpe."*[44]

Concerning Violet Sharp, Wolfe felt that her *"suicide was suspicious."* But when it came to his suspicion of Betty Gow, his mother said he *"did not like the way the nursemaid reacted to him that night…".*[45] His thoughts concerning Hauptmann were that:

> *"The New Jersey State Police had the correct perpetrator of the kidnapping with the arrest of Hauptmann, although Hauptmann was accompanied by others that night. Hauptmann was definitely not at the Lindbergh house on the night of March 1st by himself."*[46]

*In demonstrating that no fingerprints were found during Trooper Kelly's search for them while he dusted the nursery, I quoted his Official Statement, and his testimony during his first trip to the stand at Flemington.[47] To further support there was no finding of prints, I point to the Patsy Orlando investigation. Orlando had come under suspicion concerning the kidnapping once John Gronski, a man working at his Woodsville farm, provided certain information

---

[44]   Moran, Irvin. Email exchanges with Author from February 4, 2017 thru February 13, 2107. (Irvin was a graduate of Trenton State College and served 2 years as a Special Investigator with the NY State Prosecutor's Office before becoming a Special Agent with the ATF investigating cases for 29 years before he retired in 2004).

[45]   Ibid.

[46]   Ibid.

[47]   See *TDC Volume I*, pages 162-3.

to Police.[48] As a result of this investigation, Captain Lamb instructed Detective Bornmann to proceed to the State Bureau of Identification in Trenton to check Orlando's fingerprints against prints obtained from some unsolved Breaking & Entering cases.[49] While making the comparison as instructed, Bornmann discovered that the "*latent print found on the Hemerda job was found not to be distinct enough for comparison…*".[50] What this clearly demonstrates is that if a print was found, then it was taken. Whether or not it was "usable" or of "sufficient value" did not seem to matter. And so even if one were to consider Kelly's later (and quite different) testimony during his other trips to the witness chair, this example above would beg the question as to why those supposed prints weren't taken too. After all, if a print from a simple B&E was taken regardless of its value then surely the same would have been done during the most famous case in the world.

More to this point, we must consider the Lindbergh Kidnapping Evidence Review conducted by the New Jersey State Police in the late 1970's and concluding in 1980.[51] Specifically focusing on the fingerprint evidence review, we are able to get the full flavor of the situation. At the time of this investigation, the NJSP had 202 latent prints which had been turned over to Lt. Elmendorf by Capt. Gardiner on September 12, 1951, none of which were taken from the

---

[48]   Gronski, John. Statement. April 20, 1934. Made to Detective L. J. Bornmann and Trooper J. Genz, New Jersey State Police. New Jersey State Police Museum and Learning Center Archives.

[49]   Bornmann, Lewis. Detective, NJSP. New Jersey State Police Report. <u>Continued investigation of information given by John Gronski, residing at the farm of Patsy Orlando, Woodsville, N.J., given in a statement dated April 20, 1934</u>. May 7, 1934. New Jersey State Police Museum and Learning Center Archives.

[50]   Ibid.

[51]   New Jersey State Police. <u>Lindbergh Kidnapping – A State Police Review with Annexes</u>. March 15, 1980. New Jersey State Police Museum and Learning Center Archives.

nursery. There were 99 negatives of latent impressions which they had found within the Lindbergh "Trenton" files, 5 inked impressions located within the Lindbergh "Alpine" Files, 5 impressions located on the Ransom Notes, and 3 latent photographs which had not been identified with any other latent negatives.[52] For the purposes of this review, the NJSP contracted a company called Calspan Technology Products which was using the most advanced computerized fingerprint identification system in the country at the time.[53] On May 8, 1977, Lt. Barna and DSG. Demeter drove to Calspan in Buffalo, N.Y. with all the latents and fingerprint cards to determine *"the value and/or possible comparison of any latent impressions developed during the course of the original investigation."*[54] During the encoding process, many prints were found to be of *"no value"* either because of *"poor quality"* or were from the wrong area of the hand.[55] Therefore, Calspan could only use (51) partial impressions which were then encoded.[56] This proves that latents of *"no value"* were taken during the investigation because if some were of such poor quality that they could not be used by the most advanced technology in 1977, then certainly they weren't any good in the early 1930s. Simply put, if Kelly did not take what he supposedly discovered in the nursery on March 1, 1932, because they were of *"no value,"* then they were not fingerprints at all.

---

[52]   Barna, Thomas A. Lt., New Jersey State Police. New Jersey State Police Special Report. <u>Lindbergh Kidnapping Case Review (Fingerprint Comparison)</u>. September 23, 1977. New Jersey State Police Museum and Learning Center Archives.

[53]   "Calspan Computer Holmes In on Crime, Gives City Police Sherlock on Prints." *The Buffalo Evening News.* April 14, 1977. New Jersey State Police Museum and Learning Center Archives.

[54]   Barna, Thomas A. Lt., New Jersey State Police. New Jersey State Police Special Report. <u>Lindbergh Kidnapping Case Review (Fingerprint Comparison)</u>. September 23, 1977. New Jersey State Police Museum and Learning Center Archives.

[55]   Ibid.

[56]   Ibid.

The comparison with Calspan was conducted, and at its conclusion, no positive results were found compared with Bruno Richard Hauptmann; in fact, only Lt. Bornmann's right middle, ring, and little fingers were positively identified with any of those latents.[57]

*To further support the footprint evidence, and that investigators were convinced at least three people were involved, one must consider the "John Doe" indictments made by Hunterdon County Prosecutor Anthony Hauck during the September 1932 term. Here he made three indictments for: "Richard Roe," Peter Roe," and "Helen Doe." One of them is as follows:

> *HUNTERDON COUNTY, To Wit:*
>
> *THE GRAND INQUEST OF THE STATE OF NEW JERSEY, in and for the body of the County of Hunterdon, upon their respective oath PRESENT, that HELEN DOE, late of the Township of East Amwell, in the said County of Hunterdon, on the first day of March in the year of our Lord, One Thousand Nine Hundred and Thirty-two, with force and arms, at the Township of East Amwell, within the jurisdiction of this Court, did willfully, feloniously and of her malice aforethought, kill and murder, one Charles A. Lindbergh, Jr., contrary to the form of the statute in such case made and provided and against the peace of this State, the Government and dignity of the same.*[58]

---

[57] Ibid.

[58] Hauck, Anthony M. Indictment. <u>Hunterdon Oyer and Terminer.</u> September Term, A. D. 1932. New Jersey State Police Museum and Learning Center Archives. (Thanks to Wayne McDaniel for reminding me about these after reading *TDC Volume I.*)

Three separate indictments, two men and one woman. Does this mean they did not believe the female prints were Anne's at the time? Or, did they believe the double-set of footprints leading away from the house were joined there by a woman's?

*As fate would have it, a new source became available to the public on Ronelle Delmont's website after I published Volume One. It is a partial transcript consisting of several interviews with Edmund Delong, and some relate to his notes taken during an off the record interview with Schwarzkopf in June of 1932. Here Schwarzkopf revealed the footprint scenario was as I laid out in Volume One.[59] There were two sets of prints leading away from where the ladder was discovered, and a third set was found nearer to the house.

*Also in this interview DeLong revealed that on his way to Highfields on the night of the kidnapping he stopped by an all-night restaurant in Princeton. By the time he arrived, Breckinridge's chauffeur was already at the place picking up coffee.[60] This is a clear indicator that Breckinridge was at Highfields at that time, so it finally proves beyond all doubt that Blackman was there first and much sooner than Delong was.

Chapter 14 – "The Next Phase"

*A mistake that existed in my original manuscript which was corrected but either reversed or never applied concerns something mentioned in the Oscar Bush section of this chapter. The Wyckoff

---

[59]   Delong, Edmund S. Oral Interview. Interview No. 3. Interviewed by Frank Rounds, Jr. March 2, 1962. Page 90. lindberghkidnappinghoax. com/sue.html (Note: Partial transcript).

[60]   Delong, Edmund S. Oral Interview. 1962. Page 49. lindberghkidnappinghoax.com/sue.html (Note: Partial transcript which does not include specific or total citation).

Family was rather large in number and can trace its history to the area back to the late 1600s.[61] The first issue is that while many of the police reports spell the name as "Wycoff" that is not the correct spelling. Next, although related, Nelson Wyckoff and James Wyckoff were two different people. Because of Police references to Nelson being an *active guide* and *informer*, and Jim being referred to as an *active guide* and *tracker*, the word "Wyckoff" would be used by police to refer to either. The Press certainly made the mistake too, referring to James as Lindbergh's neighbor.[62] Since this mistake made it into my first volume, it is more important than ever that I correct it now. Nelson was 64 years old and lived on the second farm house north of Lindbergh Lane.[63] James "Jim" Wyckoff was 48 years old and lived with Oscar Bush in Princeton Basin. It was Jim who was solicited by a reporter to find Bush, and while Nelson had gotten to Highfields at 11:00 AM on March 2nd to act as a guide for Police, both Jim and Oscar preceded him there acting as both trackers and guides.[64]

*In a strange bit of circumstance, Nelson Wyckoff's brother, William Henry Wyckoff, had been charged with murder for the grisly "Wyckoff Murders" which occurred in Zion on February 11, 1916. He was defended by George K. Large and was acquitted.[65]

---

[61]   The Wyckoff Association In America. (1950). *The Wyckoff Family In America*. The Tuttle Publishing Company, Inc.

[62]   "2 Woodsmen Vie with Planes in Kidnap Search," *New York Herald Tribune*. March 3, 1932.

[63]   Wyckoff, Nelson. Statement. March 2, 1932. Made to Acting Captain Gauthier, Jersey City Police Department. New Jersey State Police Museum and Learning Center Archives.

[64]   **Note**: This information clears up "who was who" and "who did what" as it concerns *TDC Volume I*, pages 235-7. The point about the terminology concerning "morning" and "forenoon" applies regardless.

[65]   Dutch, Andrew K. Hysteria, Lindbergh Kidnap Case. (1975). Dorrance & Co. Page 189.

*As I wrote about Squire Johnson in this chapter, I included the fact he was paired up with Reporter George Daws under the instruction of both Governor Moore, and Commissioner Ellis.[66] (Daws is spelled "Dawes" in most of the reports). Because of their joint investigations, Daws was privy to certain information as it related to Johnson. It is this perspective that I believe can now shed light on what happened as it involved him during the course of the Lindbergh Trial. As Johnson insinuated to Governor Hoffman, would there have been a lash of official censure towards him if he testified?[67] Although Daws claimed to have come into this information "indirectly" and that it was "hearsay," he would write that Johnson was told it would be in his best interests to keep quiet with an emphasis being placed onto the fact he had a "State job."[68]

*Also in the Squire Johnson section of this chapter, I wrote about Lindbergh's claim that the dowel was *"strange to him."*[69] Taking this a step further, cross examination with Lindbergh drew this exchange:

> Q: As far as you can recall, do you recall whether or not there was a piece of wood in the library about 12 or 14 inches long?

> A: I don't recall any.[70]

This, once again, shows Lindbergh testified to something different than what the actual facts represent.

---

[66] See *TDC Volume I*, page 218.

[67] Ibid., pages 222-23.

[68] Daws, George. Letter from Geo Daws to Mr. Ellis Parker. December 6, 1935. Andy Sahol Collection.

[69] See *TDC Volume I*, page 216.

[70] Lindbergh, Charles. Testimony. The State of New Jersey vs. Bruno Richard Hauptmann, Hunterdon County Court of Oyer and Terminer, page 146, 1935. New Jersey State Law Library.

Chapter 15 – "In the Shadow of Death"

*The Prosecution came up with a creative way of charging Richard Hauptmann with First Degree Murder. With the help of Newark Attorney Harold H. Fisher, the charge was formulated with the idea the killing occurred while in the perpetration of a burglary.[71] This position was not without potential difficulty for the State…. Since the *corpus delecti* was discovered in Mercer county and Highfields was in Hunterdon county, if it could not be proven the child was murdered in Hunterdon, then the venue would be improper and the Flemington Court would have been without jurisdiction.[72] Furthermore, if the death of the child did not *"ensue from the burglary,"* (if the burglary was "complete" before the alleged blow causing the death of the child) then they were two separate crimes.[73] With this information in mind, had the Prosecution been aware of Dr. Mitchell's testimony at the Gaston Means trial?

> Q [**Rover**]: *Assuming, Doctor, that the time he was last seen alive was the first of March of that year, from your examination and your experience how long after the first of March would you say the child died?*
>
> A [**Dr. Mitchell**]: *From the amount of decomposition that existed in this child I would say that the youngster died within a very short time after its disappearance. It is rather difficult to state accurately the time, but basing*

---

[71] Fisher, Harold H. <u>Letter from Harold H. Fisher to Honorable David T. Wilentz</u>. September 27, 1934. New Jersey State Police Museum and Learning Center Archives.

[72] The State of New Jersey vs. Bruno Richard Hauptmann, <u>Hunterdon County Court of Oyer and Terminer</u>, Sur Indictment for Murder, Motion for Direction of Verdict of "Not Guilty." December Term, 1934. New Jersey State Police Museum and Learning Center Archives.

[73] Ibid.

my conclusions upon the degree of decomposition, I would say the child died within probably 48 hours, at least, following the disappearance from its home.[74]

Had Dr. Mitchell testified in this way in Flemington the case the Prosecution was pursuing against Hauptmann would have been completely ruined.[75] So why didn't he? George Hawke would learn that answer during his 1951 interview with Fred Pope. Pope brought his brother in law to the Flemington Trial with him for the morning session; however, realizing he may not be admitted again for the afternoon by the Sheriff, he had him stay in the Judge's chambers during the lunch break.[76]

"There during the noon recess the in-law heard one of the lawyers of the prosecution coaching Dr. Mitchell to make sure above all else to testify that <u>death was instantaneous</u>."[77]

As a result, Dr. Mitchell testified during the Hauptmann Trial that the child's death was caused by a fractured skull, occurring instantaneously or within a very few minutes following it.[78] When asked if that fracture was due to external force he replied that it had

---

[74] Mitchell, Charles H., MD. Testimony. United States of America vs. Gaston Bullock Means and Norman T. Whitaker, <u>The Supreme Court of the District of Columbia</u>, page 265, May 9, 1933.

[75] Hawke, George G. (1951) *Trial By Fury: The Hauptmann Trial. Princeton University Senior Thesis*. Page 112. New Jersey State Police Museum and Learning Center Archives. (Note: citing an interview with Pope on March 23, 1951.)

[76] Ibid. page 69.

[77] Ibid.

[78] Mitchell, Charles H., MD. Testimony. The State of New Jersey vs. Bruno Richard Hauptmann, <u>Hunterdon County Court of Oyer and Terminer</u>, Vol. 4, pages 1483 & 1487, 1935. New Jersey State Law Library.

every indication of it.[79] Once his role for the State was complete, Dr. Mitchell quickly submitted a bill to Assistant Attorney General Joseph Lanigan claiming:

> *"I feel that the amount of time I spent on this case including the testimony givin* [sic] *which I feel was rather essential as it prooved* [sic] *the cause of death warrants presenting a bill for $500.00."*[80]

However, Mitchell's payment was slashed and he was paid $300.00 instead.[81]

Governor Hoffman was always baffled by the State's theory. After his unofficial investigation into the matter he asserted that it was *"never proved the child was killed on the Lindbergh premises"* and that *"no one knows to this day, with the exception of those who participated in this crime"* how the child was killed or where it occurred.[82]

*I think one of the most shocking revelations was Lindbergh's demeanor during this entire event. We've always been led to believe he was stoic, serious, sad, and would do "anything" to get his child back. But as one can see documented all throughout Volume I, his actions indicated anything but. It was in this chapter that I mentioned Lindbergh's "search" with Curtis where his desire to play

---

[79]   Ibid. page 1483.

[80]   Mitchell, Chas. H. M.D. Letter from Chas. H. Mitchell to Mr. Joseph Lanigan. February 7, 1935. New Jersey State Police Museum and Learning Center Archives.

[81]   Attorney General, The State of New Jersey. Invoice. Expenses in Lindbergh Kidnaping Case. Charles H. Mitchell, M.D. February 7, 1935. New Jersey State Police Museum and Learning Center Archives.

[82]   Hoffman, Harold Giles. *The Crime - The Case - The Challenge (What Was Wrong with the Lindbergh Case?)*, Original Manuscript: Unedited & Uncorrected, circa 1937. Page 125. New Jersey State Police Museum and Learning Center Archives.

cards surpassed his interest in locating his son. To this point further, according to Curtis, Lindbergh did more sleeping than anything else.[83] Also, the original plan was to search via an amphibian plane, but Lindbergh vetoed that idea and insisted on a boat instead.[84] This despite the fact a search by sea would cover a drastically less amount of area. And of course, when awake, Lindbergh was his "usual" jovial self and pulled pranks at just about every opportunity. One time he dressed up in some ridiculous yachting costume. He also harassed Curtis about his "*brown hat*" to the point where Curtis threw it into the ocean to get him to stop.[85] But Lindbergh had the boat turned around to retrieve it! Once retrieved, he made Curtis wear it again and the jokes immediately began anew.[86] And Curtis wasn't the only victim:

> "*He played so many tricks on Bruce and Richard that they were forced to keep their cabin locked. One day, though, the Colonel found a skeleton key which enabled him to enter the room and throw a bucket of water on the sleeping Richard.*"[87]

These examples seem endless. Does any of this sound like a man who gives a damn about finding his son?

---

[83] Curtis, John Hughes. Trial Preparation Notes. —Lindbergh—. Law Office of C. Lloyd Fisher & Ryman Herr. Undated. New Jersey State Police Museum and Learning Center Archives.

[84] Ibid.

[85] Fisher, Lloyd C. "The Case New Jersey Would Like to Forget," *Liberty Magazine*. Part Four. (Aug 1936). New Jersey State Police Museum and Learning Center Archives.

[86] Curtis, John Hughes. Handwritten Notes. Undated. New Jersey State Police Museum and Learning Center Archives.

[87] Fisher, Lloyd C. "The Case New Jersey Would Like to Forget," *Liberty Magazine*. Part Four. (Aug 1936). New Jersey State Police Museum and Learning Center Archives.

Chapter 16 – "Lt. "Buster" Keaten"

*An "error" I made repeatedly in this chapter and elsewhere was spelling Keaten's name both as "Keaton" and "Keaten." As anyone who has ever done a thorough job of researching the New Jersey State Police reports can tell you, his name is spelled both ways in almost a 50/50 ratio. As a result, having read so many of these reports over the years, seeing these variations did not raise a red flag for me. It is directly because of this these spellings went from the source material into the pages of my book without a second thought.

*Robert Waverly Hicks was a criminologist from Washington, D.C. His first involvement with this case came prior to the 1932 Gaston Means trial, having been employed under the direction of both William E. Leahy and United States Attorney Leo Rover.[88] His expenses were being paid for by Evalyn Walsh McLean.[89] The purpose of Hicks's initial involvement was to find the Lindbergh child's fingerprints which would assist in disproving the Means position that the corpse discovered on May 12th in Mount Rose was not Charles Lindbergh Jr.[90] There was considerable difficulty getting Hicks into Highfields, and it had to be done secretly. This was due to the fact it was not something that had been permitted by Lindbergh.

---

[88] Hicks, Robert W. Letter from Robert W. Hicks to J. Joseph Barse, Esq. November 7, 1978. New Jersey State Police Museum and Learning Center Archives.

[89] Hicks, Robert W. Deposition. Harold Roy Olson vs. United States Department of Justice, Federal Bureau of Investigation, and William H. Webster. United States District Court District of Connecticut, Civil Action No. B-78-24, page 21, August 9, 1978. New Jersey State Police Museum and Learning Center Archives.

[90] Ibid., page 22.

Ultimately, arrangements were made between Rover and Hunterdon County Prosecutor Anthony Hauck.[91] According to Hicks:

> *"There was only one person there and it appeared that no one wanted to talk with me because they knew they were double-crossing Breckinridge and the colonel. I was like poison ivy almost. It sounds strange, but that's the way it was."*[92]

Hicks was able to develop many prints from books, blocks, and on the banister outside of the nursery which he believed were the child's.[93] He contacted Mrs. McLean concerning these prints and a meeting was set up where Hicks, McLean, J. Edgar Hoover, and Clyde Tolson met at Friendship to determine whether or not the prints were "workable."[94] In looking over the prints, Hoover said they were "usable" then ordered Hicks to continue giving McLean his reports and warned him against allowing these prints to "float" around.[95] As the men began to speak more freely, Hicks asked Hoover *"well, what do you think of the case?"* to which JEH responded that he told Special Agent in Charge Connelley:

> *"I mentioned to Connolly that I thought it was an inside job."*[96]

---

91 Hicks, Robert. Handwritten Notes. Undated. New Jersey State Police Museum and Learning Center Archives.

92 Hicks, Robert W. Deposition. Harold Roy Olson vs. United States Department of Justice, Federal Bureau of Investigation, and William H. Webster. <u>United States District Court District of Connecticut</u>, Civil Action No. B-78-24, page 27, August 9, 1978. New Jersey State Police Museum and Learning Center Archives.

93 Ibid., page 38.

94 Ibid., page 40.

95 Ibid., page 41.

96 Ibid., page 42.

*Also in this chapter, some very important information was developed from the documentation showing Keaten, Lamb, and Walsh's personal beliefs contrary to the official version of events. To complement Keaten's position further, his grandson Michael's memories dovetail almost perfectly with it. More to this point, Lt. Keaten's daughter, Lydia, told me that while her father never mentioned his beliefs to her, he did however express a strange position to her friend Marge one day.[97] Marge told her he spoke at length about the crime then slipped in something like... *"they got the wrong man"* after which he *"got quiet"* ending the conversation.[98] Lydia also mentioned that when the subject came up in conversation with her husband Bill, she was surprised to hear him say her father mentioned something along similar lines to him as well.[99] As to his paperwork being burned, it was her understanding that some things actually did get turned over the NJSP.[100] However, the fact that once her father died the papers were supposed to be burned was *"something we all knew was supposed to happen"* but she did not know *"where it came from but we all just knew."*[101]

---

[97]   Bowen, Lydia Keaten. Telephone Interview with author. October 13, 2016.

[98]   Ibid.

[99]   Ibid.

[100]   Ibid.

[101]   Ibid.

2

The Woodlawn Experience

Much has been written over the years about the "intermediary" John F. Condon. Was his involvement sincere, open, and honest? The evidence says no. He rarely said the exact same thing twice, and his stories seemed to evolve based upon what he was hearing from police, reading in the newspapers, or possibly from a source yet to be named. As a result of these constant contradictions, lies, and misdirections, an entire book could be written just on this man himself. Having said this, many researchers don't see a red flag here and make excuses for what they do not like but then point to whatever version Condon may have said which they do like. This, and not the other versions, are what they consider the truth so there is no need in their minds to consult or consider anything else he may have said. For me, this line of thought is completely irrational. In fact, bolstering, embellishing, lying, or padding his information in order to be believed or distract from the truth is evidence of only one thing. I will give facts and circumstances to exemplify this by focusing on specific slices of time during his involvement which are by no means everything.

Phone Call(s)

We will never know how many phones calls were made to Condon's house by the Kidnappers. Furthermore, we will never know exactly the dates and times they were made. One of Condon's first accounts of any phone calls made by the Kidnappers was that he received a call *"two or three days"* after placing the ad *"Money is Ready –Jafsie"*…

> *"…from a person announcing himself as John, instructing me to remain at home for a period of one week between six and twelve P.M., and during this time I would receive a letter."*[102]

In continuing, Condon claimed that a communication came to him *"that evening"* after this phone call.[103] Later during this account, he told Inspector Walsh that there were *"two"* phone calls made to him during the negotiations and that in both he was told he would receive written communication from the Kidnappers and that both times *"there were a number of people talking, they were directing John in the same room."*[104] It was during one of these calls that the man told him he was calling from *"West Chester."*[105] Four days later during his Grand Jury testimony in the Bronx, Condon once again asserted that both the phone call and the note arrived on the same day with the call coming in about 3 in the afternoon and the note being delivered a *"few minutes after 8…"*[106]

---

[102] Condon, Dr. John F. Statement. May 13, 1932. Made to Inspector Harry W. Walsh. New Jersey State Police Museum and Learning Center Archives.

[103] Ibid.

[104] Ibid.

[105] Ibid.

[106] Condon, John F. Testimony. <u>Bronx Grand Jury</u>. May 20, 1932. New Jersey State Police Museum and Learning Center Archives.

> *"...as nearly as I can remember, a telephone message came from Westchester stating that they had seen the advertisement in the paper and wanted to know if I would be home from 6 o'clock to 10, or 6 o'clock to 12 every night for the week and that I will get a communication."*[107]

In response to a Juror's question Condon answered:

> *"He told me that is the only way, the one who was speaking with a foreign accent and was surrounded by a number of people who are talking told me I am phoning from Westchester where you are known."*[108]

In January 1934, Special Agent Manning interviewed Condon about this subject once again. Condon essentially gave the same account of the phone call and this appears to be the basis for the information included in what's known as the "FBI Summary Report."[109] It was in this interview with Condon that he clarified this call was not coming in from "Westchester County" but that John had told him he was calling "*from a station on Westchester Square in the Bronx.*"[110] A couple of months after this interview, Condon met with Special Agent Seykora to go over his account which concerned several angles that he was involved in. Concerning the phone call, he said it came

---

[107]   Ibid.

[108]   Ibid. continued after King.

[109]   Sisk, T. H. DOI (FBI) et. al., DOI Report. <u>Summary</u>. NY File No. 62-3057, p. 171. February 16, 1934. National Archives at College Park Maryland.

[110]   Manning, J. J. Special Agent, DOI. USBOI Report. <u>Kidnaping And Murder Of Charles A. Lindbergh, Jr</u>. January 19, 1934. National Archives at College Park Maryland. (Note for future reference: The FBI had changed its name from USBOI to DOI by this time but the heading on this particular report still says "United States Bureau of Investigation")

in *"about 3:00 P. M. on March 12, 1932"* from an unknown man *"who stated he was calling from Westchester Square."*[111] However, Condon furnished information with this new wrinkle:

> *"Dr. Condon stated that this man spoke with an Italian accent and stated that Dr. Condon was selected as a go-between and instructed him to remain at home in the evenings. Dr. Condon further stated that during this telephone conversation, he heard other Italian voices apparently speaking to the others in the room, telling them, "Stat Zit" (phonetic), which he stated was an Italian expression meaning, "Shut up"."*[112]

Shortly thereafter, at the request of the FBI, Condon was asked to prepare a detailed transcript of any phone calls to be forwarded to them for their consideration.[113] In late June 1934, Condon was interviewed by Corporal Leon of the New Jersey State Police and it is during this interview even more details began to emerge. Here, Condon said that on the morning of *"March 8, 1932, just before 9:00 o'clock"* his wife answered a call from one of the Kidnappers asking to speak with him.[114] According to Condon she told him to call back at 6 PM and this man did but he still was not available and the caller

---

[111] Seykora, J. E. Special Agent, DOI. DOI Report. <u>Kidnaping and Murder of Charles A. Lindbergh, Jr</u>. March 8, 1934. New Jersey State Police Museum and Learning Center Archives.

[112] Ibid.

[113] Sisk, T. H. Special Agent, DOI. <u>Letter from T. H. Sisk to Director</u>. June 4, 1934. National Archives at College Park Maryland.

[114] Leon, Samuel J. Cpl. New Jersey State Police. New Jersey State Police Report. <u>The following is the result of an interview with Dr. John F. Condon at his home at 2974 Decatur Avenue, Bronx, N.Y., as to how the kidnappers of the Lindbergh Baby knew his name and address when he signed his name "Jafsie"</u>. June 26, 1934. New Jersey State Police Museum and Learning Center Archives.

was once again told by Mrs. Condon to call back at 7:00 PM. Again they called sometime after 7 and Condon was home eating dinner at the time when his wife let him know the same man calling him twice earlier was on the phone again. Condon told Cpl. Leon:

> *"I then answered the phone, the man on the other end said, 'Is this you Mr. Doctor', and I said that it was. He said 'Did you gotted* [sic] *our note'? 'Did you take it to Col. Lindbergh and what did he say'? I told him that I did get the note and that I did take it to Col. Lindbergh and that he wanted me to act as the Go-between. While this man was talking to me on the phone I could hear other voices on the other end which I am sure was Italian. I was then told by this man not to go out during this week and to stay home every night and that I would get a message. I stayed home and the following Saturday night, a taxicab driver came to my home and gave me a note."*[115]

Somewhere around the time Condon was being interviewed by Cpl. Leon the transcripts of these calls were completed. Consistent with what he told Leon, they show three separate calls coming in at 9 AM, 6 PM, and 7 PM. However, they show these calls were received on either *"March 10th or 11th, 1932."*[116] This document records the call to Condon was made by a man having a *"Scandinavian or German accent."* It also reveals Condon heard *"what appeared to be Italian voices coming from the place where man was calling"* and that he *"distinctly heard someone, not the man he was talking to, say:*

---

[115] Ibid.

[116] Condon, John F. Transcript. <u>Telephone conversation had by Mrs. John F. Condon with unknown man, believed to be kidnaper, either March 10th or 11th, 1932.</u> Undated. New Jersey State Police Museum and Learning Center Archives.

"Statti citto!""[117] These transcripts were attached to a letter Agent Sisk wrote to J. Edgar Hoover in which he wrote that Mrs. Condon corroborated *"that the kidnapper "John" was a foreigner or German or Scandinavian extraction"* and that there was a *"distinct possibility that Italians are involved in the crime because of the Italian voice overheard by Dr. Condon while speaking with a man believed to be "John.""*[118]

Joseph Perrone

On March 12, 1932 between the hour of 7:45 and 8:30 PM taximan Joseph Perrone was cruising east on Gun Hill Road and when he came to Knox Place a man *"came running off the sidewalk"* hailing him.[119] It appeared to Perrone that this man had *"come out of an apartment house on the Southwest corner...."*[120] According to Perrone, the man was wearing a brown overcoat and fedora, about 35 years old, had a *"very fair complexion and light hair"* while weighing about 175 or 180 lbs. and standing about 5'9" tall.[121] The odd thing about him was that some of what he said was *"very good English"* yet, in other parts he had a foreign accent. This led Perrone to believe he was *"putting on"* or in other words, believed *"him to be native born*

---

117   Ibid.

118   Sisk, T. H. Special Agent, Division of Investigation. Letter from T. H. Sisk to Director. August 18, 1934. New Jersey State Police Museum and Learning Center Archives.

119   Perrone, Joseph. Testimony. Bronx Grand Jury. May 17, 1932. New Jersey State Police Museum and Learning Center Archives.

120   Zapolsky, A. Sgt. New Jersey State Police. New Jersey State Police Report. Investigation of the Lindbergh Kidnaping and Murder Case regarding an interview with one Joseph Perrone, 1410 Rowland Street, Apartment 3-C, Bronx, N.Y., Taxi driver who delivered a note to Dr. Conodn on the night of March 12th, 1932. November 29, 1932. New Jersey State Police Museum and Learning Center Archives.

121   Perrone, Joseph. Testimony. Bronx Grand Jury. May 17, 1932. New Jersey State Police Museum and Learning Center Archives.

and had feigned this accent in the speech to mislead" him.[122] The man asked Perrone to deliver a letter to *"2974 Decatur Avenue"* which Perrone agreed to do with the man then giving him a dollar for the 50¢ fare on the trip. The man then backed up, took out a piece of paper to write down Perrone's license plate number, and waved him on his way.[123]

Ever since Condon received a phone call from the Kidnappers, he waited for their contact at his home. At about 8:30 PM on March 12, the doorbell rang. Condon opened the door and there stood Joseph Perrone. Condon asked why he was calling and was informed he was there to deliver a note. Condon had him step inside then began quizzing Perrone by asking where he had gotten the note, requesting a description of the man who gave it to him, and even asking *"is he German?"*[124] About that time Milton Gaglio came running down the steps and Condon told him to give Perrone a tip as he *"went into another room with the letter in his hand."*[125] Gaglio asked Perrone if he was given this note at *"Bainbridge and Gunhill Road."*[126] Interestingly enough, Gaglio would deny that he ever asked this when interviewed by police.[127] Gaglio then followed Perrone outside and took down *"the cab driver's number from the shield and asked him his name."*[128] Perrone then got into his cab and drove away.

---

[122]   Ibid.

[123]   Ibid.

[124]   Ibid.

[125]   Perrone, Joseph. Statement. May 21, 1932. Made to Detective James Fitzgerald, Jersey City Police Department. New Jersey State Police Museum and Learning Center Archives.

[126]   Ibid.

[127]   Gaglio, Milton P. Statement. May 25, 1932. Made to James Fitzgerald, Police Department, Jersey City; Andrew Zaplosky, New Jersey State Police, Trenton, N. J.; E. J. Connelley, Special Agent in Charge, U. S. Bureau of Investigation, Department of Justice, New York City. New Jersey State Police Museum and Learning Center Archives.

[128]   Ibid.

Milton Gaglio & Max Rosenhain

When asked, Gaglio told police the reason he was there at that time was because Condon told him that he *"expected a note or a call on that night"* so he remained with him that evening with his car, thinking he may have to drive him someplace.[129] This is an interesting claim. How would Condon know that a communication was coming that very night if what he told police about this call was true? And if he did know then why wasn't that information ever shared with police? Why did he tell them something much different? For those "supporters" of Condon this would be shrugged off as either a fabrication made by Gaglio or a "mistake" on his part. However, neither of these explanations are adequate. We know this because Condon told Max Rosenhain the same thing:

> *"I guess March 9th was on a Tuesday if I am not mistaken. Condon received a telephone call on Thursday after we came back on the same week and the telephone message was very short, I wasn't present when it came, but Condon told me about it and said that between 8 and 9 the following night of Friday March 12th he would receive a communication or whatever it was, that he would receive a communication."*[130]

So it's obvious Condon had specific information he was sharing with these men that he was hiding from the cops. It became clear that the question Gaglio posed to Perrone came from information shared with him by Condon before Perrone arrived. Gaglio's denial he ever said it only proves that he should not have known – but he did.

---

129 Ibid.
130 Rosenhain, Max. Testimony. <u>Bronx Grand Jury</u>. May 17, 1932. New Jersey State Police Museum and Learning Center Archives. (Note: March 9th was on a Wednesday and March 12th was on a Saturday).

Al Reich

Meanwhile, upon opening this communication, it was revealed that Condon was instructed to proceed to a frankfurter stand near Woodlawn Cemetery where it was indicated he would find another note.[131] Numerous sources say that Reich was at Condon's home when the note arrived.[132] Condon even testified to this in Flemington:

> Q: *And how soon thereafter did you start?*
> A: *Fifteen minutes to a half an hour, as soon as we got ready.*
>
> Q: *With whom?*
> A: *With Alfred J. Reich.*
>
> Q: *Where was he? Where had he been?*
> A: *At my home.*
>
> Q: *Did he drive his car?*
> A: *He drove his car following directions in the note.*[133]

As if we don't have enough contradiction and controversy, Al Reich seemed to be telling a different story. Once officially interviewed by police, he claimed that:

---

[131] Sisk, T. H. DOI (FBI) et. al., DOI Report. <u>Summary</u>. NY File No. 62-3057, p. 213. February 16, 1934. National Archives at College Park Maryland.

[132] Connelley, E. J. Special Agent in Charge, Bureau of Investigation. <u>Letter from E. J. Connelly to Director Re: Kidnaping and Murder of Charles A. Lindbergh Jr</u>. June 23, 1932. National Archives at College Park Maryland.

[133] Condon, John F. Testimony. The State of New Jersey vs. Bruno Richard Hauptmann, <u>Hunterdon County Court of Oyer and Terminer</u>, pages 607, 1935. New Jersey State Law Library.

> *"Sometime about the middle of March Dr. Condon*
> *got in touch with me and asked me if I would drive*
> *him to a refreshment stand about 100 ft. north of the*
> *last station on the Jerome Av. Subway and I told him I*
> *would. He stated that he had received a note from the*
> *kidnappers instructing him to drive to this stand and*
> *get a note from under a rock there, which would give*
> *instructions where to meet the kidnappers."*[134]

Reich's version seems very much supported by Gaglio's because it doesn't make sense he'd be waiting around to drive Condon somewhere if Reich was already there for that purpose. What could be the meaning of this? According to Gregory Coleman, after the note delivered by Perrone was read, everyone agreed that *"no time should be lost"* and that Breckinridge *"insisted that Dr. Condon be protected"* so Reich was *"pressed into service."*[135] Still, why did Condon lie about Reich already being there?

The Notes

Mr. Condon

> *We trust you but we will note come in your Haus it is*
> *to danger. even you can note know if Police or secret*
> *servise is watching you follow this instruction. Take a*
> *car and drive to the last supway station from Jerome*
> *Ave. here 100 feet from the last station on the left seide*

---

[134] Reich, Alfred. Statement. Made to Det. Robert Coar and Det. S. J. Leon. May 13, 1932. New Jersey State Police Museum and Learning Center Archives.

[135] Coleman, Gregory. *"Vigil."* Manuscript: Unpublished and Undated (1932?). Pages 14-5. New Jersey State Police Museum and Learning Center Archives.

*is a empty frankfurther stand with a big open porch
around. you will find a notise in senter of the porch
underneath a stone.*

*this notise will tell you
were to find uss.*

act accordingly

*after 3/4 of a houer be
on the place. bring mony with you.*[136]

Having read this note, it was Breckinridge's opinion that the "*time limit in which*" Condon had to complete this mission was to "*obviate the possibility of a plant.*"[137] He believed that being directed to the second note under the rock would give the Kidnappers the ability to "*observe*" and identify so once satisfied could continue "*in keeping the contact further.*"[138]

Frankfurter Stand

In following the instructions contained within the note, Reich drove Condon up to the front of the stand "*just northwest of the extreme end of the Jerome Avenue subway*" then parked his car.[139] According

---

[136] Exhibit S-48. New Jersey State Police Museum and Learning Center Archives.

[137] Breckenridge, Colonel Henry. Testimony. <u>Bronx Grand Jury</u>. May 17, 1932. New Jersey State Police Museum and Learning Center Archives.

[138] Ibid.

[139] Condon, John F. Statement. Made to Assistant District Attorney Edward F. Breslin. May 14, 1932. New Jersey State Police Museum and Learning Center Archives.

to Reich, they arrived at *"about 8:45."*[140] Once Condon got out of the car, he walked to the *"porch"* and *"found the note under the rock where they had said it would be."*[141] After this Condon…

> *"…stood under the arc light which was located directly beside the automobile and read the same out loud, the purpose of this being to attract the attention of the kidnappers, should they be concealed in the vicinity."*[142]

This note read:

> *"cross the street and follow the fence from the cemetery.*
>
> *direction to 233 street*
>
> *I will meet you."*[143]

According to Breckinridge, it was *"inferred that Dr. Condon was recognized by a confederate of the kidnapers [sic] while securing the note from under the stone."*[144]

---

[140] Peacock, Robert, Assistant Attorney General of New Jersey. Trial Preparation Notes. Statement Of Facts Which Alfred J. Reich Will Testify To: Undated. New Jersey State Police Museum and Learning Center Archives.

[141] Reich, Alfred. Statement. Made to Det. Robert Coar and Det. S. J. Leon. May 13, 1932. New Jersey State Police Museum and Learning Center Archives.

[142] Seykora, J. E. Special Agent, DOI. DOI Report. Kidnaping and Murder of Charles A. Lindbergh, Jr. March 8, 1934. New Jersey State Police Museum and Learning Center Archives.

[143] Exhibit S-51. New Jersey State Police Museum and Learning Center Archives.

[144] Breckinridge, Col. Henry. Statement. Undated. New Jersey State Police Museum and Learning Center Archives.

Dodge

A New Jersey State Police Memorandum which was assembled sometime after the child's body was discovered, records that both Condon and Reich told them about a car that was nearby. Quoting the document:

> "*Condon tells of auto coming to watch him get note.*
> *Al Reich confirms this – at El. terminal*"[145]

This could explain what Breckinridge meant in his statement above. However, as I wrote earlier, John Condon's stories were fluid. This fluidity was based upon what he was overhearing among police, and he would incorporate this information into his own accounts, bolstering them and giving them added credibility. Obviously someone sincere or honest doesn't need to engage in these devious tricks designed to fool law enforcement. As an example, in the fall of 1933, the police were revisiting Ben Lupica's sighting of the "*black Dodge Sedan*" with ladders inside the car near Lindbergh's home on March 1, 1932.[146] Police then conducted experiments with the 1929 Dodge Six by putting a ladder like the one left behind at Highfields in the car through the "*front door window and having it rest on the front of back seat*" to see if it could have fit – and it did with "*about six*

---

[145] New Jersey State Police Memorandum. Untitled. Undated (1932). New Jersey State Police Museum and Learning Center Archives. (Note: During Gov. Hoffman's re-investigation if certain documents were found to be of importance his team gave it an Exhibit Number. This was given "Ex. No. 11").

[146] Lupica, Sebastian Benjamin. Statement. Made to Detective L. J. Bornmann of the New Jersey State Police. September 9, 1933. New Jersey State Police Museum and Learning Center Archives.

inches" to spare.[147] It was just after these investigations that, during an interview with Special Agent J. J. Manning, Dr. Condon suddenly recalled he saw an *"old Dodge car believed to be a Sedan, parked at the Jerome Avenue entrance"* to Woodlawn Cemetery.[148] Then, true to form, during an interview with Special Agent Sandberg months later, Condon told him he *"did not recall that it was a Dodge,"* in fact he would tell Sandberg that:

> *"he did not know what make of car it was; that he was sure it was not a sedan but that it was a touring care with a brown canvas top…"*.[149]

Sandberg, aware of what Condon had told Special Agent Manning, followed up by questioning Condon *"how far it was from the Jerome Avenue entrance to Woodlawn"* but Condon once again contradicted what he told Manning by answering that *"he did not even know there was an entrance to the cemetery across from the frankfurter stand."*[150] This is what happens when people are untruthful: after the fact they cannot remember the exact version of lies they've told earlier. After learning about the "Department of Justice" recent interview with

[147] Bornmann, L. J. Detective, New Jersey State Police. New Jersey State Police Report. <u>Verification as to whether or not the ladder used in the Lindbergh kidnapping could have been carried in a 1929 Dodge Sedan as stated by Sebastian Benjamin Lupica who stated that he saw such a car carrying a ladder on the night of the kidnapping.</u> October 5, 1933. New Jersey State Police Museum and Learning Center Archives.

[148] Sisk, T. H. Special Agent, DOI (FBI). Division of Investigation Report. <u>Kidnaping and Murder of Charles A. Lindbergh, Jr.</u> December 8, 1933. (Period for which made: November 22, 27, and December 4, 1933). New Jersey State Police Museum and Learning Center Archives.

[149] Sandberg, E. Special Agent, DOI (FBI). United States Bureau of Investigation Report. <u>Kidnaping and Murder of Charles A. Lindbergh Jr.</u> August 14, 1934. New Jersey State Police Museum and Learning Center Archives.

[150] Ibid.

Dr. Condon, the State Police sent over Corporal Leon to interview him and find out just what was being discussed. Condon told Leon that Agent Sandberg had been by to ask him "*in reference to people, automobiles, etc., that were in the vicinity of the Woodlawn Cemetery on the night that he first contacted "John.*""[151] According to Leon Condon furnished the following:

> "*...that directly across the street on the cemetery side from the Frankfurter stand about 200 feet from the end of the elevated structure, there was a dark open car with a light canvas top parked, he does not know the make of the car nor did he see anyone in said car.*"[152]

Meanwhile, Agent Sandberg following up his Condon interview, sought out what Al Reich remembered "*with reference to the Dodge car supposed to have been seen by Dr. Condon near the Jerome Avenue entrance to the Woodlawn cemetery on the night of March 12, 1932.*"[153] Al Reich remembered:

> "*...seeing a car parked across the street from a frankfurter stand with two or three people in it, but he thinks it was a Coupe, the make of which he does not recall, and that it was parked just north of the entrance to the Woodlawn Cemetery on Jerome Avenue. He*

---

[151] Leon, Samuel J. Cpl., New Jersey State Police. New Jersey State Police Report. <u>Interview with Doctor John F. Condon re: new developments or information that he may have on Lindbergh case.</u> August 25, 1934. New Jersey State Police Museum and Learning Center Archives.

[152] Ibid.

[153] Sandberg, E. Special Agent, DOI (FBI). United States Bureau of Investigation Report. <u>Kidnaping and Murder of Charles A. Lindbergh Jr.</u> September 4, 1934. New Jersey State Police Museum and Learning Center Archives.

stated that his car was facing south on Jerome Avenue when he stopped in front of the frankfurter stand."[154]

This car came up during cross examination in the Flemington trial as well. Here Condon changed up his story again:

> A: *Now I saw an automobile and it seemed to me that somebody was in that automobile. Does that answer your question?*
>
> Q: *How far away was that?*
> A: *Maybe, rough guess, forty feet.*
>
> Q: *Was there anything to indicate to you that anybody in that automobile wanted to attract your attention?*
> A: *Nothing whatever.*
>
> Q: *How many people in the automobile would you say?*
> A: *I only saw one sticking out, his head out, in the front.*
>
> Q: *Now, was there anything else, or was there any other person in that neighborhood at that time that attracted your attention?*
> A: *Yes, sir.*
>
> Q: *All right. Tell us about that?*
> A: *There was another automobile which seemed to be a country automobile. It had a canvass covering. I was exceedingly careful while I was investigating and I noticed that that [sic] was a sort of country automobile; that is, it was not one of these polished automobiles*

---

[154]   Ibid.

that we see in the City of New York, for instance, and in Flemington.

Q: *How far away was that from you?*
A: *40. Across the way. I should judge the road is at least a 100 feet road, but I saw the automobile.*

Q: *Was the lighting good there that night?*
A: *Splendid.*

Q: *Did you take the number of the automobile?*
A: *I did not, because I was sideways or cater-cornered to it. I couldn't see any number there.*[155]

Woodlawn Cemetery

So after reading the instructions found under the rock, Condon got back into the car, and as directed by this note, Reich drove *"to 233rd Street and Jerome Avenue, in front of the Van Cortlandt entrance to the cemetery"* parking next to the curb.[156] It was at this point that Condon got out of the car and *"stood in the center of the small triangle at the gate"* waiting for contact while Reich remained in the car.[157] Condon waited for about *"ten or fifteen minutes"* but saw no-one so he returned to the car then told Reich that he was *"wondering if they*

---

[155] Condon, John F. Testimony. The State of New Jersey vs. Bruno Richard Hauptmann, <u>Hunterdon County Court of Oyer and Terminer</u>, pages 741-2, 1935. New Jersey State Law Library.

[156] Seykora, J. E. Special Agent, DOI. DOI Report. Kidnaping and Murder of <u>Charles A. Lindbergh, Jr</u>. March 8, 1934. New Jersey State Police Museum and Learning Center Archives.

[157] Ibid.

were coming."[158] Condon said to Reich "*I don't know, maybe they have been scared away.*"[159] It was then that "*a fellow came walking down what would be the sidewalk in our direction...*".[160]

The Look-Out

As the man approached, Reich told Condon "*you had better get out, maybe this is your man coming.*"[161] As Condon got out of the car to return to his position, he noticed a man wearing a "*brown fedora*" and "*brown overcoat*" walking slowly past as he held "*a handkerchief to his face.*"[162] Although being dressed the same as the man who employed Perrone to deliver the note, this man was described by Condon as "*apparently being a Calabrese Italian*" and that he was also both "*short and swarthy.*"[163] Condon added that he was walking "*noticeably stooped*" but that he didn't know if this was a "*peculiarity*

---

[158] Reich, Alfred. Statement. Made to Det. Robert Coar and Det. S. J. Leon. May 13, 1932. New Jersey State Police Museum and Learning Center Archives.

[159] Peacock, Robert, Assistant Attorney General of New Jersey. Trial Preparation Notes. <u>Statement Of Facts Which Alfred J. Reich Will Testify To:</u> Undated. New Jersey State Police Museum and Learning Center Archives.

[160] Reich, Alfred. Statement. Made to Det. Robert Coar and Det. S. J. Leon. May 13, 1932. New Jersey State Police Museum and Learning Center Archives.

[161] Peacock, Robert, Assistant Attorney General of New Jersey. Trial Preparation Notes. <u>Statement Of Facts Which Alfred J. Reich Will Testify To</u>: Undated. New Jersey State Police Museum and Learning Center Archives.

[162] Sisk, T. H. DOI (FBI) et. al., DOI Report. <u>Summary</u>. NY File No. 62-3057, p. 260. February 16, 1934. National Archives at College Park Maryland.

[163] Seykora, J. E. Special Agent, DOI. DOI Report. <u>Kidnaping and Murder of Charles A. Lindbergh, Jr.</u> March 8, 1934. New Jersey State Police Museum and Learning Center Archives.

or whether the man leaned to that side in order to turn around and look at the automobile."[164] Both Reich and Condon agreed this man appeared "*well fed and healthy looking.*" While Reich could only offer that this man was a "*medium sized Italian*" both he and Condon held the belief this man was:

> "*...in that vicinity for the purpose of observing Condon find the note and subsequently follow its directions, and to see if the police were near.*"[165]

This notion was further backed up by Breckinridge's assertion that:

> "*Al Reich is of the opinion that a medium-sized Italian was the individual who observed the Doctor when he removed the note from under a stone at the frankfurter stand and that this Italian gave to "John" the signal verifying the identity of Dr. Condon.*"[166]

This was the one thing Reich told everyone to whom he spoke: he was convinced that this man was an "*accomplice.*"[167] This man

---

[164] Sisk, T. H. Special Agent, DOI. USBOI Report. Kidnaping and Murder of Charles A. Lindbergh Jr. June 26, 1934. New Jersey State Police Museum and Learning Center Archives.

[165] Sisk, T. H. DOI (FBI) et. al., DOI Report. Summary. NY File No. 62-3057, p. 260. February 16, 1934. National Archives at College Park Maryland.

[166] Manning, J. J. Special Agent DOI. USBOI Report. Kidnaping and Murder of Charles A. Lindbergh Jr. December 8, 1933. National Archives at College Park Maryland.

[167] Matteson, Leigh. Unpublished Manuscript. *Lone Wolf Versus Lone Eagle.* Page 40. (1936) New Jersey State Police Museum and Learning Center Archives

continued to walk *"and upon reaching the corner of 233rd and Jerome he turned right, which was the last Dr. Condon saw of him."*[168]

There have been many researchers over time who simply reject the idea that this man was a "look-out." Some claim he was just a random person walking by without any idea of the event. Others claim this man actually *was* Cemetery John since neither man was seen together or at the exact same time. Still others have pointed to where Condon told Inspector Walsh that he *"saw no one other than the man who called himself John"* as proof this man was not involved or may not even have existed at all.[169] However, Condon told Agent Sisk the look-out was not Cemetery John, and that with the exception of "John" he *"never saw the same man twice on any occasion."*[170] In "supposing" Condon was telling the truth, this led Agent Sisk to suggest a possibility which may *"eventually prove of importance"*:

> *"That the lookout observed by Dr. Condon and Al Reich at Woodlawn Cemetery was involved in the case and was "John's" accomplice."*[171]

[168] Sisk, T. H. Special Agent, DOI. USBOI Report. Kidnaping and Murder of Charles A. Lindbergh Jr. June 26, 1934. New Jersey State Police Museum and Learning Center Archives.

[169] Condon, Dr. John F. Statement. May 13, 1932. Made to Inspector Harry W. Walsh. New Jersey State Police Museum and Learning Center Archives.

[170] Sisk, T. H. Special Agent, DOI. USBOI Report. Kidnaping and Murder of Charles A. Lindbergh Jr. June 26, 1934. New Jersey State Police Museum and Learning Center Archives.

[171] Sisk, T. H. Special Agent, Division of Investigation. Letter from Special Agent Sisk to Director. August 18, 1934. New Jersey State Police Museum and Learning Center Archives.

This lookout would be mentioned again by Dr. Condon after Hauptmann's arrest. Condon, having failed to identify him as being Cemetery John, confided in Agent Turrou that he had:

> "...*studied the photograph of Isidore* [sic] *Fisch which appeared in the newspapers and that it is* [his] *belief now that when on March 12, 1932 he went to meet "John" at the Woodlawn Cemetery he saw a party strongly resembling the features and description of Isidore* [sic] *Fisch pass the car in which he and Al Reich were sitting."*[172]

Cemetery John

As the look-out passed Condon and then disappeared from sight, Condon resumed his position in the triangle...

> "...*maybe 5 minutes after that a man inside of the cemetery fence shook his handkerchief and I called out, "I see you. It is all right.", and I walked over to the cemetery fence."*[173]

This man shaking the handkerchief was inside of the "*big iron gate*" which appeared to Condon to be locked.[174] He was directly behind this gate "*with his face very close to the bars*" and he asked "*Did you*

---

[172] Turrou, L. G. Special Agent Division of Investigation. Memorandum. Memorandum for Special Agent T. H. Sisk. October 5, 1934. National Archives at College Park Maryland.

[173] Condon, John F. Testimony. Bronx Grand Jury. May 20, 1932. New Jersey State Police Museum and Learning Center Archives

[174] Condon, John F. Statement. Made to Assistant District Attorney Edward F. Breslin. May 14, 1932. New Jersey State Police Museum and Learning Center Archives.

got my note?" to which Condon replied that he had.[175] According to
Condon, he expressed doubt that this man was the right party which
caused "John" to ask "*didn't you get the signature?*" which supposedly
satisfied Condon.[176] During this encounter, Condon noticed "John"
was wearing a "*brown fedora hat*" with a "*dark brown band*" and a
"*snap rim*" along with a "*black coat, light in fabric*" with his trousers
being "*pepper and salt*" colored.[177] Condon also described him as
being "*Scandinavian*" and "*30 yrs.*" old with a "*medium complexion,*"
standing "*5'9'*" tall weighing between "*158 to 165*" pounds with an
"*oval shaped face*" and a "*prominent forehead.*"[178] Next, according
to Condon's statement to District Attorney Breslin, he said the
following…

> "*…he said, "Well, what about it, have you got the
> money?" I said, "No, I can't bring that money up
> here without some evidence". He said, "I can get you
> evidence; I can get you the sleeping suit of that baby."
> From inside sources I found out today the man was
> betraying their trust.*"[179]

According to this same source it was at this point in time the
Cemetery Guard approached, interrupting their conversation and
causing Cemetery John to flee.

---

[175] Ibid.

[176] Condon, Dr. John F. Statement. May 13, 1932. Made to Inspector
Harry W. Walsh. New Jersey State Police Museum and Learning Center
Archives.

[177] Avon, James A. Officer, New York City Police Department. New York
City Police Department Report. July 19, 1932. New Jersey State Police
Museum and Learning Center Archives. (Note: Amended version to his
report of May 21, 1932).

[178] Ibid.

[179] Condon, John F. Statement. Made to Assistant District Attorney Edward
F. Breslin. May 14, 1932. New Jersey State Police Museum and Learning
Center Archives.

The problem is we do not know exactly the timing of everything due to Condon's contradictions and the discrepancies in his accounts. For example, in some sources, Condon's conversation at the gate was merely "*a few minutes*" long before Robert Riehl arrived scaring him off.[180] From the amount of conversation exchanged between Condon and Cemetery John in those sources it seems to fit. However, if we look at what he said before the Bronx Grand Jury, Condon testified the conversation at the gate lasted about "*25 minutes*" making the claim that he demanded that John take him as a "*hostage*" to see the child when John claims he could not because "*they will scratch me out.*"[181] So we see that very early on Condon was confusing the location of where things were supposed to have been said, and presented different variations of the same conversations as well. The expression in Condon's statement to Breslin (as one example) was that Cemetery John claimed they would "*smack me out*" and another, the conversation about being a "*hostage*" was said <u>after</u> John fled the cemetery and then later made while sitting on the park bench, not at the gate.[182] Remember, these are merely examples, and in fact, it happens just about everywhere. So it appears quite obvious Condon's memory was either quite flawed or the man wasn't telling the truth because he couldn't keep his lies in order.

---

[180] Sisk, T. H. DOI (FBI) et. al., DOI Report. <u>Summary</u>. NY File No. 62-3057, p. 172. February 16, 1934. National Archives at College Park Maryland.

[181] Condon, John F. Testimony. <u>Bronx Grand Jury</u>. May 20, 1932. New Jersey State Police Museum and Learning Center Archives.

[182] Condon, John F. Statement. Made to Assistant District Attorney Edward F. Breslin. May 14, 1932. New Jersey State Police Museum and Learning Center Archives.

The Cemetery Guard

Robert Riehl was a police officer for the Woodlawn Cemetery Police Department.[183] The main job for the police officers of this department was to "*keep anyone from robbing graves and damaging the property.*"[184] As mentioned above, history records that he interrupted the negotiations between Cemetery John and John Condon at the Van Cortlandt Gate.

Al Reich's Version

In trying to continue to establish a time-line, it's important to note that Reich believed Condon had approached the gate (to speak with Cemetery John) at "*about 9:30PM.*"[185] Since he had both the door and the window closed, Reich could not hear anything.[186] He also couldn't see anyone inside the cemetery but could see that Condon was talking to someone through this gate. However, after "*maybe ten minutes,*" he saw a fellow jump off the gate, land near Condon, then

---

183   Zapolsky, A. Sgt, NJSP, and Fitzgerald, J. Det., Jersey City Police Department. New Jersey State Police Report. Attempting to obtain statement from Robert Riehl, Police Officer of Woodlawn Cemetery, New York City, who is supposed to have seen one of the kidnapers jumping over fence at the time Dr. Condon (Jafsie) had meeting with kidnapers at that place. July 15, 1932. New Jersey State Police Museum and Learning Center Archives.

184   Jones, Edward C. Letter from Edward C. Jones to Attorney General David Wilentz. January 11, 1935. New Jersey State Police Museum and Learning Center Archives.

185   Reich, Alfred. Statement. Made to Det. Robert Coar and Det. S. J. Leon. May 13, 1932. New Jersey State Police Museum and Learning Center Archives.

186   Reich, Alfred Jacob. Testimony. The State of New Jersey vs. Bruno Richard Hauptmann, Hunterdon County Court of Oyer and Terminer, page 570, 1935. New Jersey State Law Library.

run across the street into Van Cortlandt Park.[187] Reich testified he could see that Condon followed "John" to a point about 100 yards away where there was a park bench located near a "shack" and it was at this location where they both sat down.[188] Reich claimed he waited for *"about an hour"* before Condon returned to his car.[189]

John Condon's Version(s)

As noted above, after Condon approached the gate he either had a very short conversation with John lasting only a couple of minutes, or had one lasting up to 25 minutes before John's vault over the gate. If the conversation was only a minute or two this puts the timing somewhere around 9:30 PM if Reich's statement is to be considered truthful. On the other hand, if it lasted the full 25 minutes then it puts the jump around 10:00 PM, except this would mean Reich was either wrong or untruthful when he claimed Condon's conversation at the gate lasted maybe ten minutes. It's a catch-22.

Moving up in time to when Riehl approached… One of Condon's earliest accounts was as follows:

> *"At this time the cemetery guard in uniform appeared on the inside of the fence and he said "Oh! there is someone, or there is a cop" and climbed the fence which is approximately twelve to fourteen feet high and ran across 233rd St., into the woods. I said wait, don't run, you are my guest, nobody will interfere with you and I*

---

[187]   Ibid. Pages 570-1.
[188]   Ibid. Pages 571-2.
[189]   Ibid. Page 573.

followed him across 233rd St., into the woods, I called
him again while he was running and he stopped."[190]

It was the next day during his interview with District Attorney
Breslin that his account was amended to include his interaction
with Riehl. Condon revealed the guard was *"about 25 feet"* away
when John, still standing on the inside talking through the bars,
"caught ahold of the gate," climbed, then jumped over the fence *"in*
two seconds" at which time Condon said to him: *"Don't run away,*
you are my guest" explaining to the DA that he did not want to lose
him, and continued by telling John *"nobody will touch or harm you"*
as John continued to run *"into the woods."*[191] Once the question
was posed about what the guard said, Condon continued with this
information:

> *"He came over to me and said, "What's the matter with*
> *that fellow?" I said, "He was a little frightened being*
> *inside with an officer near." That's all that passed*
> *between us. He went in the woods and I said, "Hold*
> *on, you are my guest", and he half turned, then turned*
> *all the way, and started back toward me a little."*[192]

About two years later during an interview with Corporal Leon of the
New Jersey State Police, Condon gave this version of these events:

> *"At this time a cemetery guard appeared in the bushes*
> *and he said 'There is a cop'. He then climbed over the*

---

190 Condon, Dr. John F. Statement. May 13, 1932. Made to Inspector
     Harry W. Walsh. New Jersey State Police Museum and Learning Center
     Archives.

191 Condon, John F. Statement. Made to Assistant District Attorney Edward
     F. Breslin. May 14, 1932. New Jersey State Police Museum and Learning
     Center Archives.

192 Ibid.

fence, jumped down in front of me and started to run north across 233rd Street. I said, 'Hay don't run away, you are my guest, do you want to run away and leave me here to be drilled', but he did not stop. Just then the guard said to me, 'What is the matter with him'. I told the guard that I did not know but that maybe he was frightened, then I ran after him and caught up to him in the woods. He asked me if I sent the cop, I told him that I did not and that I wouldn't do anything like that because I had given him my word."[193]

Then during the Flemington Trial, there is some interesting testimony that Condon gave which must be reviewed considering what he told authorities earlier about what he said to John as he ran away:

A: *Jumped down in front of me.*

Q: *Then what happened?*
A: *"Did you sended the cops?" "No, I gave you my word that I wouldn't do that, and I kept my word." He then said "It is too dangerous" and started to run in a northernly direction. He reached 233rd Street, because we had a part of that plaza in front of the gate to go, he reached 223rd Street and kept on running, and I said – is it alright for me to say that?*

Q: *Yes, go ahead.*

---

[193] Leon, Samuel J. Cpl. New Jersey State Police. New Jersey State Police Report. The following is the result of an interview with Dr. John F. Condon at his home at 2974 Decatur Avenue, Bronx, N.Y., as to how the kidnappers of the Lindbergh Baby knew his name and address when he signed his name "Jafsie". June 26, 1934. New Jersey State Police Museum and Learning Center Archives.

A: *I said, "Hey, come back here. Don't be cowardly."*

Q: *Yes.*
A: *"Here I am a poor school teacher up here in the
cemetery and you leaving me here to be drilled."*

Q: *Then what happened?*
A: *"You are my guest." He kept on running.*

Q: *What did you do?*
A: *I followed him.*[194]

Robert Riehl

Special Patrolman Robert Riehl had been employed for over five
years at Woodlawn Cemetery. On March 12, 1932, he was working
the 4:00 PM to Midnight shift. Starting at 7:00 PM he was required
to make a walking tour of the grounds, stopping to make "rings" at a
different box every hour at one of the various gates. On this night, at
9:00 PM Riehl made his ring opposite the frankfurter stand, which
he identified later as being *"mentioned and pictured in the newspapers,
but did not observe anyone near same."*[195] Shortly before 10:00 PM, he
went to make his hourly ring on box 442, which was located at the
gate of 223rd Street & Jerome Avenue.[196] As Riehl approached, he saw
"a man sitting on top of the stone column of the gate, talking to the other

---

[194] Condon, John F. Testimony. The State of New Jersey vs. Bruno Richard
    Hauptmann, <u>Hunterdon County Court of Oyer and Terminer</u>, page 623,
    1935. New Jersey State Law Library.
[195] Avon, James A. Officer, New York City Police Department. New York
    City Police Department Report. <u>People State of New Jersey</u>. May 21,
    1932. New Jersey State Police Museum and Learning Center Archives.
[196] Ibid.

fellow who was on the outside of the gate."[197] As Riehl got to within 75 feet, the man on top of the column saw him when at that point "*he hollered to the other man who was on the outside of the gate.*"[198] According to his April 13, 1932, interview, Riehl quoted the man as saying "*here comes a cop*" before jumping onto the ground outside of the gate then running "*across Jerome Avenue and into Van Cortlandt Park.*"[199] In his official statement made July 19, 1932, Riehl told police the man sitting on the column yelled "*to the other man who was outside of the gate*" that "*there's the Cop coming*" at which time he jumped down off the column landing on the outside of the gate, got up, then ran "*into the park and disappeared.*"[200] At this point obvious questions come to mind: Why didn't Reich see this man sitting on top of that stone column, and why did Condon claim "John" had only been on the ground speaking to him through the bars? It's also interesting to note two of Riehl's other observations made here....
One that he immediately thought the man on the column may have broken his leg from the jump (until he got up to run), and that during this event – "*the other man did not answer at all.*"[201]

Take note: "*the other man did not answer at all.*"

---

[197]   Riehl, Robert. Statement. Made to Sgt. A. Zapolsky, of N.J. State Police, and Det. James Fitzgerald, of Jersey City Police. July 19, 1932. New Jersey State Police Museum and Learning Center Archives.

[198]   Ibid.

[199]   Avon, James A. Officer, New York City Police Department. New York City Police Department Report. People State of New Jersey. May 21, 1932. New Jersey State Police Museum and Learning Center Archives.

[200]   Riehl, Robert. Statement. Made to Sgt. A. Zapolsky, of N.J. State Police, and Det. James Fitzgerald, of Jersey City Police. July 19, 1932. New Jersey State Police Museum and Learning Center Archives.

[201]   Ibid. (Note: This observation destroys any notion that, if Cemetery John actually was the kidnapper who had been climbing down the ladder at Highfields, he fell off the ladder injuring his leg as was alleged Hauptmann had been during his trial in Flemington).

What did Cemetery John look like according to Riehl? In his April interview, he told police this man was "*22 years, 5 feet-3inches, 135 lbs., slim build.*"[202] In his later July statement Riehl claimed he "*could not describe his face*" or "*color of his hair*" because it "*was to* [sic] *dark to see it.*"[203] However, in his "*best judgement*" he said he was...

> "*...about 5'6" or 7" inches, in ht. wt. about 130 or 135 lbs., and from his action while running I would judge him to be about 23 or 24 yrs. old, dressed with dark pants, white shirt, no coat on, and wearing a cap.*"[204]

Another significant observation from Riehl was that "*when this man hollered I did not notice Foreign accent in speech.*"[205] This is important because Riehl was not only of German heritage, he was born there, so one might expect he would have been able to identify a German accent coming from this man. Something else of interest is the indication that this young man was yelling a warning to the individual standing outside the gate. And since this man, according to Riehl, made no plea for him to stay (or any other comment for that matter), Condon's various (and conflicting) statements suggesting he indeed responded to the man are highly suspicious. None of them are believable, by the way, but rather what one might relate in order to appear sincere in their actions.

---

202   Avon, James A. Officer, New York City Police Department. New York City Police Department Report. <u>People State of New Jersey</u>. May 21, 1932. New Jersey State Police Museum and Learning Center Archives.

203   Riehl, Robert. Statement. Made to Sgt. A. Zapolsky, of N.J. State Police, and Det. James Fitzgerald, of Jersey City Police. July 19, 1932. New Jersey State Police Museum and Learning Center Archives.

204   Ibid.

205   Ibid.

When police asked Riehl for a description of the man standing outside of the gate in April, he gave the following information: *"50 years, 5 feet-9 inches, 200lbs., black overcoat and black soft hat."*[206] When asked in July he said this man was:

> *"between 50 or 55 Yrs., of age, about 5'6" or 5'7" in ht., wt., about 170 lbs., clean shaven, round face, apparently American, wore a Dk., suit, Dk., over coat, collar & tie, Blk., soft hat turned up all the way around, this man spoke like a real American."*[207]

Riehl was asked point blank by Sergeant Zapolsky and Detective Fitzgerald if the man outside of the gate was John Condon. Riehl said *"no"* referring to newspaper pictures that he saw citing, among other things, that Condon had a *"different shaped face,"* and while Condon had a *"mustache"* the man outside the gate *"had none."*[208] Riehl finished by saying he could identify this man *"if I spoke to him and seen him personally..."*[209] This was probably because, unlike the fellow who was perched on top of the column, he actually spoke face to face with that man outside the gate. Just what was said between them? In April, Riehl stated that he asked this man...

> *"...whether the man who fled was trying to steal something, and the man stated he did not know, but he*

---

[206] Avon, James A. Officer, New York City Police Department. New York City Police Department Report. <u>People State of New Jersey</u>. May 21, 1932. New Jersey State Police Museum and Learning Center Archives.

[207] Riehl, Robert. Statement. Made to Sgt. A. Zapolsky, of N.J. State Police, and Det. James Fitzgerald, of Jersey City Police. July 19, 1932. New Jersey State Police Museum and Learning Center Archives.

[208] Ibid.

[209] Ibid.

*would follow him and ask him, whereupon he walked
across Jerome Avenue and vanished in the park.*"[210]

Riehl's July version of this conversation is as follows:

> "*As I went near the gate and questioned the other man
> who was on the outside, as to what the young fellow
> was doing on the top of the column, and his reply was
> (I dont [sic] know, I have no idea and if you wait a
> minute I'll go over and ask him). I made my ring at
> this gate and waited about 5 or 8 minutes and no one
> came back, so I continued on my patrol and I had no
> Idea what it was all about.*"[211]

Riehl was obviously a disinterested party and his only goal that night
was to simply do his job. There was no motive for him to lie, and in
fact, there was every reason to simply keep his mouth shut about the
entire matter. How can anyone in their right mind believe Condon's
version over his?

Governor Hoffman asked why Riehl, who was an important
eyewitness, was never called to testify in Flemington. He wrote that:

> "*Riehl, unfortunately, was not as keen as Condon.
> He could not distinguish a middleweight from a
> heavyweight, or see a tear in a man's eye on a dark
> night, or the color of his hair through a cap or hat*

---

[210] Avon, James A. Officer, New York City Police Department. New York
City Police Department Report. <u>People State of New Jersey</u>. May 21,
1932. New Jersey State Police Museum and Learning Center Archives.

[211] Riehl, Robert. Statement. Made to Sgt. A. Zapolsky, of N.J. State Police,
and Det. James Fitzgerald, of Jersey City Police. July 19, 1932. New Jersey
State Police Museum and Learning Center Archives.

pulled down, so he would not have made a good witness for the state."[212]

In conclusion he added:

"Had Riehl testified, and had his conscience not have permitted him, as in the case of so many others, to change stories between 1932 and 1935, the jury at Flemington might have been convinced that "it was two other fellows" at Woodlawn, not Hauptmann and Condon. No, Riehl's testimony just wouldn't fit."[213]

However, while this explains why Riehl was not a State witness, it does not offer any reason why the Defense did not call him. So why didn't they? During the Flemington trial it was reported that:

"State attorneys said they had spoken to Robert Riehl, the guard and had confirmed Jafsie's description of his conduct. He expressed a willingness to testify if needed, it was said."[214]

However, this report was completely dashed when a Reporter interviewed Riehl concerning the man he saw outside the gate, and he was quoted as saying "*I am positive it wasn't Dr. Condon…*"[215]

---

[212] Hoffman, Harold Giles. *The Crime - The Case - The Challenge (What Was Wrong with the Lindbergh Case?)*, Original Manuscript: Unedited & Uncorrected, circa 1937. Page 104. New Jersey State Police Museum and Learning Center Archives.

[213] Ibid. Pages 104-5.

[214] "Bruno's Double To Be Brought in By the Defense." *United Press Report.* January 12, 1935. New Jersey State Police Museum and Learning Center Archives.

[215] "Guard Is Sure He Didn't Talk to Dr. Condon." *New York Post.* January 12, 1935. New Jersey State Police Museum and Learning Center Archives.

Even before Hauptmann had been extradited to New Jersey, Riehl had been quoted in a New York paper:

> *"Nobody can tell me it was Bruno Hauptmann who talked to Dr. Condon." Riehl was quoted as saying. "I've seen pictures of Hauptmann and I've seen pictures of Isadore Fisch. I'll bet my bottom dollar that man was Fisch."*[216]

This sounds like something the Defense would really want to use. However, Hauptmann was still being represented by James Fawcett at that time. In fact, once Reilly took over the case, he had one of the PIs working for the Defense check Riehl's story out. Frank Pettit of the Pettit Detective Agency sent R. C. Cashin to Riehl's home on 1892 Guerlain Avenue to interview him in December before the trial. Once there, Cashin showed Riehl the various newspaper clippings and after looking them over he said the following:

> *"I don't like to give any more stories or further stories as the Cemetery Officials advised me, that I had no right to give any statement, and it would be advisable if I care to keep my job to hold my tongue too and to not make any more statements. My Captain was sore too for he told me that it was none of my business. These newspaper stories are a lot of lies and they have caused me a lot of trouble and annoyance."*[217]

---

[216] "Says Fisch, Not Hauptmann, At Ransom Tryst." *United Press Report.* October 14, 1934. New Jersey State Police Museum and Learning Center Archives.

[217] Pettit, Frank P., Private Investigator, Pettit Detective Agency. <u>Report on Robert Riehl Special Guard at Woodlawn Cemetery</u>. December 22, 1934. New Jersey State Police Museum and Learning Center Archives.

Despite this, Cashin was able to get a signed statement from Riehl. In this statement Riehl claimed while he was *"150 feet away"* he saw that a *"tall thin man"* sitting on the cemetery fence post talking to a *"short stocky man standing on the outside of the fence"* and once he was spotted the fellow yelled out *"There comes the Cop"* then jumped down and ran toward 233rd Street.[218] Riehl stated: *"...the other party stood still and did not run after him or holler at him"* and that he approached this man and spoke with him.[219] Riehl asked *"what do you want? Does he want to jump in the Cemetery?"* and the man replied *"Wait I'll find out"* then went toward 233rd Street never to be seen again.[220] In conclusion, Riehl once again stated that the man on the outside of the fence *"was not Dr. Condon"* and he also said that he did not see the other man's face because it was *"very dark."* However, Riehl had seen photos of both Hauptmann and Fisch but did not believe either was the man he saw sitting on top of the column that night.[221] The idea that Cemetery John was not Fisch wasn't appealing to Reilly. Furthermore, it was Pettit's belief that Riehl would attempt to "protect" Condon because...

> *"...some City Officials must have reached the Captain of the Guards and had them to threaten Mr. Riehl or the have reached the Official of the Cemetery and had them to do the same thing."*[222]

---

[218] Riehl, Robert. Statement. Made to Operative R. C. Cashin of the Pettit Detective Agency. December 22, 1934. New Jersey State Police Museum and Learning Center Archives.

[219] Ibid.

[220] Ibid.

[221] Ibid.

[222] Pettit, Frank P. Pettit, Private Investigator, Pettit Detective Agency. <u>Report on Robert Riehl Special Guard at Woodlawn Cemetery</u>. December 22, 1934. New Jersey State Police Museum and Learning Center Archives.

The "Chase"

It was Riehl's observations that Cemetery John ran away then "*disappeared*" in the park. As this occurred, we must remember that Riehl had a brief conversation with the man outside the fence, after which this man walked into the park and also "*vanished.*" These two points are more that do not match up with the versions Condon told. So is big Al Reich the tie-breaker? Was his position in the car better suited to see the events in Van Cortlandt Park than Riehl, or was he simply part of the ruse? Reich testified that it was a "clear night" so clear in fact, that he was able to see that both men sat on the bench with as much distance between them as possible.[223] Despite what Reich claimed he could see, if all that Condon asserted occurred, it's rather easy to determine who is telling the truth....

Starting from the beginning, whether or not it was Condon whom Riehl encountered, it is quite obvious Condon portrayed this event as one he was involved in with Reich backing him up. So even if it wasn't him, they wanted police to believe it was. Next, if we are to believe Condon that Cemetery John was actually in fear that he had set him up because of Riehl's approach, it's hard to fathom the idea that he stuck around after running into the park. To get around this obstacle, Condon claimed that after his communication with Riehl, he was able to call to John as he was in full flight and it was this action which convinced him to stop. Are we to believe this old man could catch this guy running, by Condon's own admission, "*fast*?"[224] This is supposed to be the man who is running for his life and, in Condon's own words, claimed got over that fence in "two

---

[223]   Reich, Alfred Jacob. Testimony. The State of New Jersey vs. Bruno Richard Hauptmann, <u>Hunterdon County Court of Oyer and Terminer</u>, pages 572-4, 1935. New Jersey State Law Library.

[224]   Condon, John F. Testimony. The State of New Jersey vs. Bruno Richard Hauptmann, <u>Hunterdon County Court of Oyer and Terminer</u>, page 748, 1935. New Jersey State Law Library.

seconds" and was blaming <u>him</u> for the cop's approach. Not only that, Condon did not chase him right away and was handicapped by the delay his conversation with Riehl created. It is absurd of course. Additionally, John's warning, yelled to the man outside the fence, is even greater indication that Condon and John were in a very trusting relationship. If in fact it was even Condon at all.

According to Condon he called to John as he ran, assuring him he was safe, and this caused him to stop. Condon *"asked him to sit down on the bench"* and John complied.[225] However, on the very next day Condon adjusted this version to show he was a little more forceful with John by telling Breslin that: *"He come back a few steps and I caught him by the arm."*[226] Clearly this makes a little more sense if John was truly suspicious of Condon and alarmed by the situation. It explains that John didn't actually fully comply but was influenced by some physical force or interaction. However, about a week later Condon seems to have forgotten about this tid-bit and resorted back to his earliest version where he claimed:

> *"I called to him to come back that he was my guest now and that nobody would touch him or harm him. He turned and walked slowly back to where I walked in the woods and then I asked him to sit on the bench. He sat on the bench next to me."*[227]

---

[225] Condon, Dr. John F. Statement. May 13, 1932. Made to Inspector Harry W. Walsh. New Jersey State Police Museum and Learning Center Archives.

[226] Condon, John F. Statement. Made to Assistant District Attorney Edward F. Breslin. May 14, 1932. New Jersey State Police Museum and Learning Center Archives.

[227] Condon, John F. Testimony. <u>Bronx Grand Jury</u>. May 20, 1932. New Jersey State Police Museum and Learning Center Archives.

No force, just a trusting Kidnapper willing to risk arrest at the mere request of Condon. Since we have Riehl's account of the man running into the woods, it is quite clear he waited for Condon (or whoever it was) there. Then by the time of the Flemington Trial Condon reverted back to the story of his forceful influence over John:

> A: *I followed him into a little clump of trees near a shack on the opposite side of the way from the cemetery, and I went over and got a hold of his arm and said, "Hey, you mustn't do anything like that; you are my guest."*
>
> Q: *Then what did you do?*
> A: *I brought him back—*
>
> Q: *All right.*
> A: *I didn't bring him back, I led him back to the seat by the small shack.*[228]

---

[228] Condon, John F. Testimony. The State of New Jersey vs. Bruno Richard Hauptmann, <u>Hunterdon County Court of Oyer and Terminer</u>, page 623, 1935. New Jersey State Law Library.

Park Bench in Van Cortland Park
Where Condon spoke to Cemetery John after he ran away from Robert Riehl
(Courtesy NJSP Museum)

Gregory Coleman

In June of 1934, Special Agent Sisk had several conversations with Lt. Keaten, during which he came to understand Keaten's assessment of Condon. It was Keaten's belief that not only was Condon involved, he contradicted himself too many times to be believable and could not be relied on.[229] And Sisk also learned Inspector Walsh was:

---

[229] Sisk, T. H. Special Agent, Division of Investigation. Memorandum for the Director. <u>Unknown subjects Kidnapping and murder of Charles A. Lindbergh, Jr</u>. June 23, 1934. National Archives at College Park Maryland.

*"positively convinced that Dr. Condon is involved in
the crime and it is obvious from the talk of officers of
the State Police that they also are convinced."*[230]

In light of this, Sisk sought to find a source for Condon's earliest
recollection of events in order to compare them with his later stories
about what occurred. Fortunately, Sisk was able to find exactly what
he was looking for:

*"Recently I determined that Mr. Gregory Coleman
of the Bronx Home News was the first person to
thoroughly interview and question Dr. Condon after
his meeting with the kidnaper* [sic] *at Woodlawn
Cemetery March 12, 1932. Mr. Coleman saw Dr.
Condon the following day, March 13, and made notes
as to the Doctor's conversation with the kidnaper,
when the matter was fresh in the Doctor's mind."*[231]

It was these notes that Coleman used to assist in writing his
unpublished story about Condon titled *Vigil*.[232] To underscore
the importance of this source, I will quote Sisk here: *"We are also
obtaining other details from Mr. Coleman, who seems to know more*

---

[230] Sisk, T. H. Special Agent, Division of Investigation (FBI). Memorandum
For The Director. <u>Unknown Subjects Kidnapping and Murder of Charles
A. Lindbergh, Jr</u>. June 29, 1934. National Archives at College Park
Maryland.

[231] Sisk, T. H. Special Agent, Division of Investigation (FBI). Memorandum
For The Director. <u>Unknown Subjects Kidnapping and Murder of Charles
A. Lindbergh, Jr</u>. July 27, 1934. National Archives at College Park
Maryland.

[232] Gardner, Lloyd C. June 2004. *The Case That Never Dies*. Rutgers
University Press, pages 430-1. (Note: His book was the first to mention
this source that I know of).

about the ransom negotiations than the Police.[233] In *Vigil* Coleman describes Cemetery John's flight in a more realistic scenario. It reads that as John fled, Condon had been "*fearful that his first man-to-man contact with the abductors was permanently broken off.*"[234] Condon called after the man but he "*darted across 233rd St.*" and disappeared out of sight. Here it claims Condon remained on the avenue, and was "*pacing up and down until finally the man appeared again.*"[235] The manuscript also says Condon told Coleman that he suggested the two walk into a secluded section of Van Cortlandt Park and out of sight for the purpose of gaining the Kidnapper's trust. At that point both Condon and John "*walked a distance of two blocks until they arrived at a deserted work-shack and sat down upon a bench in front of it.*"[236]

The Bench

It was on this bench that Condon, ad nauseam, told so many versions about what was exchanged between him and Cemetery John. They are included in just about every book in one form or another. In light of this, I did not want to waste the time of the reader and I am just going to focus on some of the things that reveal the most about the situation. The very first thing is the amount of time it took for this conversation to occur. In his earliest account to police,

[233] Sisk, T. H. Special Agent, Division of Investigation (FBI). Memorandum For The Director. Unknown Subjects Kidnapping and Murder of Charles A. Lindbergh, Jr. July 27, 1934. National Archives at College Park Maryland.

[234] Coleman, Gregory F. *Vigil*. Unpublished Manuscript. Page 17. Undated (circa 1932). New Jersey State Police Museum and Learning Center Archives.

[235] Ibid.

[236] Ibid.

Condon claimed it took *"about an hour and forty minutes."*[237] He also testified in the Bronx that he returned home at *"quarter to 12 or near it."*[238] As mentioned above, Al Reich testified in Flemington that this conversation lasted *"about an hour"* and his statement is also consistent with this testimony. Breckinridge testified in the Bronx that Condon had held John in a period of conversation that lasted *"certainly an hour"* and arrived back to his home *"between 11 and 12."*[239] Condon himself testified in Flemington that he spoke with John *"for more than one hour."*[240] The account in *Vigil* says *"they talked for more than an hour and fifteen minutes, despite the chilly winds that swept by them."*[241] Obviously, this is quite a period of time for a killer to be sitting around speaking with someone who was supposed to be delivering the ransom money but did not. Furthermore, any length of time near an hour leads one to believe quite a lot was said. To me, it's simply more proof these men trusted one another. In one version of the conversation, Condon quotes John as saying:

---

[237] Condon, Dr. John F. Statement. May 13, 1932. Made to Inspector Harry W. Walsh. New Jersey State Police Museum and Learning Center Archives.

[238] Condon, John F. Testimony. Bronx Grand Jury. May 20, 1932. New Jersey State Police Museum and Learning Center Archives.

[239] Breckenridge, Colonel Henry. Testimony. Bronx Grand Jury. May 17, 1932. New Jersey State Police Museum and Learning Center Archives.

[240] Condon, John F. Testimony. The State of New Jersey vs. Bruno Richard Hauptmann, Hunterdon County Court of Oyer and Terminer, page 624, 1935. New Jersey State Law Library.

[241] Coleman, Gregory F. *Vigil*. Unpublished Manuscript. Page 17. Undated (circa 1932).

> *"Our number two man says he knows about you and you can be trusted. That's why I come, but who is that man over in the auto?"*[242]

This comes from a man who was just surprised by a cop walking towards him inside the fence? Who supposedly ran away because he believed Condon set him up? Also consider that Condon claimed in another source that he believed John was pointing a gun at him from inside of his pocket during this conversation.[243] But again, in the previous source he quotes John as saying:

> *"Number two knows you and we all 'drust' [sic] you. The gang has faith in you that you vouldn't [sic] tell."*[244]

So why was John pointing a gun at him then? Or was that made up too? No matter how one looks at this it's a contradiction. The FBI viewed these accounts as considerably important to their investigation. They believed this because…

> *"…of the distinct possibility that the kidnapper, during the rather lengthy discussions with Dr. Condon may have uttered certain truths which may materially aid the investigation and possibly furnish a clue which will aid in identifying him. Undoubtedly the kidnapper "John" falsified many of his statements and deliberately*

---

242 Condon, John F. Transcript. <u>At Woodlawn Cemetery – about 9:00 P. M., March 12, 1932</u>. Undated (March 1934). New Jersey State Police Museum and Learning Center Archives.

243 Condon, Dr. John F. Statement. May 13, 1932. Made to Inspector Harry W. Walsh. New Jersey State Police Museum and Learning Center Archives.

244 Condon, John F. Transcript. <u>At Woodlawn Cemetery – about 9:00 P. M., March 12, 1932</u>. Undated (March 1934). New Jersey State Police Museum and Learning Center Archives.

sought to mislead Dr. Condon. However, worried by fear of arrest and under a great nervous strain he may not have had sufficient mental alertness to concoct misleading and untruthful replies to all of the many questions directed to him by Dr. Condon."[245]

But what if Condon was making up the conversations himself? Giving police what he thought they would accept as true all the while protecting the identities of the Kidnappers? Might what the FBI mentioned above apply to Condon? In fact, mixing in certain truths could actually have been a method to protect himself later on whereby he could point to them as proof that he was cooperating with authorities. But is there proof Condon was doing this? I say yes. In fact, even the FBI did not believe he was being 100% truthful in his recollections of these conversations:

"It is believed that Dr. Condon may have magnified, imagined, and "dressed up" some of the statements attributed to the kidnapper and also his own remarks."[246]

As I've mentioned above, there is only one reason why someone in Condon's position would do this.

Was John Alone?

As I've already proven above, the look-out was not Cemetery John. "History" tells us this man walked away then disappeared from the rest of the events stemming from the meeting at Woodlawn and

---

[245] Sisk, T. H. Special Agent, Division of Investigation. <u>Letter from Special Agent Sisk to Director</u>. August 18, 1934. New Jersey State Police Museum and Learning Center Archives.

[246] Ibid.

Van Cortlandt Park. However, there is an interesting part of the conversation between John and Condon while on the bench that was revealed to Coleman and exists only through him. According to *Vigil*, Condon was attempting to get John to bring him to the baby. "*You are armed*," he told him, "*you could shoot me or your friends could shoot me*" – this Condon believed was as good a reason as any to convince John it would be okay to "*let*" him "*see the child*" for himself.[247] It was then the shocking details emerged – they were <u>not</u> alone:

> "*At this point, the shivering thug looked out towards Jerome Ave. as though trying to see someone on the lighted avenue. Dr. Condon queried: "Your friend is with you? Yes, I know; why not call him? I will go with both of you. Two against one is fair. The only thing I want is the baby." But the skulking figure before the venerable Doctor was adamant. "No, I must not call my friend under any circumstances. He would kill me."*[248]

For those cynics who may believe parts of this manuscript were dressed up, the "control" <u>here</u> would be Coleman's Grand Jury testimony…

> "*…and Dr. Condon had told the kidnapper that they would not give that money without seeing the baby and he pleaded with the man in the cemetery and in Van Courtlandt [sic] Park to be brought to the baby, and the man in the cemetery indicated that there was another man some distance away, and he said, "he wont [sic] let me" one expression he used, "he will*

---

[247] Coleman, Gregory F. *Vigil*. Unpublished Manuscript. Page 18. Undated (circa 1932).

[248] Ibid.

*smack me down" and Dr. Condon argued with him
and he said he wants his fare, and he said, "can you
drive a car, you can take me to the baby, you can kill
me" and a conversation along those lines."*[249]

As anyone can see, this testimony supports the scenario above as
written in *Vigil*. It is not represented like this anywhere else. Very
interesting when one considers what Sisk revealed in his investigation
concerning Coleman's knowledge.

The Conscientious Kidnapper

If all of this craziness wasn't enough, consider how John, the
supposed Kidnapper, tried to assist Red Johnson, and Betty Gow!
While on the bench terrified that he would be arrested or worried
that he was going to get "smacked out" by the gang for not returning
with the $70,000, he still found the time to exonerate those he felt
were falsely accused of the crime. To me, this is an important clue
which must be properly evaluated.

On May 14, 1932, during an interview with Assistant DA Edward
Breslin, Condon told about his interaction with Cemetery John at
Woodlawn Cemetery where he brought this out…

> *"…and he said "One of our fellows is in trouble
> already, and only five of us left." He said, "You can't
> get – what do you call it – immunity". I surmised that
> he referred to Red Johnson, which again was verified
> in a minute or two because he said, "Red Johnson is
> innocent, and so is the girl"; he meant Betty Gow. I*

---

[249]   Coleman, Gregory. Testimony. <u>Bronx Grand Jury</u>. People vs. Hauptmann.
September 24, 1932. New Jersey State Police Museum and Learning
Center Archives.

said, "John" – he had given his name as John – 'if he is innocent I can help him'". He told me Red Johnson and the girl had nothing to do with it. A couple of days after that he was taken over to Ellis Island. They looked upon Johnson as a kind of a leader, and among the Scandinavians they thought he was dreadfully abused; so did the Scandinavian papers."[250]

Only six days later, during Condon's sworn testimony before the Bronx Grand Jury, the exchange went as follows:

[Breslin]: *Did you have any conversation with him or during the conversation with him did he suggest to you the name of Johnson?*

[Condon]: *Yes, but not in connection with the ransome [sic]. I said to him, "You say you got two nurses." He said the men were to have 20,000 and the other 3 10,000. We didn't expect so much expense. You told me one of them was in trouble? Yes. What will you do with that one? Is that Red Johnson? No Red Johnson and Betty Gow are innocent would you help. I certainly would if they were innocent.*

Q: *Did he make some reference to the fact or mention that Red Johnson was getting a rough deal from the police?*

A: *Not only rough deal, but it was so mean, and something ought to be done. I said, "John, I will tell*

---

[250]   Condon, John F. Statement. Made to Assistant District Attorney Edward F. Breslin. May 14, 1932. New Jersey State Police Museum and Learning Center Archives.

you what I will do, I will help him by stating that you say he is innocent."[251]

Another interesting account comes from the detailed transcript of the conversation created by Dr. Condon for the FBI in the early summer of 1934.[252] Here is the relevant part:

Condon: "What about Red Johnson?"

Man: "He is innozent – the girl has nuttin to do wid it. Betty Gow is innozent too."

Condon: "If Red Johnson is innocent I can help him."

Man: "He had nuttin to do wid it, he should be freed. I have to be going now. It was worth my life to come here, and it seems you can't trust me. They will do something to me because I haven't got the money."[253]

While these three accounts differ, the main points within them remain the same. That is, both Red Johnson and Betty Gow are innocent. Next, that Red was mistreated and should be helped. Finally that Condon offers his assistance to them. Now, is this really coming from John? If so why in the hell would a Kidnapper not want the attention of the police on two innocent people instead of him and his gang? It makes no sense unless Betty or Red were actually connected in some way. But this assumes Condon is being

---

[251] Condon, John F. Testimony. Bronx Grand Jury. May 20, 1932. New Jersey State Police Museum and Learning Center Archives.

[252] Sisk, T. H. Special Agent, DOI. Letter from T. H. Sisk to Director. June 4, 1934. National Archives at College Park Maryland.

[253] Condon, John F. Transcript. At Woodlawn Cemetery – about 9:00 P. M., March 12, 1932. Undated (March 1934). New Jersey State Police Museum and Learning Center Archives.

truthful. What if he was making this up? Assuming he was, how would he know whether Betty or Red were not involved? So if he did not know, what reason could he possibly have to obstruct justice in this way?

Adding to this, once we review some of Condon's testimony which mentions Red Johnson, we see more problems concerning what John supposedly told him. Here is some testimony on January 9th:

> [Reilly]: *Then why did you pick out a local Bronx Borough paper, with a circulation of 150,000 with all of New York's six million people to insert your ad?*
> [Condon]: *Because those papers all led toward one poor miserable fellow that I thought was innocent. His name was Arthur Johnson.*[254]

So what Condon is testifying to here is that he already believed Red was innocent prior to his interaction with Cemetery John.

> Q: *Did you know Red Johnson?*
>
> A: *I did not.*
>
> Q: *Then why should you, a Doctor of Philosophy, an A.B., a Professor of Fordham, suddenly decide that you would protect Red Johnson, a sailor on a yacht, unless you knew him?*
>
> A: *I'll tell you why: because I always hated to see an underdog, and always give him a chance throughout my life, and I heard that Arthur Johnson had nothing*

---

254 Condon, John F. Testimony. The State of New Jersey vs. Bruno Richard Hauptmann, <u>Hunterdon County Court of Oyer and Terminer</u>, page 694, 1935. New Jersey State Law Library.

to do with it, from many people. I was at the time going in among them and questioning them concerning the probabilities of the case.

Q: *What people told you Red Johnson had nothing to do with it?*

A: *A number of sailors. I visited every single shipyard there; went to every sailor I that could find and found out that Arthur Johnson was not that kind of fellow.*[255]

If what Condon is now testifying to in Flemington is true, then there is no doubt he made up the notion of Cemetery John uttering the claim of Red and Betty being innocent. His testimony is crazy in another way too… Consider that Hauptmann's wife and friends all said he wasn't the type to kidnap a baby yet Condon is willing to take the words of sailors to make up something coming from the Kidnappers. Yet, in referring back to his previous statements/ testimony given in the Bronx, he seemed to be leading authorities to think he held no opinion during that time regarding Red's involvement, or possibly thought he might be involved, and that the opinion of innocence was Cemetery John's. This was exactly Breckinridge's position, and having spoken with Condon about this exact point testified to this in the Bronx:

[Breslin]: *"It is a fact to [sic] isn't it in this conversation that Dr. Condon had with this man known as John some reference was made to Red Johnson?"*

[Breckinridge]: *"Yes he said that Red Johnson was innocent and some woman that was mentioned in the newspapers in connection with Red Johnson was*

---

[255] Ibid.

> *also innocent. He wasn't referring to Betty Gow, that*
> *led the doctor to believe quite the contrary, it was his*
> *assertion that the Johnson man was innocent, made*
> *him think they were guilty."*[256]

Coleman would also demonstrate that Condon believed Johnson was involved during this process. He asserted he was present in Dr. Condon's home when it was decided to give an *"impression"* that *"Johnson had been absolved of all knowledge of the crime."*[257] Coleman stated that John's concern about Johnson aroused a heightened suspicion of him by Lindbergh and his advisors *"although the colonel never lost his faith in Betty Gow and trusted her implicitly."*[258] To further muddy the waters, Coleman wrote:

> *"So convinced was Dr. Condon that Johnson had some*
> *knowledge of the kidnaping* [sic] *and of the man he met*
> *in Woodlawn Cemetery, that he made frequent trips*
> *to City Island in the hope of locating some of Johnson's*
> *friends during a lull in the ransom negotiations."*[259]

The controversy doesn't end here. Returning to the cross examination of Condon by Reilly in Flemington, another bombshell occurred:

> Q: *Did you learn that he phoned Betty Gow at half*
> *past eight the night of the kidnaping?*
>
> A: *I knew that the night of the kidnaping.*

---

[256] Breckenridge, Colonel Henry. Testimony. <u>Bronx Grand Jury</u>. May 17, 1932. New Jersey State Police Museum and Learning Center Archives.

[257] Coleman, Gregory F. "The Story of Jafsie Brought Down to Date." *Bronx Home News.* October 3, 1934. New Jersey State Police Museum and Learning Center Archives.

[258] Ibid.

[259] Ibid.

Q: *How did you know it if you were not in contact with him?*

A: *I will tell you how I knew it. I knew it because it was spread around all through that—*

Q: *The night of the kidnaping?*

A: *Now your English again—*

Q: *The night of the kidnaping? Answer the question. That is what you said, the night of the kidnaping.*

A: *Ask your question.*

Q: *You said you knew that the night of the kidnaping.*

A: *That occurred the night of the kidnaping.*

Q: *No. You said you knew it the night of the kidnaping.*

A: *Did I say that?*

Q: *Yes, you did.*

A: *I said that—when you spoke that he, Arthur Johnson, had telephoned to Betty Gow on the night of the kidnaping, but I had never seen it, I add it again, I had never seen Red Johnson, as called, I mean Mr. Arthur Johnson.*[260]

---

[260] Condon, John F. Testimony. The State of New Jersey vs. Bruno Richard Hauptmann, <u>Hunterdon County Court of Oyer and Terminer</u>, page 695, 1935. New Jersey State Law Library.

Condon's testimony would continue into January 10th. It was during Wilentz's redirect where he attempted to neutralize the damage from the above exchange:

[Wilentz]: *Just a minute now. My recollection is that your testimony was: "I knew that, the night of the kidnaping." Now, is that correct?*

[Condon]: *No. I knew that was so on the night of the kidnaping.*

Q: *When did—*

A: *I did not know it on the night of the kidnaping.*

Q: *When did that information come to you?*

A: *Will you pardon my distinction there?*

Q: *All you have got to do, sir, is come along with me and we will finish in a minute.*

A: *Yes.*

Q: *When did you ascertain that – not accurately; to the best of your recollection.*

A: *It was after my meeting with John at Woodlawn Cemetery on March 12th, 1932.*

Q: *Where did you get the information, in other words?*

A: *From John.*

Q: *About the newspapers?*

A: *No.*

[Reilly]: *Do not lead him, Mr. Attorney General, please.*

[The Witness]: *No.*

[Reilly]: *Go ahead. I've been waiting to hear this.*

Q: *What I want to know is this, sir: at some time or other you learned that Miss Gow had received a telephone call from Mr. Johnson?*

A: *Yes.*

Q: *When did that information come to you and how did it come to you if you remember?*

A: *It came to me through general gossip and the newspapers.*[261]

Clearly Condon had been led through this testimony by Wilentz. Furthermore, during re-cross Reilly suggested that after Condon's testimony was made on the 9th, he was coached after conferring with a member of Prosecution about how to testify on the 10th. Condon denied this and claimed it was merely a mistake in English.[262]

Moving on to another example of the conscientious Kidnapper which I earlier referenced in Governor Hoffman's point above, we see a real sensitive side as it concerns his mother:

---

[261] Ibid. Pages 816-7.
[262] Ibid. Pages 819-20.

> ""*What is your name?" He said, "Call me John." Well, John, did you ever think of your own mother?" Yes, and a tear came to his eye, which I saw on the night on the northerly side of the large gate of the cemetery."*[263]

One cannot deny the inconsistencies here. Condon's assertions change whenever and however he needs them to.

$1000

Among the kindnesses exhibited by John was the fact that he told Condon he could keep his $1000 offer included in his appeal to the Kidnappers in his letter in the Bronx Home News.[264] According to Condon, the exchange between them went as follows:

> [Condon]: *"This is just a source of trouble to me; I am getting no money, I am just trying to help the baby. Please take me to the baby, you can blindfold me. Show me you are all right. I will give you my own $1000. as reward, which is all that I have now, in addition to the $70,000."*

> [Man]: *"You can't, they won't let you. You can't see the baby this time, but you can come later wid [sic] the Colonel, after we make a get-away. Number two*

[263] Condon, John F. Testimony. Bronx Grand Jury. May 20, 1932. New Jersey State Police Museum and Learning Center Archives.
[264] Condon, John F. Letter from John F. Condon to Editor of Home News. March 7, 1932. New Jersey State Police Museum and Learning Center Archives.

says you're a fine fellow and we shouldn't take any of your money."[265]

So while they raised the ransom by $20,000 on Lindbergh, they forgave Condon's debt to them. It does not make sense that a group of Kidnappers who attempted to collect on a murdered baby wouldn't gladly accept every scrap available to them. It might have been a good thing too, that they did not try to collect it, because it did not appear that he had the money available to offer in the first place. In the late fall of 1933, while waiting at Condon's home for his return to interview him, Special Agent Manning had a quick conversation with his wife. According to Manning, Mrs. Condon was suffering from *"mental discomfort"* as a result of her husband's involvement in the case and couldn't make sense as to why he would offer $1000 reward:

> *"Although the Condon family has considerable of its money tied up in real estate, the assets are virtually frozen, and at the present time the Condon cash is quite depleted, Mrs. Condon explaining that the Doctor is encountering considerable difficulty in straightening out his mortgages and tax payments on many of his real estate holdings."*[266]

[265] Condon, John F. Transcript. <u>At Woodlawn Cemetery – about 9:00 P. M., March 12, 1932</u>. Undated (March 1934). New Jersey State Police Museum and Learning Center Archives.

[266] Manning, J. J. Special Agent DOI. USBOI Report. <u>Kidnaping and Murder of Charles A. Lindbergh Jr</u>. December 8, 1933. National Archives at College Park Maryland.

The Dead Baby

History records that John asked Condon *"vould* [sic] *I burn if the baby was dead, if I didn't kill it!"*[267] However, this question is suspiciously absent from many of Condon's other accounts. Did he forget about this shocking question? Was it ever actually asked of him? Or had Condon made it up? It strikes me as an invention meant to offer John a defense if he was ever apprehended. After all, who in their right mind asks such a question … most especially <u>before</u> the ransom for a live baby is paid?

How John Got Involved

Condon informed Inspector Walsh that Cemetery John said to him:

> *"They picked me because I had no record, but they got something on me." In other words that he had been in something and they knew it and he wished that he had not started in it.*"[268]

This was similar to the testimony he gave in the Bronx where he claimed John said:

---

[267] Leon, Samuel Cpl. New Jersey State Police. New Jersey State Police Report. <u>The following is the result of an interview with Dr. John F. Condon at his home at 2974 DeCatur Avenue, Bronx, N.Y., as to how the kidnappers of the Lindbergh Baby knew his name and address when he signed his name "Jafsie"</u>. June 26, 1934. New Jersey State Police Museum and Learning Center Archives.

[268] Condon, Dr. John F. Statement. Made to Inspector Harry W. Walsh, Sgt. Warren T. Moffatt, Lieut. A. T. Keaton and Detective Horn. June 2, 1932. New Jersey State Police Museum and Learning Center Archives.

> *"Well, I was brought in on this, they had something on me. I didn't want to come into it and I wish I was out."*[269]

Was Condon talking about John, or was he really explaining the reason for his own involvement and talking about himself? Next, at various times, Condon would quote John as saying the *"leader is a very high official"* who was *"very smart"* and *"in the government service."* Whether true or not, this information seems designed to emphasize the level of danger these men now find themselves in.[270] Once again it appears to me that Condon is attempting to build a defense for John, and if not John – for himself.

The "Curtis" Hoax

According to Condon, Cemetery John also brought up John Hughes Curtis during their conversation on the bench:

> *"He told me the baby is not in Norfolk, Virginia, nor in the north, and he said, "We relay the baby from one boat to another.""* [271]

What we see is that while John was attempting to protect Betty and Red by proclaiming their innocence, here he is also attempting to protect Lindbergh by exposing Curtis. This recollection by Condon was not unique. He told Corporal Leon the following:

---

[269]   Condon, John F. Testimony. <u>Bronx Grand Jury</u>. May 20, 1932. New Jersey State Police Museum and Learning Center Archives.

[270]   Condon, John F. Transcript. <u>At Woodlawn Cemetery – about 9:00 P. M., March 12, 1932</u>. Undated (March 1934). New Jersey State Police Museum and Learning Center Archives.

[271]   Condon, John F. Statement. Made to Assistant District Attorney Edward F. Breslin. May 14, 1932. New Jersey State Police Museum and Learning Center Archives.

> "*At this time he told me to tell Col. Lindbergh not to pay any attention to the other gang, meaning Curtis, as they were not the right parties, and told me that he would send me evidence to prove that they had the baby.*"[272]

Condon also provided this information in his transcript of the conversation he had with John at Woodlawn which he created for the FBI:

> "*Tell Colonel Lindbergh he's wasting his time with those people down soud; they are not the 'ride' parties. In order that you might know as how we are the 'ride' parties I will send you Lindbergh's son's sleeping garment and he will know we are the 'ride' ones. You will see the Colonel and he will know if it is the garment the baby was in, that will prove we are the 'ride' parties. The colonel is off the track, those others are not the 'ride' parties on the case.*"[273]

To fully understand the weight of what Cemetery John was supposedly saying we must review certain facts that are attached to the Curtis angle of the case. Curtis claimed his first contact was

---

[272] Leon, Samuel Cpl. New Jersey State Police. New Jersey State Police Report. <u>The following is the result of an interview with Dr. John F. Condon at his home at 2974 DeCatur Avenue, Bronx, N.Y., as to how the kidnappers of the Lindbergh Baby knew his name and address when he signed his name "Jafsie"</u>. June 26, 1934. New Jersey State Police Museum and Learning Center Archives.

[273] Condon, John F. Transcript. <u>At Woodlawn Cemetery – about 9:00 P. M., March 12, 1932</u>. Undated (March 1934). New Jersey State Police Museum and Learning Center Archives.

made by "Sam" on the night of March 9, 1932.[274] The next day Curtis then brought Dean Peacock into his confidence and the two men made a phone call to Highfields. According to Curtis he believed he spoke with "*Mr. Rosner*" who gave the men "*little satisfaction*."[275] After this, Peacock wrote a letter to Mrs. Morrow, who he knew from Mexico City, on the night of March 11, 1932.[276] No word was ever received as a result of this letter.[277] This led the men to get in touch with Admiral Burrage on March 19, 1932, who called Hopewell. A return message was promised for the next morning but never came.[278] On March 20th, Burrage wrote a note to Lindbergh announcing they would arrive in Hopewell on March 22nd. The men arrived at Highfields on the 22nd at 5:45 PM and were escorted to Lindbergh where a brief conversation took place with Lindbergh in which he "*stated emphatically that he must have positive proof that he was dealing with the right people. That they must show him clearly that he was dealing with the kidnappers and not with one of the hundreds of imposters*."[279]

It was these facts above which led Governor Hoffman to conclude that Condon lied claiming "*it was not until March 19 that Curtis first made his appearance in the case, or the Norfolk angle was ever*

---

[274] Curtis, John Hughes. Statement. Made to Captain Lamb and Mr. Frank Wilson, Federal Agent. May 13, 1932. New Jersey State Police Museum and Learning Center Archives.

[275] Ibid.

[276] Peacock, H. Dobson, Rector of Christ Church (Episcopal). Letter from H. Dobson Peacock to Mrs. Dwight Morrow. March 11, 1932. New Jersey State Police Museum and Learning Center Archives.

[277] Curtis, John Hughes. Statement. Made to Captain Lamb and Prosecutor Hauck. May 14, 1932. New Jersey State Police Museum and Learning Center Archives.

[278] Ibid.

[279] Ibid.

mentioned."[280] Lloyd Fisher, the attorney who represented Curtis at his trial in Flemington, wrote in his notes "*it is a significant fact that the name of Curtis and his associates never ~~entered~~ were mentioned in the Lindbergh case until the 23rd of March 1932...*".[281] Simply put, on March 12, 1932, Curtis wasn't even known to Lindbergh, and he had no role in any negotiations during that time to be warned away from.

Ravages of Disease

Condon observed many details about John. One such observation was the man was sick. In fact, as Condon recalled to Inspector Walsh, John "*shivered with cold and told me he was sick*" which led the saintly Dr. Condon to offer the additional service to "*go and get medicine.*"[282] Oddly on the very next day, Condon told Assistant District Attorney Breslin that as John pulled his collar away from his face (which allowed him to get a glimpse) John "*coughed*" prompting Condon to tell him "*...you got a severe cold; I will go and get you some medicine.*"[283] Immediately after this interview, Condon told Officer Avon that John was "*Scandinavian*" who "*acted very nervous,*" and

---

[280] Hoffman, Harold Giles. *The Crime - The Case - The Challenge (What Was Wrong with the Lindbergh Case?)*, Original Manuscript: Unedited & Uncorrected, circa 1937. Page 93. New Jersey State Police Museum and Learning Center Archives.

[281] Fisher, C. Lloyd. Typed Notes. <u>Subjects to be covered in examination of Condon</u>. Undated. New Jersey State Police Museum and Learning Center Archives.

[282] Condon, Dr. John F. Statement. May 13, 1932. Made to Inspector Harry W. Walsh. New Jersey State Police Museum and Learning Center Archives.

[283] Condon, John F. Statement. Made to Assistant District Attorney Edward F. Breslin. May 14, 1932. New Jersey State Police Museum and Learning Center Archives.

"was continually coughing."[284] A week later while under oath during the Bronx Grand Jury testimony, Condon seemed to give more detail concerning John's sickness:

> *"He took down his coat for a moment and that was the first time and only time I got a glance of the full face. His hat, fedora and was down over his forehead. He looked to be Scandinavian type and his face with rather high cheek bones came down to almost a pointed chin, smooth face no blemishes, or blotches. It seemed to me inroads of disease would make it that shape."*[285]

The next relevant account came when Inspector Walsh, feeling strongly that Condon was involved, decided to put the "screws" to him.[286] This was the notorious interview where the men walked along the Palisades and Walsh asked Condon if he didn't feel like throwing himself off the cliffs.[287] Condon told Walsh that John *"had a hacking cough"* and that *"his skin was smooth and it gave me the impression that disease had started its inroads into his body."*[288] This observation was no secret, and he made sure to impress it upon Lindbergh too, writing him a letter which included: *"I thought that he was subject*

---

[284] Avon, James A. Officer, New York City Police Department. New York City Police Department Report. July 19, 1932. New Jersey State Police Museum and Learning Center Archives. (Note: Amended version to his report of May 21, 1932).

[285] Condon, John F. Testimony. Bronx Grand Jury. May 20, 1932. New Jersey State Police Museum and Learning Center Archives.

[286] See *TDC Volume I*, pages 332-3.

[287] Sisk, T. H. Special Agent, Division of Investigation. Memorandum for the Director. Unknown subjects Kidnapping and murder of Charles A. Lindbergh, Jr. June 23, 1934. National Archives at College Park Maryland.

[288] Condon, Dr. John F. Statement. Made to Inspector Harry W. Walsh, Sgt. Warren T. Moffatt, Lieut. A. T. Keaton and Detective Horn. June 2, 1932. New Jersey State Police Museum and Learning Center Archives.

to a pulmonary disease when I saw him."[289] Condon continued with this position for the entire length of the investigation. He later gave the FBI this information in the transcript as coming from John: *"No, I could not. I got a cold." (Coughing – coughed frequently during conversation).*[290] So again, while we see the fact of John frequently coughing, we also see Condon revert back to crediting John with the claim he was sick. In Flemington, during direct examination he seemed to echo these claims:

> [Condon]: *"…I have two coats, I will give you one if you are in want." Then he coughed. It is what they call a hollow cough. I don't want to imitate that.*
>
> [Q]: *It was a cough?*
>
> [A]: *He coughed, I said, "The inroads of pulmonary disease—" shall I?*
>
> [Q]: *Go ahead.*
>
> [A]: *"—seem to start." Let me go over and get you some medicine….*[291]

However, as cross examination continued into the next day of January 10th, Condon was asked about this again:

---

[289]   Condon, John. <u>Letter from Jafsie to Colonel Lindbergh</u>. July 12, 1932. New Jersey State Police Museum and Learning Center Archives.

[290]   Condon, John F. Transcript. <u>At Woodlawn Cemetery – about 9:00 P. M., March 12, 1932</u>. Undated (March 1934). New Jersey State Police Museum and Learning Center Archives.

[291]   Condon, John F. Testimony. The State of New Jersey vs. Bruno Richard Hauptmann, <u>Hunterdon County Court of Oyer and Terminer</u>, page 627, 1935. New Jersey State Law Library.

[Q]: *And that he had a cough that indicated to you that he was suffering from consumption?*

[A]: *No, sir.*

[Q]: *Or pulmonary trouble?*

[A]: *Yes, sir.*

[Q]: *Was it a hard cough?*

[A]: *No.*

[Q]: *Was it a soft cough?*

[A]: *No.*

[Q]: *Was it a cough that appeared to you to come from his lungs?*

[A]: *Yes, sir.*

[Q]: *And you suggested that he take something for the cough?*

[A]: *No, I didn't.*

[Q]: *Well, what did you suggest?*

[A]: *I suggested that I go to the drug store and get some medicine, I said.*

[Q]: *And how far away was the nearest drug store?*

[A]: *Oh, I couldn't tell you that now, but I could find it; I know all the places there.*[292]

But before this topic was over, Condon was asked: *"And he only coughed once?"* to which he replied: *"That is all."*[293] And so we see by this example, here too, Condon was no stranger to telling lies.

Cemetery John's Strange Thumb(s)

There was something else about John that Condon noticed too. Although exactly where and when it was noticed – if noticed or that it existed at all – is a matter for debate. But it is a definite fact that Condon, at some point, told police John had a strange lump at the base of one of his thumbs or possibly both. The first important point about Condon's claim is that the NJSP were the last to know about it:

> *"During the conversation with Lt. Keaton [sic] there was considerable discussion relative to the description of John the kidnaper [sic] given by Dr. Condon. During the discussion agent mentioned the right thumb of the kidnaper which had been mentioned by Dr. Condon to the writer as having a growth on it, and Lt. Keaton [sic] stated that he had never heard of this and stated that he realized of course it was very important. I might add that Lt. Finn is aware of this fact and it seems surprising that Lt. Keaton was ignorant of it."*[294]

---

[292]   Ibid. Page 751.
[293]   Ibid. Page 752.
[294]   Sisk, T. H. Special Agent, Division of Investigation. Memorandum for the Director. <u>Unknown subjects Kidnapping and murder of Charles A. Lindbergh, Jr</u>. June 23, 1934. National Archives at College Park Maryland.

Of course we must consider that Lt. Keaten was, as he had been known to do on occasion, feigning ignorance about this subject. What we do know is that during the joint investigations that included members of the NJSP, at the point in time when Condon seemingly recalled this detail for authorities, these men were in fact checking every suspect's hands. However, if Keaten was personally unaware, it underscores the position that Condon was not consistent with his stories and in fact, this is highlighted by the fact that Special Agent Manning created a *"supplemented"* description of John. In this description, Manning wrote that John had *"eyebrows medium heavy and in a straight line across forehead"* as well as the fact *"he did not walk lame,"* and *"could run fast."* He added that John had *"unusually large"* ears, and that John had an *"unusually large muscular or fleshy development on inside thumb of left hand."*[295] After Manning left the FBI, he was replaced by Special Agents Seykora and Sandberg who continued investigations relative to Condon and other subjects relating to this crime. Sandberg interviewed Condon on July 19, 1934. It was during this interview that Condon gave him a description of John which included that John's eyes *"resembled those of a Chinaman or Japanese,"* his eyebrows ran in a straight line *"almost joining each other,"* his ears were not only *"unusually large"* but that they were *"protruding somewhat."* When it came to the defect, Condon told Sandberg that the *"peculiarity"* John had was *"unusually large muscular or fleshy development on the inside at the base of the thumbs of both hands"* and indicated that *"Dr. Condon has submitted a penciled sketch showing this unusual development."*[296]

---

[295] Manning, J. J. Special Agent, DOI. USBOI Report. <u>Kidnaping And Murder Of Charles A. Lindbergh, Jr.</u> January 19, 1934. National Archives at College Park Maryland.

[296] Sandberg, E. Special Agent, DOI. USBOI Report. <u>Kidnaping And Murder Of Charles A. Lindbergh, Jr.</u> July 24, 1934. New Jersey State Police Museum and Learning Center Archives.

The sketch referenced by Sandberg was enclosed inside of a letter Dr. Condon mailed to the New York Office received on July 16, 1934. The sketch itself was of *"the kidnapper's left hand"* and he referred to the hand as *"the mutton chop."* Condon made several *"notations on the margin"* some of which were:

> *"Fingers flat, pointed, thin fingers; heavy thumb base muscle.*
>
> *Such a hand seems to be that of a painter or sailor. It signifies great power and quickness to <u>grab</u>.*
>
> *'The mutton chop' hand. Thumb base most prominent feature."*[297]

These weren't the only notations. Condon drew "an arrow" towards the *"finger tips"* then made the following *"notation alongside of the arrow"*:

> *"Extension of 'John's fingers….long…..ordinary hand…..stops here where curved strokes are drawn across the fingers."*[298]

In yet another notation concerning the *"finger tips"* Condon wrote as follows:

> *"Just as if disease, such as a pulmonary inroad would cause."*[299]

---

[297] Sisk, T. H. Special Agent, DOI. USBOI Report. <u>Kidnaping And Murder Of Charles A. Lindbergh, Jr</u>. July 27, 1934. National Archives at College Park Maryland.

[298] Ibid.

[299] Ibid.

What exactly do we see here? We have an important characteristic added to John's description. Had it been forgotten earlier? Once remembered, we see it goes from right thumb, to left thumb, to both thumbs, back to left thumb. This is classic Condon as is his tendency to tie something in with a known or accepted fact mentioned previously. From my perspective it is something very unique not unlike the "secret symbol" on the ransom note, and in fact, probably even more close to the three holes which positively identify the real Kidnappers. But the way I see it, although cut from the same cloth, its purpose seems to be just the opposite as it relates to John. What do I mean? It is a way to rule someone <u>out</u> instead of rule someone in; therefore, if John were caught they could look for this unique characteristic then use it to disqualify him. If I am right, and I believe I am, this "*fleshy development*" never existed in the first place and it acted as a safety net for Condon to protect the Kidnappers' true identity from police.

To continue on this line of thought, Condon also made the claim that John's "*pronunciation of the word "perfect" was unusually noticeable in that "John" is alleged to have pronounced this word as "perfet"*" giving him yet another unique characteristic by which to identify (or not identify) him.[300]

The Departure

As we examine more of the conversation on this bench between Condon and John we learn that John claimed to be from "*Boston.*"[301]

---

[300] Cullen, T. F. Special Agent In Charge DOI (FBI). <u>Letter from T. F. Cullen to Director (J. Edgar Hoover)</u>. September 12 1933. New Jersey State Police Museum and Learning Center Archives.

[301] Condon, John F. Statement. Made to Assistant District Attorney Edward F. Breslin. May 14, 1932. New Jersey State Police Museum and Learning Center Archives.

The child was being kept on a boat and it would take "*six hours to get in touch with them and six more hours to make a getaway.*"[302] John said he could signal the boat from shore, "*and when I wave my handkerchief, they stop and I go aboard.*"[303] It was for this reason, supposedly, that there could be no "one for one" trade of the baby and ransom. So a compromise was struck. By all accounts John agreed to send the child's sleeping suit as proof they indeed had possession of the child.[304] At the end of this very long meeting, the men parted ways and John disappeared into the darkness.

[302] Ibid.

[303] Ibid.

[304] Condon, Dr. John F. Statement. Made to Inspector Harry W. Walsh. May 13, 1932. New Jersey State Police Museum and Learning Center Archives.

Woodlawn Cemetery Gate (Where Condon first met Cemetery John)
(Courtesy NJSP Museum)

Depicting how Cemetery John appeared to Condon when they met
(Courtesy NJSP Museum)

3

Suspicious Events and Strange Encounters

During the negotiations, Condon *"made it a practice to admit to the house anyone who came there hoping for some sort of a contact."*[305] Sometime after the Woodlawn Cemetery meeting, but before the Saint Raymond's Cemetery rendezvous, two separate men visited Condon's home.

The Needle Salesman

One such visitor to the home was a "Needle" Salesman. Like everything else, there are several versions of this visit.

Henry Breckinridge's Version

Breckinridge claimed that after the Woodlawn meeting but before the sleeping suit was received, he was sitting on the couch in the front

---

[305] Breckinridge, Henry. Memorandum. re: Needle-seller and Scissor-grinder. December 8, 1933. New Jersey State Police Museum and Learning Center Archives.

room of the Condon home when someone approached the door and *"looked in both directions,"* appearing *"nervous"* before he rang the bell.[306] This man was *"in his early forties,"* an *"Italian"* standing at *"5 feet 7 or 8 inches"* and *"shaven but with a dark beard – one of those dark Italian complexions with the face covered with small visible red veins."*[307] He was *"wearing gold rimmed spectacles,"* had on a *"felt hat,"* a *"dark overcoat with velvet collar,"* and was also *"wearing gloves."*[308] While he noticed these clothes were *"shabby"* the man was not *"unkempt."* This man said he was there to peddle needles and *"complained of hard times."* Condon and Breckinridge told the man they would buy a package and invited him in.[309] As Breckinridge started to pay him fifteen cents, Condon instead gave him a quarter. It was at this point Breckinridge noticed the man acting *"peculiar"* by not removing his gloves while he *"fumbled around in his vest pocket, took out some change and gave the Doctor back a dime."*[310] Breckinridge said this man's *"demeanor seemed to me to be furtive"* and once he left the house, Breckinridge watched as the man departed toward Bedford Park Blvd, *"accosted one passing woman and then proceeded out of the street."*[311] Breckinridge *"often"* stated to police that he was *"suspicious"* of this man.[312] In fact, he added the following to his memorandum about the encounter:

---

[306] Ibid.

[307] Ibid.

[308] Ibid.

[309] Ibid.

[310] Ibid.

[311] Ibid.

[312] Sisk, T. H. Special Agent, Division of Investigation. Memorandum for the Director. <u>Unknown subjects Kidnapping and murder of Charles A. Lindbergh, Jr.</u> June 23, 1934. National Archives at College Park Maryland.

"The needle seller more or less fit the description given by Al Reich of the man he saw hovering around Dr. Condon's first meeting at Woodlawn Cemetery."[313]

FBI Summary Report

The only real difference in the Summary Report from Breckinridge's account is that it says the Needle Salesman was *"25 years of age."*[314] The other point was that this man *"walked off the block entirely without making any effort to sell needles at neighboring houses"* which of course agrees with Breckinridge's Memo although he did not specifically emphasize it there.[315] From the context it appears their information is coming from both Condon and Breckinridge.

John Condon's Version

On March 6, 1934, Special Agent Seykora interviewed Dr. Condon concerning the Needle Salesman who called his house *"on or about March 15th, 1932."*[316] Condon *"described"* this man as follows: *"Age about 27, 5'5", stocky build, dark hair, dark eyes, apparently Italian, Peculiarities: Poorly dressed."*[317]

---

[313] Breckinridge, Henry. Memorandum. re: Needle-seller and Scissorgrinder. December 8, 1933. New Jersey State Police Museum and Learning Center Archives.

[314] Sisk, T. H. DOI (FBI) et. al., DOI Report. Summary. NY File No. 62-3057, p. 177. February 16, 1934. National Archives at College Park Maryland.

[315] Ibid.

[316] Seykora, J. E. Special Agent, DOI. DOI Report. Kidnaping and Murder of Charles A. Lindbergh, Jr. March 8, 1934. New Jersey State Police Museum and Learning Center Archives.

[317] Ibid.

"Dr. Condon stated that this needle salesman could possibly be the same man as the suspected "lookout" at Woodlawn Cemetery although he did not recognize him as such when he saw him."[318]

During April 2nd thru the 4th, 1934, Special Agents Sisk and O'Leary were following up a lead that required they learn more about the Needle Vendor. In his report Sisk wrote:

"It is pointed out that during the ransom negotiations, in the Lindbergh case, an unknown individual called at the Condon residence and under rather suspicious circumstances, sold someone in the house a package of needles. There is a possibility that this needle vendor might have been a lookout or scout for the kindapers [sic]."[319]

They stopped at the Condon residence to interview him concerning the Needle Salesman. During this interview:

"Dr. and Mrs. Condon stated that neither of them were at home when the needle vendor called; however, that Myra Condon Hacker, their daughter, was the one who went to the door and purchased the needles and that Colonel Breckinridge was also present in the front room at the time, but did not go to the door."[320]

So while both Breckinridge and Condon himself said he was there, at this latest interview he now claimed he was not. How then could

[318] Ibid.

[319] Sisk, T. H. Special Agent, DOI. USBOI Report. Unknown Subjects. Kidnaping and Murder of Charles A. Lindbergh, Jr. April 6, 1934. New Jersey State Police Museum and Learning Center Archives.

[320] Ibid.

he make any comparison of this man or offer any description if he never even saw him? Which version is true? Is Breckinridge lying? If so why?

Myra Condon Hacker's Version

Once interviewed, Myra told Sisk and O'Leary that both she and Breckinridge were sitting in the front room "*about two weeks before the ransom was paid*" and were "*talking about the case when the bell rang*" causing her to get up and answer the door.[321] There stood a man "*holding a single package of needles in his hand*" and asked if she wanted to buy them:

> "*Mrs. Hacker stated that the man seemed to be appraising her so intently and also seemed to be peering into the house, that she became suspicious and told him to wait just a minute and then she went in and talked to Colonel Breckinridge, who in the meanwhile was peering through the window at the man. Colonel Breckinridge suggested that she buy needles from the man, but make him give her some change. She went back to the door and handed the man twenty-five cents. Her recollection was that the needles were fifteen cents, which necessitated him giving her ten cents change. Mrs. Hacker stated that the man seemed "stunned and surprised" and not prepared to make change; however, that he fumbled around in his lower right hand vest pocket with his right hand and finally gave her ten cents changes.*"[322]

---

[321]   Ibid.
[322]   Ibid.

She described him as *"well dressed, with nice clothes, and did not in any way resemble the different peddlers and vendors she had been in the habit of seeing."* She did not recall exactly how he was dressed except that she believed he wore a soft felt hat, a dark overcoat under which was a black suit and tie. They appeared *"fairly expensive and bore no evidence of wear."*[323] She said this man *"positively was not an Italian but a German or Austrian,"* had no foreign accent, and *"was about fifty years of age"* but not any younger. He wore gloves and she also noticed he kept his *"left arm"* held *"close to his side"* which she believed meant it was *"paralyzed"* or possibly a *"wooden arm"* and that he held his head slightly tilted to the right side.[324] Other observations she had were that his face was *"queer,"* but with considerable *"strength,"* sharp eyes, *"not a laboring man,"* impressed her as *"clever,"* the *"unusual"* type of individual and appeared like someone *"used to giving orders."*[325] Mrs. Hacker further stated:

> *"...the man had only the one package of needles in his hand. She stated that she can remember from past experience, that needle vendors usually have a little kit with them and several different varieties of needles and this man was the first who ever approached her in such a fashion, and with only the one package of needles under such circumstances. Mrs. Hacker further stated that she had always regarded this man with great suspicion, in fact, with more suspicion than anyone else she had seen since the case started. She stated she could not understand why no one had ever questioned her about this, as it was common knowledge to the police*

---

[323] Ibid.
[324] Ibid.
[325] Ibid.

and other investigating authorities that both the needle vendor and scissors grinder had been at the house."[326]

The Scissors Grinder

Another visitor to the Condon home on this day was made by a Scissors Grinder.

Henry Breckinridge's Version

Breckinridge claimed another encounter, *"on the same afternoon"* as the Needle Vendor visit, with a *"scissor grinder and umbrella mender"* who *"stopped in front of the house with his paraphernalia"* then *"came straight up to the door and rang the bell."*[327] Breckinridge *"answered the bell"* and:

> *"...gave him a pocket knife to sharpen and sent for Dr. Condon who brought out three table knives. Having completed his job and conversed a little, he went off down Decatur Avenue toward Bedford Park Boulevard, left Decatur Avenue and went to no other house on the block."*[328]

He described this man as an *"Italian"* who was possibly *"Sicilian"* somewhere between 21 and 23 years old, *"slender,"* and stood about *"5 ft. 6 or 7."* Both Condon and his wife mentioned to Breckinridge that they *"could not remember any scissor grinder or needle seller coming*

---

[326] Ibid.

[327] Breckinridge, Henry. Memorandum. re: Needle-seller and Scissor-grinder. December 8, 1933. New Jersey State Police Museum and Learning Center Archives.

[328] Ibid.

to their house" prior to that day and that *"none has come since."*[329] This is in agreement with what Condon told Agents Sisk and O'Leary during their visit in early April '34 that *"...in the year 1932 they were rather uncommon, and in fact, none of the Condon household could recall any needle salesmen having stopped at the house prior to the individual in question..."*.[330]

Among his final observations, Breckinridge wrote:

> *"I inferred that these two men were send-ins who came to look the place over and see if there were any police around and find out what was going on. They impressed me that I would recognize them immediately if I saw them."*[331]

FBI Summary Report

This report once again is mostly in agreement with the Breckinridge account. Something new is that it says the Scissors Grinder appeared at Dr. Condon's home *"about an hour after"* the Needle Salesman.[332] It confuses the accounts of who *"fumbled"* in the vest pocket for change attributing this action to the Scissors Grinder instead. It also complements Breckinridge's suspicion by explaining:

---

[329]   Ibid. (Note: Considering this memo was written on 12/8/33.)

[330]   Sisk, T. H. Special Agent, DOI. USBOI Report. Unknown Subjects. Kidnaping and Murder of Charles A. Lindbergh, Jr. April 6, 1934. New Jersey State Police Museum and Learning Center Archives.

[331]   Breckinridge, Henry. Memorandum. re: Needle-seller and Scissor-grinder. December 8, 1933. New Jersey State Police Museum and Learning Center Archives. (Note: "Two men" meaning the Scissor Grinder and Needle Salesman)

[332]   Sisk, T. H. DOI (FBI) et. al., DOI Report. Summary. NY File No. 62-3057, p. 177-8. February 16, 1934. National Archives at College Park Maryland.

> *"Colonel Breckinridge expressed an opinion either the needle vendor or the scissors grinder or both were emissaries of the kidnapers [sic] employed for the purpose of visiting Dr. Condon's house to determine whether there was a "plant" in the house and to determine accurately just how well the police were guarding the house."*[333]

The report continues by expressing the belief that Breckinridge's suspicions were a possibility.[334] But while the FBI may have believed this, Lt. Keaten expressed doubt by telling Sisk he *"could not feature the kidnaper [sic] openly going to the Condon residence."*[335]

John Condon's Version

On March 6, 1934, during the same investigation made by Special Agent Seykora concerning the Needle Salesman, he interviewed Dr. Condon concerning the Scissors Grinder. Condon told Seykora this man was *"about 45 years of age"* and *"apparently Italian"* but that he should interview *"Colonel Breckinridge"* for a *"more complete"* description.[336] Condon added that *"about two weeks ago"* there was another *"scissors grinder"* who came to his home and that *"it may have been the same one that called before, although he is not certain."*[337]

---

[333]   Ibid. Page 178.

[334]   Ibid.

[335]   Sisk, T. H. Special Agent, Division of Investigation. Memorandum for the Director. Unknown subjects Kidnapping and murder of Charles A. Lindbergh, Jr. June 23, 1934. National Archives at College Park Maryland.

[336]   Seykora, J. E. Special Agent, DOI. DOI Report. Kidnaping and Murder of Charles A. Lindbergh, Jr. March 8, 1934. New Jersey State Police Museum and Learning Center Archives.

[337]   Ibid.

On April 3, 1934, Special Agent O'Leary interviewed Condon with the intent, among other things, to get a better description of the Scissors Grinder. Although Condon could not place the exact time of this visit, he did tell O'Leary he was *"quite sure that it was before the visit of the needle vendor."*[338] Despite the cloudy memory concerning this man only a month earlier, this time Condon had a lot to offer. He described him as follows:

> *"Age 38–42, 5'8", 150 or less, medium build, Weather beaten complexion, dark hair, Mid-European; possibly an Austrian, Hungarian or Italian, no accent noticed. Peculiarities Very stoop-shouldered as if in the scissor grinding business for some years. This man wore a long dark overcoat, either black or dark blue and a soft felt hat."*[339]

Condon explained that this man was passing by his house when he, desirous of having a *"pocket knife sharpened,"* *"went out and stopped the scissors grinder and that the man would not have stopped at the house otherwise."*[340] This new version of events went even further:

> *"Dr. Condon stated that he is convinced that this man actually was a scissors grinder and that when he had the knife sharpened, the man appeared to know his business thoroughly. Dr. Condon state that he judged this by the way the man operated the foot treadle of the grinding machine and by the way he held the knife from the grinding wheel, and that upon the completion*

---

[338] O'Leary, J. M. Special Agent, DOI. DOI Report. <u>Kidnaping and Murder of Charles A. Lindbergh, Jr.</u> April 5, 1934. New Jersey State Police Museum and Learning Center Archives.

[339] Ibid.

[340] Ibid.

of the grinding, the man tested the knife upon his thumb as if he knew what he was doing."[341]

Condon offered even more by giving specific details about the man and his equipment:

> "*The grinding outfit was old and apparently had been in use for some years. It contained a large and a small grinding wheel, operated by a foot treadle. The outfit was painted blue and the man pushed it along in front of him. Apparently the outfit was equipped with wheels. Dr. Condon states that he spoke to this man and that although the man was very reticent, he did reply and Dr. Condon noticed at the time that the man spoke without any noticeable accent and he gathered from this that the man must have been in this country for some years."*[342]

Finally, Sisk interviewed Condon again in June 1934. It was during this interview he asked about the Scissors Grinder who came to his house in the middle of March 1932. Condon stated he could not remember the exact date and that this man:

> "*...did not come up to the house voluntarily but that he, Condon, happened to be standing in front of his residence when the grinder happened along and he thereupon invited him in to sharpen some knives. Dr. Condon stated that the man did not appear suspicious to him...*"[343]

---

[341] Ibid.

[342] Ibid.

[343] Sisk, T. H. Special Agent, DOI. USBOI Report. <u>Kidnaping and Murder of Charles A. Lindbergh Jr</u>. June 26, 1934. New Jersey State Police Museum and Learning Center Archives.

Condon gave a description of this man to include that he was *"Italian,"* 40 years old, of a *"stout"* build, 150lbs., black hair, dark skin, *"medium length arms; left arm held close to side,"* dark suit, dark overcoat, ragged clothes, grey fedora hat, and a *"stooped"* carriage.[344]

Once again, if Breckinridge isn't telling the truth what's his motivation? And if Condon is — which version is true and which is not?

Regarding his latest version it is irresistible not to conclude Condon was borrowing a trait given by his daughter to the Agents concerning the Needle Salesman. This time, though, the tightly held left arm belonged to a different man. What I see here is a consistent pattern of lies, distractions, and misdirections given by Condon to authorities with his daughter, Myra, possibly attempting to protect him. *"My father will think as I think and say as I say"* she would be quoted "snapping" off sometime later.[345]

Now, if anyone is to be believed about these events it can only be Breckinridge.

The Sleeping Suit

On March 16, 1932, a package arrived by mail at Condon's home.[346] Condon testified in Flemington that it had been placed on top of his mailbox.[347] What are the actual facts? All the accounts about this

---

[344] Ibid.

[345] Gardner, Lloyd C. June 2004. *The Case That Never Dies*. Rutgers University Press. Page 375.

[346] Breckinridge, Henry. <u>Memorandum.</u> (Attached to letter from Henry Breckinridge to Colonel H. Norman Schwarzkopf). August 29, 1932. New Jersey State Police Museum and Learning Center Archives.

[347] Condon, John F. Testimony. The State of New Jersey vs. Bruno Richard Hauptmann, <u>Hunterdon County Court of Oyer and Terminer</u>, page 758, 1935. New Jersey State Law Library.

situation seem to differ on almost every point. Condon told ADA Breslin that this package came on *"Tuesday about 10:00 o'clock; that is, the 10:00 o'clock mail in the morning."*[348] Tuesday fell on the 15th. Six days later he testified that it came *"in the morning, 10:40..."*[349] By the time of his Flemington testimony, the time became 10:30 AM, so it's somewhat of a safe bet it came around that time. On May 13th, Condon told Inspector Walsh that after the brown parcel came: *"...I opened it and a sleeping suit was wrapped up and inside"* and that he *"...sent for Colonel Breckenridge [sic]...".*[350] Importantly, Condon gave a similar account to Breslin the very next day:

> *"The sleeping suit was rolled up in the package and I opened it out and I sent word to Colonel Lindbergh and to Colonel Breckenridge [sic] as I had promised, in case anything come [sic] up."*[351]

The only difference here seems to be that in one account it is hard to know where Breckinridge was, but in the next he appears to clear this up by implying neither were present at the time. The problem is that Breckinridge was present. In fact, he testified that:

> *"When that package came I directed the doctor not to touch it and then with gloves we opened the package because I wanted it preserved in case it might have*

---

[348] Condon, John F. Statement. Made to Assistant District Attorney Edward F. Breslin. May 14, 1932. New Jersey State Police Museum and Learning Center Archives.

[349] Condon, John F. Testimony. <u>Bronx Grand Jury</u>. May 20, 1932. New Jersey State Police Museum and Learning Center Archives.

[350] Condon, Dr. John F. Statement. Made to Inspector Harry W. Walsh. May 13, 1932. New Jersey State Police Museum and Learning Center Archives.

[351] Condon, John F. Statement. Made to Assistant District Attorney Edward F. Breslin. May 14, 1932. New Jersey State Police Museum and Learning Center Archives.

*finger prints somewhere on it and then Colonel
Lindbergh was informed that we had the package and
it was delivered to him."*[352]

According to Coleman's *Vigil*, Condon showed him the "*baby's
coverall sleeping garment*" in the afternoon, and "*Col. Breckinridge
had described the garment over the telephone to Colonel Lindbergh...*"
when it was originally "*...suggested that the garment could be brought to
him, but he insisted that he would call himself.*"[353] Sabotaging any hope
of clarification on the matter, Condon testified in Flemington that
both Lindbergh and Breckinridge were "*present*" when he opened
the large brown envelope containing sleeping suit in his parlor.[354]
But how could this be? According to Condon's own testimony in
the Bronx on May 20, 1932, Lindbergh did not arrive to his home
until that "*evening.*"[355] That would mean they didn't open it until
much later. But how could Condon show Coleman this suit in the
afternoon? Furthermore, if this package arrived around 10:30 AM,
why did it take Lindbergh so long to arrive to inspect it? And apply
this point in spades once considering that *Vigil* claims Lindbergh
did not even leave his home until "*shortly before 11:00 o'clock on
Wednesday night*" and it wasn't until 1:30 AM Thursday morning
that he arrived with Captain William Galvin as they "*hurried up the*

---

[352] Breckenridge, Colonel Henry. Testimony. <u>Bronx Grand Jury</u>. May 17, 1932. New Jersey State Police Museum and Learning Center Archives.

[353] Coleman, Gregory F. *Vigil*. Unpublished Manuscript. Page 25. Undated (circa 1932). New Jersey State Police Museum and Learning Center Archives.

[354] Condon, John F. Testimony. The State of New Jersey vs. Bruno Richard Hauptmann, <u>Hunterdon County Court of Oyer and Terminer</u>, page 634, 1935. New Jersey State Law Library. (Note: Exhibit S-53)

[355] Condon, John F. Testimony. Bronx Grand Jury. May 20, 1932. New Jersey State Police Museum and Learning Center Archives.

steps" to Condon's home.[356] Why hurry now? It was nearly 15 hours after the package was received! Coleman explained the reason for the delay was caused by the fact that "*his every move was observed by the large army of newspapermen*" and it wasn't until that time he could "*succeed in getting away.*"[357] In any event, during Condon's redirect by Wilentz he, as he often did, disagreed with himself. Here he was asked once again who was present when the package was opened. This time he could only remember "*Colonel Breckinridge.*"[358] This prompted a leading question from the AG causing Condon to agree that his daughter, Myra, was also there at the time.[359] Also during the Flemington trial, Breckinridge (once again) testified that he was present when the package arrived.[360] Interestingly, this was also brought out during his testimony:

Q: "*Who was present when that package was opened?*"

A: "*Dr. Condon, Mr. Ralph Hacker, and myself.*"

Q: "*Was it opened in your presence?*"

A: "*It was, sir.*"[361]

---

[356] Coleman, Gregory F. *Vigil.* Unpublished Manuscript. Page 28. Undated (circa 1932). New Jersey State Police Museum and Learning Center Archives.

[357] Ibid.

[358] Condon, John F. Testimony. The State of New Jersey vs. Bruno Richard Hauptmann, <u>Hunterdon County Court of Oyer and Terminer</u>, page 814, 1935. New Jersey State Law Library.

[359] Ibid.

[360] Breckinridge, Henry. Testimony. The State of New Jersey vs. Bruno Richard Hauptmann, <u>Hunterdon County Court of Oyer and Terminer</u>, page 825, 1935. New Jersey State Law Library.

[361] Ibid. Page 826.

Is this a "typo" in the trial transcripts, or was Breckinridge claiming Condon's son-in-law was there?

Next to the stand was Condon's daughter Myra. She testified that she was there when the package arrived "*around ten-thirty.*"[362] She also testified that along with Breckinridge and her father, she was present when the package was opened.[363] When asked what time Lindbergh arrived, she replied: "*Well, I couldn't say – a few hours.*"[364]

How Many Notes?

A mystery first brought up in Dr. Lloyd Gardner's book *The Case That Never Dies* was the question as to how many notes were inside of the package containing the sleeping suit.[365] One thing that is known with certainty is there was one note with writing on both sides.[366] Gardner suggests there may have been a phone call to Condon a few days before receiving the package, and that call could possibly have later confused the issue.[367] Were there two notes, a note and a call, or just one note? Over the years I have accumulated just about everything I believe there is to find in order to properly evaluate this situation.

[362] Hacker, Myra Condon. Testimony. The State of New Jersey vs. Bruno Richard Hauptmann, <u>Hunterdon County Court of Oyer and Terminer</u>, page 849, 1935. New Jersey State Law Library

[363] Ibid. Page 846.

[364] Ibid.

[365] Gardner, Lloyd C. June 2004. *The Case That Never Dies.* Rutgers University Press. Page 69.

[366] Exhibit S-52. New Jersey State Police Museum and Learning Center Archives.

[367] Gardner, Lloyd C. June 2004. *The Case That Never Dies.* Rutgers University Press. Page 69-70.

The first thing I have done is completely disregard any notion there was a phone call on March 14th. The fact is there is nothing about such a call from any source, official or otherwise, outside of Condon's *Liberty* Articles from which his book *Jafsie Tells All!* was later created.[368] In fact, Condon told ADA Breslin that after Woodlawn, he "*did not hear from him again*" until he received the sleeping suit package.[369] So what is mentioned, as well as what I've previously outlined, shows if such a call was made then Condon would have brought it up at some point to police. If it did occur, and he chose not to inform anyone, then he was concealing it which makes no sense. Next, we must examine what Condon said, and when, in order to get to the bottom of this. In his May 13th statement he told Inspector Walsh that "*…I opened it and a sleeping suit was wrapped up and inside the sleeping suit was a note telling me it was Baby Lindbergh's sleeping suit.*"[370] In trying to tie Condon in to definitely saying there was "only" <u>one</u> note in that package, this falls short. The next source is the May 14th statement and one that Dr. Gardner also mentions in his book. Here I wanted to look at what Condon said a little more closely…. Condon said that package came "*…and the letter addressed to me was on the inside.*" According to Condon this letter said:

> "*This is Colonel Lindbergh's baby's sleeping suit I talked to you about; I don't think there will be any*

---

[368] Condon, Dr. John F. "Jafsie & the sleeping suit." *Liberty Magazine.* February 8, 1936. New Jersey State Police Museum and Learning Center Archives.

[369] Condon, John F. Statement. Made to Assistant District Attorney Edward F. Breslin. May 14, 1932. New Jersey State Police Museum and Learning Center Archives.

[370] Condon, Dr. John F. Statement. Made to Inspector Harry W. Walsh. May 13, 1932. New Jersey State Police Museum and Learning Center Archives.

doubt about that; send it to Colonel Lindbergh and tell him the longer he delays, the amount will be bigger."[371]

As Dr. Gardner wrote, this is different from what was written in the *"actual note."*[372] It appears to me that, in the event it is not a different and separate note he was attempting to recollect, it could be a quick summary of the March 16th note, combined with both the March 21st and 29th notes. However, if we move on to a further point in this statement Condon also stated:

"Then it was arranged that Colonel Lindbergh would come to my house; he came and took supper, and after supper I showed him that sleeping suit and the letters; he asked if he might take that with him, and I said, "Colonel Lindbergh, it is your baby; I want to help you in any way I can"; and he seemed pleased."[373]

Here he says *"letters"* which clearly shows he's talking about more than one. However, six days later during the Bronx Grand Jury, Condon testified that *"the following Tuesday there is that time I am not positive about that a large brown rough wrapping paper with a package and a letter on the inside."* Condon claimed to have read the letter first, then *"...opened that and saw that it was a little baby's sleeping suit."* This letter read, or as Condon put it *"words to that effect"*:

[371]   Condon, John F. Statement. Made to Assistant District Attorney Edward F. Breslin. May 14, 1932. New Jersey State Police Museum and Learning Center Archives.
[372]   Gardner, Lloyd C. June 2004. The Case That Never Dies. Rutgers University Press. Page 69.
[373]   Condon, John F. Statement. Made to Assistant District Attorney Edward F. Breslin. May 14, 1932. New Jersey State Police Museum and Learning Center Archives.

"I promised you this sleeping suit of the baby. Col. Lindbergh will now pay. See that he gets it."[374]

It is beginning to appear that Condon claimed only one letter was inside of this package. He does it in his testimony again here:

Q: *You indicated before, a few days after that you received in the mail a sleeping garment together with a letter?*

A: *Yes.*[375]

Once again this seems to be further proof that Condon was claiming there was only one letter inside of this package. What came next is puzzling. There was a volley of questions concerning where all of the notes in this case had gone. One question in particular seemed to come out of left field:

Q: *You didn't retain possession any* [sic] *of the communications?*

A: *I didn't retain any of these. I wrapped them up and handed them to Col. Breckenridge* [sic]*, he was Col. Lindbergh's representative.*[376]

At this point, the mystery appears to have been solved, and the confusion seems to have come from Condon's usual contradictions or "mistakes." But nothing ever goes as it should. In a letter written by SAC Connelley to J. Edgar Hoover regarding a ransom note evidence review on June 23, 1932, he noted the following:

---

[374] Condon, John F. Testimony. Bronx Grand Jury. May 20, 1932. New Jersey State Police Museum and Learning Center Archives.
[375] Ibid.
[376] Ibid.

> *"Apparently there was another note enclosed with
> the sleeping suit which does not seem to have been
> submitted to Mr. Osborn and according to the Bronx
> Home News story this note read in substance as follows:*

>> *"Mr. Lindbergh will find ouer program in enclosed
>> letter. If you are willing you may confer with Mr.
>> Lindberg [sic] about it."*[377]

Oddly enough, on June 22, 1932, Condon was being transported
to Newark Headquarters to view "Rogues Gallery" photos by Sgt.
Moffatt of that department along with Corporal Horn of the New
Jersey State Police. During this ride the men were surprised to hear
a new story come from Condon who was in the back seat where
he began to talk about *"a mysterious note that was left at his home
previous to paying the Ransom money."*[378]

> *"He stated that on this occasion, himself and Al Reich
> were in his home one evening when the doorbell rang.
> He said that Reich was looking out a front window and
> he was standing in the hallway looking out the door
> which was closed, when the doorbell rang, Condon
> immediately opened the front door and stepped out on
> the porch but could see no one in sight. He also stated*

---

[377] Connelley, E. J. Special Agent in Charge, Bureau of Investigation. Letter from E. J. Connelly to Director Re: Kidnaping and Murder of Charles A. Lindbergh Jr. June 23, 1932. National Archives at College Park Maryland.

[378] Moffatt, Warren T. Sgt., Newark Police Department and Horn, William F. Cpl., New Jersey State Police. New Jersey State Police Report. Conversation with Dr. John F. Condon in the presence of Maurice Silken, residence 15 Wadsworth Avenue, Bronx, N.Y. on June 6th, 1932 at Audubon Avenue and 181st Street, New York City. July 8, 1932. New Jersey State Police Museum and Learning Center Archives.

that he looked for an automobile but could not see any. Upon looking down at the door mat he saw a piece of paper and picked up same and entered the house where he read the note and found it to be a note from the Lindbergh Baby kidnapers [sic]. *Condon said he was so surprised at this occurance he could not understand how anyone could get upon the front porch to leave this note and ring the bell without Al Reich or himself seeing them.*"[379]

A few months later, on October 13, 1932, Lt. Keaten placed a call to Lindbergh. It was during this call that it was revealed there had been a *"missing"* ransom note. Lindbergh informed him that he had *"received"* the missing note and if he would come down to the Morrow Estate he could pick it up.[380] Keaten added:

"(This note was mailed on March 16th, 1932 when Dr. Condon received the Denten [sic] *suit worn by Charles A. Lindbergh, Jr. at the time he was kidnaped* [sic]. *This note was supposed to have been enclosed in this package, and had later disappeared.)"*[381]

The report mentions that Keaten would be turning this note over to Col. Schwarzkopf who in turn would send it to *"Dr. Osborn"* so that he could compare it to the other ransom notes.[382] Judging

---

[379] Ibid.

[380] Keaten, Arthur T. Lieut., New Jersey State Police. New Jersey State Police Report. <u>Investigation by Lieut. Arthur T. Keaten Concerning the Kidnaping and Murder of Charles A. Lindbergh, Jr. of Hopewell, N. J. on the night of March 1st, 1932 between the hours of 8-00 P. M. and 10-00 P. M.</u> October 13, 1932. New Jersey State Police Museum and Learning Center Archives.

[381] Ibid.

[382] Ibid.

from the correspondence, Lt. Snook, who ran the State Bureau of Identification within the New Jersey State Police at that time, contacted Osborn Sr. and it appears this *"ransom note"* was delivered to Osborn on October 19th to be examined.[383]

As mentioned in Dr. Gardner's book, the situation did not end there, and he cites a NJSP report that is in my possession.[384] And so five days later Cpl. Leon and Cpl. Horn, as was the custom, went to Condon's home to show him photographs of various suspects in an attempt to identify Cemetery John. While there, Condon had blurted out that he recently turned over a ransom note to Col. Breckinridge to be given to Col. Lindbergh.[385] In order for the reader to properly understand Condon's tactics, it is necessary for me to quote the confusing story in its totality as reported by these officers:

> *"That at the time that he received the Baby's Sleeping Garmet* [sic] *from the alleged kidnapers* [sic]*, he also received a note which asked in effect, 'Did you Got the note which was thrown in your garden?' Dr. Condon stated that he looked in his garden and all in back of his house but failed to find the note. About five weeks ago he received in the mail, a note containing the same symbols used on the other ransom notes, and he*

---

[383] Osborn, Albert S. Letter from A. S. Osborn to Lieut. R. A. Snook. October 17, 1932. New Jersey State Police Museum and Learning Center Archives.

[384] Gardner, Lloyd C. June 2004. *The Case That Never Dies*. Rutgers University Press. Page 132.

[385] Leon, Samuel J. Cpl. And Horn, William F. Cpl., New Jersey State Police. New Jersey State Police Report. Memorandum of story told to the undersigned by Dr. John F. Condon in reference to Ransom note that was supposed to be with the Lindbergh Baby's sleeping garmet previous to the payment of the Ransom money. October 18, 1932. New Jersey State Police Museum and Learning Center Archives.

> *understands that this was the same note, mentioned in*
> *the note he received with the Baby's Sleeping Garmet*
> *[sic], but that same was not thrown in his garden but*
> *on his front lawn.*"[386]

Although not specified in Lt. Keaten's report, this shows that Condon was the obvious source of the missing ransom note which he had picked up from Lindbergh at the Morrow Estate. But what's to be made of this? Was this note the one which would later be exhibit S–52, or was it the mysterious second note that had been in the Sleeping Suit package? And, as Dr. Gardner pointed out, what about this new note Condon described by Horn & Leon? These investigators must have been completely dumbfounded. They concluded:

> "*The above story is not quite clear to the undersigned,*
> *due to the fact that we do not understand how Dr.*
> *Condon knows that the note he received about five*
> *weeks ago, is the same one that was supposed to have*
> *been thrown in his garden, and which he now claims*
> *was thrown on his front lawn. We did not clear this*
> *thing up because we did not wish to cause Dr. Condon*
> *to become alarmed by questioning him.*"[387]

However, Cpl. Leon would interview Condon again in June of 1934. Although the confusing situation above is not mentioned, we do see, once again, that Condon was claiming there were two notes inside of the sleeping suit package:

> "*A few days after this I received a package through*
> *the mail with the baby's sleeping garment in same*

---

[386]   Ibid.

[387]   Ibid.

and two notes, which garment was identified by Col. Lindbergh as that which the baby wore."[388]

It was only a couple of days prior to this interview that Lt. Keaten specifically told Special Agent Sisk that:

"...Dr. Condon kept one of the original ransom notes for eight months after he received it unknown to the State Police; that when they found out about it and asked him why he retained the note, he stated that he did not know he had it; that he had discovered it out in the bushes in front of his house."[389]

Neither of the investigators believed the explanation and they speculated that he may have kept the note as a *"souvenir of the case."*[390]

Is there any evidence in Condon's Flemington testimony which clears any of this up? Hardly. Under direct examination Condon was asked about what this package contained and he responded: *"The baby's sleeping suit, with two letters."*[391] Ensuring that this was no slip of the tongue or mistake of any kind we see Condon continued with this

---

[388] Leon, Samuel J. Cpl. New Jersey State Police. New Jersey State Police Report. The following is the result of an interview with Dr. John F. Condon at his home at 2974 Decatur Avenue, Bronx, N.Y., as to how the kidnappers of the Lindbergh Baby knew his name and address when he signed his name "Jafsie". June 26, 1934. New Jersey State Police Museum and Learning Center Archives.

[389] Sisk, T. H. Special Agent, Division of Investigation. Memorandum for the Director. Unknown subjects Kidnapping and murder of Charles A. Lindbergh, Jr. June 23, 1934. National Archives at College Park Maryland.

[390] Ibid.

[391] Condon, John F. Testimony. The State of New Jersey vs. Bruno Richard Hauptmann, Hunterdon County Court of Oyer and Terminer, page 633, 1935. New Jersey State Law Library.

assertion under cross examination. Reilly asked Condon whether there were one or two notes inside of the sleeping suit package to which Condon replied: "*Two, two.*"[392] Since one of those notes had been entered into evidence (S–52), Reilly inquired as to "where" the second note was. It was not in Court and no one seemed to know where it was. For the first time, this very exchange led to a more detailed explanation: "...*One was addressed to Colonel Lindbergh and one was addressed to me.*"[393] After examining S–52 Condon claimed that was the note which was addressed to him, but the one addressed to Lindbergh had been "*within the package in which the sleeping suit was folded.*" When asked how he knew that letter had been addressed to Lindbergh Condon replied, "*Because I opened the package and it was inside the package with the sleeping suit*" and as best he could remember it was addressed "*Colonel Lindbergh.*"[394] Condon claimed he left the note in the open package on top of his piano, and that he had "*never seen it since.*"[395] In fact, he testified that Lindbergh specifically took away "*both*" of the ransom notes included in that package.[396] If true, what note did he turn over to Breckinridge sometime in October 1932? If what Lt. Keaten wrote in his report is true, then Condon is perjuring himself.

One could assume calling Breckinridge to the stand might clear this up. If so, they would assume wrong. Under direct examination the following exchange occurred:

> Q: *And when it was opened in your presence what was found there?*

---

[392] Ibid. Page 759.
[393] Ibid.
[394] Ibid.
[395] Ibid. Page 760.
[396] Ibid. Page 764.

A: *There was found in it the sleeping garment of the baby and at least one letter.*[397]

Who answers a question in this way unless they are uncertain as to what they saw once the packaged was opened? But was that the case?

Q: *And one letter that you remember?*

A: *Yes, sir.*

Q: *Do you recollect whether there was any other note besides the one letter?*

A: *I do not.*

Q: *Whatever it was that was in that package when it was opened you saw, did you not?*

A: *Yes, sir.*

Q: *And whatever it was that was in there and which you saw, what happened to it? To whom was it delivered?*

A: *To Colonel Lindbergh.*[398]

This exchange is quite amazing. Wilentz disproves his own witness's testimony while leading the trail to Lindbergh. On that path it essentially dead-ends the issue without any harm to Condon.

---

[397] Breckinridge, Henry. Testimony. The State of New Jersey vs. Bruno Richard Hauptmann, <u>Hunterdon County Court of Oyer and Terminer</u>, page 826, 1935. New Jersey State Law Library.

[398] Ibid.

However, all of this is undone once Condon's daughter Myra came to the stand next.

> Q: *Was there or was there not a note in there?*
>
> A: *Yes, sir.*
>
> Q: *Have you any recollection as to whether it was one or two notes.*
>
> A: *(No answer.)*
>
> Q: *Give us your best recollection.*
>
> A: *My best recollection is that there were two notes.*
>
> Q: *That is your best recollection?*
>
> A: *Yes, sir.*[399]

How does Wilentz solve this problem? He engages in the exact same tactic he used with Breckinridge…

> Q: *Whatever was in that package, what was done with it – notes, package, and all?*
>
> A: *It was completely turned over to Colonel Lindbergh, when he arrived.*[400]

Unfortunately, we are no closer to the truth with this testimony, are we? Whatever was in that package, it seems clear to me from

---

[399] Hacker, Myra Condon. Testimony. The State of New Jersey vs. Bruno Richard Hauptmann, <u>Hunterdon County Court of Oyer and Terminer</u>, page 846, 1935. New Jersey State Law Library.

[400] Ibid.

everything referenced above that Myra did not remember – or may have never even known in the first place.

Was It Real?

The actual Sleeping Suit itself was a Dr. Denton #2 which was purchased *"some weeks before"* the kidnapping in NYC on Fifth Ave. at *"Altman's Department Store,"* and *"had been worn only a few times."*[401] Something that seems important to address is whether or not the Sleeping Suit was the actual garment the child had on when he was supposedly abducted. In Coleman's *Vigil*, the scene is described as follows:

> *"There was no time lost in presenting the sleeping garment to the Colonel, who inspected it minutely, and as Dr. Condon said, Lindbergh "noted the size, form, color and use like an adept in English composition." Tears came to the eyes of the distracted father as he inspected each button, put two fingers in the little pocket and then remarked: "This is my boy's dress." Almost shyly, Col. Lindbergh asked the Doctor whether he could have his own child's garment and in an effort to break the tension Dr. Condon remarked: "In the condition that 'Jafsie' is now, you can have the house." Col. Breckenridge then showed Lindbergh the latest letter from the kidnapers [sic]. Col. Lindbergh realized more than ever that "Jafsie" had established contact with the kidnapers [sic].*[402]

---

[401] Sisk, T. H. Special Agent, USBOI (FBI). Memorandum For The Director. Unknown Subjects Kidnapping and Murder of Charles A. Lindbergh, Jr. October 27, 1934. National Archives at College Park Maryland.

[402] Coleman, Gregory. *"Vigil."* Manuscript: Unpublished and Undated (1932?). Page 29. New Jersey State Police Museum and Learning Center Archives.

Obviously this account has been embellished but before the point is lost, Coleman clearly claims that Lindbergh identified the sleeping suit as authentic. So much so that it *"established"* that Condon was dealing with the real kidnappers. The side point is that Coleman mentions that Lindbergh was shown the *"latest letter"* which is yet another source for further confusion on this point. Also, there was Condon's statement to police that Lindbergh had *"identified the sleeping suit as that of his baby's, he asked me if he might take it with him, which he did"* which, minus all of the drama, is in agreement with what Coleman wrote.[403] In fact, combine this with what he said to Breslin on May 14th, along with what he told Cpl. Leon in June of '34, it all seems to agree rather nicely. Breckinridge's Grand Jury testimony also seemed to back up Condon's assertion. When asked if Lindbergh was *"definitely satisfied that was the identical sleeping garment"* he replied:

> *"As far as he could be he was, the literal statement of the fact would be that it was the exact counterpart of the sleeping garment which the baby had when taken including mark of the identification etc."*[404]

Unfortunately, nothing about any of Condon's stories ever fit nicely. On May 18, 1932, Colonel Schwarzkopf held a joint law enforcement conference that included both the Treasury Department and Department of Justice representatives. During this meeting, he informed the men that while the sleeping suit was a Doctor Denton's #2, same kind as the baby was wearing before he disappeared, *"there was nothing to positively identify it"* therefore, it was *"not accepted as*

---

[403] Condon, Dr. John F. Statement. Made to Inspector Harry W. Walsh. May 13, 1932. New Jersey State Police Museum and Learning Center Archives.

[404] Breckenridge, Colonel Henry. Testimony. <u>Bronx Grand Jury</u>. May 17, 1932. New Jersey State Police Museum and Learning Center Archives.

conclusive."[405] While in front of the Bronx Grand Jury Condon's testimony now seemed to follow Schwarzkopf's line of thought on this point:

> *"Yes, and I spilled it out on the piano and he looked*
> *at it for a while, and I think he became sadder in*
> *appearance, the face became more drawn and he said,*
> *"It looks like my son's garment."*[406]

On the very same day of Condon's testimony, Lindbergh gave an official statement to police. In it he says that Condon *"received a package containing a sleeping suit identical with the one worn by the baby when he was kidnaped* [sic]."[407] This statement seems to support Condon's original claim solidifying any question about it. However, during the Gaston Means trial Lindbergh completely clears this matter up. While under cross examination:

> [Tomlinson]: *"Was a piece of garment given to you?"*

> [Lindbergh]: *"Prior to that, a piece of garment had been returned."*

> [Q]: *"Did you identify it as being a part of your son's clothing?"*

> [A]: *"It was similar. In all probability it was the same."*

---

[405] New Jersey State Police Board of Strategy Meeting Minutes. Conference regarding the Lindbergh case held in the offices of Colonel H. Norman Schwarzkopf, Superintendent, New Jersey State Police. Page 8. May 18, 1932. New Jersey State Police Museum and Learning Center Archives.

[406] Condon, John F. Testimony. Bronx Grand Jury. May 20, 1932. New Jersey State Police Museum and Learning Center Archives.

[407] Lindbergh, Charles A. Statement. Made to Inspector Harry W. Walsh. May 20, 1932. New Jersey State Police Museum and Learning Center Archives.

[Q]: *"Are you entirely satisfied in your own mind about it?"*

[A]: *"Not without doubt. There is no question in my mind about the identity of the notes."*[408]

In the late summer of 1934, Lt. Keaten went over the scene and discussed the various pieces of evidence with Special Agent Sisk. It was during this time they reviewed the facts that concerned the discovery of the dead baby's remains. Keaten told Sisk that while the *"flannel garment made by Betty Gow"* was still on the corpse, the sleeping suit *"was gone."*[409] For what it's worth, the State used Anne Lindbergh to identify the sleeping suit (S-15) in Flemington:

[Q]: *"And it is the sleeping suit then that your son wore that night as he went to bed?"*

[A]: *"It is."*[410]

No hesitation. No qualifiers. And no doubt. It's an interesting bit of testimony.

---

[408] Lindbergh, Charles A. Testimony. United States of America vs. Gaston Bullock Means and Norman T. Whitaker, The Supreme Court of the District of Columbia. Criminal Division No. 2, Criminal No. 53134. Tuesday, May 9, 1933.

[409] Sisk, T. H. Special Agent, USBOI (FBI). Memorandum For The Director. Unknown Subjects Kidnapping and Murder of Charles A. Lindbergh, Jr. October 27, 1934. National Archives at College Park Maryland.

[410] Lindbergh, Anne Morrow. Testimony. The State of New Jersey vs. Bruno Richard Hauptmann, Hunterdon County Court of Oyer and Terminer, page 70, 1935. New Jersey State Law Library.

Forensic Reviews

With all of the screw-ups and bungling throughout this investigation, one of the things done right was the submission of certain pieces of evidence for scientific evaluations. The Sleeping Suit was one such item which was scrutinized in this way. In fact, it was inspected on three separate occasions.

E.R. Squibb & Sons

On May 16, 1932, Sgt. Kubler of the NJSP drove over to the Squibb Laboratory in New Brunswick, New Jersey, and dropped off several pieces of evidence including the "*baby's Denton sleeping suit*" to its director Dr. John F. Anderson for analysis.[411] The examination of this suit was made by H. A. Holaday and B. G. Thomas and revealed that the suit was in overall "*good condition*" and that it had been recently "*laundered*." There were "*no holes*" and they noted "*all buttons intact excepting left outside back button at hip pulled out with piece of fabric and piece from strip of cloth sewed under fabric as button reinforcement*."[412] Also interesting was "*seven out of the nine button holes show no evidence of having been used since the garment was washed*." Those holes that had a "*slight spread*" belonged to the "*center button hole back flap and third button hole from top in back*."[413] There were some stains found. A "*yellowish brown stain on the front of left shoulder immediately below neck band*," and three

---

[411]   Kubler, Louis E., Sgt. New Jersey State Police. New Jersey State Police Report. <u>Special Report</u>. May 16, 1932. New Jersey State Police Museum and Learning Center Archives.

[412]   Anderson, John F., M.D., Director, E. R. Squibb & Sons Biological Laboratories. <u>Letter from John F. Anderson to Colonel H. Norman Schwarzkopf</u>. May 27, 1932. New Jersey State Police Museum and Learning Center Archives. (Note: See Report IV attached to this letter)

[413]   Ibid.

more "*faint*" or "*small*" stains which were described as "*yellowish.*" They reported that "*none*" of those stains had the "*appearance of blood stains.*" Despite this, the yellowish-brown stain was cut away from the suit then:

> "...*submitted to Dr. Leonard who extracted the material with physiological salt solution and conducted tests for blood which were reported as negative.*"[414]

Chief Medical Examiner's Office Essex County, New Jersey

Similar to the 1932 Squibb examinations, NJSP officers drove up to Newark, New Jersey, at various times and dropped off several pieces of evidence to be evaluated by Doctor Albert E. Edel who worked in the Chemical and Toxicological Laboratory of the Chief Medical Examiner's Office in Essex County. Some of Dr. Edel's findings included that "*the garment shows wear and has a button missing.*"[415] In addition to noting it had "*been washed,*" another notable find was:

> "*The right sleeve has an impression 1 inch to 1 1/8 inch from the edge and running parallel to it. This impression was caused by some external force other than the normal wear of the garment.*"[416]

---

[414] Ibid.

[415] Edel, Dr. Albert E., Analytical Chemist. Chief Medical Examiner's Office, Essex County, New Jersey. Chemical And Toxicology Report. State of New Jersey VS. Bruno Richard Hauptmann, Case No. 7741. December 31, 1934. New Jersey State Police Museum and Learning Center Archives.

[416] Ibid.

New Jersey State Police
Central Laboratory
Forensic Science Bureau

In the Fall of 1976, the New Jersey State Police began a "review" of the Lindbergh Kidnapping evidence. Officially, "Phase I" began in April 1977 and was a "*forensic analysis of specimens pertinent to the identification of the body of Charles A. Lindbergh Jr.*"[417] Two examinations were made of the Sleeping Suit during phase one, both of which were made by Sr. Chemist Alan T. Lane. During the first, Lane inspected the suit for "*foreign material*" whereby "*macroscopic and low power microscopic examinations*" were made. The suit was found to be "*clean*" and "*no significant foreign material was recovered.*"[418] The second was a search specifically for the presence of blood. The sleeping suit was "*tested with luminal reagent, examined microscopically, and selected areas treated with benzidine*"; however, "*no blood was detected.*"[419] Their final position concerning their evidence review of S–15 was that "*there were no significant findings.*"[420]

[417] Peterson, Vincent M. Lt., New Jersey State Police. Forensic Science Bureau Report. Lindbergh Evidence Review. Phase I (April – June 1977). L77311932. Undated. New Jersey State Police Museum and Learning Center Archives.

[418] Lane, Alan T., Sr. Forensic Chemist. Department of Law and Public Safety, Division of State Police. Laboratory Report. Lindbergh Kidnap/Murder. Laboratory No. L77311932. May 25, 1977. New Jersey State Police Museum and Learning Center Archives.

[419] Lane, Alan T., Sr. Forensic Chemist. Department of Law and Public Safety, Division of State Police. Laboratory Report. Lindbergh Kidnap/Murder. Laboratory No. L77311932. May 26, 1977. New Jersey State Police Museum and Learning Center Archives.

[420] Peterson, Vincent M. Lt., New Jersey State Police. Special Report. Examination of Evidence Re: L77311932. March 17, 1978. New Jersey State Police Museum and Learning Center Archives.

Where Was It Mailed?

Something that has come to be accepted as "fact" concerns where the Sleeping Suit was mailed from. The FBI Summary Report matter of factly states:

> "...a freshly laundered Dr. Denton's Sleeping Suit #2, purporting to be that of the Lindbergh Baby, was received by Dr. Condon through the mails in a package wrapped in brown paper, the postmarked Station "E", Brooklyn, N. Y. (2581 Atlantic Avenue)."[421]

As with anything that comes from that Summary Report, we must always try to find its original source. That source appears to be SAC Connelley's letter written to J. Edgar Hoover on June 23, 1932. Concerning this exact point that letter says:

> "Apparently as a result of the conversation of Condon with John on March 12th there was mailed to Dr. John E. [sic] Condon, 2974 Decatur Avenue, New York, in plain brown wrapping paper a bundle containing what was alleged to be the sleeping suit worn by the baby at the time it was taken, same being mailed apparently March 15th and received March 16th and, according to news accounts, was mailed at Station E, Atlantic Avenue, Brooklyn."[422]

---

[421] Sisk, T. H. DOI (FBI) et. al., DOI Report. <u>Summary</u>. NY File No. 62-3057, p. 178. February 16, 1934. National Archives at College Park Maryland.

[422] Connelley, E. J. Special Agent in Charge, Bureau of Investigation. <u>Letter from E. J. Connelly to Director Re: Kidnaping and Murder of Charles A. Lindbergh Jr</u>. June 23, 1932. National Archives at College Park Maryland.

Since it was not uncommon for the FBI to rely on newspaper accounts during this case when they had no other source, it appears this is indeed what their summary concerning this point is based upon. During the Bronx Grand Jury both Condon and Breckinridge were asked where this package had been mailed from. Condon's testimony was as follows:

> [Q] *Do you recall where that package was mailed, was it from a local post office?*

> [A] *I would state that just now* [sic] *because I have been the recipient of thousands of letters. I kept the paper and handed it to Col. Lindbergh.*

> [Q] *Isn't it a fact that all these communications received through the mail were mailed in the post office throughout the Greater City?*

> [A] *Yes, throughout the Greater City of New York.*[423]

When Breckinridge was asked his reply was: "*No sir, I am sorry I don't know, but it was from some New York station.*"[424]

In *The Case That Never Dies*, Dr. Gardner makes yet another interesting observation. He concludes that the presence of a single ten-cent stamp on this package meant it had been weighed at the post office for the "*precise postage.*" This he calls a "*risky enterprise*" and also suggests the possibility that it could have been mailed by an

---

[423] Condon, John F. Testimony. <u>Bronx Grand Jury</u>. May 20, 1932. New Jersey State Police Museum and Learning Center Archives.

[424] Breckenridge, Colonel Henry. Testimony. <u>Bronx Grand Jury</u>. May 17, 1932. New Jersey State Police Museum and Learning Center Archives.

"accomplice."[425] Would people who were used to dropping letters into a mail box, or who used Perrone to deliver a ransom note, be so bold as to walk into a Post Office anywhere in the City of New York and risk having a package weighed for delivery to John "Jafsie" Condon?

At Flemington during cross examination, Condon was shown S–53, and was again asked where the package had been mailed from:

> [Reilly] *Can you tell from the stamp, cancellation mark, what station—*

> [Condon] *Pardon me?*

> [Q] *—is on the envelop?*

> [A] *What station? I will take a look at that. I see New Jersey first.*

> [Wilentz] *You mean the cancelled stamps?*

> [A] *You mean the cancelled stamps? Well just a minute. (Examines paper.) As it stands, as it stands, on account of it being blurred, I could not tell you at present.*[426]

So here we see for the first time someone being asked this question with the envelope in hand. Fact is, that postmark was "blurred" and in fact, the NJSP were always of the opinion that the postmark

---

[425] Gardner, Lloyd C. June 2004. *The Case That Never Dies.* Rutgers University Press. Page 70.

[426] Condon, John F. Testimony. The State of New Jersey vs. Bruno Richard Hauptmann, <u>Hunterdon County Court of Oyer and Terminer</u>, page 758, 1935. New Jersey State Law Library.

could not be identified.[427] However, during an examination made by Document Examiner and Handwriting Expert John F. Tyrrell, his conclusion was that the postmark was: "*STAM*" and "*CONN*" meaning it had actually been mailed from Stamford, Connecticut and not Brooklyn.[428] This type of new information often meets with "resistance" from Lindbergh kidnapping enthusiasts. One researcher, Robert Purdy, set out to prove for himself once and for all where this package was mailed. Over the course of his research, he obtained a copy of the postmark from the NJSP Archives in West Trenton. He then sent it off...

"...*to 5 postal historians and postmark dealers. I asked them – without prompting – if they could tell me where it was from. The unanimous opinion was Stamford, Connecticut.*"[429]

Bizarre Bazaar

Another possible accomplice had come to be known to history as the "Lady of Tuckahoe." What exactly are the true facts and how can we use them to determine what the truth really was? According to the FBI Summary Report it was on March 19, 1932:

"*Dr. Condon said to have received verbal instructions from unknown woman in Charity Bazaar conducted by him 394 East 200th Street in the Bronx, to meet*

---

[427] Tyrrell, John F., Document Examiner. Letter from John F. Tyrell to Col. H. Norman Schwarzkopf. December 12, 1934. New Jersey State Police Museum and Learning Center Archives. (Note: This letter quotes Schwarzkopf from a previous communication).

[428] Ibid.

[429] Purdy, Robert "Rab." Internet Work. *Stamford/Sleeping Suit*. March 5, 2006. http://lindberghkidnap.proboards.com.

*him the following Wednesday, March 23, 1932 at
Railway Station, Tuckahoe, N.Y."*[430]

This report continued that on March 23, 1932:

> *"Dr. Condon accompanied by Al Reich (former
> pugilist and alleged bodyguard of Dr. Condon) meets
> unknown woman at Tuckahoe, N.Y., is instructed by
> her to continue advertising."*[431]

This account seems clear. It obviously points to a female confederate
relaying a message to Condon from the Kidnappers. Another
interesting fact is that newspapers were also carrying accounts of
these meetings. For example, the United Press version read as follows:

> *"Shortly after Dr. Condon inserted one of his
> advertisements, he was at his bazar [sic] in the
> Bronx when a woman entered and started pricing
> a violin. She did not seem greatly interested in the
> violin and finally said: "Nothing can be done until the
> excitement is over. Meet me at the depot at Tuckahoe
> on Wednesday at 5 p.m. I will have a message for you."*
>
> *AGAIN MEETS WOMAN*
>
> *Dr. Condon went to the Tuckahoe station and again
> met the woman. She then said: "You will get a message
> later."*[432]

---

[430] Sisk, T. H. DOI (FBI) et. al., DOI Report. <u>Summary</u>. NY File No.
       62-3057, p. 22. February 16, 1934. National Archives at College Park
       Maryland.
[431] Ibid. Page 23.
[432] "Woman Linked With Kidnapers by Go-Between." *Salt Lake Telegram*.
       April 12, 1932. Utah Digital Newspapers, J. Willard Marriott Library.

Since both accounts virtually agree, the question now becomes what source the FBI used for the specific information they included in their report. Was it the newspapers, Condon, or someone else? One thing for sure, there was a flurry of investigations concerning this event on the heels of most of the newspaper accounts. In fact, the New Jersey State Police were actively investigating at Tuckahoe, N.J., and it's clearly mentioned in a Special Report that this investigation was triggered by "...*an article in the newspaper.*"[433] This source also indicated it was the first time the NJSP were hearing about this. Meanwhile, the NYPD also began an investigation beginning on April 14, 1932, into this at the Central Railroad Station in Tuckahoe, N.Y. Here too, the NYPD report mentions that they did so because "...*it was stated in newspapers that Dr. Condon had met a woman there at about 9–00 P. M. March 23rd, 1932.*"[434] The New Jersey venue was eventually ruled out as having any possible connection by police. In light of this, what did the officers in New York turn up? Officer Avon and Detective Thompson interviewed Louis Tenore, a "*signal maintainer*" at the Rail Road Station, who told them he worked during that time, "*was about,*" and "*did not observe Dr. Condon whom he knows from pictures, talk to any woman.*"[435] Also interviewed was August Maday, the ticket agent on duty "*on March 23rd*" from "*2–40 P.M. to 10–40 P.M.*" who claimed he "*did not observe Dr. Condon meet any person thereat.*"[436] On May 17th, a lead came in that Emil Hecht, a stationery store proprietor on Main Street in Tuckahoe may

---

433 De Winne, G. T. Tpr., New Jersey State Police. New Jersey State Police Report. <u>Lindbergh kidnapping. Re: alleged contact between Kidnap Gang and Dr. Condon known as (Jafsie) at Tuckahoe R. R. Station, Tuckahoe, N. J.</u> April 13, 1932. New Jersey State Police Museum and Learning Center Archives.

434 Avon, James A. Officer, New York City Police Department. New York City Police Department Report. <u>People State of New Jersey.</u> May 21, 1932. New Jersey State Police Museum and Learning Center Archives.

435 Ibid.

436 Ibid.

have witnessed Condon speaking to a woman at the R.R. Station on March 23rd. However, during his interview with Detective Thompson he completely denied ever seeing Dr. Condon at all.[437]

At the time of the Bronx Grand Jury this matter was still fresh in the minds of the Authorities. Breckinridge was asked about it on May 17, 1932, and this was the reply he gave:

> "*I never paid much attention to that, I think you can imagine, if you don't know the man* [sic] *of phoney approaches to the doctor and also a number of sincere approaches about perfectly legitimate business that might be well misinterpreted by the doctor or myself, for instance I listened on his extension phone one night to a long conversation from a fellow that wanted to buy a violin, he went down and opened this bazaar up that was with the theory that somebody might come there that might not want to come to the house, that he would go down there and let him in and talk to him and on this one occasion I think this woman phoned him and then she came down to the store and saw him, and I think he was supposed to meet her over in Tuckahoe, and I think he went over to Tuckahoe and didn't meet her or see her, that is my recollection, but I never paid very much attention to that, that particular one case for the fellow that would call up about a violin or viola, there is a long conversation between a fellow that wanted a gumundi violin, now the doctor himself worked on that, he thought that the viola was the party and the violin was the money.*"[438]

---

[437]   Ibid.
[438]   Breckenridge, Colonel Henry. Testimony. <u>Bronx Grand Jury</u>. May 17, 1932. New Jersey State Police Museum and Learning Center Archives.

So we see from Breckinridge's recollection the woman approached Condon at the Bazaar; however, when Condon went to keep the appointment she did not show up. As previously referenced, Condon testified before the Bronx Grand Jury on May 20, 1932. Here was Breslin's chance to get the desired information about this event straight from the horse's mouth:

[Q] *Now doctor it has been mentioned in the public press at at* [sic] *one time during your negotiations with the alleged kidnappers that you visited Tuckahoe to get a suppose communication or make an appointment with some unknown woman, are those reports correct?*

[A] *They are absolutely false, I saw no one at Tuckahoe, except my own relatives I never went to Tuckahoe to see anybody about anything.*

[Q] *Were you in Tuckahoe at anytime while these negotiation were going on?*

[A] *I think I went there with my family, that needs an explanation on account of the false statements in the press, my son a lawyer is married, he has a little baby girl. I think this is rather irrelevant if you want to stop me and I go to New Rochelle College lecturing, have done that every Monday for about 20 years, on the way back I stopped at Pelham Terrace that is around Boston Shore road south of New Rochelle and bring some little token to the child, it is possible that coming back I may have ridden with them in the automobile to come down to my home but never on any errand of any kind where anybody was concerned at all, nor where the case bore and in justice to the departments I volunteered when requested to come to Yonkers and*

White Plains, Mt. Vernon I had to answer questions concerning that that [sic] was new to me, no I never had anything to do with that.[439]

To make matters more confusing (if not worse) Coleman gave an entirely different account. The first thing he wrote about was the Bazaar itself. It was located in the O'Hara Building at Bedford Park Blvd. and Webster Avenue before the kidnapping to raise money for a *"new Chapel on Harts Island."* Condon would occupy his time there *"between his lectures at Fordham College and the College of New Rochelle."*[440] During the kidnapping, and while Condon was *"negotiating with the kidnapers [sic]"* Coleman claimed he often *"met the Doctor there."*[441] Coleman mentioned the following encounter which completely contradicted Condon's Grand Jury testimony:

"...Dr. Condon's curiosity was aroused by a woman at the bazaar who said she desired to purchase one of the many violins on sale. It was evident that she wasn't particularly interested in Dr. Condon's sales talk and something she said in the course of the short conversation proved to the Doctor that she didn't want to buy a violin. She said: "Nothing can be done until the excitement is over. There is too much publicity. Meet me in the depot at Tuckahoe on Wednesday at 5 o'clock. I will have a message for you." Dr. Condon sought more information but the woman hurried away."[442]

---

[439] Condon, John F. Testimony. <u>Bronx Grand Jury</u>. (Continued after King) May 20, 1932. New Jersey State Police Museum and Learning Center Archives.

[440] Coleman, Gregory F. *Vigil*. Unpublished Manuscript. Page 24. Undated (circa 1932). New Jersey State Police Museum and Learning Center Archives.

[441] Ibid.

[442] Ibid. Page 34.

Knowing that it was Condon himself who was giving this information to Coleman creates a matter that is difficult to understand. Why was Condon giving two different stories, and if he perjured himself before the Grand Jury what would be the reason? The next question Coleman seemed to answer is whether Condon met the woman at Tuckahoe:

> "*On Wednesday evening, Dr. Condon and Al Reich went to the Tuckahoe depot of the New York, Westchester and Boston R. R. to keep the appointment with the "violin prospect," but this trip accomplished little except to solidify the hopes of the vigil party. The woman was there all right, but she merely announced, "you will get a message later—keep advertising in the Home News until you hear" and hastened away. No attempt was made to follow her, for Dr. Condon was under orders that he must do nothing to arouse distrust among the kidnappers. The safety of the child was always the first consideration.*"[443]

It is important to note that Coleman's account is almost identical to what Inspector Walsh wrote in his Jersey Journal article about this event.[444]

Since the FBI Summary was finished on February 16, 1934, any source after could contain new information. But would their Agents learn anything later to complement or refute what's written in their earlier summary about this matter? They certainly would. On March 6, 1934, Special Agent Seykora interviewed Condon and took that

---

[443] Ibid. Page 36.

[444] Walsh, Harry W. Inspector. "The Inside Story Of The Lindbergh Case." *The Jersey Journal.* November 11, 1932. New Jersey State Police Museum and Learning Center Archives.

opportunity to ask him about the woman who called at the *"charity bazaar"* on *"March 19th, 1932."* Condon told him this woman…

> *"…remarked that it was "too noisy" (apparently meaning that there was too much publicity concerning the case at the time), and that he would receive a message in the future and that he should meet her at the railway station at Tuckahoe on the following Wednesday; that he, Dr. Condon did not inform anyone of this meeting at the time and on the following Wednesday, had his daughter-in-law, Mrs. Jack Condon, drive him to a place north of Tuckahoe for the purpose of visiting friends and on this occasion he stopped at the railway station but did not see anything of the woman who had called at the bazaar and has never seen this woman since that time."*[445]

We see in this version, despite his insistent denial on May 20, 1932, that Condon said the encounter with this woman did in fact occur at the bazaar. However this time, just like Breckinridge's recollection of the event, this woman did not show at Tuckahoe. Also, we see that a new person drove him there. Al Reich had transformed into Kay Condon! Condon also gave Seykora a description of this mysterious woman…

"…appeared to be about twenty-five years of age, of medium height, dark complexion, black hair, bobbed and worn in somewhat of a "Gypsy" fashion, that is, coming down on the forehead and down on the ears and possibly split curls."[446]

---

[445]   Seykora, J. E. Special Agent, DOI. DOI Report. Kidnaping and Murder of Charles A. Lindbergh, Jr. March 8, 1934. New Jersey State Police Museum and Learning Center Archives.

[446]   Ibid.

Also taking advantage of his April 3, 1934, interview with Condon, Special Agent O'Leary inquired about the *"woman who called at the bazaar."* Condon told him the woman *"was alone"* and came into the bazaar *"around 1 or 2 in the afternoon."*[447] Condon explained there was some talk about the purchase of a violin *" for some time"* when she said *"too many people. You will get a message. Wait."*[448] Condon told O'Leary the woman told him to *"meet her at the Tuckahoe Station at 5 P.M. on the same day."*[449] Condon gave him the following description of this woman as:

> *"Age 30, 5'6", 125 – 130 lbs., plump build, dark hair, dark eyes, dark complexion, spoke with noticeable accent. Clothing – dark; Dr. Condon cannot describe. Dr. Condon states that the woman was very quietly dressed and apparently of some education and refinement."*[450]

It was not even a month later and the story had changed again. The woman was now five years older and told him to meet her at Tuckahoe *on the same day*. Also, for the first time, we see this woman had a *"noticeable accent."* If it was so noticeable, why hadn't he mentioned it before? One thing he did stay consistent about is that he tells O'Leary that he *"went to the railroad station at Tuckahoe at the designated time but the woman failed to appear."* [451] So at least he seemed to remember part of what he told Seykora, though perhaps not what he told Coleman.

---

[447] O'Leary, J. M. Special Agent, DOI. DOI Report. <u>Kidnaping and Murder of Charles A. Lindbergh, Jr.</u> April 5, 1934. New Jersey State Police Museum and Learning Center Archives.

[448] Ibid.

[449] Ibid.

[450] Ibid.

[451] Ibid.

It was in June of 1934 that Condon gave yet another differing account to Special Agent Sisk concerning this woman. Sisk's report records the following information:

> *"It appears that Dr. Condon was in his bazaar alone during the afternoon about the middle of March, 1932. A young Italian woman came in and started talking to him about violins. After a few remarks about these instruments she made some remark about it being dangerous to talk there and suggested that Dr. Condon meet her the next day at noon time at Tuckahoe, New York, which is approximately twenty miles from the Bronx. Dr. Condon proceeded to Tuckahoe the next day with his daughter-in-law, Kay Condon, who has red hair. The latter fact is noted here because some of the newspapers carried reports that Dr. Condon was seen at Tuckahoe with a red-haired woman who was believed to be an emissary of the kidnappers. Dr. Condon stated that he and Kay waited around the Tuckahoe railroad station which was the meeting place designed by this unknown woman, but no one showed up. After waiting two hours they returned home. Dr. Condon stated he brought Kay Condon along with him because he could not drive a car himself and she acted as his chauffeur."*[452]

It's easy to see why the police threw their hands up at this type of stuff! What happened to visiting friends? Why did he use Kay instead of Reich? Or did he use Reich as the earlier accounts state? Which day did he go to Tuckahoe? The same, the next, the 23rd,

---

[452] Sisk, T. H. Special Agent, DOI. USBOI Report. <u>Kidnaping and Murder of Charles A. Lindbergh Jr</u>. June 26, 1934. New Jersey State Police Museum and Learning Center Archives.

or did he even go? As useless as it may be, Condon also gave Sisk a description of this woman as well... She was "*25*" years of age, "*5'6*", had "*straight black*" hair, her build was "*rather stout*" with an "*old*" face, and "*dark*" eyes. She had "*dark*" skin, "*full*" cheeks; he believed her to be a "*native-born Italian*" speaking with "*some accent*" and wearing "*new, of rather expensive make*" clothing, being "*nicely dressed*" in a "*dark dress*" along with "*a sort of turban hat*" and also wearing a "*cape or shawl over her dress but no furs.*"[453]

The differences here are too many to list. Too many authors and researchers alike seem to rely on Condon's book *Jafsie Tells All!* It's unimaginable to me. Use it as a source, yes, but to rely on it for anything seems beyond incredible. It's in his book he gives a fantastic account of the Bazaar incident, and it is downright depressing to see all of the differences in this new story he tells. After all, this is the same man who identified Hauptmann sending him to the electric chair...

> "*Late that afternoon, a short-middle-aged woman with the oval face and olive skin of an Italian, came into the bazaar. Plainly dressed in dark clothes, she looked about her a bit timidly, now at the customers, now at the merchandise exhibited for sale, now at me.*"[454]

A short middle-aged woman? Plainly dressed? Does this sound anything like the woman Condon described to any of the investigators?

> "*She stepped close, began to speak rapidly, in a whisper: "Nothing can be done," she said, tumbling the words out clearly, "until the excitement is over. There is too much publicity. Meet me at the depot at Tuckahoe*

[453] Ibid.
[454] Condon, John F. (1936). *Jafsie Tells All!* Jonathan Lee. Pages 120-1.

> *Wednesday at five in the afternoon. "I will have a*
> *message for you!"*[455]

Here her words are in line with previous accounts plus Condon changes the meeting date again, back to the original Wednesday at 5. Original, that is, if you don't believe his Bronx Grand Jury testimony. The book continues:

> *"Al Reich was busy that day, and since I do not drive*
> *a car myself, I asked one of my daughters-in-law*
> *to drive me to Tuckahoe. She knew nothing of the*
> *incident of the woman who had come to the bazaar*
> *four days previously. She merely knew that I had an*
> *appointment of some sort."*[456]

So here we now have an explanation for why Reich did not drive him. But is this true when nothing else seems to be? Perhaps we should all be grateful that he attempted to make sense of at least this one mystery. Of course it does not explain why Coleman would say Reich drove him especially when we know that Condon was his source, and that he imparted to him this information during the negotiations and always within 24 hours after any contact or event such as this. It also doesn't agree with what Reich told police when he said:

> *"...I was at Dr. Condon's home every day since the*
> *day after the doctor received the first message from the*
> *kidnappers, going home around two or three o'clock*
> *every morning...".*[457]

---

[455]   Ibid. Pages 121-2.

[456]   Ibid. Page 129.

[457]   Reich, Alfred. Statement. Made to Det. Robert Coar and Det. S. J. Leon. May 13, 1932. New Jersey State Police Museum and Learning Center Archives.

And again, it omits the earlier story about "visiting friends" he gave to Agent Seykora also. In closing the chapter on this event, here are Condon's final words concerning whether or not he met her at Tuckahoe:

> *"The truth of the matter is that the woman never appeared. I saw nothing of her again at any time. What is the true explanation of her? To this day I do not know. Of the many mysterious fantastic incidents that occurred in the famous Lindbergh case, this one ranks high among those that have baffled students of the case. She did appear at the bazaar, did cautiously give me a message, did make a definite appointment and failed to keep it."*[458]

Baffled? Yes! But not at the story, rather, at Condon's inability to tell the truth. Baffled at how one man can obstruct justice while no one does anything about it.

A Special Delivery?
(The 2nd Taxi Driver Mystery)

The ransom drop off would take place on April 2, 1932. The instructions arrived, according to Condon, by *"another taxi man"* who brought a note to his home at *"about eight o'clock."*[459] As is always the case, anything that involved Condon took on a life of its own where anything and everything had movable parts. People, places, dates, descriptions and certain "facts" would all change over time. Sometimes slightly, sometimes drastically, and at times would even revert back to their original forms. As Leon Ho-age would accurately describe…

---

[458] Condon, John F. (1936). *Jafsie Tells All!* Jonathan Lee. Page 129.

[459] Condon, Dr. John F. Statement. Made to Inspector Harry W. Walsh. May 13, 1932. New Jersey State Police Museum and Learning Center Archives.

"...that the Doctor is very consistent at being inconsistent. He has a most peculiar habit of differing with himself."[460]

And so it goes that we are, as were the police at the time, held hostage by his version of events and can only get to the truth by evaluating each and every thing he ever said. Before getting into the depth of Condon's tale about this event, I believe it's very important to point out how much time and energy went into investigating it. Almost immediately, the New Jersey State Police, along with those officers on loan to them from the Jersey City Police, began an exhaustive search for this unknown "taxi driver" who delivered the note to Condon on April 2nd. The *"New York Police had also worked on this"* and there was an *"immense amount of work"* done by police as it concerned this angle.[461]

The Leads

Authorities began by pulling a page out of the Bronx phone directory then investigated each and every taxicab company listed there. After that they moved on to every cab company in Brooklyn as well. During this meticulous investigation and search for the "Missing Taxi Driver" the only "leads" which the police turned up I have ever been able to find include these three possibilities:

---

[460] Ho-age, Leon. Analysis. *"The Story of Doctor John F. Condon "Egoist" Extraordinary."* March 4, 1936. New Jersey State Police Museum and Learning Center Archives. (Note: see page 197 in V1 of TDC for more information on Ho-age).

[461] Sisk, T. H. Special Agent, Division of Investigation. Memorandum for the Director. Unknown subjects. <u>Kidnapping and murder of Charles A. Lindbergh, Jr</u>. June 23, 1934. National Archives at College Park Maryland.

Eugene W. Casey

On June 20th, the owner of the Knickerbocker Fleet Owners Taxi Association, Harry Hyman, had reported that he received an anonymous telephone call indicating that Eugene Casey was the Taxi Driver who delivered the note to Dr. Condon.[462] Police tracked him down then began to question him. Casey told the police that "*he knew where DeCatur Avenue was and knew the Bronx quite well, but that he did not deliver any notes to Dr. Condon.*"[463] However, Casey did tell investigators a wild story involving two men and a woman that was supposed to have occurred sometime in April of that year. It began on Valentine Avenue where he picked up a man with "*mixed gray hair*" between the age of "*39 and 40.*" They drove to a place near a tennis court then picked up a girl with a "*cream colored spring coat with a belt and blue beret, looked as if she was working in a soda fountain as she had a white apron on.*"[464] From here he was instructed to drive up the concourse under the tunnel then stopped at an apartment house where he picked up his third passenger...

> "*...this man got in saying, "My own mother would not know me in this make up." The man had on an artificial nose, false eye-brows, his hair seemed to be*

---

[462] Zapolsky, A. Sgt, NJSP, and Fitzgerald, J. Det., Jersey City Police Department. New Jersey State Police Report. <u>Continuation of investigation endeavoring to locate 2<u>nd</u> Taxi Driver who delivered note to Dr. Condon on April 2, 1932</u>. June 20, 1932. New Jersey State Police Museum and Learning Center Archives.

[463] Zapolsky, A. Sgt, NJSP, and Fitzgerald, J. Det., Jersey City Police Department. New Jersey State Police Report. <u>Continuation of investigation regarding Eugene Walter Casey, Taxi Driver who is supposed to have delivered the second note to Dr. Condon on April 2, 1932</u>. June 22, 1932. New Jersey State Police Museum and Learning Center Archives.

[464] Ibid.

dark but he had false hair which looked red which was not neatly kept. He also had a Charley [sic] *Chaplin Mustache which was also false.*"[465]

They all spoke to each other in a *"whisper"*; however, Casey told police the man in the disguise, as well as the woman, both spoke with an *"English accent."*[466] He was directed to drive to the main gate at *"Woodlawn Cemetery"* and once there the man wearing the disguise got out and walked north down Central Avenue. The other man asked Casey *"what train to take"* in order to get to the *"Fort Lee Ferry"* so as to get to *"Englewood."*[467] Just after coming out of Van Cortlandt Park, the girl got out of the cab to leave for the subway, but not before dropping a *"pink handkerchief"* that had a *"red boarder* [sic] *around it"* as well as the *"initial "S" in a circle on a corner"* which Casey noticed when he picked it up and handed to the girl."[468] The original passenger was then driven back to Valentine Avenue, and Casey was given five dollars on a three dollars and some cents fare. Casey was later brought to Alpine Station to have his official statement taken. While there, he was shown a picture of two women and asked if either had been the woman in question who had been in his cab that night. Casey replied *"I am almost sure the girl that is sitting down is the one that rode in my taxi cab on that particular night."*[469] The picture was of both Edna and Violet Sharp, and Violet was the one who was seated.[470]

---

465 Ibid.

466 Ibid.

467 Ibid.

468 Ibid.

469 Casey, Eugene Walter. Statement. Made to Detective Salvatore Rizzo, New York Police Department, Detective James Fitzgerald, Jersey City Police Department, and Sgt. Andrew Zapolsky, New Jersey State Police. June 22, 1932. New Jersey State Police Museum and Learning Center Archives.

470 Ibid.

The next day both Zapolsky and Fitzgerald continued to investigate by searching for Casey's cab records as well as driving him around to look at the various places he was supposed to have picked up and dropped off these passengers. At some point Casey asked the men *"why his name was not in the papers."*[471] After being told they didn't think he wanted his name mentioned Casey told them his original story was false and that he picked up the first man on Webster Avenue, drove to Decatur Avenue to pick up the girl, drove to Dickerson Avenue to pick up the man in disguise, drove to Woodlawn to drop him off, then drove to the subway to drop off the girl, and would eventually return to Decatur to drop off the first man at the end of the trip.[472] Casey was brought to Captain Oliver's office where he was interrogated by both Oliver and Inspector Lyons and they concluded Casey was just *"looking for publicity."*[473] However, despite this, it did not end the investigation. The next day investigators attempted to verify anything Casey said with trip tickets which they secured from Buda Garage Corporation, his employer at the time. None of the trip cards showed a fare that terminated at Decatur Avenue.[474] Casey attempted to explain that the trip was off the books so he could pocket the money but the Cops were finished with him

---

[471] Zapolsky, A. Sgt, NJSP, and Fitzgerald, J. Det., Jersey City Police Department. New Jersey State Police Report. Continuation of investigation regarding Eugene Walter Casey, Taxi Driver who is supposed to have delivered the second note to Dr. Condon on April 2, 1932. June 23, 1932. New Jersey State Police Museum and Learning Center Archives.

[472] Ibid.

[473] Ibid.

[474] Zapolsky, A. Sgt, NJSP, and Fitzgerald, J. Det., Jersey City Police Department. New Jersey State Police Report. Continuation of investigation regarding Eugene Walter Casey of 49 East 133rd Street, New York City, who is supposed to have delivered the second note to Dr. Condon on April 2, 1932. June 24, 1932. New Jersey State Police Museum and Learning Center Archives.

at that point and had enough. They concluded Casey *"was not of sound mind"* and believed he *"made up the story."*[475]

Isidore Lowenthal

The next lead originated from a letter written to Schwarzkopf from Harry Leibowitz, the general manager of the Archer Cab Corporation which stated that he may have some information concerning the "missing" taxi driver.[476] Fresh off of their wild goose chase with Casey, Sgt. Zapolsky and Detective Fitzgerald were detailed to investigate on July 5th. Leibowitz told the men that he had been approached by one of his chauffeurs, Isidore Lowenthal, after requesting via posted notice that anyone with information to report to him.[477] According to Leibowitz, Lowenthal told him he observed the activity in front of Condon's home on April 2, 1932.[478] Three days later police meet with Lowenthal and at that time took down his official statement. According to Lowenthal, *"on or about the last day of March 1932"* while he stood *"opposite of Dr. Condon's house"* at about *"6-00 or 6-30 P.M."* he saw a *"Brown General Cab"* pull up and stop.[479] Lowenthal continued:

---

[475] Ibid.

[476] Leibowitz, Harry, General Mgr., Archer Cab Corp. <u>Letter from Harry Leibowitz to Col. H. N. Schwarzkopf</u>. June 10, 1932. New Jersey State Police Museum and Learning Center Archives.

[477] Zapolsky, A. Sgt, NJSP, and Fitzgerald, J. Det., Jersey City Police Department. New Jersey State Police Report. <u>Investigation of attached communication, addressed to Col. H. Norman Schwarzkopf of the New Jersey State Police, Trenton, N.J., sent by Harry Leibowitz...</u>. July 5, 1932. New Jersey State Police Museum and Learning Center Archives.

[478] Ibid.

[479] Lowenthal, Isidore. Statement. Made to Detective James Fitzgerald, Jersey City Police Department, and Sgt. Andrew Zapolsky, New Jersey State Police. July 8, 1932. New Jersey State Police Museum and Learning Center Archives.

> *"The driver of this cab stepped out and took off his Chauffeur's cap and long duster and placed them on the driver's seat, closed the door and walked across the street and up to Dr. Condon's house. While he was walking up I looked at the cab and saw the back of a man and woman sitting in his cab. He put his hand into his inside pocket and took something out and handed it to someone at the door of the house and walked right back to the cab. I do not know to whom he handed the thing he pulled out of his inside coat pocket. He came back to the cab, sat right down and drove away."[480]*

Lowenthal could not give a description of the man, except that he wore a "*derby*," or of the woman, except that she wore a "*dark turban*." However, he gave a detailed description of the cab driver which include that he was "*apparently Italian*," who was "*dark complected*," with "*side-boards*," between the ages of "*30 and 35*," walked with a "*decided limp*," weighed about "*150 to 155lbs.*," and while he did not get the license number of the cab he told police he had "*positively seen him before on a Taxi Cab*."[481] On July 9th, the officers met Lowenthal and showed him "*1900 photographs of Hack Drivers*" and he picked out the photos of "*Victor Cragnotti*" and "*Anthony Mazzi*."[482] On July 11th, Lowenthal was able to see Mazzi in person then ruled him out.[483] On July 15th, investigators brought Lowenthal to see Victor Cragnotti and his cab, and after

---

[480] Ibid.

[481] Ibid.

[482] Zapolsky, A. Sgt, NJSP, and Fitzgerald, J. Det., Jersey City Police Department. New Jersey State Police Report. <u>Continuation of investigation endeavoring to locate second Taxi Driver who delivered the note to Dr. Condon on April 2, 1932 at about 8-00 P. M.</u> July 11, 1932. New Jersey State Police Museum and Learning Center Archives.

[483] Ibid.

carefully looking him over told police he was not the man he saw either.[484] Probably still smarting from the Casey hoax, it was after this event that these officers noted in their report that Lowenthal "*has not seen anyone delivering a note to Dr. Condon, but has made up a story for some reason unknown.*"[485] About a month and half later Lowenthal's name resurfaced but Zapolsky recommended his "*angle of this investigation be closed*" due to the fact "*investigators have come to the conclusion that this man was looking for publicity, thinking that this would help him to get his job back in a Cabaret as a singer.*"[486]

Kenneth & Carl DaCosta

One of the last possible leads came from Special Agent Sisk almost two years later. He was surprised to learn the "missing" taxi driver had not been discovered so it was decided the Bureau would pick up this angle and continue to investigate. In doing so, Sisk found that a man named Kenneth DaCosta resided at "*the corner of 188th St. and Marion Ave.*," which suggested the possibility he might have been the person in question.[487] It was also learned this address was "*only*

---

484 Zapolsky, A. Sgt, NJSP, and Fitzgerald, J. Det., Jersey City Police Department. New Jersey State Police Report. <u>Continuation of investigation endeavoring to locate second Taxi Driver who delivered the note to Dr. Condon on April 2, 1932 at about 8-00 P. M.</u> July 15, 1932. New Jersey State Police Museum and Learning Center Archives.

485 Ibid.

486 Zapolsky, A. Sgt, NJSP. New Jersey State Police Report. <u>Attached report re: Isidore Lowenthal, 797 Jennings Street, Bronx, N. Y.</u> August 31, 1932. New Jersey State Police Museum and Learning Center Archives.

487 Sisk, T. H., Special Agent, DOI (FBI). USBOI Report. Unknown Subjects. <u>Kidnaping and Murder of Charles A. Lindbergh Jr.</u> June 28, 1934. National Archives at College Park Maryland.

a few blocks distant from Rosenhain's Restaurant."[488] We will see later
in this chapter exactly why this address is significant. As a result,
the NYPD "*Hack Bureau*" arranged for an interview with both
Kenneth and his brother Carl DaCosta, who "*hack in the vicinity
of 201st Street and DeCatur Avenue, Bronx, N. Y.*"[489] While at the
46th Precinct for this interview, "*Hack Inspector Thompson*" vouched
for these men by stating that "*he has known the DaCosta brothers
for several years; that their record is good and they are considered to be
hard working, reliable taxi drivers.*"[490] While being interviewed by
Lt. Finn, these men both readily admitted to being "*active in the
vicinity of Dr. Condon's home*" for a "*number of years*" and that "*on
numerous occasions*" they had driven him to various places such as the
"*Polo Grounds, to the Yankee Stadium, to City Island, etc;*" however,
they had "*never on any occasion delivered any note or message to Dr.
Condon.*"[491] They added that from the time of the kidnapping to
the payment of the ransom money "*there was a good deal of activity
noticeable around Dr. Condon's home*" and that it "*was generally
known among the taxi drivers in that vicinity that there were many
newspaper reporters watching Dr. Condon's house.*"[492] However, before
the interview ended, Carl added something that piqued the interest

---

[488] Sandberg, E. Special Agent, DOI (FBI). United States Bureau of
Investigation Report. Kidnaping and Murder of Charles A. Lindbergh
Jr. July 20, 1934. New Jersey State Police Museum and Learning Center
Archives.

[489] Horn, William F. Cpl., New Jersey State Police. New Jersey State Police
Report. Report of investigation concerning attempt to locate taxi-cab
driver who delivered eleventh note to Dr. Condon, re: Lindbergh Case.
July 13, 1934. New Jersey State Police Museum and Learning Center
Archives.

[490] Sandberg, E. Special Agent, DOI (FBI). United States Bureau of
Investigation Report. Kidnaping and Murder of Charles A. Lindbergh
Jr. July 20, 1934. New Jersey State Police Museum and Learning Center
Archives.

[491] Ibid.

[492] Ibid.

of the investigators, and would also pique the interest of Governor Hoffman and his investigators as well once his "re-investigation" learned of it. Carl DaCosta stated that:

> "...in the Spring of 1932, he could not recall the approximate date nor whether it was before, during or after the ransom negotiations, he drove Dr. Condon from his home to St. Raymond's Cemetery on East Tremont Avenue; that Dr. Condon got out of the cab, as he recalls, on East Tremont Avenue near Whitmore Street; that Dr. Condon was carrying a medium sized satchel or suitcase and that when he got out of the cab he has an impression that Dr. Condon began talking with some laborers who were working on the street in front of the cemetery."[493]

This was as close as any police officer had ever gotten to this mysterious Taxi Driver. So what was the complete story about this event and why weren't they able to locate him?

The Myriad of Stories

In the first version Condon gave to police about this event, he claimed this taxi man told him the note had been given to him by "*a man at 188th St. & Madison Ave.*" to deliver to him. Condon told police that both Lindbergh and Breckinridge were at his home at the time and that Lindbergh "*had in his possession $70,000.*"[494] The

---

[493] Ibid.

[494] Condon, Dr. John F. Statement. Made to Inspector Harry W. Walsh. May 13, 1932. New Jersey State Police Museum and Learning Center Archives. (Note: The story later changed from "Madison" to "Marion" in his other accounts. Whether this was a misunderstanding is unknown.)

very next day, DA Breslin solicited more information from Condon about this encounter…

> "…and in about three or four more nights I got a second message from a taxi man, who claimed that he came from 188th Street and Marion Avenue, and that a man wearing a brown overcoat sent him. He described the overcoat as having one button and from the description, or near the same description, I felt it was the same party. The taxi man said he got a dollar from the man."[495]

As I've researched this case for almost two decades now, I've seen what I believe to be a pattern in the stories Condon told. If something was known or accepted, he sometimes attempted to "piggyback" off of that scenario and by applying it to a new one, it seems to me, he thought the new scenario would be more believable to the Authorities. Unless what he said above is true, he is borrowing what happened from his encounter with Perrone in order to show it's the same man doing the same thing as it applies to this taxi driver as well. But if it isn't true why would he do this? Keep this question in mind as you read on… As in his version he gave to police on the 13th, he told Breslin that "Lindbergh was there, Colonel Breckenridge [sic] was there, Al Reich and myself" and additionally, "there happened to be a local newspaper man around and the reporter got that scoop."[496] More information was drawn out as well, including that this second taxi man arrived sometime "between 8:00 and 8:15 in the night" and also that he "said he was up around Rosie's all the time."[497] When asked

---

[495] Condon, John F. Statement. Made to Assistant District Attorney Edward F. Breslin. May 14, 1932. New Jersey State Police Museum and Learning Center Archives.

[496] Ibid.

[497] Ibid.

if he could *"recognized that taxi drive* [sic]*"* if he ever saw him again Condon responded by saying:

> *"I couldn't describe him so well, I was more interested in the note and transactions that* [sic] *I was in the taxi driver."*[498]

During Condon's grand jury testimony, we get the timing of this event from him as *"about 8 o'clock or a little after 8."* He stayed consistent with the location being *"188th and Marion"* but added a little more to it this time: *"I went to the door and asked him where he got it, what kind of a man. He said, "Not richly dressed, brown fedora."*[499] Condon continued that when it came to this taxi driver *"personally I didn't get his name,"* but that *"someone attempted to get his name and address."*[500] After a pause involving the stenographer, Condon's testimony resumed. He was asked *"who"* went to the door when the second taxi man arrived and he replied *"I went to the door both times."*[501] More to the point here:

> [Q] *Was Colonel Breckinridge with you or was anyone else there at the time?*
>
> [A] *At the front door?*
>
> [Q] *Yes?*
>
> [A] *Not at the front door he was there but not at the front door.*

---

498 Ibid.

499 Condon, John F. Testimony. Bronx Grand Jury. May 20, 1932. New Jersey State Police Museum and Learning Center Archives.

500 Ibid.

501 Ibid. continued after King.

[Q] *Was there anybody else present while you were talking to the taxicab driver?*

[A] *I am not positive whether a little man reputed to belong to the secret service was there or not at that particular time — he came many many* [sic] *times, I think not.*[502]

As the exchange continued, it was brought out that Condon had only "*half*" opened the front door, and that he did not let him into the house. This appears to be Condon's explanation why, if hypothetically Breckinridge (or anyone else) happened to be in the hallway behind him, the taxi man at the door wouldn't have been seen.[503]

The next logical step is to examine what Coleman may have written about this event. Unfortunately, there's very little to be learned from it:

"*A little respite from the business of heart-rending theorizing was being enjoyed at the "headquarters" at 7.45 o'clock on Saturday evening when the door bell rang. A taxi driver stood at the door—with a message for "Mr. Dr. John Condon."*"[504]

During the course of this investigation, Condon was reinterviewed by Inspector Walsh and Lt. Keaten. He told the men "*he had not been able to learn anything about this man and that he did not know where he was from*" and when Keaten asked him if he "*had taken*

502   Ibid.
503   Ibid.
504   Coleman, Gregory F. *Vigil*. Unpublished Manuscript. Page 48. Undated (circa 1932). New Jersey State Police Museum and Learning Center Archives.

ever taken down the Registration of the Taxi Cab" Condon told him he had not.[505] However, he gave them a complete narrative about the encounter:

> *"He was in his home on April 2nd, 1932 when his doorbell rang, he went out and answered the bell and upon opening the door, was confronted by a Taxi Cab Driver who handed him a sealed Envelope. This man then walked off the porch into the street and got into his car and rode away, and being excited because he had just received a letter he forgot to get the registration of this car. Condon, however, stated that this fellow, apparently was a Jew, around 5'6", and had long side-boards. He further stated that if he ever seen this man again he would be able to identify him as the man who gave him the second note."*[506]

Two days later Cpl. Leon and Detective Coar returned to follow up on this matter at Condon's home. The version of events he gave these men is as follows:

> *"Lindbergh and Breckenbridge [sic] was at his home in the Bronx and that they three were sitting in the dining room when the doorbell rang. He went to the front door and a Taxi Cab Driver handed him an Envelope, Condon being excited took the envelope and went back to Col. Lindbergh and Col. Breckenbridge [sic], who were still in the dining room, then Col. Lindbergh and*

---

[505]   Walsh, Harry W. Inspector, Jersey City Police Department and Lt. Arthur T. Keaton, NJSP. New Jersey State Police Report. <u>Conversation with Dr. Condon in reference to unknown Taxi Driver and "John" the Kidnaper.</u> July 7, 1932. New Jersey State Police Museum and Learning Center Archives.

[506]   Ibid.

> *Condon returned to the front door, but the Taxi Cab*
> *Driver disappeared. He did not know what Company*
> *Cab it was, and did not get the registration. The only*
> *description that he could give in regards to the Taxi*
> *Driver was that he was a Jew and had long side-boards*
> *and that he had dark hair and Condon would be able*
> *to identify the Taxi Driver."*[507]

Here we now see a drastic change from what Condon told Breslin on May 14th. How did he go from not being able to describe him to giving a detailed description about three weeks later? How does he say he could not identify this man then later tells Keaten, Walsh, Leon, and Coar that he <u>could</u> if he ever saw him again? It is one or the other yet Condon tells authorities - both? Is it any wonder police were never able to locate this individual?

While the records at the New Jersey State Police Archives seem to indicate the search for this "Missing Taxi Driver" began to wane and sputter by late 1932, Special Agent Frank J. Wilson of the Treasury Department believed this to be a valuable clue as noted here:

> *"Another note was delivered to Mr. Condon by a*
> *taxicab driver on the evening of April 2, 1932, but*
> *the New York City and Jersey City Police officers*
> *were unable to locate the driver. It is possible that the*
> *missing driver was an accomplice in the crime and it*

---

[507] Leon, Samuel J. Cpl., New Jersey State Police and Det. Robert Coar, Jersey City Police Department. New Jersey State Police Report. <u>Conversation with Dr. Condon about the Taxi Driver who delivered the Second note to his home</u>. July 9, 1932. New Jersey State Police Museum and Learning Center Archives.

is thought that taxicab drivers coming under suspicion should be carefully investigated."[508]

The FBI Summary recounts the official story about this driver without any mention of the taxi driver's description. This can only mean, up until the time of its creation, the FBI was never updated or communicated to with the additional information provided to police by Condon after his original accounts. Therefore, by reading what's written, we get a better understanding concerning what Condon's original story was:

> "*During the course of that day, the eleventh ransom note of this case was delivered to Dr. Condon at his home on Decatur Avenue, allegedly by a taxicab driver. At the time of the delivery of this note Colonel Breckinridge was in the back room of Dr. Condon's house, and Colonel Lindbergh was also in the house, but neither saw the person who delivered the note. Dr. Condon is the only one who saw the man, and according to him, the man arrived driving a taxicab. Condon could give description of either the man or the taxicab.*"[509]

What we can also see is that authorities were not altogether "sold" on this version either. The Summary adds that "*...the surrounding circumstances relative to the delivery of this particular note are still*

---

[508] Wilson, Frank J. Special Agent, United States Treasury Department. <u>Memorandum relating to certain details not covered in body of report and some feature of the investigation not referred to in report.</u> SI-6336-M. November 8, 1933. New Jersey State Police Museum and Learning Center Archives.

[509] Sisk, T. H. DOI (FBI) et. al., DOI Report. <u>Summary.</u> NY File No. 62-3057, p. 182. February 16, 1934. National Archives at College Park Maryland.

in dispute."[510] In addition, this summary says Condon stated the note had been delivered "*shortly after 8 o'clock on that evening*" and provides more important details concerning what he said here:

> "*Condon further adds that he believed someone then in the house attempted to get the name and address of this taxi driver but these efforts were without success although just why he did not know. In Condon's recollection, Gaglio was not present in Condon's at the time of the delivery of this note. Condon has said he cannot identify this taxi driver of April 2nd, nor does he think he could identify or recognize him if he saw him again, giving as his reason therefor [sic] that at the time of the appearance of the taxi driver, Condon was interested only in the note from the kidnapers [sic] and was not careful to note the description of this man or his taxi.*"[511]

In June of 1934, Special Agent Sisk, Seykora, and Sandberg pursued the identity of the "Missing Taxi Driver" by conducting a series of investigations into him. During this time, Sisk had thoroughly questioned Condon who relayed to him this version of events:

> "*Dr. Condon stated that when the unidentified taxi driver arrived at his residence, there were present in the house besides himself Colonel Lindbergh, Colonel Breckinridge and Al Reich; that the taxi driver arrived between 8 and 8:05 P.M.; that when the doorbell rang he (Condon) went to the door, leaving Al Reich*

> *sitting in the front room and Colonels Lindbergh and*
> *Breckinridge in the kitchen in the rear of the house.*"[512]

Condon further stated to Agent Sisk:

> "*...that none of the others present in the house came*
> *to the door or saw the taxi driver; of this fact he is*
> *positive.*"[513]

So we also see that at times Condon actually is <u>positive</u> about something. Also, as sometimes Condon would do, he provided Sisk with the actual conversation that ensued between them:

> "*Man : Are you Dr. Condon?*
> *Dr. C: Yes.*
>
> *Man : Here is a note for you.*
> *Dr. C: Where did you get it?*
>
> *Man: Near 188th Street and Marion Avenue. A man*
> *asked me to give it to Dr. Condon.*"[514]

Sisk asked for more information regarding the above conversation, but Condon claimed he could not add anything other than what he quoted above. Sisk had possession of the Bronx Statement as well as the Bronx Grand Jury testimony and pointed out that the differences were probably due to them having been "*fresh*" in his memory compared to his own interview.[515] (While it sounds possible,

---

[512] Sisk, T. H., Special Agent, DOI (FBI). USBOI Report. <u>Unknown Subjects. Kidnaping and Murder of Charles A. Lindbergh Jr</u>. June 28, 1934. National Archives at College Park Maryland.

[513] Ibid.

[514] Ibid.

[515] Ibid.

shouldn't this explanation apply everywhere? If he could not identify him when his memory was "fresh" how then could he completely change this assertion only about a month later? How many days removed from an event does one's memory become "stale," or in this example, "fresher" over time?) Sisk's interview had once again sought to uncover the taxi driver's identity. His report states:

> *"Dr. Condon is not positive but he believes he overlooked getting the taxi driver's name, and address. He stated he may have asked the man for same but in the excitement forgot to make a note."*[516]

Although prefaced with not being positive, this is yet another change in his earlier version. Did he ask or didn't he? Did someone else try or didn't they? Did no one try? His versions are on a sliding scale. Normally, if one doesn't remember they do not remember. Here, it appears, he was attempting to remember what he said earlier – he is clearing guessing at what that was. In discussing Condon's failure to obtain the registration with his peers in both the NJSP and NYPD Sisk learned:

> *"Captain Lamb and Lieutenants Keaton [sic] and Finn stated they could not understand why Dr. Condon did not get this man's name and address when he delivered the note; that when they questioned Condon at Alpine, N.J. in April, 1932 his explanation was that he overlooked obtaining the man's name and address due to the excitement of the moment; that in his desire to see the contents of the note he forgot all about the taxi driver."*[517]

---

[516] Ibid.

[517] Sisk, T. H. Special Agent, Division of Investigation (FBI). Memorandum For The Director. Unknown Subjects. <u>Kidnapping and Murder of Charles A. Lindbergh, Jr</u>. June 29, 1934. National Archives at College Park Maryland.

Here we see what was probably Condon's first recollection to police, and despite being unbelievable, it is obviously the simplest and best explanation. Yet, due to the fact he could not remember it fully, and faced with a situation where it was possibly never true in the first place, we see a story that varies and changes somewhat with each and every new version of it.

Continuing with his interview, Sisk wanted a description of this man prompting Condon to explain since the event was so far removed he "*could not furnish a detailed description*" of the man other than "*possibly about 30 years of age and either Italian or Jewish.*"[518] Condon also told Sisk that he "*would be unable to identify*" this man by photograph; however, he may be able to "*remember*" him if he saw him "*in the flesh.*"[519] What does seem very important is the fact that Condon was "*positive*" this man was a "*taxi driver.*"

> "*...he was wearing a chauffeur's cap and had every appearance of being a taxi driver and also the man stated he was a taxi driver. When questioned as to whether he (Dr. Condon) saw a taxicab in front of the house, he stated that he did not notice a taxi and, in fact, made no effort to see whether or taxi was parked in front of the house as it was dark and the bushes and trees in front of his house obscured the view; further, that he had no reason to doubt the man's work. Condon stated, however, that he has a vague recollection of having observed the lights of a car through the bushes and of hearing a motor running.*"[520]

---

[518] Sisk, T. H., Special Agent, DOI (FBI). USBOI Report. Unknown Subjects. Kidnaping and Murder of Charles A. Lindbergh Jr. June 28, 1934. National Archives at College Park Maryland.

[519] Ibid.

[520] Ibid.

Earlier in May, Special Agent Seykora had investigated the area of 188th Street and Marion Avenue only to learn there had *"never been a taxi stand"* at that corner, that it was *"principally residential"* and for that reason *"no taxicabs"* were in *"the practice of cruising in that vicinity."*[521]

Another important revelation would come in July when both Agents Seykora and Sisk were discussing with Condon his Grand Jury testimony concerning the "missing" taxi driver mentioning *"Rosie's."* Condon hadn't remembered testifying about this, and told the Agents that *"if he had so stated in testifying that was his impression at the time."*[522] However, later when they discussed this same point again, *"Dr. Condon stated that he believed the taxi driver said in effect that he knew some of the taxi drivers around Rosenhain's restaurant."*[523]

On July 11, 1934, Special Agent Sandberg interviewed Condon yet again about the April 2nd taxi driver episode. Condon stated to him that the only parties *"present at that time were Colonel Lindbergh, Colonel Breckinridge, Al Reich, and himself."*[524] However the very next day, for the very first time ever, his daughter Myra told Agent Sandberg that she was present at the house that night."[525] Sandberg asked Condon if Myra had been there that night but noted in his report that *"Dr. Condon does not remember that his daughter Myra*

---

[521] Ibid.
[522] Sandberg, J. E. Special Agent, DOI. USBOI Report. Kidnaping And Murder Of Charles A. Lindbergh, Jr. July 20, 1934. New Jersey State Police Museum and Learning Center Archives.
[523] Ibid.
[524] Sandberg, E. Special Agent, DOI. USBOI Report. Kidnaping And Murder Of Charles A. Lindbergh, Jr. July 11, 1934. New Jersey State Police Museum and Learning Center Archives.
[525] Sandberg, E. Special Agent, DOI. USBOI Report. Kidnaping And Murder Of Charles A. Lindbergh, Jr. July 24, 1934. New Jersey State Police Museum and Learning Center Archives.

was at his home on the night of April 2, 1932…".[526] Noticing this new development, Sandberg quickly pursued it by interviewing Myra. It was during this interview that Myra not only said she was there, but that…

> *"…when the party who delivered the ransom note on that night appeared on the front porch of her father's home she saw this party through the glass in the front door; that she approached the door but did not open it and then returned to the other room as her father answered the door."*[527]

Why did this information come out for the very first time now? Had Condon "forgotten" about it, or was he trying to "protect" his daughter by omitting her from the scenario? If the latter, what caused him to even bring her into the conversation on this occasion instead of flatly saying she had not been there? Sandberg sought a description of this taxi driver from Myra:

> *"She stated this party appeared to have dark skin, like that of an Italian; that he was slim and of medium height; that he was dressed in an ordinary dark suit and was not dressed like a taxi driver. She further stated that he did not appear to be over 25 years of age and could possibly have been as young as 19 years of age."*[528]

This situation where Myra suddenly appears in a scenario so late in the case is eerily similar to the Needle Salesman event. If what she said was true, then Condon was lying the entire time about the man being a Taxi Driver; however, it confirms someone did come to the

---

[526]   Ibid.

[527]   Ibid.

[528]   Ibid.

house that night. But was she merely injecting herself in a way to protect or "save" her father from himself? It's a move that is hard to comprehend because in both situations she had actually proven that her father had lied – if in fact she was telling the truth herself. While testifying in Flemington, Myra told Wilentz that she had been there when the man delivered the note on April 2ⁿᵈ. She said, to the best of her recollection, that he was "*five feet six or seven, very slim*" then followed it up by saying he was "*very dark.*"[529] Under cross-examination it was brought out that she believed the man was in his "*twenties*" with "*dark hair,*" a "*dark complexion,*" but refused to guess at his "*nationality*" referring instead to what she told the "*Department of Justice*" when it was "*fresher*" in her mind.[530] Wow! So her mind was "fresh" for well over two years after the event, but in about six months' time afterwards that specific recollection became "stale." Dr. Condon's testimony needs to be mentioned as well. When asked by Wilentz who was in his home after the ransom "*money was ready*" he testified "*Colonel Lindbergh, Colonel Breckinridge, Alfred J. Reich, Mrs. Condon, of course, and my children.*"[531] This is also new. Supposing Myra is one of these children … which others were there? Under cross-examination the wheels came off. When asked who accompanied him to the door on April 2ⁿᵈ he replied "*Milton Gaglio*" and when asked if his daughter went with him to the door he explained that he could not remember then added "*If she accompanied me she was behind me; I didn't see her.*"[532]

---

[529] Hacker, Myra Condon. Testimony. The State of New Jersey vs. Bruno Richard Hauptmann, <u>Hunterdon County Court of Oyer and Terminer</u>, page 847, 1935. New Jersey State Law Library.

[530] Ibid. Page 850.

[531] Condon, John F. Testimony. The State of New Jersey vs. Bruno Richard Hauptmann, <u>Hunterdon County Court of Oyer and Terminer</u>, page 644, 1935. New Jersey State Law Library.

[532] Ibid. Pages 669-70.

The Breckinridge Account
(Ransom Money Pick-Up)

When it came to April 2nd Breckinridge, by his own admission, was in a very sticky situation. Although I digress here, it is important to point out by example what he was willing to say or do. During the Hauptmann Bronx Grand Jury testimony, he was asked if he had been part of the "chain" who handled the ransom money. He responded by testifying:

> *"Well do you mind if I saw [sic] this that I am in this peculiar situation, although frankly I must admit that it would make no difference to me if I went to jail or was disbarred, I know it that it was something which a lawyer should not do in those circumstances."*[533]

After some reassuring by DA Foley, he replied with this confusing answer:

> *"Nevertheless I try to be cagey and not be in a position as to the actual handling of the funds that were going to be turned over to a criminal in an extortion, although I saw frankly that I was morally responsible just as much as anybody else, I didn't not actually handle this fund but I was with the people who did handle that and we went down and I was a party to the transaction that turned it over to Dr. Condon and I was there while he turned it into a vault."*[534]

---

[533] Breckinridge, Henry. Testimony. Grand Jury. People vs. Hauptmann. September 25, 1934. New Jersey State Police Museum and Learning Center Archives.

[534] Ibid.

171

Now if this sounds like he's not answering the question with the whole truth, yet again, you are not alone in this belief. Foley pointed this out then tried once more. Breckinridge then responded for a third time:

> *"I think one bunch came in Al Reich's car and perhaps Col. Lindbergh brought some of it himself. I think that Dr. Condon and Al Reich could remember that better than I, or perhaps Francis Bartow one of the Morgan partners knows, we got it out of his business."*[535]

However, when checking out Breckinridge's Bronx Grand Jury testimony in May of 1932 about this event, his memory was a little less fuzzy...

> *"...I motored down to where the money was. Colonel Lindberg* [sic] *got the money and brought it up, went down, I went down with Al Reich and Al and I came back in one car and Col. Lindberg* [sic] *came back in another."*[536]

Got that? So Lindbergh in one car and Breckinridge and Reich in the other. Now by the time of the Flemington trial, Breckinridge is perfectly clear about this situation. But this time Al and Lindbergh are in the same car but Breckinridge by himself:

> *"The money was brought in two separate packages in two separate conveyances, from the house of Mr. Francis Bartow, $50,000 of it in an automobile in which were Colonel Lindbergh and Mr. Al Reich; the*

---

[535] Ibid.

[536] Breckenridge, Colonel Henry. Testimony. <u>Bronx Grand Jury</u>. May 17, 1932. New Jersey State Police Museum and Learning Center Archives.

other one by myself, the $20,000 by myself in another automobile."537

The Breckinridge Account
(The Missing Taxi Driver)

With this in mind, once back to the "Missing Taxi Driver" we see that during his Bronx Grand Jury testimony, Breckinridge was asked about the delivery of the note on April 2, 1932. He said that note was delivered at "*7:40 or 7:45*" and that Colonel Lindbergh was also there at the time it was delivered.538 He explained:

> "*From carelessness they got no information from this taxi driver, they were so excited about going through with this thing, they didn't question that fellow, didn't take his name...*".539

Since upon receiving this note, Condon walked it to the back room to show the note to Breckinridge and Lindbergh, it seems reasonable to believe that they got the very first narrative concerning its delivery. So who was he referring to when he said "*they?*" One gets the impression from the context of his answer that it was Reich. Later in the testimony another question was asked as to whether or not "any steps" had been taken to identify the second taxi driver to which Breckinridge responded "*none whatever, I chided them for that, the doctor came to the door and grabbed the note.*"540 Not only does

537   Breckinridge, Henry. Testimony. The State of New Jersey vs. Bruno Richard Hauptmann, <u>Hunterdon County Court of Oyer and Terminer</u>, page 828, 1935. New Jersey State Law Library.
538   Breckenridge, Colonel Henry. Testimony. <u>Bronx Grand Jury</u>. May 17, 1932. New Jersey State Police Museum and Learning Center Archives.
539   Ibid.
540   Ibid.

he use another plural pronoun ("*them*") here it also appears he was unaware of any conversation whatsoever between the second taxi driver and Condon. Sometime later, Col. Schwarzkopf requested Breckinridge to provide him with a written record of events and this was done with the emphasis that it was his "*recollection*" of what transpired after Condon's visit to Hopewell.[541] Included in this memorandum of events was his description of the April 2nd delivery as follows:

> "*On the evening of Saturday, April 2nd another note was delivered to Dr. Condon's residence. I was in a back room of the house and cannot state that the note was delivered by a taxi driver though this was reported as fact.*"[542]

During his Flemington testimony, Breckinridge said after the money was in Condon's home the men waited for word from the Kidnappers based upon the contents of the previous ransom note: "*The situation, all I can say is that it was such as one would expect, people waiting for such an event.*"[543] Next, Breckinridge testified that at "approximately" 8 o'clock:

> "*I think that Dr. Condon received the note in the presence of his daughter, Mrs. Hacker, brought it back*

---

[541] Breckinridge, Henry. Letter from Henry Breckinridge to Colonel H. Norman Schwarzkopf. August 29, 1932. New Jersey State Police Museum and Learning Center Archives.

[542] Breckinridge, Henry. Statement. Unsigned. Undated. New Jersey State Police Museum and Learning Center Archives. (Note: This statement is mentioned by Agent Manning on December 8, 1933, therefore, it existed prior to this report).

[543] Breckinridge, Henry. Testimony. The State of New Jersey vs. Bruno Richard Hauptmann, Hunterdon County Court of Oyer and Terminer, page 831, 1935. New Jersey State Law Library.

> *to the rear room where the rest of us were, the rear*
> *room of Dr. Condon's house."*[544]

Breckinridge further testified that he heard the door bell ring, agreed that Condon "*immediately*" brought back an unopened note that was opened in his presence, and that within "*fifteen*" minutes both Condon and Lindbergh departed with the ransom money.[545] Under cross examination, Breckinridge shared the information that Myra had given a description of this taxi driver to police although he is not sure when that occurred.[546] Could that have been the impetus for Breckinridge to change his original story to include "Mrs. Hacker," or was she the party he spoke of "chiding" when he used the word "they" in his Bronx testimony?

The Lindbergh Account
(Ransom Money Pick-Up)

Charles Lindbergh's statement concerning the ransom money delivery was that on the "*afternoon of April 2ⁿᵈ, 1932, I carried $50,000 to Doctor Condon's home. I sent a package of $20,000. in another car.*"[547] In his Hauptmann Bronx Grand Jury testimony, Lindbergh said: "*I took the package from downtown New York, I took a package of $50,000 to Dr. Condon's house and I had that package in my possession the entire time.*"[548] When asked if he "*received*" the money "*from the banking house yourself*" Lindbergh responded "*I*

---

[544] Ibid. Page 832.

[545] Ibid. Pages 832-3.

[546] Ibid. Page 841.

[547] Lindbergh, Charles A. Statement. Made to Inspector Harry W. Walsh. May 20, 1932. New Jersey State Police Museum and Learning Center Archives.

[548] Lindbergh, Charles A. Testimony. Grand Jury. People vs. Hauptmann. September 26, 1934. New Jersey State Police Museum and Learning Center Archives.

received it in New York from the banking house and from that time on it wasn't out of my possession."[549]

The Lindbergh Account
(The Missing Taxi Driver)

His statement concerning the "Missing Taxi Driver" only contains a simple sentence that *"I remained at Doctor Condon's house until evening when a taxicab delivered a message from the kidnapers* [sic]*."*[550] According to a late July 1934 memo written by Special Agent Sisk, Lindbergh told Lt. Keaten that…

> *"…he, Col. Breckinridge, Dr. Condon and Al Reich were the only ones present at the Condon residence during the evening of April 2nd when the taxi driver arrived with the eleventh ransom note; that he and Col. Breckinridge were in the kitchen and Al Reich was in the front room when the door bell rang; that Dr. Condon went to the door alone and Al Reich, who had been sitting in the front room, got up and went to the rear of the house so as to leave Condon alone to handle the situation. Condon came back in a few seconds holding the ransom note in his hand and simply stated that a taxi driver had brought it without going into any details."*[551]

---

[549]   Ibid.

[550]   Lindbergh, Charles A. Statement. Made to Inspector Harry W. Walsh. May 20, 1932. New Jersey State Police Museum and Learning Center Archives.

[551]   Sisk, T. H. Special Agent, Division of Investigation (FBI). Memorandum For The Director. Unknown Subjects. Kidnapping and Murder of Charles A. Lindbergh, Jr. June 29, 1934. National Archives at College Park Maryland.

In Flemington, Lindbergh's testimony was that he was there when the note arrived: *"The doorbell rang in the home; Dr. Condon went to the door and returned with this note."*[552] Being in the back of the house he did not see who delivered that note. When questioned concerning who was there when the note was read, Lindbergh testified *"Colonel Breckenridge* [sic] *was there and I believe Mr. Reich was there"* then he corrected himself by saying *"Mr. Reich was there."*[553] He further testified that as a result of reading this note both he and Condon departed the house at *"approximately half past eight."*[554] Under cross examination Lindbergh agreed that Condon went out of room, went to the door once the bell rang, then returned with a note and it was *"within ten minutes probably of the receipt of that note"* that they left the house.[555]

The Reich Account
(Ransom Money Pick-Up)

Concerning the ransom money pick-up, Reich told Lt. Finn that…

> *"…Breckenridge* [sic] *and I drove down there to Mr. Batow's* [sic] *office, there was some kind of parade, army day or navy day or something, it was on a Saturday, I don't think Lindbergh was there at all. I think it was just Breckenridge* [sic] *and myself."*[556]

---

[552] Lindbergh, Charles. Testimony. The State of New Jersey vs. Bruno Richard Hauptmann, <u>Hunterdon County Court of Oyer and Terminer</u>, page 106, 1935. New Jersey State Law Library.

[553] Ibid.

[554] Ibid.

[555] Ibid. Page 189.

[556] Reich, Alfred J. Statement. Made to Acting Lieutenant James J. Finn, M.O.D. October 8, 1934. New Jersey State Police Museum and Learning Center Archives.

After picking up the money, Reich remembered: *"I was under the impression that Breckenridge* [sic] *and I left and went to Breckenridge's* [sic] *house."*[557] From there the men met *"with Colonel Lindbergh"* and Reich left with him in his Franklin while Breckinridge left in his Ford Touring Car separately *"to Condon's home."*[558] During his Flemington testimony he gave a much different story when he agreed with the question posed that he went with Breckinridge to Mr. Bartow's house, *"met Colonel Lindbergh down there"* where they *"got some money."*[559] Reich testified *"...we took the fifty in Colonel Lindbergh's car and Colonel Breckinridge took the twenty in his car."*[560] This echoed the contents of Peacock's trial preparation notes:

> *"He will testify that on April 2, 1932 he went to Mr. Bartow's house on 66th St. with Col. Breckinridge. Col. Lindbergh was there. They stayed there for quite some time, and finally he left with Col. Lindbergh and had the package which contained the $50,000. They left in Col. Lindbergh's Franklin to go to Dr. Condon's home. Col. Breckinridge took the other package of $20,000 and left in his Ford and he met them at Dr. Condon's home."*[561]

---

[557]   Ibid.

[558]   Ibid.

[559]   Reich, Alfred Jacob. Testimony. The State of New Jersey vs. Bruno Richard Hauptmann, <u>Hunterdon County Court of Oyer and Terminer</u>, page 579, 1935. New Jersey State Law Library.

[560]   Ibid.

[561]   Peacock, Robert, Assistant Attorney General of New Jersey. Trial Preparation Notes. <u>Statement Of Facts Which Alfred J. Reich Will Testify To</u>: Undated. New Jersey State Police Museum and Learning Center Archives.

Francis Bartow
(Ransom Money Pick-Up)

Prior to trial, Bartow was interviewed by Frank Wilson concerning the chain of custody as it involved these ransom money packages. Bartow explained that "*on the afternoon of April 2ᵈ* [sic]" Colonel Breckinridge arrived with Al Reich at his home for the purposes of picking up the money.[562] Bartow also told Wilson that he "...*did telephone Colonel Lindbergh and received his authority to make the delivery.*"[563] At that time he removed the package from his closet and brought it down to the library where, in the presence of Breckinridge and his partner H. P. Davidson, he "*surrendered it to Mr. Reich.*"[564] Bartow's Flemington testimony is nearly identical:

> "*Colonel Breckinridge called at my house, introduced me to a man by the name of Al Reich, request that — he stated that it was Colonel Lindbergh's request that I deliver the money to him. In order to verify that I called Colonel Lindbergh on the phone, who authorized me to make the delivery to him, and I did it.*"[565]

So while one would think the truth would come out at trial, we see as evidenced by this event, Lindbergh seems to have been in two places at the exact same time. Remove Breckinridge's fear of disbarment, remove the fact that Lindbergh wasn't at Bartow's house, and remove the fact they made a trip to Breckinridge's place. Why? Also, why

---

[562] Bartow, F. D. Interrogation. Questioned by Special Agent in Charge Frank Wilson, U.S. Internal Revenue Bureau, Intelligence Unit. December 17, 1934. New Jersey State Police Museum and Learning Center Archives.

[563] Ibid.

[564] Ibid.

[565] Bartow, Francis D. Testimony. The State of New Jersey vs. Bruno Richard Hauptmann, <u>Hunterdon County Court of Oyer and Terminer</u>, page 1517, 1935. New Jersey State Law Library.

claim Lindbergh was at Bartow's house? Perhaps it makes it "easier" for the Prosecution to navigate? Maybe it eliminated the problems concerning the chain of custody of this ransom money? Whatever the reason, we only know the truth because of what Reich told Lt. Finn which is only supported by Bartow's truthful version of events.

The Reich Account
(The Missing Taxi Driver)

During Reich's original questioning by police, he told them he was present in Condon's home when the second taxi cab driver delivered the note. However, he told police he "*did not see the taxicab*" make the delivery and only knew "*what was told to me by Dr. Condon*."[566] In late August 1934, Reich told Special Agent Sandberg that he was at Condon's place when the (Sandberg referred to it as "*supposed*") "*taxi driver delivered the ransom note on the night of April 2, 1932, but that he did not see this party.*"[567] He also claimed during this interview that besides himself, Condon, Lindbergh, Breckinridge, Mrs. Condon, "*and he believed Myra Hacker*" were all present during this event. He further stated that:

> "*...Myra Hacker was there so much that he could not be sure just which days she was there and which days she was not there. He also stated that Mrs. Condon stayed in her room on the second floor most of the time.*"[568]

---

[566] Reich, Alfred. Statement. Made to Det. Robert Coar and Det. S. J. Leon. May 13, 1932. New Jersey State Police Museum and Learning Center Archives.

[567] Sandberg, E. Special Agent, DOI (FBI). United States Bureau of Investigation Report. <u>Kidnaping and Murder of Charles A. Lindbergh Jr.</u> September 4, 1934. New Jersey State Police Museum and Learning Center Archives.

[568] Ibid.

However, according to his testimony in Flemington, in addition to himself on the evening of April 2, 1932, Condon, Mrs. Condon, Colonel Lindbergh, Colonel Breckinridge, Ralph Hacker, and Myra Hacker were all present in the Condon home.[569]

The Surveillance

There was no surveillance from the New Jersey State Police. It was Schwarzkopf's original suggestion that his men follow Condon to any meeting he was to have with the Kidnappers; however, those ideas were *"rebuffed"* by Lindbergh.[570] Schwarzkopf complied, as always, and insured there would be no interference from his organization. (It's important to note that Captain Lamb told Special Agent Sisk in July 1934 that because of this, his organization specifically blamed Lindbergh for the failure to reach a solution by that time.)[571]

Prior to April 2, 1932, Lindbergh had gone to see Commissioner Mulrooney and *"requested that the police stay out of the case until the ransom negotiations were completed"* and Mulrooney agreed to comply with this request.[572] One might ask "why" he would agree. It turns out that after the second ransom note had been received, Mulrooney had decided to have his men make *"twenty-four-hour"* stakeouts of the scores of mailboxes he suspected might be used to mail the next letter. They would watch and then check any box after a letter was dropped into it to see if it had been addressed to either

---

[569] Reich, Alfred Jacob. Testimony. The State of New Jersey vs. Bruno Richard Hauptmann, <u>Hunterdon County Court of Oyer and Terminer</u>, page 577, 1935. New Jersey State Law Library.

[570] Coakley, Leo J. *Jersey Troopers*. (1971) Rutgers University Press. Page 116.

[571] See *TDC* Volume I, page 342.

[572] Sisk, T. H. Special Agent, Division of Investigation (FBI). Memorandum For The Director. Unknown Subjects. <u>Kidnapping and Murder of Charles A. Lindbergh, Jr</u>. June 29, 1934. National Archives at College Park Maryland.

Condon or Lindbergh. If one was discovered, they would follow the sender before they disappeared from view.[573] Lindbergh "*vetoed*" this idea and claimed his son could be killed if such a move was made. "*Mulrooney argued the letter writer need never know he was under surveillance*," but Lindbergh still said "*no*" and added…

> "…*if Mulrooney went ahead anyway, he, Lindbergh, would use his influence to see that Mulrooney was broken.*"[574]

Fearing Lindbergh's power Mulrooney not only acquiesced, he never challenged Lindbergh's authority again.

The Bureau was kept completely in the dark but was secretly informed with what they referred to as "hear-say" information regarding the negotiations which they received from Thomas G. Lanphier.

Special Agent F. J. Lackey

In addition to becoming what amounted to the FBI's "informant," Lanphier had been suspicious of Condon which resulted in the request from the FBI to investigate Condon's background. He also requested that SAC Connelley arrange "*to have Agents located near Condon's residence in the Bronx should sudden emergency demand their presence.*"[575] This was done, and according to the available

---

[573]   Hynd, Alan. *Violence in the Night*. Fawcett Publications. (1955) Page 10.

[574]   Ibid. Pages 10-11.

[575]   Keith, J. M. Special Agent-In-Charge, BOI. BOI (FBI) Memorandum For The Director. <u>RE: Kidnapping of Charles A. Lindbergh Jr</u>. April 6, 1932. National Archives at College Park Maryland.

documentation, without the knowledge of Lindbergh or any of the police.[576]

> *"In an undercover manner an Agent was placed in a room across the street from Condon's residence, and two other Agents were placed in a room about a block away, to be reached by Connelley on the telephone should any sudden emergency require their presence."*[577]

The man stationed across from Condon's home was Special Agent Lackey. According the SAC Keith, on the night of April 2, 1932, Lackey observed:

> *"…the tan colored Franklin convertible sedan of Col. Lindbergh drive up to Condon's residence shortly before 9:50 P.M. Lindbergh and Breckenridge [sic] and a third man whose identity is unknown, were in the car. They went into the residence, carrying with them two black bags and extra overcoats. At 9:50 P.M., April 2nd, Lindbergh, Breckenridge [sic] and the unknown party left Condon's residence with the black bags and the extra overcoats, driving away in a northerly direction. The Condon residence remained lighted until 1:00 A.M., at which time the lights were extinguished and activity ceased."*[578]

---

[576] Sisk, T. H. Special Agent, Division of Investigation (FBI). Memorandum For The Director. Unknown Subjects. Kidnapping and Murder of Charles A. Lindbergh, Jr. July 27, 1934. National Archives at College Park Maryland.

[577] Keith, J. M. Special Agent-In-Charge, BOI. BOI (FBI) Memorandum For The Director. RE: Kidnapping of Charles A. Lindbergh Jr. April 6, 1932. National Archives at College Park Maryland.

[578] Ibid.

This narrative seems to be an eyewitness account concerning the end of the event. The next official account of Lindbergh's Franklin came from Elmer Irey. He was the chief of the Intelligence Unit within the Internal Revenue Bureau. According to his account, SAC Hugh McQuillan, SAC Madden, and Irey were all at the Hotel Taft when "*at 11:00 p.m.,*" the Franklin pulled up to pick him and Madden up for a meeting at the Morrow Apartment on East 72nd Street where Lindbergh, Breckinridge, and Condon currently were waiting for their arrival.[579] Al Reich and Captain Galvin were the only men in the Franklin when it pulled up.[580]

However, in a letter written in the summer of 1932 to J. Edgar Hoover, SAC Connelley wrote:

> "*However, from reliable source it was definitely known that four persons left the Condon home at about 10:00 p.m. with a package on Saturday night, April 2, 1932 for the purpose above indicated, the other two parties being, it is understood, Wilson and Irey or Wilson and Madden of the Intelligence Unit.*"[581]

Since this letter was written in 1932, it seems to me his source was most likely Agent Lackey since they were unaware of any other surveillance at the time. So while we know the men he claims were

---

[579] Irey, Elmer L. <u>Memorandum in re: Trip with Colonel Lindbergh, Colonel Breckenridge and Dr. Condon on April 2, 1932</u>. April 4, 1932. New Jersey State Police Museum and Learning Center Archives. (Note: His men were the Treasury Agents or sometimes referred to as "T-Men" (although they were sometimes referred to as "G-Men" as well).

[580] Ibid.

[581] Connelley, E. J. Special Agent in Charge, Bureau of Investigation. <u>Letter from E. J. Connelly to Director Re: Kidnaping and Murder of Charles A. Lindbergh Jr</u>. June 23, 1932. National Archives at College Park Maryland.

the "other two parties" were incorrect, the fact that another car with two more people was involved is worthy of serious consideration.

Detectives Itschner and Clune

Despite the standing orders not to interfere, Captain Oliver violated those department instructions by planting *"two detectives at the Condon residence."*[582] This fact came to the attention of Agent Sisk when confidentially given to him by Captain Leahy. Sisk was also told because of this violation the men made no official reports although he believed notes may have been taken. However, the information about these detectives seemed to have been known to Lt. Keaten as well who told Sisk…

> *"…that he was almost sure that two New York detectives had the Condon residence under surveillance on April 2nd and that he could not understand why these detectives did not get the license number of the taxicab."*[583]

Almost simultaneously, Special Agent Sandberg was being informed by Lt. Finn that on the day the ransom was paid Detectives Tim Clune and Fred Itschner had covered Condon's home in an unofficial capacity.[584] This, Finn explained, was due to Lindbergh's *"request that the police stay away that day"* and he also confirmed that as a

[582] Sisk, T. H. Special Agent, Division of Investigation (FBI). Memorandum For The Director. Unknown Subjects. Kidnapping and Murder of Charles A. Lindbergh, Jr. June 29, 1934. National Archives at College Park Maryland.

[583] Ibid.

[584] Sandberg, E. Special Agent, Division of Investigation (FBI). Memorandum For File. Unknown Subjects. Kidnapping and Murder of Charles A. Lindbergh, Jr. July 12, 1934. National Archives at College Park Maryland.

result no official report had been written.[585] It had been because of this information that Sandberg interviewed both Clune and Itschner who readily admitted they...

> "*...covered the Condon home all day April 2, 1932 and that they did not observe a taxi or any other car drive up to the Condon home on this date.*"[586]

In fact, their position was put in very clear terms by Special Agent Sisk in his memorandum to Hoover in June of '34:

> "*I might state that the New York office has recently learned the identity of the detectives who did have the house under surveillance and that these detectives claim they positively did not see a taxicab pull up in front of the Condon home that evening.*"[587]

The detectives had offered Sandberg an alternative possibility to consider though...

> "*...that it could have been possible for a party to have walked up to the Condon home and delivered the message without their seeing him.*"[588]

---

585   Ibid.

586   Ibid.

587   Sisk, T. H. Special Agent, Division of Investigation (FBI). Memorandum For The Director. Unknown Subjects. <u>Kidnapping and Murder of Charles A. Lindbergh, Jr</u>. June 29, 1934. National Archives at College Park Maryland.

588   Sandberg, E. Special Agent, Division of Investigation (FBI). Memorandum For File. Unknown Subjects. <u>Kidnapping and Murder of Charles A. Lindbergh, Jr</u>. July 12, 1934. National Archives at College Park Maryland.

These men also shared an interesting observation they had made in which they claimed that at about 4:45 PM a man they believed was Arthur O'Sullivan came to the Condon home and stayed there until:

> *"Dr. Condon went out that night to pay the ransom money and that O'Sullivan then followed Dr. Condon in his car around the block; that the large car and the reporter's car circled the block about 8:00PM April 2, 1932."*[589]

Something mentioned to Sisk that was not covered in the Sandberg interview was Captain Leahy's assertion that these detectives…

> *"…tried to tail Lindbergh and Condon when they started out for St. Raymond's Cemetery to pay the ransom money. However, that the detectives' car broke down."*[590]

Was this true or was it confusion concerning the second car these men watched tail the car Condon was in? Lt. Keaten had asked Lindbergh whether or not he was tailed that night. Lindbergh told him that…

> *"…he does recall that one and possibly two cars followed him and Dr. Condon when they left to pay the ransom money; however, that he succeeded in eluding these cars."*[591]

---

[589] Ibid.

[590] Sisk, T. H. Special Agent, Division of Investigation (FBI). Memorandum For The Director. Unknown Subjects. <u>Kidnapping and Murder of Charles A. Lindbergh, Jr</u>. June 29, 1934. National Archives at College Park Maryland.

[591] Ibid.

Another version of this would come to light in early 1936. Former Assistant United States Attorney Dan Cowie claimed that he was introduced to Lindbergh by United States Attorney George Medalie and that Lindbergh specifically told him...

> *"...that the night of the pay-off, he drove Dr. Condon and was followed by Colonel Irey of the Intelligence Unit and Colonel Breckenridge* [sic] *in another car."*[592]

Seeking an independent source for this information, I discovered a detailed memorandum written by J. Edgar Hoover which indicates the meeting between Lindbergh and Cowie did occur.[593]

Arthur O'Sullivan

In another strange twist, O'Sullivan had himself been accused of kidnapping. In 1931 he was arrested for *"posing as an official"* for taking Walter Dickerson to Flushing to question him regarding the death of Benjamin P. Collings which occurred aboard his yacht.[594] The charges against him were eventually dismissed.

In an earlier interview, Dr. Condon had told Special Agent Sandberg that on April 2, 1932, *"he received no 'phone calls' that day from any*

---

[592] Cowie, Dan B. Letter from Dan B. Cowie to Hon. Harold Hoffman. January 13, 1936. New Jersey State Police Museum and Learning Center Archives.

[593] Hoover, J. Edgar, Director, United States Bureau of Investigation. Memorandum For The Files. January 26, 1933. National Archives at College Park Maryland.

[594] "Veteran Reporter Wins Dismissal in Kidnaping." *The Washington Post.* November 13, 1931. New Jersey State Police Museum and Learning Center Archives.

reporters or anyone else that he recalled."[595] Condon said the same thing to Lt. Keaten as well, telling him "*no 'phone calls' received that day*" and also he "*advises no reporters in his house on April 2, 1932.*"[596] Was Condon lying – again? Since the police placed O'Sullivan in or near Condon's home, Sandberg sought him out to see what could be learned from him.

Once located, O'Sullivan told Sandberg that he had been detailed to cover the Condon home and was "*undoubtedly in the vicinity*" on April 2nd; however, he did not remember "*that particular day as being outstanding from any other day.*"[597] He explained that he had only been in Condon's home once at the onset of his assignment and that he spoke to him for possibly "*an hour or an hour and a half.*" He also claimed that Condon told him to "*keep away from the house*" so he typically stayed at the drugstore nearby, the restaurant on the west side of the street, or stayed in his car which he parked in various places so that he had a view of the home. O'Sullivan also told Sandberg that he would "*two or three times a day*" call the home looking for developments sometimes speaking with Condon directly and sometimes with whoever picked up the phone. He also said that there actually had been "*several times he went up to the house and rang the bell and other members of the family answered,*

[595] Sandberg, E. Special Agent, DOI. USBOI Report. Kidnaping And Murder Of Charles A. Lindbergh, Jr. July 11, 1934. New Jersey State Police Museum and Learning Center Archives.

[596] Keaten, Arthur T., Lieut., New Jersey State Police. New Jersey State Police Report. Re: report of investigation of Agent E. Sandberg of the Department of Justice in reference to an interview with Arthur O'Sullivan, reporter for Daily News in 1932, who covered Dr. Condon's residence during the negotiations for the return of the Lindbergh Child. July 11, 1934. New Jersey State Police Museum and Learning Center Archives.

[597] Sandberg, E. Special Agent, DOI. USBOI Report. Kidnaping And Murder Of Charles A. Lindbergh, Jr. July 11, 1934. New Jersey State Police Museum and Learning Center Archives.

and stated that nothing new had happened...".[598] O'Sullivan also told Sandberg that during his entire assignment he *"did not recall ever having seen a taxi drive up to Dr. Condon's house at any time during the ransom negotiations."*[599] He admitted that he, as well as other reporters had "trailed" Reich's car and that they had even solicited the local druggist, Harry Schwarzler, to assist in tailing him.[600] He also gave Sandberg a list of at least eleven other reporters who were in the vicinity of the Condon home part of the time during the ransom negotiations, and added that:

> *"it was the practice of the reporters to question anyone who entered or left the Condon residence, to make a note of all license numbers of cars which pulled up in front of the house, and to call in to the City Desk and obtain listings on the license numbers."*[601]

This fact was echoed by Lt. Keaten when he told Special Agent Sisk...

> *"...that a large number of newspaper men were around the Condon residence during the day and night of April 2nd and that the reporters would undoubtedly have copied down all license numbers of cars which pulled up to the house and would have bombarded with questions anyone who entered or left the house."*[602]

---

[598] Ibid.

[599] Ibid.

[600] Ibid.

[601] Ibid.

[602] Sisk, T. H. Special Agent, Division of Investigation (FBI). Memorandum For The Director. Unknown Subjects. <u>Kidnapping and Murder of Charles A. Lindbergh, Jr</u>. June 29, 1934. National Archives at College Park Maryland.

Another tip provided to authorities was that it was *"general knowledge that a Mr. Bender of the United Press had secured a room directly across from Dr. Condon's through which he kept the residence under surveillance continuously night and day...."*[603] A further point from O'Sullivan was that the only reporter *"who enjoyed Dr. Condon's confidence was Gregory Coleman of the Bronx Home News."*[604]

Detective Phillip Creamer

The FBI also learned that in addition to the two New York detectives watching the Condon home, they had detailed a detective from the *"undercover squad"* to place a *"tap on the Condon telephone during April 2nd and 3rd, 1932."*[605] Special Agent Sandberg was able to ascertain from Lt. Finn that the detective in question was Phillip Creamer, and he came in to recount what he had learned from these wire taps to both Finn and Sandberg. Creamer stated that he had tapped this line from April 2, 1932, from 9 AM to April 3, 1932, ending at 9 P.M. The first call that came in was from Ralph Hacker

---

[603] Haussling, E. A. Sgt., New Jersey State Police. New Jersey State Police Report. Received of letters, etc. from the Department of Justice, and interview with Mr. Arthur O'Sullivan at the Department of Justice Headquarters, this date. July 10, 1934. New Jersey State Police Museum and Learning Center Archives.

[604] Sandberg, E. Special Agent, DOI. USBOI Report. Kidnaping And Murder Of Charles A. Lindbergh, Jr. July 11, 1934. New Jersey State Police Museum and Learning Center Archives.

[605] Sisk, T. H. Special Agent, Division of Investigation (FBI). Memorandum For The Director. Unknown Subjects. Kidnapping and Murder of Charles A. Lindbergh, Jr. June 29, 1934. National Archives at College Park Maryland.

to Myra at about 9:45 AM[606] Concerning O'Sullivan, Creamer stated that he called several times in the "forenoon" beginning about 10:10 AM speaking sometime with Condon, Myra, or Reich.

> *"About 4:45 P.M. the same date Arthur O'Sullivan called again and wanted to come to the house and Condon said he would be on the front porch; that about 5:30 P.M. that day O'Sullivan called again and Condon said there was nothing new; that O'Sullivan then told Dr. Condon he would be covering Curry's dinner at Hotel Commodore that night, also told Dr. Condon that his brother Ray was the secretary to Tammany Hall."*[607]

Creamer added that O'Sullivan called several more times that night with Reich answering once and claiming nothing new had happened. Other calls he noted came at 1:00 PM from Coleman of the Bronx News *"and Condon promised him the first "break" in the case."*[608] Another party named Bartow called but no one answered. A little while later he called again and when Condon picked up Bartow told him *"the black bag was down in his office and Condon said Reich is fixing a tire on the Packard."*[609] At approximately 2 PM two men from the United Press, Bender and Bieckel, called and were told *"nothing new had happened"* but a little while later Condon called Bender and *"during the conversation promised him the first "break"*

---

[606] Sandberg, E. Special Agent, Division of Investigation (FBI). Memorandum For File. Unknown Subjects. <u>Kidnapping and Murder of Charles A. Lindbergh, Jr</u>. July 12, 1934. National Archives at College Park Maryland.

[607] Ibid.

[608] Ibid.

[609] Ibid.

in the case.[610] Also sometime during the day Al Reich called an auto repair shop to have the tire fixed.

Aside from confirming Condon a liar, Creamer's wiretap also proved O'Sullivan could not have been in Dr. Condon's house at the time Detective Clune indicated. Furthermore, this is also backed up by O'Sullivan himself having claimed to Sandberg that…

> "…he positively did not follow Dr. Condon or anyone else around the block on April 2, 1932, the night the ransom money was paid. He stated he would have been very glad to have had such an opportunity but that he positively did not do so."[611]

Since O'Sullivan was obviously misidentified, who was the person these men saw? One of the last things Detective Creamer noted was that:

> "Myra Hacker left the house about 7:00 P.M. the same date but that Mrs. Condon stayed there all the time."[612]

Since by all accounts the supposed "taxi driver" delivered the note at 8 PM (give or take a few minutes), this proves beyond all doubt that Myra was <u>lying</u> about seeing the man who delivered this note. It also explains why no one placed her there prior to her declaration which she made for the first time in the summer of 1934.

---

610 Ibid.
611 Ibid.
612 Ibid.

Captain Oliver

As previously written, Captain Richard Oliver was under Commissioner Edward Mulrooney's order that *"the territory above 125th Street and the Harlem River was forbidden ground to all New York detectives."*[613] As also seen written above, he defied these orders.

After the child's dead body was discovered on May 12, 1932, the New Jersey State Police considered Condon a suspect.[614] As a result, Schwarzkopf requested that Mulrooney provide some of his men to cover the Condon home for the *"purpose of ascertaining all visitors"* to see him:

> *"We are anxious to find out the identity, home addresses and business addresses of these visitors, just who they are and whether or not they are connected with the people whom Doctor Condon was negotiating with just prior to the time the ransom money was paid. We are particularly interested in getting this information, should any persons of Scandinavian or German extraction call on Doctor Condon or be seen in the vicinity of his home acting in a suspicious manner.*
>
> *This information has been telephoned direct to your Captain Oliver who requested it be brought to your attention in the form of a communication which we hasten to do herewith."*[615]

---

[613] Waller, George. *Kidnap: The Story of the Lindbergh Case.* (1961) The Dial Press. Page 78.

[614] Coakley, Leo J. *Jersey Troopers.* (1971) Rutgers University Press. Page 119.

[615] Schwarzkopf, H. Norman, Colonel and Superintendent, New Jersey State Police. <u>Letter from H. Norman Schwarzkopf to Commissioner Mulrooney</u>. May 14, 1932. New Jersey State Police Museum and Learning Center Archives.

As suspicion of Condon heightened, the state police asked Mulrooney for assistance in their search for the "Missing Taxi Driver," which they were given as evidenced in the preceding pages of this book. They also seemed to discover that Condon's place had been surveilled as noted here:

> "*See Captain Oliver in reference to the covering of Condon's house the night the second note was delivered there.*"[616]

Resulting from this investigation was a five-page typed document of all events and concerns as it related to John Condon.[617] Among the items listed within this memo was something extremely important as it related to the "missing" taxi driver:

> "*Dick Oliver says no cab came to Dr.'s. on Apr. 2.*"[618]

One would expect a fact like this to receive prominent attention in each and every book on this case. It certainly isn't new. In fact, Governor Hoffman pointed this out in his Liberty Article Series.[619] It was also brought up again in Andrew Dutch's book written in

---

[616]   Lamb, J. J. Captain, New Jersey State Police. <u>Memorandum for Colonel Schwarzkopf</u>. July 6, 1932. New Jersey State Police Museum and Learning Center Archives.

[617]   New Jersey State Police Memorandum. Untitled. Undated (1932). New Jersey State Police Museum and Learning Center Archives. (Note: During Gov. Hoffman's re-investigation if certain documents were found to be important it was given an Exhibit Number in preparation for presentation to the Court of Pardons. This was given "Ex. No. 11").

[618]   Ibid.

[619]   Hoffman, Harold Giles. *The Crime - The Case - The Challenge (What Was Wrong with the Lindbergh Case?)*, Original Manuscript: Unedited & Uncorrected, circa 1937. Page 109. New Jersey State Police Museum and Learning Center Archives.

1975.[620] So if Oliver even gets mentioned at all somewhere, why would anyone omit this very important <u>fact</u>? Regardless of why certain authors might choose to omit certain facts while also pushing fiction as history, it seems logical to conclude that Oliver made this statement based upon the Clune and Itschner observations. However, a new version emerged, and one that placed Oliver himself as surveilling the Condon home on April 2, 1932.[621] This story originates with Dr. Dudley Shoenfeld. In his book he wrote:

> *"To overcome the resultant confusion, Colonel H. Norman Schwarzkopf was given sole charge. Actually, however, Colonel Lindbergh, advised by Colonel Breckinridge, completely dominated all police work. The New York police, not extended full confidence, retired from the scene. The others remained and agreed to restrict their activities to the prescribed regulations."*[622]

According to Shoenfeld, on the evening of April 2nd Oliver *"shadowed"* the home then followed Lindbergh and Condon to St. Raymond's Cemetery in an *"old automobile."*[623] As the story goes, Oliver was not only *"dressed like a derelict,"* Lindbergh noticed he was being followed and took evasive measures to lose him and believed he had been successful. However, Shoenfeld wrote they had not lost Oliver and he had actually witnessed Condon leaving the car to pay the ransom. What was Oliver's plan at that point? According to Shoenfeld, Oliver would *"kidnap"* John or *"pretend to be a member of another gang"* which would allow him to be led back to the *"hideout."*

---

[620] Dutch, Andrew K. *Hysteria, Lindbergh Kidnap Case.* (1975). Dorrance & Co. Page 59.

[621] Shoenfeld, Dudley D. *The Crime and the Criminal: A Psychiatric Study of the Lindbergh Case.* (1936). Covici-Friede. Page 30.

[622] Ibid. Page 21.

[623] Ibid. Page 30.

Ridiculous? No, absolutely absurd. Regardless, Shoenfeld asserted that Oliver talked himself out of the idea, not because it was crazy or stupid or would have gotten himself killed, but because if the baby had been alive at the time his actions could have resulted in his death.[624] It should be noted here that Waller had a version of this event involving Oliver as well. The only main difference was that Oliver was dressed in *"plain clothes"* and mentioned that while observing the scene he was *"well hidden."*[625]

Is there any truth to this story? I searched the NJSP Archives from top to bottom at least three full times in my life.[626] Aside from that I have been through certain collections at least ten or more times. While I must admit I often find items I "missed" in places I have previously viewed on several different occasions, I can say without hesitation there has been only one document that has any hint of such a scenario. This occurred during a "Nellie" search when information came to police that a man named *"Ernest Smith"* was the owner of a boat with that name.[627] The source for this information was *"obtained indirectly from a man who in turn receives it from an unknown girl."*[628] After Oliver interviewed this *"man whose name is unknown"* they were able to locate this *"girl."* From this *"girl"* they were able to learn her informant was a different man named *"Tony"* who lived in the *"Bronx."* The girl also said that *"Tony"* told her...

---

[624] Ibid. Page 31.

[625] Waller, George. *Kidnap: The Story of the Lindbergh Case.* (1961) The Dial Press. Page 78.

[626] Strange as it may sound, I have been told I am the only researcher to have ever done it – even once.

[627] Walsh, Harry W. Inspector, Jersey City Police Dept. and Keaton, A. T. Lieut., N. J. State Police. New Jersey State Police Report. Report on investigation of the kidnaping of Charles Lindbergh, Junior. April 7, 1932. New Jersey State Police Museum and Learning Center Archives.

[628] Ibid.

> "...*that Captain Oliver could have apprehended one of*
> *the kidnapers* [sic] *at the time he met the intermediary*
> *at the cemetery.*"[629]

The "*girl*" gave one last bit of information which was "*that the*
Lindbergh child is still alive and in good health and is concealed
somewhere in the Brownsville section of New York."[630] Nowhere else is
anything mentioned despite the fact both Lt. Keaten and Lt. Finn
had no problem revealing to the FBI that Oliver had disobeyed
orders by planting his men and tapping the phone lines.

Here we must ask ourselves what makes sense – and what does
not. To me it seems Oliver is responsible for all that's in the official
documentation: Detectives watched the house, a detective listened to
phone calls, detectives attempted to follow (but the car broke down).
These activities are no less troubling than if he had actually gone to
the cemetery to meet Cemetery John. And yet, everything we know
DID occur is suspiciously absent from both Schoenfeld and Waller.

---

[629]   Ibid.
[630]   Ibid.

4

The Ransom Drop Ruse

After Condon pretended to receive the new ransom note from a taxi driver, he brought it back to the kitchen area to show Lindbergh, Breckinridge, and Reich. Here Lindbergh had possession of the $70,000 dollars that had been shoved into the "ransom box." As we all know, the box which the ransom note writer asked for seemed to have been designed for only $50,000, so once the demand increased by $20,000 the box could not hold the full amount. Reich explained that he, Condon, and Lindbergh had all attempted to force *"the extra twenty thousand"* in and they *"broke the box."*[631] Reich told police the only way the money may have fit is if they took the box apart first. So in the end, Reich said they simply *"put a piece of paper around it"* and made do to ensure no money would spill out.[632] Lindbergh, however, said *"the box itself was wrapped with cord to hold it together."*[633]

---

[631] Reich, Alfred J. Statement. Made to Acting Lieutenant James J. Finn, M.O.D. October 8, 1934. New Jersey State Police Museum and Learning Center Archives.

[632] Ibid.

[633] Lindbergh, Charles A. Sr. Statement. Made to Inspector Harry W. Walsh. May 20, 1932. New Jersey State Police Museum and Learning Center Archives.

The Decision
(Lindbergh's Version)

The note was read, and it directed them to drive to *"Bergen Greenhauses florist"* on *"3225 east Tremont Ave."* where there would be another note waiting. On the flip side it gave them a time limit of *"3/4 of a houer"* while also warning them not to speak to anyone, that the kidnappers would be listening for any police radio alarm, claiming they had the same equipment.[634] At that time both Condon and Reich were about to go when Lindbergh spoke up and stopped them. He was *"somewhat suspicious"* that both he and Breckenridge were to be left behind while they took the ransom money, so he told them he would drive instead of Reich, then said Reich would remain at the Condon residence with Breckinridge.[635] According to Lindbergh:

> *"Condon stalled a bit and remarked to Colonel Breckenridge [sic] that he, Condon, feared that Colonel Lindbergh might use firearms were he, Lindbergh, present."*[636]

However, Lindbergh insisted. The fact that Lindbergh did not trust Condon is extremely important. When recalling his version of events to Special Agent Larimer during a 1933 meeting, he told the investigator that...

> *"...were Dr. Condon a younger man he would be immediately suspicious of him. However, in spite of*

---

[634] Exhibit S-66. New Jersey State Police Museum and Learning Center Archives.

[635] Larimer, Hugh Special Agent, USBOI. USBOI (FBI) Report. Unknown Subjects. Kidnapping of Charles A. Lindbergh Jr. March 4, 1933. New Jersey State Police Museum and Learning Center Archives.

[636] Ibid.

Condon's age there were several little things which raised doubt as to Condon's sincerity."[637]

During his meeting with Dan Cowie, Lindbergh made similar remarks claiming that *"he had absolutely no confidence in Dr. Condon...."*[638] However, Lindbergh would contradict himself on this point when asked by a Juror during his Bronx Grand Jury testimony if he ever doubted *"the honesty"* of Condon to which he responded *"I had no reason to."*[639] Why was Lindbergh saying one thing to some people but something very different to others? In the end, Lindbergh's own statement that he had no reason to doubt Condon led to the relationship being viewed by history as a trusting one (despite the fact of Lindbergh not trusting him) and would be used to bolster Condon's credibility.

Regardless, in response to Lindbergh's insistence that he go and Reich stay back, Reich reasoned they should still make use of his car and explained...

"...the first contact was made by Dr. Condon and me in my ford coupe and Colonel Lindbergh was going to make this contact. I said "take my car because they may be suspicious if they see another car."[640]

---

[637] Ibid.

[638] Cowie, Dan B. Letter from Dan B. Cowie to Hon. Harold Hoffman. January 13, 1936. New Jersey State Police Museum and Learning Center Archives.

[639] Lindbergh, Charles A. Testimony. Grand Jury. People vs. Hauptmann. September 26, 1934. New Jersey State Police Museum and Learning Center Archives.

[640] Reich, Alfred J. Statement. Made to Acting Lieutenant James J. Finn, M.O.D. October 8, 1934. New Jersey State Police Museum and Learning Center Archives.

The decision was made and, depending on which account Lindbergh made in Flemington one believes, about 8:15 PM or about 8:30 PM Lindbergh was behind the wheel of Reich's ford coupe when both he and Condon departed with the $70,000 enroute to the flower shop.[641]

(Condon's Version)

Condon's spin on this was much different. He told Gregory Coleman that he…

> "…*had arranged for Col. Lindbergh to drive him to the kidnapers* [sic] *with the money in Al Reich's coupe, if that plan proved feasible and consistent with the expected directions from the kidnapers* [sic]."[642]

After the note was delivered by the "taxi driver," Condon immediately recognized it as authentic by the "*blue and red ink of the ominous signature.*" It directed him to the florist shop with no time to spare.

> "*Col. Lindbergh donned his hat and coat and carrying the box of money walked to Al Reich's coupe in front of the Condon home. He drove the Doctor to the nursery at top speed.*"[643]

---

[641] Lindbergh, Charles. Testimony. The State of New Jersey vs. Bruno Richard Hauptmann, <u>Hunterdon County Court of Oyer and Terminer</u>, pages 106 & 193, 1935. New Jersey State Law Library.

[642] Coleman, Gregory. "*Vigil.*" Manuscript: Unpublished and Undated (1932?). Page 47. New Jersey State Police Museum and Learning Center Archives.

[643] Ibid. Page 49.

(Breckinridge's Version)

Breckinridge testified they had all been at Condon's because they "*knew things were coming to a head on the second of April*."[644] According to Breckinridge Lindbergh...

> "...*insisted on going with Dr. Condon for two reasons, one of them was that if the doctor was going to be bumped off for ransoming his child that he had just the same right to get bumped off and the second reason was Dr. Condon was in a hot spot first the $70,000 and then the taking out of the $20,000 and if there was any suspicion on the doctor it would be said that the man that put up the money was there when the transaction took place. After all those phases and that reasoning was discussed the Colonel decided to go with him which he did...*"[645]

What to make of this explanation? It disagrees with Condon's version, and most importantly Lindbergh's version as well. So now we have three totally different scenarios to choose from. Unfortunately, if what Breckinridge was testifying to was true, they already knew before it actually happened the $20,000 would be removed ahead of time. So what he appears to be spelling out is that Lindbergh went with him as a pre-emptive measure to protect Condon from any accusations which would result from that money being removed. Hard to believe but there it is nevertheless. Did he misspeak? Is what he said a misunderstanding of some sort?

---

[644] Breckinridge, Henry. Testimony. <u>Grand Jury</u>. People vs. Hauptmann. September 25, 1934. New Jersey State Police Museum and Learning Center Archives.

[645] Ibid.

St. Raymond's Cemetery
Lindbergh's Version

Following the instructions in the note, Lindbergh and Condon proceeded to the florist shop on Tremont Avenue near Whittemore *"and parked directly opposite its entrance."*[646] *"This was about 8:40 P.M."*[647] Lindbergh testified he believed that it took *"a little over a half an hour to drive"* there from the house.[648] Condon then told Lindbergh the note instructed him to look beneath a table under a rock so Condon got out of the car and walked in the direction of the floral shop. Lindbergh remained seated in the car and noticed several people walking along the sidewalk. This distracted his attention and he did not watch Condon closely at this time.[649] Condon returned to the car with a note, then while remaining outside of the car, leaned over using a flash light so they could both read what was written on the new note. Lindbergh said Condon took an unusual amount of time which he explained to Lindbergh was being done to give the kidnappers the *"opportunity to identify him."*[650] As Condon was reading the note, Lindbergh's attention was drawn to a man who...

"...appeared walking along the sidewalk opposite to the direction in which the car was stationed. He walked

---

[646] Lindbergh, Charles A. Sr. Statement. Made to Inspector Harry W. Walsh. May 20, 1932. New Jersey State Police Museum and Learning Center Archives.

[647] Larimer, Hugh Special Agent, USBOI. USBOI (FBI) Report. Unknown Subjects. <u>Kidnapping of Charles A. Lindbergh Jr.</u> March 4, 1933. New Jersey State Police Museum and Learning Center Archives.

[648] Lindbergh, Charles. Testimony. The State of New Jersey vs. Bruno Richard Hauptmann, <u>Hunterdon County Court of Oyer and Terminer</u>, page 195, 1935. New Jersey State Law Library.

[649] Ibid.

[650] Lindbergh, Charles A. Sr. Statement. Made to Inspector Harry W. Walsh. May 20, 1932. New Jersey State Police Museum and Learning Center Archives.

with an unusual gait rather awkwardly and with a pronounced stoop. His hat was pulled down over his eyes."[651]

As he approached the car he was eventually *"nearest enough to see him clearly."*[652]

> *"As he passed the car he covered his mouth and the lower part of his face with a handkerchief, and looked at Doctor Condon and at me. He continued along Tremont and passed out of sight. This man wore a brown suit and a brown felt hat. He was about 5' 8" or 9" tall, weight about 150 to 160 lbs. I am unable to give a more detailed description with any degree of accuracy. I formed the impression, however, that this man was not over 30 years of age and that his complexion was dark. He wore no topcoat. He was averagely dressed.*"[653]

Lindbergh had given Lt. Keaten an almost identical description *"shortly after the incident occurred,"* with the only difference being that he was more specific about the "unusual gait" which he described *"as rolling"* and *"somewhat similar to sailor's walk and somewhat awkward."*[654] Lindbergh would later testify to the Grand Jury that

---

[651]   Ibid.

[652]   Lindbergh, Charles A. Testimony. Grand Jury. People vs. Hauptmann. September 26, 1934. New Jersey State Police Museum and Learning Center Archives.

[653]   Lindbergh, Charles A. Sr. Statement. Made to Inspector Harry W. Walsh. May 20, 1932. New Jersey State Police Museum and Learning Center Archives.

[654]   Sisk, T. H. Special Agent, DOI. USBOI Report. Kidnaping and Murder of Charles A. Lindbergh Jr. June 26, 1934. New Jersey State Police Museum and Learning Center Archives.

he felt *"sure"* this man *"was one of the actual group of kidnappers or connected with them..."*[655] And, as we shall see, he was right. The note Condon was said to have retrieved read:

"cross the street and

    walk to the next corner and follow Whittermore Ave
    to the soud

take the money with

    you come alone
      and walk
     I will meet you"[656]

Condon then walked across Tremont without the money *"to the corner of Tremont and Whittemore opposite the cemetary* [sic]*"* and approached a *"man"* and a *"little girl"* who were standing on that corner and spoke to them.[657] From there he walked across Whittemore then waited a *"few moments."* After that he began to walk back to the car, but after about half way back across Whittemore *"a voice from the cemetary* [sic] *called 'Ay Doctor'"* which Lindbergh could hear *"distinctly and Doctor was pronounced with a definite accent."*[658] Condon, hearing the voice, turned around, walked back to the corner of the cemetery, then down Whittemore out of sight. Also, once the voice called out...

---

[655] Lindbergh, Charles A. Testimony. <u>Grand Jury</u>. People vs. Hauptmann. September 26, 1934. New Jersey State Police Museum and Learning Center Archives.

[656] Exhibit S-68. New Jersey State Police Museum and Learning Center Archives.

[657] Lindbergh, Charles A. Sr. Statement. Made to Inspector Harry W. Walsh. May 20, 1932. New Jersey State Police Museum and Learning Center Archives.

[658] Ibid.

> "...*the man with the little girl previously mentioned
> turned quickly, watched Doctor Condon pass down
> Whittemore, and then walked rapidly out of sight
> along the cemetary* [sic] *side of Tremont Avenue.*"[659]

The time was now about 9 P.M.[660] "*A few minutes later*" Condon
returned to the car and told Lindbergh that "'*John' had agreed to take
$50,000 instead of $70,000*" so he "*told*" Lindbergh to "*take out of
the box the $20,000.*"[661] Lindbergh removed the $20,000 and gave
the box containing $50,000 back to Condon, who then proceeded
to corner of the cemetery once again. This time however, instead
of walking back down Whittemore Avenue (from where he had
just come) he continued down Tremont and "*out of sight.*"[662] "*A few
minutes later he came into view walking back along Tremont on the
cemetery side and turned down Whittemore and again passed out of
sight.*"[663]

This little peculiarity generated doubt concerning the ransom
payment in both Lindbergh and Breckinridge. According to the
FBI Summary Report...

> "...*after Condon's obtaining this money he departed
> the parked car and again returned to the cemetery to
> recontact "John." On this return trip, however, instead
> of taking the first turn off East Tremont Avenue into
> St. Raymond's Cemetery, Condon passed the entrance
> and walked down another block completely outside of
> the sight of Colonel Lindbergh, then Condon turned
> around, walked back and walked into the cemetery*

---

[659]   Ibid.
[660]   Ibid.
[661]   Ibid.
[662]   Ibid.
[663]   Ibid.

with box apparently under his arm. It is not known to Colonel Lindbergh or Colonel Breckinridge nor has Condon explained it satisfactorily just why he went one block further down the cemetery before he returned and entered it, to contact "John" the second time on the night of April 2nd."[664]

About 15 minutes after Condon had disappeared back down Whittemore Avenue, another strange event took place. The peculiar man in the brown suit who Lindbergh had noticed originally eyeing him up was back. This time he...

"...appeared on the cemetary [sic] side of Tremont running in the direction of Whittemore. When he came to Whittemore he stopped running and when midway across Whittemore he hesitated, looked down Whittemore back along Tremont and then continued in a walk along Tremont passing the car on the opposite side of Tremont. As he passed the car he covered his face with a handkerchief and blew his nose so loudly that it could be distinctly heard across the street where I was parked and undoubtedly a considerably greater distance."[665]

This eyewitness account of this "look-out" is so important that I want to give Lindbergh's Grand Jury version offered up in his testimony there as well:

---

[664] Sisk, T. H. DOI (FBI) et. al., DOI Report. Summary. NY File No. 62-3057, p. 195. February 16, 1934. National Archives at College Park Maryland.

[665] Lindbergh, Charles A. Sr. Statement. Made to Inspector Harry W. Walsh. May 20, 1932. New Jersey State Police Museum and Learning Center Archives.

"Just before Dr. Condon returned from having met the man and made the payment this same man came running back on the other side of the street on the cemetery side, he stopped or paused then as he crossed Wittemere [sic] street looking first backward at the car and then around and then in all directions, he then began walking rapidly so he passed the car again, this time on the otherside of the street going in the other direction covering his face with the handerchief [sic] and he blew his nose very loudly after he had passed far enough I had no direct view of his face, he removed the handkerchief and with a quick motion threw it down with his left hand into a lot an open lot opposite the side of Tremont from the Florist shop...".[666]

Lindbergh had told Lt. Keaten that he believed *"the man was giving a signal that the coast was clear"* because *"it would have been a simple matter for anyone to have concealed himself"* within the *"trees and shrubbery"* and *"observe the man give the signal with his handkerchief."*[667] And just as Lindbergh had told Inspector Walsh in his official statement, he also told Special Agent Larimer that this lookout was a *"young man of average size, wearing a brown suit and a brown felt hat with a snap brim pulled down in front"* and had a *"stooped posture"* which may have been *"real or assumed."*[668] He also

---

[666] Lindbergh, Charles A. Testimony. <u>Grand Jury</u>. People vs. Hauptmann. September 26, 1934. New Jersey State Police Museum and Learning Center Archives.

[667] Sisk, T. H. Special Agent, DOI. USBOI Report. <u>Kidnaping and Murder of Charles A. Lindbergh Jr</u>. June 26, 1934. New Jersey State Police Museum and Learning Center Archives.

[668] Larimer, Hugh Special Agent, USBOI. USBOI (FBI) Report. Unknown Subjects. <u>Kidnapping of Charles A. Lindbergh Jr</u>. March 4, 1933. New Jersey State Police Museum and Learning Center Archives.

told him that he *"spoke of this individual to Condon, but Condon stated he had not seen the man."*[669]

According to Lindbergh, after this man blew his nose, it was *"at this time Doctor Condon reappeared walking up Whittemore."*[670] Condon got into the car and told Lindbergh that he had *"persuaded "John" to give him directions as to where the baby would be found. He said these directions were given him on his promise not to open them for two hours."*[671]

James Bergen

Before delving into Condon's version of what happened at St. Raymond's, I think it's important to inject another eyewitness account. Having been detailed to investigate by Inspector Bruckman, Detective Thompson and Officer Avon interviewed the owner of Bergen's nursery. James A. Bergen told the officers that on April 2nd he arrived at his shop at *"8-00 P. M."* and observed…

> *"…a closed automobile parked in front of same, near curb, facing west, with a man standing on curb, with his head in car talking to an occupant. He further stated that man on curb wore dark clothes, and as he did not pay any attention to them he could not furnish us with any further descriptions. He informed us that he turned on the lights, stayed a few minutes, then left to mail letters at a box at E. Tremont & Puritans Avenues which was about 100 feet away. Upon return*

---

[669] Ibid.

[670] Lindbergh, Charles A. Sr. Statement. Made to Inspector Harry W. Walsh. May 20, 1932. New Jersey State Police Museum and Learning Center Archives.

[671] Ibid.

to nursery he observed man and automobile still there, that he then extinguished light in nursery and left for home. He stated that he did not observe anything unusual, neither did he observe man and woman standing at Whittemore and E. Tremont Avenues, as mentioned and pictured in the newspapers. He also informed us that he knows Dr. Condon, but that he did not observe him in the vicinity that night."[672]

After Hauptmann's arrest, Bergen was brought in to the Bronx County District Attorney's Office to be interviewed again. Bergen explained that although his store was already closed, he returned there from his home on Puritan Avenue between "*7:45 and 8:15*" ("*as near as he could judge*") to the florist shop to pick up and mail some letters that were there.[673] As he approached he noticed a "*small*" car on Tremont Avenue in front of the shop's door with a man "*standing on the curb and seemed to have his head and shoulders in the car talking to someone in the car.*"[674] He entered the shop and put the light on thinking it might have been someone interested in entering the store. He waited about six or seven minutes then left the shop and walked to the mail box located at Puritan and Tremont then returned. According to Bergen, "*they were awhile there and I went in and put out the light and went on.*"[675] Bergen also told the men he had known Dr. Condon "*for a good many years*" but could not tell

---

[672] Avon, James A. Officer, New York City Police Department. New York City Police Department Report. July 19, 1932. New Jersey State Police Museum and Learning Center Archives. (Note: Amended version to his report of May 21, 1932).

[673] Bergen, James A. Statement. Made to Assistant District Attorney Breslin, Capt. Lamb, N.J. State Police, Agent Seykora, Dept. of Justice and Stenographer King. October 3, 1934. New Jersey State Police Museum and Learning Center Archives.

[674] Ibid.

[675] Ibid.

if the man leaning in the car was him because "*his back was to me, I couldn't see his face.*"[676]

Several questions emerge from this account. Was this Lindbergh and Condon? The car was small and pointed in the place and direction Lindbergh claimed. A man was leaning in the car just as Lindbergh claimed Condon was doing. However, the timing does not fit. Could Bergen have been wrong about the time? If so, how didn't Lindbergh notice someone going in and out of the florist shop and turning the light on and off? Or, if Bergen was right about the time, was this the Kidnappers preparing/rehearsing for the upcoming ransom drop?

Bergen Greenhauses Florist
(Courtesy NJSP Museum)

---

[676]   Ibid.

John F. Condon's Version

We know from Condon's statement to Breslin that he was fully aware the police would not be interfering with the ransom drop:

> *"Colonel Lindbergh did not want any interference from the police; he laid down the law; he said that if he was interfered with in this case, being that it meant so much to him, they would hear from him personally."*[677]

Since the men were under a 45-minute time limit to arrive, we must rely on their recollections in order to establish a timeline of events. The timing of one thing determined the timing of the other – when they received the note, when they left Condon's house, when they arrived at the florist shop, etc.

Condon told Breslin that the whole thing lasted about an hour and five minutes when he claimed they left his house about *"9:00 o'clock"* and at *"10:05 I was back."*[678] Just the day before Condon had told Inspector Walsh almost the exact same thing.[679] During his Bronx Grand Jury testimony just six days later, a slightly amended but equally confident explanation emerged when he claimed they actually arrived: *"About five minutes past 9, I had just looked at my watch to see the time."*[680]

---

[677] Condon, John F. Statement. Made to Assistant District Attorney Edward F. Breslin. May 14, 1932. New Jersey State Police Museum and Learning Center Archives.

[678] Ibid.

[679] Condon, Dr. John F. Statement. May 13, 1932. Made to Inspector Harry W. Walsh. New Jersey State Police Museum and Learning Center Archives.

[680] Condon, John F. Testimony. Bronx Grand Jury. Continued after King. May 20, 1932. New Jersey State Police Museum and Learning Center Archives.

Condon claimed that upon their arrival at the florist shop, he found the note with a stone on it under a table. Apparently it was too dark to read the note there, so Condon brought the note back to the car, read it, then handed it to Lindbergh, who had stayed in the automobile, to read himself.[681]

The Look-Out

It was at this time Lindbergh witnessed the "look-out" walking by. As previously stated, Lindbergh had said when he eventually spoke about this man to Condon, Condon told him he had not seen him. Condon explained this further to Special Agent Sisk:

> "*Dr. Condon stated he did not see this man but that Colonel Lindbergh did see him; that he, Dr. Condon, had gone to get one of the ransom notes in front of Bergen's Greenhouse and returned with it and was showing it to Lindbergh with the aid of a flashlight when this man walked by the car, going east on Tremont Avenue; that Colonel Lindbergh saw him but was not able to give a very good description due to the fact that the man had his face partly covered with his handkerchief, as if he were blowing his nose.*"[682]

Condon claimed to have then walked across the street to the corner of East Tremont and Whittemore and, despite the warning in the note supposedly given to him by the unknown taxi driver not to speak to anyone, did exactly that anyway.

---

[681]   Ibid.

[682]   Sisk, T. H. Special Agent, DOI. USBOI Report. <u>Kidnaping and Murder of Charles A. Lindbergh Jr</u>. June 26, 1934. New Jersey State Police Museum and Learning Center Archives.

The Man & Girl

It was while standing on this corner that Condon saw:

> "*a man and a little girl on the corner and asked if they knew where Witmore* [sic] *street or avenue was. I didn't look at the sign up to that time, they didn't know.*"[683]

However, Condon would respond to a question posed to him by Inspector Walsh only 13 days later by saying he "*met the man and woman there and said "Do you know where Widdeman* [sic] *Street is?*"[684] So what we see here is the "little girl" just transformed into a "woman." The FBI Summary Report goes into a little more depth and detail...

> "...*Condon walked down to the corner to East Tremont Avenue to the Whittemore Avenue entrance of St. Raymond's Cemetery, where he saw a man and a little girl on the corner and from them he inquired as to whether they knew where Whittemore Avenue was. Condon states that in making this inquiry he had only one purpose in view and that being his effort to find out whether these individuals were any persons known to him. Condon states he cannot describe either the man or the girl from whom he made this inquiry, both being unknown to him. Up to that time Condon did not look at the street sign, it being assumed that because*

[683] Condon, John F. Testimony. <u>Bronx Grand Jury</u>. Continued after King. May 20, 1932. New Jersey State Police Museum and Learning Center Archives.

[684] Condon, Dr. John F. Statement. Made to Inspector Harry W. Walsh, Sgt. Warren T. Moffatt, Lieut. A. T. Keaton and Detective Horn. June 2, 1932. New Jersey State Police Museum and Learning Center Archives.

*of his familiarity with that territory he knew the exact
location of Whittemore Avenue. However, he states
that after making inquiry of the above mentioned man
and girl they advised him that they did not know the
location of East Whittemore Avenue."*[685]

And so the "woman" has reverted back to a "little girl." Not long
after this report was written Special Agent O'Leary spoke to Condon
about these figures in the case. Condon told him that between
"9 and 9:15 P.M." he noticed *"a man and a little girl standing on
the corner facing the street as if waiting for a street car."*[686] It should
be noted that after hearing this new revelation, Agent O'Leary
investigated this possibility but discovered *"there is no street car stop
at that intersection."*[687] Condon said that he walked up to the back
of the man and girl then…

> *"…he asked them "could you tell me whether this is
> Whittemore Avenue or not?" The man is alleged to
> have made a half turn and remarked over his shoulder
> "No, we couldn't or "No, we are strangers here."*[688]

Condon described the little girl as being *"about 12 years of age,
wearing a light dress and a light coat."* He described the man as being
"about 35, height 5'6" or 5' 7'", had on *"dark clothes and a soft hat"*
and *"native born"* based on his voice. He added that he associated
them as *"father and daughter"* and estimated the age of this man

[685] Sisk, T. H. DOI (FBI) et. al., DOI Report. Summary. NY File No.
62-3057, p. 185. February 16, 1934. National Archives at College Park
Maryland.

[686] O'Leary, J. M. Special Agent, DOI. DOI Report. Kidnaping and Murder
of Charles A. Lindbergh, Jr. April 5, 1934. New Jersey State Police
Museum and Learning Center Archives.

[687] Ibid.

[688] Ibid.

accordingly. He also claimed that since this man's back was turned, and that he was *"standing in the shadow of a telegraph pole,"* he could not give a very accurate description.[689] Condon also claimed that he did not see from what direction they had come or where they went after he spoke to them but was certain he had never seen them before or since. A later interview with Condon, as well as a separate discussion with both Captain Lamb and Lt. Keaten about these two individuals, came from Special Agent Sisk. It was during this interview with Sisk that Condon told him that:

> *"he did not believe that this man was in any way connected with this case as a lookout or in any other capacity as the man acted perfectly normal in every way...".*[690]

This observation wouldn't have necessarily seemed strange if he was making this assertion from the beginning. However, it is a weird thing to declare for the very first time years later. Also, if the man was acting as he described, that in my opinion was not normal at all. In yet another one of Condon's contradictions, the one he told Sisk during this interview was a doozy...

> *"...that he reached the corner of Tremont and Whittemore Avenues but not being sure exactly where Whittemore Avenue was located at that time he inquired of a man who was standing on the corner with a little girl as to where this Avenue was located."*[691]

---

[689] Ibid.

[690] Sisk, T. H. Special Agent, DOI. USBOI Report. Kidnaping and Murder of Charles A. Lindbergh Jr. June 26, 1934. New Jersey State Police Museum and Learning Center Archives.

[691] Ibid.

Again, this is yet another clear indicator that Condon could not keep up with the lies he had previously told. Condon did however repeat to Sisk what he told O'Leary:

> "*The man did not turn completely around and face him, stated Dr. Condon, but merely turned half way around so that he had a side view of the face, and he then informed the Doctor that he did not know where Whittemore Avenue was located, after which Dr. Condon went about his business and paid no more attention to this man.*"[692]

Condon went on to describe this man as being "*calm*" with an "*erect carriage,*" age "*45,*" height "*5' 7",*" with a "*stout build,*" "*black hair,*" "*dark skin,*" "*small mouth,*" "*smooth shaven,*" with "*short*" legs and neck being either "*Austrian or Italian,*" wearing a dark "*fedora,*" with "*old*" and "*dark*" clothes, and had an appearance of a "*working man.*"[693] Sisk was skeptical of this description and noted in his report:

> "*It is of course a question whether Dr. Condon could remember the description of this unknown man for such a long period of time, when he had only seen the man for a few seconds in semi-darkness, however he insists that the description furnished is accurate.*"[694]

He gave a description of the little girl as being "*between the ages of nine and twelve.*"

Sisk next spoke with Captain Lamb and Lt. Keaten about this subject. They advised him that they had spoken with Condon about this man and little girl on several occasions but that he was "*unable*

---

[692] Ibid.

[693] Ibid.

[694] Ibid.

to remember what the man looked like or to give a description of him."
Also:

> "Lieutenant Keaton [sic] and Captain Lamb stated
> that Dr. Condon told them that the person with this
> unknown man was a young lady and not a little girl,
> but on another occasion Dr. Condon indicated that it
> was a little girl."[695]

Not long after this Condon was interviewed again, this time by
Corporal Sam Leon of the NJSP. According to Leon's report:

> "He stated that he walked across East Tremont Avenue
> to Whittemore and there was a man and girl standing
> on the corner, apparently waiting for a trolley car. He
> stated that he asked this man if this was Whittemore
> Avenue and the man stated that he did not know as he
> was not acquainted around there. This man spoke very
> good English and was commonly dressed and looked
> like a laboring man, wearing a dark soft hat, dark
> overcoat. He was dark complected and about 35 years
> of age. The girl was about 10 or 11 and wore light
> clothing. This is all that was said to this party"[696]

Condon's Flemington testimony indicates the girl was "about 12"
and what's most interesting is that he continued to state that he asked
the man he encountered where Whittemore Avenue was because he

---

[695] Ibid.

[696] Leon, Samuel Cpl. New Jersey State Police. New Jersey State Police
Report. The following is the result of an interview with Dr. John F.
Condon at his home at 2974 DeCatur Avenue, Bronx, N.Y., as to how the
kidnappers of the Lindbergh Baby knew his name and address when he
signed his name "Jafsie". June 26, 1934. New Jersey State Police Museum
and Learning Center Archives.

himself did not know, to which the man replied "*no, we are strangers here.*"[697] According to Condon's testimony made under oath:

> "*I looked up at the avenue sign and saw "Whittemore Avenue." The first time I knew that name pertaining to it.*"[698]

Since Condon had originally informed the FBI that his only goal in asking the man "where" Whittemore Avenue was located was an effort to learn if he was known to him, and the fact he had repeatedly told them that "*several members of his family had been buried in St. Raymond's Cemetery,*" they had always accepted that he was familiar with this area and knew where Whittemore Avenue was.[699] So with this in mind, as well as what's clearly instructed in the note, it is quite obvious Condon is merely repeating his second version and most recent fabrication made to authorities.

"Hey Doc"

According to Condon's earliest official statement to the police, he left Lindbergh in the car with the money then walked over to the corner where he "*waited about five minutes*" before he started to walk back to the car. As he did so, he heard someone yell from the cemetery "*Hey! Doc, here I am,*" which Condon responded to by saying "*alright,*" then walked over near the cemetery fence where he thought someone might be behind a tomb stone "*but I could see no*

---

[697] Condon, John F. Testimony. The State of New Jersey vs. Bruno Richard Hauptmann, <u>Hunterdon County Court of Oyer and Terminer</u>, page 652, 1935. New Jersey State Law Library.

[698] Ibid.

[699] Seykora, J. E. Special Agent, DOI. DOI Report. <u>Kidnaping and Murder of Charles A. Lindbergh, Jr</u>. March 8, 1934. New Jersey State Police Museum and Learning Center Archives.

one."[700] A week later his wait on that corner had gotten longer once Condon testified that he waited there "*about ten minutes or may be 15 minutes walking around there…*," and the voice which called to him from the cemetery said less with only a "*hey doc.*" Though he responded the same way in this rendition with "*alright,*" after he looked around and did not see anyone he asked "*where are you*" but did not get a reply.[701] About two weeks later the story changed again. This time he told Inspector Walsh that while waiting he spoke out loud "*so that anyone around could hear it,*" proclaiming "*I don't see anybody, I guess there's no use,*" but once he started back for the car heard someone say "*Doc*" to which he responded "*all right, I hear you*" and then walked toward the voice and said "*where are you?*"[702] Since these are the three earliest versions I think it's best to avoid mentioning the later ones as it concerns this angle. These versions are enough to compare with what Lindbergh said he saw and heard. Of course his version could be doubted as well; however, it is important to note the differences to give us the best chance to figure out what the truth might have been.

The first important fact is whoever "yelled" did so loud enough that Lindbergh, parked fifty yards away from where Condon was standing, could hear. What was the need for that other than to impress Lindbergh himself? Next, despite Condon's declaration that he said something "*so that anyone around could hear,*" if he did, it apparently wasn't loud enough for Lindbergh to hear. So if what

---

[700] Condon, Dr. John F. Statement. Made to Inspector Harry W. Walsh. May 13, 1932. New Jersey State Police Museum and Learning Center Archives.

[701] Condon, John F. Testimony. <u>Bronx Grand Jury</u>. Continued after King. May 20, 1932. New Jersey State Police Museum and Learning Center Archives.

[702] Condon, Dr. John F. Statement. Made to Inspector Harry W. Walsh, Sgt. Warren T. Moffatt, Lieut. A. T. Keaton and Detective Horn. June 2, 1932. New Jersey State Police Museum and Learning Center Archives.

Condon asserted he said was true, even if we knew which direction Condon faced, then it can only mean "John" was much closer to Condon than Condon to Lindbergh.

Cemetery John

As Condon wandered down Whittemore Avenue, supposedly in search of the voice he heard, he noticed there were "*no lights*" and it was "*dark*" as he proceeded toward a border hedge.[703] Once there, he heard a voice from behind that hedge say "*here I am*" which Condon claimed to have recognized "*to be John whom I had met at Woodlawn Cemetery on the previous occasion.*"[704] At this point John asked if Condon had the money and Condon told him it was in the automobile but that he would not turn it over without a "*receipt.*" Before the Bronx Grand Jury he testified he was asking for this because his "*object*" behind that request was really to "*see the handwriting.*"[705] According to Condon, John told him "*we sent you the sleeping suit*" and promised to also provide him "*directions in six hours in order they might have a getaway,*" which John indicated they thought would be enough. But due to Condon's insistence, while he did not have any receipt, he "*could get that in two minutes*" and told Condon to retrieve the money while he did so.[706] However, it was at this time Condon decided to haggle with John over the ransom amount! He told John about how hard times were for everyone

---

[703] Condon, John F. Testimony. <u>Bronx Grand Jury</u>. Continued after King. May 20, 1932. New Jersey State Police Museum and Learning Center Archives.

[704] Condon, Dr. John F. Statement. Made to Inspector Harry W. Walsh. May 13, 1932. New Jersey State Police Museum and Learning Center Archives.

[705] Condon, John F. Testimony. <u>Bronx Grand Jury</u>. Continued after King. May 20, 1932. New Jersey State Police Museum and Learning Center Archives.

[706] Ibid.

including Lindbergh. At some point in the conversation it was agreed that "John" would accept $50,000 instead of the $70,000.[707] In the version he told to Inspector Walsh in June, Condon claimed John said *"we have concluded to take fifty thousand."*[708] Not only is it crazy to think anyone would be immediately willing to take $20,000 less, this statement suggested that John had conferred with his confederates about it. But how? Inspector Walsh obviously wanted to know, so he asked Condon about it when taking his statement:

[Q] *At the time that you made payment of the fifty thousand dollars in the St. Raymond cemetery how many men did you see there?*

[A] *One.*

[Q] *Did you ever have any reason to believe that there was more than one?*

[A] *From what he said.*

[Q] *What did he say?*

[A] *He said there were other men there but I did not see them.*

[Q] *Did he stop to consider somebody else before finally agreed* [sic] *to fifty thousand dollars payment?*

---

[707] Condon, Dr. John F. Statement. Made to Inspector Harry W. Walsh. May 13, 1932. New Jersey State Police Museum and Learning Center Archives.

[708] Condon, Dr. John F. Statement. Made to Inspector Harry W. Walsh, Sgt. Warren T. Moffatt, Lieut. A. T. Keaton and Detective Horn. June 2, 1932. New Jersey State Police Museum and Learning Center Archives.

[A] *No.*

[Q] *Did he give you the impression that he had interviewed somebody else?*

[A] *He couldn't because he was standing as near as you are.*[709]

So the question remains why John would have said "we" when accepting the lesser amount. According to Condon's Bronx Grand Jury testimony John's response was slightly different: "*I suppose if we cannot get 70 I will take 50.*"[710] But does this response make sense when Condon not only always alleged John was not the leader, but that he was quite fearful of him? Although it isn't mentioned anywhere else, during the Board of Strategy Conference held by Colonel Schwarzkopf on May 18, 1932, he gave the following details…

> "*…he recognized it was John by this talk. He said to them at this time you must tell me where we can get the baby and they said we will let you know, he said no you must tell me and John said I will have to talk to my partners and he went off to two men standing in the background some distance off and he came back and said all right if you will promise not to open this for two hours I will give you a letter telling you where the baby is…*".[711]

---

[709] Ibid.

[710] Condon, John F. Testimony. <u>Bronx Grand Jury</u>. Continued after King. May 20, 1932. New Jersey State Police Museum and Learning Center Archives.

[711] New Jersey State Police Board of Strategy Meeting Minutes. <u>Conference regarding the Lindbergh case held in the offices of Colonel H. Norman Schwarzkopf, Superintendent, New Jersey State Police</u>. Pages 14-5, May 18, 1932. New Jersey State Police Museum and Learning Center Archives.

Schwarzkopf would not have mentioned this to all the Law Enforcement present if he did not believe it himself. So where did this information come from? It could have only come from one of three places... Either Condon gave this version to Law Enforcement at some point prior to the conference, or he made this claim to Breckinridge or Lindbergh. If made to Breckinridge, he would have informed Lindbergh, who in turn would report this information back to Schwarzkopf as if he had been informed by Condon himself.

As retold by Condon, the conversation between the two men started off small but with each passing version over time continued to grow. This can be seen by comparing Condon's initial statement against his recreated version (a recording) of the supposed dialogue made for the FBI on March 23, 1934.[712] In his initial statement there are two quick verbal exchanges recounted, but by the time of his recorded version the typed transcript reveals three pages worth of conversation and isn't the rambling mess he presented to the Bronx Grand Jury. But can any of it be trusted? The consensus of sources indicates that after it was agreed the gang would accept $50,000, Condon would return to the car for the money, while "John" went to get the "receipt." Condon walked back to the car where Lindbergh was sitting with the ransom money and...

> "...told him I was pleased to state that they had reduced after consideration and conversation to make the deal for $50,000. instead of $70,000. whereupon Colonel Lindbergh took a package containing $20,000. from the box and handed the box with $50,000. to me to give to the kidnaper [sic], which I carried to the hedge and asked him for directions. He asked me to take a

---

[712] Long, H. B., Administrative Division, FBI. Memorandum To Mr. Harbo. Lindbergh Kidnaping Case, Bureau File #7-1. January 15, 1947. National Archives at College Park Maryland.

*sealed note and to promise him that I would not open
it for two hours. I took the note back and handed it to
Colonel Lindbergh.*"[713]

If his initial story was true, then he knew Cemetery John by his
voice. Yet, at Bronx Grand Jury his testimony grew legs. Upon
returning to the hedge with the $50,000 "John" was there "*crouching
down*" and since Condon could not get a "*good glimpse at the man*"
told him to "*stand up.*" John apparently complied and it was then
that he recognized him as "John."[714] But in this version it doesn't
end there... Condon quizzed John by asking "*where did I ever see
you before?*" which prompted a reply from John that "*I am the one
that spoke to you at the other cemetery.*"[715] Why wasn't this method of
identification recalled a week earlier to police? Why was it different?
Something else too that Condon noticed was that John's "*voice
seemed to change and his English changed.*"[716] Dr. Gardner was the first
to recognize this "observation" as the same as one Perrone had made
concerning the man who flagged him down to deliver his note.[717]
He seems to believe it shows they both may have dealt with the same
person. However, I see it differently. What I see is Condon adding to
and spinning a tale which he wants to be "believable." For Condon,
taking something known and adding it to his story contributed to
that end. As his tale became "bigger" he needed to add "facts" to
make it appear true and unimpeachable. Condon continued in his

---

[713] Condon, Dr. John F. Statement. Made to Inspector Harry W. Walsh.
May 13, 1932. New Jersey State Police Museum and Learning Center
Archives.

[714] Condon, John F. Testimony. <u>Bronx Grand Jury</u>. Continued after King.
May 20, 1932. New Jersey State Police Museum and Learning Center
Archives.

[715] Ibid.

[716] Ibid.

[717] Gardner, Lloyd C. June 2004. *The Case That Never Dies.* Rutgers
University Press. Page 81.

testimony that John asked if he had the money, and Condon in turn asked for the receipt. Instead of the quick exchange as told by his original statement, there was this long drawn out nonsensical back and forth:

> "*they have agreed to go through this and your work was perfect, you used no C in the name*" *and I said* "*what is that*" *and he said* "*your work was perfect they are pleased.*" "*well I kept my word.*"[718]

<u>Translation</u>: John is telling Condon his work is "perfect" but was pronouncing it "*perfet.*" The gang is very pleased with Condon, and Condon responded that he keeps his word.

> "*everyone trust you, one of them knows you*" "*bring them out*" "*no, no*" *he said,* "*he could not come no matter what happened it is too dangerous, it is 30 years, John he would be in an awful position*" "*I want the baby that is all that I care about*" "*would the Colonel let it go at that*" "*Give me the baby and the Colonel will not press the charge against you, he has given you all that he had, why don't you give the receipt, where can I get the baby*" "*it is in the note, would you not like to meet John, you know they all like you*" *and again he used the word perfect*"[719]

<u>Translation</u>: First of all, Condon seems to forget he's talking to "John" and instead has John either calling himself "John," the Leader "John," or maybe even both. Next, again John is heaping praise on Condon, that the others could not come out because they are looking

---

[718]   Condon, John F. Testimony. <u>Bronx Grand Jury</u>. Continued after King. May 20, 1932. New Jersey State Police Museum and Learning Center Archives.

[719]   Ibid.

at 30 years for this crime if caught. However, he also seems to be asking if Condon wants to meet him. "John" asked if Lindbergh will now let this go, and Condon says if the baby is returned he was willing to. John told him that the information they need to get the baby is in the note.

> *"I said 'come up here if you want it, come up here take it' 'how much is it' '$50,000 John, don't double cross me' 'no, no, they would not do that, I have the note right here, I hand you that when you hand the money' I tried to catch some German accent and said, 'do you specken deutch' 'no you can't speak German' Scandinavian, was the same man."*[720]

<u>Translation</u>: Condon tells John to come closer to accept the box. John asks how much. Condon tells him it's $50,000 but not to double cross him. John says they would never double cross him. Condon plays a trick to try to catch a German accent, it does not work, which convinced him that John was Scandinavian just like the man at Woodlawn. But he already knew that – didn't he?

At this point Condon handed over the box while John handed over the note and Condon said he saw John go *"down through the cemetery, in a little distance I could see it was very dark and went towards the Westchester Creek…"*.[721]

In his June statement he ended the conversation a little differently:

> *"I said now you won't cross me or you won't go back on me. He said we are all satisfied that you have done your part all right and he put his hand out over the hedge to shake hands with me, which I did. He said*

---

[720] Ibid.

[721] Ibid.

"Let me see this, let me count this, let me investigate to see if it is all right. They would smack me out if they think I had gypped some of the money. He got there and took out some [illegible] from the box. It was not locked."[722]

So if John hadn't spoken with his gang about the reduction, how could this have made any sense at all to Condon? He would be returning with $20,000 less. Why wouldn't they suspect it had been stolen by John? How could they possibly know they weren't *"gypped?"*

Once Condon received the note and supposedly watched John walk away, he returned to Lindbergh who was still waiting in the car. *"We rode back to my home and enroute to my home stopped and noted the contents of the letter which directed us to go to Bay Head, Horses Neck Beach and Elizabeth Islands where the baby was on the boat Nellie."*[723] This note actually read:

*"The boy is on B oad Nelly
it is a small Boad 28 feet
long two person are on the
Boad the are innosent.
You will find the Boad between
Horseneck Beach and gay Head
Near Elizabeth Island."*[724]

[722] Condon, Dr. John F. Statement. Made to Inspector Harry W. Walsh, Sgt. Warren T. Moffatt, Lieut. A. T. Keaton and Detective Horn. June 2, 1932. New Jersey State Police Museum and Learning Center Archives.
[723] Condon, Dr. John F. Statement. Made to Inspector Harry W. Walsh. May 13, 1932. New Jersey State Police Museum and Learning Center Archives.
[724] Exhibit S-70. New Jersey State Police Museum and Learning Center Archives.

There was a funny thing about this note as well. If John was caught off guard, although the secret symbol was missing, it certainly didn't look hastily written or scrawled out without thought or preparation. In fact, according Special Agent Seykora:

> "*Dr. Condon was of the impression that the 13ᵗʰ ransom note which John handed to him after receiving the money had already been written and was already in John [sic] possession when he first met "John" that evening, basing this opinion on the fact that the note apparently had been carefully written and showed no evidence of having been written on top of a tombstone in the dark, and further that it is not likely that "John" or any other person would have risked using a flashlight in a cemetery at that time of the night, for the purpose of writing a note.*"[725]

If what Condon noted to Agent Seykora was true, then you had better believe police noticed it too. So here again is something that supports the notion Condon never had any conversation with John requesting a "receipt" since it is very clear he already had one. Now if someone already had such a note, why would they? After all, they had already sent the sleeping suit as proof they had the child, and according to Condon, that was all the proof they felt was needed. The fact is the evidence points to the Kidnappers knowing to bring a receipt – as proof he actually handed over the ransom money – which would then prove to Lindbergh he hadn't been gypped. The only person to benefit from this arrangement was Condon.

So now the question becomes: How'd they know ahead of time to bring it?

---

[725] Seykora, J. E. Special Agent, DOI. DOI Report. <u>Kidnaping and Murder of Charles A. Lindbergh, Jr</u>. March 8, 1934. New Jersey State Police Museum and Learning Center Archives.

Ransom Drop Location
(Where Condon said the money was handed over the hedge)
(Courtesy NJSP Museum)

Secret Symbol

Since they obviously had the letter ahead of time, another question might be why there was no symbol on it. Condon seemed ready for that question. In a letter written to J. Edgar Hoover he offered up his *"personal deduction"* that *"the leader stole the "symbol."*[726] Then in a later communication to Hoover, Condon seemed to move this "deduction" along further when he wrote...

---

[726]   Condon, John F. Letter from John F. Condon to Hon. J. Edgar Hoover. October 20, 1933. National Archives at College Park Maryland.

"...and John's letter (in your possession) stated that a leader among them went away with their "sign" so they would not write to me anymore."[727]

Was this true? Did Hoover have such a letter or was this simply a ruse Condon could later dismiss by saying he gave it to someone else? That could certainly have been, considering his next act which completed the conversion of his "deduction" into a solid "fact," attributing it to something "John" had actually (supposedly) told him:

"One of our men I told you is in trouble now. He took our things away with the signature and while he's alive it's dangerous. We can't send you any more signals. There are only 'fife' of us left."[728]

It seems to me Condon was worried that authorities might have questioned the receipt's authenticity because the symbol wasn't on it. I believe Condon overheard investigators or was privy to a conversation about this note. If it was not authentic it cast suspicion on Condon himself. So he went with the lesser of two evils, and adjusted his story so that an explanation could be made.

The $20,000

The Treasury Department agents were first brought into this case on March 7, 1932, after Lindbergh had phoned the Secretary of the Treasury, Ogden Mills, asking for help concerning Al Capone's

[727] Condon, John F. Letter from John F. Condon to Mr. Hoover. February 5, 1934. National Archives at College Park Maryland.
[728] Condon, John F. Transcript. At Woodlawn Cemetery – about 9:00 P. M., March 12, 1932. Undated (March 1934). New Jersey State Police Museum and Learning Center Archives.

recent offer of assistance.[729] The next day Elmer Irey arrived at Hopewell, and along with SAC Arthur Nichols, conferred with Lindbergh then told him *"that the offer of Alphonse Capone of Chicago to cooperate should be entirely disregarded."*[730] During Irey's involvement, it was noted:

> *"There were so many investigators working on this case, often at cross purposes, that Lindbergh himself had the final say-so when a major investigative move was contemplated."*[731]

The Treasury Agents' involvement did not end here however. It was on March 3rd that Lindbergh had gone on the radio to offer immunity to the Kidnappers as well as a promise the ransom money would not be marked.[732] In one of their meetings sometime after the sleeping suit had been received, according to Irey:

> *"I told Lindbergh that every single bill should be listed and a record kept of the serial numbers. Lindbergh argued stubbornly against it; he did not want to break his promise (sic). It seemed extraordinary ethics to all of us."*[733]

Irey had already made it clear to Lindbergh that if *"he couldn't see where any good would be accomplished by the Unit unless some phase*

---

[729] Irey, Elmer L. Chief, Intelligence Unit, Internal Revenue Service, Treasury Department. <u>Memorandum Regarding Matter That The State May Desire Mr. Elmer L. Irey To Testify With Reference To</u>. January 16, 1935. New Jersey State Police Museum and Learning Center Archives.

[730] Ibid.

[731] Hynd, Alan. *The Giant Killers*. R.M. McBride. (1945). Page 144.

[732] Sisk, T. H. DOI (FBI) et. al., DOI Report. <u>Summary</u>. NY File No. 62-3057, p. 15. February 16, 1934. National Archives at College Park Maryland.

[733] Irey, Elmer L. *The Tax Dodgers*. Greenberg. (1948). Page 75.

developed that was practically in line with the Unit's investigative procedure," he would pull his men off the case. "*Lindbergh seemed surprised at the attitude of Irey, probably because Irey was the only investigator who had been called into the picture who didn't jump at the chance of staying in it.*"[734] True to his word, Irey would not back down. He delivered an "*ultimatum*" to Lindbergh by telling him that "*unless he complied and permitted the Treasury to record the serial numbers the department would have to withdraw…*" because he could not stand by and allow Lindbergh to "*compound a felony*" or to have his Unit have any part in it.[735] Lindbergh, Irey wrote, "*pursed his lips and said nothing, and as far as we were concerned we were out of the case.*"[736] However, the next day Captain Galvin called Agent Madden to inform him that he was "*speaking for Breckinridge and if Madden went to J.P Morgan & Company office a new set of ransom money would be drawn up as we wanted it arranged.*"[737] Clearly, once Irey spoke in terms of a crime being committed, Lindbergh went to Breckinridge who advised this course of action be taken.

Although it did not come easy, this represented one of the few but huge victories for Law Enforcement. They now had a major tool to assist in tracking down and bringing the culprits to justice once this money was delivered. However, that victory would be nearly undermined….

Many circumstances developed which caused police to question Condon's motives and the removal of the $20,000 was among them. He fell under heavy suspicion since police believed removing that 20K was evidence of willfully aiding the Kidnappers. It was that separate package which contained the most identifiable bills (the

[734] Hynd, Alan. *The Giant Killers*. R.M. McBride. (1945). Page 144.
[735] Tully, Andrew. *Treasury Agent The Inside Story*. Simon And Schuster. (1958) Page 168.
[736] Irey, Elmer L. *The Tax Dodgers*. Greenberg. (1948). Page 75.
[737] Ibid.

FIFTIES), and the ones Treasury Agents firmly believed would draw the most attention and lead to the arrest of the criminals. The severity of Condon's actions was reflected in Frank Wilson's own words:

> *"Two hours later Jafsie told me how he had saved Lindy a lot of money. Lindbergh was there and I didn't want to say anything at the time, but I was boiling inside. When I got Art Madden alone, I said, "What in the hell did Jafsie take out the fifties for? Now it is going to be a hundred times harder to trace that money." Actually I was understating it."*[738]

Elmer Irey was mad as hell too and much less polite upon hearing the news. Once he learned, he stared Condon down then told him *"I could shoot your head off."*[739] This sentiment would also come out during Inspector Walsh's line of questioning in June:

> [Q] *...If the man to whom you paid the money is arrested or if a person is arrested who is betrayed by one of the kidnappers in the event of their arrest might come forward and say Condon knew all about this. We told him?*

> [A] *It might be embarrassing, Chief.*

> [Q] *We didn't bring you here to molest you, to injure you?*

---

[738] Wilson, Frank J. (as told to Howard Whitman) *Undercover Man II: Inside The Lindbergh Kidnapping.* Collier's. May 10, 1947. New Jersey State Police Museum and Learning Center Archives.

[739] Tully, Andrew. *Treasury Agent The Inside Story.* Simon And Schuster. (1958) Page 170.

[A] *I believe that.*

[Q] *I believe that you know who these people are?*

[A] *No.*

[Q] *I say you are between two fires and if I were in your place I'd pick the one that would do the least damage?*

[A] *I did, before the Grand Jury, before the District Attorney and to everyone I have told the truth.*

[Q] *The Grand Jury is the best example of fiasco that I met in my life. From the circumstances of this case as I know them you know more than you have told us?*

[A] *No.*[740]

The questioning would get to the specifics about that $20,000, and it revealed an important theory the police seemed to have believed:

[Q] *Who suggested the fifty thousand?*

[A] *They did. I did not suggest any amount. I said it was such hard scraping. They had fifty thousand in the first note.*

[Q] *The first noe* [sic] *wants fifty thousand, the second note said we have to raise it because we have to take somebody else, in; then along comes the pay day and*

---

[740] Condon, Dr. John F. Statement. Made to Inspector Harry W. Walsh, Sgt. Warren T. Moffatt, Lieut. A. T. Keaton and Detective Horn. June 2, 1932. New Jersey State Police Museum and Learning Center Archives.

> *its cut down twenty thousand again, and the very first thing they know they can't produce at all and a short time later the baby is found dead. The person whom they took in and who made it necessary to elevate the ransom twenty thousand evidently became aware of the fact that the baby was dead and couldn't be produced and said that he didn't want any of this money. That person couldn't have been anybody but you?*
>
> [A] *That is a mistake. It is not true.*[741]

Despite Condon's denials Walsh pressed on:

> [Q] *This crime has been too perfect, to be going on the way it has been without some protector?*
>
> [A] *I believe that.*
>
> [Q] *There's nothing left for me to do but hold you up as their protector?*
>
> [A] *It's not true Chief.*[742]

It's a very telling exchange because it is clear Walsh is now "on to him" and accusing him of being involved. It is also another example that shows Condon could not keep track of his lies. Note the discrepancy between the preceding conversation and the following snippet with regard to who reduced the ransom demand. It was, in fact, during his recreation of his conversation with "John" at St. Raymond's that Condon revealed this:

---

[741]   Ibid.
[742]   Ibid.

Man: (Stands up). "Did you get the sleeping suit I sent you? Did the Colonel say it was his son's?

Condon: "Yes, the Colonel says it was his son's, but it is a time of depression, Colonel Lindbergh doesn't have as much money as everyone thinks. He feels the depression too. Besides you bargained for $50,000. and now you want $70,000. Give me the baby now and I will give you $50,000."[743]

Scandinavian vs. German

Another thing Walsh did not "like" was Condon's assertion that "John" was "Scandinavian."

[Q] *What makes you think this John is a Scandinavian?*

[A] *He told me, and his accent. He doesn't use the word perfect. He has no "c" in it. Perfet.*

[Q] *They exhibited a strain of deceit from the time they stole the baby up to the present time so why shouldn't you accept his statement that he was of Scandinavian birth as a matter of deceit too?*

[A] *That might be. That's all that I had to judge from, his conversation and the statement he made to me.*

---

[743] Condon, John F. Transcript. <u>At St. Raymond's Cemetery, about 8:30 or 9:00 P. M., April 2, 1932</u>. Undated (March 1934). New Jersey State Police Museum and Learning Center Archives.

[Q] *With your experience as an educator you have had different languages. You said he said he was a Scandinavian. Could you say of you own knowledge?*

[A] *I figure he was not a German and I figure he was what he said he was from the way I've heard them speak and from the way that he spoke to me.*[744]

Further chaos is added to this point if we examine what Condon testified to in Flemington about Riehl.

[Q] *Did you see the guard?*

[A] *I did.*

[Q] *Describe him, please?*

[A] *Describe him? It was rather dark there and all that I could tell about him would be that he was Riehl. That is his name. Excuse me, that is his name, and of German extraction because I spoke to him; and a rather stout man – I would call it portly – a heavyweight.*[745]

What this testimony did was show that Condon attempted to prove Riehl had seen him and not someone else. However, by doing so he also proved that someone who uttered a few words to him would convince them they were of *"German extraction."* This means if

---

[744] Condon, Dr. John F. Statement. Made to Inspector Harry W. Walsh, Sgt. Warren T. Moffatt, Lieut. A. T. Keaton and Detective Horn. June 2, 1932. New Jersey State Police Museum and Learning Center Archives.

[745] Condon, John F. Testimony. The State of New Jersey vs. Bruno Richard Hauptmann, <u>Hunterdon County Court of Oyer and Terminer</u>, page 744, 1935. New Jersey State Law Library.

Condon was being truthful on the stand here, then he had always lied to authorities by claiming he believed "John" was Scandinavian.

That Strange Detour

Special Agent J. J. Manning would discover that Lindbergh described a peculiar detail about Condon's unusual decision to detour his return trip with the ransom money from Whittemore down East Tremont. During the course of his interactions with him during late 1933, and early 1934, he questioned Condon directly about this event. Condon provided him with three separate explanations...

> "...that on his second trip back to the cemetery on the night of April 2nd in passing the entrance he thought he saw some shadows behind the tombstones and thinking possibly that someone had concealed himself there, he would "stick him up" and take the ransom money from him, he walked down another block to give this matter serious thought before he turned around and entered the cemetery. Condon's second explanation for his walking the extra block is that he did so to give him sufficient time in which to say a prayer. His third explanation is in substance that he was confused, and did not know exactly where he was going, since he may have been a little excited at the time."[746]

---

[746] Sisk, T. H. DOI (FBI) et. al., DOI Report. Summary. NY File No. 62-3057, p. 196. February 16, 1934. National Archives at College Park Maryland.

Gregory Coleman's Version

Although hearsay, since it is well documented that Condon was providing Coleman with the "inside" scoop, I believe it is important to see how he told the story of this event. One thing Coleman pointed out was as the men pulled up to the front of Bergen's nursery, *"the setting was almost identical to that of Dr. Condon's first rendezvous with the kidnaper-messenger."*[747] He mentioned how Condon found the note under the stone and then took it over to Lindbergh. However, once Condon walked across the street as directed by the note…

> *"…he met a man and woman at the corner who either sensed the fact that he was puzzled about the street for which he was heading, or were assisting in directing him to the kidnappers. The woman remarked: "This is Whittemore Ave." and walked away with her male escort."*[748]

Again, this is important because Coleman's only source for his information is Condon himself and this fact was cemented in Coleman's Grand Jury testimony…

> *"…Dr. Condon was directed to proceed to the otherside of the street and walk on Wittemore [sic] Avenue and when he walked over he told me that there was a man and woman who passed by and I never was able to conclude whether they first spoke to the doctor or the*

---

[747] Coleman, Gregory F. *Vigil*. Unpublished Manuscript. Page 49. Undated (circa 1932). New Jersey State Police Museum and Learning Center Archives.

[748] Ibid.

doctor first spoke to them, but they told him that this was Wittemore [sic] Avenue…".[749]

Coleman explained the scene as if standing on Whittemore:

> *"That street forms the western border of the cemetery and is bordered on the east side by a high, stone retaining wall. The street is about 40 feet in width and extends alongside the cemetery down to the swamplands directly in the rear of the garbage dumps on 177th St., and by way of it, one may reach the Westchester Creek, which enters Long Island Sound about a mile away. A few blocks in from Tremont Ave., Balcom Ave. also enters Whittemore Ave. and affords another means of entering the cemetery grounds from Tremont Ave."*[750]

Having looked over the scenario himself, Coleman believed that a *"group of the kidnapers [sic]"* could have easily remained *"in the cemetery"* observing anyone *"on the lighted Tremont Ave."* while at the same time remaining *"hidden in the darkness"* among the *"innumerable tombstones"* which provided *"excellent hiding places."*[751] According to Coleman, Condon had waited on the corner but did not make contact. As a result, he turned to leave when he heard a cry *"Hey doctor"* which stopped him. Condon walked down Whittemore towards a *"heavy six-foot evergreen bush"* which acted as a border wall, and *"saw movement in the bush."* Condon called out *"where*

[749] Coleman, Gregory. Testimony. <u>Bronx Grand Jury</u>. People vs. Hauptmann. September 24, 1932. New Jersey State Police Museum and Learning Center Archives.

[750] Coleman, Gregory F. *Vigil.* Unpublished Manuscript. Page 50. Undated (circa 1932). New Jersey State Police Museum and Learning Center Archives.

[751] Ibid.

are you?" and to this question a *"soft"* voice replied, *"here I am."*[752] The conversation between these men began where John asked if he had the money. Condon replied: *"Yes, but I need a receipt to show the Colonel that I gave you the money."*[753] In response to this:

> *"The kidnaper-messenger* [sic] *then stated:* "Wait, I give you directions where to find the baby" *and the man walked back a distance and was shielded from the Doctor's view by the tombstones. He returned minutes later, bearing an envelope. "When you give me the money, I give you the letter."*[754]

But the conversation did not end there because, as Coleman referred to it, Condon used *"psychology"* on John. Condon wanted to take his time to garner as much information as possible but recognized that John was *"anxious"* and wanted *"the business over quickly."* Here Condon seized on the opportunity to reduce the amount of ransom. John *"made it plain that he wanted to get away and in his nervous haste, he exclaimed, "We will be satisfied with $50,000"."*[755] Condon returned to the car, informed Lindbergh of the situation, and *"they took $20,000 out of the box..."*.[756] Once Condon returned with the money he...

> *"...opened the box over the hedge and the kidnaper* [sic] *peering covetously at its contents, fingered the bills. "Thanks, that's fine," the kidnaper* [sic] *remarked,*

---

752   Ibid.
753   Ibid.
754   Ibid. Pages 50-51.
755   Ibid. Page 51.
756   Coleman, Gregory. Testimony. <u>Bronx Grand Jury</u>. People vs. Hauptmann. September 24, 1932. New Jersey State Police Museum and Learning Center Archives.

hastily declining Dr. Condon's offer to light a match so he could see the money."[757]

Along with the ransom money, Condon had also inserted *"a long note appealing to the kidnapers* [sic] *to play fair."* This note was said to have said *"As long as you play fair with me, I will play fair with you."*

> *"And to further assure the kidnapers* [sic] *of his "good intentions" the Doctor handed the messenger two telegraph blanks addressed to himself. He told the messenger in case they needed lawyers, to simply wire him and he would provide them."*[758]

With the note in hand, assured by John of the gang's trustworthiness and that the women on *"Nellie"* were *"innocint* [sic]*,"* the men shook hands, then Condon watched him disappear with the *"box clutched tightly in his arm."*[759]

Henry Breckinridge's Version

Like Coleman, Breckinridge was in a position to hear the versions of events, not only from Lindbergh, but from Condon as well. Again, while whatever he recalls is hearsay, it is important to learn what he knew as it was told to him from both men who were actually there. The first unusual difference occurred when John met Condon...

> *"...John shouted so loud that Colonel Lindberg* [sic] *heard it to* [sic] *and then John walked down inside of*

---

[757] Coleman, Gregory F. *Vigil*. Unpublished Manuscript. Page 52. Undated (circa 1932). New Jersey State Police Museum and Learning Center Archives.

[758] Ibid. INSERT on page 52.

[759] Ibid. Page 52.

the cemetery wall where it starts there on the corner of Tremont Avenue and Witmore [sic] Avenue, the doctor on the outside and John on the end, John leaps over, he climbs up on the wall and gets down into the road and crosses the road and vaults over the low wall into the second portion of the cemetery and contacts the doctor at the hedge…".[760]

The details here clearly indicate that he wasn't making this version up, and that it could have only come to him from Condon. According to Breckinridge *"Condon argued with "John" on the subject of the amount."*[761] Once John agreed to take fifty thousand instead of the seventy thousand, he indicated that *"we will communicate with you in the morning"* but that Condon balked at this by demanding a *"receipt"* and then ordered John to *"give me that letter and instructions now."*[762] And so the original intent was for the kidnappers to *"mail"* the note *"in the morning"* so they would have had *"plenty of time to get away."*[763] Condon returned to the car, and the $20,000 was extracted. Breckinridge in his Grand Jury testimony added *"the $20,000 was in a separate package accidentally, it was in a separate package and could be easily extracted."*[764] Condon returned to the spot, then exchanged the *"box of money for the letter and John asked him if he would shake hands goodbye and they shook hands and good*

---

[760] Breckenridge, Colonel Henry. Testimony. Bronx Grand Jury. May 17, 1932. New Jersey State Police Museum and Learning Center Archives.

[761] Breckinridge, Henry. Statement. Unsigned. Undated. New Jersey State Police Museum and Learning Center Archives. (Same statement previously referenced).

[762] Breckenridge, Colonel Henry. Testimony. Bronx Grand Jury. May 17, 1932. New Jersey State Police Museum and Learning Center Archives.

[763] Breckinridge, Henry. Statement. Unsigned. Undated. New Jersey State Police Museum and Learning Center Archives. (Same statement previously referenced).

[764] Breckenridge, Colonel Henry. Testimony. Bronx Grand Jury. May 17, 1932. New Jersey State Police Museum and Learning Center Archives.

bye [sic]."[765] Prior to this, John told Condon "*that he must not open this missive for two hours*" but Breckinridge said "*of course we opened it anyway.*"[766]

The Authorities

Various men of Law Enforcement visited the scene to get a sense of what had occurred. Upon being ordered to summarize the facts and observations of the crime Frank Wilson revealed this about the "look-out" at St. Raymond's:

> "*During the time Colonel Lindbergh was parked in front of the florist shop and while Dr. Condon was making the payment to the kidnapper, Colonel Lindbergh observed a man pass the auto with a handkerchief to his face. He later observed him running along East Tremont Avenue and when the man reached a point on East Tremont Avenue which could be observed from the point on Whittemore Avenue where Dr. Condon was handing the money across a hedge surrounding the cemetery, the man threw a handkerchief on the ground. In all probability the handkerchief was a signal to the person receiving the money (John), and the man dropping it was an accomplice in the crime who was observing all persons in the vicinity to see if they were police officers and to observe if any attempt*

---

[765]   Ibid.

[766]   Ibid.

[sic] *were being made to apprehend the person with whom Dr. Condon conducted his business."*[767]

If what Wilson writes here is true, then this "look-out" is in a place where both Lindbergh and Condon could see him, yet also where Condon and Lindbergh could not see each other. So while the observation that police believed this man was a confederate is important, it's also something they were not impressed with as it related to Condon's sincerity. Police paid particular attention to Lindbergh's account of Condon walking down East Tremont after retrieving the ransom money from the car and before Condon eventually returned to once again travel down Whittemore. Here they evaluated Condon's movements as they related to the "look-out" and formulated an interesting theory as outlined in a New Jersey State Police memorandum....

The first thing noted was that Condon *"stands there while man in brown suit passes."* Another comment listed was that *"Dr. did not notice man in brown suit – strange."* From there it is noted that this *"man disappears to the East"* (down East Tremont). The memo notes that Condon, once in possession of the ransom money, *"goes East on Tremount* [sic] *out of site* [sic] *– (Same as Bn. Man),"* before he *"returns – turns down Whittemore – out of site* [sic]*"* and also *"He could have met man in Brown East on Tremont. They were both down there at the same time."*[768] They noted that:

---

[767] Wilson, Frank J., Special Agent, Internal Revenue Service. Internal Revenue Report. SI-6336. In re: Kidnapping and murder of Charles Augustus Lindbergh, Jr. page 5. November 11, 1933. New Jersey State Police Museum and Learning Center Archives.

[768] New Jersey State Police Memorandum. Untitled. Undated (1932). New Jersey State Police Museum and Learning Center Archives. (Note: During Gov. Hoffman's re-investigation if certain documents were found to be of importance his team gave it an Exhibit Number. This was given "Ex. No. 11").

"Man in brown suit comes back running.
Slows down before getting to Whittemore.
At Whittemore stops – looks all around –
Looks hard down Whittemore – continues west on
Tremount [sic].
Blows nose when passing car.
Had handkerchief up to face when passing car first
time.
About same time he drops handkerchief, Dr. appears
at Whittemore.
Comes to car – says he has note." [769]

Police were also suspicious about the *"peculiar & accurate synchronization Dr. & Brn. Man."*[770] So what to make of all of this? It was during my research at the NJSP Archives into the "Missing Taxi Driver" investigations that I discovered a memorandum written by Captain Lamb somewhere around June or July of 1932. Among the items listed in this memo were the following:

"See Commissioner Mulrooney for a thorough check on Taxi Drivers, New York City re: delivery of the second note.

Report on check of Condon's and Reich's safe deposit boxes.

The Colonel to see all reports of investigations submitted by the New York Police Department. See Captain Oliver in reference to the covering of Condon's house the night the second note was delivered there.

Obtain all signatures of holders of safe deposit boxes now in possession of the New York City Police Department.

---

[769]   Ibid.
[770]   Ibid.

See Prosecutors Marshall and Hauck re: indictments John Doe and Jane Doe."[771]

What makes this memo especially important is the drawing at the bottom which can be safely assumed was sketched by either Lamb or Schwarzkopf. Here it shows the scenario of the ransom drop concerning East Tremont, Bergen's flower shop, the car, and Whittemore with several "x"s marking specific spots. One such spot is an "x" way down at the bottom of East Tremont. There can be no doubt that this "x" marks where police believed Condon actually exchanged the ransom.[772] If this theory is true, it would mean the real meeting took place there, the money was removed, and Condon returned back up the street with an empty box under his arm before turning down Whittemore. Another interesting piece of information found on this memo is a handwritten note next to this sketch which says *"Details on talk to Officer at* [illegible] *meeting."*[773]

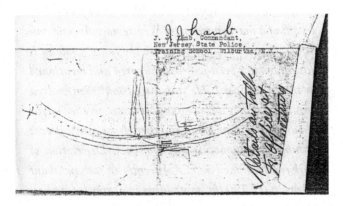

Ransom Drop Sketch (Found at bottom of Captain Lamb's Memorandum)
(Courtesy NJSP Museum)

---

[771] Lamb. J. J. Commandant, Training School, New Jersey State Police. <u>Memorandum for Colonel Schwarzkopf.</u> Undated (1932). New Jersey State Police Museum and Learning Center Archives.

[772] Ibid. (See sketch at bottom).

[773] Ibid. (see hand written notation at bottom)

Bernard Uebel

While continuing their investigation into the ransom money exchange, police went to see Clarence Schultz, the Superintendent of St. Raymond's cemetery on April 14, 1932. He was in his home on 3254 East Tremont Avenue, across the street from Bergen's flower shop but slightly closer to the corner of Whittemore. Unfortunately, Schultz told the investigators he did not observe anything and could not furnish the men with any information. Police then sought out Bernard Uebel, the Special Officer (badge 1097) at St. Raymond's Cemetery. The investigators soon learned that Uebel did see something, and he had a story to tell that would completely turn this situation upside down.

Uebel claimed that he was working on April 1st when at about "*1–30 P. M. he saw…*"

> "*…a dark complexioned man with three or four others get out of a maroon sedan on Whittemore Avenue and St. Raymond's Cemetery (where the ransom money is alleged to have been passed as pictured and mentioned in the newspapers). He stated that said men walked around as if they were looking for someone, they stayed about three or four hours and then drove away, license number of automobile unknow* [sic]. *Description of dark complexioned man: Apparently an Italian, about 38 yrs, 6'0", 190 lbs, protruding jaw, grey fedora hat, back band, black overcoat.*"[774]

---

[774] Avon, James A. Officer, New York City Police Department. New York City Police Department Report. July 19, 1932. New Jersey State Police Museum and Learning Center Archives. (Note: Amended version to his report of May 21, 1932).

The possibilities here run wild. Just as Woodlawn's officer, Robert Riehl, altered the narrative of events, here too Uebel seemed to be doing the same. He continued:

> "Uebel further stated that on April 2nd, at about 2–30 P. M. while operating a cement mixed [sic], he observed Dr. Condon park his auto, at section 5 on Whittemore Avenue (same location as others parked on previous day) with a man driving him, car was faced east. Both alighted from car and Dr. Condon walked over to a Ford touring car, painted Green, no license obtainable, with side curtains drawn, containing several men, said car having driven up after Dr. Condon's and they parked behind his auto on Whittemore Avenue facing south. Dr. Condon talked to them a few minutes and rejoined his friend, they both walked south on Whittemore Avenue, in the meantime the gree [sic] touring car with men, turned about and drove away. When Dr. Condon and friend reached section 8, Dr. Condon left him, walked across Balcom Avenue into marshes, then walked in an easterly direction in marshes alongside of ditch for about four city blocks, then came out at a red barn in the cemetery, rejoined his friend in section 8, walked back to his parked car taking a course on the inside of the hedge, parallel to Whittemore Avenue. His friend got into the automobile but Dr. Condon walked to Ford touring car which had again parked in same place. Dr. Condon took a large white envelope out of his pocket and handed it to an occupant of said automobile. He then walked back to his car and got in it with his fiend [sic], backed up and drove north on Whittemore Avenue toward E. Tremont Avenue and Ford, T. C. followed. Uebel stated that he was

on a mexer [sic] *about three hundred yards* [sic] *from parked automobile and he observed everything that took place as he had field glasses with him. He alos* [sic] *stated that he spoke to Dr. Condon as he passed, as he knew him. Uebel could not describe Condon's friend or any occupant of the Ford, T. C. He also said he could not observe anything that Dr. Condon did while walking in the marshes."*[775]

What's interesting here is the detail of Uebel's account. This seems indicative of someone who had recently witnessed these events. And what Uebel witnessed did not end with these two accounts, and there was another bombshell which he dropped on the men:

"Uebel stated that at about 7–45 A. M. Monday April 11th, 1932 he saw the maroon automobile again, no license number obtainable, drive up and park on Whittemore Avenue, at the same location, with the dark complexioned man sitting alongside the driver. He observed the dark complexioned man walk to a box-wood bush in the rear of 3254 E. Tremont Avenue, which is about 75 feet west of Whittemore Avenue, reach into bush, take out a box and put it under his coat, go back to automobile and drive away. When asked the size of the box, he stated that it was about the size of the box mentioned in the newspapers, namely 6 X 7 X 14 inches, as mentioned in the Lindbergh case. Description of chauffeur of said automobile: 29 yrs, 5'9", 160 lbs, light complexioned, black derby, tan raincoat with belt, he further stated he could identify this man and that this car had a N. Y. State Registration. He further stated that he

---

[775] Ibid.

*observed this transaction while at cemetery barn about
200 feet away."*[776]

We see there were three separate "events" that Uebel witnessed. This
last account would fully explain why police believed the ransom
transaction did not occur on Whittemore but instead on East
Tremont. Under this scenario, the box was empty upon Condon's
return, and the idea of the exchange occurring where history records
it took place was a ruse designed to buy time for the kidnapper (who
actually received it earlier and at a different place) and ensure a clean
getaway. As a result, the empty box was stashed in the bush to give
the appearance that Condon had turned it over once he returned to
the car empty handed.

This was a brilliant move, and while it showed these men were no
fools, it also left no doubt that Condon was a confederate in this
extortion.

Everything about this account appeared believable – except the
dates. Authorities were fairly certain Condon was accountable for
his whereabouts on both April 1st and 2nd however, they wanted to
re-check this to make sure. In the meantime, on April 18th, Det.
Thompson went back to St. Raymond's upon learning that Uebel
had once again seen the maroon colored automobile and this time
he got the plate number: *"5–U–4949 N. Y."* This car traced back to
Gregory Coleman's *"1928 Hupmobile, brougham painted maroon."*[777]
Coleman was brought down to see ADA Breslin and *"stated that
he had visited the cemetery on several occasions in the automobile in
question, with Dr. Condon."*[778] This proves beyond all doubt Uebel
was not lying. Although I haven't been able to find an official

---

[776]   Ibid.

[777]   Ibid.

[778]   Ibid.

transcript of that interrogation, I think Coleman's explanation to Breslin can be deduced from his later testimony:

> *"My recollection was distinctive because I went up with Dr. Condon to St. Raymond's cemetery after the ransom was paid and I went up there Monday morning around noon and Dr. Condon pointed out just what had transpired there and it was very distinct in my mind and he stood on one side of the hedge and the man to whom he spoke stood on the other side."*[779]

Since Monday was April 4th, perhaps Uebel got his days mixed up. This of course would in no way invalidate any of Uebel's eyewitness account except for the timing of what he saw. In fact, what Uebel describes happening on *"April 2nd"* seems to be the basis for what Coleman wrote in *Vigil*.[780] It must also be remembered that it was that same maroon car to which Uebel attached the removal of the ransom box from its stash spot in the bush. So, at the very least, Uebel saw someone retrieve the ransom box which was hidden in that bush.

There are two cars and several people in Uebel's sightings. Looking closely at these in an attempt to establish a time-line, we already know the maroon car was Coleman's. Although mistaken for an Italian, and slightly undersized by his description, the man with the noticeable "jaw" could certainly be Al Reich. Also, Breckinridge was driving a Ford touring car at the time of the ransom negotiations. When it came time for the Bronx Grand Jury testimony in May of that year, Uebel's account was still fresh in Breslin's mind. We know this because of the questions he asked Breckinridge....

---

[779] Coleman, Gregory. Testimony. <u>Bronx Grand Jury</u>. People vs. Hauptmann. September 24, 1932. New Jersey State Police Museum and Learning Center Archives.

[780] See earlier account above.

Concerning his car:

> [Q] *You own a Ford car do you not?*
>
> [A] *Yes sir.*
>
> [Q] *That is rather ancient vintage?*
>
> [A] *About two years old, it looks older, the truth of the matter was that my hack hire the first 30 days was $1000 and I sent to the farm and got my Ford.*[781]

Concerning where Condon was during the afternoon of April 2nd:

> [Q] *Getting down to the afternoon of April 2nd are you in the position to tell us whether Condon left his home at anytime in the afternoon of April 2nd?*
>
> [A] *No, I don't know.*
>
> [Q] *So that you are in a position to tell us whether Dr. Condon left the house that afternoon?*
>
> [A] *No, but I am conscious of him having been there, my impression is that we were altogether from the time that the Colonel got there with the money until the money was paid over.*
>
> [Q] *Do you know whether or not Dr. Condon at anytime shortly prior to the delivery of the money visited the scene of the transfer of the money?*

---

[781]   Breckenridge, Colonel Henry. Testimony. <u>Bronx Grand Jury</u>. May 17, 1932. New Jersey State Police Museum and Learning Center Archives.

[A] *Of the St. Raymonds cemetery I wasn't, but he was desirous I should visit the scene at Woodlawn on one or two occasions, he was constantly on the move trying to pick up information from the moment on March 12th. It is obvious to us that this gang were expert in the geography of the Bronx.*[782]

Concerning if/when he went to St. Raymond's cemetery:

[Q] *After April 2nd and after your return from the vicinity of Marthias* [sic] *vineyard did you go to St. Raymonds cemetery at anytime?*

[A] *Yes sir.*

[Q] *Do you recall what time that was, Monday or Tuesday?*

Breckinridge made a rambling reply beginning with:

"You see I asked the doctor immediately, the first thing we did we went over to this, I have an April calendar here, I asked the doctor as a matter of fact I was going to ask the doctor to go to St. Raymond's cemetery and follow the route of John to see if there might be anything that would give us an inkling as to his identity or build up evidence, you see we took the numbers of all...".[783]

As he continued, he claimed *"...but I found the doctor had already done that, so we went up, and the doctor said there was three foot prints that belonged to John...".*[784] I will get to the footprints later, but for now

---

[782]   Ibid.

[783]   Ibid.

[784]   Ibid.

we see Breckinridge testified that he asked to go to St. Raymond's for the purpose of looking for clues but found that Condon "*had already done that.*" However, according to this testimony they go together anyway. If this testimony is accurate, it means Condon preceded Breckinridge to St. Raymond's and went with him there – again. We see more testimony on this subject from Breckinridge during his 1934 Bronx Grand Jury testimony. The problem here seems to be that he is describing the trip there to cast the footprint – so he could be speaking in general terms when he starts out by saying:

> "*...When we came back from this airoplane* [sic] *ride I took the doctor to the place where this John the kidnapper as we always called him was at the time, you remember the layout there, the old part of the cemetery and there is thena* [sic] *fence there and you cross a paved road and there is another section of the cemetery...*".[785]

He could also be combining events as I have learned through my research that people tend to do at times. This could be an attempt at evasion too; however, it could also be the fault of those who asked the questions by not drawing out the desired specifics.

Breslin also asked about Coleman:

> [Q] *Did anyone accompany Colonel Lindberg* [sic] *and Dr. Condon to St. Raymond's cemetery?*

> [A] *No sir, not that I know of.*

---

[785] Breckinridge, Henry. Testimony. <u>Grand Jury</u>. People vs. Hauptmann. September 25, 1934. New Jersey State Police Museum and Learning Center Archives. (Foley not Breslin is asking him the questions here)

[Q] *It is true is it not that a newspaper man known as Coleman was apprised of the developments as they occurred?*

[A] *Yes sir, that is a funny story too, but by compunction of accident and design not in on what was transpiring at the beginning of Dr. Condon's contact anyhow he saw one of those notes and he knew, it would be impossible to proceed with the doctor's contact and the doctor made arrangements with Mr. Coleman if Mr. Coleman would promise not to divulge it to anybody else of the press and not to molest him or annoy him in carrying out his enterprise, but that is a story the Home News beat.*[786]

This line of questioning from Breslin did not end with Breckinridge. While Condon was on the stand before the Bronx Grand Jury, he testified about the men leaving his home on April 2nd "*before noon*" to get the money and not returning until "*about four or five.*"[787] Breslin then seized on this opportunity:

[Q] *Had you gone out that afternoon, Doctor?*

[A] *I don't recollect that, I wasn't with them.*

[Q] *I mean by yourself?*

[A] *I don't know whether I stayed there or not, I don't know.*[788]

---

[786]   Breckenridge, Colonel Henry. Testimony. <u>Bronx Grand Jury</u>. May 17, 1932. New Jersey State Police Museum and Learning Center Archives.

[787]   Condon, John F. Testimony. <u>Bronx Grand Jury</u>. May 20, 1932. New Jersey State Police Museum and Learning Center Archives.

[788]   Ibid.

Later in his testimony, Condon said the search for the "*boat Nellie*" ended in his return to New York on Sunday. Breslin then asked:

> [Q] *And did you go back up there again in company with Colonel Lindbergh?*
>
> [A] *No.*
>
> [Q] *Now on the following day, doctor, Monday?*
>
> [A] *Yes Sir.*
>
> [Q] *Did you go to St. Raymond's Cemetery again?*
>
> [A] *Within a day, Monday, Monday, yes Monday morning.*
>
> [Q] *And in company with a newspaper reporter Mr. Coleman?*
>
> [A] *Yes sir, Gregory Coleman.*[789]

The last question posed to Condon was asked by a Juror who wanted to know if Lindbergh had been "*in a position*" to see him through the "*wind shield.*" Condon replied:

> "*Until I went down the middle of the road and turned down with him he stayed in there and didn't want to be seen and I tried to shield him.*"[790]

Whether or not authorities believed Condon stayed home on Saturday afternoon is not known, but two things are. First, they

---

[789] Ibid. continued after King.
[790] Ibid.

did <u>not</u> believe he was on the level. Second, they had testimony and statements which indicated the situation Uebel described had occurred on Monday the 4th. The question remains whether his first account which he said occurred on the 1st was actually the trip on the 4th or had instead occurred on Sunday the 3rd. That seems to be what Breslin was attempting to learn when he asked Condon about possibly returning to St. Raymond's with Lindbergh on Sunday.

Unfortunately this question would never be answered despite Uebel's account being resurrected by Governor Hoffman after his re-investigation team was able to go through all of the documentation. Once they read Officer Avon's report, Robert Hicks sent his private investigator, William Dillon, to interview Uebel and get a statement. As Uebel was questioned, he told Dillon *"that he had known Condon since he was a boy"* and that:

> *"To the best of my recollection, I remember seeing him*
> *in the cemetery near Whittemore and Balcom Ave. on*
> *April 1, 1932 between 2 and 3 o'clock in the afternoon.*
> *I remember because it was payday."*[791]

From this statement alone we already can see the effects of time on Uebel's original eyewitness account. While he had not placed Condon among those he saw on that date in his earlier version, this later account had him there on that day. Regardless, as a result of this statement, and the results of Officer Avon's previous investigation, Hoffman announced to the press on February 20, 1936, that he had a witness who placed "Jafsie" at St. Raymond's prior to the ransom

---

[791]   Uebel, Bernard. Statement. Made to Wm. D. Dillon, Private Investigator. January 29, 1936. New Jersey State Police Museum and Learning Center Archives.

delivery there.[792] Later that year, there was a follow up interview/investigation made by the team of Trooper William Lewis and Leon Ho-age, who reviewed some of the information Uebel had provided to Avon. Uebel confirmed that most everything they said was correct.[793] However, he did not *"remember saying a white envelope had been passed and does not remember having seen that happen."*[794] Uebel offered that he was *"sure"* of the April 1ˢᵗ date because it was *"pay day."* Because of the length of time that had elapsed, they both decided it was a good idea to give Uebel some time to refresh his memory and would return to see if there was anything new he could remember the following week.[795]

Eight days later, the investigators returned to speak to Uebel. Uebel immediately told them he wanted to make *"corrections of the statements given"* to Officer Avon, that the second date in Avon's report that he spoke of was a *"Monday,"* and that *"he is sure of the Monday."*[796] His next assertion was that the first date was either *"March 31ˢᵗ or April 1, 1932 (whichever date was pay day at the cemetery)."* However, on this occasion he seemed to have mis-remembered the actions witnessed at the second event as being the first. He further recalled the event of the man with a *"lantern jaw"* having retrieved the box, arriving in a Green Ford (five passenger) car on the second occasion which fell

---

[792] "Witness Throws Doubt On Jafsie Story At Trial" Paper Unknown. February 20, 1936. New Jersey State Police Museum and Learning Center Archives.

[793] Hoage, Leon and Wm Lewis. Report. <u>Visit made by Leon Hoage and William Lewis to check report of Invest. Officer James A. Avon of a call he made with Det. Thompson of N. Y. on Bernard Uebel Spec. Officer at St. Raymond's cemetery – on April 14 1932</u>. August 4, 1936. New Jersey State Police Museum and Learning Center Archives.

[794] Ibid.

[795] Ibid.

[796] Hoage, Leon and Wm Lewis. Report. <u>Bernard Uebel Special Officer at St. Raymonds</u>. August 12, 1936. New Jersey State Police Museum and Learning Center Archives.

on a Monday.[797] So what we see is that he remembered one day based upon whenever "*pay day*" was. We also see that he omitted the first occurrence reported to Avon and Thompson, then shifted the second into the first time slot. Next, he moved the ransom box retrieval from the third event into the second. However, his stories are extremely consistent as he retold what he saw except for two things… the car used in the box retrieval, and the fact that the passenger and not the driver had been the one to retrieve the box. Something else that is important to note is that Uebel said the "*box-wood*" bush was "*near the shop,*" and a map was drawn to give a scenario of events. This is valuable because that bush is further away from the "*rear of 3254 E. Tremont Avenue*" than the general description may suggest. As recorded in their report, both Ho-age and Lewis were impressed with Uebel as having been "*honest,*" noted he "*apparently takes some offense at his story being in any way questioned,*" added that he "*did not at the time know that Condon was Jafsie,*" and that he "*did not know that what he saw at the time was of such importance until after he had heard of money being paid.*"[798]

Clearly any discrepancies made by Uebel in 1936 are consistent with the time that had passed from April 1932 to August 1936. I firmly believe that Uebel's original eyewitness accounts were completely true and, at worst, his only mistakes may have been the actual dates on which he believed they occurred. Certainly, we had several people who claimed that what he originally described as occurring on April 2nd actually happened on April 4th, without any knowledge of what Uebel said he saw, and (equally important) without Uebel having knowledge about what they told police. Thus, it would make sense if Condon told Coleman what had occurred (that he may have visited the scene on Sunday April 3rd without Condon) prior to the Monday visit. Finally, if police were correct and the ransom drop

---

[797]   Ibid.
[798]   Ibid.

happened further down on East Tremont before Condon returned to Whittemore, then he would have stashed that box before returning to Lindbergh. Uebel witnessed a car return days later, possibly with Reich, and saw a man leave that car to retrieve the box. This all fits in perfectly with that theory, especially since Uebel doesn't offer any such theory himself, and in fact, doesn't appear to have one at all but is simply recalling what he had seen to the best of his ability. It is also supported by the fact the ransom box was never recovered by police. This would explain fully why they had not and why Hauptmann did not have it along with the ransom money found in his garage.

The only thing missing now is to show that Condon lied about the Ransom Box in some way. And that will be clearly shown in the coming pages....

A view near the boxwood bush toward and where the ransom drop supposedly occurred (Courtesy NJSP Museum)

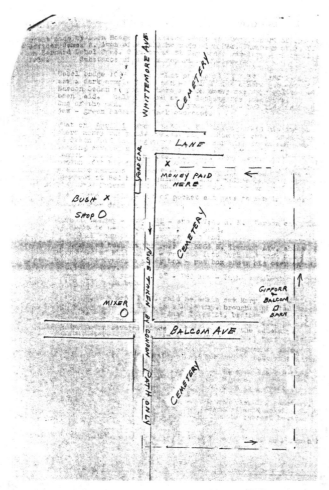

Map attached to Lewis/Ho-age report dated August 12, 1936
concerning interview with Bernard Uebel
(Courtesy NJSP Museum)

Footprints

Condon testified to the Grand Jury that on *"Monday morning"* he had returned to St. Raymond's with Gregory Coleman and answered affirmatively when asked if he had found *"a certain foot print or foot*

prints" in the "*vicinity*" on this occasion which led him to believe
they were made by John:[799]

> [Q] *And that one particular foot print that was well
> defined an impression was taken later on by the police
> authorities?*
>
> [A] *Yes sir, I was there, yes.*[800]

As mentioned above, Breckinridge testified that while he visited the
cemetery...

> "...*the doctor said there was three foot prints that
> belonged to John because when he came down the
> cemetery along the wall bordering Witmore* [sic]
> *Avenue, climbed over that fence and dropped down
> into the road, as he dropped into the road fortunately
> one of his feet hit the soft earth before the macadam
> starts, the heel of the right foot hit that soft earth but the
> rest of the right foot was on the hard macadam, leaving
> no traces, he crossed that road and he vaulted over a
> low fence, that is a thing you frequently experience if
> you ever jumped horses, it was low, in other words that
> second portion of the cemetery is lower than the street,
> so this little fence on the street side probably only two or
> three feet high and then on lower side it is a foot or two
> lower and one on a new made grave where the earth
> was mounted over, we wanted to take some pictures
> of that and measured some foot prints, my idea at the
> time being to check that up with the footprints down*

---

[799] Condon, John F. Testimony. <u>Bronx Grand Jury</u>. Continued after King.
   May 20, 1932. New Jersey State Police Museum and Learning Center
   Archives.

[800] Ibid.

there at Jersey and I appealed to the authorities for
somebody to accompany me there and that was very
kindly done as they co-operated in every single way
and we went down there and got some quick setting
surgeons plaster and we made a cast of the foot print on
the earth of this new made grave, very fortunate for if
he put his foot in the grave you would not get anything
and it was sent down to Jersey to be compared with
whatever data they had of those foot prints they had
around the window there."[801]

Breslin followed this information up with a question asking what was
found out about the comparison to which Breckinridge responded,
"they do checkup well, it was pretty hard to see foot prints so as to see if
they are inclined to be identical."[802] Breckinridge testified similarly
during the Bronx Grand Jury testimony involving Hauptmann:

"…John the Kidnapper was down the side of the fence
and according to Dr. Condon's statement jumped over
the first wall and landed in this road, now that road
was a surface road and he landed with his left foot on
the paved surface and his right foot on the shoulder
of the road, the first thing we did we went out there
that night and measured the heel on the shoulder of
the road and it tallied exactly with the impression on
the new made concrete. We didn't try to take a plaster
of paris form of that first heel because it was too faint,
and then later an excellent impression of that foot print
according to the story of the doctor of what John did

---

[801] Breckenridge, Colonel Henry. Testimony. <u>Bronx Grand Jury</u>. May 17, 1932. New Jersey State Police Museum and Learning Center Archives.
[802] Ibid.

that it would indicate that it was the foot print of John the kidnapper."[803]

The FBI Summary report recorded that after the payment of the ransom, Breckinridge and *"officers from the New Jersey State Police returned to the cemetery"* at which time Condon pointed out approximately where *"John was standing at the time of the ransom payment."*[804] As a result a *"footprint was discernable near a new grave"* and a *"plaster cast was made of same by Colonel Breckinridge..."*. The report goes on to say...

> *"...with respect to this particular footprint, Corporal William Horn advised former Special Agent J. J. Manning, that the plaster cast of this print was of little value inasmuch as the ground in which the impression was imbedded was so soft that it spread under the mold; on the other hand, Colonel Breckinridge and Corporal Horn on a previous occasion advised that the closest approximation indicates the footprint was about a size eight, although this is merely their opinion."*[805]

In an attempt to find out exactly which members of the NJSP were present, I combed through multiple documents and quickly discovered a report by Corporal Wilton. He wrote *"...I do not know how many prints were made on the baby's clothes or the footprints in the cemetery because there was no report"*; however, his report

---

[803] Breckinridge, Henry. Testimony. <u>Bronx Grand Jury</u>. People vs. Hauptmann. September 25, 1932. New Jersey State Police Museum and Learning Center Archives.

[804] Sisk, T. H. DOI (FBI) et. al., DOI Report. <u>Summary</u>. NY File No. 62-3057, p. 107. February 16, 1934. National Archives at College Park Maryland.

[805] Ibid.

clearly indicated that "*Sgt. Kubler*" took those pictures.[806] This led to the discovery of a report written by Sgt. Kubler which stated that on "*April 19, 1932*" he had been detailed by Schwarzkopf to "*St. Raymond's Cemetery*" in the Bronx to "*photograph foot print in grave at scene where ransom money had been paid.*"[807] I figured the date had to be a mistake, and what was written in this report further seemed to support my conclusion:

> "*This investigation was of secretive nature and only verbal report was made to Col. Schwarzkopf. Exact number of prints received not known at this time.*"[808]

As I continued to search, I found a cover card included with the photographs of footprints. On this card was <u>typed</u>:

"*Foot Prints Cemetry* [sic] *Lindbergh Case*"

"*Sgt. Kubler 4/5/32*"

<u>Handwritten</u> on the card was:

"*Done*"

"*No Report*".[809]

---

[806] Wilton, G. G. Corporal, Photo Section, Bureau of Identification Trenton, N. J. New Jersey State Police Report. <u>Report on Photographs, Lindbergh Case</u>. August 11, 1934. New Jersey State Police Museum and Learning Center Archives.

[807] Kubler, Louis Sgt. Identification Bureau. New Jersey State Police Report. <u>Report on photographs, Lindbergh case</u>. August 11, 1934. New Jersey State Police Museum and Learning Center Archives.

[808] Ibid.

[809] New Jersey State Police Picture Files. Cover Card. New Jersey State Police Museum and Learning Center Archives. (Many of the sets of pictures include these cards which give information about them).

So it seemed that Sgt. Kubler had been among the group who set upon St. Raymond's for the purpose of documenting these footprints. Was this Trooper's presence what Breckinridge meant when he testified that he "appealed to authorities for somebody to accompany" him there? The answer is no. I can say this with certainty based upon a NYPD report which stated the following:

> "On April 6th, 1932 at 1– A. M. the Police Commissioner called the 43rd Squad and stated that a man by the name of Bronson would call and that I was to go with him where ever he went and to see that he was not interfered with. At 1–50 A. M. a man who gave his name as Bronson called in a New Jersey car with three other men."[810]

I've always believed "Bronson" was really "Brandon" which was Breckinridge's code name at the time. The report continued:

> "We went to St. Raymond's Cemetery. Led by Doctor John F. Condon who was in a Ford Coupe driven by Al Reich we went down (South) on Whittemore Avenue to first path off Whittemore Avenue running East. On the north side of said path there is a cement wall about five foot high and against said wall, even with the first path on top of said wall East of Whittemore Avenue, and running in a Northerly direction, there was two foot prints.
>
> On Southerly side of path running East from Whittemore Ave., there is a cement wall that drops

---

[810] Gunset, Edward Detective. Investigating Officer. New York City Police Report. Report from New York Police Headquarters. July 19, 1932 (May 26, 1932). New Jersey State Police Museum and Learning Center Archives.

down four foot and on top of said wall there is a wooden fence three foot high. On first grave East of Whittemore Avenue, and South of above mentioned path there was a foot-print. This foot-print was photographed and a plaster cast made of same.

Dr. Condon stated that "He saw 'him' run down path (path running same as Whittemore Avenue) and jump over fence (fence mentioned above.)"[811]

Here we can finally get an exact date and time when this visit occurred. Also, what's most notable about this event is that Condon's narrative is remarkably different where these footprints are concerned. All of this running, jumping, and vaulting only seems to be recalled as pertaining to this specific investigation.

What more can we "learn" from Condon's perspective? On March 6, 1934, he accompanied Special Agents Sisk and Seykora to St. Raymond's and gave them a tour of the scene pointing out the different places and events which had occurred there on the night of April 2nd. Among the many details learned during this trip Seykora noted:

"Dr. Condon stated that he was of the impression at that time that "John" had entered the cemetery further east and had walked on between the graves and had jumped over the retaining wall down to the lower slope. Dr. Condon further stated that when he first located "John", he told "John" to stand up from behind the hedge and "John" replied, "My father wouldn't let me", which remark was apparently meaningless to Dr. Condon; that upon leaving John for the purpose of

> *returning to Col. Lindbergh to get the money, "John"*
> *apparently walked back into the cemetery three or four*
> *rows of graves. Dr. Condon did not hear any voices*
> *whatever and saw no lights and as it was very dark*
> *"John" disappeared into the darkness at that time."*[812]

In evaluating what Condon told investigators, I must repeat that it is obvious he didn't always remember all of the details he previously gave. Additionally, when he "rambled" or talked in circles this was a purposeful act of evasion or of buying time to think about what or how to answer. I also have come to recognize that he "adds in" or sometimes "takes out" certain truths to his story for reasons that I can best attribute to the possibility these facts can be pointed to as an insurance policy in the event his lies are discovered. It's like he does not want to reveal too many actual facts, but does not want the entire story to be all lies either. It is also clear to me that he did "slip up" in certain places. It's in these places the normal reaction would be to dismiss or shrug off what he said but, in my opinion, that would be a mistake. It's those new, bizarre, or out of place comments which I believe are most revealing and give one a peek into what really went on in his mind. Barring the fact he sometimes forgot certain lies, there are reasons why he said what he said – none of which I attribute to dementia.

In continuing with their tour, Seykora reported:

> *"A couple of days after the money was paid, Dr.*
> *Condon noticed a grave near Balcom Avenue and*
> *Whittemore Avenue in the cemetery, which appeared*
> *to have recently been dug into. Dr. Condon was of the*

---

[812] Seykora, J. E. Special Agent, DOI. DOI Report. <u>Kidnaping and Murder of Charles A. Lindbergh, Jr</u>. March 8, 1934. New Jersey State Police Museum and Learning Center Archives.

*impression that possibly the box containing the ransom
money had been concealed in this grave."*[813]

This is a perfect example of what I describe above. Exactly what
would be the reason for Condon to see a freshly dug grave in a
cemetery, then consider the possibility that the ransom box was
buried there? Hauptmann hadn't been arrested yet so there is no
innocent way to know he will not be in possession of it. It's my belief
that he's tipping his hand because he <u>knew</u> the box and the money
had become separated. Agent Seykora continued:

> *"Within several days after the payment of the ransom
> money, Dr. Condon found a foot print on a fresh grave
> near the aforementioned retaining wall over which
> "John" was believed to have jumped. On the theory
> that this foot print had been made by "John" at the
> time he jumped, a plaster cast was taken of the foot-
> print by Ralph Hacker in the presence and with the
> assistance of Dr. Condon, Al Reich, Col. Breckinridge
> and a representative of the New Jersey State Police and
> a patrolman of the New York Police Department who
> was assigned there for the purpose of preventing police
> interference with the party."*[814]

A day or two later, Agents O'Leary and Seery spoke with both Reich
and Condon. Reich told these men…

> *"…that due to the extreme softness of the earth on
> the grave and the fact that the party making the
> foot-print impression had apparently jumped from
> some height, that the size and shape of the foot print
> were [sic] somewhat distorted and would not give an*

---

[813] Ibid.
[814] Ibid.

indication of the true size or shape of the shoe making the impression."[815]

Upon hearing Reich's opinion about this, Condon offered up that he *"was of the impression that the shoe was a working man's shoe of about size nine."*[816] Some months later in August, Special Agent Sandberg spoke with Condon again and revisited this issue. After Condon was read the contents of Officer Gunset's 1932 report, Condon made some comments concerning the scenario. He went over who was present, and apparently confused the Jersey Trooper for the man referred to as "Bronson" in Gunset's report. It was at this point Condon told the Agent that *"he did not know the name of the party who took the plaster paris cast of the foot print..."*.[817] Next Sandberg wrote:

> *"Dr. Condon stated that he and Gregory Coleman were at the St. Raymond's Cemetery, probably during the daytime of the day preceding the night that the plaster cast was taken of the foot print in St. Raymond's Cemetery; that they were there for the purpose of looking over the situation..."*.[818]

Special Agent Sisk

When putting together the FBI Summary Report in February 1934, some of the information Sisk relied on about this footprint

---

[815]   Ibid.

[816]   Ibid.

[817]   Sandberg, E. Special Agent, DOI (FBI). United States Bureau of Investigation Report. Kidnaping and Murder of Charles A. Lindbergh Jr. September 5, 1934. New Jersey State Police Museum and Learning Center Archives.

[818]   Ibid.

came from Special Agent J. J. Manning's interaction with both Breckinridge and Corporal Horn of the New Jersey State Police. In a letter to J. Edgar Hoover written by SAC Fay which predates the summary, he wrote:

> *"Agent Manning also inquired of Corporal Horn with reference to this plaster footprint cast, with a view of determining the particular size of the shoe which would fit therein. Corporal Horn stated in reply to this inquiry that although this plaster cast is a fairly good job, it was made under a great handicap in view the extreme softness and condition of the ground at the particular time."*[819]

However, Horn also explained the cast wasn't something a shoe could be properly fitted into because he said that various sizes could all fit:

> *"This is due, stated Corporal Horn, to the slopping sides of the plaster cast, caused as mentioned above by the extremely soft mud in St. Raymond's Cemetery at the time the cast was made by Colonel Breckinridge."*[820]

Sisk had the unenviable distinction of having graced the stand during the Flemington trial on four separate occasions. He was quizzed by Reilly several times about St. Raymond's cemetery, to which he made several surprising replies. The first involved the claim that Condon had family members buried there:

---

[819] Fay, F. X. Special Agent in Charge, U.S. Bureau of Investigation (DOI). Letter from F. X. Fay to Director. January 18, 1934. National Archives at College Park Maryland.
[820] Ibid.

[Q] *Now, Condon, Dr. Condon, was very familiar with St. Raymond's Cemetery, wasn't he?*

[A] *Well, I don't know that he was very familiar with it, no.*

[Q] *Well, didn't—*

[A] *I never heard that.*

[Q] *Didn't your investigation disclose that several member's of Dr. Condon's family were buried in St. Raymond's Cemetery?*

[A] *No. Our investigation did not disclose that. We had received information that some of them were buried there, but investigation disproved that fact.*

[Q] *Well, wasn't it Dr. Condon that advised you – I am now reading from your official report –*

[A] *That is not my report.*

[Q] *Well, it was made by one of your agents?*

[A] *Yes. I read it before I gave it –*

[Q] *Who made this report?*

[A] *Special Agent Seykora.*[821]

---

[821] Sisk, Thomas H. Testimony. The State of New Jersey vs. Bruno Richard Hauptmann, <u>Hunterdon County Court of Oyer and Terminer</u>, pages 3413-4, 1935. New Jersey State Law Library.

If the report that Sisk handed over to Reilly before this questioning was the same report I've cited previously, it clearly states this information came to them from Condon himself. What's even more fascinating was Sisk's footprint testimony:

> [Q] *Now, from the information that you have learned officially on this case as an agent of the Department of Justice investigating the case, have you learned that a plaster cast of the footprint in the cemetery of the man who received the money from Dr. Condon was taken?*
>
> [A] *I learned that a footprint, a plaster cast of a footprint was taken, but there is no positive connection between that footprint and the man who received the ransom money.*
>
> [Q] *How do you know? You were not there when the ransom money was paid?*
>
> [A] *It is a matter of speculation.*[822]

This is especially interesting because of the obvious inferences in the documentation mentioning the footprint, particularly since they were relying on what Condon was telling them in order to trust this print was legitimate evidence. After Hauptmann's arrest, Agent Sisk's mindset was reflected in what Hoover wrote in a memo:

> "*I inquired if there was such a footprint, and Mr. Sisk advised that there was; that the footprint was at the corner of the hedge and the railing of the cemetery – about ten feet from the point where Dr. Condon met the kidnaper* [sic]*, and the supposition is that the kidnaper* [sic] *followed behind Dr. Condon as he*

---

[822] Ibid. Page 1965.

walked down the dark road, and then jumped over the fence onto the fresh burial plot."[823]

Reilly had also asked Sisk where Condon had been standing in relation to this footprint when the money was passed and Sisk replied *"about fifteen or twenty feet from that point, I believe."*[824] But questioning about the print itself revealed this:

> [Q] *Did you also learn that this footprint was apparently made by a person who had jumped from some height and that the size and shape of the footprint was distorted?*
>
> [A] *Yes, sir.*[825]

I've seen this mentioned in a couple of other places. One source came from Lt. Keaten as he explained the situation to Agent Sisk:

> *"They stated that the footprint found at St. Raymond's Cemetery of which a plaster cast was made was approximately a size 8 or 8½; that in jumping over the cement wall to where he met Dr. Condon the kidnaper [sic] skid in the soft ground thus the impression left was not absolutely accurate."*[826]

---

823 Hoover, John Edgar, Director. Memorandum For Mr. Tamm. September 25, 1934. National Archives at College Park Maryland.

824 Sisk, Thomas H. Testimony. The State of New Jersey vs. Bruno Richard Hauptmann, Hunterdon County Court of Oyer and Terminer, pages 1965-6, 1935. New Jersey State Law Library.

825 Ibid. Page 3412.

826 Sisk, T. H. Special Agent, Division of Investigation (FBI). Memorandum for the Director. Unknown Subjects Kidnapping and Murder of Charles A. Lindbergh, Jr. June 23, 1934. National Archives at College Park Maryland.

The only other source I have was in the Hoover memo where it is written:

> *"When Mr. Hacker made the mold the police, as well as Dr. Condon, and Detective Compton of the Bronx, were present. Mr. Sisk said this information had been brought to our attention, and it was estimated that the size of the foot was about 8½. Hauptmann wears a size nine shoe."*

> *"Mr. Sisk said that whoever made the footprint on the grave had skidded due to the fact that the ground was soft, and this print really is of little value. Mr. Sisk said that the New York papers merely stated that it is understood the authorities have a footprint. He said Mr. Hacker had taken the print because he is an architect and is familiar with handling plaster casts."*[827]

There is a lot to consider and process here. If the person "skidded" why didn't Corporal Horn, Breckinridge, or any other person there mention this before? And if the print is longer, as a result of a skid, how does that help identify Hauptmann whose shoe size is bigger than the distorted print? Another confusing issue is who made the cast. Several sources credit different people with making it. Lastly, we see a new name associated with the New York Cop who was present. Was this a mistake or was someone else there in addition to Detective Gunset? Reilly also asked Sisk about the identity of the police officer who was there, and despite the fact he appeared to be Hoover's source, answered differently on the stand:

---

[827] Hoover, John Edgar, Director. <u>Memorandum For Mr. Tamm</u>. September 25, 1934. National Archives at College Park Maryland.

[A] *I asked him, but he did not know the name of the officer.*

[Q] *He couldn't remember?*

[A] *No.*

[Q] *Did he say whether or not he had a description of the police officer from which he could point him out?*

[A] *I didn't ask him that.*

[Q] *Did you attempt to find out who the police officer was?*

[A] *Well, no, I did not.*[828]

Moving on, according to Detective Gunset's report, there were seven men, including him, who went to the cemetery for the purpose of documenting these footprints. So far, I've identified Gunset, Breckinridge, Condon, Reich, Hacker, and Kubler. So who was the other man?

A. P. Madden

As previously mentioned, A.P. Madden was an SAC in the Intelligence Unit of the Treasury Department's Internal Revenue Service. At about 9:45 PM on April 5th Breckinridge called him on the phone requesting him to come to Condon's home. Once there, he found a group of people assembled which included Breckinridge, Reich,

---

828   Sisk, Thomas H. Testimony. The State of New Jersey vs. Bruno Richard Hauptmann, Hunterdon County Court of Oyer and Terminer, pages 3411, 1935. New Jersey State Law Library.

Sgt. Kubler, Ralph Hacker, *"one of Jafsie's sons,"* Condon, and his *"daughter."* Prior to his arrival, *"a group"* had been at St. Raymond's cemetery in relationship to the foot prints. Madden wrote:

> *"...I was told they had created some disturbance at or near the cemetery, and had decided to leave. The principal subject under discussion after my arrival was had around the dining room table, and related to the advisability or inadvisability of going back to the cemetery. At that time, it was not generally known that the ransom had been paid. Brandon appeared to be particularly anxious to go back to the cemetery, and the others present were evidently willing to follow his plan, although no one other than Brandon was very aggressive about the matter. It was about midnight before any definite decision had been reached."*[829]

Madden was worried that the whole group could be arrested if they returned and suggested that Breckinridge call Mulrooney to ask for one of his men to accompany them. The arrangements were made, then along with Condon, Breckinridge, Hacker, Reich, and Kubler, they picked up the NY officer then drove to the cemetery.[830]

> *"My recollection is that there was a good heel print on the edge of the road where the contact man had jumped over the wall. Measurements of the heel print were made. My recollection is that Brandon took the measurements and perhaps also Ralph Hacker and the identification expert. I think that the paster [sic] of Paris cast was made largely by Ralph Hacker and the*

---

[829] Madden, A. P. Special Agent in Charge, Intelligence Unit, Internal Revenue Service. <u>Letter from A. P. Madden to Mr. Frank J. Wilson.</u> November 13, 1934. American Heritage Center, University of Wyoming.
[830] Ibid.

*identification expert with the assistance of Al Wright
[sic]."*[831]

Since this was all going on around 1 AM, Madden was still worried
that someone might *"make a commotion over people being in the
cemetery with flash lights at that hour."*[832] After they left Madden
recalled:

> *"...that Brandon stated that it was a very fine cast
> and might at some time in the future prove to be very
> valuable. I expressed some doubt regarding it because as
> I observed the pouring of the plaster of Paris, it seemed
> to me that it was pulling in earth from the sides with
> the result that the cast was probably larger than the
> print. I stated that, in my opinion, the measurements
> if any of this material was to be of any value, would
> be worth more than the cast."*[833]

As it related to Hauptmann's arrest, Madden's position seems
particularly important:

> *"It is my recollection that the newspapers have reported
> that an old pair of Bruno's shoes were found in his
> home or in his garage. I am very curious to know
> whether or not the measurements of the foot print
> coincide with the measurements of any shoes that may
> have been examined thus far."*[834]

All of Hauptmann's shoes had been confiscated by police. When
Anna Hauptmann had been by to see the shoemaker who *"used to*

---

[831] Ibid.
[832] Ibid.
[833] Ibid.
[834] Ibid.

fix" her husband's shoes, he informed her that he had been visited by the police "*to look over the size*" of Hauptmann's shoes and was told by them "*that it didn't fit the print they found up there*."[835] The NJSP eventually turned over all of his shoes to Dr. Albert Edel for examination and analysis on December 21, 1934.[836]

Neither his shoes nor any foot print cast was ever offered as evidence against him.

[835] Stockburger, H. Tpr. New Jersey State Police. New Jersey State Police Report. <u>Conversation between Mr. and Mrs. Hauptmann at the Hunterdon County Jail in Flemington N.J. on November 17th, 1934</u>. November 17, 1934. New Jersey State Police Museum and Learning Center Archives.

[836] Edel, Dr. Albert E., Analytical Chemist. Chief Medical Examiner's Office, Essex County, New Jersey. <u>Letter from Albert Edel to Captain John J. Lamb</u>. March 14, 1935. New Jersey State Police Museum and Learning Center Archives.

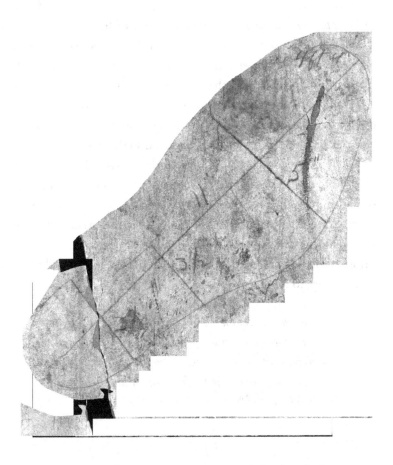

Saint Raymond's Footprint Measurements (taken by police)
(Courtesy NJSP Museum)

283

Ransom Box

With Uebel's solid eyewitness account in mind, the Ransom Box seems to be a vital clue. According to Coleman the mere request for such a box made it *"evident that the kidnapers* [sic] *had planned a hiding place for the money."*[837] He also claimed that the box itself was kept with the ransom money at the Corn Exchange Bank *"until two days before the final negotiations."*[838] Another interesting fact which came from Coleman was that the box was *"specially"* constructed. Condon made a brilliant decision that while it would be made to the exact specifications as outlined in the ransom note, he would have it constructed with different kinds of wood so that there would be *"no difficulty in recognizing it."* As a result, the *"top and bottom was made of mahogany and the sides of white maple."*[839] So once again we see something "unique," a method of identification, which originated from Condon. It's interesting to note that the other person who was spending a lot of time with Condon and had all of the inside information had made this claim as well. In fact, Breckinridge added a little more to it when he testified…

> *"…we constructed a special box, it was mahogany top and bottom on the sides special twins and special paper wrapping up that bundle, it would be indestructible in case they burned it up from fire and left it behind somewhere…".*[840]

---

[837] Coleman, Gregory F. *Vigil*. Unpublished Manuscript. Page 8a. Undated (circa 1932). New Jersey State Police Museum and Learning Center Archives.

[838] Ibid.

[839] Ibid. Insert "A" page 47.

[840] Breckenridge, Colonel Henry. Testimony. <u>Bronx Grand Jury</u>. May 17, 1932. New Jersey State Police Museum and Learning Center Archives.

So while there were two different positions offered concerning what might happen to the box, they both agreed about the different wood, one being mahogany.

It was after a conversation which Special Agent Manning had with Lt. Finn sometime in September 1933 that his interest in the Ransom Box was renewed. Manning visited with Condon on September 7th, and what Condon told him is reflected in a subsequent report:

"...Dr. Condon stated in one instance that a furniture dealer, who is a very close friend of his, made up this box for him to comply in minute detail with the specifications given in the ransom note...".[841]

However, Manning also noted...

> *"...on another occasion, Dr. Condon began a conversation relating to the preparation of this box and remarked that his son-in-law Hacker had seen the ransom note describing the box with dimensions and thereafter drew his own dimensions more accurately with the view to making up the box himself. No further comment was offered by Condon relative to this angle of the case, and after making the above remark he immediately switched over to the discussion of his relations with Al Reich...".*[842]

The next day that Manning returned and once again engaged Condon about the box. This conversation convinced Manning that *"Hacker"* made the *"set of plans from which this packet or box"*

---

[841] Manning, J. J. Special Agent, DOI. USBOI Report. <u>Kidnaping And Murder Of Charles A. Lindbergh, Jr</u>. September 11, 1933. National Archives at College Park Maryland.

[842] Ibid.

would be constructed.[843] Condon then explained to Manning that he obtained various kinds of wood from which the box was to be made, then brought them along with the plans to his old friend, who he could "*not recall*" at the time, to have it built. He further stated that he was quite clear that "*not even Lindbergh*" knew the person who made the box "*nor the place at which it was made*."[844] Condon claimed the box also had an "ordinary cabinet lock" on it and that he still had both the key and the plans in his possession. Agent Manning wrote:

> "*It seems from Condon's statements that the poplar, white pine and boxwood (mahogany) were glued together by the cabinet maker and the box made from the combined materials. This Condon said he did only for the reason that in the event the box showed up at a later date he would be able to identify it.*"[845]

Manning coaxed Condon into his car for the purpose of locating his "friend" who made the box. As they drove around Condon pointed out a vacant store on Webster Avenue and told Manning that the "*man who made the box used to have his business in there.*"[846] Condon called out to a man on the street then inquired about that business. When the man replied that it was "*Perretty,*" Condon remarked that "*Old man Peretty is the man who made the box*" and that it cost Condon "*$3.25.*"[847] About a week later, Manning, accompanied by Lt. Finn and Sgt. Zapolsky, tracked down Frank Peremi Jr. and interviewed him. One important bit of information learned was that

---

[843] Manning, J. J. Special Agent, DOI. USBOI Report. <u>Kidnaping And Murder Of Charles A. Lindbergh, Jr</u>. September 15, 1933. National Archives at College Park Maryland.

[844] Ibid.

[845] Ibid.

[846] Ibid.

[847] Ibid.

Frank Peremi Sr. *"died in October, 1931"* so he could not have made the box.[848] Next, he told the investigators that both Condon and Reich had been in to see *him* about making a box. *"Peremi stated that he advised Condon of his willingness to make the box, providing he was paid $3.50 for such service,"* but that Condon remarked *"$3.50 was too much for such a job"* and left, stating *"he would probably return in about an hour"* but never did.[849]

Having determined that Peremi had not made the box, it was clear to Manning that Condon was being *"untruthful."*[850] Despite this (or possibly because of this) the matter seemed to go cold. Yet, oddly enough, in another conversation in late November 1933 with a *"Special Agent,"* Condon claimed the box was a *"family heirloom."*[851] Also during late November, Condon turned over to Manning several letters he had recently received. One of those letters, dated November 6, 1933, was written by "Gus Liskis" and Manning was especially interested in one particular line:

> *"Professor how we going to get back and restore the confidence to send you the Ransom Box to your family."*[852]

---

[848]   Manning, J. J. Special Agent, DOI. USBOI Report. <u>Kidnaping And Murder Of Charles A. Lindbergh, Jr</u>. September 29, 1933. National Archives at College Park Maryland.

[849]   Ibid.

[850]   Cullen, T. F. Special Agent in Charge, Division of Investigation. <u>Letter from T. F. Cullen to Director</u>. October 6, 1933. National Archives at College Park Maryland.

[851]   Sisk, T. H. DOI (FBI) et. al., DOI Report. <u>Summary</u>. NY File No. 62-3057, p. 193. February 16, 1934. National Archives at College Park Maryland.

[852]   Manning, J. J. Special Agent, DOI. USBOI Report. <u>Kidnaping And Murder Of Charles A. Lindbergh, Jr</u>. December 8, 1933. National Archives at College Park Maryland.

Manning wrote:

> *"Considerable significance is attached to this quoted sentence in view of the fact that the box containing the ransom money paid by Dr. Condon over the hedge in the St. Raymond Cemetery, Bronx, New York City, has never been returned to Dr. Condon; in fact, very few individuals who have not had an active interest in the details of this case have knowledge that the ransom money was contained in any particular box at the time of its payment."*[853]

The FBI would lose a valuable tool at this point in their investigation as Special Agent J. J. Manning left the Division. For whatever reason, on March 5th, 1934, Lt. Keaten detailed Cpl. Leon to find out from Condon the name and address of the man who made the ransom box. Exactly why he did not send Sgt. Zapolsky, who had been with Agent Manning during his interview with Peremi, is unknown. Upon Leon's arrival, Condon told him that he had the *"box made on Webster Avenue, but he did not know the man's name who made same."*[854] And so Leon and Condon retraced almost the exact sequence of events by driving to Webster, learning that it was Peremi, and that the shop had closed, etc. Once again, Condon recalled that he paid *"Peremi $3.25 for the making of this box."* However, he added a new detail when he retold this story to Leon…

> *"…he told Peremi to make the box in such a way that he would be able to identify it at a later date. He also*

---

[853]   Ibid.

[854]   Leon, Samuel J. Cpl., New Jersey State Police. New Jersey State Police Report. <u>Questioning Dr. Condon as to name and address of person that made the Box in which the Lindbergh Ransom Money was in at the time of the pay-off</u>. March 5, 1934. New Jersey State Police Museum and Learning Center Archives.

> *stated that Peremi gave him pieces of the wood that was
> used in the construction of this box. He stated that the
> box was made according to orders received in one of
> the ransom notes as to size, etc."*[855]

The very next day several Agents from the FBI arrived at Condon's house and prodded him with multiple questions concerning his involvement. At some point the identity of the ransom box maker came up, and once again everyone piled into a car but this time, armed with Special Agent Manning's reports, headed straight for Frank Peremi's apartment. There, Condon asked Peremi directly *"of what materials he had made the box for him."*[856] Peremi told him he did not make the box, and once again, explained how Condon left saying his quoted price was too much without ever returning. A conversation ensued whereupon Condon blurted out that he recalled *"the man who made the box had a shop, the windows of which had some fancy inlaid cabinet work."* Peremi believed this may have been a cabinet maker by the name of *"A. Samuelsohn"* whose new shop was now at 3037 Webster Avenue.[857] The next day Agents O'Leary and Seery brought Condon to Samuelsohn's store. Upon arrival Samuelsohn immediately identified Condon and stated *"I remember you. I did a little job for you a couple of years ago."* Samuelsohn located his documentation about the job in his records where it was recorded *"3/25, one box, maple, 7x6x14 — $3.00."* Samuelsohn said the box was maple, 5-ply veneer, tongue and groove but could not recall if a lock had been placed in it.[858]

---

[855] Ibid.

[856] Seykora, J. E. Special Agent, DOI. DOI Report. <u>Kidnaping and Murder of Charles A. Lindbergh, Jr.</u> March 8, 1934. New Jersey State Police Museum and Learning Center Archives.

[857] Ibid.

[858] Ibid.

In early April 1934, Special Agent O'Leary shared this new information with Lt. Keaten. Keaten immediately sent Cpl. Leon to verify this information which Leon did by interviewing Abraham Samuelsohn, who told him that he did make the box.[859] Leon walked away from this investigation furious. He reported what he learned back to Lt. Keaten. But instead of Law Enforcement making a unified effort to learn from Condon exactly why he had lied about who built the box, and why he had lied about the materials used in it, something very strange occurred. According to Special Agent Sisk…

> "…*Trooper Leon expressed to Dr. Condon considerable indignation at what they termed his failure to inform them of the identity of the box maker in question, intimating to Condon that he was favoring this Division in furnishing it information not furnished the State Police.*"[860]

Sisk then learned:

> "*With further reference to the Division's contact with Dr. Condon, it was recently confidentially reported to Agent Sisk by Lieutenant Finn that the State Police were endeavoring to "poison Dr. Condon's mind against this Division." Lieutenant Finn wants it strictly understood that he is not to be quoted, regarding this statement.*"[861]

---

[859] Leon, Samuel J. Cpl., New Jersey State Police. New Jersey State Police Report. <u>Investigation of person and place where Dr. Condon had box made in which the Lindbergh Ransom Money was passed</u>. April 3, 1934. New Jersey State Police Museum and Learning Center Archives.

[860] Sisk, T. H. Special Agent, Division of Investigation. Memorandum. <u>Memorandum For The Director</u>. June 8, 1934. National Archives at College Park Maryland.

[861] Ibid.

So while everyone was now more certain than ever that the case could be solved through Condon, instead of a united front in getting to the necessary information, there was an all out competition to, instead, win his favor and the red carpet was rolled out for him. In fact, the New Jersey State Police instantly began the tactic of patting Condon on the back about everything and *"treated him like a king."*[862]

In one of the smarter moves made concerning this angle, Cpl. Leon drove over to see Mr. Samuelsohn again and once there placed an order for an *"exact duplicate of the box."* [863] About a month later, the box was forwarded to the Training School in West Trenton.[864] However, no one seemed to have ever told Breckinridge. This is clear from what he told the Grand Jury after Hauptmann had been arrested:

> *"... a special box was to be made which Dr. Condon had made, the doctor did that very cleverly, it had several sorts of wood in that box...".*[865]

Once on the stand in Flemington, it became evident that no one had told Condon not to continue to lie about it. This was well illustrated during the cross examination by Reilly:

---

[862] Hoover, J. Edgar. Director, Division of Investigation. <u>Memorandum For Mr. Tamm</u>. June 8, 1934. National Archives at College Park Maryland.

[863] Leon, Samuel J. Cpl., New Jersey State Police. New Jersey State Police Report. <u>Obtaining an exact duplicate of the box in which the Ransom Money was paid</u>. May 22, 1934. New Jersey State Police Museum and Learning Center Archives.

[864] Receipt. Received by J. J. L. (Captain Lamb) *"1 Box of 5 Ply Maple, 7"x 6"x 14", inside measurements."* June 22, 1934. New Jersey State Police Museum and Learning Center Archives.

[865] Breckinridge, Henry. Testimony. Grand Jury. <u>People vs. Hauptmann</u>. September 25, 1934. New Jersey State Police Museum and Learning Center Archives.

[Reilly]: *Who made the box?*

[Condon]: *A wood carver on Webster Avenue, near 198th Street or 200th Street.*

Q: *What was his name?*

A: *I couldn't tell you.*

Q: *What?*

A: *I can't tell you, but I would know it if you would recall it to me.*[866]

Another question we now all know the answer to, but which Condon lied about:

Q: *Has the box ever been found?*

A: *I do not—*

Q: *As far as you know.*

A: *I do not know.*[867]

And finally, Condon returns to his original and biggest lie:

Q: *Now, what was the box made of?*

A: *That is what I meant by planning.*

---

[866] Condon, John F. Testimony. The State of New Jersey vs. Bruno Richard Hauptmann, <u>Hunterdon County Court of Oyer and Terminer</u>, page 767, 1935. New Jersey State Law Library.

[867] Ibid. Page 769.

Q: *Just tell us.*

A: *I took whitewood — yes, I am telling you— I took whitewood, and they call that poplar, they call it honeysuckle, that is the same wood. I took whitewood and mixed it with other styles of wood until I got the color and the kind of a box that I wanted.*[868]

John's Dead

Was John dead? Could he have been murdered, or killed? After much time had passed, police believed the possibility existed. As a result, in the summer of 1933, Lt. Keaten decided to have Condon do something a little different than the usual mug-shot reviews.[869] On this occasion…

"*…he viewed New Jersey State Police photos of dead persons, dating from approximately from the first of March, 1932, to date. The purpose being that the "John" mentioned by him, in the Lindbergh Case, might be among them. He failed to identify any of the pictures as being "John". The undersigned, in company with Detective Fred Itschner of Capt. Oliver's Office, then proceeded to the New York City Police Gallery, Headquarters Building, and where Dr. Condon viewed all pictures of dead persons, on file at*

---

[868] Ibid.

[869] Leon, Samuel J. Cpl. And Horn, William F. Cpl., New Jersey State Police. New Jersey State Police Report. Making arrangements with Doctor Condon, to have him look over photographs of unidentified dead, at Office of Capt. Oliver, N.Y. City Police Headquarters, re. Lindbergh Case. July 12, 1933. New Jersey State Police Museum and Learning Center Archives.

that place, dating from approximately the first day of March, 1932, to date."[870]

About a month later, while Condon was chatting with a New York Times reporter, he made a startling admission. According to the article that resulted:

> *"No further word came from the mysterious "John," who had carried on negotiations with Dr. Condon, but the retired school teacher said he had received a letter since informing him that the man to whom he gave the money had "died a sudden death."*[871]

Was he doing that "thing" again? That "thing" where he borrows certain facts in order to bolster his own account? Whether he was or not, it was in any case a believable scenario, that is, aside from the coincidence that police first injected the idea. And if Condon was "in league" with the Kidnappers, it would be a very convenient fact for John to have died – particularly if he was actually still alive. That would get both him and John "off the hook." And why not? He invented the "lump" on the thumb for just this purpose, so why not a similar tactic here?

Another year later mid–1934, the idea that John may have died was still circulating among the NJSP. After all, it was their idea in the first place. In fact, while going over certain ideas about the case with Agent Sisk:

---

[870]   Leon, Samuel J. Cpl. And Horn, William F. Cpl., New Jersey State Police. New Jersey State Police Report. <u>Report of investigation re having Dr. Condon look over pictures of unidentified dead; re Lindbergh Case.</u> July 14, 1933. New Jersey State Police Museum and Learning Center Archives.

[871]   "Condon Recalls Ransom Payment." *The New York Times.* August 3, 1933.

> *"Colonel Schwarzkopf and Lt. Keaton [sic] stated that in their opinion there is a distinct possibility that John, to whom Condon paid the ransom money, is dead, possibly having been "bumped off" by his associates in the crime; that for this reason they had tried to obtain the records of all unidentified dead since April 2, 1932, whever [sic] possible procuring pictures and exhibiting them to Dr. Condon and Joseph Perrone."*[872]

There is however also a chance Condon did receive such a letter, and if it came to him before the cops brought it up, he would look all the more credible. So when did he claim he received it? It just so happens that during an interview with Agent Sandberg Condon explained the details:

> *"During Agent's conversation with Dr. Condon he advised that he received an anonymous letter about two weeks after the ransom money was paid, stating it was useless for him to look for "John", as "John" was killed two days after the money was paid. He quoted from the letter as follows: "You gave a description of "John." I could do better myself." Dr. Condon stated that he turned this letter over to Detective Thompson of the 43rd Precinct, New York Police Dept., Bronx, N.Y."*[873]

---

[872]   Sisk, T. H. Special Agent, Division of Investigation (FBI). Memorandum for the Director. <u>Unknown Subjects Kidnapping and Murder of Charles A. Lindbergh, Jr.</u> June 23, 1934. National Archives at College Park Maryland.

[873]   Sandberg, E. Special Agent, DOI (FBI). United States Bureau of Investigation Report. <u>Kidnaping and Murder of Charles A. Lindbergh Jr.</u> August 14, 1934. New Jersey State Police Museum and Learning Center Archives.

It was a couple of weeks later that Sandberg followed up this lead with Detective Thompson…

> *"…who stated that Dr. Condon never gave him any anonymous letters, stating that John had been killed two days after the money was paid."*[874]

There was something else that Det. Thompson wanted to set the record straight about. Despite the fact that Condon was telling everyone he was a *"distant relative, fifth or sixth cousin,"* it was not true, and *"he was not in any way related to Dr. Condon."*[875] As a direct result of what was learned in this interview, Sandberg questioned Condon again. Once enlightened, Condon claimed…

> *"…that if he did not give this letter to Detective Thompson, he must have given it to some representative of the New Jersey State Police, or to one of Captain Oliver's men of the New York Police."*[876]

Starting to get the picture? Sandberg sure was. And as a result he set up a gallery of photos consisting of *"unidentified dead"* for Condon to peruse. However, unknown to Condon at the time, these people had all been alive in 1932 and had only been killed in the years 1933, and 1934.[877] Sadly, this little trick did not bear fruit as Condon proclaimed John was not among them.

---

[874] Sandberg, E. Special Agent, DOI (FBI). United States Bureau of Investigation Report. <u>Kidnaping and Murder of Charles A. Lindbergh Jr.</u> September 4, 1934. New Jersey State Police Museum and Learning Center Archives.

[875] Ibid.

[876] Ibid.

[877] Ibid.

Vaclav Simek

Vaclav Simek had been arrested in Detroit in 1924 related to the charge of extortion for threatening to kidnap and blind Edsel Ford Jr. if he was not paid $1,000,000.[878] He was picked up at a church which was the designated drop point for the ransom. Later convicted and sentenced to 1 to 2 years, he was eventually deported on April 29, 1925, to Czechoslovakia.[879] According to Treasury Agent Frank Wilson, information had been secured by an "informant at Detroit" that Simek was involved in this case, and that as a result he secured a photo of Simek from the office of the Counsel for Czechoslovakia at New York City.[880] Wilson wrote that several other unrelated pictures were mixed in with Simek's photo then submitted to Dr. Condon for his consideration to see if any could be "John."

> *"He picked out the picture of Simek and said, "Boys, you are hot, I want to see that man", but he would not definitely state that Simek was the kidnapper to whom he had made the ransom payment. From time to time Dr. Condon had been shown a great number of pictures and this was the first occasion that*

---

[878] Snook, R. A. Lieut. New Jersey State Police. New Jersey State Police Report. <u>Investigation of Vaclav Simeck, suspect Lindbergh case, in cooperation with Inspector Wm. J. Collins, Detroit Police Department and Asst. Prosecutor John Collins, Detroit.</u> July 22, 1932. New Jersey State Police Museum and Learning Center Archives.

[879] Sisk, T. H. DOI (FBI) et. al., DOI Report. <u>Summary.</u> NY File No. 62-3057, p. 369. February 16, 1934. National Archives at College Park Maryland.

[880] Wilson, Frank J., Special Agent, Internal Revenue Service. Internal Revenue Report. SI-6336. <u>In re: Kidnapping and murder of Charles Augustus Lindbergh, Jr.</u> page 13. November 11, 1933. New Jersey State Police Museum and Learning Center Archives.

*he indicated we were on the right track and we were
therefore very anxious to locate Simek."*[881]

Condon was informed that the picture he had selected was the
"Detroit suspect" and then "*his excitement increased.*"[882] Two men
present from Detroit during this event were Inspector William Collins
of the Detroit Police Department along with Assistant Prosecutor
John Collins. Prosecutor Collins declared that he was positive Simek
had committed the crime.[883] He had samples of Simek's handwriting
which he went over with Snook and advised that it was a match of
the handwriting in the ransom notes. Snook's opinion was that while
Simek's handwriting displayed "*foreign characteristics,*" he did not
believe there was a connection.[884] As a result, it was decided that A.
S. Osborn would make an examination. The next day, Osborn made
a very careful examination of the writing but concluded they had
not been written by the same man...

> "*...he supported his decision by stating that the writer
> in 1924 showed signs of education and culture and
> that eight years later his writing would not be similar
> to the writing in the Lindbergh notes, which writing
> indicated a certain illiteracy.*"[885]

However, the fact Simek was now ruled out as the ransom note
writer did not deter Lt. Snook:

---

[881]   Ibid. Page 14.

[882]   Snook, R. A. Lieut. New Jersey State Police. New Jersey State Police
        Report. <u>Investigation of Vaclav Simeck, suspect Lindbergh case, in
        cooperation with Inspector Wm. J. Collins, Detroit Police Department
        and Asst. Prosecutor John Collins, Detroit</u>. July 22, 1932. New Jersey
        State Police Museum and Learning Center Archives.

[883]   Ibid.

[884]   Ibid.

[885]   Ibid.

"In my opinion the handwriting decision in this case merely indicated that the suspect did not with his own hand write the Lindbergh notes. This fact does not eliminate him as a possibility and it would appear that there are sufficient grounds to continue the investigation of the suspect to the very end."[886]

As a result, Lt. Snook secured Simek's photographs along with his fingerprints. Snook wrote *"the fingerprints will be checked against the fingerprints taken from the scene of the crime and they will also be searched in our files (State Bureau)."* [887] The FBI noted that Simek's description did not match up with Condon's previous descriptions of "John."[888] As a result, all available methods of investigation in the states were conducted jointly by the NJSP and the Treasury Department. The Department of State was asked to conduct an investigation outside of the country. It was determined that Simek had been in Santo Domingo working for *"Compania Electrica at Salto Jimenoa."*[889] The records of this corporation were examined and it was proven that Simek was working there *"during the time"* the *"crime was committed."*[890] Police later re-visted Condon with a

---

886 Ibid.

887 Ibid.

888 Sisk, T. H. DOI (FBI) et. al., DOI Report. <u>Summary</u>. NY File No. 62-3057, p. 370. February 16, 1934. National Archives at College Park Maryland.

889 Brown, James E., Jr. Secretary of Legation. <u>Letter from James E. Brown Jr. to The Honorable Secretary of State</u>. September 29, 1932. New Jersey State Police Museum and Learning Center Archives.

890 Wilson, Frank J., Special Agent, Internal Revenue Service. Internal Revenue Report. SI-6336. <u>In re: Kidnapping and murder of Charles Augustus Lindbergh, Jr</u>. page 14. November 11, 1933. New Jersey State Police Museum and Learning Center Archives.

photograph of Simek, and Condon now "*failed to identify same.*"[891] However, the story does not end there. Corporal Leon visited Condon in the later summer of 1934. Condon shared with him that Prosecutor Collins from Detroit, Michigan, had been by to see him the day before. When asked about the details one of the things Collins shared with him was that...

> "...*Vaclav Simek, whom Dr. Condon identified the picture of as that of "John", and whom he learned through his investigation, was in San Domingo City, several years before the kidnapping and was there at the time of the kidnapping, has two brothers who look exactly like him and one of them is his twin brother. One of these brothers is supposed to be living in Hopewell, N.J., and formerly was employed by a riding academy in the vicinity of Hopewell, N.J.*"[892]

Arthur Barry

A notorious jewel thief, Arthur Barry, had stolen over $2 million in gems and jewelry from Connecticut and Long Island homes.[893] His life of crime seemed halted once he was arrested on June 5, 1927, at the Ronkonkoma railroad station based on a tip possibly provided to

---

[891] Leon, Samuel J. Cpl. And Horn, William F. Cpl., New Jersey State Police. New Jersey State Police Report. The showing of Vaclav Simek's photograph to Dr. John F. Condon for identification, re: Lindbergh Case. January 18, 1933. New Jersey State Police Museum and Learning Center Archives.

[892] Leon, Samuel J. Cpl., New Jersey State Police. New Jersey State Police Report. Interviewing of Dr. John F. Condon at his home, Bronx N.Y., in reference to further evidence or suggestions that he may have information that may be of assistance in the solution of the Lindbergh Crime. August 15, 1934. New Jersey State Police Museum and Learning Center Archives.

[893] "National Affairs: Barry Trapped." *Time.* October 31, 1932.

police by one of his many girlfriends.[894] He later confessed and was sentenced to 25 years in prison. However, on July 28, 1929, there was a riot at Auburn State Prison where Barry was incarcerated which led to his escape.

In July of 1931, Otto Reuter and his wife decided to place an ad for a "roomer" in a paper called the Rural New Yorker in an effort to assist with the taxes on their farm in Byram Township.[895] Responding to this ad was a man named "James Toner" and a woman named "Ann" whom he referred to as his "wife." They agreed to the $2 per week terms then selected the front room on the second floor.[896]

After the kidnapping, many people contacted the NJSP with their suspicions that Barry had been the perpetrator. Among them came a letter from a man who had previously driven down to Highfields and spoken with Schwarzkopf personally. He wrote:

> *"In my searchings today I have found that a man named Arthur Barry is the actual kidnaper* [sic] *of the baby, but have not yet found out his present where abouts, further found out that you must have ordered the house searched that we spoke about."*[897]

---

[894] "Boston Billy Shot By L.I. Cop." *The Suffolk County News.* July 8, 1927. www.fultonhistory.com

[895] Leon, Samuel J. Cpl. New Jersey State Police. New Jersey State Police Report. <u>Continued investigation on Arthur T. Barry in reference to his connection with the Lindbergh Kidnaping and Abduction Case.</u> October 24, 1932. New Jersey State Police Museum and Learning Center Archives.

[896] Ibid.

[897] Schneck, George. <u>Letter from George Schneck to Mr. Schwarzkopf.</u> May 24, 1932. New Jersey State Police Museum and Learning Center Archives.

Another came from the night editor at the New York Daily News. He sent a telegram which claimed Barry had been spotted at "Salvi's speakeasy" and that:

> "At the New Grill, Salvie's W. 41ˢᵗ St speakeasy, where mobsters congregate, the consensus is that a professional pulled the Lindbergh job. They point out, too, that Barry is an expert sneak thief, with many Long Island porch climbing gem robberies to his credit, and that the Lindbergh kidnaping [sic] bears all the ear marks of his work."[898]

Eventually, the Newark Police Department was provided intelligence from an informant who claimed to have overheard Barry planning other kidnappings, and specifically mentioning that *"Lindbergh took him out of the newspaper headlines and that it would be a great joke if he (Lindbergh) put him, (Barry) back in the headlines again."*[899] On October 21, 1932, the Newark Police had learned Barry was *"hiding on the farm of one Otto Reuter"* and requested state police assistance in his apprehension. The next day, State Police Corporals Leon and Horn accompanied Newark Detectives Fallon and Carr and they arrested Barry sometime after 8:30 PM on the farm that night.[900] The entire house was searched but nothing was found to implicate

[898] Burke, Jefferson D. Postal Telegraph Cable Company Press Telegram. March 15, 1932. New Jersey State Police Museum and Learning Center Archives.

[899] Sisk, T. H. DOI (FBI) et. al., DOI Report. Summary. NY File No. 62-3057, p. 344. February 16, 1934. National Archives at College Park Maryland.

[900] Leon, Samuel J. Cpl. And Horn, William F. Cpl., New Jersey State Police. New Jersey State Police Report. Apprehension of Arthur T. Barry, Jewel Thief, Woodport – Andover Road, Byram Township, Sussex County, N. J. re: his possible implication in the Lindbergh Case. October 22, 1932. New Jersey State Police Museum and Learning Center Archives.

him. Back at the station, he was fingerprinted then questioned. Barry maintained his innocence and gave the alibi that he was on the farm the entire night of March 1st.[901] Once questioned, Reuter was shocked to learn that the nervous and sickly man he knew as "Toner" was the infamous Barry. When asked about Barry's comings and goings, Reuter claimed the last time he left the farm was on Thanksgiving 1931, and the only visitors he received during the year 1932 were his "wife" and his brother about whom Reuter stated:

> "...there was no question about this young fellow being Toner's brother because they look exactly alike."[902]

Reuter had never seen any guns in Toner's possession, said he was a very likeable guy, and said he had been on the farm "*on the night of the Lindbergh Crime*" the entire night.[903] He remembered the time of the event well because he read about it in the New York Times that Toner received at the home every morning.

With the fact that Barry might be ruled out as a suspect, the police decided to show Condon pictures of Barry. Three days after his arrest, Cpl. Leon and Sgt. Zapolsky arrived at Condon's home. Upon their arrival and before he was shown any pictures, Condon informed them that...

---

[901] Ibid.

[902] Leon, Samuel J. Cpl. New Jersey State Police. New Jersey State Police Report. Continued investigation on Arthur T. Barry in reference to his connection with the Lindbergh Kidnaping and Abduction Case. October 24, 1932. New Jersey State Police Museum and Learning Center Archives.

[903] Leon, Samuel J. Cpl. And Horn, William F. Cpl., New Jersey State Police. New Jersey State Police Report. Apprehension of Arthur T. Barry, Jewel Thief, Woodport – Andover Road, Byram Township, Sussex County, N. J. re: his possible implication in the Lindbergh Case. October 22, 1932. New Jersey State Police Museum and Learning Center Archives.

> *"…he had read full accounts of this subject in the newspapers and he would be safe in saying that Barry had no connection whatsoever with his negotiations, and it is Dr. Condon's personal opinion that Barry had nothing to do with the receiving of the Ransom money."*[904]

The police decided to show him a photo anyway, and as predicted, Condon told the men Barry *"in no way resembled the man known as "John" and in fact he, Dr. Condon, had never seen Barry personally before."*[905] Despite this, police were still not ready to rule Barry out, and the next day returned to the Reuter farm and confiscated *"all wearing apparel"* and *"one pair of old worn out black oxford shoes"* specifically to compare *"with plaster cast."*[906] In a strange twist, Olly Whateley requested to look over Barry and stated to police that his pictures *"slightly resembled a man who had visited the Princeton home of the Lindberghs about a year ago."*[907] Two days later Olly and Elsie Whateley were transported to Newark Police Headquarters where they looked Barry over but claimed they had never seen him

---

[904] Zapolsky, A. Sgt. And Leon, Samuel J. Cpl. New Jersey State Police. New Jersey State Police Report. <u>To the home of Dr. John F. Condon, Decatur Avenue, Bronx, N.Y. for the purpose of showing him photograph of Arthur T. Barry, Notorious Gem Thief, who was apprehended on the night of October 22nd, 1932 at the farm of Otto Reuter, Byram Township, Sussex County, N.J.</u> October 25, 1932. New Jersey State Police Museum and Learning Center Archives.

[905] Ibid.

[906] Horn, William F. Cpl., New Jersey State Police. New Jersey State Police Report. <u>Further investigation of Arthur T. Barry, regarding any connection he might have with the Lindbergh Case.</u> October 26, 1932. New Jersey State Police Museum and Learning Center Archives.

[907] Haussling, E. A. Sgt. New Jersey State Police. New Jersey State Police Report. <u>Inspection of Arthur Barry by Mr. and Mrs. Ollie Whateley.</u> October 28, 1932. New Jersey State Police Museum and Learning Center Archives.

before.[908] Finally, on November 2nd, Condon was transported to those same headquarters to view both Barry and the woman who was supposed to be his wife, Ann Blake. Barry was brought out in a line up mixed in with newspaper men and detectives. Condon looked the men up and down then proclaimed none were "John."[909] After he said this he picked out Barry then stated he "*knew him from seeing his picture in the newspaper.*"

> "*Dr. Condon then asked Barry several questions and asked him to pronounce several words such as: perfect, They will smack you out, and other words that was used by "John." He then looked over Ann Blake and stated that Barry nor Ann Blake were not* [sic] *the people whom he was in contact with in regards to the paying of the ransom money.*"[910]

Were not the *people*? This account harkens back to Schwarzkopf's claim during the police board of strategy meeting doesn't it? And it was only a couple of months earlier that Condon made virtually this same claim in a response to Attorney Nat J. Patterson's letter to him which asked if his client were to furnish the location of the men involved whether he'd be able to identify them. Condon responded: "*Although I am not a policeman I believe that I could identify one or*

---

908   Ibid.

909   Leon, Samuel J. Cpl. And Horn, William F. Cpl., New Jersey State Police. New Jersey State Police Report. <u>The transporting of Dr. John F. Condon from his home in the Bronx, N.Y. to the Newark Police Headquarters for the purpose of identifying Arthur T. Barry and Ann Blake who is supposed to be Barry's wife</u>. November 2, 1932. New Jersey State Police Museum and Learning Center Archives.

910   Ibid.

two of the men."[911] The press, who had been on hand for this entire Barry event, wrote the following in an Associated Press report:

> *"The man I gave the money to," said Dr. Condon,*
> *"was much taller," he looked at Barry's hands. "Those*
> *are not his hands," he said. "I saw his hands as I*
> *handed him the money, and received a receipt which*
> *is now in Colonel Lindbergh's possession." Barry looked*
> *relieved."*[912]

As an aside, despite being completely cleared of this crime at this time, the FBI was still receiving both tips and information as late as December 1949 that Barry had in fact been involved.[913]

Identifying Hauptmann

Just as history records, on September 20, 1934, Hauptmann was placed in a line up at the Greenwich Street station among 13 police officers. The purpose of this was to see if Condon could identify him as the man he came to know as "John." At 5:30 PM Condon entered the room. Condon asked for permission to speak with those in the lineup and it was granted. Then...

> *"Dr. Condon walked back and forth along the line three*
> *times. The third time he stopped at 3a, Hauptmann,*

---

[911] Condon, John F. <u>Letter from John F. Condon to Mr. Nathaniel J. Patterson</u>. August 23, 1932. New Jersey State Police Museum and Learning Center Archives.

[912] "Jafsie Clears Suspect Held For Kidnaping." *Winona Republican-Herald.* November 3, 1932. Winona State University Archives.

[913] Logue, J. T. Federal Bureau of Investigation. Office Memorandum. <u>J. T. Logue to Mr. Pennington</u>. December 6, 1949. National Archives at College Park Maryland. (Note: It's possible they extended beyond that but this is as far as my research has yielded me.)

and scrutinized him carefully, then he walked down the line to #13."[914]

Condon then requested to "eliminate" some and selected four among the men, one of whom was Hauptmann. But instead of an elimination, they were requested to "step forward" after which Condon made an announcement:

> *"When I saw you I gave you my promise that I would do all I possibly could for you if you gave me the baby. The only way in the world I think you can save yourself at all is to tell the truth. I gave you a promise heard that day. Follow that promise."*[915]

Condon requested these four selected men show him their hands, and they put their hands out with their palms up. Condon then *"examined the palms of the hands of the four men."*[916] Condon asked the men if they ever saw him before and they all answered "*no*." Then he walked to *"Bruno Richard Hauptmann,"* handed him a slip of paper, then asked him to read it aloud:

> *Hauptmann: I stayed already too long. The leader would smack me out. Your work is perfect."*

> *Dr. Condon: I could not quite hear those last three lines. You read "The leader would"* –

---

[914] Duane, J. J. Detective, MOD. Transcription. <u>Line Up Conducted in Office of Second Deputy Police Commissioner, 156 Greenwich Street, N.Y.C. – 5:30 p.m. September 20, 1934</u>. September 21, 1934. New Jersey State Police Museum and Learning Center Archives.

[915] Ibid.

[916] Ibid.

Hauptmann: The leader would smack me out. Your work is perfect.[917]

A back and forth ensued with Condon asking if Hauptmann had ever seen him before, and of course with Hauptmann maintaining that he hadn't. Condon then said "*let me see your hands*" and Hauptmann once again held them out.[918] Up to this point it is clear Hauptmann was not mis-pronouncing "*perfect*" as "*perfet*" as John had supposedly done, and did not have any type of fleshy "*lump*" or development on either hand. These were supposed to be the two clear identifiers that John possessed, yet Hauptmann did not have them. And Condon clearly attempted to use them here. The question is whether he did so sincerely or as an attempt to disqualify the man he knew to actually be John. Condon then moved on from Hauptmann specifically to address all four men. But he then suddenly focused on and addressed Hauptmann again:

"*I gave the money I promised to help out in case the baby was restored to me, do you remember that?*

Hauptmann: No."[919]

Another round of back and forth continued, Hauptmann was told to put on a hat, and his denials continued. Finally, Inspector Lyons stepped in and asked Condon if he would say Hauptmann "*was the man.*"

Dr. Condon: I would not say he was the man.[920]

Inspector Lyons: You are not positive?

---

[917] Ibid.
[918] Ibid.
[919] Ibid.
[920] Ibid.

Dr. Condon: I am not positive.[921]

Hauptmann was again given something to read: "*What would your mother say. She would not like it. She would cry,*" and more back and forth continued. Eventually Condon asked: "*Nine years up there; you don't know me?*" to which Hauptmann, like everything else, answered "*no.*"[922] Finally, the quizzing and conversation came to an end when Inspector Lyons once again asked Condon "*is that the man?*" The transcript reveals the following:

> *He is the one who would come nearer to answering the description than anybody I saw. You gave me no hint and I picked him out. He is a little heavier. Can I go over and talk to him? – I couldn't say he is not the man.*
>
> *Inspector Lyons: It looks like him?*
>
> *Dr. Condon: Yes.*
>
> *Inspector Lyons: But you cannot identify him?*
>
> *Dr. Condon: No, I have to be very careful. The man's life is in jeopardy.*[923]

After this charade, Condon was led into a side room by Special Agent Turrou, who was acting under instructions by assistant director Hugh Clegg to "*be close to Condon at all times and not to permit*

---

[921] Ibid.

[922] Ibid.

[923] Ibid.

him to talk to any strangers."[924] Turrou remained with Condon until midnight, and during the early stages of this time together Condon began fishing for information. Condon questioned Turrou about the "*details concerning Hauptmann's arrest,*" and also asked "*how much money had been found in his possession,*" but Turrou wasn't falling for it and refused to provide him "*any information of the sort.*"[925] Turrou explained to Condon that he in no way wanted to influence him concerning his incomplete identification of Hauptmann. If was after this that Condon started to make unusual comments:

> "*Dr. Condon then stressed to Agent the facility with which he had picked Hauptmann out from a line of fifteen men. Several times he asserted to me that he could never forget the features and the accent of the man to whom he had talked at Woodlawn Cemetery on several occasions. He said that the outstanding words which he had asked Hauptmann to read while he was in line, such as the words "particularly" and "perfect", were pronounced by Hauptmann in the same way as he had heard John say them when he talked to him at the cemetery.*"[926]

Unfortunately, the transcript does not bear this out or support his claim. Even more important information would come to Turrou from the unpredictable Dr. Condon:

> "*Dr. Condon several times had boasted to me of the remarkable memory he possesses and that he could*

---

[924] Turrou, L. G. Special Agent, Division of Investigation. Memorandum For File. Re: Unknown Subjects – Kidnaping and Murder of Charles A. Lindbergh, Jr. September 21, 1934. New Jersey State Police Museum and Learning Center Archives.

[925] Ibid.

[926] Ibid.

never make an error in identification. As the evening went along Condon became very impatient and asked me why he was being detained. He said that were it not for the Department of Justice, with whom he had at all times heartily cooperated, he would have put his hat on and walked right out. He cast several uncomplimentary remarks against the New York Police and the New Jersey State Police."[927]

Here we see the divide and conquer strategy Condon employed so often to his advantage. However, reality seemed to cause Condon to sober up, and by 9:30 PM...

"...Dr. Condon rather dejectedly told Agent that his life now wasn't worth five cents; that "They" are going to kill him. He added that he was glad, however, that the case was finally solved. He said he was aware of the fact that numerous insinuations were cast to the effect that he, Dr. Condon, received a part of the Lindbergh ransom money, and that he was further accused of withholding the real truth from the authorities investigating the case."[928]

We see from this a man who was afraid, and this is a repeat of something said earlier. That occurred on April 13, 1932, when Condon made a comment to reporters which they included in their article:

"I have never identified them nor said a word against them." Condon vowed after returning home during the night from another of his mysterious errands. "I value

---

[927]   Ibid.

[928]   Ibid.

my life. They value theirs. I know my life wouldn't be worth anything if I said anything against them."[929]

So we see that Condon, from these two additional examples, was once again referring to multiple people being involved. We also see that he admitted he's fully aware of the police accusations. If that is the case, then his antics could not have been based upon any mental lapses or maladies. In short, this admission proves he knew what he was doing. Turrou's memo continued…

> *"He said that now at last the case has been solved and that he is vindicated in the eyes of the public. He remarked that he does not expect a reward for the part he had taken in the solution of this case. From the tone of Dr. Condon's conversation, it appeared that Dr. Condon had picked Hauptmann out from the line as the man whom he knew as John."*[930]

We can see Turrou listening and evaluating every word and action. Who among us can doubt what he says? Condon is working his way to the ultimate conclusion, even if it kills him. But no so fast! This is "Jafsie" we're talking about:

> *"In a subsequent conversation, however, he indicated that he was not going to identify the man because he was doubtful whether Hauptmann was John. He said that Hauptmann bears a great likeness to his (Hauptmann's) brother, who was the real John, and*

---

[929] "Condon Mute Because He Fears Death." *Urbana Daily Courier.* April 13, 1932. Library at the University of Illinois.

[930] Turrrou, L. G. Special Agent, Division of Investigation. Memorandum For File. Re: Unknown Subjects – Kidnaping and Murder of Charles A. Lindbergh, Jr. September 21, 1934. New Jersey State Police Museum and Learning Center Archives.

with whom he had made the contact at the cemetery. He asserted that the real John was killed long ago and that the money was taken away from him by his confederates. He intimated that the real men who are responsible for the kidnaping [sic] *and murder of the Lindbergh child are now somewhere in Long Island, around Bayshore."*[931]

John's "brother." The word "perfect." John's "dead"... Sound familiar? A precise example of how the mind of a criminal works. He is pulling everything out that he can possibly think of that came up in the investigation to give him credibility which he believes would support him in NOT identifying Hauptmann. Does this exemplify someone eccentric, crazy, or "slipping" due to age? If Hauptmann <u>was</u> John, and Condon is saying he is not, how could <u>any</u> other elimination decision made by Condon be trusted?

As Condon was led away to the District Attorney's office he *"intimated"* to Turrou that *"he was not going to identify Hauptmann and that he would tell the true story later on."*[932] Was a confession from Condon on the horizon? Apparently not.

The next day Condon was at it again. *"Refreshed by hours of sleep"* he declared to the press that *"the finding of the ransom money and the actual kidnaping* [sic] *were entirely separate matters."*[933] He insisted to the press that he *"did not positively identify Hauptmann"* and when asked again he replied: *"I can't talk. Really, I never said I was positive. All is in abeyance now. I did not identify Hauptmann."*[934] On the

---

[931] Ibid.

[932] Ibid.

[933] "Cash No Link To Kidnaping Says Condon." *The New York Daily News.* September 22, 1934. New Jersey State Police Museum and Learning Center Archives.

[934] Ibid.

following morning, Ralph Hacker met reporters to do a little damage control. He announced that *"everything"* his father-in-law had done as *"intermediary"* came under the advisement of what he called the *"board of control"* that consisted of *"seven or nine"* which included Schwarzkopf, Irey, and Frank Wilson among others.[935] Condon also made himself available by inviting reporters into his living room, and he made the statement that Hauptmann *"was involved but did not play a lone hand."*[936] He made the stunning accusation that *"three"* persons were involved and that he believed Fisch had been poisoned in Germany: *"I believe the body should be exhumed and an autopsy performed. I suspect foul play. I believe he was murdered."*[937] However, Condon once again relayed that he refused to identify Hauptmann as John: *"Hauptmann fits the shadowy character he talked with, in some respects, but that in others he does not."*[938] Condon then took it a step further by saying John had an *"incessant cough"* and that Hauptmann had no cough. *"This cough has caused Dr. Condon to speculate whether Fisch might be 'John,'"* according to the papers.[939] *"John,"* Condon told the men, *"talked with a German accent and his speech at time was in a falsetto."*[940]

On September 29th, Inspector Bruckman sent Bronx Home News editor Harry Goodwin to see Condon with a confidential proposal. He offered a *"private meeting between Hauptmann and Dr. Condon for the purpose of making another effort to determine whether Hauptmann"*

---

[935] "Official Advised Jafsie." *The New York Times.* September 22, 1934. New Jersey State Police Museum and Learning Center Archives.

[936] 'Jafsie' Believes 3 Took Part in Actual Kidnaping." *Winona Republican-Herald.* September 22, 1934. Winona State University Archives.

[937] Ibid.

[938] "Hauptmann Pal Slain Abroad, 'Jafsie' Fears." *The Washington Post.* September 23, 1934. New Jersey State Police Museum and Learning Center Archives.

[939] Ibid.

[940] Ibid.

was John – Condon declined.[941] On October 5th, Agent Turrou interviewed Condon. He told Turrou that his character had been particularly maligned since his failure to identify Hauptmann. However, he...

> "...*intimated to the writer that Hauptmann is the man involved in the instant crime and in all likelihood Hauptmann is the man known to him as "John." He added that in order to dispense all remaining doubt in his mind as to whether Hauptmann is really "John" he would like to have a private interview with Hauptmann for a period of a half an hour in the presence of as many officials as this office desires...".*[942]

He told Turrou because of the many "*courtesies*" shown to him by "*this office*" Condon wanted them to get the credit for his identification of Hauptmann. He even told Turrou that he sent a wire to President Roosevelt about the "*good work of this Division in connection with the apprehension of Hauptmann...*".[943]

> "*Dr. Condon pointed out that he is considerably aggrieved over the fact that he failed to identify Hauptmann the first time he was confronted with him. He attributed the failure of identification largely to the stupid manner in which the police handled the situation relative to bringing about the identification in question. He particularly deplored the fact that there were about 75 men present in the room at the*

---

[941] Turrou, L. G. Special Agent Division of Investigation. Memorandum. <u>Memorandum for Special Agent T. H. Sisk</u>. October 5, 1934. National Archives at College Park Maryland.

[942] Ibid.

[943] Ibid.

time he was confronted with Hauptmann, which he declared was wholly unwise and unnecessary."[944]

It was also during this meeting, as previously mentioned, that Condon told Turrou that the lookout at Woodlawn Cemetery strongly resembled Fisch. So once again we see Condon "adapt" his story to adjust to the changing facts which have emerged.

On October 23rd, Condon, accompanied by Gregory Coleman, was driven to Perth Amboy to go over the details of his involvement with Attorney General Wilentz.[945] If Condon was treated by Wilentz as other witnesses were who told a story he did not like, then there is no doubt he was threatened just as the others were. Regardless, the next day Condon was transported to Flemington for the purpose of having an "interview" with Hauptmann.[946] At 1:14 PM the "party" arrived at the Flemington Jail.[947] Trooper Stockburger made a detailed record of the conversation. Here is one exchange that I believe is important:

> *Hauptman: The first time I met you was in the lineup. I had nothing to do with the Lindbergh case (Hauptmann pronounced it Lindenburgh).*

> *Condon: That brings us to the middle of the story. This is divided into four parts. The house, the meeting in the*

---

[944] Ibid.

[945] Leon, Samuel J. Cpl. New Jersey State Police. New Jersey State Police Report. <u>The taking of Dr. Condon to Perth Amboy, N. J., for an interview with Attorney General David Wilentz</u>. October 23, 1934. New Jersey State Police Museum and Learning Center Archives.

[946] Ibid.

[947] New Jersey State Police Log Book. Chronological Entries. Page 20. Unsigned (entry lines are initialed). October 24, 1934. New Jersey State Police Museum and Learning Center Archives.

park, the kidnaping [sic] and the murder. The meeting in the park had nothing to do with the case, there was no crime committed, there was no money passed. I didn't have Lindbergh's money. I had $1000.00 of my money. I had $998.00 and I had to sell my pet fiddle for $2.00 to make up a $1000.00. At that time Colonel Lindbergh had $3300.00, that's all the money he had due to the stock market, and I told him if it was his brother I wouldn't do it but for the baby I tried to get the baby back. Colonel Breckinridge told me that I was afraid but I don't know such a word. I am not afraid of the police or anyone, although the whole world is against me. Fingers are pointed at me, there he goes he passed the ransom money. I am not one of the ordinary crowd, I am an educated man and was a Professor in College. John, I don't mean to call you John, I went to Canada when there was 20 inches of snow, to the swamps of Mexico and to Los Angeles. I have spent my money. If you tell the truth I will help you and I am not going to ask anyone for help. I have suffered a lot, my wife is crying everyday.[948]

Here we can plainly see that much of what Condon said was for the consumption of the authorities. Additionally, he appeared to be sending Hauptmann a message in the best way that he could under the circumstances and it is one of support: He's standing strong, under tremendous pressure, and offered "help" to Hauptmann if he decided to "*tell the truth.*" Here is man walking a very tight rope

---

[948] Stockburger, H. Trooper, New Jersey State Police. New Jersey State Police Report. <u>Conversation between Doctor John F. Condon and Bruno Richard Hauptmann at the Hunterdon County Jail in Flemington, N. J., on October 24, 1934 at about 1:00 P. M. in the presence of Colonel Schwarzkopf, Attorney General Wilentz, and Prosecutor Hauck</u>. October 24, 1934. New Jersey State Police Museum and Learning Center.

with Cops on one side, and a confederate on the other – both having him over a barrel. Step off too far on one side and he's arrested, step off too far on the other, and it could mean Hauptmann breaks and then implicates him...or worse. Which path would Condon take? Condon searched for an "out" and then injected "*Al Capone*" into the conversation. Hauptmann explained that he didn't know any "*gangsters.*"[949] The interaction ended with these parting words:

> *Hauptmann: I had nothing to do with it, if I would know just a little about the case I would tell about it.*
>
> *Condon: I believe you but the evidence is against you and only you can help yourself. Think of your mother, how happy she would be if I could send her a telegram that you are free that you are not guilty. Are you glad that I came to see you?*
>
> *Hauptmann: Yes, you are welcome.*[950]

Condon and the rest of the party then departed the jail at 2:25 PM.[951] Hauptmann had always maintained that Condon exclaimed as he left "*I can not testify against this man.*"[952] While this statement was never recorded in any official document I could find, there are other indicators that Condon had made these precise feelings known to authorities. Additionally, during a visit with her husband two days later, Anna told Hauptmann that the newspaper "*came out with a*

---

[949] Ibid.

[950] Ibid.

[951] New Jersey State Police Log Book. Chronological Entries. Page 20. Unsigned (entry lines are initialed). October 24, 1934. New Jersey State Police Museum and Learning Center Archives.

[952] Hauptmann, Richard B. Letter from B. Richard Hauptmann to Governor Harold G. Hoffman. December 12, 1935. New Jersey State Police Museum and Learning Center Archives.

big headline Hauptmann identified by Condon."[953] At this one would expect stress and alarm – yet, Hauptmann shrugged it off saying "*you can expect almost anything from the news papers.*"[954] Hauptmann was not worried. On the other side of it, reporters showed the headlines to Condon claiming he had made such an identification. On this occasion, Condon did not give his usual verbal runaround or pat himself on the back in any way. This time he simply responded… "*No comment to make. If there is any information to be given out, it will be from New Jersey authorities.*"[955] No comment? Well that's says it all doesn't it?

The Condon Investigation

On November 1st, multiple newspapers ran articles quoting Hauptmann's attorney, James Fawcett, as saying that Hauptmann told Fawcett's associate Bernhardt Meisels that Condon did not identify him during their recent meeting in the Flemington Jail.[956] This, it seemed, was salt in the wound and the authorities had had enough. It was clear they believed Condon was protecting Hauptmann and they weren't going to sit around and do nothing about it. After all, it was Condon himself who had asserted to police that Cemetery John "*couldn't be a resident of the Bronx without my*

---

[953] Stockburger, H. Trooper, New Jersey State Police. New Jersey State Police Report. <u>Conversation between Mr. and Mrs. Hauptmann at the Hunterdon County Jail in Flemington on October 26, 1934 at about 3:00 PM</u>. October 26, 1934. New Jersey State Police Museum and Learning Center.

[954] Ibid.

[955] "No Comment By Condon." *The New York Times.* October 26, 1934. New Jersey State Police Museum and Learning Center.

[956] "Lindy Suspect Denies Condon Identified Him." *The Washington Post.* November 2, 1934. New Jersey State Police Museum and Learning Center.

having seen him before."[957] As a result, on November 6th, Schwarzkopf designated Corporal Leon to investigate both Condon and Reich and attempt to turn up any evidence to show that Condon and Hauptmann knew each other prior to the Lindbergh Case.[958] He also designated Sgt. Zapolsky to investigate whether *"any yachts or boats Red Johnson worked on was ever in any of the shipyards in City Island or in the East River."*[959] It was a little late in the game, however, if Condon was to testify for the Defense; that could have a devastating effect on the State's case against Hauptmann. But the question remained… why would they have to look any further than Perrone to make this connection? It was Sgt. Zapolsky and Det. Patterson who wrote that…

> *"…Perrone stated that a few days after he attended the Bronx County Grand Jury, he had taken a passenger to City Island, and there had observed Dr. Condon talking to a man whom he thought was the man that gave him the note."*[960]

Had they forgotten, or, as I will show later, was it because the State Police had little faith in Perrone? Either way, they would nevertheless

---

[957] Condon, Dr. John F. Statement. Made to Inspector Harry W. Walsh, Sgt. Warren T. Moffatt, Lieut. A. T. Keaton and Detective Horn. June 2, 1932. New Jersey State Police Museum and Learning Center.

[958] New Jersey State Police Memorandum. Memorandum For Detective Leon. Unsigned. November 6, 1934. New Jersey State Police Museum and Learning Center.

[959] Schwarzkopf, H. Norman. Memorandum For Sergeant Zapolsky. November 6, 1934. New Jersey State Police Museum and Learning Center Archives.

[960] Zapolsky, A. Sgt. And Patterson, Claude Det. New Jersey State Police. New Jersey State Police Report. Interviewing Joe Perrone, Taxi Driver, who delivered note to Dr. John F. Condon on the night of March 12th, 1932, re Lindbergh Case. March 1, 1934. New Jersey State Police Museum and Learning Center Archives.

use him in Court to testify against Hauptmann so why not utilize him to this end as well?

Instead, acting on something just about everyone who has ever looked into this case to this day questions, the NJSP also believed the nexus between Condon and Hauptmann existed on City Island. After all, Condon had a place on City Island for 40 years, Reich lived there for 12 years, and by now it was a well known fact that Hauptmann paid to have his canoe stored at Dixon's Boat House which was located in that small Island community. With the countless trips Hauptmann made to Hunter's Island in his canoe it seemed almost impossible the men hadn't met, or at least, seen each other from time to time in passing. This was the first place Leon went to investigate.

It was on November 7th that Leon interviewed John Dixon and his brothers. They all knew both Condon and Reich, but had never seen them in the company of Hauptmann.[961] They recalled Hauptmann as a man of few words, and the only real information they could offer was that on numerous occasions Anita Lutzenberg would come to the Boat House "*inquiring for Hauptmann and would wait at the boat house until he returned from Hunter's Island.*"[962] This is interesting because Dixon had told Special Agent Turrou and Detective Wallace of the NYPD at his first interview that "*on numerous occasions*" he had observed "*Mrs. Henkel*" in his company and would be away with her for a considerable amount of time when he was.[963] He also

---

961   Leon, Samuel J. Cpl. New Jersey State Police. New Jersey State Police Report. Investigating life of Dr. John F. Condon at City Island, N.Y., and the possibilities of him meeting Bruno Richard Hauptmann before the Lindbergh Case. November 7, 1934. New Jersey State Police Museum and Learning Center Archives.

962   Ibid.

963   Turrou, L. G. Special Agent, Division of Investigation. Memorandum. Memorandum For File. September 22, 1934. National Archives at College Park Maryland.

told the men that *"apparently"* Mrs. Henkel was *"a married woman"* and that they appeared *"quite intimate."*[964] Could it have been for the sake of Mrs. Henkel's reputation that he didn't bring this up again to Leon? In continuing his investigation on the 7th, Leon interviewed Condon and inquired about Dixon and his Boat House. This obviously sent a very clear message to him as it suggested what the investigation was all about. Condon explained that he knew Dixon, had never been to his boat house, and remembered that he last spoke with him about 15 years ago.[965] The next day, this time accompanied by Det. Thompson of the New York City Police, Leon returned to Dixon's boat house to check Hauptmann's locker for evidence. They were informed that Officers had previously seized a pair of Hauptmann's sneakers but had left other items behind.[966] The investigators then moved on to Condon's *"shack"* which was located *"at the foot of Beach St. and King Avenue"* where they noted *"a full view of Hunter's Island could be had at this point."*[967]

The next day the investigators returned to Condon's home on Decatur Avenue and began to question him about any carpenters he may have employed but nothing of value came from it. However, it was during this interview that Condon was *"unable to recall ever seeing Hauptmann before the negotiations in reference to the Ransom money."* It's yet another sure sign that Condon was fully aware of

[964] Ibid.

[965] Leon, Samuel J. Cpl. New Jersey State Police. New Jersey State Police Report. Investigating life of Dr. John F. Condon at City Island, N.Y., and the possibilities of him meeting Bruno Richard Hauptmann before the Lindbergh Case. November 7, 1934. New Jersey State Police Museum and Learning Center Archives.

[966] Leon, Samuel J. Cpl. New Jersey State Police. New Jersey State Police Report. Continuing investigation on the life of Dr. John F. Condon and the possibilities of meeting Bruno Richard Hauptmann before the Lindbergh Crime. November 8, 1934. New Jersey State Police Museum and Learning Center Archives.

[967] Ibid.

what these men were attempting to find. So, true to form, Condon revealed something both new and interesting to the men about a man named George S. Miller:

> *"...that Miller told him that he knew Colonel Lindbergh and that Colonel Lindbergh use to work with him in a shipyard near City Island, and that they used to call Lindbergh at that time "Slim" and "Axle." Dr. Condon stated that Miller might have known Hauptmann and also thought that it would be a good idea to question Miller in reference to the conversation about Colonel Lindbergh..."*[968]

Was this a diversion? Was Condon pushing investigators toward Lindbergh? If he actually believed Miller should have been looked at, why did he wait until now to reveal this information to the police? The investigators moved on to Al Reich; however, police wrote that he *"was unable to give us any information that would connect Hauptmann with Dr. Condon."*[969] There had been a report in a local paper that Condon had been seen eating with Hauptmann at Bunnie's Fry Shop, so on the next day they proceeded there to investigate. While there, they weren't able to verify this story and it seemed based solely on a rumor. However, while interviewing the owner, Preston Parry, he told them that Condon was *"very talkative,"* and a *"big*

---

[968] Leon, Samuel J. Cpl. New Jersey State Police. New Jersey State Police Report. <u>Continuation of investigation in reference to the life of Dr. John F. Condon and the possibilities of Bruno Richard Hauptmann meeting him before the Lindbergh Case</u>. November 9, 1934. New Jersey State Police Museum and Learning Center Archives.

[969] Ibid.

faker.[970] Parry claimed Condon would come into the restaurant, and if no one noticed him would loudly announce something about the Lindbergh Case in order to draw attention to himself which caused others to immediately engage him in conversation.[971] On November 13th, Leon and Thompson were finally able to interview George Miller. What Miller told was a very strange story that appeared to be a case of mistaken identity. Yet it also shows that Condon gave them something real to look into instead the "usual" nonsense where cops would interview people who had no idea what they were talking about. But was that the point? Could it have been a signal to them that he was on the level? Could it have been meant as a wild goose chase to tie them up and waste their time? Or could there be something to the story that Condon wanted them to legitimately check out? The story went like this…

> "…that back about 1916 he worked in the shipyard at City Island and there was a young man there about 14 years of age working in the same gang. This boy had a Masonic Lodge ring on his finger and one of the men in the gang asked him what he was doing wearing the ring, because he had to be 21 years of age before he the Masonic Ring could be worn. To this the boy stated that it belonged to his father. Mr. Miller stated that he is not positive but he thinks that this boy was Col. Lindbergh as a few years ago he state [sic] Col. Lindbergh joined the Masonic Lodge at Brooklyn, N.Y. and before he was 21 years of age. He stated that he told Dr. Condon about this. Mr. Miller further stated

[970] Leon, Samuel J. Cpl. New Jersey State Police. New Jersey State Police Report. <u>Report of continued investigation in reference to Dr. John F. Condon and the possibilities of Bruno Richard Hauptmann knowing him before the Lindbergh Crime</u>. November 10, 1934. New Jersey State Police Museum and Learning Center Archives.
[971] Ibid.

*that he has never seen Bruno Richard Hauptmann on
the Island...".[972]*

It was also on this same day that papers were running yet another story
about Condon which indicated he had not identified Hauptmann:

> *"Defense Attorney Lloyd Fisher, quoting Hauptmann,
> on his interview with Condon said his client had told
> him, 'Dr. Condon indicated to me that he knew I
> had nothing to do with the kidnaping [sic] or with the
> procuring of the ransom money.'"[973]*

It was yet another open handed smack in the face to New Jersey and
a reminder that they were running out of time. In the meantime,
separate and apart from Leon and Thompson's investigation, other
police officers were busy chasing down the clues that were discovered
in the Hauptmann's apartment. If a name, address or phone number
was found, they would send an officer to find out the connection
to him. One such item was a slip of paper found on September
19th which had the name *"George V. Villiers"* written on the slip
along with his *"address"* and *"some numerals written on the back."*[974]
Detective Patterson drove over to 4441 Park Avenue and found
Villiers, a 45 year old unemployed auto mechanic there. When
questioned about the piece of paper he said it was his and that it was

[972] Leon, Samuel J. Cpl. New Jersey State Police. New Jersey State Police
Report. Continuation of investigation of Dr. John F. Condon and Al
Reich and the possibilities of them knowing Bruno Richard Hauptmann
before the Lindbergh Crime. November 13, 1934. New Jersey State Police
Museum and Learning Center Archives.
[973] "Hauptmann Says 'Jafsie' Clears Him." *The Washington Post.* November
13, 1934. New Jersey State Police Museum and Learning Center Archives.
[974] Patterson, Claude Detective, New Jersey State Police. New Jersey State
Police Report. Continued investigation of Bruno Richard Hauptmann
and associates, re: Lindbergh Case. November 13, 1934. New Jersey State
Police Museum and Learning Center Archives.

a page that *"came out of a note book"* which he kept in his car. He claimed he had no idea how Hauptmann came into possession of it, and that the handwriting with his name and address on it was not his. However, the numbers written on the back were his, and where he recorded the mileage for his trip to Atlantic City *"about a year ago"* in order to know when to have his oil changed.[975] He insisted he did not know or ever see Hauptmann or any of his associates. However, Condon's name came up, and yes, Villiers did know him, in fact, he had been a *"former pupil"* of his when he *"attended school #12, but has not seen Condon for a period of 5 years...".*[976]

The very next day Leon and Thompson went to Lane's Bathing Beach on Minnieford Ave on City Island. There they met a woman named Etta Lane who claimed to have known Condon since before he was married. She explained that, during his younger days when he taught at the public school on East 128th Street, he was *"quite the lady's man"* and that *"all the school teachers used to argue as to whom was going to walk home with him."*[977] However, she also referred to Condon as *"a big faker"* who was *"a lover of publicity"* who would *"do anything to get his name and picture in the newspaper."*[978] Lane agreed to act as an informant for the police and made efforts to turn up information which she could possibly turn over to them later on.

Over the next three weeks, Leon and Thompson continued their investigation on City Island, Hunter's Island, Throggs Neck, and the surrounding areas. They combed through the various boating and

---

[975] Ibid.

[976] Ibid.

[977] Leon, Samuel J. Cpl. New Jersey State Police. New Jersey State Police Report. <u>Continuation of investigation of Dr. John F. Condon and Al Reich and the possibilities of them knowing Bruno Richard Hauptmann before the Lindbergh Crime</u>. November 14, 1934. New Jersey State Police Museum and Learning Center Archives.

[978] Ibid.

German clubs but rarely found anyone willing to admit they knew Hauptmann. Those few that did had little to offer, and none ever claimed to have seen him with Condon.[979] However, on November 26th, Condon was picked up at 2 PM at his home then hauled into the NJSP Station at Alpine where he was *"interviewed by Attorney General Wilentz and other superior officers assigned to the Lindbergh investigation."*[980] Nothing seemed to occur after this "interview" and both Leon & Thompson continued on with their investigations into the possible Condon/Hauptmann connection. The men had seemed to spin their wheels and returned to some of the same places they had previously visited. They dropped in from time to time to see Etta Lane and she had nothing to give. Then, on December 6th, the investigators made a trip to see Chief Special Agent McCabe, of the New York Telephone Company. They were investigating the Condon phone number changes and wanted to get the exact details about it. They learned that on April 12, 1932, a woman called at the Kingsbridge Road Telephone Office and stated...

> *"...she was Mrs. Condon and that she wanted their phone disconnected or the number changed as they are being annoyed by people calling them. Mr. Fink stated that he talked Mrs. Condon into having her number changed to a Non-Published number, and according to the Telephone Records the number was changed*

---

[979] Note: Detective Joseph Meade's investigation into Emil Mueller which began on December 6, 1934, was a totally separate investigation.

[980] Leon, Samuel J. Cpl. New Jersey State Police. New Jersey State Police Report. <u>Continuing investigation on Dr. John F. Condon and Al Reich and the possibilities of Bruno Richard Hauptmann knowing them previous to the Lindbergh Crime</u>. November 26, 1934. New Jersey State Police Museum and Learning Center Archives.

*from Sedgwick 3-7154 to a Non*Published number,
Sedgewick 3-1177."*[981]

It seems significant that the Condons were willing to *disconnect*
their phone on April 12, 1932, because the child had not yet been
recovered. Furthermore, even after being *convinced* to a number
change, what if Kidnappers wanted to call as they were said to have
done before? Why would they want to cut off a possible method of
communication prior to the discovery of that child? On December
10th the men were once again on City Island speaking with Etta
Lane. Little did they know, Condon had packed up and taken off
for parts unknown with two friends, Eben Reilly, and Milton Page,
both from City Island.[982] This clearly looked like an attempt by
Condon to flee from his current predicament.

The Unexpected Trip

With the date of the trial rapidly approaching, Wilentz must have
had a serious case of heartburn upon hearing the news of Condon's
sudden departure. However, he received a post card a few days later
from Condon on which was written:

*"My dear Attorney General
At Columbia, Augusta Ga,*

[981] Leon, Samuel J. Cpl. New Jersey State Police. New Jersey State Police Report. <u>Investigation of Dr. John F. Condon and Al Reich and the possibilities of Bruno Richard Hauptmann knowing them before the Lindbergh Crime</u>. December 6, 1934. New Jersey State Police Museum and Learning Center Archives.

[982] Leon, Samuel J. Cpl. New Jersey State Police. New Jersey State Police Report. <u>Re: interview with Dr. John F. Condon in reference to his trip to Miami, Florida, and what other information he may have of value on this Lindbergh Investigation</u>. December 26, 1934. New Jersey State Police Museum and Learning Center Archives.

On road to Miami Fla.
On Radio at Columbia
J.F.C."[983]

Then, if that wasn't bad enough, Condon surfaced at Palm Beach, Florida, where he gave an interview to a reporter named B. B. Lewis in a place called Wertz coffee shop. The bad news for Wilentz was that he told this man Hauptmann would "*not be convicted.*"[984] The good news was that Condon also told Lewis "*he would return to New Jersey in time for the beginning of Hauptmann's trial.*"[985] Or was this, in light of the bad news – more bad news? Was this little "excursion" meant to be a way to avoid any attempt by authorities to continue to tamper, pressure, and/or intimidate him prior to this testimony? It sure looked that way. Condon would turn up in Miami at the home of Al Capone looking to speak with his wife who was out at the time. Condon refused to reveal the nature of his visit only to say it was "*good news*" based on a letter he received from a woman he would not name.[986] Interesting in more ways than one. Capone's name came up at the beginning of this case, and it was a fact that was widely publicized – even making it into Coleman's manuscript *Vigil*.[987] It looks like, yet again, Condon had reached back into the depths of this case in order to find a "valid" distraction: First during his conversation with Hauptmann in the Flemington Jail,

---

[983] Condon, John. <u>Postcard from J.F.C to Hon. David Wilentz</u>. December 11, 1934. New Jersey State Police Museum and Learning Center Archives.

[984] Lewis, B. B. "'Jafsie' Thinks Hauptmann Will Not Be Convicted." *The Palm Beach Post*. December 15, 1934. New Jersey State Police Museum and Learning Center Archives.

[985] Ibid.

[986] "'Jafsie' With 'Good News,' Call On Mrs. Al Capone – Who's Out." *The Washington Post*. December 16, 1934. New Jersey State Police Museum and Learning Center Archives.

[987] Coleman, Gregory F. *Vigil*. Unpublished Manuscript. Page 44. Undated (circa 1932). New Jersey State Police Museum and Learning Center Archives.

and now again in Miami. However, Condon's next stop can only be considered mind boggling by any measure.

Samuel Garelick

Sam Garelick was a WWI Veteran from Bayonne, New Jersey, and had recently moved to Miami, Florida, in search of employment. While in Miami, a conspiracy formed between Fred Gray, Roy Gray, and Warne Millard to kidnap a wealthy Cuban refugee named Dr. Santiago Claret.[988] Samuel Garelick was later brought into the conspiracy and the plan by the four men resulted in a failed attempt. However, *"several days later"* a second attempt was made, and Dr. Claret was abducted when he was thrown into his car…

> *"…his eyes and mouth bandaged and taped, and then carried about 15 or 16 miles. He was taken from his car, forced upstairs to the third floor of an old dilapidated, isolated and unoccupied apartment building and forced to sign a check for $16,000 and write a note to the First National Bank of Miami directing them to cash the check for his chauffeur, about whom they had some knowledge. He was then left there with his eyes and mouth securely taped, prone on the floor, with his hands and feet bound to the structural frame work of the building."*[989]

---

[988] Worley, G. A., State Attorney Eleventh Judicial Circuit of Florida. Letter from G. A. Worley to Honorable David Sholtz. July 1, 1935. New Jersey State Police Museum and Learning Center Archives.

[989] Hawthorne, Vernon, State Attorney Eleventh Judicial Circuit of Florida. Letter from Vernon Hawthorne to Honorable Harold G. Hoffman. March 26, 1935. New Jersey State Police Museum and Learning Center Archives.

The kidnappers told Dr. Claret that once the check was cashed he would be released, and he was then left alone. However, after *"about four or five hours"* he was able to manipulate *"the release of one hand from the small ropes that bound him,"* and as a result complete his *"release and escape."*[990] Authorities were convinced the Kidnappers did not plan to return to release Dr. Claret, and had it not been for his escape, he would have been *"left to die."*[991] Garelick was arrested on December 10, 1934, and taken to Dade County Jail to await trial.

On December 16th, Condon suddenly appeared at the jail and requested to speak with Garelick. The Sheriff, D. C. Coleman, *"assumed it had some connection with"* the *"Lindbergh Case"* so he granted him access to the prisoner.[992] Garelick was removed from his cell and taken to the Sheriff's office where he saw Condon waiting and knew immediately who he was because he had seen his picture in the papers. Condon began to question Garelick, asking him if he was *"German,"* where he was from, if he could *"speak German,"* whether he knew *"where Hopewell was,"* *"where Flemington was,"* where *"Saint Raymond Cemetery is at,"* and asked him to *"say different words in German,"* etc.[993] At some point Garelick saw where this line of questioning was going and he *"stood up and said to him why ask me those questions, when they got the man with the money and you have identified him as the man you gave it to. [sic]"*[994] According to Garelick:

---

[990] Ibid.

[991] Ibid.

[992] Coleman, D. C. Dade County Sheriff. <u>Western Union from D. C. Coleman to Honorable Harold G. Hoffman, Governor</u>. March 6, 1936. New Jersey State Police Museum and Learning Center Archives.

[993] Garelick, Samuel. Affidavit. Sworn to H. M. Richards at Raiford, Union County, Florida, Witnessed by Lt. Robt W. Hicks, and C. J. Godwin. March 20, 1936. New Jersey State Police Museum and Learning Center Archives.

[994] Ibid.

"His answer to me was if I was sure that he was the right man I would of not come [sic] down here and question you about it. Then he started to ask more questions."[995]

According to the affidavit, the questions turned into more about who he knew. For example, he was asked if he knew *"Harry Walsh Police Inspector?"* Did he *"know any of your City officials?"* When Garelick answered in the affirmative Condon wanted to know why he knew them so well. Garelick answered that he had been on the *"Board of Election for many years."*[996] Condon seemed to wind up the questioning by asking him *"do you know any ball players in Bayonne or Jersey City?* then offered some parting words *"to play ball with the people down here"* as he left.[997] According to Hauptmann's attorney Lloyd Fisher:

"Garelick is a very short man, approximately five feet two in height, and bears no resemblance – facial or otherwise – to Hauptmann."[998]

The Return Home

After learning that Condon was back in the Bronx, Leon and Thompson rushed over to his home to interview him. Condon told the men that he had only left for *"a little vacation and rest,"* and that *"nothing in particular took him to Miami."*[999] Condon clearly

[995] Ibid.

[996] Ibid.

[997] Ibid.

[998] Fisher, Lloyd C. Notes. <u>Samuel Garelick</u>. Undated. New Jersey State Police Museum and Learning Center Archives.

[999] Leon, Samuel J. Cpl. New Jersey State Police. New Jersey State Police Report. <u>Re: interview with Dr. John F. Condon in reference to his trip to Miami, Florida, and what other information he may have of value on this Lindbergh Investigation</u>. December 26, 1934. New Jersey State Police Museum and Learning Center Archives.

lied to them. He next told them that he had been "*pestered*" by newspaper men but that he "*told them nothing in reference to the Lindbergh Case.*"[1000] Yet another lie. Finally, he explained that he left his companions "*down there*" by jumping onto a "*Grey Hound Bus*" and arrived in New York on the 22nd.[1001]

Had Jafsie been on the lam, or was he in Miami to specifically find a patsy to replace Hauptmann? Regardless of which, it is quite clear this was no "vacation." And with his return, the specific investigations into the possibility that Hauptmann and Condon knew each other came to a screeching halt. Was it because Condon himself was now ready to "*play ball?*" On January 3, 1935, one day into the trial, a New York Times article, citing anonymous but "*official sources,*" claimed that while Condon did not "*announce any identification,*" he had "*promised*" Hauptmann that he "*would intercede with President Roosevelt for clemency*" if he would name others involved "*in the crime.*"[1002] The article added that while Condon pleaded with Hauptmann to "*take him into his confidence,*" Hauptmann only "*sat motionless and silent.*"[1003] Finally, this article made it clear that Condon was "*expected to point out Hauptmann as 'John'*" once he took the stand and added "*Jail officials may be summoned to corroborate "Jafsie's" story.*"[1004]

On January 9th, Condon was called to the witness stand by the prosecution. According to Hauptmann's attorney Lloyd Fisher:

> "*Condon had refused to the day of his testimony in Flemington to identify Hauptmann. He was given*

1000 Ibid.

1001 Ibid.

1002 "Condon Offer To Prisoner." *The New York Times.* January 4, 1935. New Jersey State Police Museum and Learning Center Archives.

1003 Ibid.

1004 Ibid.

careful attention by the press, but perhaps his attraction lay in the gamut of contradictory views he gave to the press. In any case, Attorney General Wilentz was very concerned about what Condon would say when he took the stand."[1005]

That moment had finally come:

[Wilentz]: *Who is John?*

[Condon]: *John is Bruno Richard Hauptmann.*[1006]

Governor Hoffman described his response a little differently than as reflected in the trial transcripts:

"JOHN," he said, "IS BRUNO RICHARD HAUPTMANN!"[1007]

[1005] Hawke, George G. *Trial By Fury: The Hauptmann Trial.* Princeton University Senior Thesis. (1951) Page 66. New Jersey State Police Museum and Learning Center Archives. (Note: citing an interview he conducted with Lloyd Fisher on April 7, 1951.)

[1006] Condon, John F. Testimony. The State of New Jersey vs. Bruno Richard Hauptmann, <u>Hunterdon County Court of Oyer and Terminer</u>, page 593, 1935. New Jersey State Law Library.

[1007] Hoffman, Harold Giles. *The Crime - The Case - The Challenge (What Was Wrong with the Lindbergh Case?)*, Original Manuscript: Unedited & Uncorrected, circa 1937. Page 88. New Jersey State Police Museum and Learning Center Archives.

5

The Skeletons In The Closet

Once word was out that John F. Condon had been involved in the kidnapping negotiations, there was an anonymous letter writing frenzy against him. Many accusations of terrible things were made. One was about a "half-breed" Indian who he reportedly swindled, and another about him stealing a woman's purse on board a ship only to pretend he returned the purse as a Good Samaritan so as to deflect the blame for being the actual thief once it was learned the Captain was not going to dock until the purse was discovered. But while these accusations involved theft and deception, the absolute worst of the bunch accused Condon of having sexually abused a little girl. One letter writer wrote:

> "I know John F. Condon. Years ago when I was a pupil of P.S. #68, located at 128 Street, between 7th and Lenox Avenues, Harlem, N.Y.C. Condon taught one of the class [sic] in the first grade (then the highest) classes.
>
> I would not trust Condon with five dollars much less $50,000.

Twenty years or so ago I read in the papers that he was in jail for raping a young girl, a minor, but through politics and religion he got out of it I believe.

Watch your step with him…."[1008]

Another disturbing letter came from a letter writer who supposedly visited a teacher "*who worked under Dr. Condon at P.S. 12 for approximately (25) years*":

"*…What action, if any, was taken about the alleged accusations of a fourteen year old girl, a pupil of P.S. 12 during Condon's employment as principal of said school, who became pregnant?*"[1009]

And these stories did not just come from anonymous sources:

"*Dr. Condon is alleged to have a past record supposedly arrested in 1904 for impairing the morals of a minor in New York.*"[1010]

Of course none of this means such an incident ever occurred, but suspicions were raised, and on April 15, 1932, Sgt. Moffatt placed a call to Capt. Oliver for verification. Captain Oliver returned the call and "*stated that John F. Condon had been checked up and that he knew of the case mentioned…*" but did not elaborate or mention anything

[1008] "Hiram." Letter from Hiram to Colonel Lindbergh. April 13, 1932. New Jersey State Police Museum and Learning Center Archives.

[1009] Anonymous. Anonymous Letter. Date unknown. New Jersey State Police Museum and Learning Center Archives.

[1010] Coughlin, Walter J. Lt., New Jersey State Police. Teletype. (Confidential) Teletype from Lieut Coughlin to Col. Schwarzkopf. April 11, 1932. New Jersey State Police Museum and Learning Center Archives.

further.[1011] On the same day, Cpl. Horn paired up with Sgt. Moffatt and they made an investigation on City Island. It appeared that during this investigation they had a conversation with a Detective who worked out of Captain Oliver's office, and the following was recorded by Horn:

> *"Detective Lieutenant John Brennan of Capt. Oliver's staff is very familiar with this section of the City Island, having lived there since he was 15 years of age. He knows Mr. John F. Condon personally as well as Al Reich and states that Condon is a man who has always been interested in the welfare of young boys in this vicinity, coaching them in different athletics, preferably baseball and boxing. He further states that Condon is a great man for seeking publicity and as to his criminal record Brennan does not know if such a record exists, but knows an old man in that section who is very well acquainted with Condon and Brennan will talk to this man in an effort to check up on information received that Condon some years back had raped a young girl."*[1012]

While I have never found a report which mentions what Brennan did or did not turn up, it seems obvious whatever it was had been

---

[1011] Moffatt, W. T. Sgt., Newark Police. Newark Police Report. <u>Telephone conversation by the undersigned with Capt. Oliver, of N. Y. Police.</u> April 15, 1932. New Jersey State Police Museum and Learning Center Archives.

[1012] Horn, W. F. Cpl, New Jersey State Police and Moffatt, W. T. Sgt., Newark Police. New Jersey State Police Report. <u>Investigation of a letter received at these Headquarters Apr. 14, 1932 from L. S. Albert stating that certain information in his possession relative to one John F. Condon should be investigated.</u> April 15, 1932. New Jersey State Police Museum and Learning Center Archives.

passed on to Lt. Keaten and Inspector Walsh as evidenced by their line of questioning put to Condon here:

> [Q] *Is there or was there ever any criminal character connected with your life?*
>
> [A] *Why no.*
>
> [Q] *Were you ever arrested?*
>
> [A] *No.*
>
> [Q] *Never?*
>
> [A] *No.*
>
> [Q] *On no complaint?*
>
> [A] *Not that I remember and I would remember if I were.*
>
> [Q] *Were you ever suspected of a crime?*
>
> [A] *Not to my knowledge.*
>
> [Q] *Were you ever questioned concerning your participation in a crime?*
>
> [A] *I was questioned about that little girl, if that's what you mean. Well I was questioned by an official of the Board of Education and a committe [sic] composed of Dr. Maxwell and Thomas O'Brien. I thought it was from a newspaper that had brought that into consideration through a man. This is surmise, but I think it's correct. There was a principal who lost his*

position and they appointed me to take his place. I think he died under very peculiar circumstances.

[Q] *What constituted the complaint?*

[A] *That I had improper liberties with this little girl. Her old sister came back, a girl of about thirty.*

[Q] *What was the age of the girl involved?*

[A] *Fourteen or fifteen.*

[Q] *What was the disposition by the committee?*

[A] *That it was all right and I was exonerated.*

[Q] *What school was that in?*

[A] *P. S. 12, in the Bronx.*

[Q] *Are you still attached to that school?*

[A] *I just retired, honorably, the year before last. Then on the second of October I was appointed lecturer at Fordham University.*

[Q] *What was the girl's attitude concerning the complaint? Was she inclined to withdraw or press it?*

[A] *She was inclined to withdraw it. Her older sister spoke to me later and said she was sorry.*[1013]

[1013] Condon, Dr. John F. Statement. Made to Inspector Harry W. Walsh, Sgt. Warren T. Moffatt, Lieut. A. T. Keaton and Detective Horn. June 2, 1932. New Jersey State Police Museum and Learning Center.

The FBI took an interest in this subject as well. However, the "hot and cold" relationship they had with the NJSP really hampered their ability to properly investigate certain aspects. But once back in the good graces of the NJSP, they were meticulous in recording whatever information was given to them. It was during one of their cordial conversations that this specific matter came up. Lt. Keaten had information about this situation that he shared with Agent Sisk which he felt might be surprising:

> *"Lt. Keaton* [sic] *stated that in spite of the fact he is suspicious of Condon he does not believe the rumor circulated by Lt. Finn and other New York Police officers to the effect that Condon was guilty of sexual abnormalities with small children in New York. He stated that he had never seen any criminal record on Condon although Lt. Finn made allusions, at times, to such a record. He stated that when he and Harry Walsh questioned Condon they asked him about this alleged sexual abnormality and Condon explained it by saying that when he was principal of a grammar school in the Bronx the mother of one of the girls made a complaint against him and he had a hearing before the Board of Education as result of which he was completely exonerated. Subsequently the sister of the girl came to him and apologized admitting that there was nothing to the charge."*[1014]

A few days later the subject came up again. This time there was a little more information added and shared:

[1014] Sisk, T. H. Special Agent, Division of Investigation. Memorandum for the Director. <u>Unknown subjects Kidnapping and murder of Charles A. Lindbergh, Jr</u>. June 23, 1934. National Archives at College Park Maryland.

"There has been considerable talk floating around to the effect that Dr. Condon had a criminal record. This matter was put up squarely to Capt. Lamb and Lieutenant Keaton, [sic] and to Lieutenant Finn and Captain Leahy. The New Jersey men stated that they had never been able to locate any criminal record on Condon and the New York men stated they had no record of him in their files. Lieutenant Finn stated, however, that when Condon was teaching in a public grammar school many years ago a woman made a complaint to the Board of Education that Condon had been guilty of indecent actions with her daughter, a minor. After a hearing Condon was completely exonerated of this charge and later the mother of the girl apologized to Dr. Condon admitting that she had a motive for making the charge. Lieutenant Keaton [sic] stated that he and Harry Walsh asked Condon about this when they grilled him at Alpine and that he gave the explanation as above set forth; that they checked the matter and found that Condon's story regarding it was correct."[1015]

There was another source which came from a Condon family member that backed this up. This came from a man named Dennis Doyle whose mother was Condon's first cousin. During his interview the matter surfaced:

[Q] *What was the family's reaction to the press story about Dr. Condon and the young girls?*

[1015] Sisk, T. H. Special Agent, Division of Investigation (FBI). Memorandum For The Director. Unknown Subjects Kidnapping and Murder of Charles A. Lindbergh, Jr. June 29, 1934. National Archives at College Park Maryland.

[A] *It was never discussed. All I knew about it, it was in the newspapers. I recall asking my mother one time whether she ever heard anything about it. She said it was just some girl looking for publicity. I said it seems funny to bring up insinuations at this time. When Mr. Lockwood asked me if I knew anything about Dr. Condon I told him he was very well liked in the community.*[1016]

Could it be that Condon had been falsely accused? If so, this was a horrible situation for anyone to face, and it would seem like a good idea to dispel it here and now. However, there are always two sides to every story, and there appears to have been at least one alleged victim. I can only imagine how impossible it would have been back then for any minor to come forward with such a terrible accusation against a Principal of their school. Fortunately, Governor Hoffman was able to get the girl's side of the story, and it was not the same version that had been told. This information came to light when the radio host of "Voice of Experience," Dr. Marion Sayle Taylor, wrote a letter to Hoffman and provided him a copy of a letter written to the show by the sister of an actual victim.[1017] The sister, Mrs. Willis S. Meigs wrote the following, the sincerity of which I will leave up to the reader to decide:

[1016] Doyle, Dennis. Statement. Taken at Harts Island, Bronx County, New York, in the presence of Capt. J. J. Appel, Detective Ralph Lewis of the New York Police and Corporal William F. Horn of the New Jersey State Police, 5:00 P. M. May 28, 1936. New Jersey State Police Museum and Learning Center Archives.

[1017] Taylor, Dr. Marion Sayle. Letter from Dr. Marion Sayle Taylor to His Excellency Governor Harold G. Hoffman. April 7, 1936. New Jersey State Police Museum and Learning Center Archives. (Note: Thanks to both Wayne McDaniel and Margaret Sudhakar for bringing this letter to my attention).

"Dear Voice of Experience:

I don't know if this can do any good, as after all it is not my story. I could write to Gov. Hoffman, but that would perhaps be folly, so I'm writing you, as I know you will not divulge my name. This concerns the Hauptman [sic] case, or rather John Condon.

I know that man personally, and before God I swear him to be as big a liar and menace to womanhood as ever lived. My little sister was a pupil in the Westchester P. S. while he was the Principal of that school.

My sister was as sweet a child as ever lived, pretty as a picture, but—she lost her happy go lucky way and would sit and cry, refusing to eat. And refusing, with terror to confide in our mother.

One night my Mother overheard my sister confiding in her chum (Florence Tomlinson, now the wife of Ed Shields of the N. Y. Police force). Mother heard Florence say, "If you won't tell your Mother I will"—naturally— my Mother entered the room and faced the girls and the story was told of how Condon would send for this girl or that, and very often the girl was my sister. They went—to have the key turned in his office door and he would start his devilishness. He did not do her any bodily injury but he would "play" with her body and make her do likewise with him, and then warning her not to dare tell a soul, for the girls were always blamed, and he would never be blamed because he was too well known. Can you imagine such a fiend as he, turning saint—oh no.

343

He would simply go to his Pirest [sic] *and I dare say he wouldn't confess even to him. My parents took the matter to the school board but nothing was done because Sigrid had not been bodily injured, and that happened at about the time that Condon smilingly denied he had had* [sic] *any trouble with his teachers.*

He's a scoundrel, never the kindly old man so many think him to be.

All through the trial my sister told me, she sat at the radio—fearing her name might be mentioned in connection with Condon. I had hoped she'd be brave enough to face Condon, but she had a most lovely family and I can understand so well how she hates to bring this horror to light before her children's eyes—horror—yes, its [sic] *been a nightmare to her all through these years.*

The Lindbergh killing was an act of mercy in comparison to what Condon did to my sister's mind. I don't know if you could use this knowledge to help Hautman [sic] *without mentioning names, for as you see it isn't my story, but I feel so certain that Condon is deeply mixed up with this case, as a confederate, not as a man of mercy.*

Sincerely,
(signed) Mrs. Willis S. Meigs,
113 E. Main St.,
Avon, Mass."[1018]

[1018] Mrs. Willis S. Meigs. <u>Letter from Mrs. Willis S. Meigs to Voice of Experience</u>. Undated. New Jersey State Police Museum and Learning Center Archives.

Mrs. Condon

Condon's wife is an enigma. Always present, almost never seen, and rarely heard from. However, the few times she is mentioned or spoken with it seems very important information is revealed. I've always wondered why law enforcement did not sit down with her more often. In fact, for each trip to the Condon home to interview him, why didn't they interview her as well?

The FBI realized there was still very much to learn late in the case, surprised that the most basic and elementary methods which should have been employed, and assumed were, had never been. As a result, they began to turn over those stones in late 1933. While their efforts were a boon for anyone like me who ever cared to know what actually happened - as they relate to Mrs. Condon they were still lacking. However, by late summer of 1934, Agent Sandberg began to run down and finally compile a complete family tree for the Condon family. In doing so he asked Mrs. Condon about her side of the family. Sandberg wrote the following in his report:

> *"Mrs. Condon, wife of Dr. John F. Condon, advised that all the relatives on her side of the family are dead."*[1019]

Was this true? It was never followed up, and in all honesty, who would think she'd lie about something like this to a Federal Agent? But she had lied, so it appears her husband wasn't the only one hiding something. Her brother, Robert Browne, was still alive.[1020] In fact, police had actually been to see him earlier in the case...

[1019] Sandberg, E. Special Agent, DOI. USBOI Report. Kidnaping And Murder Of Charles A. Lindbergh, Jr. July 24, 1934. New Jersey State Police Museum and Learning Center Archives.
[1020] Thanks to Rab Purdy and Siglinde Rach for helping me verify that Browne had not died until October 23, 1934.

That investigation began when the New York City Police Department received an anonymous letter which read:

DEAR COLONEL

"JAFSIE'S MONEY
WILL BE FOUND AT BROWNES
1777 LEXINGTON AVE N.Y.

As a result, an officer went over to this address. It was an almost vacant four-story brick building with its only occupants in the ground floor apartment. That apartment was occupied by its owner, Robert Browne, and his wife. Browne's actions were odd. He told the officer he was an *"attendant in the Supreme Court, New York County,"* and that his wife was *"bedridden for the past seven years."*[1021] It was learned that Browne was the brother-in-law of Dr. Condon but stated to the investigator that he had not seen him *"in the past three years, nor his sister, wife of Dr. Condon, in the past year, and knows of no reason why he should be mentioned in this case."*[1022] Had there been a falling out? This information was never pursued. Had the officer searched for the money in the building? No. In fact, as noted in the letter:

> *"He would not allow anyone to visit the vacant apartments in the building, and held conversation with our officer through the window."*[1023]

[1021] O'Brien, John, Chief Inspector, City of New York Police Department. Letter from John O'Brien to H. Norman Schwarzkopf, Esq. June 1, 1932. New Jersey State Police Museum and Learning Center Archives.
[1022] Ibid.
[1023] Ibid.

I've found no evidence of follow up. And while we see New York shared this information with New Jersey, it was obviously never shared with the FBI.

Harold C. Keyes

Although often portrayed as a failure by those who wish it had been, Governor Hoffman's re-investigation was a monumental success, considering the amount of time they had and its chaotic nature. Researchers now have a tremendous amount of information to consider, then apply to, their knowledge of this case as a result of the material that investigation produced. The problem that most will face is that they do not know enough about the case prior to diving into that material. And so of course, if you don't know what you are reading then it will have little to no value. Or if you do know a lot about the case, then the Hoffman investigation is a challenge to understand and integrate – which has led some to call it a failure operated by, in essence, a motley crew of misfits. This position bolsters the notion that the State was completely legit, while anyone outside of that circle was a fraud, kook, or an idiot. But this is completely disingenuous. Fact is, many who assisted with Hoffman's investigation had also been connected to the State at one time or another. Lt. Robert W. Hicks, and Leo Meade, as examples, both worked for the Hunterdon County Prosecutor's Office *in relation to this case* prior to their involvement with Hoffman. It's not possible to judge these men as inept while working for Hoffman but as competent while working for the State. To judge them differently is a contradiction that in this case is illogical and unacceptable. In order to judge these men as incompetent while working for Hoffman, we would have to judge them similarly in their work for the State. But we do not. We cannot because they did an irrefutably good job for the State. See how that reasoning works? Interestingly, denying the good work done for Hoffman, in effect, pushes the Lone Wolf theory. So, whether this contradiction persists through ignorance or by ruse, I do not think anyone serious about the solution of this crime has time for it.

Among those who assisted Hoffman was Harold C. Keyes. Keyes had worked for the Secret Service Division of the Treasury Department from 1918 to 1924 before being asked to resign because of "*unethical conduct.*"[1024] It was during his employment with the Secret Service that he used the code name "*Operative K-4*" or "*Kay-4.*" After his departure from that agency, Keyes made rounds as a speaker and would lecture to audiences about his past experiences as a Secret Service Operative, to include "*guarding*" the "*President.*"[1025] The Treasury Department felt these appearances were not appropriate and sought to end his lectures, their position being that Keyes had only acted in that capacity "*once or twice*" in his career.[1026] However, whatever efforts they made to silence Keyes failed, and he continued to give talks where he asserted he had guarded "*Presidents Wilson, Harding and Coolidge*" during his employment with the Secret Service.[1027] Simultaneous to these events, Keyes had worked as an investigator for the Jennings-Foley Detective Agency.[1028] Keyes then moved on to the job of the Chief Investigator for the Unemployment

[1024] Treasury Department, Secret Service Division. <u>Bulletin No. 120</u>. November 1, 1930. New Jersey State Police Museum and Learning Center Archives.

[1025] "Keyes Discusses Presidents' Lives." *The Hempstead Sentinel.* December 12, 1929. New Jersey State Police Museum and Learning Center Archives.

[1026] Treasury Department, Secret Service Division. <u>Bulletin No. 120</u>. November 1, 1930. New Jersey State Police Museum and Learning Center Archives.

[1027] "How to Foil Assassin Explained by Former Secret Service Man." *The Brooklyn Daily Eagle.* February 19, 1933. New Jersey State Police Museum and Learning Center Archives.

[1028] Keyes, Harold C. Private Investigator, Jennings-Foley Detective Agency. <u>Letter from Harold C. Keyes to Colonel Charles A. Lindbergh</u>. March 8, 1932. New Jersey State Police Museum and Learning Center Archives.

Relief Committee, and spent his time investigating and arresting fraudulent relief claims.[1029] It was sometime after this job that he started his own detective agency called the *"Bureau of Secret Service"* which had offices in both New York City and Louisville, Kentucky. By the time he was employed by Lloyd Fisher as a defense investigator, Keyes had accumulated an *impressive* list of references some of which included:

> Vincent Astor, Harvey W. Gibson, Peter S. Duryee, Serge Obolensky, Sebastian Kresge, Max D. Steuer, George W. Ferris, Sanford Cohen, Col. William Hayward, Harold Content, James H. Cullen, Mark Eisner, L. Stewart Gatter, Abraham I. Menin, Maxwell S. Mattucks, Stephen P. Anderton, Solomon Badesch, Roland L. Redmond, Joab H. Banton, George Z. Medalie, Henry Breckinridge.[1030]

It's hard to imagine that Keyes would list any of the above men if they would not have recommended his services. Included in the work he did for Lloyd Fisher was his investigation of Condon's trip to Becket, Massachusetts. Fisher found the work on this angle to be worthwhile and very interesting.[1031] However, as time wore on and money became tight, Fisher found Keyes was not producing and began to suspect he was withholding information, possibly to sell to

---

[1029] "Relief Food Fraud Sends Pair To Jail." *The Brooklyn Daily Eagle.* March 11, 1933. New Jersey State Police Museum and Learning Center Archives.

[1030] Keyes, Harold C. Bureau of Secret Service Letterhead. 1936. New Jersey State Police Museum and Learning Center Archives.

[1031] Fisher, Lloyd. Letter from Lloyd Fisher to Miss Elizabeth McLaughln. March 12, 1936. New Jersey State Police Museum and Learning Center Archives.

the press; at that time his employment for the defense concluded.[1032]
Almost immediately after this separation, Keyes offered his services
to Hoffman's efforts and they were accepted.

When I first began researching this case, I discovered that much of
the information in the Keyes reports was mentioned by, or included
in, other sources. It was this fact which made me pay close attention
to whatever he reported back to Governor Hoffman because it
was proof to me that he was doing at least some quality work.
The possibility that Keyes was leaking information however was
quite real, and this unfortunate situation was a potential problem
for just about anyone who ever involved themselves in this case –
including the police and any other authority attached to it. Leaking
information to the press for money, though, does not mean that
information was not real and does not constitute reason not to
pursue it further. Moreover, from the amount of information he
was providing Hoffman, I could not imagine that he was "holding"
anything back - at that point.

Keyes had a lot to say about Condon. There are two unverifiable
pieces of information that I believe should be shared. The first is that
a "*reliable source*" told him that sometime in June of 1934, Condon's
"*son*" drew up an application to have him committed to an "*insane
asylum.*"[1033] His unnamed source also advised that the rest of the
family "*rebelled*" and caused the effort to fail.[1034] Keeping in mind
that Condon's sons John Jr. and Lawrence were both Lawyers, it
seems possible one of them may have attempted to do this. If true,

---

[1032] Fisher, Lloyd. <u>Letter from Lloyd Fisher to Hon. Harold G. Hoffman.</u>
February 5, 1936. New Jersey State Police Museum and Learning Center
Archives.

[1033] Keyes, Harold C. Report. Untitled. Undated. (Attached to a letter to
Governor Hoffman dated January 10, 1936.) New Jersey State Police
Museum and Learning Center Archives.

[1034] Ibid.

would it have been done because they believed he was legitimately insane, or as a defense against certain charges his son may have believed he'd likely face? Also, from what I've written earlier about Myra's attitude, it seemed very likely that had this attempt actually occurred, she would never have allowed it. It all does makes sense; however, that does not make it true.

The second item of interest was that *"Al Reich, a former pugilist"* was a *"man that has been identified at times with the narcotic traffic in New York."*[1035] This is something that caught my eye because of the fact the files contain a woefully inadequate amount of information on this man. It's hard to believe that someone so close to this matter did not attract a lot more attention.

However, what's most unique about Keyes is that he had an "inside" connection with Henry Breckinridge. So, whatever he wrote concerning what Breckinridge told him should be accurate. The Governor could have easily determined whether or not this relationship had in fact existed. Judging from my experience with his investigation, he would have, prior to accepting Keyes to assist, and would have noted had Keyes ever been discredited for this reason. But no such document exists. Instead, all indications are that he was satisfied with Keyes's efforts. However, it is important to add that it does not mean Keyes's interpretation of what was told to him was correct either.

According to Keyes, his involvement in the Lindbergh case began as follows:

> *"In the early stages of my investigative work I was recommended to Colonel Schwarzkopf by Colonel Breckinridge and several other prominent men and*

[1035] Ibid.

through their efforts, Governor Moore made an appointment for me to see Schwarzkopf. I offered my services to Schwarzkopf in the investigation and was willing to make available to him information that I had acquired in my investigation. I asked Schwarzkopf if he would either give me a temporary appointment in his service or else cooperate with me in the matter of making available certain files of his department. Schwarzkopf very candidly informed me that he would do neither."[1036]

This information checks out with everything I've learned through my research concerning similar outside offers made to Schwarzkopf of this nature. Moving past this original interaction, Keyes also wrote that Breckinridge had told him that he spent many weeks "*at the home of Condon*" and "*during the many months prior to the arrest of Hauptmann I frequently consulted with him on the various angles of my investigation directed toward solving the Lindbergh kidnapping.*"[1037] It was during a conversation with Breckinridge that Keyes learned…

"That he had questioned Jafsie time after time trying to catch him in an inconsistency. Breckinridge at this conference said that he believed Condon was mixed up in the kidnapping in some manner. That he believed this so firmly that he, Colonel Breckinridge prepared two ransom letters as near in character as possible as those that had been coming to Condon and that he had mailed these letters to Condon, but Condon, although he had been very willing to discuss with Breckinridge everything partaking to the case, for some strange reason, never mentioned receiving these two letters.

[1036] Ibid.
[1037] Ibid.

Whether he subsequently turned these letters over to the police is a question. Colonel Breckinridge at the time felt that Jafsie had identified the letters sent by him as a trap and that he determined this because he probably had knowledge of where the genuine letters were coming from and was in a position to determine that the two sent by Colonel Breckinridge were phonies...".[1038]

This fact, recounted to him personally, proved to Keyes that Breckinridge's public position of having "*high regard*" for Condon was untrue. There was also the issue of the specific line of questions Reilly made during cross examination that concerned "*decoy letters.*" Keyes said Breckinridge "*lied.*" Here is that exchange:

[Reilly] *Yes. And I assume as a member of the Bar, and of your experience that you did question in your mind the insertion of his appeal in the Bronx News?*

[Breckinridge] *Yes, sir.*

[Q] *It gave you some thought?*

[A] *It did, yes, sir.*

[Q] *Is it true, Colonel, that you caused to be written to him or did you write two letters to him bearing counterfeit symbols at any time?*

[A] *No, sir, I did not.*

[Q] *Do you know of any letters being written to him—*

[1038] Ibid.

[A] *No, sir.*

[Q] *-any decoy letters?*

[A] *No, sir, not that I know of.*[1039]

Now the question becomes "who" Reilly's source was for this information. Keyes does not claim to be that source, and if he is not, then it is further evidence to support his claim that Breckinridge lied.

The Mysterious Al Reich

It seems incredibly odd that while Reich seemed to have been in the middle of everything, he was never "pressed" by police at the level he should have been. In fact, it should be recalled that Lindbergh himself was suspicious of him on the night of the ransom drop, and it was that suspicion which caused him to replace Reich. These points are reflected in Special Agent Sisk's letter to Hoover concerning his conversations with both Captain Lamb and Lt. Finn:

> *"Regarding Al Reich, the New Jersey State Police seem to know next to nothing, inasmuch as Captain Lamb asked me if I happen to know how Al Reich makes his living. Notwithstanding this remark on Captain Lamb's part, he had previously stated that his organization is very suspicious of Al Reich. Lieutenant Finn, who incidentally has never talked to either Al Reich or Condon, has frequently stated that he was suspicious of Al Reich and he believed Reich associated*

[1039] Breckinridge, Henry. Testimony. The State of New Jersey vs. Bruno Richard Hauptmann, <u>Hunterdon County Court of Oyer and Terminer</u>, page 839, 1935. New Jersey State Law Library.

with dope peddlers and might himself be in the drug trade."[1040]

So what Sisk found was that in late June of 1934, while both the NJSP and NYPD were very "suspicious" of Al Reich, neither had taken any meaningful steps to pursue those suspicions. It is evident from this paragraph that Keyes was not inventing information. Further, since the FBI Summary Report, which had been assembled months earlier, claimed that "*inquiry*" had "*failed to find him* [Reich] *involved in any criminal enterprise*" we see that what's contained in the report cannot always be completely trusted.[1041] Clearly, this is a matter that should have been looked at more closely. In fact, Sisk during that very conversation pressed for more information on the facts concerning Reich's personal involvement in the drug trade, and Lt. Finn responded by telling him it was only a "*rumor*" at that point.[1042] If he felt it worthwhile to mention it, why wasn't it investigated? Sisk attributed this to "*overlook apparently through lack of organization.*"[1043] In a previous conversation with Lt. Keaten, he had expressed that no one, as far as he knew, had ever gone thoroughly through Reich's life, and he wanted to assign one of

---

[1040] Sisk, T. H. Special Agent, Division of Investigation (FBI). Memorandum For The Director. Unknown Subjects Kidnapping and Murder of Charles A. Lindbergh, Jr. June 29, 1934. National Archives at College Park Maryland.

[1041] Sisk, T. H. DOI (FBI) et. al., DOI Report. Summary. NY File No. 62-3057, p. 159. February 16, 1934. National Archives at College Park Maryland.

[1042] Sisk, T. H. Special Agent, Division of Investigation (FBI). Memorandum For The Director. Unknown Subjects Kidnapping and Murder of Charles A. Lindbergh, Jr. June 29, 1934. National Archives at College Park Maryland.

[1043] Ibid.

his men to work with the "Division" on that angle.[1044] It seems completely insane that this late in the game they hadn't covered the basics but at least something was finally being contemplated albeit at the eleventh hour.

By the time my friend Lloyd Gardner's book came out in 2004, I had read at least once everything the NJSP Archives held. However, there is just so much information that it is impossible to remember everything, and for the same reason it is possible that some information is simply missed. One such item exists in <u>The Case That Never Dies</u> and deserves mention. Once I read about Gardner's suggestion that Condon may have encountered Hauptmann at the boxing clubs, I never forgot about it.[1045] I had the Huddleson Report in my possession but had somehow overlooked where Hauptmann mentioned seeing if he was fit to be a boxer.[1046] My immediate reaction was to think Reich would have higher odds of running into Hauptmann than Condon. After his retirement, Reich continued to "*keep busy as a licensed referee for professional wrestling and boxing matches in New York State.*"[1047] It is hard to resist the idea that Reich would have appeared at the various boxing clubs in the area. With this in mind, is it possible that *he* could have been the link between Hauptmann and Condon? After all, one of the several versions

---

[1044] Sisk, T. H. Special Agent, Division of Investigation. Memorandum for the Director. <u>Unknown subjects Kidnapping and murder of Charles A. Lindbergh, Jr</u>. June 23, 1934. National Archives at College Park Maryland.

[1045] Gardner, Lloyd C. June 2004. *The Case That Never Dies*. Rutgers University Press. Page 246.

[1046] Huddleson, Dr James H. Report to Mr James M. Fawcett: <u>Examination of Bruno Richard Hauptmann</u>; p.7, October 3, 1934. New Jersey State Police Museum and Learning Center Archives. (Thanks to Siglinde Rach for pointing this out to me).

[1047] Falzini, Mark W. (2008). *Their Fifteen Minutes*. Iuniverse Inc. Page 48.

Condon gave police about how he became friendly with Reich was that…

> "…while Condon was actively engaged in tutoring
> young boys in athletics throughout the Bronx, he struck
> up an acquaintanceship with Al Reich and thereafter
> associated himself with Reich in numerous real estate
> transactions in City Island particularly, and to a small
> degree in the Borough of Queens at New York."[1048]

So what we see is they met through "athletics" and that they also became tied together financially after their acquaintance.

Boad Nelly

The Boad Nelly note. A terrible hoax or a valuable clue? I say valuable clue, and a very valuable one. That is because whoever worded that note had specific knowledge about the areas mentioned that most people just did not have. An attorney by the name of Noah Browning wrote a letter to Schwarzkopf explaining that he did have knowledge concerning the area, and it was due to the fact that he *"sailed to the Vineyard Sound and sometimes to Cuttyhunk and through Quick's Hole"* and that *"not one in ten thousand"* people would have the knowledge to write what was written in that note.[1049] Browning believed the author of this note could have been familiar as a resident or visitor to Martha's Vineyard, or from Cuttyhunk, or a sailor

---

[1048] Manning, J. J. Special Agent, DOI. USBOI Report. <u>Kidnaping And Murder Of Charles A. Lindbergh, Jr</u>. September 11, 1933. National Archives at College Park Maryland.

[1049] Browning, Noah. H. <u>Letter from N. H. Browning to Col. H. Norman Schwarzkopf</u>. June 23, 1932. New Jersey State Police Museum and Learning Center Archives.

from the sea, and believed these clues could "*help narrow the field of search.*"[1050] He explained:

> "*Nobody ever sees Gay Head except from Cuttyhunk or from the sea. No passenger boats go within sight of it. Cuttyhunk has a small all the year round population and there is a Club there occupied in summer. The westerly end of Martha's Vineyard is practically uninhabited, but there is a light house at Gay Head. The large summer colonies on Martha's Vineyard are on the eastern end of the island. Passenger boats to the Vineyard and Nantucket go through Woods Hole from Buzzard's Bay and not within view of Gay Head. Sailing yachts usually go through Quick's Hole. I never heard of Horseneck beach, if there is such a place on Marthas [sic] Vineyard. There is no such place as Elizabeth Island. The Elizabeth Islands are in a line from Cuttyhunk to Woods Hole and except Cuttyhunk have no permanent population and little, if any, summer population.*"[1051]

Could this have been Hauptmann? This question was not lost to police, and Schwarzkopf specifically ordered Sgt. Zapolsky to investigate "*fishing boats*" to see if Hauptmann "*ever went up toward Martha's Vineyard*" and if so, "*find out if Hauptmann was friendly with the crew.*"[1052] However, nothing was ever learned to connect him along this line. Aside from a canoe he used from City Island to get to his favorite recreation spot on Hunter's Island, there is no evidence that he would have such knowledge as outlined above. Of

---

[1050] Ibid.

[1051] Ibid.

[1052] Schwarzkopf, H. <u>Norman. Memorandum For Sergeant Zapolsky.</u> November 6, 1934. New Jersey State Police Museum and Learning Center Archives.

course those who believe Hauptmann was a "Lone-Wolf" always fall back on the excuse of "blind luck" and I am quite sure their excuse would be that, in this instance, he threw a dart at a map. But as we've seen time and time again there is something bigger going on. The fictional spot where the baby was being kept could have been anywhere. With the money paid, why make it so close, and why make the note as accurately detailed as it was? Furthermore, why not hand over a blank piece of paper sealed in an envelope? Once opened, if the paper was blank, who looks suspicious? Condon. Since their need for him was over why would they care?

Special Agent Sisk saw it too. And he wrote this interesting observation in a letter to Hoover on August 18, 1934:

> "*Rather strong indications that "John" or one of his associates was connected in some way with boats because of "John's" apparent "boat consciouness" [sic] while conversing with Dr. Condon and because of the statements in the thirteenth ransom note; also, because of his statement that he was a sailor, and his mention of places which would be known to sailors and boatmen.*"[1053]

So looking past the idea that Hauptmann was somehow both brilliant and dumb, two people immediately come to mind who might have such knowledge. The first would be Hauptmann's "nephew" Hans Mueller who I will get to later. The next would be none other than John "Jafsie" Condon. Condon all but proves this during an interview Corporal Leon had with him in June 1934. During this interview Condon suggested to Leon that he interview one "*Captain Ailes*" of City Island. Condon explained Ailes might

---

[1053] Sisk, T. H. Special Agent, Division of Investigation. <u>Letter from Special Agent T. H. Sisk to Director</u>. August 18, 1934. New Jersey State Police Museum and Learning Center Archives.

possess information on the boat *"Nellie"* because the last he heard of him *"he was cooking on a boat at Cuttahunk* [sic] *Island in the vicinity of Woodshole, Gayhead, Horseneck and New Bedford, Mass."*[1054] Condon made sure to mention that he did not suspect Ailes of being involved, and also disclosed that the boat he worked on was owned by a *"Lieut. Cornell"* who *"is well known by Col. Breckinridge."*[1055] Does any more need to be shown to prove that Condon did possess what Browning suggested? As is always the situation when doing research, these facts run into others that seem important so they too must be told. A couple of days later, Leon returned to see Condon, who told him he was considering going to Bristol, R.I., to assist a friend named Robert Barry. The purpose was to deliver sails made by a City Island sailmaker named *"Ratsey,"* *"for yachts that were entered in the International Boat races."*[1056]

It was days later, on July 10th, that Special Agent Sandberg made a quiet attempt to interview both of Condon's mail carriers. Thomas Rafferty and John Cole had both delivered mail to Condon's home during the year 1932 during which there were three daily deliveries made... 7:15 to 7:30 AM, 10:30 to 10:45 AM, and 2:20 to 2:35 PM, with one man making the morning tours and the other making the

---

[1054] Leon, Samuel Cpl. New Jersey State Police. New Jersey State Police Report. Interview with Dr. John F. Condon for the purpose of finding out what he knew about John Ailes, alias John Beatie, and what connections he had with the Lindbergh Case. June 26, 1934. New Jersey State Police Museum and Learning Center Archives.

[1055] Ibid.

[1056] Leon, Samuel Cpl. New Jersey State Police. New Jersey State Police Report. Interview with Dr. John F. Condon in reference to Burlington County Detective, Ellis Parker, and also other information that he may have, which would be of value to the Lindbergh case at this time. June 28, 1934. New Jersey State Police Museum and Learning Center Archives.

afternoon tour but each week rotating these tours.[1057] Both men told Sandberg that Condon was a "*fiend for notoriety*" and was considered in the neighborhood to be a "*nitwit.*"[1058] They also claimed that most of his neighbors consider him an "*old fool*" and apparently they ignored him and he ignored them. They said he would often be seen walking up to people asking "*do you know who I am?*" and calling the carriers back to his house if they passed by without delivering any mail to let them know he was expecting "*important mail*" and ask if they did not have it.[1059] They added that before this crime Condon had gotten "*very little mail.*"[1060] Rafferty recalled a conversation with him at a time when Condon "*was being accused of complicity*" when he told him "*I am a wealthier man than Lindbergh myself.*"[1061]

Leon learned after his last interview with Condon that he did in fact take the trip with Barry to Rhode Island and left City Island with him on "*Friday night, July 6, 1934, about 10:00 P. M.*"[1062] On Saturday, upon arrival at the shipyard around 7:00 AM, he noticed a sailor who resembled "John" although he was not quite sure it was him and did not see this man again thereafter.[1063] On Sunday morning, while on the dock at Newport, Condon walked down among the Sailors when...

1057 Sandberg, E. Special Agent. Division of Investigation. USBOI Report. Unknown Subjects. Kidnaping and Murder of Charles A. Lindbergh, Jr. July 12, 1934. New Jersey State Police Museum and Learning Center Archives.

1058 Ibid.

1059 Ibid.

1060 Ibid.

1061 Ibid.

1062 Leon, Samuel Cpl. New Jersey State Police. New Jersey State Police Report. Interview with Dr. John F. Condon in reference to his trip to Bristol, R. I. July 13, 1934. New Jersey State Police Museum and Learning Center Archives.

1063 Ibid.

> "...one of them asked Mr. Barry if Dr. Condon were
> not "Jafsie", and Barry told him that he was; that this
> fellow then came over and sat down by Dr. Condon on
> a carpenter's wooden horse and asked him if he wasn't
> "Jafsie" in the Lindbergh case and Dr. Condon told
> him that they did call him that."[1064]

According to what Condon told Sandberg, this sailor introduced
himself as "*Sorenson*" and claimed to have known Condon from City
Island when he worked on "*Plant's yacht*" at the same time that Red
Johnson was working for "*Durant*" at City Island. Condon also told
Sandberg that he stated to Sorenson that "*he didn't think Johnson had
anything to do with the Lindbergh case, and Sorenson said that he didn't
either.*"[1065] However, during his interview with Leon, he...

> "...went on to state that Sorensen told him that he
> was on a yacht owned by Mr. Plant and was anchored
> at City Island the same time that Red Johnson was
> on the Lamont yacht at that place and that he knew
> Johnson very well, and said that Johnson, to his
> personal opinion, did not have anything whatsoever
> to do with the Lindbergh Crime, as he was not that
> type of fellow."[1066]

[1064] Sandberg, E. Special Agent. Division of Investigation. USBOI Report.
Unknown Subjects. Kidnaping and Murder of Charles A. Lindbergh,
Jr. July 24, 1934. New Jersey State Police Museum and Learning Center
Archives.

[1065] Ibid.

[1066] Leon, Samuel Cpl. New Jersey State Police. New Jersey State Police
Report. Interview with Dr. John F. Condon in reference to his trip
to Bristol, R. I. July 13, 1934. New Jersey State Police Museum and
Learning Center Archives

So what we are getting out of both versions is that Red was innocent and that he and Sorenson were at City Island – a place where Sorenson knew who Condon was from the time he was there. The story does not end here. After his conversation with the big Swede Sorenson, Condon walked over to a man named Captain Robbins of Rockport, Maine. Captain Robbins apparently knew Condon was Jafsie, then informed him that he was associated with *"Grant"* as a boatman.[1067] Mr. Grant was in charge of the Morrow Boat in Maine according to Robbins.[1068] Robbins then claimed to Condon that he was not only at the "Boatman's Ball" when both Gow and Red were there, but that he actually danced with Gow several times.[1069] Robbins also told Condon that…

> *"…the Lindbergh kidnaping* [sic] *was supposed to have been "hatched" at the Boatman's Ball. Robbins further stated that everyone around the Morrow place in North Haven, Maine, believes it was an inside job."*[1070]

[1067] Sandberg, E. Special Agent. Division of Investigation. USBOI Report. Unknown Subjects. Kidnaping and Murder of Charles A. Lindbergh, Jr. July 24, 1934. New Jersey State Police Museum and Learning Center Archives.

[1068] Leon, Samuel Cpl. New Jersey State Police. New Jersey State Police Report. Interview with Dr. John F. Condon in reference to his trip to Bristol, R. I. July 13, 1934. New Jersey State Police Museum and Learning Center Archives.

[1069] Ibid.

[1070] Sandberg, E. Special Agent. Division of Investigation. USBOI Report. Unknown Subjects. Kidnaping and Murder of Charles A. Lindbergh, Jr. July 24, 1934. New Jersey State Police Museum and Learning Center Archives.

Robbins also recommended that Grant *"may have some information that might be of value to the Lindbergh Case."*[1071]

The Family Connections

Another angle to be explored was whether someone known to the family had been involved. An eventual effort was made to identify possible connections, indirect or otherwise, to members of the Morrow staff. The "go to" source for any information along these lines was the secretary to the estate Arthur Springer. Springer told Special Agent Seykora that *"twenty-five"* years ago Senator and Mrs. Morrow *"had a summer home for one or two seasons on the island of Martha's Vineyard near East Chop, in the vicinity of Oak Bluffs, in the northwest section of the island,* and that *"General Morrow also visits friends on Martha's Vineyard occasionally."*[1072] Springer told investigators that he *"usually spends his summer vacations"* on Martha's Vineyard with his wife, but that they do not have a boat, and they *"are not familiar with the boating and yachting activities in that vicinity."*[1073] Springer did point out that there was an "important Government lighthouse located at Gay Head," which was an *"excursion point"* for many of the summer residents, and also pointed out there was a *"small Indian Reservation"* located at *"Gay Head"* as well.[1074]

[1071] Leon, Samuel Cpl. New Jersey State Police. New Jersey State Police Report. <u>Interview with Dr. John F. Condon in reference to his trip to Bristol, R. I</u>. July 13, 1934. New Jersey State Police Museum and Learning Center Archives.

[1072] Seykora, W. F. Special Agent, USBOI (FBI). USBOI Report. Unknown Subjects. <u>Kidnaping and Murder of Charles A. Lindbergh Jr</u>. May 10, 1934. National Archives at College Park Maryland. (Note: The FBI had changed its name from USBOI to DOI by this time but the heading on this particular report still says "United States Bureau of Investigation")

[1073] Ibid.

[1074] Ibid.

As mentioned in the FBI Summary report, Mrs. Rhoderick Cecil Henry Grimes-Graeme also spent vacations at a summer cottage belonging to a friend located at the Oak Bluffs portion of Martha's Vineyard.[1075] This report identifies that friend as Mrs. W. Lillian Chignault. At issue here is the fact this information came from, as indicated in that summary, an "*informant*." That "*informant*" was T. J. Cooney of The Thiel Service Company, a private detective agency typically used by the FBI at that time. Although most of what is reported in the summary is word for word, Cooney wrote in his memo that this summer cottage was owned by "*a woman friend in New York*."[1076] Since the summary indicated that Chignault was living in Hartford, and Springer indicated he "*did not recall*" the name of the friend himself, it is hard to know for sure if Chignault was the actual owner of this cottage. By the time of Springer's interview, Agent Seykora was merely relying on the summary report, a report which itself relied on the information in Cooney's memo.[1077]

Another revelation made by Springer to Agent Seykora was that...

"...*when the Col. And Mrs. Lindbergh were on their honeymoon, they purchased a twenty-five foot motor boat and cruised in it from Long Island through Long Island Sound, past Block Island and Martha's*

[1075] Sisk, T. H. DOI (FBI) et. al., DOI Report. <u>Summary</u>. NY File No. 62-3057, p. 98. February 16, 1934. National Archives at College Park Maryland.

[1076] Cooney, T. J. Assistant General Manager, The Thiel Service Company. Memorandum. January 24, 1933. New Jersey State Police Museum and Learning Center Archives.

[1077] Seykora, W. F. Special Agent, USBOI (FBI). USBOI Report. Unknown Subjects. <u>Kidnaping and Murder of Charles A. Lindbergh Jr.</u> May 10, 1934. National Archives at College Park Maryland. (Note: The FBI had changed its name from USBOI to DOI by this time but the heading on this particular report still says "United States Bureau of Investigation")

> *Vineyard, to the Morrow summer estate on the island of North Haven, Maine.*"[1078]

During this trip Anne had written they were discovered at "*Woods Hole*" by the Press.[1079] So this honeymoon trip clearly indicates they were quite familiar with all of the points indicated in the "Boad Nelly" note. Furthermore, a fellow researcher and friend unselfishly shared this information with me:

> "*I had thought that Anne and Charles had embarked on their cruise with no training whatsoever. Not So!!! In the summer of 1928 several close-mouthed executives of Elco had spent two months training Charles in how to operate, navigate, and maintain a chartered 38' Elco Charles had chartered. It was true that they never set foot on Mouette prior to the cruise. As a long time boater and member of the United States Power Squadron since 1972, that made me feel better about that aspect of the voyage.*"[1080]

The Discovery

Like many other things involving this case, history paints fiction into a corner disguised as truth to forever remain there fooling everyone. In this case we've all been led to believe the "Nellie" had never been found. But that is not true.

[1078] Ibid.

[1079] Lindbergh, Anne Morrow. (1973). *Hour of Gold, Hour of Lead*. Harcourt Brace Janovich. p43.

[1080] Sasser, John. Email to Author. "*Various Data re Honeymoon and boat...*" August 22, 2005.

We all know about the fruitless search conducted by air and sea as described by those who were with Lindbergh during his search over the area described in the note. While there is a little story in a couple of books written before this one which claims Lindbergh did not eat, he did in fact eat both lunch during the search and dinner at the Long Island Aviation Country Club after it was over.[1081] Such false information is meant to promote the desired narrative. But what is "desired" isn't always factual. Instead, the true story is very different. Lindbergh's behavior was his usual jovial demeanor. This is best exemplified by Elmer Irey's eyewitness account:

> "*The take-off was perfect, Lindbergh's hands and nerves were obviously under full control. After we had sufficient altitude, Breckinridge asked to take over the controls. He, too, was a flyer and this seemed an opportunity to get in some flying time. As Breckinridge flew, Lindbergh quietly crossed controls and wires and in no time Breckinridge was baffled to find the plane rising when he wanted to lose altitude and turning right when he wanted to turn left. His amazement amused Lindbergh. It was quite a scene, Lindbergh playing practical jokes, Breckinridge wondering if he was crazy, and Jafsie yowling excerpts from the Song of Solomon.*"[1082]

And nothing disproves the desired narrative more than the fact that the boat Nelly actually had been discovered. We already know from the sources which were previously written that several Coast Guard ships had joined in the hunt. These boats were requested to "*fly a*

[1081]   Irey, Elmer L. <u>Memorandum in re: Trip with Colonel Lindbergh, Colonel Breckenridge and Dr. Condon on April 2, 1932</u>. April 4, 1932. New Jersey State Police Museum and Learning Center Archives.

[1082]   Irey, Elmer L. *The Tax Dodgers*. Greenberg. (1948). Page 79. (Thanks to Mark Falzini for pointing this out.)

signal" if they discovered any information, while Lindbergh flew his plane with the other men "*in the entire vicinity, examining closely every boat which*" they sighted.[1083] Since there was no signal waiting for them at the Coast Guard Station at Cuttyhunk they abandoned their search at 7 PM, and this is what eventually led Lindbergh to phone his wife Anne the news of their "*failure.*"[1084]

The actual facts concerning this matter include that Treasury Agent Kelleher had been assigned to investigate this angle apart from Irey's involvement. Kelleher was the perfect man for the job. He worked out of the Boston Office, lived in Lawrence, Mass., and was intimately familiar with the areas mentioned in that note.[1085] Furthermore, the Coast Guard at that time fell under the Treasury Department and their cooperation was at his disposal. What can be learned from Agent Kelleher is quite shocking. He first learned that "*a boat named "Nellie" about forty-five feet long and colored green*" had been seen on "*April 2nd, about 4 P. M.*" off "*Cuttyhunk headed East toward Woodshole or Vineyard Haven.*"[1086] The only difference was this boat was about forty-five feet long instead of the 28 feet as described in the note. This fact did not seem to deter Agent Kelleher, and he pursued this lead:

[1083] Irey, Elmer L. <u>Memorandum in re: Trip with Colonel Lindbergh, Colonel Breckenridge and Dr. Condon on April 2, 1932</u>. April 4, 1932. New Jersey State Police Museum and Learning Center Archives.

[1084] Ibid.

[1085] Kelleher, D. A. Special Agent, Internal Revenue Service. Memorandum. "<u>No Man's Land</u>." Undated (April 12, 1932). New Jersey State Police Museum and Learning Center Archives.

[1086] Kelleher, D. A. Special Agent, Internal Revenue Service. <u>Memorandum of Message from Dave Kelleher at New Bedford, Massachusetts, at 9:45 A. M. on April 9th</u>. April 9, 1932. New Jersey State Police Museum and Learning Center Archives.

"The original inquiry upon which I proceeded to Woods Hole was in regard to the "Nellie", a boat which was searched by the Coast Guard on Sunday afternoon, April third, at Edgartown. This boat was searched by two crews of Coast Guards and nothing suspicious was found by either. It was again searched by me on Sunday, April tenth, about nine o'clock when encountered off Cuttyhunk, proceeding in the direction of New Bedford. The search revealed a full load of flounders. The living quarters, the engine room, and all available places of concealment were inspected and nothing suspicious was found. This boat is registered from Point Judith, Long Island, but is from Stonington, Connecticut. Its owner and master is Albert E. Jones of Mystic, Connecticut."[1087]

And so armed with the knowledge that a boat "Nellie" was where it was supposed to be on April 2nd, we see the information in this note was not a "complete" farce at all. Breckinridge would later brush this fact off when testifying before the Bronx Grand Jury for two reasons: The child was not found on board, and the boat was bigger than described in the note.[1088] However, there were just too many coincidences to dismiss. Along the lines of the information Noah Browning provided, not only did the writer know about the area, they also seemed to know that a boat with that name would be there. And, as usual, the story does not end there....

[1087] Kelleher, D. A. Special Agent, Internal Revenue Service. Memorandum. "No Man's Land." Undated (April 12, 1932). New Jersey State Police Museum and Learning Center Archives.

[1088] Breckenridge, Colonel Henry. Testimony. Bronx Grand Jury. May 17, 1932. New Jersey State Police Museum and Learning Center Archives. (Note: This testimony is the source for the information in the FBI Summary Report).

Another Name Surfaces

As I will show later, after Hauptmann's arrest, Special Agent Frank Wilson seriously considered that Isador Fisch may have passed Lindbergh Ransom money. It was during this period of time that Wilson realized the boat "Nellie" was traced back to Stonington – a place tied to Fisch. As a result, he immediately sought out the names of the men who conducted the search of "Nellie" at Edgartown Harbor on April 3, 1932. As it turned out, one man was Chief Boatswain's Mate Theodore Trei who was stationed at the Coast Guard Depot in South Baltimore at the time of the request.[1089] Another man, John J. Quickert, who searched the "Nellie" on both April third and seventh, was Chief Boatswain's Mate at the time of the search but had been "discharged" and was living in Louisville, Kentucky, on the date of the request.[1090] What Wilson did with this information I have never been able to discover. One thing I do know is that the Defense was never made aware of it.

The ties between the boat "Nellie" and Fisch would come to Governor Hoffman in a very odd way. Not through the law enforcement channels we would expect, but through reporter Bob Conway who sent him a brief note which read in part:

> *"I've broken yarn about a link between the boat Nellie of the Lindbergh ransom notes and Isador Fisch. I know you (or the Governor) may have some of this*

[1089] Kelleher, D. A. Special Agent, Internal Revenue Service. <u>Letter from Dave Kelleher to Special Agent Frank Wilson</u>. January 4, 1935. New Jersey State Police Museum and Learning Center Archives.

[1090] Ibid.

stuff, but it may be that we have additional dope you'd be interested in."[1091]

As a result, Governor Hoffman instructed Bill Lewis (who was still a private investigator at the time and not yet reinstated as a NJ Trooper), paired with Detective William S. Mustoe (who was on loan to Hoffman by the Monmouth County Prosecutor's Office), to visit Stonington, Conn. There they discussed the situation with Sergeant Arthur Whitmarsh who promised his full support in chasing down any facts he could find.[1092] Whitmarsh would later learn that the boat "Nellie" did in fact exist and was owned by Albert E. Jones who, at the time of the investigation now lived in Newport, R. I., and had this boat since it was built.[1093] In a memo to Hoffman, investigators Lewis and Mustoe made it clear that this "Nellie" was *claimed to be non-existent by investigation authorities at the time.*"[1094] The connection between Stonington and Fisch was a friend and business associate by the name of Erich Schaefer who had known Fisch since he landed in America in 1925.[1095] It was during a pre-trial statement that Schaefer told Prosecutor Peacock that Fisch

[1091] Conway, Bob. Type Note. Note from Bob Conway to Bill Conklin. Wednesday 9:30 P. M. Undated (1936). New Jersey State Police Museum and Learning Center Archives.

[1092] Lewis, William, Investigator. Meade Detective Bureau Report. Investigation of Erich Schaeffer, Stonington, Connecticut. February 26, 1936. New Jersey State Police Museum and Learning Center Archives.

[1093] Adams, Walter C. Sgt. Stonington Police Department. Letter from Walter C. Adams to Mr. Meade. March 4, 1936. New Jersey State Police Museum and Learning Center Archives.

[1094] Meade, Leo And Mustoe, Leo. Memo. Respectfully referred to HGH for his information. Undated (March 1936). New Jersey State Police Museum and Learning Center Archives.

[1095] Schaefer, Erich. Statement. Made to Mr. Peacock. December 10, 1934. New Jersey State Police Museum and Learning Center Archives.

enjoyed a *"wonderful – very good reputation"* and that other people *"thought the world of him."*[1096]

The Mystery of the Stolen Purse

One of the strangest stories about Condon involved both theft and deception. The old man's habit was to tell multiple versions of a story, never relating the exact same tale twice. The FBI Summary Report gives one a flavor of this and is a good place to start. In this report they mention the story...

> *"...that on August 14, 1888 he misappropriated a purse containing $300 belonging to a passenger on board a boat sailing between New York and Vancouver, B.C., nothing tangible has been developed to date upon which to predicate the statement that or has had criminal tendencies."*[1097]

This seems to exonerate the man of all possible wrong doing doesn't it? It was the summary of all evidence they had available at that time. Or was it? There was, as I have demonstrated, much to be learned.

In the summer of 1932, a version of this story was presented to Prosecutor Hauck by William Jones. Jones was a firearms expert from Manhattan and because of his profession was acquainted with the law enforcement community. He explained that his friend, John Roche, brought his daughter to see him specifically to tell him her story. Miss Roche had been on this very boat and had recognized Condon from his picture in the paper as the man she had met

---

[1096] Ibid.

[1097] Sisk, T. H. DOI (FBI) et. al., DOI Report. <u>Summary</u>. NY File No. 62-3057, p. 159. February 16, 1934. National Archives at College Park Maryland.

there.[1098] She explained that Condon did *"all the talking,"* *"wanted to entertain the passengers,"* and was the one to *"start games"* to keep everyone occupied.[1099] Her story continued:

> *"When the ship was getting near New York a lady lost three hundred dollars and Condon got is* [sic] *some way and the Officers of the ship made him turn it over to her after some trouble. Then he said that she could not identify it and made some words about it to justify his keeping it."*[1100]

Since the FBI Summary was written long after this information was communicated to Hauck, one might conclude the girl's story was investigated and dismissed. How untrue that is. First there is no evidence the FBI was even aware of this letter or the information it contained. Next, a "meaningful" interview with Condon about this matter did not come until the summer of 1934. Here it is in its entirety:

> *"Another interview was had with Dr. Condon at his home, and he stated that about August, 1930, he took a trip from New York to the Pacific Coast by bus and returned by water through the Panama Canal on the S. S. "California"; that there were possibly over three hundred people aboard; many of whom were school teachers; that he was elected chairman of the entertainment committee, and that during the voyage a man by the name of Hennessey, who stated that he was a clerk of the court in New York City, found a*

[1098] Jones, William A. <u>Letter from William A. Jones to Hon. Anthony M. Hauck, Jr.</u> August 1, 1932. New Jersey State Police Museum and Learning Center Archives.

[1099] Ibid.

[1100] Ibid.

pocketbook with ten dollars in it, and that he brought it to Dr. Condon, as chairman of the entertainment committee, to see if he could ascertain the owner of the same; that Dr. Condon announced the finding of the pocketbook, and that it was finally ascertained that the pocketbook belonged to a Miss Cummings, who, he believed, was a teacher from the West. Dr. Condon stated that he introduced Mr. Hennessey to Miss Cummings and Miss Cummings offered Mr. Hennessey a five-dollar reward, for finding her pocketbook, but Hennessey refused the reward. Dr. Condon further stated that in an inner compartment of said pocketbook there was the sum of three hundred dollars, but that it was all returned to Miss Cummings. Dr. Condon stated that he remembers that Hennessey was a good musician and that he played the piano several times while the rest of the people sang and danced."[1101]

It was after hearing this version that Special Agent Sandberg decided he would track down Hennessey and interview him about events on this 1930 trip.[1102] By August, Sandberg's attempts at finding Hennessey were met with negative results. He returned to Condon who now told a different story and indicated the trip had occurred in *"August 1931."*[1103] Armed with this new version of the trip, Sandberg

---

[1101] Sandberg, E. Special Agent. Division of Investigation. USBOI Report. Unknown Subjects. Kidnaping and Murder of Charles A. Lindbergh, Jr. July 24, 1934. New Jersey State Police Museum and Learning Center Archives.

[1102] Ibid.

[1103] Sandberg, E. Special Agent, DOI (FBI). United States Bureau of Investigation Report. Kidnaping and Murder of Charles A. Lindbergh Jr. September 4, 1934. New Jersey State Police Museum and Learning Center Archives.

went directly to the Panama-Pacific Company then examined their records and ascertained…

> "…*that said ship sailed from San Francisco, Saturday, August 29, 1931, from Los Angeles, Calif., August 31, 1931, and that Mr. John F. Condon is listed as a tourist passenger on said ship, but that there is no such party as Hennessey listed either as tourist or first class passenger on said ship. Further investigation will be made to ascertain if Dr. Condon knows the correct name of the party who found said purse.*"[1104]

The Shady Deal

There is another reference in the FBI Summary report that mentioned "*rumors*" concerning Condon and his involvement in "*shady real estate transactions in the Bronx and City Island…*".[1105] Among these "rumors" was one which the police had been alerted to by one Leonard Albert, whose mother, Mrs. Michelina Albert, was one of Condon's neighbors on City Island, living on 532 Minnieford Avenue. Leonard had informed police that Condon had swindled a former resident of City Island out of a large sum of money.

> "…*Leonard Alberts informed the undersigned that this Condon does not bear a good reputation on City Island where he owns a summer home located on the next corner from the Alberts home. He stated that some years back there was a half breed Indian who owned a home in City Island and John F. Condon*

[1104] Ibid.

[1105] Sisk, T. H. DOI (FBI) et. al., DOI Report. <u>Summary</u>. NY File No. 62-3057, p. 159. February 16, 1934. National Archives at College Park Maryland.

was his adviser and acted for him in negotiating a real estate deal where this property was sold, also consisted of valuable antiques. Later this Indian died and the proceeds of this sale, amounting to $22,000, which in some manner unknown to the informant, reverted to John F. Condon, although this Indian had several relations still living in this vicinity. This is one of Condon's deals which makes these people feel very suspicious of this man."[1106]

On April 18th, a letter arrived at Hopewell addressed to the Lindberghs. This letter claimed that Condon had "*never*" had the "*respect of the community*" and that he was commonly known as "*windy Jack.*"[1107] The purpose of this letter was to warn the family by bringing up the incident involving a "*mentally incompetent*" man named "*Jacob Stinnard*" [sic]. It went on to claim that Stinard "*willed all his property to Condon just one week before his death*" and that this caused "*quite a sensation on City Island.*"[1108] This letter further claimed his heirs contested the will, among them "*David Stinnard* [sic] *of Mt. Vernon;*" that the rumor about Stinard having "*Indian blood*" came from Condon himself who bragged about all the money left to him, and that Stinard "*never had a drop of Indian blood.*"[1109]

[1106] Horn, W. F. Cpl, New Jersey State Police and Moffatt, W. T. Sgt., Newark Police. New Jersey State Police Report. Investigation of a letter received at these Headquarters Apr. 14, 1932 from L. S. Albert stating that certain information in his possession relative to one John F. Condon should be investigated. April 15, 1932. New Jersey State Police Museum and Learning Center Archives.

[1107] Anonymous. Letter to Mrs. and Mrs. Lindbergh. April 18, 1932. New Jersey State Police Museum and Learning Center Archives.

[1108] Ibid.

[1109] Ibid.

This "rumor" came to the attention of Hugh McQuillan, SAC for the Intelligence Unit of the Treasury Department's IRS Division. Upon returning to New York from Hopewell he, along with Special Agent Harvey, investigated this story and learned the "*old Indian*" was a man named "*Jacob Steinard* [sic]."[1110] The neighbors cast doubt on Stinard's "*Indian*" heritage but confirmed that Condon "*was his only friend*."[1111]

In order to get to the bottom of this, I contacted a good friend Siglinde Rach who has spent a considerable amount of time researching this angle (among many others). She was kind enough to share what she had discovered with me:

> "Condon's real estate activities on City Island went back to at least 1899. During his many years there he befriended a local resident named Jacob Stinard, about 12 years his senior, a lifelong bachelor and colorful character who made his living peddling clams with his sister in Yonkers for over thirty years. Because of his occupation, Jacob was known as Jake the Clam Man. After his sister's death in 1916, Jake sold their home on City Island to a family named Albert and settled into a home on 341 Walnut Street in the Nodine Hill section of Yonkers, where his sister had spent her final months. This address, coincidentally, was only a short walk from 11 – 13 Oak Street, where Peter Birrittella's family ran a bakery. On May 12, 1917, Jacob Stinard sold another one of his real estate holdings, one located at 603 Baker Avenue in the Bronx, to his good friend John F. Condon, of 1403 Washington Avenue, for one dollar. Two weeks later, on May 26, Jake the Clam

---

[1110] McQuillan, H. Special Agent in Charge, Intelligence Unit, Internal Revenue Service. Letter from H. McQuillan to Elmer Irey. May 20, 1932. New Jersey State Police Museum and Learning Center Archives.
[1111] Ibid.

> *Man was dead. He died, along with his parrot, in a*
> *fire from the explosion of an oil stove, which he had lit*
> *in the kitchen of his home on Walnut Street. Stinard*
> *tried to extinguish the blaze but was unable to do so,*
> *being quickly engulfed by the flames. He managed to*
> *drag himself to the door, collapsing on the threshold.*
> *When he was found, he had about $2,800 dollars in*
> *cash and gold pieces sewn into his undershirt.*"[1112]

A search of the newspaper articles at the time reveal the following:

> *"Steinard* [sic] *owned considerable property in the*
> *Nodine Hill district. He left a will, which it is believed*
> *bequeaths all his property to John A. Condon, an*
> *attorney of New York. So far as can be learned he*
> *leaves no relatives though he is said to have a sister and*
> *two nephews living in Mount Vernon. The property*
> *in which Steinard* [sic] *met his death was transferred*
> *to the New York attorney only last week. Condon had*
> *been a close friend of the victim and had transacted all*
> *his legal business for him.*"[1113]

And also:

> *"The last will of Jacob Stinard of 341 Walnut Street,*
> *Yonkers, has been filed for probate in the surrogate's*
> *office. The petition states that he left $4,250 of personal*
> *property but his estate is believed to be much more. The*
> *petition also states that he left no heirs at law. He leaves*
> *all his property to his friend, John F. Condon of 1403*

[1112] Rach, Siglinde. *Jake the Clam Man.* Unpublished Research. 2018. Author's possession.

[1113] "Nodine Hill Character Is Burned To Death." *Yonkers Daily News.* May 26, 1917. New Jersey State Police Museum and Learning Center Archives.

*Washington Avenue, in the Bronx, "In consideration
of the many services and kindnesses he has rendered
me during my lifetime." He also appoints Mr. Condon
executor of the will, which was dated Nov. 8, 1916.
It is said by some who knew him that he had relatives
living at City Island, Larchmont and Pelham, who
may appear to contest the will."[1114]*

So it appears Condon had in fact inherited his dead friend's fortune.
Was it a "swindle" or was it merely a man disinheriting his remaining
family members, for whatever reason, to reward his only friend?

*"The timing of Jake's death and the financial windfall
for Condon certainly provided fertile ground for such
a rumor to have sprung up, one with enough strength
to persist for decades.*

*Jacob Stinard is buried in Pelham Cemetery on City
Island, with other members of his family, in a grave
marked by a large obelisk. His father lies buried in
a Quaker cemetery the Bronx. The native American
heritage is unsubstantiated but not impossible, as the
family had lived in the region for many decades."[1115]*

The "Jafsie No. 2" Letters

Sometime in the beginning of 1934, the FBI became interested
in Condon's handwriting. Special Agent Charles Appel Jr. was
the document examiner who had worked out of the Criminology

[1114] "Pelham Resident An Heir." *New Rochelle Pioneer.* June 9, 1917. Siglinde
Rach Collection.

[1115] Rach, Siglinde. *Jake the Clam Man.* Unpublished Research. 2018.
Author's possession.

Laboratory since its inception on November 24, 1932.[1116] It was Appel who on February 2nd was given the task of comparing Condon's handwriting to the Lindbergh Ransom Notes. After careful examination Appel wrote in his report:

> *"The inconspicuous characteristics appearing in the Lindbergh extortion letter which seem to furnish individual characteristics of the writer are absent from the writing of Condon. It is believed for this reason that he did not write the extortion letters."*[1117]

With the conclusions of Appel, who had been doing professional document examinations for nearly four years for the FBI, it seemed this question was now answered for good. Soon after this, however, a new matter arose when the Editor of the Daily Times in Chicago forwarded two suspicious letters to the FBI. The letters were postmarked February 28th, and March 1st, 1934, and had both been signed *"Jafsie No. 2."* These letters were immediately forwarded to Agent Appel for examination. Appel issued a report which included the following:

> *"It is definitely concluded that John F. Condon wrote these letters to the Times."*[1118]

This conclusion now created some doubt about his earlier decision that Condon had not written the Lindbergh Ransom Notes:

[1116] "The Story of Charles A. Appel, Jr., Founder of the FBI Laboratory. *The Grapevine.* March 2015. www.socxfbi.org

[1117] Appel, C. A. Special Agent, Division of Investigation. Laboratory Report. <u>Case: Unknown Subjects, Charles A. Lindbergh Jr., Victim; Kidnaping</u>. February 7, 1934. National Archives at College Park Maryland.

[1118] Appel, C. A. Special Agent, Division of Investigation. Laboratory Report. <u>Case: Unknown Subjects, Charles A. Lindbergh Jr., Victim; Kidnaping</u>. March 7, 1934. National Archives at College Park Maryland.

> *"In making this comparison it was observed that the letters to the Times are clearly disguised and that various means of disguise are carried through almost all of the writing. This is very unusual and indicates ability. These disguises, however, which are from the normal writing of Condon are in the direction of those used in writing the Lindbergh extortion letters. For this reason a comparison was made of the letters to the Times and of specimens of Condon's writing with photographic copies of the Lindbergh extortion letters. There were observed many normal writing habits which are alike in all three specimens. In order to be certain it is necessary to make a very thorough examination especially in order that it can be determined whether sufficient of these similarities in normal writing habits exist to prove identity and to prove the writing of each of the Lindbergh letters instead of possibly only the latter ones. This is an important consideration determining whether his entrance in the case was before or after the kidnapping. Such an examination requires original specimens."*[1119]

This report sent the Agents scrambling. As this was going on, they asked another government document examiner, Dr. Wilmer Souder from the Bureau of Standards, to conduct his own examination of the *"Jafsie No. 2"* letters and they were sent to his laboratory in Washington D.C.[1120] On March 16th, his efforts were completed, and he walked over to the FBI office to report his findings verbally to John J. Edwards of that office:

[1119] Ibid.

[1120] Coffey, E. P. Chief of the Criminology Laboratory, Division of Investigation. <u>Memorandum For The Director</u>. April 4, 1934. National Archives at College Park Maryland.

> *"Dr. Souder stated that he could not make a positive identification, but there were many similarities between the letter in question which should not be overlooked. He further stated that he had not seen any of Dr. Condon's handwriting before and that he made a comparison of the letters addressed to the Division with the notes in the Lindbergh case and that there were several similarities."*[1121]

Dr. Souder was enthusiastic about his comparison between the Ransom Notes and Condon's handwriting.[1122] He recommended that everything be sent together to the *"best expert in the United States for examination, and recommended Mr. Albert S. Osborn and Mr. Stein."*[1123] Dr. Souder was interested to learn about Condon's background *"particularly as to education"* and asked for an interview with Special Agent Sisk who he would travel to New York to see.[1124]

The observations of both Appel and Dr. Souder immediately caused SAC Cowley to call Special Agent Sisk about setting up surveillance of Condon and attempt to check any of his expenditures against the Lindbergh ransom money list.[1125] Sisk was advised to take precaution and avoid any suspicion because they did not want Condon to

[1121] Edwards, John J. Division of Investigation. <u>Memorandum For The Director</u>. March 16, 1934. National Archives at College Park Maryland.

[1122] Coffey, E. P. Chief of the Criminology Laboratory, Division of Investigation. <u>Memorandum For The Director</u>. April 4, 1934. National Archives at College Park Maryland.

[1123] Edwards, John J. Division of Investigation. <u>Memorandum For The Director</u>. March 16, 1934. National Archives at College Park Maryland.

[1124] Coffey, E. P. Chief of the Criminology Laboratory, Division of Investigation. <u>Memorandum For The Director</u>. April 4, 1934. National Archives at College Park Maryland

[1125] Cowley, S. P. Special Agent in Charge, Division of Investigation. <u>Memorandum For The Director</u>. March 20, 1934. National Archives at College Park Maryland.

know he was being watched. Cowley also requested there be made an attempt to secure a room near the Condon home to be used for this purpose.

In the meantime, as ordered, Special Agent Sisk turned over the Daily Times letters to Osborn to be compared with specimens of Condon's handwriting and also to have his handwriting compared with the Lindbergh Ransom Notes.[1126] On March 20th, both Albert S. Osborn, and his son, Albert D. Osborn, turned over written reports with their findings.

According to Albert D. Osborn's report concerning the comparison between Condon's handwriting and the Times letters, he found *"consistent"* differences among the small "s"s, and these along with *"other differences"* made him *"doubt"* Condon wrote those letters.[1127] His conclusion concerning whether Condon had written the ransom note was as follows:

> *"The specimens written to Mr. Hoover, when compared with the original Lindbergh notes, show little similarity. Of course, the writer of these specimens is a good writer and has sufficient skill to write the Lindbergh notes, but it is hard to believe that one could adopt such a consistent and thorough disguise."*[1128]

To any layperson this certainly sounds legitimate. The only problem is that he would later claim Hauptmann had done exactly

---

[1126] Sisk, T. H. Special Agent, Division of Investigation. <u>Letter from T. H. Sisk to Director</u>. March 20, 1934. National Archives at College Park Maryland.

[1127] Osborn, Albert D. <u>Letter from Albert D. Osborn to Mr. F. X. Fay</u>. March 20, 1934. National Archives at College Park Maryland.

[1128] Ibid.

that – adopted a consistent and thorough disguise. [1129] Osborn Jr. added that he also believed that whoever wrote the Times letters did not write the Ransom Notes.[1130] Albert S. Osborn concluded that Condon "*did not write*" the "*anonymous writing to the Chicago Daily Times.*"[1131] Osborn Sr. also wrote…

> "*…I will add that, in my opinion, Mr. Condon did not write the original Lindbergh kidnaping* [sic] *notes, and in my opinion the writer of the letters to the Chicago Daily Times was not the writer of the original notes.*"[1132]

Special Agent E. P. Coffey was perplexed by the differences observed by the experts. He wrote to J. Edgar Hoover:

> "*It would appear to be difficult to reconcile the reports submitted by the Osborns with the earlier findings of Mr. Appel and Dr. Souder. The reports submitted by the Osborns are not sufficiently detailed to permit them to be carefully weighed. The reports of both the Osborns in substance are that the Chicago Times letters, the Lindbergh ransom notes, and the writings of Dr. Condon are all dissimilar. Yet, both the Osborns agree the Chicago Times letters are 'carefully and painstakingly disguised throughout.*'"[1133]

[1129] Osborn, Albert D. <u>Letter from Albert D. Osborn to Joseph Lanigan, Esq</u>. November 28, 1934. New Jersey State Police Museum and Learning Center Archives.

[1130] Osborn, Albert D. <u>Letter from Albert D. Osborn to Mr. F. X. Fay</u>. March 20, 1934. National Archives at College Park Maryland.

[1131] Osborn, Albert S. Osborn. <u>Letter from Albert S. Osborn to Mr. F. X. Fay</u>. March 20, 1934. National Archives at College Park Maryland.

[1132] Ibid.

[1133] Coffey, E. P. Chief of the Criminology Laboratory, Division of Investigation. <u>Memorandum For The Director</u>. April 4, 1934. National Archives at College Park Maryland.

It was also discovered that a fingerprint had been obtained from one of the letters written to the Times and that it belonged to a woman named *"Frances King."*[1134] King had previously been arrested by New York City Police for blackmail against *"Bruce Barton,"* a writer and republican political figure.[1135] The only problem was that King had been *"continuously incarcerated since August of 1933,"* therefore, she could not have authored these letters without jail authorities knowing about it. Furthermore, Agent Appel examined King's handwriting and determined it was *"not identical with either the Chicago Times letters or the original Lindbergh ransom notes."*[1136] At some point, Dr. Souder contradicted his verbal observations and wrote that he was *"unable to connect the Jafsie No. 2 handwriting with that of John F. Condon,"* an action which Coffey chalked up to Dr. Souder being *"ultra-conservative in his opinions in his written report."*[1137] Finally, in light of the Osborn team conclusions, as well as the fact that King's fingerprint was located on a letter written to the Times, S.P. Cowley advised Agent Sisk that no surveillance of Condon should be attempted or maintained *"until some information has been obtained indicating Condon's implication in this case."*[1138]

[1134] Ibid.

[1135] Fried, Richard. *The Man Everybody Knew: Bruce Barton and the Making of Modern America.* Ivan R. Dee. 2005. See pages 139-141.

[1136] Coffey, E. P. Chief of the Criminology Laboratory, Division of Investigation. Memorandum For The Director. April 4, 1934. National Archives at College Park Maryland.

[1137] Ibid.

[1138] Cowley, S. P. Special Agent in Charge, Division of Investigation. Memorandum For The Director. March 23, 1934. National Archives at College Park Maryland.

Berryman Sketch

One of the best ideas the FBI ever had was to get an artist to have a sketch made up of Cemetery John. The New York Times reported that *"James T. Berryman, cartoonist for The Washington Star"* had created the sketch, and that it was based on *"the descriptions given to the artist"* from both *"Dr. Condon and Perrone."*[1139] The article also quoted Attorney General Homer S. Cummings as saying the sketch bore *"an amazingly striking resemblance to Bruno Richard Hauptmann, the man now held."*[1140] An actual picture of that sketch was included in another article on the same day, alongside of Hauptmann's photograph.[1141] The most interesting part about this wasn't what was being said, but rather that the sketch was not the one boasted by the FBI as having been made by Berryman, the one we all recognize.[1142] When I discovered this fact, I headed to the NJSP Archives to dig deeper and learn what was going on. Unfortunately, that led to more questions than answers. There I discovered the Berryman Sketch was a frontal facial composite alongside a ¾ profile sketch. They are not what is (or was) located on any of the FBI. gov websites over the years. So what I learned, apparently, was that there were two different sets of sketches attributed to Berryman. Since the earliest version of the sketch I could find was the one I discovered at the NJSP Archives, it appeared this had been the first to be drawn, at least the first of the two sets I was now aware of but I sought further clarification. I thumbed through Robert Peacock's unpublished and undated manuscript, and noted that his version of the Berryman Sketch also matched the one in the NYT, as well as

---

[1139] "Artist Portrayed Unknown Suspect." *The New York Times*. September 23, 1934. New Jersey State Police Museum and Learning Center Archives.

[1140] Ibid.

[1141] "Attorney General Cumming's Review of Kidnapping Case." *The New York Times*. September 23, 1934. New Jersey State Police Museum and Learning Center Archives.

[1142] www.fbi.gov/history/famous-cases/lindbergh-kidnapping

the one at the NJSP Archives. My next encounter was the Lt. James Finn Liberty Magazine article which included the most famous version of the sketch.[1143]

I continued to search for as much documentation as possible. One of the earliest sources came from an FBI Memo:

> "*Relative to the sketches being made by the artist Berryman of the kidnaper* [sic]*, Lieutenant Keaton* [sic] *and Captain Lamb stated that they thought it a very good idea. However, they have also stated that they thought we ought to discuss with Colonel Schwarzkopf the extent to which it will be used and for what purposes. It would have been almost impossible to have preserved the making of this sketch as a secret from the State Police. Dr. Condon very possibly might have told them about it had we not, and if we used it to any extent at all the State Police would have learned of its existence, and trouble would have resulted.*"[1144]

This source reveals that the FBI did not actually want to share this information with New Jersey. It also doesn't mention Perrone as a possible source for it and Sisk uses the word "sketches" which to some may indicate several "versions." That could be; however, I consider the possibility that it could have simply referred to both the face and the profile. Also, this memorandum was written on July 27, 1934. If, at the time of writing this, the sketch was "*being made*" that means

---

[1143] Finn, James J., Lieutenant. "How I Captured Bruno Hauptmann." *Liberty Magazine.* October 19, 1935. New Jersey State Police Museum and Learning Center Archives.

[1144] Sisk, T. H. Special Agent, Division of Investigation (FBI). <u>Memorandum For The Director</u>. Unknown Subjects. Kidnapping and Murder of Charles A. Lindbergh, Jr. July 27, 1934. National Archives at College Park Maryland.

it would have been impossible for it to have been shown to anyone previous to this date. Another FBI source is informative, but in no way solves the mystery concerning why there were two different sketches and why only one was presented throughout history as being the actual sketch:

> "*Three months before Hauptmann who was eventually executed as the kidnaper-murderer* [sic] *of the Lindbergh baby by the New Jersey State authorities was ever heard of or suspected in connection with the Lindbergh Kidnaping* [sic] *Case, Mr. Hoover, as Director of the Federal Bureau of Investigation, sent a cartoonist for a Washington newspaper to New York City to work with Dr. Condon or "Jafsie" who paid over the $50,000 ransom money to somebody in a cemetery one night. Dr. Condon described and redescribed that individual. The cartoonist, drew and redrew his features from Dr. Condon's oral description hundreds of times, the eyes, the nose, the ears, the mouth, the teeth, the forehead, then two composite pictures, for more than two days, until Dr. Condon said, 'That's the man to whom I paid the ransom money.'"*[1145]

Here too, this could all mean there were several versions of this sketch that resulted from the sessions with Berryman. Or it could simply mean it was the final version of the full face and profiles individually. But I do wonder – Why didn't Condon identify Hauptmann? The

---

[1145] Drane, W. H. Lester Major, Assistant Director, Federal Bureau of Investigation. <u>Address to Thirteenth Meeting of the International Criminal Police Commission in London, England</u>. "Modern Trends In Criminology In The United States Of America." June 8, 1937. Federal Bureau of Investigation, Record/Information Dissemination Section, Winchester, Virginia.

"later" sketch, for lack of a better term, looks more like Hauptmann than the other. And if it was so striking, and Condon proclaimed that was *the man,* why wasn't it so striking to him once they met in the police station?

In the end the questions still remain. Was the sketch truly based on BOTH Condon and Perrone? As to the different versions of this sketch I can draw no conclusions. I simply do not have enough information. What is important, and why I wrote about this, is to point out there is more to this than what history has presented.

"Original" Berryman Sketch
(Courtesy NJSP Museum)

389

Gang of Five

During the time when Lloyd Gardner was conducting research for his book, *The Case That Never Dies*, we communicated often. One thing that stands out in my memory was his interest in the relationship between Arthur O'Sullivan and Condon. It was O'Sullivan who took down Condon's fantastic story about being "*rowed out to a vessel off Throggs Neck, blindfolded, about a week after the meeting at Woodlawn cemetery.*"[1146] However, going back to the beginning of the story to get the full flavor, it started with Condon looking over the "*Rogue's gallery at headquarters*" for the "*quintet who "threatened to get him without fail,*" but "*he shook his head*" no.[1147]

> "*They are not here*", he told detectives. "*Maybe they are arrested. I'd be able to recognize four of them in a minute, but I am not so sure about the fifth. I ought to know them. They had me in a mighty tight spot.*"[1148]

There appear to be different "versions" of this story, though once they are gathered together and examined, it is clear they all came from one source with the various papers/editors deciding which piece to include in their stories and which not to.

[1146] Gardner, Lloyd C. June 2004. *The Case That Never Dies*. Rutgers University Press. Page 85.

[1147] Deuell, Harvery, The News, Managing Editor. <u>Letter from Harvey Deuell to Mr. William Conklin</u>. December 16, 1936. New Jersey State Police Museum and Learning Center Archives.

[1148] Ibid.

> *"When the bandage was taken from his eyes he said he*
> *found himself surrounded by five armed men. They*
> *made an effort to conceal their faces, he said."*[1149]

There among those men stood *"John"* who was a *"German,"* an *"Italian"* named *"Doc,"* a third man who was *"Spanish,"* and two other *"shadowy figures."*[1150] Condon ordered *"put down your guns"* explaining *"I am not armed. I've been a baseball umpire most of my life and I'm used to settling arguments without weapons."*[1151] They all lowered their weapons except for "Doc."

> *"'That's all right', he said, "but there is a penalty for*
> *the crime we've committed – fifty years. We aren't*
> *going to take any chances."*[1152]

Condon recognized "John" as the man he previously dealt with.

> *"I asked John when he was going to show me the baby,"*
> *he said. "But he said they had decided the day before to*
> *transfer the child to a hiding place ashore."*[1153]

The fullest version of the story adds that Condon was told...

[1149] "Jafsie Guarded From Five He Met On Kidnap Boat." *Newark Evening News.* May 16, 1932. New Jersey State Police Museum and Learning Center Archives.

[1150] Gardner, Lloyd C. June 2004. The Case That Never Dies. Rutgers University Press. Page 86.

[1151] "Gang Of Five Seen By Jafsie On Boat." *The Washington Post.* May 16, 1932. New Jersey State Police Museum and Learning Center Archives.

[1152] Deuell, Harvery, The News, Managing Editor. <u>Letter from Harvey Deuell to Mr. William Conklin</u>. December 16, 1936. New Jersey State Police Museum and Learning Center Archives.

[1153] "Jafsie Guarded From Five He Me On Kidnap Boat." *Newark Evening News.* May 16, 1932. New Jersey State Police Museum and Learning Center Archives.

> "...that the gang had two women associates, one of whom the newspapers identified as the woman who called on him in the Bronx with a message and later met him by appointment at the Tuckahoe, N.Y. railroad station with further instructions."[1154]

The day after Jafsie told this new story police and reporters swooped in. However, Condon flatly denied it all.[1155] This may have turned the situation into a "he said – he said" situation with Condon being pitted against O'Sullivan. One could easily rationalize siding with O'Sullivan. However, O'Sullivan wasn't without his own bit of history to contend with.

As mentioned earlier, in 1931 O'Sullivan was arrested along with two other men for kidnapping a man named Walter Dickerson who they believed had been involved in the slaying of Benjamin P. Collins on his yacht "*Penguin*" on September 9, 1931.[1156] They were charged with "*posing as an official*" in order to pick up Dickerson and bring him to Flushing to question him, which they believed would solve the murder and make them heroes.[1157] O'Sullivan's charge was later dismissed.[1158]

Unfortunately for Condon, there is another source which calls into question his denial. The source was someone I mentioned earlier: Dennis Doyle. The thing that stands out to me is that when Doyle

---

[1154] "Gang Of Five Seen By Jafsie On Boat." *The Washington Post*. May 16, 1932. New Jersey State Police Museum and Learning Center Archives.

[1155] Gardner, Lloyd C. June 2004. The Case That Never Dies. Rutgers University Press. Page 86.

[1156] "Veteran Reporter Wins Dismissal in Kidnaping." *The Washington Post*. November 13, 1931. New Jersey State Police Museum and Learning Center Archives.

[1157] Ibid.

[1158] Ibid.

was asked about Condon, he told authorities "*he was very well liked in the community.*"[1159] That is an answer I would expect to see coming from his relative, and it makes what Doyle told them about this story more believable:

> "*Certain instances which occurred after talking to Dr. Condon, I met him in a restaurant. I saw the story in the papers and when he told me he met several men on a boat, I took it with a grain of salt. This was in Bickford's Restaurant. This is a locality where everyone knows everyone else. Someone said "Jafsie" was around the corner and I went around to see him. I sat down and had a talk with him. He said you know I'm mixed up in the Lindbergh case, and he talked to me. We talked about twenty minutes and we talked about our folks. I didn't question him, I was just listening in about the four men and the baby on the boat. It is just simply a question and makes me more or less libel as far as Condon is concerned. A thing is either the truth or a lie. Condon can't tell two stories and have them both the truth. It is a mix-up. Then there was another angle about two months after having spoken to Condon, I noticed a clipping in the Daily News, in which it stated that he had met four men on a boat and referred to them by the name of Doc.*"[1160]

[1159]   Doyle, Dennis. Statement. Taken at Harts Island, Bronx County, New York, in the presence of Capt. J. J. Appel, Detective Ralph Lewis of the New York Police and Corporal William F. Horn of the New Jersey State Police, 5:00 P. M. May 28, 1936. New Jersey State Police Museum and Learning Center Archives.
[1160]   Ibid.

The Rowboat Incident

I've often wondered if the "Rowboat incident" wasn't somehow the genesis for the "Gang of Five" story. It began on April 18, 1932, when Condon made a statement via a *"newsreel microphone"* that contact with the culprits had been *"reestablished"* saying *"we are in contact with the kidnappers, and the baby will be returned soon, I hope."*[1161] On April 19th he climbed into a boat and rowed around Pelham bay supposedly in an attempt to *"make another contact."*[1162] Upon his return his boat capsized at the dock and Condon fell into the water. He then *"scrambled ashore"* and announced to the press *"I got a message."*[1163] Sometime later, Condon sent along a picture that was a...

> *"...close resemblance to the ship which he saw pass while he was in rowboat off Fort Schuyler, while he was endeavoring to make connections concerning the Kidnaping [sic] of the Lindbergh Child."*[1164]

Breckinridge was even asked about the "row boat incident" during the Grand Jury testimony:

> *"The main thing that the doctor has had has been the so called contacts with the so called underworld, he*

[1161] "'Jafsie Claims New Contacts." *Salt Lake Telegram.* April 18, 1932. Utah Digital Newspapers (digitalnewspapers.org).

[1162] ""Jafsie" Gets Ducking on Mystery Trip, but Asserts, "I Got a Message."" *Salt Lake Telegram.* April 20, 1932. Utah Digital Newspapers (digitalnewspapers.org).

[1163] Ibid.

[1164] Leon, Samuel J. Cpl., And Horn, William F., Cpl., New Jersey State Police. New Jersey State Police Report. <u>Attached picture received from Dr. John F. Condon and is supposed to be a close resemblance to the one Dr. Condon saw while he was in a rowboat off Fort Schuyler.</u> December 9, 1932. New Jersey State Police Museum and Learning Center Archives.

thought that was a very bad thing to have anything to do with these fellow [sic], and he was still convinced that water rats had something to do with this thing so he began to circle around them and enlarge his acquaintance among them, he had this boat and he turned over in the water there as a matter of fact and got himself wet with the idea the people would let him alone, so he went over there and got out of his boat and in getting out of his boat he got quite wet and they took him in and dryed [sic] him out and he made friends with them and they turned around and let him loose and he went around to find this boat that John was supposed to use, the doctor reminds me of a man named David Sayer, this was before the Civil War and he asked my grandfather to give him a letter of introduction to a banker which he did, it said, "if you talk to him you think he is a fool and if you do business with him you will think you are one."[1165]

Coal Barge John

So considering Condon's penchant for being less than truthful, telling stories, and outright lies, the fact that two other independent people say he told this "Gang of Five" story, leads me to conclude that he did. While in Flemington, we see that Reilly somehow had this information at his disposal…

> Q: *Were you taken blindfolded aboard a boat at any time?*

[1165] Breckenridge, Colonel Henry. Testimony. <u>Bronx Grand Jury</u>. May 17, 1932. New Jersey State Police Museum and Learning Center Archives.

A: *I was never blindfolded by anybody in my life.*[1166]

Reilly knew that Condon had lied and came back to the point again:

Q: *I asked you whether you were blindfolded and you said no.*

A: *Never, never.*[1167]

In an attempt to possibly "jog" Condon's memory, Reilly posed the question "*did you ever visit a boat anchored just above Throgg's Neck?*" to which Condon surprisingly answered, "*many times.*"[1168] Condon went on to explain that while he was in his pilot boat he saw men on a boat and spoke to them, but did not get on board.[1169] Reilly asked for a description and Condon answered that one of the men was "*Coal Barge John.*"

> "*A man who has been working on those boats for years. Right above Throgg's Neck, you said, didn't you? I mean in a northerly direction. When I say "above" I distinguish the words "northerly direction," and "above" is that fair? Yes, north of Throgg's Neck. Yes.*"[1170]

Reilly wanted to know how many men Condon saw. Condon answered he did not know but that he saw "*two at least.*" The last question Reilly asked about it was this:

[1166] Condon, John F. Testimony. The State of New Jersey vs. Bruno Richard Hauptmann, <u>Hunterdon County Court of Oyer and Terminer</u>, page 786, 1935. New Jersey State Law Library.

[1167] Ibid.

[1168] Ibid. Page 787.

[1169] Ibid.

[1170] Ibid. Page 788.

Q: *How many boats did you visit after you paid – and
I am not talking about steamboats that you rode on or
the rowboats that you rowed in; how many boats did
you visit after you paid ransom money in connection
with this case?*

Mr. Wilentz: Excluding steamboats and rowboats?

*Mr. Reilly: I don't want anything he rode on. I
want boats he went to visit.*

*The Witness: I don't recollect – one. One that I
told you about was the only thing I visited, and
then I did not go aboard.*[1171]

So he visited a boat on Throgg's Neck *"many times"* but only once?
And by the way, just who the hell was "Coal Barge John?" He is not
mentioned in any police investigation or interview with Condon.
Nobody knew, and apparently neither did Condon himself. Why?
Because what he was testifying to was not only untrue it was
impossible. There again, even on the stand in Flemington, Condon
was doing "it" again.

Captain John Tritton

Captain Tritton had become fairly well known for his experiences
on the auxiliary schooner Nomad. He had been its Captain in 1929
and abruptly quit, along with his two man crew, once they docked
at Charleston, South Carolina.[1172] Tritton claimed the Nomad's

[1171] Ibid. Page 789.
[1172] "Ex-Skipper Denounces Owner of Yacht in Sea Death Mystery; Charges
Ross Threatened Life." *Brooklyn Daily Eagle.* April 5, 1929. fultonhistory.
com/Fulton.html

millionaire owner, Leland Ross, had failed to properly relieve him for 48 hours straight during their journey from Havana, and once he finally did, he fell asleep at the wheel, leaving all on board in peril. Captain John C. Schofield was hired as Tritton's replacement; however, the schooner was later found disabled and drifting, with Ross explaining that Captain Schofield had been thrown overboard by rough seas.[1173]

On June 26, 1936, Captain John Tritton wrote a confidential letter from his Jersey City home to Governor Hoffman. He asked that his letter and his name be given no publicity, but felt compelled *"after long and serious consideration"* to write to him regarding what he believed was an injustice.[1174] *"I have decided to give you information, with which Dr. Condon can be charged with gross perjury, in part of his testimony against Richard Bruno Hauptman* [sic]*."*[1175]

> *"According to Dr. Condon, when he was looking for "Coal barge John" there was a coal barge anchored North of Trogs* [sic] *Neck for several years. Dr. Condon is a native of that locality, – why did he perjure him self* [sic]*, – why did he falsify his testimony, what it is the reason back of this crooked-cock-eyed swearing to facts testimony.*
>
> *Dear Governor, I hearby stake my thirty odd years (since 1901) knowledge of those waters, that there never was, and never be a coal barge anchored in those waters.*

[1173] Ibid.

[1174] Tritton, John Captain. <u>Letter from John Tritton to Hon. Harold G. Hoffman</u>. June 26, 1936. New Jersey State Police Museum and Learning Center Archives.

[1175] Ibid.

First, there is not enough water for coal barge to anchor. Second, – it is wide open waters, and particularly against North East weather. Please be reminded, that the above can be substantiated through the New York Harbor Masters office, – coraborated [sic] *by the Light House keepers on Throgs* [sic] *Neck, and innumerable other sources, to* [sic] *many to be mentioned here."*[1176]

Back to O'Sullivan

In discussing O'Sullivan with Dr. Lloyd Gardner further, he told me he wished he knew Governor Hoffman's source for his Liberty Article concerning the woman that had visited Condon who asked for his *"protection."*[1177] He further described his fruitless search through the Hoffman Collection at the NJSP Archives for it. I had been through that entire collection myself and hadn't recalled ever seeing the source. Of course that didn't mean I was 100% sure it wasn't there, only that if it was then I missed it. It was shortly after this interaction that I was at the NJSP Archives and asked my good friend Mark Falzini, the Archivist at the NJSP Museum, what was in a group of grey boxes nearby the Hoffman Collection. He told me it was additional paperwork that had belonged to Governor Hoffman but that it was mostly non-kidnap related. I asked permission to look through some boxes and he told me *"be my guest, that will make you the first person since I've been working here."* That was all the motivation I needed. As I began to comb through those boxes, I was initially discouraged. I found, just as Mark had told me, tons of political and non-related material. However, as I progressed I

[1176] Ibid.

[1177] Hoffman, Harold Giles. *The Crime - The Case - The Challenge (What Was Wrong with the Lindbergh Case?)*, Original Manuscript: Unedited & Uncorrected, circa 1937. Page 109. New Jersey State Police Museum and Learning Center Archives.

did find there was some material about the crime, and some as it related to Ellis Parker. And so I continued. Before long, bingo (!!!), an affidavit made by Arthur J. O'Sullivan. What are the odds?! To be clear, Lloyd later informed me that he wound up discovering a copy in the main collection, and I do now have two separate copies, one a negative, so there seem to be two different places where it can be found. It was, however, this sequence of events that sticks out in my mind the most, and it meant I had in fact missed it my first time through that collection. The hunt for the elusive in this case is monumentally frustrating; only persistence and good luck would reward me.

Attached to the affidavit was an interesting little memo to the Governor:

> "O'Sullivan was the legman who talked with Condon at the time he said he had been threatened with indictment by District Attorney McLaughlin of Bronx County."[1178]

I strongly believe the affidavit should be published in its entirety:

> "Arthur J. O'Sullivan says that on or about May 15th, 1932, he was employed as a reporter for THE NEWS and that on the above date and the day before, May 14th, 1932, his particular assignment was to interview Dr. John F. Condon, in connection with the Lindbergh Kidnaping [sic] case. He says that he had read the articles printed in THE NEWS on those dates and that the portions quoting the said Dr. Condon are true entirely.

[1178] Conklin, Bill. Memo. <u>Memo from Bill Conklin to the Governor.</u> Undated (1936). New Jersey State Police Museum and Learning Center Archives.

He further says that said Dr. Condon talked freely with him on divers occasions and that on May 14th, 1932, he did say the following, in the parlor of his Decatur Ave., Bronx, home, to this reporter, to wit:

"Supposing there were a family in which most of the members were bad but one of them was very good and, suppose that the good one came to you and went down on her knees, asking your protection. Wouldn't you do everything to shield her name?"

He says that in this interview the said Dr. Condon informed him that this was precisely the thing that precipitated his entry into the Lindbergh kidnaping [sic]. When the reporter asked the said Dr. Condon if he would ever, under any circumstances, reveal the name of the woman who had come to him (at his home, he said) the said Dr. Condon replied in substance, "No, I'll carry her name a secret to the day I die."

He states that he makes this statement without ill feeling or prejudice against the Bronx educator and says that he has only made this statement believing same will be placed before the Governor of New Jersey, with a view of clearing up undisclosed angles in the Lindbergh kidnaping [sic] and ransom."[1179]

It was soon after my discovery of this affidavit that I spoke with Dr. Gardner again. His first question to me was "*do you think this woman was the same one Silken brought to his house?*"

[1179] O'Sullivan, Arthur J. Affidavit. April 8, 1936. New Jersey State Police Museum and Learning Center Archives.

Maurice Silken

The question posed to me by Lloyd Gardner was something I hadn't even considered. I had been fixated on Condon's assertion that it was the reason for his entry into the case, knowing it was a contradiction from other reasons he had given. With that in mind, I wanted to know exactly what that reason was, and there was where my full attention was focused. This startling question is a perfect example of how Lloyd's brilliant mind works - with nothing distracting him from considering all of the possibilities surrounding every aspect or an event or clue. He's relentless and thorough to a fault.

Silken was another strange character who graced the stage of events. He used his position as a taxi driver to observe and report in hopes of assisting police in cracking this case with his endgame being a reward.[1180] As a result, he wrote a lot of letters which concerned many observations that he actually made, but he also speculated about or asserted things, making "leaps of faith" which were impossible or untrue. Nevertheless, there was one thing which he wrote to Lindbergh about that was true:

> *"On March 7, about noon, a woman, about forty years old; five foot, two inches tall; weighing approximately 150 pounds; hired my taxicab at 181 Street and Amsterdam Avenue, N. Y. C. She handed a slip of white paper to me with the address, 2974 Decatur, on it, and she seemed to be very nervous at the time. When I arrived at the address, I drove slightly past the house, and she scolded me for driving past the house.*

[1180] Horn, W. F. Cpl, New Jersey State Police and Moffatt, W. T. Sgt., Newark Police. New Jersey State Police Report. Interview with Maurice Silken, 15 Wadsworth Avenue, Apt. #-2-C Bronx, N. Y., concerning attached communication. July 8, 1932. New Jersey State Police Museum and Learning Center Archives.

*I told her not to be so excited, and that I would back
the car down to the house. It was then that I noticed
that she spoke with a foreign accent. I also noticed that
Dr. Condon's "Jafsie" advertisement was printed in the
newspaper on March 8, the next day."*[1181]

Another reason this trip stood out in Silken's mind was that he was
yelled at for passing the house. He thought because of her reaction
he was going to get *"gypped"* out of his tip. It was not until June 3,
1932, that Schwarzkopf sent men to investigate the various claims
Silken had been making. On June 6th, Cpl. Horn along with Sgt.
Moffatt of the Newark Police Department took Silken to meet with
Condon. During this meeting Silken retold the story concerning the
woman he drove from Amsterdam Ave. on the *"morning of March
7th, 1932 at about 11–00 o'clock"* to the Condon home for which he
was *"paid $1.00 for the trip and $.15 tip"* with the woman being in a
"highly nervous condition" and having a *"foreign accent."*[1182] After he
briefly questioned Silken, Condon told police that he was telling the
truth. Horn and Moffatt asked Condon who this woman was, and
Condon replied that *"he did not know her name"* but that she visited
him *"for the purpose of having him get some children that she could keep
at a summer camp"* she was starting at the *"Atlantic Highlands"* in
New Jersey.[1183] Silken jumped into the conversation and *"reminded"*
Condon that he had told *"Detective Hickey of Inspector Brockman's
[sic] Office in New York"* that the *"woman applied for a position as*

[1181] Silken, Maurice. Letter from Maurice Silken to Colonel Charles A.
Lindbergh. April 24, 1932. New Jersey State Police Museum and
Learning Center Archives.

[1182] Horn, W. F. Cpl, New Jersey State Police and Moffatt, W. T. Sgt., Newark
Police. New Jersey State Police Report. Continued investigation of
information furnished by one Maurice Silken, Residence 15 Wadsworth
Avenue, Apartment #-2-C. June 6, 1932. New Jersey State Police Museum
and Learning Center Archives.

[1183] Ibid.

a housekeeper" for him.[1184] Upon hearing this, Condon appeared "*somewhat confused*," but admitted that was "*the truth*" then proclaimed that "*it was not right for these New York Detectives to be giving out information concerning this investigation.*"[1185] These men noted in a later report that:

> "*When Silken heard this explanation he stated that Det. Hickey of the New York Police, who investigated his first report of this matter, had interviewed Dr. Condon concerning the visit of this woman and Hickey told Silken that when he questioned Condon about this woman's visit Condon told him that this woman had applied to him for a position in his home as a housekeeper, although he did not advertise for any housekeeper, he could not understand why this woman, whom he does not know, visited him inquiring for that position. Condon could give no further information concerning this woman's identity or her present whereabouts.*"[1186]

Silken himself gave even more details about this encounter in a later letter which he wrote to Lindbergh:

> "*Mr. Condon said to me that this woman was a swedish music teacher from Atlantic Hylands* [sic]*, who spoke with a swedish accent and that this women*

[1184] Ibid.

[1185] Ibid.

[1186] Horn, W. F. Cpl, New Jersey State Police and Moffatt, W. T. Sgt., Newark Police. New Jersey State Police Report. <u>Conversation with Dr. John F. Condon in the presence of Maurice Silken, residence 15 Wadsworth Avenue, Bronx, N. Y. on June 6th, 1932 at Audubon Avenue and 181st Street, New York City</u>. July 8, 1932. New Jersey State Police Museum and Learning Center Archives.

*told him that she scolded me, which I have stated in my
information to the police. Mr. Condon at this meeting
was questioned by Sargent [sic] Moffatt as how long
he knew this woman, and if he knew her name. He
said that he cannot recollect her name just then, but
he said he knew her for about eight years, and that he
would try to locate her.*"[1187]

By July of 1934, Condon was still stringing along investigators by
agreeing to assist Special Agent Sandberg in an attempt to *"ascertain
the name of the woman who was taken to"* his house on March 7,
1932, by Maurice Silken concerning the *"Atlantic Highlands."*[1188]
Sandberg wrote *"if successful"* he intended to interview her *"relative
to her visit."*[1189] In an attempt to further pursue this matter, Sandberg
consulted both Lt. Keaten and Captain Lamb. Concerning the
woman in reference to the *"Atlantic Highlands"* they told him *"there
was not enough information to institute a check of the women"* and
that *"if such a woman had actually been taken"* to Condon's house
"they were satisfied she had nothing to do with" the case.[1190] Sandberg
wrote that he thought it might have been possible that the woman
in question was actually Myra Hacker.[1191]

[1187] Silken, Maurice. Letter from Maurice Silken to Mr. C. A. Lindbergh.
October 1, 1934. New Jersey State Police Museum and Learning Center
Archives.
[1188] Sandberg, E. Special Agent. Division of Investigation. USBOI Report.
Unknown Subjects. Kidnaping and Murder of Charles A. Lindbergh,
Jr. July 24, 1934. New Jersey State Police Museum and Learning Center
Archives.
[1189] Ibid.
[1190] Sandberg, E. Special Agent, DOI (FBI). United States Bureau of
Investigation Report. Kidnaping and Murder of Charles A. Lindbergh
Jr. August 14, 1934. New Jersey State Police Museum and Learning
Center Archives.
[1191] Ibid.

There was even more information which was revealed just prior to the Hauptmann execution. Governor Hoffman sent William Lewis over to New York on April 2, 1936, to locate then get a complete statement from Silken about everything he had to say. This statement included information about the March 7th event. Here he clearly misremembered something saying that Condon "denied" what he told Detective Hickey, but as previously shown above he did not and conceded it was true. Next, and probably most interesting, he brought this new information up:

> *"On July 16th, 1932, Ben Papker, a taxi driver who occasionally worked his own cab at the corner of 181st Street and Amsterdam Avenue, told me that on that day he had driven a woman to 2974 Decatur Avenue, Bronx, at about 10:30 A.M. He told me that this woman must have been one of my stady [sic] riders, because when she got in his cab she said to him, "Are you the driver who drove me here before?" He described this woman as about 5 ft. 6 in. in height, about thirty (30) years of age, and of fair complexion, and that she paid him one dollar ($1.00) for her fare and gave him thirty cents (30¢) tip. Papker told me that she spoke very good English. This trip was made about five weeks after I had spoken to Dr. Condon, as herein related.*
>
> *Some time after this Chris Christenson, a taxi cab driver that works steadily on this corner, told me that he also drive [sic] a woman from 181st Street and Amsterdam Avenue to Dr. Condon's residence. The trip Christenson made was later than the one made by Papker, but he could not give a very good description of the woman he took, except that she spoke good English. I believe that the two latter women passengers were sent to this particular taxi stand for the purpose*

*of furnishing an alibi for the woman I had taken
from that point to Dr. Condon's home on March 7th,
1932."*[1192]

With this in mind, could it have been Myra Hacker as Keaten and
Lamb suggested to Agent Sandberg? If she did not take Silken's cab
on the morning of March 7th, then could she be the one taking the
other trips and for the purpose Silken suggested? Or was this all pure
guess-work and coincidence?

The Offer

In Hoffman's *Liberty* series, he wrote that Condon...

*"...told, at Lynn, Massachusetts, a fantastic story of
having been offered $250,000 to change his testimony
and throw the blame for the Lindbergh crime on Isidor
Fisch."*[1193]

This claim appears to be backed up by the numerous newspaper
articles which revealed Condon making these claims. One such
claim from the Associated Press quoted Condon and ran as follows:

*" "I have been approached several times with offers
of sums—really great sums—if I would go to the
authorities to have Hauptmann taken off that death*

[1192] Silken, Maurice. Statement of Mr. Maurice Silken, 26 Post Avenue,
Apartment 32, New York City, N. Y. Signed and sworn to William Lewis.
April 2, 1936. New Jersey State Police Museum and Learning Center
Archives.

[1193] Hoffman, Harold Giles. *The Crime - The Case - The Challenge (What
Was Wrong with the Lindbergh Case?)*, Original Manuscript: Unedited &
Uncorrected, circa 1937. Page 109. New Jersey State Police Museum and
Learning Center Archives.

> *sentence," he declared. "One man, in fact, approached*
> *me, and afterwards the offers ranged from $10,000 to*
> *$250,000."*

> *Dr. Condon added that he believed Hauptmann to*
> *be guilty of the crime and that he would not favor*
> *commutation of his sentence."*[1194]

Upon hearing about these stories, Governor Hoffman sent telegrams
and looked to confirm that Condon had actually said these things.
A reporter for the Lynn Item replied by Western Union that he had
interviewed Condon, and yes, he did make statements that he had
been offered a large sum of money by a man who "*had a prominent
part in*" a "*hockey game in New York*" as well as "*several offers before
that.*"[1195] Condon claimed the man associated with hockey "*assured*"
him the "*money*" would be "*paid in cash*" and also that several
other reporters had interviewed Condon and they all would say the
same.[1196]

Once Condon caught wind that Governor Hoffman had sent
telegrams asking for confirmation that he had made statements about
the bribes he quickly back peddled. According to his "spokesman:"

> *"A man came up to my real estate office in City Island*
> *on Long Island and said he was a hockey player. He*
> *was slightly inebriated and he began to sympathize*
> *with Hauptmann. He said he felt that Hauptmann*
> *was being persecuted and declared: 'It's a shame. You*
> *ought to be on the other side. It would be worth a*

[1194] Associated Press Clipping. Untitled. December 13, 1935. New Jersey
State Police Museum and Learning Center Archives.
[1195] Peabody, Arthur B. Western Union. Received at NAM67 2/163-. Undated.
New Jersey State Police Museum and Learning Center Archives.
[1196] Ibid.

quarter of a million dollars for you if you were on the other side."[1197]

Condon also claimed, through this same "spokesman," that he did not know the man's identity or take the offer seriously and considered it just flippant talk.[1198] However, the Lynn Item reported that those in the audience during his vaudeville appearance in Lynn, as well as reporters who interviewed him, took exception to this explanation....

> "...*they said, he made the comment apparently in a serious vein and did not make any reference to any "inebriate." Local newspapermen who also interviewed him and who claim he made the statements before them, said that he not only appeared serious in referring to the alleged "bribe," but also declared that the offers came in telephone conversations and by letter.*"[1199]

Fred J. Tangney of the Union Leader in Lynn wrote a letter to William C. Conklin in response to the Governor's request. He backed up what was written in the Lynn Item and even pointed out that paper was "*friendly to that theatre, from a business viewpoint, whereas a statement from me alone might be misinterpreted based on the fact that we would not accept advertising from the theatre that sponsored "Jafsie's visit.*"[1200] Tangney also wrote:

[1197] ""Jafsie" States Bribe Offer Was By An Inebriate." *Lynn Item*. January 8, (1936). New Jersey State Police Museum and Learning Center Archives.

[1198] Ibid.

[1199] Ibid.

[1200] Tangney, Fred J. <u>Letter from Fred J. Tangney to Wm. C. Conklin</u>. January 9, 1936. New Jersey State Police Museum and Learning Center Archives.

"It was not necessary to seek out Dr. Condon for an interview while he was in Lynn, as he made almost daily appearances outside the theatre, giving statements and answering questions."[1201]

John F. Condon
(Courtesy NJSP Museum)

[1201]   Ibid.

John F. Condon
(Courtesy NJSP Museum)

6

Hans Mueller

Hans Mueller was Maria Mueller's husband, and Maria was Anna Hauptmann's niece. Very little has been mentioned about Mueller (if anything) in most of the books on this case, a fact which makes it doubly important to mention him here.

On September 19, 1934, Mueller arrived at the Hauptmann apartment. He spoke to both his wife and Anna in German and the conversation was overheard by Det. Sgt. Haussling of the N.J. State Police but he reported that *"nothing of interest was spoken."*[1202] Mueller claimed to Haussling that he had known Hauptmann for seven years, worked as a waiter at Schwartz's Restaurant, and was the father of a three year old child. The next thing he told him was very interesting:

> *"Muller* [sic] *advanced the opinion that the $20.00 gold bill found on Hauptmann had been received by Hauptmann when he was collecting gold certificates*

[1202] Haussling, E. A. Det. Sgt. New Jersey State Police. New Jersey State Police Report. <u>Guard at home of B. Richard Hauptmann, 1279 East 222nd Street, Bronx, New York</u>. September 19, 1934. New Jersey State Police Museum and Learning Center Archives.

> *about the time of the gold embargo and he further*
> *stated that Hauptmann told him he had about*
> *$400.00 worth of gold notes* [sic] *Muller* [sic] *also*
> *stated that he was indebted to Hauptmann for about*
> *$175.00."*[1203]

I've always viewed this as suspicious. How did Mueller know anything about Hauptmann's gold note collecting habits? Next, his "debt" to Hauptmann could be explained by any number of reasons, one being to protect him from any accusation in the event Hauptmann were ever caught. Certainly, as I will later prove, Hauptmann had considered what he'd say if indeed he was ever picked up. This alone showed he prepared for the occurrence of certain negative possibilities. The next day at noon, Haussling went to Schwartz's Restaurant, picked up Mueller, then brought him to police headquarters on Greenwich Street for questioning. The Mueller apartment was searched, and certain memorandum books and business cards were confiscated.[1204]

On September 21, 1934, at 6:30 AM Anna and Hans Mueller arrived back at the Hauptmann apartment. Anna told authorities that they had been released and allowed to go home. Maria had been watching Manfred, along with her own daughter Ruth, and they were all together now. Police noted the condition of the apartment, which was in complete disarray due to their searches, and suggested they depart for the Mueller's apartment on Marion Avenue. As they were gathering belongings, Hans collapsed into

---

[1203] Ibid.

[1204] Haussling, E. A. Det. Sgt. New Jersey State Police. New Jersey State Police Report. <u>Apprehension of and search of apartment of Hans Muller, 2701 Marion Avenue, Bronx, N.Y.</u> September 20, 1934. New Jersey State Police Museum and Learning Center Archives.

a state of unconsciousness.[1205] Police called for an ambulance, administered first aid, and Mueller *"came around"* in *"about five minutes."*[1206] According to the report, it was learned from the hospital that Mueller had suffered a dislocated shoulder from his fall, and had been diagnosed as having a *"seizure"* as a result of *"an epileptic fit."*[1207] I've always wondered to myself whether or not Mueller simply passed out due to the stress. And if so, was it because of his worry for Hauptmann? Or possibly even for himself? But that is just speculation, and the report as written seemed to show that the man was an epileptic. Nothing in it shows any suspicion towards him; in fact, police seemed more worried that his condition might be attributed to them, so it was made clear this event occurred when none of their ranks were in the apartment.

It was later that evening that Mueller, along with Anna and Maria, were picked up again and brought to District Attorney Foley's office for more questioning. However, something written in a memo the very next day showed the FBI was already suspicious of Mueller:

> *"With regard to Hans Mueller, I told Mr. Clegg that this is the brother-in-law who came in and spoke German to her* [Anna Hauptmann] *the other night and told her what to say when she was questioned. Mr. Clegg stated this was correct and also he was permitted by the police to walk out without any interference."*[1208]

[1205] Breed, P. M. Special Agent, And Kavanaugh, J. S. Special Agent, Division of Investigation. Memorandum For The File. <u>Re: Unknown Subjects Kidnaping And Murder of Charles A. Lindbergh, Jr</u>. September 21, 1934. New Jersey State Police Museum and Learning Center Archives.

[1206] Ibid.

[1207] Ibid.

[1208] Tamm, E. A. Division of Investigation. <u>Memorandum For The Director</u>. September 22, 1934. National Archives at College Park Maryland.

While everyone was at the DA's office at this time, the Mueller apartment was empty, and Detective James Cashman took the opportunity to search it again.[1209] It was specifically noted that this residence was only *"one and one half blocks removed from the residence of Dr. John F. Condon."*[1210] While Cashman was searching he found a *"small pocket diary"* that had been…

> "…*wrapped in a portion of the outer page of the New York Evening Journal, issue March 25, 1932, the top headlines being "***STOR NEGOTIATES FOR LINDY BABY."*[1211]

Police seized all newly discovered relevant items and documents from the apartment and brought them down to the station for investigation. Among the documentation seized were indications that Mueller had a criminal record, and further investigation revealed he *"was arrested several times"* for violations of the *"Prohibition Laws."*[1212] Also among the mountain of items seized on this occasion was an interesting item torn from the "Q" page of his address book. Written on this page was *"4U13–41"* which was Hauptmann's license plate number.[1213] Why would Mueller need to write down Hauptmann's

---

[1209] Seery, W. F. Special Agent, Division of Investigation. United State Bureau of Investigation Report. Unknown Subjects. <u>Kidnaping And Murder of Charles A. Lindbergh Jr</u>. September 24, 1934. New Jersey State Police Museum and Learning Center Archives.

[1210] Ibid.

[1211] Ibid.

[1212] Dickerson, J. H. Detective, New Jersey State Police. New Jersey State Police Report. December 29, 1934. New Jersey State Police Museum and Learning Center Archives.

[1213] Purdy, Robert "Rab." Email to Author. November 10, 2003.

license plate number? Police made a note of it which seemed to indicate their interest in this as well.[1214]

As Police combed through this material they searched the addresses that were found anywhere on any item they collected. They were also looking into Hauptmann in the exact same way with police checking through his Address, Financial Logs, and Memorandum books. Anything mentioned was to be investigated. While thumbing through one such item, police were surprised to see a notation written:

> *"Capt. H. Mueller, N.Y.", "Marquita, c/o Harlem Yacht Club, City Island, N.Y."*[1215]

Was this the "Boad Nelly" connection to Hauptmann the police sought? Or was it the Hauptmann/Condon connection the police were also seeking at that time? As police investigated, it took them to Johnson's Boat Yard on City Island. There they met Mr. Johnson who informed them that he remembered the *"Marquita"* as being a 50 foot sail boat which had been turned into a *"party boat."* He remembered that Hans Mueller was the *"caretaker"* and called himself the *"captain."*[1216] Police then began to follow up any leads they had concerning Mueller with more interest, and they also wanted to obtain any and all information regarding his connection to the Marquita. One such lead took them to his old apartment on

---

[1214] Seery, W. F. Special Agent, Division of Investigation. United State Bureau of Investigation Report. <u>Unknown Subjects. Kidnaping And Murder of Charles A. Lindbergh Jr.</u> September 24, 1934. New Jersey State Police Museum and Learning Center Archives.

[1215] Zapolsky, A. Sgt. New Jersey State Police. New Jersey State Police Report. <u>Investigation re: Bruno Richard Hauptmann, re: Lindbergh Case.</u> November 13, 1934. New Jersey State Police Museum and Learning Center Archives.

[1216] Ibid.

300 East 159th Street where he had resided from the summer of 1933 to May of 1934. Police interviewed the former janitor, Ferdinand Profitlich, who told police a simple story...

> "...Muellers had a party in their apartment and he had received complaints from other tenants about the noise and he went up to Mueller's apartment and asked them to quiet down, but instead Mueller became abusive and he was forced to call a policeman who ordered Mueller to quiet down, and Mueller then came down to his apartment and invited him out to settle the matter, but that he did not pay any attention and Mueller moved out of the apartment shortly after."[1217]

In the meantime, the NJSP had learned that the FBI had already conducted a thorough investigation into the transfer of title of the *"Mariquita"* [sic] which had been sold numerous times.[1218] This investigation seemed to have been done on the heels of Mueller telling Inspector Bruckman that he had worked on the *"Mariquetta"* [sic].[1219] Now, armed with Agent Austin's report, the NJSP sought out Henry Reimers who owned the boat at the time Mueller had worked on it. Reimers told police that he purchased the *"Marquita"* from Frank Lewinski of Clason Point in 1925, and that Lewinski

---

[1217] Ibid.

[1218] Austin, R. M. Special Agent, Division of Investigation. Memorandum For Special Agent T. H. Sisk. Re: Bruno Richard Hauptmann with alias and Unknown Subjects. Kidnaping and Murder of Charles A. Lindbergh Jr. October 2, 1934. New Jersey State Police Museum and Learning Center Archives.

[1219] Muller, Hans. Questioning. Questioned by Inspector Bruckman. October 1, 1934. New Jersey State Police Museum and Learning Center Archives.

recommended Mueller for the job as caretaker so he hired him.[1220] Reimers said that Mueller had been active at Clason Point spending a lot of time with a relative there. He also said that Mueller "*did not have any knowledge of navigation, and was not permitted to operate the boat*"; however, during the year "*1928 or 1929*" he had taken Mueller with him on...

> "*...boat trips to Port Washington, Hempstead Harbor, Glen Cover and other point in that direction, but at no time did they take any of Mueller's friends on these trips.*"[1221]

Police sought out Frank Lewinski but discovered he had died. However, they learned his son Alfred was residing on Clason Point so they went to interview him. Alfred told police that they sold the "*Marquita*" somewhere around 1925 to Henry Reimer.[1222] Alfred also told them that Mueller had "*jumped ship about a year previous and that he was hanging out at the Peterson Boat Yard*" and "*kept after him for a job*" so when the boat was sold he asked Reimers to hire him.[1223] He also added that "*Peterson*" was supposed to be Mueller's relative, and that Mueller "*knew nothing about navigation*" and that "*he only worked on the boat as a deck hand and doing odd jobs.*"[1224]

[1220] Zapolsky, A. Sgt. New Jersey State Police. New Jersey State Police Report. Continued report of Investigation with reference to Bruno Richard Hauptmann, re: Lindbergh Case. November 15, 1934. New Jersey State Police Museum and Learning Center Archives.

[1221] Ibid.

[1222] Leon, Samuel J. Cpl., New Jersey State Police. New Jersey State Police Report. Investigation of Frank Lewinski, Clason Point, Bronx, N. Y., who recommended Hans Mueller to Henry Reimer for a job on the boat "Marquita", re: report of Sgt. Zapolsky, dated November 15, 1934. November 21, 1934. New Jersey State Police Museum and Learning Center Archives.

[1223] Ibid.

[1224] Ibid.

Days later, police proceeded to 300 Zerega Avenue to Peterson's boatyard. There they interviewed Gustave Peterson who explained he had been at this boatyard since 1930, and before that spent seven years at Clason Point. He told police that Hans Mueller had come to his place in the spring of 1927, and that he worked for him doing "*odd jobs.*"[1225] Peterson also indicated he had not known at the time that Mueller had jumped ship, and they were related because Mueller's brother had been married to his sister back in Germany but they had since divorced. He then explained to them it was during the time that Mueller worked for him that he bought a "*motor launch*" for $15.00 from one of Peterson's customers and this event caused a serious argument between the men.[1226] This occurred because Mueller failed to pay the man, so Peterson took the $15.00 out of Mueller's pay then gave it to the customer owed the money. Mueller left his employ, actually sued him for the $15.00, and Peterson claimed he had not seen him since.[1227]

What became of the boat Mueller purchased? Had he taken it out? Was he familiar with the areas written in the "Boad Nelly" note? Unfortunately, it does not appear that police ever followed up with any of this. Something else interesting is that during the Treasury Intelligence Unit's investigation of the boat "Nellie" back in April of 1932, their investigation took them to Boston. While there, Special Agent Kelleher investigated "*Lighter Number Ten of the American Agricultural and Chemical Company*" tied to pier 45 at Mystic Wharf. During the course of that investigation he learned that a boat from New York named the "*Marguerite*" had been docked alongside of it

[1225] Leon, Samuel J. Cpl., New Jersey State Police. New Jersey State Police Report. Continuing investigation of Frank Lewinski, Clason Point, Bronx, N. Y., re: report of November 28th, 1934. November 30, 1934. New Jersey State Police Museum and Learning Center Archives.
[1226] Ibid.
[1227] Ibid.

and there had been "*suspicious movements*" observed on that boat.[1228] Although Kelleher wrote that arrangements had been made to search the "*Marguerite*" there is no further documentation about that event which I could find. Was the "Marguerite" the "Marquita?" It seems rather unlikely. Mueller had left the boat when Reimers still owned it, and he had no idea that it had been sold to Fred Jenks on April 11, 1930.[1229] In fact, Mueller was under the impression that Reimers was still the owner when he was being interviewed in 1934.[1230] However, police weren't finished learning more about Mueller as it related to something else....

In December of that year, police had a new source of information: Charles Schleser. He was a "mole" for Attorney General Wilentz. It was at his urging that Schleser pretended to be a Defense Witness and attended meetings held friendly to the Defense so that he could learn everything that was being discussed then report it back to the State.[1231] There was one tip he provided that had something to do with Hauptmann's car accident.... Since there was evidence of blood on the ransom money, Schleser suggested perhaps either Hauptmann or Mueller had bled on that money because of that accident. As a result, Schleser brought police to see Martin Kunz, who had worked at the "*York Bar and Grill*" from September of

---

[1228] Kelleher, D. A. Special Agent, Internal Revenue Service. Letter from Dave Kelleher to Special Agent in Charge. April 14, 1932. New Jersey State Police Museum and Learning Center Archives.

[1229] Austin, R. M. Special Agent, Division of Investigation. Memorandum For Special Agent T. H. Sisk. Re: Bruno Richard Hauptmann with alias and Unknown Subjects. Kidnaping and Murder of Charles A. Lindbergh Jr. October 2, 1934. New Jersey State Police Museum and Learning Center Archives.

[1230] Muller, Hans. Questioning. Questioned by Inspector Bruckman. October 1, 1934. New Jersey State Police Museum and Learning Center Archives.

[1231] Gardner, Lloyd C. June 2004. *The Case That Never Dies*. Rutgers University Press. Page 262-5.

1932 until February of 1934 when it closed. Kunz told police that he had worked there with Mueller, and in fact, along with another waiter named *"Paul,"* he and *"Hans Mueller contemplated buying the restaurant"* and entered into negotiations with one of the owners.[1232] It was during these negotiations that Kunz claimed Mueller had *"between one and two thousand dollars on his person which Mueller contended came from his rich uncle who was speculating in stocks."*[1233] If this story was true, did Mueller really believe that's where the money came from, or was he actually involved with Hauptmann concerning ransom money in some way? With regard to the car accident, Kunz told them Mueller explained to him that no one in the car had been injured. Suddenly, Kunz was the source that kept on giving.... He let the cops know that Mueller...

> *"...knew all the "gorillas" of the neighborhood and when pressed with some of the names he gave the following: Tobin and his brother, John Basterbo, a bookmaker, and Coxie. Kunz stated that Hauptmann always came into the place alone and when Fisch frequented the resort he was generally in the company of 3 or 4 other German Jews, but never in the company of Hauptmann."*[1234]

And Kunz was not finished giving information. He told investigators that owner of the York Bar and Grill *"Samuel Kirsh at one time saw about $3,000 in gold certificates in the possession of Mueller."*[1235] Kunz also said that *"Mueller once owned a cabaret on East 86ʰ Street known as the "Diele."* And lastly, Kunz stated...

[1232] Haussling, E. A. Det. Sgt. New Jersey State Police. New Jersey State Police Report. Continued investigation re: Isidor Fisch. December 27, 1934. New Jersey State Police Museum and Learning Center Archives.

[1233] Ibid.

[1234] Ibid.

[1235] Ibid.

*"...that sometime last winter Mueller had told him
that he had bought a gun from a former bar tender at
the "Diele", he did not describe the gun."*[1236]

The Gun

It was during the search of Hauptmann's garage on September 26,
1934, that police decided to move the bench away from the right
side and knock out the various pieces of 2 x 4s in the wall that were
used to reinforce the building. One such piece showed signs of
having been previously removed. Police pried this piece out which
revealed that it had been used as a "safe" to conceal tightly rolled up
Lindbergh Ransom Money. This board also concealed a....

*"...small automatic revolver, nickel plated, stamped
"Liliput" Kal. 4.25 Model 1926 fully loaded with
seven shells, trigger guard number 2975 with one ivory
butt grip, the left grip being missing."*[1237]

This gun was immediately brought over to District Attorney Foley's
office, and it was shown to Hauptmann during his questioning at
11:45 AM on the very same day. Hauptmann made it clear that
he kept the existence of the ransom money concealed there from

---

[1236] Ibid.

[1237] Bornmann, Lewis Detective, New Jersey State Police. New Jersey State
Police Report. <u>Searching apartment of Bruno Richard Hauptmann's
Home and garage located at 1279 East 222nd Street, Bronx, N. Y. for
evidence in connection with the kidnapping of the Lindbergh baby on
March 1, 1932</u>. September 25, 1934. New Jersey State Police Museum
and Learning Center Archives. (Note: This is a report covering multiple
days beginning with September 25.)

authorities <u>because</u> of the presence of that gun, and he also told them it had *"always"* been loaded and that he *"never used it."*[1238]

> [Foley]: *What did the pistol have to do with the money?*

> [Hauptmann]: *Nothing, but I was afraid about the pistol.*

> [Q]: *How long did you have the pistol?*

> [A]: *About 10 years.*

> [Q]: *Where did you get it?*

> [A]: *I bought it from a German fellow.*

> [Q]: *Did you buy it in America?*

> [A]: *Yes.*[1239]

During Hauptmann's extradition hearing this pistol was brought up again. Once again Hauptmann explained that the reason he did not reveal where the additional ransom money was had to do with

[1238] Hauptmann, Bruno Richard. Statement. Made to District Attorney Foley, Inspector Bruckman, County Detective Hanley, Captain Lamb, Lieut. Keaten, Joseph Lanagan, Ass't Attorney General. September 26, 1934 at 11:45 A. M. New Jersey State Police Museum and Learning Center Archives.

[1239] Ibid.

that pistol being in the same place.[1240] Eventually we come to an interesting question posed by Wilentz;

> [Q]: *That was not a hunting gun, was it? You did not use that for hunting, did you?*

> [A]: *Yes, I did.*[1241]

That is a hard one to believe, especially since he told Foley he never used it. There appears to be another time where Hauptmann lied about this gun during this hearing:

> [Q]: *When did you put that gun away?*

> [A]: *Thirty-one.*

> [Q]: *Thirty-one what?*

> [A]: *1931.*

> [Q]: *What month?*

> [A]: *October.*

> [Q]: *You put that gun away with the bullets?*

> [A]: *Yes.*

[1240] Hauptmann, Bruno Richard. Testimony. The People State of New York ex rel. Bruno Richard Hauptmann, v. John Hanley, Sheriff of Bronx County. <u>Supreme Court, Bronx County, Special Term Part I</u>. page 70. October 15, 1934. New Jersey State Police Museum and Learning Center Archives.

[1241] Ibid.

[Q]: *Is that when you fixed up that board that is Exhibit B for identification?*

[A]: *Yes.*[1242]

Unless there was a misunderstanding of some kind, and there does not appear to be, this cannot be true. Hauptmann did not move into his apartment until October 12, 1931.[1243] It wasn't until "*four or six weeks*" later that Hauptmann built that garage.[1244] Under re-direct by his attorney, more information about this pistol was learned:

[Fawcett]: *Regarding the revolver, will you be good enough to tell us why you hid that revolver in the garage?*

[A]: *I did not have any license to carry a revolver, and I did not like to keep it in the house, and I did not like to throw it away either, so I concealed it in the garage.*

[Q]: *And did you like to tell the name of the person you got that revolver from?*

[A]: *No, I cannot.*

[Q]: *I say you did not want to tell that did you?*

[1242] Ibid. Page 71.

[1243] Bornmann, L. J. Detective, New Jersey State Police. New Jersey State Police Report. <u>Interviewing Max Rauch, joint owner with his mother of the premises occupied by Bruno Richard Hauptmann at 1279 East 222nd Street, Bronx, New York</u>. October 11, 1934. New Jersey State Police Museum and Learning Center Archives.

[1244] Zapolsky, A. Sgt. New Jersey State Police. New Jersey State Police Report. <u>Continued investigation re: Bruno Richard Hauptmann, re: Lindbergh Case</u>. November 26, 1934. New Jersey State Police Museum and Learning Center Archives.

[A]: *No, I cannot remember; I bought it on 86th Street someplace.*

[Q]: *You did not want to get the person in trouble that you bought that revolver from, did you?*[1245]

Hauptmann would later use his autobiography as a way to "clear up" the matter of this gun. It is there that he explained the gun was purchased in "1930" after planning to go on his cross-country trip.[1246] He wrote further:

> *"I thought that some weapon was necessary because we intended to sleep in the open. I did know that it was against the law to have a pistol, but I felt conscience-free because I had no criminal thoughts."*[1247]

Hauptmann wrote that once he had hidden the gun inside the piece of wood that it never left *"this place."*

> *"At first I wanted to hide it in the house but my wife would not permit me. She told me to throw it away, but I did not want to do that."*[1248]

[1245] Hauptmann, Bruno Richard. Testimony. The People State of New York ex rel. Bruno Richard Hauptmann, v. John Hanley, Sheriff of Bronx County. Supreme Court, Bronx County, Special Term Part I. page 102. October 15, 1934. New Jersey State Police Museum and Learning Center Archives.

[1246] Hauptmann, Richard. Autobiography: Unedited & Uncorrected (Translated). The Story of My Life. Page 148. May 4, 1935. New Jersey State Police Museum and Learning Center Archives.

[1247] Ibid.

[1248] Ibid. Page 165.

Clemens Kaiser

On November 9, 1934, Detective Patterson, along with Detective James Cashman of the NYPD, noticed a car parked outside of the Hauptmann apartment. They went over to find Hans Mueller there, and asked him who owned the car in question. Mueller told police it *"was owned by a friend of his."*[1249] Police traced the tag, and it came back to a woman named *"Gretal Kaiser, 2800 Bainbridge Avenue, Bronx, N.Y."*[1250] Once the information was turned over to Lt. Keaten he ordered an immediate investigation be conducted on this individual. They quickly learned that Gretal was married to Clemens Kaiser. Their investigation into Kaiser led them to Toms River, New Jersey, where they interviewed a man named William Van Kirk.

Van Kirk was the owner of *"Capt. Kidd's Inn"* located in Money Island, New Jersey. He employed Rudy Schmidt on the weekends and Schmidt sometimes brought his nephew, Clemens Kaiser, with him to *"help out."*[1251] In November 1933, Schmidt left for other employment but Van Kirk hired Kaiser as a bartender and his wife to work in their household from December 1933 to June 1934. Van Kirk grew suspicious of Kaiser, who only made $10 a week, yet seemed to be doing a lot of...

[1249] Patterson, Claude Det. New Jersey State Police. New Jersey State Police Report. Investigation of Bruno Richard Hauptmann and associates, re: Lindbergh Case. November 9, 1934. New Jersey State Police Museum and Learning Center Archives.

[1250] Ibid.

[1251] Van Kirk, William. Statement. Made to Sgt. John Wallace, New Jersey State Police. November 14, 1934. New Jersey State Police Museum and Learning Center Archives.

> *"...running around in the car through the state of Jersey and New York City and seemed to be able to sport a little in the speakeasy's and cabaret's."*[1252]

Van Kirk would explain to the NJSP what else he learned about Kaiser while he was in his employ. Kaiser told Van Kirk that when he returned to New York...

> *"...about five years ago" he brought back "with him two small German Luger guns. One of these he left his uncle Rudy have, and later returned the gun too [sic] Clements [sic], while he was here, and Clemens showed it to me about March."*[1253]

Sometime in October 1934, Kaiser returned to Money Island and visited Van Kirk along with his wife and his in-laws who were visiting the country. Van Kirk noticed Kaiser was extremely *"nervous and shaken up"* so he asked him what the problem was. Kaiser told him *"that he had men trailing him in New York City, around his home and around where he was employed as a bartender."*[1254]

> *"He said, "I want to speak to you about the gun I showed you." He stated he got afraid of the men trailing him, and was afraid they would search his home and person, he said he threw the gun in the river because he was afraid they would find this gun and connect it with the other gun like it, to which I ask [sic], what other one? [sic] and he replied the one he gave Hauptmann [sic] nephew and in turn he said Hauptmann [sic] nephew sold it to Hauptmann. He visits Hauptmann's nephew frequently, most every day, also they had*

[1252] Ibid.

[1253] Ibid.

[1254] Ibid.

visited Hauptmann's house, but I don't recall him ever mentioning Hauptmann's nephew [sic] name, but they are all supposed to be very close friends. He also told me that the defense wanted him to take the stand on behalf of Hauptmann and testify, and I asked him what questions, and he would not say, and I told him, if it was not the truth, not to do it, and he replied that they had nothing on Hauptmann and he did not think they could convict him. I then told him if that was all he had on his chest, to go to Col. Schwarzkopf at Trenton, N.J. and tell him all he knew about the guns and the Hauptmann case, otherwise they would get him into it sooner or later and deport him back to Germany on account of smuggling the guns into the country."[1255]

Van Kirk told police he was *"willing to testify for the State if needed."*[1256]

On November 20, 1934, Clemens Kaiser was picked up and brought to the Greenwich Street Station for questioning. While being grilled, he was asked:

[Q]: *Now did you have any conversation with William Van Kirk and will you tell me what your conversation was?*

[A]: *So far as I remember I told Mr. Van Kirk that I came into possession of two German guns in 1930 which arrived in a Christmas present package from my mother. I told him that I had one of these guns in my possession*

[1255] Ibid.

[1256] Wallace, John Sgt.-Det. New Jersey State Police. New Jersey State Police Report. <u>Investigation of Clemens Kaiser, formerly of Longfellow Avenue, Money Island, Toms River, N.J.</u> November 14, 1934. New Jersey State Police Museum and Learning Center Archives.

*in New Jersey when the Hauptmann case came up –
when Hauptmann was arrested in other words. That I
disposed of it in the Bronx, New York. That is all.*"[1257]

[Q]: *That is the only conversation you had with him?*

[A]: *After that he advised me I should go to Colonel
Schwarzkopf which I did not think was necessary.
That is all I remember about the conversation.*

[Q]: *Do you remember telling Van Kirk the story about
the gun which Hauptmann had hidden in his garage?*

[A]: *Yes I do.*

[Q]: *Now you do remember – Now will you tell me
what disposition was made of the gun – whose hands it
was in until it arrived in Hauptmann's possession – as
far as you know?*

[A]: *As far as I know both guns came into my possession
as I stated before, in a Christmas package which came
from the other side. Through a defect in the wrapper of
a little package inside I detected the package contained
two guns, German made Lilliput 4.25. I was supposed
to send this package without opening, to a Chicago
address. My uncle advised me not to send this package
through the mail and I followed his advice and kept
one for myself and one I gave to my uncle. This was in
1930. I kept the gun which was in my possession until
1931 and then gave it to a bartender which worked in
the place of my uncle on 86th Street.*

[1257] Kaiser, Clemens G. J. Statement. Made to Sgt. John Wallace. November
20, 1934. New Jersey State Police Museum and Learning Center Archives.

[Q]: *What is his name – the name of the bartender who received the gun?*

[A]: *The only name I knew was Martin.*[1258]

He told Wallace he gave "Martin" the gun in the beginning of March 1931. It is so painfully obvious that Kaiser was lying that it's almost hard to read. And to be sure, Sgt. Wallace wasn't being fooled either. He asked more questions about *"Martin,"* learning that he was between *"35 and 40"* but that unfortunately, Kaiser *"never saw him again after that."*[1259] However, Kaiser told Wallace that it was after Hauptmann was arrested, to his surprise, that he learned that *"Martin"* had given the gun to *"Hans Muller* [sic] *and from Hans Muller* [sic] *it came into the possession of Hauptmann."*[1260] The only way Kaiser found out about this was because Mueller told him. Kaiser admitted being introduced to Hauptmann by Hans Mueller in August of 1934 and that he had only ever been around him *"twice."* Kaiser claimed Mueller told him that Hauptmann had lent Fisch money, but that he never told Van Kirk he was willing to testify for the Defense. Finally, Kaiser denied knowing when Mueller gave over this gun to Hauptmann.[1261] According to the reports, both Kaiser and his wife were released but ordered to return to Police Headquarters at 1:00 PM the next day on the 21st.[1262] Mr. and Mrs. Kaiser arrived as instructed, and Gretel was then questioned.

1258 Ibid.
1259 Ibid.
1260 Ibid.
1261 Ibid.
1262 Wallace, John Sgt. New Jersey State Police. New Jersey State Police Report. <u>Investigation of Clemens & Gretal Kaiser, 2800 Bainbridge Ave. Bronx, N.Y. formerly of Money Island, Toms River, N.J.</u> November 23, 1934. New Jersey State Police Museum and Learning Center Archives.

> *"A verbal statement was taken by Mrs. Gretel Kaiser*
> *& she advised that she had seen a small gun while she*
> *& her husband were living in Elberon, N.J. in 1932.*
> *She stated while she was in Germany she remembers*
> *Clemens writing to his Mother & stating that he had*
> *never received the Xmas Package & later he wrote &*
> *stated that he received it & he had thrown the two guns*
> *in the River."*[1263]

Clemens was once again interviewed and asked to explain what he was going to testify to on behalf of the Defense, but he once again denied that he had agreed to do so. He did, however, admit to meeting Harry Whitney at Hans Mueller's home after Hauptmann's arrest.[1264] There is no evidence that the police made any effort to recover the gun. As a result, it probably lies at the bottom of the East River to this day.[1265]

I could never understand why Mueller and Kaiser were not arrested. Here the police had evidence of a crime and that both were involved. Despite Kaiser's eventual admission in giving up Mueller as the man who got the gun, it is clear he did not tell the total truth. Since he was willing to flip on Mueller, it seems obvious that with a little more pressure, Kaiser would have eventually told them everything that he knew. On top of that, there are clear indicators that Mueller

---

[1263] Ibid.

[1264] Ibid. (Whitney was "related" to Anna and acted as an Investigator for Fawcett. Although Fawcett would deny this connection, there are sources which prove they had that relationship at one time).

[1265] Wallace, John Det. Sgt. New Jersey State Police. New Jersey State Police Report. <u>Investigation of one Gretel Kaiser, owner of Ford Tudor Sedan, Registration # ON-2882 N.J. residing at 2800 Bainbridge Ave. Bronx, N.Y. formerly living on Longfellow Ave, Money Island, Toms River, N.J.</u> November 13, 1934. New Jersey State Police Museum and Learning Center Archives.

potentially knew much more about what was going on than what he was telling police. Why didn't authorities use this gun charge as leverage? It is interesting to note that neither of the men testified in Flemington. Perhaps a deal was struck to ensure neither of these men would testify for the Defense?

Anna, Hans Mueller, and Maria Mueller
outside of court in Flemington, NJ circa 1935
(Author's Collection)

"Gun found in Hauptmann's garage"
(Courtesy NJSP Museum)

7

Vacations, Finances, and Ransom Money

The California Trip

Something that has always struck me as "funny" was Hauptmann's cross-country trip to California. It was something he had always wanted to do, and in fact, had attempted to do after he and Anna were married. Yet in 1931 Hauptmann left his job despite the fact the economy was in the tank and work was almost impossible to find. It was at that time that Hauptmann decided to buy a new car and take that trip. He also gave up his apartment and placed all of his belongings into storage. The Prosecution's position on this event was that despite the fact his...

> "...financial reserves were running at a low ebb in 1931, he nevertheless did not hesitate to use up the last of their savings on an automobile pleasure trip to California in that year because he was expecting to

> *recoup his fortunes in the near future by obtaining the*
> *$50,000 ransom payment from Lindbergh.*"[1266]

This is a major eye-opening observation. It would mean Hauptmann was so sure of his success, that even before it happened, he would risk financial ruin in the months leading up to the very crime itself. To me that doesn't make any sense. If he were to send himself into ruin, how could he carry out a plot while homeless? However, it does seem to indicate that he was taking this trip at that time as a sort of "bucket list" event. Not a good sign to anyone who may believe Hauptmann was completely innocent. But, if it's an indicator of guilt, then it shows a commitment to the crime – at that very point in time. Furthermore, while the Prosecution seemed to think he was spending money in anticipation of an event, could this expenditure instead be an indicator that he may have already come into money? Since I've always believed people were hired to participate in this crime, it doesn't seem farfetched to believe those agreeing to participate had been given something up front prior to the event. To further support this theory, here again is Robert Peacock's position which I believe backs up the idea:

> *"One of his notes stated – and he repeated these words*
> *to Condon – 'this kidnapping was planned a year*
> *already." How true this was.*"[1267]

So how can this be reconciled with the idea that Hauptmann, having planned the crime for a year, would strike out to Hopewell when the family was not supposed to be there? The answer is an obvious one: he either had "help" from the inside or, alternatively, he was

---

[1266] Peacock, Robert. *Guilty As Hell – At Last, The Truth About The Hauptmann Case.* Manuscript: Unpublished and Undated (1935?). Pages 47-8. New Jersey State Police Museum and Learning Center Archives.

[1267] Ibid. Page 40.

somehow assisting someone on the inside. It can only be one or the other if what Peacock writes is true.[1268]

In a quick review of this event: On March 3, 1931, that Hauptmann walked into Williamsbridge Motors and wound up placing an order for a new Dodge Sedan by leaving a down payment of $27.00 in cash with the balance of $710.00 due upon delivery of the car.[1269] According to the salesman Victor Montauari, he originally wanted to buy a "clean used car" but went with the new Dodge after he was told no used cars were available.[1270] The car was eventually delivered to Hauptmann on March 10th and he paid the balance in cash at that time.[1271] The day before, Hauptmann had withdrawn $640.00 from his account at Central Savings Bank leaving his balance on this date at $371.74.[1272] While it's impossible to say this withdrawal was for the car, I do believe it's a reasonable conclusion to draw. So this purchase does not seem to show added wealth directly.

Next, while working for Alfred Grizzle on a job as a carpenter, Hauptmann informed him a week before finishing he wouldn't be

[1268] See *TDC Volume I*, pages 88-9.
[1269] Zapolsky, A. Sgt. New Jersey State Police. New Jersey State Police Report. Report of continued investigation concerning Bruno Richard Hauptmann, re: Lindbergh Case. November 9, 1934. New Jersey State Police Museum and Learning Center Archives.
[1270] Zapolsky, A. Sgt. New Jersey State Police. New Jersey State Police Report. Report of continued investigation concerning Bruno Richard Hauptmann, re: Lindbergh Case. November 10, 1934. New Jersey State Police Museum and Learning Center Archives.
[1271] Zapolsky, A. Sgt. New Jersey State Police. New Jersey State Police Report. Report of continued investigation concerning Bruno Richard Hauptmann, re: Lindbergh Case. November 9, 1934. New Jersey State Police Museum and Learning Center Archives
[1272] Hauptmann, Anna & Richard. Central Savings Bank Card for transactions from 3/17/30 thru 12/3/31. (Note: Provided to me by Researcher Rab Purdy who obtained it from the NJSP Archives.)

able to stop down to see him on Saturday to pick up his pay because he was leaving on a trip to California. He told him:

> *"I have a sister I haven't seen in 12 years, and now I saved up a little money and I bought the car and I am going to make the trip out there to see her since I have a little money."*[1273]

If this is true, then his savings account does not back him up. However, his wife does. A couple of months before this trip Anna told her friend Louise Wollenberg that they had a savings of *"about ten or twelve thousand dollars."*[1274] During the trial Hauptmann was asked by Ed Reilly about how much cash he had prior to his trip. He answered that he estimated his cash at home totaled about $4,000 while his total in the bank, again he could not exactly recall, but believed it was about $500, saying he believed the grand total between the two to be "more" than $5,000.[1275] When confronted by the Prosecution that there was no reference to the cash in the house in his books, Hauptmann made the claim this was money he was hiding from his wife.[1276] Was he saying this to protect his wife, or was it true? If it was true, how then could what Anna said to Mrs. Wollenberg also be true? As he was pressed further about this extra cash in the house, it was developed from Hauptmann that he kept it

---

[1273] Grizzle, Alfred A. Statement. Made to Assistant District Attorney Breslin, Officer Albrecht, N.J. Sate Police, Det. Wallace, N.Y. Police and Stenographer King. November 5, 1934. New Jersey State Police Museum and Learning Center Archives.

[1274] Seykora, J. E. Special Agent, DOI (FBI). Division of Investigation Report. Bruno Richard Hauptmann, with alias and Unknown Subjects; Kidnaping and Murder of Charles A. Lindbergh, Jr. October 11, 1934. New Jersey State Police Museum and Learning Center Archives.

[1275] Hauptmann, Bruno Richard. Testimony. The State of New Jersey vs. Bruno Richard Hauptmann, Hunterdon County Court of Oyer and Terminer, page 2430, 1935. New Jersey State Law Library.

[1276] Ibid. page 2569.

in a locked trunk, at the bottom, concealed under some blankets.[1277] Hauptmann further claimed that, as a rule, he was not spending that particular stash.[1278] In examining his finances, Treasury Agent Frank used the mortgage, stock, and bank records to show a grand total of the Hauptmann's assets to be worth exactly $4,814.76 on 1/1/32.[1279] For those counting this amount, combined with the 4K in cash Hauptmann claimed, it put their net worth very near the amount Anna was telling Mrs. Wollenberg about a couple of weeks prior to their trip.

Before they left for California, Hauptmann said, he removed this cash from the trunk then placed it into a locked satchel which was left with Anna's uncle, Fred Gleiforst, for safekeeping; he also claimed Gleiforst had no idea what was in it.[1280] In a strange way, this sounds a lot like the "Fisch Story" in that a trusted person left a package full of cash with an unsuspecting individual. Gleiforst would also figure into Hauptmann's stock trading when, in 1933, investments were made on his behalf which resulted in small but favorable earnings.[1281] This does, at the very least, display a degree of trust both men had in each other.

[1277] Ibid.

[1278] Ibid. page 2626.

[1279] Frank, William E. Special Agent, United States Treasury Department. Internal Revenue Service Special Report. Financial Activities of Bruno Richard Hauptmann and his wife, Anna Hauptmann, neé Schoeffler, 1279 East 222nd Street, Bronx, New York City. January 8, 1935. Page 8. New Jersey State Police Museum and Learning Center Archives.

[1280] Hauptmann, Bruno Richard. Testimony. The State of New Jersey vs. Bruno Richard Hauptmann, Hunterdon County Court of Oyer and Terminer, pages 2781-2. 1935. New Jersey State Law Library.

[1281] Genau, J. A. Special Agent, United States Bureau of Investigation (FBI). USBOI Report. Kidnaping And Murder Of Charles A. Lindbergh, Jr. October 8, 1934. New Jersey State Police Museum and Learning Center Archives.

Accompanying them on this trip was Hauptmann's good friend Hans Kloppenburg who, as agreed, shared in the expenses along the way. According to Kloppenburg they *"went away 6 of July and come back 3 of October."*[1282] It was an amazing trip which took them to Philadelphia, then to Niagara Falls, Lake Erie, Chicago, Yellow Stone National Park, Los Angeles, Arizona, New Mexico, Texas, Florida, and finally back to New York.[1283] Kloppenberg claimed his share of the trip was *"about $250. or $300."*[1284] Hauptmann would claim his part of the expenses for this trip ran him *"approximately $400 or $500."*[1285] While at Yellowstone National Park, the group met up with Hauptmann's sister, Emma Gloeckner, who he had not seen in 23 years and who had driven to the park from Los Angeles along with her husband Charles and daughter Mildred.[1286] The group would eventually all go back to California to spend about ten days together, after which they left to spend time with Kloppenberg's

---

[1282] Kloppenberg, Hans. Statement. Taken at the District Attorney's Office in the presence of Assistant District Attorney Breslin, Captain Appel, and Stenographer King. October 8, 1934 at 8:30 P. M. New Jersey State Police Museum and Learning Center Archives.

[1283] Kloppenberg, Hans. Questioning. Conducted by Inspector John A. Lyons "and others." September 19, 1934. New Jersey State Police Museum and Learning Center Archives.

[1284] Ibid.

[1285] Hauptmann, Bruno Richard. Statement. December 6, 1934. New Jersey State Police Museum and Learning Center Archives.

[1286] Hauptmann, Anna. *The Story of Anna Hauptmann*. Manuscript. Page 26. September 1935. New Jersey State Police Museum and Learning Center Archives.

relatives in a town near San Francisco before departing for their long trip home.[1287]

Upon returning home, the Hauptmanns were now faced with no jobs, no place to live, and their belongings still in rented storage. One of the first things Hauptmann did was to get in touch with Mr. Grizzle to see if he could be rehired but was told there was no work.[1288] Having given up their apartment, they took a temporary furnished room at a friend's place on East 174th street in lieu of finding a new rental. It was at this very point the Authorities theorized that Hauptmann was in complete financial dire straits. This position relies heavily on the attempt by Special Agent Frank of the Treasury Department (IRS) to piece together a forensic accounting report concerning Hauptmann's finances. Here Agent Frank points to the fact that...

> "...during the year 1931 Hauptmann earned very little, lost practically his entire investment in securities and was living on his wife's earnings from her employment in the Fredericksen bakery. Also, their resources, except for the $3,750 mortgage, were almost exhausted."[1289]

[1287] Kneen, H. J. Special Agent, USBOI (FBI). USBOI Report. <u>Changed: Bruno Richard Hauptmann Unknown Subjects</u>. September 25, 1934. New Jersey State Police Museum and Learning Center Archives. (Note: The FBI had changed its name from USBOI to DOI by this time but the heading on this particular report still says "United States Bureau of Investigation")

[1288] Hauptmann, Richard. Autobiography: Unedited & Uncorrected (Translated). <u>The Story of My Life</u>. Page 163. May 4, 1935. New Jersey State Police Museum and Learning Center Archives.

[1289] Frank, William E. Special Agent, United States Treasury Department. Internal Revenue Service Special Report. <u>Financial Activities of Bruno Richard Hauptmann and his wife, Anna Hauptmann, nee Schoeffler, 1279 East 222nd Street, Bronx, New York City</u>. January 8, 1935. Page 8. New Jersey State Police Museum and Learning Center Archives.

Another point of fact Agent Frank would reference was Carleton and Mott's margin call of $74.89 on his account in May of '31. On May 25th Hauptmann deposited $50.00, failing to cover the entire amount. Hauptmann left this "small" amount of $24.89 in abeyance until December 2, 1931, when he withdrew $25 amount from his bank account to finally cover the balance. However, in doing so, he reduced the balance in his bank account to $75.96. Concerning this Agent Frank wrote:

> *"these circumstances indicate to me that Hauptmann was down to the end of his resources at the beginning of 1932 and that he was actually in desperate need of money."*[1290]

I see a couple of problems with this conclusion. As I mentioned earlier the actual trip itself is something I view as problematic to Frank's conclusion. The other issues I see concern the money required to pay for their temporary stay upon their return. Even if someone let them stay for "free" meaning they did not have to pay at all for room or electricity, they certainly still had to pay for food. Next, once the Hauptmanns found a new apartment on 1279 East 222nd Street, they rented it from Max Rauch for $50 per month on Columbus Day bringing their furniture from storage with them.[1291] Their previous apartment on Needham Avenue was 3–rooms at a

---

[1290] Ibid. Page 10.

[1291] Zapolsky, A. Sgt., New Jersey State Police. New Jersey State Police Report. <u>Continued investigation re: Bruno Richard Hauptmann, re: Lindbergh Case</u>. November 26, 1934. New Jersey State Police Museum and Learning Center Archives. (Note: According to Hauptmann's Autobiography cited in this book, page 163, he claimed he only paid $20 security for the first month in exchange for building the garage).

cost of $35 per month.[1292] So for a family in need of money it doesn't quite make a lot of sense to "upgrade" their living arrangements while also paying their fee for storage – if that scenario is to be believed. Yet another simple example of how this does not seem right is that Hauptmann sent his niece Mildred $5 for Christmas during that very December in 1931 when they were supposed to be so starved for cash.[1293] I look at all of this then conclude there must be a different explanation.

One of the most notable things about Hauptmann's fastidious financial keeping was the fact that he abruptly ended this practice altogether on July 4, 1930. This made it impossible for Agent Frank to definitely establish Hauptmann's true net worth and forced him to rely solely on the official documents and bank records for his estimates. Furthermore, as previously indicated by Assistant Attorney General Robert Peacock above, Agent Frank expounded this point, indicating that the date when Hauptmann stopped making records was significant. In his report he wrote the following:

> *"Thereafter no record of either his own or Mrs. Hauptmann's earnings appears and when asked the reason for this absence of records, Hauptmann replied that due to the depression he worked irregularly after that date and that his earnings were so small he did not think it worthwhile to keep a record of them. While this statement probably is true and may be the only reason for Hauptmann's failure to keep records of his*

[1292] Zapolsky, A. Sgt., New Jersey State Police. New Jersey State Police Report. Report of continued investigation concerning Bruno Richard Hauptmann, re: Lindbergh Case. November 9, 1934. New Jersey State Police Museum and Learning Center Archives.

[1293] Kneen, H. J. Special Agent, USBOI (FBI). USBOI Report. Changed: Bruno Richard Hauptmann Unknown Subjects. September 25, 1934. New Jersey State Police Museum and Learning Center Archives

earnings from July 1930 on, attention is called to the
fact that the Lindbergh baby, who was twenty months
old when kidnapped on March 1, 1932, was born just
at the time Hauptmann ceased keeping his records. It
is believed that the newspaper carried considerable
publicity concerning the birth of the baby and in view
of the statement in one of the ransom notes to the
effect that the kidnapping had been planned carefully
over a long period of time, it is my opinion that some
significance can be attached to Hauptmann's change in
procedure just at that time. In other words, I believe an
inference can be drawn that Hauptmann, reading in
the newspapers of the baby's birth on June 22, 1930,
then formulated the plan to kidnap the child, began
planning the details of the crime, and, consequently,
neglected his regular employment and discontinued
keeping a record of his small earnings because his mind
was fixed on obtaining a large sum of money through
illegal means."[1294]

So once again, if Hauptmann had indeed been planning this crime for all of this time, how does it explain why he would strike on a night when his planning should have clearly indicated that the child would not be there? And why would he have waited so long to do so if he was in such a situation which demanded he get money?

Agent Frank also made the following observation concerning the California trip:

[1294] Frank, William E. Special Agent, United States Treasury Department. Internal Revenue Service Special Report. <u>Financial Activities of Bruno Richard Hauptmann and his wife, Anna Hauptmann, nee Schoeffler, 1279 East 222nd Street, Bronx, New York City.</u> January 8, 1935. Page 6. New Jersey State Police Museum and Learning Center Archives.

"*Nevertheless, in spite of these unfortunate economic circumstances, Hauptmann and his wife on July 6, 1931 left New York with their friend, Hans Kloppenberg, and made an extended auto tour of the United States, going as far as Los Angeles, California, and not returning to New York until October 3, 1931. For a man of Hauptmann's pervious frugal and industrious habits, it seems most unusual that he would go on a pleasure trip with his finances in such poor shape unless he had in mind the obtaining of money in the near future from some other source.*"[1295]

Then there is this little tidbit worthy of note included in the report...

"*...it might be argued that Hauptmann had cash concealed at home or other resources not discovered by investigators. Of course it is always possible that an individual might have secret savings or hidden funds which cannot be brought to light by ordinary investigative methods.*"[1296]

[1295] Ibid. Page 8.
[1296] Ibid. Page 9.

California Trip - Hauptmann with his sister Emma Gloeckner.
(Courtesy NJSP Museum)

California Trip – Hauptmann, Anna, Mildred Gloeckner (niece),
Charles Gloeckner (brother-in-law), and Emma Gloeckner (sister).
(Courtesy NJSP Museum)

The Florida Trip

Another automobile trip took place on January 16, 1933, when Hauptmann and his wife left New York for Florida, returning on February 10, 1933. I think it is important to take a closer look at some of the facts which surrounded this trip to get a better idea of what might be going on with the ransom money as it relates to Hauptmann. The State believed this trip was the product of ransom money, and it has been described over the years since as, in essence, a luxurious trip. Special Agent Frank, for example, originally assigned the cost of this "holiday" as $250.00.[1297] However, at the end of Frank's final forensic accounting report he drastically cuts this figure down to $100.00.[1298] This amount agrees with what Anna wrote saying they stayed at "tourist camps" most of the time and bragged that the entire cost of this trip *"did not exceed $100."*[1299] So while we might say the impetus for this trip was "enrichment," it also seems to show evidence of Hauptmann's tendency to be frugal. Why? Next, wouldn't this have been a perfect opportunity to launder ransom money? Yet, no ransom money ever turned up during this time, which strongly suggested Hauptmann did not pass any during his

---

[1297] Frank, William E. Special Agent, United States Treasury Department. Divisions SI 6336M & SI 12262F. Internal Revenue Service Special Report. (Tentative) Re: Bruno R. Hauptmann, Schedule of misc. Expenses 4/2/32 to 9/19/34. November 25, 1934. New Jersey State Police Museum and Learning Center Archives.

[1298] Frank, William E. Special Agent, United States Treasury Department. Internal Revenue Service Special Report. Financial Activities of Bruno Richard Hauptmann and his wife, Anna Hauptmann, nee Schoeffler, 1279 East 222nd Street, Bronx, New York City. January 8, 1935. Page 6. New Jersey State Police Museum and Learning Center Archives.

[1299] Hauptmann, Anna. *The Story of Anna Hauptmann.* Manuscript. Pages 28-9. September 1935. New Jersey State Police Museum and Learning Center Archives.

trip.[1300] In fact, the only event which involved a possible ransom money sighting occurred in Newtown, Pennsylvania, "on or about February 1st," when a dark complected man about 30–35 years of age, between 5'6" and 5'7" and weighing about 150 lbs, drove a car with New York tags from store to store attempting to make small purchases in order to spend a $20.00 bill.[1301] No one in town was falling for this ploy and nobody accepted the bill in question, causing the man to pretend he'd return for the items later but never did. One witness claimed to have gotten a tag number which was traced to a man the Police claimed had been picked up in Philadelphia by the Secret Service as of the date of writing the report.[1302] The bill in question was never recovered, and there is no follow up report presently at the NJSP Archives to consult.

Barring the above occurrence, the fact that Hauptmann was not spending ransom money during this vacation is a double edged sword. On one hand, if he were a ransom passer we'd expect him to have done exactly that during this time, yet, it could be argued that no one else was passing this money while he was gone so he must have been the only one involved. What facts do we have that can help us determine the truth? I turn first to Hauptmann's actions just before this trip.

One such activity would be the Hauptmann's $3,750.00 mortgage purchase which was recorded in Anna's name on January 3, 1933.

[1300] Recapitulation of Ransom Money. Unsigned. Undated (May 1935). New Jersey State Police Museum and Learning Center Archives.

[1301] Zapolsky, A. Sgt. New Jersey State Police. New Jersey State Police Report. Investigation of attached communication sent in by Robert B. Hance, Jr., Bank Teller of the Newtown Title and Trust Company, Newtown, Penna., stating that an attempt was made to pass a $20.00 Bill of the Lindbergh Ransom Money in that town. February 10, 1933. New Jersey State Police Museum and Learning Center Archives.

[1302] Ibid.

This purchase was actually made when Hauptmann and his wife arrived at the office of Attorney Joseph Burkard in Rosedale, Long Island, on December 31, 1932. Here they turned over this amount, in cash, despite the fact there were no withdrawals from any bank or brokerage accounts.[1303] This would mean he had this amount of cash on hand, and Hauptmann's two most recent withdrawals, one from Mount Vernon Trust for $500 by Richard on December 12th, and the other for $800 on December 7th from their joint account at Central Savings Bank by Anna, would only account for $1300. On January 10th there was significant financial activity as Hauptmann deposited $139 dollars in coins into his Mount Vernon Trust account.[1304] Important to note is that at this time large amounts of coin deposits typically came from shopkeepers or slot machines.[1305] From 1924 to April 2nd, 1932, Hauptmann and Anna had only deposited $1.47 in coins and this came at a time when Anna was *"employed as a waitress and might be expected to have received*

[1303] Frank, William E. Special Agent, United States Treasury Department. Internal Revenue Service Special Report. <u>Financial Activities of Bruno Richard Hauptmann and his wife, Anna Hauptmann, nee Schoeffler, 1279 East 222<u>nd</u> Street, Bronx, New York City</u>. January 8, 1935. Page 11. New Jersey State Police Museum and Learning Center Archives.

[1304] Genau, J. A. Special Agent, United States Bureau of Investigation (FBI). USBOI Report. <u>Kidnaping And Murder Of Charles A. Lindbergh, Jr.</u> Page 48. October 8, 1934. New Jersey State Police Museum and Learning Center Archives.

[1305] Frank, William E. Special Agent, United States Treasury Department. Internal Revenue Service Memo. <u>In re: Account of Richard Hauptmann with Mt. Vernon Trust Company</u>. December 27, 1934. New Jersey State Police Museum and Learning Center Archives. (Note: Another possibility was gambling activity).

considerable" coins "*in form of tips.*"[1306] So for Hauptmann, someone who had become a full time stock trader, any large coin deposits should have been deemed highly suspicious and possibly considered the proceeds of money laundering activity.[1307] Having said that, it appears someone laundering ransom on a scale grand enough to generate large amounts of coin deposits would need a formulated laundering method and considerable amount of time to implement it. Could this have been Hauptmann himself? According to William Mulligan, it seems highly unlikely. Mulligan was employed with Steiner, Rouse & Company as a "Customers Man," and worked with Hauptmann to execute trades which started on August 17, 1932, shortly after Hauptmann had opened a brokerage account there.[1308] Mulligan stated that Hauptmann...

> "...*came to the office almost daily, and stayed there practically all day long during all the time that the accounts were opened, and only left in periods of minutes to go out to lunch.*"[1309]

[1306] Frank, William E. Special Agent, United States Treasury Department. Internal Revenue Service Special Report. <u>Financial Activities of Bruno Richard Hauptmann and his wife, Anna Hauptmann, nee Schoeffler, 1279 East 222nd Street, Bronx, New York City</u>. January 8, 1935. Page 22. New Jersey State Police Museum and Learning Center Archives.

[1307] Purdy, Robert. E-mail to Author. August 12, 2005.

[1308] Mulligan, William P. Statement. Made to Frank J. Wilson, Special Agent in Charge, Intelligence Unit, Treasury Department, and Richard Stockton, 3rd Assistant Attorney General, in the presence of Acting Lieutenant James J. Finn, Main Office Division. December 13, 1934 at 11:30 A. M. New Jersey State Police Museum and Learning Center Archives.

[1309] Mulligan, William. Statement. Made to Jos. A. Genau, Special Agent, Division of Investigation, U.S. Department of Justice, and J. L. Dalton, Special Agent, Division of Investigation, U.S. Department of Justice. September 21, 1934. New Jersey State Police Museum and Learning Center Archives.

Also on January 10th, Hauptmann made a $1400 deposit consisting of $1287 in bills, $112.50 in checks, and $0.50 in silver to his joint account in Central Savings Bank.[1310] This deposit seems very different from the deposit made on the same day to Mount Vernon Trust. Why were the coins going into one account while the bills seemed to be going into the other? It was also on this day that Hauptmann rented his safe deposit box in Central Savings Bank.[1311] Then on January 16th, the very day they left for Florida, Hauptmann deposited another $186 in coins to his Mount Vernon Trust account.[1312] If this figure represents the proceeds of laundered ransom, then in less than six days' time we see a system that is producing a sizable amount of money just in coins. If ransom money is being spent, we must assume it's producing clean bills as well; however, one can only guess as to that amount since we have only the coin deposit to consider. But what's obvious is, if it's Hauptmann laundering this money alone, a quick purchase here or there cannot possibly produce this kind of result, so he must have been doing it *after* trading hours, on the weekends, or on rare occasions when he was not at the brokerage house watching the board. It's a monumental task, unless of course, we consider the possibility that someone else assisted in this process.

[1310] Genau, J. A. Special Agent, United States Bureau of Investigation (FBI). USBOI Report. <u>Kidnaping And Murder Of Charles A. Lindbergh, Jr.</u> Page 44. October 8, 1934. New Jersey State Police Museum and Learning Center Archives.

[1311] Ibid. Page 46.

[1312] Ibid. Page 48.

Victor Schussler

The Schussler family moved into the other Rauch home apartment on August 1, 1932.[1313] Schussler was German and worked as an Upholsterer at the Prince George Hotel. Just prior to the Hauptmanns departing for their trip to Florida, their apartment keys were given to the Shusslers so that they could water the plants and look after the place.[1314] Upon their return, Hauptmann gave Schussler a baby alligator as a gift, and the two men worked together to build a pond for it.[1315] These men became friendlier as a result with Schussler showing Hauptmann how to grow dahlias, which became the impetus for Hauptmann growing and maintaining a garden ever since.[1316] Schussler had Hauptmann's permission to use the garage and was never at any time told not to go in. In fact, it was Hauptmann's suggestion that he store his chairs and other items in there so he didn't have to go up and down the steps to the cellar.[1317] Schussler explained that while most of the time the garage was locked, he simply used his pen knife to open the door to go in.[1318] On some occasions Schussler would borrow Hauptmann's

[1313] Patterson, Claude Det., New Jersey State Police. New Jersey State Police Report. <u>Continuation of investigation of Bruno Richard Hauptmann and associates, re: Lindbergh Case</u>. December 14, 1934. New Jersey State Police Museum and Learning Center Archives.

[1314] Ibid.

[1315] Schussler, Victor. Statement. Made to Assistant District Attorney Breslin, Capt. Lamb, New Jersey State Police and Agent Sisk, Department of Justice. Steno. King. September 28, 1934. New Jersey State Police Museum and Learning Center Archives.

[1316] Ibid.

[1317] Ibid.

[1318] Patterson, Claude Det., New Jersey State Police. New Jersey State Police Report. <u>Continuation of investigation of Bruno Richard Hauptmann and associates, re: Lindbergh Case</u>. December 14, 1934. New Jersey State Police Museum and Learning Center Archives.

tools, and claimed that: "*...when I wasn't working I go in there.*"[1319] After the police confiscated Hauptmann's tools, it was necessary for Schussler to go to West Trenton to claim his "small awl" and "six point webbing stretcher" which had been among those tools seized.[1320]

We must now ask ourselves whether or not the ransom money which was discovered in Hauptmann's garage after his arrest was there when he went to Florida. It has been pointed out by some researchers that Schussler's access to the garage supports the famous "Fisch Story," while others counter that the timing of the safe deposit box rental would imply the money was there during the trip. That said, this box remained rented and was active at the time of Hauptmann's arrest.[1321] So, if the safety deposit box was used, we are now left with the question of why Hauptmann did not continue to use this box as storage for the ransom instead of moving it into the garage – a place where Schussler had unlimited access. But then again if the "Fisch Story" actually was true, why would he keep this money in the garage while this safe deposit box existed?

[1319] Schussler, Victor. Statement. Made to Assistant District Attorney Breslin, Capt. Lamb, New Jersey State Police and Agent Sisk, Department of Justice. Steno. King. September 28, 1934. New Jersey State Police Museum and Learning Center Archives.

[1320] Dickerson, J. H. Det., New Jersey State Police. New Jersey State Police Report. Questioning of Victor Schussler, re: Lindbergh Case. December 20, 1934. New Jersey State Police Museum and Learning Center Archives.

[1321] Genau, J. A. Special Agent, United States Bureau of Investigation (FBI). USBOI Report. Kidnaping And Murder Of Charles A. Lindbergh, Jr. Page 46. October 8, 1934. New Jersey State Police Museum and Learning Center Archives.

The Return

One would expect since Hauptmann had purchased the mortgage, made two bank deposits (which combined make a sizable amount), then gone on a trip to Florida where they did not pass ransom money, that upon their return there would be withdrawals from their accounts and a sudden flurry of ransom money turning up. Did this happen?

The first notable item was that a $10 ransom gold certificate had been discovered at the Federal Reserve Bank on Liberty and Nassau Streets in New York City on June 13, 1933. As this bill was investigated, police traced it all the way up to East Springfield, New York, to a farmer named John O'Neil.[1322] Lt. Finn learned from O'Neil that he received the bill in question from the National Central Bank of Cherry Valley, New York, "*on or about the 10th of February, 1933.*"[1323] Although passed on the day of or very near Hauptmann's return from Florida, based on the distance from New York City, what is the likelihood that Hauptmann had been the one to pass it? If it was spent prior it could not have been him. If it was spent on that day it could not have been him. If it was spent a day or two after, then I believe we have only a slight possibility it was. The next provable monetary activity occurred when Hauptmann walked into Mount Vernon Trust on February 15th but not to make

---

[1322] Zapolsky, A. Sgt. New Jersey State Police. New Jersey State Police Report. <u>Investigation of $10.00 Gold Certificate of the Lindbergh Ransom money, A-79742843-A, which was sent by the First National Bank of Cooperstown, N. Y., on June 9th, 1933, to the Federal Reserve Bank of New York, and found there by Mrs. Purcel, 2042 Tyler Avenue, Union City, N. J. on June 13, 1933</u>. June 16, 1933. New Jersey State Police Museum and Learning Center Archives.

[1323] Manning. J. J. Special Agent, United States Bureau of Investigation (FBI). USBOI Report. <u>Kidnaping And Murder Of Charles A. Lindbergh, Jr</u>. Page 44. August 22, 1933. National Archives at College Park Maryland.

a withdrawal as one might expect. Instead he deposited $230 in fit bills there![1324] Two days later he deposited another $60 in clean bills in their Central Savings Bank account.[1325] Hauptmann received a margin call for $100 on February 24th, one for $300 on February 25th, and another for $300 on February 27th for his account at Steiner, Rouse and Company, at which time he paid $700 in cash to cover it.[1326] Withdrawals were made in this timeframe which appear to be directly related. On February 26th, he withdrew $500 from the Mt. Vernon Bank and on February 27th, withdrew another $500 from their Central Savings Bank account.[1327] However, without any further corresponding withdrawals from his accounts, he deposited another $850 into his Steiner, Rouse and Company account on March 1st.[1328]

Philip Alsofrom

On March 1st, 1933, sometime between 12 PM and 1 PM, a light complected "tall" man approximately 40 years of age with a "long thin face" wearing a soft hat and dark clothing walked into the

[1324] Genau, J. A. Special Agent, United States Bureau of Investigation (FBI). USBOI Report. Kidnaping And Murder Of Charles A. Lindbergh, Jr. Page 48. October 8, 1934. New Jersey State Police Museum and Learning Center Archives.
[1325] Ibid. Page 45.
[1326] Mulligan, William. Statement. Made to Jos. A. Genau, Special Agent, Division of Investigation, U.S. Department of Justice, and J. L. Dalton, Special Agent, Division of Investigation, U.S. Department of Justice. September 21, 1934. New Jersey State Police Museum and Learning Center Archives.
[1327] Genau, J. A. Special Agent, United States Bureau of Investigation (FBI). USBOI Report. Kidnaping And Murder Of Charles A. Lindbergh, Jr. Page 52. October 8, 1934. New Jersey State Police Museum and Learning Center Archives.
[1328] Ibid.

United Cigar Store on 181 Clinton Street in NYC and made a purchase with a $10 gold certificate ransom bill.[1329] The police had almost immediately discovered it on March 3rd after its being noticed by a Teller at the Main Branch of the Guaranty Trust Company, and as a result the Manager of the cigar shop, Philip Alsofrom, still had a fresh recollection of the event when interviewed. This wasn't the first time someone, either knowingly or unknowingly, passed a ransom bill at a cigar shop. On October 27, 1932, a $10 ransom bill was traced back to United Cigar Stores Company in Queens.[1330] However, no one interviewed by police could recall anything to assist them. Yet another $10 ransom bill was traced back to a purchase on December 21, 1932 at the United Cigar Store on Third Avenue in Manhattan.[1331] Unfortunately here too, the employees could not remember anything surrounding this event. Lt. Finn, seeing a possible pattern developing, ordered men from the Bureau of Criminal Information Squad to "cover" the United Cigar Store on Clinton Street; however, nothing resulted from this action.[1332] On the same date police were interviewing Alsofrom,

[1329] Finn, James J., Acting Lieutenant, M.O.D. New York City Police Report. Lindbergh Ransom Bill $10 Gold Certificate A 13447722 A. October 28, 1932. New Jersey State Police Museum and Learning Center Archives.

[1330] Finn, James J., M.O.S., New York City Police Department. 18th Division Report. Cooperation accorded by Banks re: Lindbergh Ransom Money. January 23, 1934. New Jersey State Police Museum and Learning Center Archives.

[1331] Recapitulation Of Ransom Money. Unsigned. Undated (May 1935). New Jersey State Police Museum and Learning Center Archives.

[1332] Finn, James J., M.O.S., New York City Police Department. 18th Division Report. Cooperation accorded by Banks re: Lindbergh Ransom Money. January 23, 1934. New Jersey State Police Museum and Learning Center Archives.

March 3rd, Hauptmann walked into Mount Vernon Trust Bank and deposited $55 into his account there.[1333]

Alsofrom would re-emerge when Special Agent Turrou visited the cigar shop to interview him on October 2, 1934. Turrou showed him a photo of Hauptmann which had recently been taken by the New York City Police, and after looking it over...

> "...*readily identified it as the person who passed the $10 bill to him on March 1, 1933. Mr. Alsofrom stated that he could never forget the features of the individual who passed the bill, and, particularly, his eye and, if confronted with Hauptmann in the flesh, he believes that he could then make a positive identification.*"[1334]

As a result of this interview, Alsofrom was asked to appear at Chief Assistant District Attorney Breslin's office for questioning. If Alsofrom identified Hauptmann, it would be a crushing blow to his Defense and a much needed eyewitness account of Hauptmann passing ransom money before his supposed discovery of funds per his now-famous "Fisch Story." However, almost immediately into the questioning Alsofrom seemed to be giving Breslin the runaround recalling that he told Lt. Finn the man's description who passed the ransom bill was as follows:

[1333] Genau, J. A. Special Agent, United States Bureau of Investigation (FBI). USBOI Report. Kidnaping And Murder Of Charles A. Lindbergh, Jr. Page 51. October 8, 1934. New Jersey State Police Museum and Learning Center Archives.

[1334] Turrou, L. G., Special Agent, United States Bureau of Investigation (FBI). USBOI Report. Kidnaping And Murder Of Charles A. Lindbergh, Jr. October 3, 1934. New Jersey State Police Museum and Learning Center Archives.

"His eyes were sunken in his face and had sort of a long face, not very long, dark complexion, not very dark complexion and that is about all I told him."[1335]

If this answer didn't bother the authorities, his answer about whether or not pictures of Hauptmann indicated he was the man who passed him that ransom bill must have:

"Yes I saw pictures in the paper and I saw a picture and imagined I saw it as I told Mr. Turau [sic] it was sort of I knew the man but whether I have seen him or not I am not positive. That man looks familiar to me."[1336]

As a result, Breslin arranged for Alsofrom to come back the next day on October 3rd and view Hauptmann while he was in court. After the opportunity to see Hauptmann face to face Alsofrom was re-interviewed:

[**Breslin**]: *Did you see anyone in the court room this morning who resembled the person who passed that bill?*

[**Alsofrom**]: *This person I was looking at is Hauptmann and he resembles the fellow I had in mind, and as I said I didn't look at the fellow too long, all I saw was a glimpse.*

[**Breslin**]: *You told us last night you had a conversation with him?*

[1335] Alsofrom, Philip. Statement. Made to Assistant District Attorney Breslin, Capt. Lamb, N.J. State Police, and Stenographer King. October 2, 1934 at 7:45 P. M. New Jersey State Police Museum and Learning Center Archives.

[1336] Ibid.

[**Alsofrom**]: *I said, "Just a second" when I got to the register, I said, "You don't get many of these bills anymore" and gave him the change, meaning the gold certificate.*

[**Breslin**]: *Can you positively identify the man?*

[**Alsofrom**]: *I cannot positively identify the man but he certainly looks like the man who came in the store the day I got the gold certificate. After I seen the man just now his sunken eyes in the head and long jaw.*[1337]

Alexander Begg

One possibly "rare" occasion of Hauptmann not being at Steiner, Rouse & Company occurred on October 17, 1932. This was a Monday when he was with Hans Mueller, Maria Mueller, and Anna in his dodge at the intersection of 121st Street and Third Avenue. It was approximately 2:25 PM on a rainy day when Alexander Begg started to cross the street. According to Hauptmann's version on the accident report, Begg was crossing against the light when he saw Hauptmann approaching and tried to retreat back to the sidewalk but slipped in front of his car.[1338] This report further indicates that Begg suffered a broken leg as a result, but there was no noticeable damage to the car. Hauptmann immediately drove Begg to the

---

[1337] Alsofrom, Philip. Statement. Made to Assistant District Attorney Breslin, Capt. Lamb, N.J. State Police, and Stenographer King. October 3, 1934 at 12:20 P. M. New Jersey State Police Museum and Learning Center Archives.

[1338] Report of Motor Vehicle Accident. State of New York. Bureau of File, Motor Vehicle Division. Stamped: "Received Oct 19 1932". New Jersey State Police Museum and Learning Center Archives.

nearest hospital then reported the accident to authorities.[1339] After Hauptmann's arrest the police, through their investigation, learned from Begg's wife that her husband had died which she claimed was a direct result of this accident.[1340] It was also learned that Hauptmann had agreed to pay $300 to Mr. Begg, but also *"claimed poverty"* as the reason for the need to set up payment in installments. And so his...

> *"...first payment of $75 was made on December 21, 1932; The second payment of $20.00 made by money order on Jan. 5 or 5 [sic] 1933; January 17 or 18, 1933, he sent money order for $20.00; February 16, 1933, money order for $50.00; March 9, sent money order for $15.00. He then visited Mrs. Begg's home while she lived at 76 Pinehurst Avenue and again pleaded with her that he was out of work and could not meet the payments, however, he again sent a money order for $20 and on July 28, he sent $20.00 more."*[1341]

On December 4, 1933, Mrs. Begg wrote Hauptmann a letter explaining that her husband had been transferred to Pelgrim State Hospital as a *"mental patient"* and that:

[1339] Hauptmann, Richard. Autobiography: Unedited & Uncorrected (Translated). The Story of My Life. Page 182. May 4, 1935. New Jersey State Police Museum and Learning Center Archives.

[1340] Zapolsky, A. Sgt. New Jersey State Police. New Jersey State Police Report. Continued report of investigation with reference o Bruno Richard Hauptmann, re: Lindbergh Case. November 15, 1934. New Jersey State Police Museum and Learning Center Archives.

[1341] Ibid.

> *"...he will never work again nor be cured and it is merely a question of time before they expect he will pass on."*[1342]

Hauptmann wrote back the following in a letter:

> *"I received your letter and I am very sorry Mr. Begg is not well. If I had more, I would have send you the money long ago, but I try to send you ten or twenty Dollars before Christmas. My wife has a baby since five weeks and so the few Dollars I made I needed badly. As soon as I am able to I will send you the rest of the money. I wish Mr. Begg will get better soon."*[1343]

On December 22nd, Mrs. Begg then received another money order for $20.00.[1344] However, from that point on nothing further was heard from Hauptmann. Mrs. Begg wrote him again in April 1934 to explain that Alexander had died and that she needed money to pay the doctor bills but Hauptmann did not reply and no more money was ever sent again.[1345]

Earlier, on March 25, 1933, Hauptmann closed his joint account at Central Savings Brank then opened a new account in his wife's name as *"Anna Schoeffler"* by transferring the existing funds from

---

[1342] Begg, Annette. Letter from Annette Begg to Mr. R. Hauptmann. December 4, 1933. New Jersey State Police Museum and Learning Center Archives.

[1343] Hauptmann, Richard. Letter from Richard Hauptmann to A. Begg. December 9, 1933. New Jersey State Police Museum and Learning Center Archives.

[1344] Zapolsky, A. Sgt. New Jersey State Police. New Jersey State Police Report. Continued report of investigation with reference o Bruno Richard Hauptmann, re: Lindbergh Case. November 15, 1934. New Jersey State Police Museum and Learning Center Archives.

[1345] Ibid.

the closed account into it.[1346] On March 27, 1933, he opened an account at Steiner, Rouse, and Company in the name of *"Miss Anna Schoeffler, c/o Hauptmann, 1279 East 222 St., New York City"* then transferred the stocks in his account over to it on March 31, 1933.[1347] Hauptmann told Mulligan he was doing this to protect himself *"due to an accident with his car and was afraid of a lawsuit."*[1348] In evaluating these financial maneuvers, Special Agent Frank wrote the following:

> *"Attention is called to the fact that the auto accident (by Hauptmann's own records) occurred on October 17, 1932 and that a $300 settlement had been arranged on which Hauptmann started payment in December, 1932. It would seem improbable that Hauptmann would worry about the damage suit months after the settlement had been reached."*[1349]

[1346] Frank, William E. Special Agent, United States Treasury Department. Internal Revenue Service Special Report. Financial Activities of Bruno Richard Hauptmann and his wife, Anna Hauptmann, nee Schoeffler, 1279 East 222nd Street, Bronx, New York City. January 8, 1935. Page 14. New Jersey State Police Museum and Learning Center Archives.

[1347] Genau, J. A. Special Agent, United States Bureau of Investigation (FBI). USBOI Report. Kidnaping And Murder Of Charles A. Lindbergh, Jr. Page 5. October 8, 1934. New Jersey State Police Museum and Learning Center Archives.

[1348] Mulligan, William. Statement. Made to Jos. A. Genau, Special Agent, Division of Investigation, U.S. Department of Justice, and J. L. Dalton, Special Agent, Division of Investigation, U.S. Department of Justice. September 21, 1934. New Jersey State Police Museum and Learning Center Archives.

[1349] Frank, William E. Special Agent, United States Treasury Department. Internal Revenue Service Special Report. Financial Activities of Bruno Richard Hauptmann and his wife, Anna Hauptmann, nee Schoeffler, 1279 East 222nd Street, Bronx, New York City. January 8, 1935. Page 14. New Jersey State Police Museum and Learning Center Archives.

This has been the position of many researchers over the years, to show Hauptmann knew he was dealing with the proceeds of ransom money and trying to hide his activity. An alternate suggestion comes from Lloyd Gardner. He wrote that it may have been done "*to provide him with a cover for further dealings with Isador Fisch*."[1350] To me, based on Hauptmann's actions concerning his payments and lack thereof, it seems probable he did not intend on making good on his settlement with the Beggs after he sent the last $20 contribution in December. Furthermore, Hauptmann testified in Flemington he believed that something was going to come up which caused him to expect the Beggs were going to want more money.[1351] So I do not have a problem with believing this was his true motive here. However, there's certainly no limit to the reasons "why" Hauptmann may have done this, and these moves could be viewed as reasonable no matter how one looks at it. For me, the bigger question is why, if Hauptmann was flush with cash, he wouldn't have simply paid the $300 and be done with the matter? There's this long drawn out "drip, drip, drip," and "back & forth" that strikes me as completely unnecessary – if not downright risky. Finally, in the scheme of all of this, yet another question exists as to why Hauptmann opened a new savings account, in his own name, at the Manhattan Savings Institution in late August 1934.[1352]

[1350] Gardner, Lloyd C. June 2004. *The Case That Never Dies*. Rutgers University Press. Page 325.

[1351] Hauptmann, Bruno Richard. Testimony. The State of New Jersey vs. Bruno Richard Hauptmann, <u>Hunterdon County Court of Oyer and Terminer</u>, page 2643. 1935. New Jersey State Law Library.

[1352] Genau, J. A. Special Agent, United States Bureau of Investigation (FBI). USBOI Report. <u>Kidnaping And Murder Of Charles A. Lindbergh, Jr.</u> Page 49. October 8, 1934. New Jersey State Police Museum and Learning Center Archives.

John Hager

Another curious example of Hauptmann's dealings with money involved a man by the name of John Hager.[1353] It began with Karl Arnold, a shoemaker who became acquainted with Hans Kloppenburg at the First Evangelical Church, known as the "German Church" in 1930, and was later introduced to Hauptmann by Kloppenburg.[1354] In the beginning of 1933, Kloppenburg moved into the shoe shop living with both Arnold and another man named August Reiger.[1355] According to Reiger, Hauptmann would come over for lunch "*from where he make his business*" and he had "*plenty respect for him*" because he had his "*big car*" and "*he was a very good worker, good carpenter. He had a thing in the German Exhibition.*"[1356] Reiger recalled Hauptmann telling the men if they had money to give him that he could "double" it within two to three days at the stock market.[1357] In March of that year Arnold's father became so

---

[1353] Note: Special thanks to Siglinde Rach for bringing up Hager in one of our many discussions.

[1354] Arnold, Karl. Affidavit. Made to Arthur C. Johnson, Detective, Shield No. 1508, NYPD, Heinrich Petri, Polizei-Inspektor, Neustadt/Haardt, and John A. Bywater, Clerk at the American Consulate General, Frankfort-on-Main, Germany. October 16, 1934. New Jersey State Police Museum and Learning Center Archives.

[1355] Reiger, August. Statement. Made to Assistant District Attorney Breslin, Capt. Lamb, New Jersey State Police; Capt. Appel of New York Police, 8th Detective Division and Lt. Keaten, N.J. State Police. Steno King. September 28, 1934. New Jersey State Police Museum and Learning Center Archives.

[1356] Ibid.

[1357] Ibid.

sick it was necessary for Arnold to return to Germany to see him.[1358] Prior to his trip, Arnold called another shoemaker, John Hager, to see if he could fill in for him at the shop for two months while he was in Germany. Having no steady job, Hager was *"very glad"* to accept this offer.[1359] During Arnold's absence, his shop became the site for card games every Saturday night that included the Henkels, Kloppenburg, and Hauptmann.[1360] Hager worked at the shop until Arnold's return on May 2, 1933. A few days later, Hager learned of Arnold's intention to permanently return to Germany to look after his ailing father. Arnold announced he was selling the business and gave Hager *"first chance"* to buy it.[1361]

Interestingly, there are two versions of how Hager came up with the money to buy the shop. The first comes from Reiger. Arnold had lent him money while he was out of work, and Reiger regarded him as a good friend claiming that *"he is the nicest fellow what I ever met in my life"* still owing him $15 at the time of his interview

[1358] Arnold, Karl. Affidavit. Made to Arthur C. Johnson, Detective, Shield No. 1508, NYPD, Heinrich Petri, Polizei-Inspektor, Neustadt/Haardt, and John A. Bywater, Clerk at the American Consulate General, Frankfort-on-Main, Germany. October 16, 1934. New Jersey State Police Museum and Learning Center Archives.

[1359] Hager, John. Statement. Made to Assistant District Attorney Breslin, Capt. Lamb, New Jersey State Police; Agent Sandberg, Dept. Of Justice and Stenographer King. September 28, 1934. New Jersey State Police Museum and Learning Center Archives.

[1360] Arnold, Karl. Affidavit. Made to Arthur C. Johnson, Detective, Shield No. 1508, NYPD, Heinrich Petri, Polizei-Inspektor, Neustadt/Haardt, and John A. Bywater, Clerk at the American Consulate General, Frankfort-on-Main, Germany. October 16, 1934. New Jersey State Police Museum and Learning Center Archives.

[1361] Hager, John. Statement. Made to Assistant District Attorney Breslin, Capt. Lamb, New Jersey State Police; Agent Sandberg, Dept. Of Justice and Stenographer King. September 28, 1934. New Jersey State Police Museum and Learning Center Archives.

with authorities.[1362] So when asked where Hager got the money to purchase the shop, he claimed neither he nor Arnold knew, and when he inquired about it, Hager was evasive by saying *"never mind"* (where it came from).[1363] Reiger said that after the shop was sold, Hauptmann came in and acted "surprised" to hear it, and that it was only later he discovered Hauptmann had been the source for the cash when Hager finally confided this fact to both Arnold and him:

> *"First it was secret from where he got the money but Arnold didn't care where he got the money and then it is later he tell me Hauptmann lend him the money."*[1364]

Reiger was lying to authorities, and it's my guess he was doing it to insulate and protect Arnold from having known Hauptmann was the source prior to the transaction. The true version came from Hager. He had $50 in savings but needed another $400 to buy the shop. Hager asked Arnold if he knew of anyone who might lend him the remaining amount and it was actually Arnold who suggested he ask Hauptmann.[1365] Hager would approach Hauptmann during the next card game asking for a loan. However, Hauptmann told him that:

[1362] Reiger, August. Statement. Made to Assistant District Attorney Breslin, Capt. Lamb, New Jersey State Police; Capt. Appel of New York Police, 8th Detective Division and Lt. Keaten, N.J. State Police. Steno King. September 28, 1934. New Jersey State Police Museum and Learning Center Archives.

[1363] Ibid.

[1364] Ibid.

[1365] Hager, John. Statement. Made to Assistant District Attorney Breslin, Capt. Lamb, New Jersey State Police; Agent Sandberg, Dept. Of Justice and Stenographer King. September 28, 1934. New Jersey State Police Museum and Learning Center Archives.

"I have no got any money now, but if I can help you may be later on."[1366]

And so *"14 days later"* Hager asked him again. This time Hauptmann agreed and had Hager go to a lawyer to draw up the papers for the loan. The next morning, on June 6th, Hager met Hauptmann at his *"stock office"* with the paperwork and claimed Hauptmann then gave him $400 in $100 dollar bills which he removed from his pocket saying:

"I swear to highest jury he give me four one hundred dollar bills. I know for sure."[1367]

Hauptmann claiming he had *"no got any money now"* two weeks earlier seems like a strange, yet genuine, response. What happened during that gap in time such that he now had money? Furthermore, $100 bills certainly did not come from laundered $5, $10, and $20 ransom money. Arnold's account of the transaction claimed Hauptmann had given Hager the money in his presence, at the shop, at which time he immediately went to purchase his ticket to Germany and left the following midnight.[1368] Reiger told authorities he was also there when the money was paid but gave a different story. He said he watched Hager count out about *"thirty bills"* with only one being a *"big bill"* perhaps a *"$50"* but then added *"I don't*

[1366] Ibid.

[1367] Ibid.

[1368] Arnold, Karl. Affidavit. Made to Arthur C. Johnson, Detective, Shield No. 1508, NYPD, Heinrich Petri, Polizei-Inspektor, Neustadt/Haardt, and John A. Bywater, Clerk at the American Consulate General, Frankfort-on-Main, Germany. October 16, 1934. New Jersey State Police Museum and Learning Center Archives.

remember good, the rest were all different five, ten."[1369] Having just interviewed Hager, police knew these versions did not match up. This prompted a question concerning whether or not Hauptmann had been there that day, and Reiger, apparently sensing he had just been caught lying, answered with "*oh, I forgot to tell you something,*" and that yes, Hauptmann was there, but he didn't know if it was the morning or afternoon, and it was exactly at that time (as mentioned above) when he pretended not to know about the shop being sold.[1370]

In rounding out this event, Hager was asked if he paid off the debt he owed Hauptmann from this purchase. He told them he paid $50 dollars a month, but that his wife got sick so he asked Hauptmann:

> "*Mr. Hauptmann, I couldn't pay you this money, the whole money*" *and he didn't press me, and he said, "Yes, you are all right, take your time*" *and I give him since.*"[1371]

In fact, Hager still owed Hauptmann $50.00 at the time of the arrest.[1372]

[1369] Reiger, August. Statement. Made to Assistant District Attorney Breslin, Capt. Lamb, New Jersey State Police; Capt. Appel of New York Police, 8th Detective Division and Lt. Keaten, N.J. State Police. Steno King. September 28, 1934. New Jersey State Police Museum and Learning Center Archives.

[1370] Ibid.

[1371] Hager, John. Statement. Made to Assistant District Attorney Breslin, Capt. Lamb, New Jersey State Police; Agent Sandberg, Dept. Of Justice and Stenographer King. September 28, 1934. New Jersey State Police Museum and Learning Center Archives.

[1372] Ibid.

Henry Lampe (Hans Lempke)

Hans Lampke and Willie Dreissigacker had been Hans Kloppenburg's roommates on 416 East 175th Street. These men, along with a co-worker named Jaroslav Nostersky, would frequent Hunter's Island. Richard Hauptmann had made the acquaintance of Lempke through Kloppenburg and would meet Nostersky on the island in the summer of 1932. During one of his interviews with police, Nostersky mentioned how completely baffled he was to hear Hauptmann's name mentioned in conjunction with this crime:

> *"I never would think he would do anything like it. He was happy. I met him in July and he was very happy, he played a mandolin and has a boat. A policeman was walking around, and it did not seem to bother him at all. He was happy."*[1373]

One day Nostersky took Lempke to visit his brother's farm in New Jersey, and during this trip Lemke learned that a nearby property was for sale. In the summer of 1932, Lempke purchased this land in Jackson Mills with the idea of raising chickens.[1374] The "farm" started out as 26 acres of woodland which he bought for $10 per acre.[1375] Sometime later, in early September of 1933, both Kloppenburg and Hauptmann arrived in Jackson Mills to build a Log Cabin on the

---

[1373] Nostersky, Jaroslav. Examination by Lieut. A. T. Keaten, Mr. Frank Wilson and Sgt. A. Zapolsky. October 4, 1934. New Jersey State Police Museum and Learning Center Archives.

[1374] Zapolsky, A., Sgt., New Jersey State Police. New Jersey State Police Report. Investigation with reference to Henry Lampe and Jeroslav Nostersky of Jackson Mills, R. F. D., Lakewood, N.J. October 3, 1934. New Jersey State Police Museum and Learning Center Archives.

[1375] Zapolsky, A., Sgt., New Jersey State Police. New Jersey State Police Report. Investigation of Hans Lampe, Bohomel Nostersky and Joe Nostersky of Jackson Mills, R. F. D. #3, Lakewood, N. J. September 19, 1934. New Jersey State Police Museum and Learning Center Archives.

property so Lempke had a place to live.[1376] During the construction Hauptmann stayed at the Nostersky farm, and Nostersky would later state that Hauptmann had brought his tools along with him to the job.[1377] When finished the cabin was a one-room 15' by 20' building with a small attic and "no accommodations."[1378] In addition to this, Hauptmann put a roof on the chicken coop. Strangely enough, during this excursion Hauptmann asked Lempke if he needed any money. Hauptmann wound up lending Lempke $100 who remembered the cash was *"mostly 1's and 5's, and he thinks there was one 20"* but could not recall if any of the cash included gold notes.[1379] The other odd thing about this loan was that Hauptmann was not asking for any interest on it.[1380] The next time Lempke saw Hauptmann, who was accompanied by his wife at the time, he asked if he wanted his hundred dollars back to which Hauptmann responded:

[1376] Cunningham, T. H., 1st Sgt., New Jersey State Police. New Jersey State Police Report. <u>Search of Henry Lempke's property at Jackson Mills, Lakewood, New Jersey, with regard to discovering any ransom money that may be concealed there</u>. September 28, 1934. New Jersey State Police Museum and Learning Center Archives.

[1377] Nostersky, Jaroslav. Examination by Lieut. A. T. Keaten, Mr. Frank Wilson and Sgt. A. Zapolsky. October 4, 1934. New Jersey State Police Museum and Learning Center Archives. (Note: ruining any idea that Hauptmann did not use his tools after March 1, 1932.)

[1378] Cunningham, T. H., 1st Sgt., New Jersey State Police. New Jersey State Police Report. <u>Search of Henry Lempke's property at Jackson Mills, Lakewood, New Jersey, with regard to discovering any ransom money that may be concealed there</u>. September 28, 1934. New Jersey State Police Museum and Learning Center Archives.

[1379] Ibid.

[1380] Zapolsky, A., Sgt., New Jersey State Police. New Jersey State Police Report. <u>Investigation of Hans Lampe, Bohomel Nostersky and Joe Nostersky of Jackson Mills, R. F. D. #3, Lakewood, N. J.</u> September 19, 1934. New Jersey State Police Museum and Learning Center Archives.

> *"No, not now, but when you have a thousand chickens,*
> *then you can give it back and you will not feel it so*
> *much."*[1381]

As a result, at the time of Hauptmann's arrest Lempke still owed him that $100 debt.

On September 28th of 1934, police went to Lempke's place to search for ransom money. They took note that he didn't seem nervous, he was very cooperative and seemed genuinely surprised to hear of Hauptmann's involvement. According to the NJSP Report of this date:

> *"He also stated that knowing Hauptmann as he had*
> *known him before, that no one would ever think that*
> *this man could commit a crime of this kind, but he says*
> *now he don't know what to think. "Maybe it is true",*
> *he said, "I don't know, I haven't slept for a week after*
> *hearing this news and being questioned by New York*
> *Police.""*[1382]

The police were also convinced that Lempke was completely impoverished showing no signs of wealth and did *"not even possess some of the common luxuries of ordinary life."* While there, they watched him eat his dinner which consisted of *"three slices of bread"* smeared with *"lard"* and one cup of *"cold coffee."*[1383]

[1381] Cunningham, T. H., 1st Sgt., New Jersey State Police. New Jersey State Police Report. Search of Henry Lempke's property at Jackson Mills, Lakewood, New Jersey, with regard to discovering any ransom money that may be concealed there. September 28, 1934. New Jersey State Police Museum and Learning Center Archives.

[1382] Ibid.

[1383] Ibid.

Cecile Barr

Just as history records, police traced a ransom $5 bill to the Lowe's Sheridan Square Theater located on 7th Avenue and 12th street. As police investigated, it was learned this bill had been received by Cecile Barr at approximately 9:30 PM on November 26, 1933. According to Barr, while working the cashier cage a man approached bearing the following description:

> "*Apparently an American; about 30/35 years of age; slender build; 5'8" or 5'9"; about 155/160 lbs., light complexion; thin face' light brown hair' smooth shaven' high cheek bones, wearing a dark soft hat with the front pulled down and no overcoat – dark suit. This man was alone.*"[1384]

The man came up then "*threw*" a five-dollar bill in at her, which had been "*folded three times in eight parts.*"[1385] According to her testimony, the bill was folded in half, then folded length wise, then folded in half again. Police noted that these folds were "*in the manner in which previous bills which were part of the ransom money were folded.*"[1386] It was exactly how the bill was folded up which made Barr

[1384] Finn, James J., Acting Lieutenant, M.O.S. New York City Police Report. Investigation Re: U. S. Currency No. B35435796 A. November 28, 1933. New Jersey State Police Museum and Learning Center Archives.

[1385] Barr, Cecile M. Testimony. The State of New Jersey vs. Bruno Richard Hauptmann, Hunterdon County Court of Oyer and Terminer, page 1917, 1935. New Jersey State Law Library.

[1386] Horn, William F., Cpl. New Jersey State Police. New Jersey State Police Report. Report of investigation concerning a recovered $5.00 bill, which is part of the Lindbergh Ransom money, re Lindbegh Case. November 27, 1933. New Jersey State Police Museum and Learning Center Archives.

look up and take notice of this man.[1387] At the time there were three different ticket prices: 35, 40, and 60 cents.[1388] Once Barr looked up and asked the man "*what do you want*" he simply said "*one forty.*"[1389] The Authorities pressed:

> Q: *His voice, did it sound like a German?*
>
> A: *All he said was "One Forty."*[1390]

However, despite this, and despite the fact that the man had his "*dark slouch hat pulled way down over his forehead,*" Barr was certain when she saw Hauptmann in the Bronx Court House on October 3rd, 1934, that he was the man in question.[1391] She would later testify to this before the Hunterdon Grand Jury on October 8th, and again during Hauptmann's Flemington trial.

I won't go on and on about the debate which exists concerning Hauptmann's defenses against Barr's claim. They are well documented in just about every book that's ever been written on this case. However, I do believe it's important to note that when Barr

---

[1387] Barr, Cecilia. Statement. Made to Assistant District Attorney Breslin, Capt. Lamb, N.J. State Police; Lt. Finn, N.Y. Police, Mr. Sekora, Dept. of Justice. Steno King. October 3, 1934 at 12:00 P. M. New Jersey State Police Museum and Learning Center Archives. (Note: Cecile is spelled "Cecilia" in his statement)

[1388] Barr, Cecile M. Testimony. The State of New Jersey vs. Bruno Richard Hauptmann, <u>Hunterdon County Court of Oyer and Terminer</u>, page 1917, 1935. New Jersey State Law Library.

[1389] Barr, Cecilia. Statement. Made to Assistant Attorneys General Richard Stockton 3d, and Harry A. Walsh; Lieut. Finn, N.Y. Police; Sgt. Haussling, N. J. State Police. October 29, 1934. New Jersey State Police Museum and Learning Center Archives. (Note: Cecile is spelled "Cecilia" in his statement as well)

[1390] Ibid.

[1391] Ibid.

submitted a request to Governor Hoffman claiming the reward, she made the claim that in her description she told the *"peace officers"* the man's nationality was *"A foreigner, either German or Scandinavian."*[1392] This assertion is simply not true since her earliest accounts suggested this man was an *"American."* That's not to say he was, just that she had no observable information available to her to suggest otherwise at that time. Later, in an effort to bolster her chances at the reward money, she seemed to lie to the Governor about this point.

Fold & Creases

I find the important part of the Barr occurrence to be the "folds" in the money. As mentioned above, some of the ransom money had these same types of folds when recovered. This fact, that only some had these folds, was supported by Special Agent Frank J. Wilson of the Treasury Department. Both he and Lt. Keaten were involved in many of the ransom money investigations concerning *"thirty-three bills found between April 6, 1932 and May 15, 1933"* and it was his claim that *"no creases or unusual characteristics were found in any of these bills."*[1393] So in this assertion there is, at least, some evidence that only a portion of the ransom bills recovered had these "creases" which were supposed to have been caused by these "eight" part folds. Regardless, it shows the police were doing their job and staying vigilant in their attempt to identify those passing this ransom as someone actually connected to its collection. In June of 1934, the NYPD sent four $5 ransom bills recovered during that month to

---

[1392] Barr, Cecile. Affidavit. To His Excellency, Harold G. Hoffman, Governor of the State of New Jersey. April 20, 1937. New Jersey State Police Museum and Learning Center Archives.

[1393] Wilson, Frank J., Special Agent, Internal Revenue Service. Internal Revenue Report. SI-6336. In re: Kidnapping and murder of Charles Augustus Lindbergh, Jr. page 16. November 11, 1933. New Jersey State Police Museum and Learning Center Archives.

their technical research lab for analysis. The lab discovered that all four bills had this eight part fold:

> *"...resulting in a compact arrangement – apparently to fold them in such a size as to be carried in a vest pocket or a watch pocket."*[1394]

This is an interesting suggestion considering the fact the earliest police report with Barr had her remembering that the man who passed her the folded up $5 *"took this bill in question out of his pocket."*[1395]

However, there is a problem with this theory. As Dr. Lloyd Gardner was to correctly point out in his book, it was the FBI Laboratory's opinion that *"the creases indicating the three-way fold of some of the bills, are without any particular significance because they have been noted on bills in general circulation."*[1396] Another author, Richard Cahill, disagreed with Gardner's position and asked the readers of his book to experiment with their own bills to disprove this claim.[1397] I personally do not see the relevance in this idea since it disagrees with the FBI Scientists, and since the circumstances which address money and people nowadays are completely different. Even if, for example, many people did fold or crease their money in the middle, I submit a crease would, then as well as now, develop over time. Cahill

---

[1394] Finn, James J. Lieutenant. "How I Captured Hauptmann." *Liberty Magazine.* October 26, 1935. New Jersey State Police Museum and Learning Center Archives.

[1395] Horn, William F., Cpl. New Jersey State Police. New Jersey State Police Report. Report of investigation concerning a recovered $5.00 bill, which is part of the Lindbergh Ransom money, re Lindbergh Case. November 27, 1933. New Jersey State Police Museum and Learning Center Archives.

[1396] Gardner, Lloyd C. June 2004. *The Case That Never Dies.* Rutgers University Press. Page 127.

[1397] Cahill, Richard T. 2014. *Hauptmann's Ladder: A Step-By-Step Analysis of the Lindbergh Kidnapping.* The Kent State University Press, pages 148-9.

also wrote in his footnote #11 that the FBI Report cited in Gardner's book should be *"viewed with a skeptical eye."*[1398] I cannot disagree more. The Division of Investigation Laboratory Report consists of 37 pages, a 10 page narrative and 27 sheets of analysis conducted by Special Agent E. P. Coffey and Samuel F. Pickering. Pickering's specialty was chemical analysis and their entire goal was to make a detailed examination of the ransom money, currently in their possession, in order to find anything which could possibly develop into a clue. It was not written from a position of criticism toward any agency, police force, or anyone else. They were meticulous in their efforts by investigating every stain, mark, or foreign material.[1399] They chose to omit any finding of these creases because in their professional opinion they saw no value in it. There is no reason whatsoever not to trust this report because it was not created with any agenda other than developing facts and evidence, and anyone reading it could easily draw this conclusion. Next, Gardner's source concerning the FBI "rebuttal" is a different source and is attributable to the FBI "Summary" Report. As to this report I would agree with Cahill that it contains some information based upon faulty sources and should be viewed as a secondary source. However, what's recorded there is relying on the above written Lab Report so it is not a dubious position.[1400]

Based on the above, what has now been developed is that some of the ransom money had the 3–way / 8–part crease. The NYPD Lab believed this was done to fit the bill into a vest or watch pocket, and

---

[1398] Ibid. page 364.

[1399] Division of Investigation, New York Office. Laboratory Report. Unknown Subjects. Charles A. Lindbergh, Jr., Victim. August 7, 1934. New Jersey State Police Museum and Learning Center Archives.

[1400] Sisk, T. H. DOI (FBI) et. al., DOI Report. Summary. NY File No. 62-3057, p. 213. February 16, 1934. National Archives at College Park Maryland.

the FBI Lab believed these folds were not unusual or unique to the ransom money.

Edwards Sport Shop

On December 4, 1932, a $5 ransom bill was passed on 111 Nassau Street at Edwards Sport Shop.[1401] The bill had been discovered by a teller at the Central Hanover Bank on December 5th, and once investigated, police determined it originated from the sports shop. Upon arriving there, Lt. Finn interviewed a salesman, Charles Brown, under the guise that this $5 had been counterfeit.[1402] It was determined that a 6' tall light complected man with a *"German accent"* had been the one who passed this ransom $5 to the shop by removing it from a large wallet he took out from his coat pocket.[1403] Lt. Finn asked Brown to notify the police if this man were to ever return to the shop; Brown agreed, then Finn left. Upon the arrest of Hauptmann, authorities recalled Brown's description of the man as "German," then brought him in hoping he'd be able to identify Hauptmann. While at the Bronx County District Attorney's office, Brown was surprised to hear the $5 was Lindbergh Ransom money, thinking all along it had been a counterfeit bill. He was again questioned concerning this event, and it was learned that the man in question was not alone but came into the store with someone and purchased a pair of gloves and another item which Brown could not

---

[1401] Finn, James J., M.O.S., New York City Police Department. 18th Division Report. Cooperation accorded by Banks re: Lindbergh Ransom Money. January 23, 1934. New Jersey State Police Museum and Learning Center Archives.

[1402] Finn, James J., Act. Lieutenant. New York City Police Report. $5 United States Note B50869762A PAID IN LINDBERGH RANSOM MONEY. December 6, 1932. New Jersey State Police Museum and Learning Center Archives.

[1403] Ibid.

recall.[1404] This man was *"almost 6 ft. tall"* and was wearing a *"fine dark haberdine* [sic] *coat, a very good one."*[1405] Brown also made this interesting observation:

> *"...he had a foreign accent and he had a large wallet and the bill was folded over in about 8 parts and that stuck me funny and what made him stick in my mind he acted like a fairy...".*[1406]

Brown was eventually asked if this man was Hauptmann:

> [**Breslin**]: *Have you ever seen that person since?*
>
> [**Brown**]: *No.*
>
> [**Breslin**]: *Were you in the court room this morning in the Bronx?*
>
> [**Brown**]: *Yes. I saw the person they are referring to but I wouldn't swear to it. It is so long back. I would recognize any of the merchandise he might have if it came out of our store.*

A couple of observations here.... This bill fell within the range of recovered ransom money mentioned in Wilson's report, which claimed no folds or creases were found on any of those bills. I assume Wilson was either wrong about this particular bill or it showed no

---

[1404] Brown, Charles H. Statement. Made to Assistant District Attorney Breslin, Capt. Lamb, N.J. State Police, Lt. Finn, N.Y.C. Police, Agent Seykora, Dept. of Justice and Stenographer King. October 3, 1934 at 12:03 P. M. New Jersey State Police Museum and Learning Center Archives.

[1405] Ibid.

[1406] Ibid.

permanent signs to the naked eye of having been folded. Next, this man came into the store with someone else and had this bill folded up exactly like the man who passed the $5 to Barr, yet he took it out of his wallet and not a vest or watch pocket. As for being a "fairy" (homosexual), I think it's a label that if applied to Hauptmann would be very hard to stick given what we know about how he acted in public. Of course one might recall Dr. Shoenfeld's opinion that the ransom note writer had "*homosexual tendencies.*"[1407] However, if this were true of Hauptmann (and I do not believe it was) then these tendencies were latent and not overt.

Hauptmann's Arrest

On the morning of September 19, 1934, Hauptmann exited his home at about 8:55 AM. He walked into his garage, got into his car, then began to drive toward Boston Road. He was being followed by three cars:

First car – Detective Wallace, Detective Cronin, Trooper Dore, and Sgt. Wallace.

Second car – Corporal Horn, Agent Seery, and Lt. Finn.

Third car – Agent Sisk, and Lieut. Keaten.[1408]

A plan had been formulated not to arrest Hauptmann on his premises. According to Lt. Finn, the reason was so that nobody

---

[1407] Shoenfeld, Dudley D., M.D. <u>Memorandum to Captain Oliver and Lt. James Finn of the New York Police Department</u>. November 1, 1932. New Jersey State Police Museum and Learning Center Archives

[1408] Finn, James, Lieut. Statement. Made to Mr. Peacock. November 22, 1934. New Jersey State Police Museum and Learning Center Archives.

would get "*hurt*."[1409] According to Special Agent Sisk, the idea was to surveil so they could catch Hauptmann passing ransom money.[1410] There had been a prearranged signal that would be given by Lt. Finn if the need arose to pull Hauptmann over.[1411] Soon Hauptmann was seen looking in his rear view mirror and noticed he was being shadowed. As a result, he increased his speed up to 40 mph in the heavy morning traffic in an attempt to "shake" those following him.[1412] The chase was then on with Hauptmann going through lights without stopping until a milk truck got in his way.[1413] Finn then gave the signal to the first car, driven by Detective Wallace, to "*get in front of him and run him into the curb*."[1414] Trooper Dore and Sgt. Wallace jumped out of their car in front of Hauptmann's, and almost immediately both other cars arrived with all of these police "*grouped around Hauptmann and made him get out of his car*."[1415] Lt. Finn immediately started to search through his front pockets while Lt. Keaten searched his back pockets. Keaten then:

[1409] Finn, James J. Testimony. <u>Bronx Grand Jury</u>. People vs. Hauptmann. September 24, 1934. New Jersey State Police Museum and Learning Center Archives.

[1410] Sisk, T. H., Special Agent, USBOI (FBI). USBOI Report. <u>Bruno Richard Hauptmann alias Richard Hauptmann alias Richard Hoffman alias Karl Pellmeier</u>. Kidnaping and Murder of Charles A. Lindbergh Jr. October 17, 1934. National Archives at College Park Maryland.

[1411] Finn, James, Lieut. Statement. Made to Mr. Peacock. November 22, 1934. New Jersey State Police Museum and Learning Center Archives.

[1412] Tamm, E. A., Federal Bureau of Investigation. <u>Memorandum For The Director</u>. October 19, 1935. National Archives at College Park Maryland.

[1413] Finn, James, Lieut. Statement. Made to Mr. Peacock. November 22, 1934. New Jersey State Police Museum and Learning Center Archives.

[1414] Finn, J. J. Leiut. (Summary) Report. Undated. New Jersey State Police Museum and Learning Center Archives.

[1415] Dore, D. Trp., New Jersey State Police. New Jersey State Police Report. <u>Activity on the Hauptman case</u>. November 2, 1934. New Jersey State Police Museum and Learning Center Archives.

"...took a wallet from his back pocket in which there was a Twenty Dollar Gold Certificate which was checked by Agent Seery and which was found to be part of the Ransom bills."[1416]

Now here is the important part... This bill was <u>not</u> discovered folded up in any way. Moreover, none of these men ever recorded or wrote that this bill had any indication of the 8–part folds in it. Not in any report, testimony, or magazine article. Next, Wilentz never mentioned it during the trial either. This is very telling, since tying Hauptmann to ransom money *prior* to the date he asserted he found it in the shoe box Fisch had left him was a very important aspect of the State's case, and it's what made Barr's testimony so crucial. If this bill had these folds, the link between Hauptmann and the ransom prior to the known dates he passed it would have complemented Barr's eyewitness account, thereby making the State's case concerning this so much easier. Furthermore, Assistant Attorney General Peacock wrote in his unpublished manuscript, *Guilty As Hell*, the following caption under a picture of this $20:

"This note was found on Hauptmann when he was arrested."[1417]

Nothing whatsoever out about folds or creases in this bill.

Here is probably a good place to address Richard Cahill's assertion that enlargements of the $20 ransom bill found in Hauptmann's possession during his arrest show that it *"was folded in the same*

[1416] Finn, J. J. Lieut. (Summary) Report. Undated. New Jersey State Police Museum and Learning Center Archives.

[1417] Peacock, Robert. *Guilty As Hell – At Last, The Truth About The Hauptmann Case.* Manuscript: Unpublished and Undated (1935?). Insert between pages 33-4. New Jersey State Police Museum and Learning Center Archives.

manner as earlier bills."[1418] Despite the preceding information making this point moot, I think for the sake of history it should be discussed. Cahill claims that during Hauptmann's arrest Lt. Finn *"photographed the bill at the scene."*[1419] Using this point to establish when the photograph was taken, he also claimed that by examining the enlarged negatives of the photograph of this bill at the NJSP Archives it proves *"without question"* these folds existed before it was removed from Hauptmann's wallet.[1420]

These assertions must be properly reviewed.

My first reservation concerns Cahill's source for his position that Lt. Finn took the picture of this bill *"at the scene."* While this sentence is footnoted, it does not cite a source. The $20 gold certificate serial no. A35517877A was introduced in court as Exhibit Number S–172. A picture of this bill can be found in Lindbergh Photograph Binder XI. However, there is no caption, and I have never been able to find a source concerning who took the photo, where the photo was taken, or when it was taken. Although many people over the years somehow have a "knack" for reviewing documents they've never seen, I do not possess such an ability and cannot evaluate this claim without seeing the documentation to support it. I'd also like to note that I do not know if other photos were taken which no longer exist, or which are not at the NJSP Archives. Thus, how would we know if the photo in question was the first? Next, in looking at the picture myself I see that it does have a clear line down its middle. However, if the other lines I see are creases too, then there are many other creases outside of the "pattern" in this bill as well. Also, if Cahill is mistaken, or if by chance Lt. Finn did not take a picture of the bill in the condition which it was found on Hauptmann, or did not take any photo which

---

[1418] Cahill, Richard T. 2014. *Hauptmann's Ladder: A Step-By-Step Analysis of the Lindbergh Kidnapping.* The Kent State University Press, page 148.

[1419] Ibid.

[1420] Ibid.

might have predated or preceded *this* photo of the bill at the scene (or anywhere else), then we must also consider the possibility that police folded the bill themselves then showed it to Hauptmann in order to ask "why" he would fold his money in this way. This is not beyond the realm of possibility considering, for example, that they showed him the "J. J. Faulkner deposit slip" during his interrogation, asked him if he'd ever seen it before, then had him write it down on a slip of paper.[1421] That written exemplar of his handwriting was never used against him, and in fact, is nowhere to be found at the NJSP Archives. To this day it has never been located. One final but important point is that the ransom was not new money. These bills were old, and if the bills were folded so they could easily be distinguished from good money by its passer for laundering purposes, then they wouldn't have been folded for long – making it less likely for permanent creases to exist from that act.

Hauptmann's Behavior

Another fact that I've found to be important was Hauptmann's demeanor at the time he was arrested. I think all of us picture ourselves in his situation and think he must have been out of his mind with fear and panic. But no. Hauptmann was calm. The situation was best described by this Q&A between a Juror and Lt. Finn:

> [**Juror**]: *Did this man appear to be frightened when you first picked him up?*

> [**Finn**]: *No sir.*

[1421] Hauptmann, Bruno Richard. Interrogation. Conducted by Inspector John A. Lyons "and others." September 20, 1934 at 11:05 A. M. New Jersey State Police Museum and Learning Center Archives.

[**Juror**]: *He wasn't frightened at all?*

[**Finn**]: *No sir.*

[**Juror**]: *Did he suspect anything?*

[**Finn**]: *No. Apparently he was well ready with the story that he was going to tell if we picked him up.*[1422]

Lt. Finn was a seasoned cop, and this type of observation coming from him should not be ignored. One thing I've always wondered was why, if Hauptmann had pulled this off alone, he did not simply pull up stakes and move his family away. Why put up with a landlord he did not like, and an apartment that had so many problems? With the police specifically focusing on the Bronx, what kept him from passing ransom money outside of, or away from the area? Why was he "*ready with*" a "*story*" in case he was arrested? For someone this proactive, what kept him glued to the Bronx waiting for this possibility to occur? And what was the story Lt. Finn believed Hauptmann had prepared? According to Detective Wallace:

> "*Hauptmann was questioned for a short period by the other investigators present as to how he came into possession of the gold certificate and advised them that he had had* [sic] *about three hundred dollars worth of gold certificates for about two years. These gold certificates had been accumulated from time to time by him together with gold pieces and he informed the*

[1422] Finn, James J. Testimony. <u>Bronx Grand Jury</u>. People vs. Hauptmann. September 24, 1934. New Jersey State Police Museum and Learning Center Archives.

investigators that he had $120.00 in gold at his home in a strong box."[1423]

This sounds a whole lot like the story-line Mueller had ready for police once he was learned Hauptmann had been apprehended. Had Mueller been "prepared" with the same alibi?

It sure looks that way.

[1423] Wallace, J. Detective Sergeant. New Jersey State Police. New Jersey State Police Report. <u>Dismounted patrol at Fordham Road and 3rd Avenue "L", Bronx, New York for the purpose of locating a suspect who was passing the ransom money in the Lindbergh case</u>. October 6, 1934. New Jersey State Police Museum and Learning Center Archives.

8

The Panel Purchase

Some people try to paint everything as either black or white. It's a mindset that I attempt to steer those interested in the case away from because in life there are very rarely only the two choices of "one" and "the other," and this case is no exception. It is true that many who believe Hauptmann guilty will point to the following story to support their claim; yet they will also completely ignore or overlook it when they then assert he was a Lone Wolf. They accept only details that they like and completely ignore those they do not. If one points to this story to show Hauptmann's guilt, it is impossible to suggest he worked alone – and yet many people do that anyway. Obviously both positions (Lone Wolf and Guilty) cannot be true, but that is exactly how the debate proceeds. Selective observation is no way to get to the truth of anything.

On September 26, 1934, a friend of Commissioner Meany walked into the 18th Division New York City Police station with information concerning Hauptmann. He told Inspector Griffith a story that, if true, was very damaging to Hauptmann's claim that he did not know he possessed Lindbergh Ransom Money.[1424] This man explained that:

> "On or about February 14 (year not given) a man appeared at Cross, Austin & Ireland Lumber Co., Gerard Ave. & 149th St. and bought a 2" x 4" fire panel, for which he paid 60 ¢. He offered a $10. Bill in payment to a salesman named Reilly, and in conversation with him remarked he had many more of them. Said Reilly retains sales slip and noted the number of the car in which this unknown man was driving. The same number appeared in the Daily News as being the car owned by Bruno Hauptmann. From the pictures published in the papers of Hauptmann he thinks he is the same man. At the time of this visit he was accompanied by 2 other man [sic]."[1425]

As a result of this information, Detective Frank of the NYPD, paired up with Detective Meade of the NJSP, proceeded to Gerard Ave & 149th St. to interview yard superintendent, William J. Reilly, and his secretary Alice Murphy. These Detectives were told that on February 14, 1934, a Federal Department man named Arthur Koehler and another man believed to be a New Jersey State Trooper were at the yard conducting an investigation when two men arrived and one "purchased one Fir Veneer Panel 24x48 for which the price was 40

[1424] Griffith, John. Inspector, City of New York Police. Memorandum for Action Deputy Chief Inspector Bruckman. Commanding Officer, 18th Division, Bronx. Undated. New Jersey State Police Museum and Learning Center Archives.

[1425] Ibid.

cents" but the man "*tendered Mr. Reilly a ten dollar bill.*"[1426] Both Reilly and Murphy identified Hauptmann from a newspaper photo as the man in question.

Reilly told the detectives that he became suspicious of the bill, and thinking it might be counterfeit, asked "Hauptmann" if he had anything smaller. In response Hauptmann said "*you are lucky to get this and I've got a lot more of them.*"[1427] Reilly then took the bill to an inside office to get the proper change from Murphy; however, once he…

> "*…in turn offered it to Hauptmann thereupon the unknown man said 'here give him his ten dollars back and take this five;' Mr. Reilly accepted the five and gave it to Miss Murphy she after taking out the forty cents took the change and above mentioned ten dollar bill to where Hauptmann & the unknown man was standing Hauptmann thereupon snatched the ten dollars from her hand and said 'keep the panel for us we will be back. Reilly being suspicious of there* [sic] *actions watched them enter an automobile and jotted down the following license plate number 4U1341NY which is registered to Bruno R. Hauptmann.*"[1428]

During this investigation, neither Reilly nor Murphy could say whether the $10 was a gold note but did say that the men never returned for the panel. The "unknown man" was described as being 35 years old, dark hair, 135lbs., about between 5 and 5–1/2 feet

[1426] Frank, Charles. Detective NYPD AND Joseph Meade. Detective NJSP. City of New York Police Report. <u>Investigation at Cross, Austin, & Ireland Lumber Co. 118E 149th St Bronx; Mott-Haven 9-1340</u>. September 26, 1934. New Jersey State Police Museum and Learning Center Archives.
[1427] Ibid.
[1428] Ibid.

tall. Reilly told the detectives if he ever saw this man again he could identify him.[1429]

A couple of days later, Agent Sisk walked into the Bronx Assistant District Attorney's office where Captain Lamb was reading a report concerning the above matter. Lamb read about the two men buying a very small amount of lumber but tendering a ten dollar bill where it was refused and a smaller amount demanded. The report further stated that…

> "…two men in the car, one of whom was Hauptmann and the other was a man about 5'6" weight about 135, who has the appearance of an Italian or an American – dark complexioned American -."[1430]

However, as soon as Sisk's presence was noticed Lamb stopped reading the report.

On October 2nd William Reilly was picked up at the lumber yard and transported "as a witness to the Bronx County Court house to endeavor to identify Hauptmann as a man that had attempted to pass one of the Lindbergh Bills." [1431] After being allowed to view Hauptmann he was returned to the Lumber Company. Although the police report on this does not say, it was later asserted that Reilly had "identified Hauptmann as the larger of the two men who

---

[1429] Ibid.

[1430] Tamm. E. A. Division of Investigation (FBI). Memorandum For The Director. September 29, 1934. National Archives at College Park Maryland.

[1431] Kelly, W. P. Det. Sgt. New Jersey State Police. New Jersey State Police Report. Investigation of the Lindbergh Case in New York City re payment made by Hans Mueller to Dr. Jos. S. Brandstein, 2952 Marion Ave., N.Y.C. October 2, 1934. New Jersey State Police Museum and Learning Center Archives.

had purchased the panel."[1432] On the same day, the United Press ran a story which claimed Schwarzkopf was telling the press that Hauptmann had an *"accomplice in passing the ransom money"* and that they knew the *"bills he handled were 'hot'."*[1433] However, it was on this very same day that Alice Murphy had also been brought into see Assistant District Attorney Breslin, and when asked, she wasn't so sure the man was Hauptmann:

> Breslin: *You have seen pictures of this man Bruno Richard Hauptmann in the paper?*
> Murphy: *Yes, I did.*
>
> Q: *Do you recognize him?*
> A: *I couldn't swear it was him by any means.*
>
> Q: *I show you this picture of Hauptmann bearing number 19753 and ask you if you can tell me whether there is any resemblance between that man and either of the men present at the time of the events you told me about?*
> A: *Yes, I think it is he, but I am not sure.*
>
> Q: *Do you think if you saw him in person you might be able to identify him?*
> A: *I might, I couldn't say for sure.*[1434]

[1432] Tinker, Arthur A. Letter from Arthur A. Tinker to Mr. Arthur Koehler. March 29, 1935. New Jersey State Police Museum and Learning Center Archives.

[1433] "Schwartzkopf Says Hauptmann Had 'Pal'". *Salt Lake Telegram.* October 2, 1934. Utah Digital Newspapers (digitalnewspapers.org)

[1434] Murphy, Alice T. Statement. Made to Assistant District Attorney Breslin, Lt. Keaten, N.J. State Police, Agent Sisk, Dept. of Justice and Stenographer King. October 2, 1934 at 11:25 A. M. New Jersey State Police Museum and Learning Center Archives.

During this statement Miss Murphy again asserted that at the time of this event *"a Government man was in there"* and that Reilly had asked her to change a ten dollar bill.[1435] She also stated that the *"shorter of the two"* man told her not to change the ten but handed her a five instead and also claimed *"their actions were suspicious."* She further stated once they bought the panel they said:

> *"'Do you mind if we leave the panel here, we are going across the street to eat,' and they looked at the men and walked out and when my employer came in I showed him the bill and said, 'Do you think there is anything wrong with this?' and he said, 'I couldn't tell.' And they never came back for the panel and Mr. Reilly marked their number down on the panel. I think they recognized this man from the Government, Mr. Arthur Kohler [sic] and a State Policeman."*[1436]

She also said she did not notice an accent and described the second man as *"5' 5'"* with *"dark complexion"* and *"quite black hair."* She also claimed that she saw a picture of Hauptmann's friend, [Willie] *"Dreissingacker,"* in the newspaper who *"looked very much like him."*[1437] Finally, when asked to fix the date Murphy said she *"didn't know"* except it must have been *"around February"* adding that it could be verified by the date *"Mr. Kohler [sic] was in the office."*[1438] On the following day, another newspaper quoted Reilly as saying he began examining the *"yellowback"* which he hadn't seen *"for some time"* and *"the men became nervous at once."*[1439] An Associated Press newspaper article wrote that after Reilly scanned pictures of

---

[1435] Ibid.

[1436] Ibid.

[1437] Ibid.

[1438] Ibid.

[1439] "Reilly to Be Questioned Further." Newspaper Unknown. October 3, 1934. New Jersey State Police Museum and Learning Center Archives.

Hauptmann's friends, he said one of them *"resembled the mysterious companion in some ways"* but he was *"not sure enough"* to say it was him.[1440]

About a week later Special Agent Sisk wrote a Memo to Assistant Director Hugh Clegg about this matter referring to the statements made by both Reilly and Murphy. Here he wrote that on February 14, 1934:

> *"Hauptmann and another individual entered the lumber yard and purchased a small piece of lumber for fifty cents and in payment tendered a $10.00 gold certificate. The lumberyard employees mentioned were a little dubious about taking a gold certificate and were also a trifle suspicious as to Hauptmann and his companion, and they therefore manifested their reluctance to take the bill, after which Hauptmann's companion took the bill back and gave them a $5.00 bill in payment for the lumber."*[1441]

Sisk also relayed that these men left the panel behind while they went across the street to the "Ideal Lunch" and that in doing so were supposed to have walked right past Bornmann and Koehler.[1442] He continued on with this very important piece of information, which I believe holds tremendous weight since Sisk was present during Murphy's questioning:

[1440] "Pal of Hauptmann Came To Aid In Lumber Yard Sought." *Plattsburgh Daily Press.* October 3, 1934. NYS Historic Newspapers. nyshistoricnewspapers.org

[1441] Sisk, T. H. Special Agent, Division of Investigation (FBI). Memorandum For Mr. Clegg. <u>Bruno Richard Hauptmann with alias Kidnaping and Murder of Charles A. Lindbergh, Jr.</u> October 10, 1934. National Archives at College Park Maryland.

[1442] Ibid.

> *"Mr. Breslin, chief assistant to Mr. Foley, asked Miss Murphy whether she had the original piece of paper upon which she had written the license number of Hauptmann's car, but she was unable to produce same, but stated she was positive the license was 4–U–1341. (This is the 1934 registration for Hauptmann's Dodge sedan.)"*[1443]

This piece of information introduces a couple of problems to consider which surround a copy of a handwritten document I found at the NJSP Archives back in 2004. In Richard Cahill's book, *Hauptmann's Ladder*, it appears he actually located the <u>original</u> after finding it in the files of the New York City Municipal Archives.[1444] Indeed this document has written on it:

"Ex 3
District Attorney Off.
Bx. Co. 10–1–34
TJK (Steno)"

"17–Panel
24 x 48 – .40
4U–13–41"

Now, many people who research this case seem to rely heavily on Waller's book for information on this event. That is a huge mistake. Waller's account differs with the source material documentation on several key points. For example, Waller claimed Murphy wrote down Hauptmann's plate number on the *"sales slip."*[1445] However, several

---

[1443] Ibid.

[1444] Cahill, Richard T. Jr. (2014). *Hauptmann's Ladder*. Kent State University Press. Page 138.

[1445] Waller, George. (1961) *Kidnap: The Story of the Lindbergh Case*. The Dial Press. Page 210.

sources, including Murphy herself, say it was Reilly who wrote the number down. In fact, Murphy claimed in her official statement that Reilly marked it down "*on the panel*." I could never tell whether or not the original slip, the copy of which I found, may have come from the panel, but Cahill's discovery suggests that it did not. I've often thought that perhaps Murphy wrote down on a separate piece of paper what Reilly had noted on the panel. If that's true, it could account for such a scrap of paper existing and explain what Sisk noted in his memo. However, why would Breslin be asking Murphy if she had the "*original piece of paper upon which she had written the license number of Hauptmann's car*" on October 2nd when, if this piece of paper was legitimate, his own office already had it on October 1st? Another issue seems to be whether or not this original $10 offered was a gold note. The earliest sources say neither Murphy nor Reilly could say, while the later sources seemed to indicate it was. One thing is made clear by Agent Sisk though…that there had "*been no ransom bills traced to either the Ideal Lunch or the lumber yard.*"[1446]

The Police would continue to bring Reilly in to look over pictures of suspects they believed might be Hauptmann's accomplice (without success) with the last source I could find being in early November.[1447] It was sometime during this period that Koehler, having heard about this revelation, referred back to his reports to see when he had been to Cross, Austin & Ireland only to discover the documentation

---

[1446] Sisk, T. H. Special Agent, Division of Investigation (FBI). Memorandum For Mr. Clegg. <u>Bruno Richard Hauptmann with alias Kidnaping and Murder of Charles A. Lindbergh, Jr.</u> October 10, 1934. National Archives at College Park Maryland.

[1447] Patterson, Claude. Detective, New Jersey State Police. New Jersey State Police Report. <u>Investigation of attached communication from Roy J. Curtiss, Justice of the Peace, Fredericks, Oklahoma, re: Lindbergh Case.</u> November 7, 1934. New Jersey State Police Museum and Learning Center Archives.

showed his last trip there was on December 14, 1933.[1448] The fact Hauptmann was with someone else during this event was appealing to Koehler. When examining Hauptmann's tools in early October, Koehler found that while certain tools there were found to have been used in constructing the "kidnap ladder," there were others missing from the garage that must have been used in its construction. Koehler surmised that the possibility *"the ripping and planning were done in Hauptmann's garage but the notching of the rails and cross cutting the rungs to proper length"* along with the actual *"ladder assembly"* were done *"at some secluded spot"* was the only way to explain this mystery he faced.[1449] And so, eager to resolve the conflict with Reilly and Murphy's accounts, he and Detective Bornmann stopped by the lumber yard on November 20th:

> *"William J. Reilly, superintendent at the yard, showed us the purchase slip for a 3–ply ¼" fir panel 24" x 48" and the panel itself which was purchased by the party in question. The slip was dated December 14, 1933, and our reports for that day showed that we were at that yard."*[1450]

[1448]   Koehler, Arthur. U. S. Forest Products Laboratory. New Jersey State Police Report. Report on examination of the ladder used in the Lindbergh kidnapping case by Arthur Koehler, U.S. Forest Products Laboratory, Madison, Wisconsin. November 10, 1933. New Jersey State Police Museum and Learning Center Archives. (Note: this report covers the dates 11-10-33 thru 12-20-33).

[1449]   Koehler, Arthur. U.S. Forest Products Laboratory. New Jersey State Police Report. Report of examination of tools and lumber from Hauptmann's garage and house by Arthur Koehler. October 1 to 4, 1934. New Jersey State Police Museum and Learning Center Archives.

[1450]   Koehler, Arthur. Forest Products Laboratory. New Jersey State Police Report. Conference with Assistant Attorney General Peacock. November 22, 1934. New Jersey State Police Museum and Learning Center Archives.

Reilly recounted the story again explaining that "Hauptmann" had offered the ten *"yellow side down"* for the payment of the 40 cent panel and that Miss Murphy had asked if they had anything smaller; they then instead offered a five dollar bill.[1451] It was when Murphy went into the back to get change that Reilly believed these men may have noticed Detective Bornmann and become "suspicious."[1452] The story would change once more:

> *"The shorter man then laid 40 cents on the desk, but the other took the five one dollar bills in change for his five and both left without the panel. Someone called after them to take the panel. They said they would go into a neighboring restaurant first but they apparently went right out of the restaurant again and got away, however, not before Mr. Reilly obtained the license number of the car which he said agreed with that on Hauptmann's car when arrested..."*[1453]

While Koehler seemed satisfied with the truthfulness of this account, he didn't understand how Hauptmann's plate, which was different in 1933, could have matched his 1934 plate number.[1454] Looking at this new account, it seems there are several possible explanations for the difference in dates.... I consider it possible both Reilly and Murphy confused the dates by combining two separate incidents into one because they were both related. Once being told their February recollection didn't "work" it's possible they found a receipt for a similar purchase on the needed day and believed they had misremembered the date. The only other explanation is that the receipt was a fraud. Nevertheless, it's conceivable that by this time Reilly's memory began to fade as it differed from the original story

1451   Ibid.
1452   Ibid.
1453   Ibid.
1454   Ibid.

somewhat. Or again, it could be he's not remembering it correctly because it was a lie. Koehler was shown the panel, and he did not make any mention of the tag number being written there, or on the receipt itself for that matter. So if Koehler was shown the actual panel then I would submit Miss Murphy's claim asserting Reilly wrote down the tag number on it was never true.

During the Flemington trial, the Prosecution wanted nothing to do with the Lumber Yard account, having already committed to the Lone-Wolf position. While it's hard to know whether or not the Defense was aware of it, they wouldn't have wanted anything to do with it either, since William Reilly's eyewitness account obviously implicated Hauptmann.

After Hauptmann's conviction, Koehler was asked by several people who had bought into the Lone-Wolf conviction hook, line, and sinker how Reilly recorded Hauptmann's 1934 registration in 1933. With the idea of writing something up on the case, he looked to reconcile this and maintain the credibility he sought. To that end, he wrote a letter to Cross, Austin and Ireland secretary Arthur A. Tinker which asked for clarity as to why the earlier newspaper accounts said the event occurred on February 14, 1934, and also asked:

> "Did the license that Mr. Reilly took down correspond with Hauptmann's 1933 license number or did he already have the 1934 plates on his car? If the license number written down by Mr. Reilly was the number for 1933, then I suppose it was necessary first to find out what number Hauptmann had on his car that year."[1455]

[1455] Koehler, Arthur. In Charge, Section of Silvicultural Relations. Letter from Arthur Koehler to Mr. Tinker. March 22, 1935. New Jersey State Police Museum and Learning Center Archives.

On receipt of Koehler's letter, Tinker went over the details carefully with Reilly before he made his reply. His first point to Koehler was that *"at no time"* did anyone notice him wearing a badge, claiming he showed him identification *"from your pocket"* and that Murphy and Reilly *"did not know who you were."*[1456] Tinker says the date of the ticket on this purchase was *"December 14th."* then goes on to retell the story once more:

> *"They offered Mr. Reilly a Ten ($10.00) Dollar bill in payment, and as our custom is to try and sidestep Ten Dollar Bills, due to the many counterfeits, Mr. Reilly inquired whether they did not have one of smaller denomination. Both replied no. Thereupon Mr. Reilly passed the bill to Miss Murphy in the next room to look over and she proceeded to the safe to make change. Both men watched her but before she could get the money, the smaller one asked for the Ten Dollar bill back and gave her a Five Dollar bill for which Miss Murphy gave him five singles. He then produced forty cents in change from his pocket. This strange act aroused Mr. Reilly's suspicions, as he wondered why they did not give him the change in the beginning."*[1457]

Rounding out the story, Tinker explained that these men said they would come back for the panel after having something to eat "across the way" then proceeded in the direction of the "lunch wagon," during which time Reilly followed them and took down the tag number on their vehicle.[1458] *"A few moments later"* Reilly

---

[1456] Tinker, Arthur A. <u>Letter from Arthur A. Tinker to Mr. Arthur Koehler</u>. March 29, 1935. New Jersey State Police Museum and Learning Center Archives.
[1457] Ibid.
[1458] Ibid.

was *"surprised to discover the machine gone"* when he glanced out the window.[1459]

In an attempt to educate the public concerning his investigations, Koehler wrote his article for the Saturday Evening Post. Included in this article was the account of the panel purchase, occurring on December 14, 1933, as further proof Hauptmann had been involved.[1460] It was a move that may have added fuel to the sentiment that there was no way this crime was a one-man job. Strangely, also included in this article was Koehler's claim that *"it is possible that my badge may have glinted from beneath my coat that day as Hauptmann looked into the cubby office where we sat."*[1461]

As time wore on, Koehler would continue to believe Hauptmann was not alone. During a talk at the Clinton Engineers' club, Koehler shared that Hauptmann *"may have had accomplices whose identity has to date remained secret"* and then gave the lumber panel purchase as an example.[1462] On this occasion, a Reporter asked him point blank if Hauptmann was *"guilty of the kidnaping"* but Koehler *"refused to commit himself."*[1463] About a month later Koehler was still offering a similar position. In January while in Minneapolis he *"refused to express his personal opinion as to Hauptmann's guilt or innocence."*[1464] However, Koehler did admit *"some points in the case leave doubt in his*

[1459] Ibid.

[1460] Koehler, Arthur. "Who Made That Ladder?" *The Saturday Evening Post.* April 20, 1935. New Jersey State Police Museum and Learning Center Archives.

[1461] Ibid.

[1462] "Accomplices Of Hauptmann In Kidnaping?" *Tri City Star.* December 19, 1935. New Jersey State Police Museum and Learning Center Archives.

[1463] Ibid.

[1464] "Some Aspects of Case Not Clear to Koehler." *Winona Republican-Herald.* January 16, 1936. Darrell W. Krueger Library, Winona State University.

mind as the hour of Hauptmann's execution" approached.[1465] Here he brought up Violet Sharp, Isador Fisch, and the sources of lumber in the other sections of the ladder.[1466] When claims of wrongdoing and "framing" were raised concerning the notorious Rail 16 evidence, Koehler quickly called that *"absolutely ridiculous."*[1467] But when asked if Hauptmann should be reprieved he *"refused an answer."*[1468]

In answering Koehler's question to Tinker, we have to consult the actual Registration Cards. As a point of fact which I mentioned earlier, new tags were issued *"each time the car registration was renewed."*[1469] The 1933 registration shows it was renewed on December 19, 1932, with the plate number 3U3624. This shows it is possible for a car to have its new tags early and before the new year. However, Hauptmann's 1934 registration for his Dodge was not renewed until January 24, 1934. This means his tag number 4U1341 did not exist on December 14, 1933.[1470] This can only mean that if Reilly and Murphy were being truthful about this encounter, it could only have happened on the date they both originally told police it occurred – February 14, 1934.

[1465] Ibid.
[1466] "Ladder Expert, in City, Says He's Still Puzzled on Hauptmann Case." Newspaper Unknown. January 16, 1936. New Jersey State Police Museum and Learning Center Archives.
[1467] "Some Aspects of Case Not Clear to Koehler." *Winona Republican-Herald.* January 16, 1936. Darrell W. Krueger Library, Winona State University.
[1468] "Ladder Expert, in City, Says He's Still Puzzled on Hauptmann Case." Newspaper Unknown. January 16, 1936. New Jersey State Police Museum and Learning Center Archives.
[1469] Falzini, Mark W. (2008). *Their Fifteen Minutes.* Iuniverse Inc. Page 17.
[1470] Note: Both registration cards can be found at the NJSP Archives.

9

The Writing on the Wall

One of the most famous accusations made concerning manufactured evidence against Hauptmann came from Anthony Scaduto's book *Scapegoat*. The story was that both Frank Fitzpatrick and Russell "Hop" Hopstatter claimed Tom Cassidy of the New York Daily News wrote Condon's phone number in Hauptmann's closet to get a scoop for the paper, the idea being that he tipped off Inspector Bruckman because the two of them were possibly working together to perpetrate this devious act. [1471] Other books would follow and echo this position and it seems to have been etched into our history of the crime. So if this was the "black" version of the incident, then other books, like the standard bearer for the "Lone-Wolf" books, Jim Fisher's *The Lindbergh Case*, would be the "white." Fisher's book simply disposes of the matter by explaining Hauptmann had admitted he wrote it there himself.[1472] The problem is that if one wants to know what happened, they cannot simply pick one of the opposite sides as if they are the only versions to choose from. The odds of being right are never 50/50 concerning anything having to

---

[1471] Scaduto, Anthony. (1976). *Scapegoat: The Lonesome Death of Bruno Richard Hauptmann.* G. P. Putnam's Sons, pages 263 & 266.

[1472] Fisher, Jim. (1974) *The Lindbergh Case.* Rutgers University Press, pages 225-6.

do with this case. There are always various shades of truth on either side that must be explored fully – if the truth is actually what is sought.

Questions & Examples

The first question in evaluating this accusation is whether or not Police would engage in this conduct. An example which quickly delivers this answer would be the NJSP actions at the Meaney Farm in 1926. Here was one case where every example of unlawful police practice occurred and was ultimately exposed: manslaughter, conspiracy, theft, false reports, excessive force, assault, cover-up, and fabricated evidence.[1473]

Next, would Reporters commit such an act? Consider the 1933 murder of Al Lillien, the "leader" of New Jersey rumrunners. Only one year after the Lindbergh Kidnapping he was in his fortified base, the old Oscar Hammerstein mansion, when he was shot three times in the back of the head.[1474] On this matter, Governor Hoffman's Director of Public Relations, William S. Conklin, wrote a Memo to his boss which concerned the possibility of a Reporter writing Condon's phone number in Hauptmann's closet:

> *"Several years ago during the Hammerstein Mansion Murder at the Atlantic Highlands a reporter pulled the same trick, giving detectives a run-around lasting weeks."*[1475]

[1473] Falzini, Mark W. (2014) *The Siege at Jutland.* Iuniverse. (Note: All the information needed is in this book)

[1474] Joynson, George. (2010) *Wicked Monmouth County.* History Press, page 116.

[1475] Conklin, William. <u>Memo to Gov:</u> Undated (1936?). New Jersey State Police Museum and Learning Center Archives.

Another example occurred on February 24, 1938 at New Rochelle after twelve-year-old Peter Levine disappeared on his way home from school and, by that night, a ransom was demanded.[1476] Only months later, on May 29th, the child's body washed up ashore in New Rochelle with his head, hands, and feet missing.[1477] Interestingly, J. Edgar Hoover placed the blame on a Reporter who pulled a cruel trick so that he could get an exclusive for his paper:

> *"In the Levine case a reporter of a New York newspaper called the father of the Levine boy on the telephone the day after the boy had disappeared and posing as the kidnaper, obtained from Mr. Levine information of a very confidential character and then at once gave this to his paper and it was published as a scoop. This reporter later had the audacity to call Mr. Levine and admit he obtained the information under a subterfuge in order to get a story. The facts now show the Levine boy was killed at approximately this time. I am convinced that if the papers had not printed any such story, Mr. Levine might have been able to make contact with the kidnapers and have had his child returned."*[1478]

In fact, Hoover took it a step further by laying blame on the Press for the Bureau's failure to solve the Mattson, Freed, and Cash cases due to the fact that the press gave "*wide publicity to the details of the*

[1476] New Rochelle Police Department: www.nrpd.com/aboutus.htm
[1477] Ibid.
[1478] Hoover, J. Edgar Director, FBI. <u>Letter from J. Edgar Hoover to Mrs. Evelyn Walsh McLean</u>. June 4, 1938. Evalyn Walsh McLean Papers 1874-1948, Library of Congress Manuscript Division, Washington, D.C. (Notes: "kidnapping is often seen spelled "kidnaping" during this period. Also, Hoover often mis-spells "Evalyn" as "Evelyn").

cases and has harassed the families of the victims until it has been almost beyond endurance."[1479]

Another example came from Governor Hoffman himself. He claimed that:

> "*It is a known fact that newspaper reporters, often under orders to "produce a new lead daily" in sensational cases, depart from the accepted ethics of their profession to manufacture evidence that will have a news value.*"[1480]

Hoffman would claim that "a newspaper friend" told him that he personally saw "*a representative of one of the large news agencies*" pull such a stunt in the Hall-Mills murder case. Here it was claimed that a note was written and addressed to the Mills girl telling her "*not to worry*" and that she "*would be taken care of*" signing it "*Mrs. H.*"[1481] And we all know what happened in that case.

A final example comes from this case itself... Once the child's body was discovered near Mt. Rose several pieces of evidence were reported in the newspapers as being discovered at the scene. According to Lt. Keaten:

> "*...nothing of value which would lead to the identity of the kidnapers* [sic] *was found around the Mt. Rose Highway; that according to the newspapers some diapers were found near the body but the State Police had conclusive proof that these were planted*

[1479] Ibid.

[1480] Hoffman, Harold. *There Is More To Be Told*. Original Manuscript: Unedited & Uncorrected, circa 1938. Page 5. New Jersey State Police Museum and Learning Center Archives.

[1481] Ibid. page 6.

by a newspaper reporter. Also an old broken shovel was found there, but the State Police had a confession from the man who planted it and he admitted having received $5.00 from a New York reporter for making the plant."[1482]

The last question would be if Police and Reporters would team up or collude in order to create a stunt like the one of which Cassidy was accused. Here we can revisit the infamous "Wyckoff Murders" which occurred in Zion on February 11, 1916. Housekeeper Catherine Fisher was killed in a barn after her head was smashed with an iron bar, then Richard Wyckoff was murdered with an axe.[1483] The dead were discovered by William Henry Wyckoff who ran to a neighbor for help.[1484] Police, short on suspects, arrested and charged William with first degree murder for this crime although he was quickly found not guilty at his trial.[1485] Later two new suspects, Charles Hawkins and William McLaughlin, emerged.[1486] The reason these men became suspects arose from the efforts of Private Investigator Allen Myers from the Burns Detective Agency who had been brought in by local police to assist – he actually went door to door <u>posing</u> as a newspaper reporter.[1487] Hawkins was picked up and questioned but denied any involvement. Once Hawkins was released, and the prospects of a conviction slim, the Police used a

---

[1482] Sisk, T. H., Special Agent, USBOI (FBI). Memorandum For The Director. <u>Unknown Subjects Kidnapping and Murder of Charles A. Lindbergh, Jr</u>. October 27, 1934. National Archives at College Park Maryland.

[1483] East Amwell Historical Society. (2010). *East Amwell, New Jersey (Images of America Series)*. Archadia Publishing. Page 15.

[1484] Ritchie, Eleanor. "Sourlands Famous For Brutal Murder of Couple in 1916." *Hunterdon County Democrat*. January 12, 1935.

[1485] Ibid.

[1486] Ibid.

[1487] "Allen Myers Dies; Noted Detective." *The New York Times*. August 14, 1934.

"trick" in an attempt to produce a confession. Their first step was to have the Hunterdon County Democrat print up a "special edition" of their paper where a fake story of McLaughlin's confession was the headline, and then it was shown to Hawkins.[1488] This created the desired result and produced a confession from Hawkins who then implicated McLaughlin. After a quick trial, they were both found guilty and a dumbfounded McLaughlin was led away from court still proclaiming his innocence.[1489]

Another example concerned Richard Hauptmann's friend Hans Kloppenburg. When interviewed by Anthony Scaduto, Kloppenburg told him that prior to his testimony in the Bronx, officials there tried to intimidate him into not testifying. Then he continued, telling Scaduto that Wilentz did the same thing to him in Flemington prior to his testimony there when he was told "*if you say on the witness chair that you seen Fisch come in with the shoe box, you'll be arrested right away*" but Kloppenburg told Wilentz he "*had seen it.*"[1490] Kloppenburg told Scaduto further:

> "*Then a day or so later, I think it was the day before I testified, there was a story in the newspapers that police were about to arrest a second man in the kidnapping. That was me they were talking about. They were trying to scare me so I would shut up. And I was scared.*"[1491]

Scaduto's account is supported by a letter Kloppenburg wrote to Anna Hauptmann:

[1488] Ritchie, Eleanor. "Sourlands Famous For Brutal Murder of Couple in 1916." *Hunterdon County Democrat.* January 12, 1935.

[1489] Ibid.

[1490] Scaduto, Anthony. (1976). *Scapegoat: The Lonesome Death of Bruno Richard Hauptmann.* G. P. Putnam's Sons. Page 447.

[1491] Ibid. Pages 447-8.

> *"I remember so very well, how I to Wilentz said, that I*
> *would swear that I. Fisch the shoe box brought to you.*
> *To that meant Wilentz that I of that testimony alone*
> *could be arrested."*[1492]

Saving the best for last, this came out of the Garrett Schenck "kidnapping" which was another angle that arose directly from the Lindbergh Kidnapping. A few days before the Lindbergh child was discovered, Schenck, who lived in Mt. Rose at the time, claimed to have seen three cars parked very near where the body was later discovered. One, a tan car with an *"M. G."* license plate, and another a *"coupe."*[1493] On the other side of the road facing the other direction was parked a *"Ford Sedan with L license plates"* and just as he moved to pass through he saw...

> *"...two men in the field walking from opposite*
> *directions facing each other. The one walking towards*
> *Mount Rose was tall and thin with a dark complexion*
> *and looked like an Italian. The other was about 190*
> *pounds, 5'9" tall. The stout man asked, 'How is*
> *everything' and the Italian answered 'okay.' It was*
> *very near the same spot where the Italian fellow was*
> *walking that they found the Lindbergh baby."*[1494]

A Private Investigator named J. J. Devine, heard about this information and then, according to him, induced Schenck to accompany him to a summer colony north of Johnstown, PA, where

---

[1492] Kloppenburg, Hans. <u>Letter from Hans Kloppenburg to Mrs. Hauptmann</u>. (translated from German to English) August 26, 1935. New Jersey State Police Museum and Learning Center Archives.

[1493] Schenck, Garrett. Statement. May 13, 1936. Made to William S. Lutz, Executive Office. New Jersey State Police Museum and Learning Center Archives.

[1494] Ibid.

he intended to get to the bottom of what he knew.[1495] Schenck, on the other hand, claimed he was taken from Hopewell and held against his will in Johnstown, Pennsylvania, from June 10th through September 3, 1932.[1496] Devine was known to the NJSP and had approached the Troopers manning the Gate House in late April and asked to speak with Lindbergh concerning information he had relative to the kidnapping.[1497] When told he could not speak directly with Lindbergh he told them: *"O.K., that settles it, I have nothing further to say."*[1498] According to Prosecutor Anthony Hauck, Devine had called him around this time to have Lindbergh and several ranking State Police members arrested for being involved in the crime.[1499]

Once Schenck was liberated, Devine returned to Hopewell to continue to investigate. It was during this time that State Police decided they had enough of Devine's involvement and on October 24th arrested him as he was driving toward his rented bungalow in East Amwell Township for "conducting investigations without

[1495] Fisher, Lloyd. Letter from Lloyd Fisher to Miss Elizabeth McLaughlin. June 5, 1936. New Jersey State Police Museum and Learning Center Archives.

[1496] Schenck, Garrett. Statement. May 13, 1936. Made to William S. Lutz, Executive Office. New Jersey State Police Museum and Learning Center Archives.

[1497] Moffatt, W. Sgt. Newark Police Department, and Horn, Wm. Cpl. NJ State Police. New Jersey State Police Report. Interview of one J.J. Devine, residence: Johnstown, Pa. April 27, 1932. New Jersey State Police Museum and Learning Center Archives.

[1498] Ibid.

[1499] DeGaetano, N. Detective, New Jersey State Police. New Jersey State Police Report. Further investigation of Private Detective John J. Devine. October 27, 1932. New Jersey State Police Museum and Learning Center Archives. (**Note:** From everything I have researched, although his theories seemed to change, it appears Devine suspected Lindbergh early in the investigation, and believed the NJSP were helping to cover it up).

being licensed in the State of New Jersey."[1500] Devine claimed that
he was told he would be let go if "*he would get out of the State and
keep his hands out of the Lindbergh case.*"[1501] After hearing about
her husband's arrest, Devine's wife hired Lloyd Fisher who, after
learning the facts, drew out a complaint of false imprisonment
against Trooper DeGaetano.[1502] Fisher then called Assistant
Attorney General Spitz who agreed the State Police "overstepped"
and it was decided between them that both sides would withdraw
their complaints.[1503] The hearing was conducted by Justice of the
Peace George Weber, the same man who went to Highfields to
conduct the John Curtis hearing.[1504] As a result of Devine's hearing,
the charges were dismissed for "lack of evidence" and in turn, the
complaints filed against the Troopers were also dismissed.[1505] Devine
continued to investigate, and it came to the attention of State Police
that he was in the constant company with a woman named Eva
Hammlin from West Amwell.[1506] As Police attempted to learn what
Devine was developing, their investigation revealed that Hammlin

[1500] DeGaetano, N. Detective, New Jersey State Police. New Jersey State
Police Report. <u>Arrest and arraignment of Private Detective John Jas.
Devine.</u> October 24, 1932. New Jersey State Police Museum and
Learning Center Archives.

[1501] Fisher, Lloyd. <u>Letter from Lloyd Fisher to Hon. Harold G. Hoffman.</u>
May 14, 1936. New Jersey State Police Museum and Learning Center
Archives.

[1502] Ibid.

[1503] Ibid.

[1504] Ibid.

[1505] DeGaetano, N. Detective, New Jersey State Police. New Jersey State
Police Report. <u>Arrest and arraignment of Private Detective John Jas.
Devine.</u> October 24, 1932. New Jersey State Police Museum and
Learning Center Archives.

[1506] Haussling, E. A. Sgt. Det., New Jersey State Police. New Jersey State
Police Report. <u>Continued investigation regarding Miss Eva Hammlin, of
Amwell Township, Hunterdon County.</u> November 17, 1932. New Jersey
State Police Museum and Learning Center Archives.

was implicating several Locals from the area including both Don Guiness and her own husband.[1507] Police were told by an informant that Devine had turned over the material he accumulated during the course of his investigations to his Lawyers, Ryman Herr and Lloyd Fisher, and that they had been authorized to negotiate a sale of these items to the highest bidding newspaper.[1508]

The New Jersey State Police wanted those documents.

That's when Detective Bornmann, while accompanying New York Journal Reporters Henry Paynter and Lamar Ball to the Law Offices of Herr and Fisher, actually pretended to be a Reporter and represented himself as one to both Ryman Herr and Lloyd Fisher in an attempt to get this above referenced information.[1509]

In the end, Devine and eight others went to trial in Clearfield County on February 27, 1933.[1510] Less than a week later Devine was convicted of both kidnapping and conspiracy to kidnap Garrett Schenck.[1511] According to Lloyd Fisher, Devine's punishment was a *"very modest fine"* and he was later hired as an investigator with

---

[1507] Niskanen, Einar. Statement. February 13, 1933. Made to Detective L. J. Bornmann, New Jersey State Police. New Jersey State Police Museum and Learning Center Archives.

[1508] Bornmann, L. J. Detective, New Jersey State Police. New Jersey State Police Report. <u>Cooperation with investigators of the Hearst Publications of New York City.</u> February 17, 1933. New Jersey State Police Museum and Learning Center Archives.

[1509] Ibid.

[1510] "Kidnapping Trial Opens." *The Washington Post.* February 28, 1933.

[1511] "8 Convicted Of Holding Man In Lindbergh Case." *Winona Republican-Herald.* March 3, 1933. Darrell W. Krueger Library, Winona State University.

a *"very responsible position"* on the staff of Pennsylvania Attorney General Charles Joseph Margiotti.[1512]

Now to the event itself…

Inspector Henry Bruckman

As a result of investigation, interviews with witnesses, and conversations with both the Assistant Chief Inspector and Superintendent of Buildings, Bruckman appeared at the Hauptmann home on the morning of September 25, 1934.[1513] Bruckman testified he entered a room the Police were searching but noticed they hadn't "cleared" the closet.[1514] Bruckman ordered the Police Carpenters to remove the shelf and pole from this closet.[1515] He had earlier testified in the Bronx that it was necessary for these things to be removed in order to enter it and *"to get a full and unobstructed view."*[1516] Detective Maurice Tobin was among the men in the Hauptmann nursery at this time, and watched as Bruckman "squeezed" into the closet.[1517]

[1512] Fisher, Lloyd. Letter from Lloyd Fisher to Miss Elizabeth McLaughlin. June 5, 1936. New Jersey State Police Museum and Learning Center Archives.

[1513] Bruckman, Henry D. Testimony. The State of New Jersey vs. Bruno Richard Hauptmann, Hunterdon County Court of Oyer and Terminer, page 1741, 1935. New Jersey State Law Library.

[1514] Ibid.

[1515] Ibid., page 1742.

[1516] Bruckman, Henry. Testimony. The People of the State of New York ex. rel. Bruno Richard Hauptmann vs. John Hanley, Sheriff of Bronx County, and the Warden of the County Jail of Bronx County. Supreme Court, Bronx County, Special Term Part I. page 194, October 15, 1934. New Jersey State Police Museum and Learning Center Archives.

[1517] Tobin, Maurice W. Testimony. The State of New Jersey vs. Bruno Richard Hauptmann, Hunterdon County Court of Oyer and Terminer, pages 1733-5, 1935. New Jersey State Law Library.

As Bruckman "*backed up into the closet*" he saw what appeared to be a "*smudge*" on a piece of inside molding which led him to put on his glasses.[1518] He then saw written there "*2974 Decatur*" which he recognized as Dr. Condon's address, and "*3–7154*" also the letter "*S*" and "*DG*" in a word which he determined was "*Sedgwick*" which was Condon's telephone number.[1519] Something else that Bruckman discovered while inside that closet, but did not testify to, was a different set of notations on the inside of the closet door near the upper hinge:

> *$500*
> *1928 B–00007162A*
> *"B–00009272A*[1520]

When asked on the stand in Flemington if he had been in any other closet in Hauptmann's apartment Bruckman responded, "*I think that I did, with other closets in a measure, something similar to what I did here.*"[1521] However, during Detective Tobin's testimony, it was developed that two more similar closets existed within this

[1518] Bruckman, Henry D. Testimony. The State of New Jersey vs. Bruno Richard Hauptmann, Hunterdon County Court of Oyer and Terminer, page 1742, 1935. New Jersey State Law Library.

[1519] Ibid. page 1743.

[1520] Bornmann, Lewis J. Detective, N. J. State Police. New Jersey State Police Report. Searching of Bruno Richard Hauptmann's Home and garage located at 1279 E 222d Street, Bronx N.Y. for evidence in connection with the kidnapping of the Lindbergh baby on March 1, 1932. September 25, 1934. New Jersey State Police Museum and Learning Center. (Note: Actual notation is slightly different)

[1521] Bruckman, Henry D. Testimony. The State of New Jersey vs. Bruno Richard Hauptmann, Hunterdon County Court of Oyer and Terminer, page 1752, 1935. New Jersey State Law Library.

apartment, and when asked if Bruckman had squeezed into those as well Tobin answered, "*he did not.*"[1522]

Special Agent F. E. Wright

On September 25th, "shortly before noon, Agent Wright was among those present to witness Inspector Bruckman's discoveries.[1523] Wright would tell Agent Sisk that Bruckman found this evidence rather quickly and "*seemed to walk right into the room and hit directly for the closet where the number was found.*"[1524] The evidence was then removed and photographed at the scene. Upon leaving to bring the evidence to the Bronx District Attorney's office, Bruckman warned Wright against reporting these discoveries to his superiors saying that if this information were to leak to the press then he'd know how it "got out."[1525] Was this his sincere concern? Perhaps a premonition? Or could Bruckman have been setting the stage for something else? The first clue might be that upon his return to the Hauptmann apartment Bruckman...

[1522] Tobin, Maurice W. Testimony. The State of New Jersey vs. Bruno Richard Hauptmann, <u>Hunterdon County Court of Oyer and Terminer</u>, page 1739, 1935. New Jersey State Law Library.

[1523] Sisk, T. H. Special Agent, DOI (FBI). Memorandum For File. <u>Bruno Richard Hauptmann with aliases. Unknown Subjects. Kidnaping and Murder of Charles A. Lindbergh, Jr.</u> September 25, 1934. Author's Possession (Thanks to Amy35 for providing this memo to me).

[1524] Kennedy, Ludovic. (1986). *The Airman and the Carpenter.* Penguin Books, page 205. (Note: Kennedy quotes a phone conversation from a document I've never seen. However, I find it creditable because of other similar situations where I have seen the documentation – and those match.)

[1525] FBI Report. Unsigned. <u>Bruno Richard Hauptmann, with aliases; Kidnaping and Murder of Charles A. Lindbergh, Jr.</u> December 23, 1935. New Jersey State Police Museum and Learning Center Archives.

> *"...invited numerous reporters and two news photographers into the house, spelled his name out for them, and explained the occurrences in detail."*[1526]

The next day, September 26th, Wright, Bornmann, and Tobin supervised New York Police carpenters Cramer and Enkler as they were in Hauptmann's garage dismantling parts of the structure by tearing out lumber and beams searching for additional ransom money. As they pried loose a 2 x 4 near the window it was discovered it was a wall safe which had five holes and a slot bored out of it which contained *"rolls of gold certificates"* and *"a small caliber automatic pistol of foreign manufacture."*[1527] Sometime after the discovery of this money Wright:

> *"...started to leave to call the Bureau Office when Bruckman stopped him and advised him not to do it. Wright told Bruckman that he had instructions and was going to follow them, whereupon Bruckman became extremely angry."*[1528]

Sometime after Wright left to call, but prior to the evening of the 27th, Inspector Bruckman gave the story concerning the additional

---

[1526] Ibid.

[1527] Seery, W. F. Special Agent, USBOI (FBI). USBOI Report. <u>Bruno Richard Hauptmann, with alias. Kidnaping and Murder of Charles A. Lindbergh Jr.</u> October 19, 1934. National Archives at College Park Maryland. (Note: The FBI had changed its name from USBOI to DOI by this time but the heading on this particular report still says "United States Bureau of Investigation")

[1528] FBI Report. Unsigned. <u>Bruno Richard Hauptmann, with aliases; Kidnaping and Murder of Charles A. Lindbergh, Jr.</u> December 23, 1935. New Jersey State Police Museum and Learning Center Archives.

discovery of this money to the press.[1529] Wright returned to work at Hauptmann's apartment the next day expecting to again cooperate under the agreement between the law enforcement agencies. Sometime that afternoon, he heard Inspectors Bruckman and Loonan speaking but once the men saw him they moved away so that he could no longer hear them.[1530] Once these men moved upstairs with the police carpenters, Wright attempted to follow but was told Department of Justice men were no longer welcome without an NYPD escort so he had to leave the premises.[1531] Wright immediately left for a telephone to advise his office of these developments and was told by Assistant Director Hugh Clegg to return to the home and tell the Inspectors that he was taking orders from the Division, and not them, and if they wanted him escorted they would have to provide one.[1532] However, upon his return, the Inspectors had already left, and the uniformed officers working as guards would not allow him to enter the apartment. Once Wright gave the New York cops Clegg's message, a Sergeant replied by saying he too had his orders so he couldn't get in and he didn't want to hear any of his *"back talk."*[1533] This occurred right in front of Reporters, and one newspaper would carry a story entitled *"U.S. Agent Barred from Hauptmann Home."*[1534] Once advised of this outrageous treatment, Hoover himself placed a call to Commissioner Valentine to complain and threatened to

---

[1529] Hoover, John Edgar. Director, DOI (FBI). Memorandum. <u>Memorandum For Mr. Tamm</u>. September 27, 1934. National Archives at College Park Maryland.

[1530] Hoover, John Edgar. Director, DOI (FBI). Memorandum. <u>Memorandum For Mr. Tamm</u>. September 27, 1934. New Jersey State Police Museum and Learning Center Archives. (Note: Different Memo from footnote #129).

[1531] Ibid.

[1532] Ibid.

[1533] Ibid.

[1534] FBI Report. Unsigned. <u>Bruno Richard Hauptmann, with aliases; Kidnaping and Murder of Charles A. Lindbergh, Jr</u>. December 23, 1935. New Jersey State Police Museum and Learning Center Archives.

withdraw from the case completely, but Valentine claimed he had no knowledge of these events, promising an investigation into the matter, the result of which he would communicate directly to Clegg once completed.[1535] Upon calling Clegg, Valentine claimed he was told the friction arose after the press was given the story about the recent discovery of ransom money from the garage, and insinuated...

> "...*the Division had given out the information, after an agreement had been reached by all parties concerned that this specific information was not to be released.*"[1536]

Clegg could not believe what he was hearing. He responded by saying that since Valentine brought it up, it was Clegg's understanding that Inspector Bruckman had given it out:

> "...*after the above-referred-to agreement had been reached, and furthermore, we had not given it out and I* [Hoover] *had been shocked that such discoveries of evidence would be given out.*"[1537]

Upon hearing this revelation, the Commissioner once again promised to investigate.

Unfortunately, Special Agent Wright was facing a two-pronged attack. It wasn't just Bruckman and his men; he was being maligned

---

[1535] Hoover, John Edgar. Director, DOI (FBI). Memorandum. <u>Memorandum For Mr. Tamm</u>. September 27, 1934. New Jersey State Police Museum and Learning Center Archives. (Note: Yet another different Memo from the previously footnoted material).

[1536] Hoover, John Edgar. Director, DOI (FBI). Memorandum. <u>Memorandum For Mr. Tamm</u>. September 27, 1934. National Archives at College Park Maryland.

[1537] Ibid.

by the press as well. On the very same day that Wright was being locked out of the Hauptmann home, Special Agent in Charge Fay was given a tip by Amster Spiro, the City Editor of the New York American, that one of their Agents was trying to sell a picture of Hauptmann's photograph album.[1538] This position was later changed to the Agent who knew someone who had one to sell, and Clegg believed they were referring to Wright.[1539] In an attempt to get to the bottom of this, the Reporter in question, a man by the name of Livingstone, was brought in and questioned. According to Clegg, he attempted to lie, but once pressed, he admitted the following...

> "...he remarked to Agent Wright that somebody could get a lot of money for the Hauptmann photographs which were in the house, to which Agent Wright replied that he thought too much of his job and would not sell anything..."[1540]

Frank Waldrop, writer for the Washington Times-Herald, was asked for information concerning what he knew about the situation, then told Clegg he heard from the Reporters at the scene that:

> "Mr. Wright has more sense and is more alert then any of them; that several newspaper reporters had tried to "crash" the house, although the policemen were supposed to be keeping them from the house,

---

[1538] Hoover, John Edgar. Director, DOI (FBI). Memorandum. <u>Memorandum For Mr. Tamm</u>. September 27, 1934. New Jersey State Police Museum and Learning Center Archives.

[1539] Ibid.

[1540] Hoover, John Edgar. Director, DOI (FBI). Memorandum. <u>Memorandum For Mr. Tamm</u>. September 28, 1934. New Jersey State Police Museum and Learning Center Archives.

nevertheless, Mr. Wright had stepped in and kept them back…".[1541]

Both Hoover and Clegg believed they had heard enough and that this matter was closed. Clegg believed that…

"…probably a policeman would have been willing to sell the articles in the house, but would have been afraid to while Mr. Wright was there, and the newspaper men were therefore trying to get rid of him too."[1542]

In rounding out this section, Clegg called to let the Bureau know that Inspector Bruckman had shown up at the New York office in a *"very meek and humble manner"* and apologized.[1543] On the morning of the 28th, Chief Inspector Sullivan stated:

"Commissioner Valentine had given his men very specific instructions about any misunderstandings and told them he would take drastic action against every one of them if anything of this kind occurred again."[1544]

Detective Lewis Bornmann

On September 25, 1934, New Jersey State Police Detective Bornmann was detailed by Captain Lamb to proceed to Hauptmann's apartment and meet up with Bronx Detective Tobin to assist in the search of

[1541] Ibid.

[1542] Ibid.

[1543] FBI Report. Unsigned. <u>Bruno Richard Hauptmann, with aliases; Kidnaping and Murder of Charles A. Lindbergh, Jr.</u> December 23, 1935. New Jersey State Police Museum and Learning Center Archives.

[1544] Ibid.

both the house and garage.[1545] Hauptmann's apartment was in a two-story stucco house on the second floor and consisted of four rooms and a bathroom. Once there, he met Tobin along with Deputy Chief Inspector Bruckman, as well as both New York Officers Enkler and Cramer who were the carpenters assigned to assist in the search.[1546] Also among these men, according to Bornmann, was a "Department of Justice man."[1547] The men went into the middle room where they discovered the serial number notation inside the clothes closet door near the upper hinge:[1548]

> *"A perusal of the list of ransom bills in possession of the*
> *undersigned disclosed that the last four digits of this*

[1545] Bornmann, Lewis Detective, New Jersey State Police. New Jersey State Police Report. <u>Searching apartment and garage of Bruno Richard Hauptmann at 1279 East 222nd Street, Bronx, New York, for evidence which might be of value in connection with the Lindbergh case.</u> September 25, 1934. New Jersey State Police Museum and Learning Center Archives.

[1546] Bornmann, Lewis J. Detective, N. J. State Police. New Jersey State Police Report. <u>Searching of Bruno Richard Hauptmann's Home and garage located at 1279 East 222nd Street, Bronx, N. Y. for evidence in connection with the kidnapping of the Lindbergh baby on March 1, 1932.</u> September 25, 1934. New Jersey State Police Museum and Learning Center Archives.

[1547] Bornmann, State Trooper, New Jersey State Police. Statement. March 24, 1936. Made to Governor Harold G. Hoffman, R. William Lagay, Secretary to the Governor, Mr. Hoge, Colonel Schwarzkopf, Captain Snook, and Lieutenant Keaton. New Jersey State Police Museum and Learning Center Archives.

[1548] Bornmann, Lewis J. Detective, N. J. State Police. New Jersey State Police Report. <u>Searching of Bruno Richard Hauptmann's Home and garage located at 1279 E 222d Street, Bronx N.Y. for evidence in connection with the kidnapping of the Lindbergh baby on March 1, 1932.</u> September 25, 1934. New Jersey State Police Museum and Learning Center.

notation were the same as on one of the five and ten dollar ransom notes."[1549]

As they continued their search another discovery was made. On the left hand inside casing, "*in what appeared to be Hauptmann's handwriting,*" was written:

> "*"2974 Decauter"* [sic] *and underneath it the numbers "3–7154." The address was immediately known to be that of Dr. Condon, intermediary between the kidnappers of the Lindbergh baby and Colonel Lindbergh and a further check disclosed the lower numbers to be the telephone exchange of Dr. Condon at the time he acted as intermediary."*[1550]

The casing with the address and phone number on it was immediately removed and then taken to District Attorney Foley's office at the Bronx County Courthouse.[1551] Sometime later that afternoon, Bruckman instructed Bornmann to bring the door with the serial numbers on it to Foley's office, and both the door and casing were later presented to the Bronx Grand Jury by Inspector Bruckmann as evidence.[1552]

H. Bennett Salomon

On September 20, 1934, Detective Bornmann was detailed to the office of the Undercover Squad at 9 AM to guard Hauptmann, and

---

[1549] Ibid.

[1550] Ibid. (Note: Actual notation is spelled "Decatur")

[1551] Ibid.

[1552] Ibid.

wasn't relieved until 1 AM.[1553] Bornmann immediately went to the Taft Hotel for some much needed sleep with orders to report to the Bronx County Court House that morning at 9 AM for Hauptmann's hearing.[1554] Unfortunately for Hauptmann, there was no such luxury and he was brought before District Attorney Sam Foley at exactly 4:05 AM to be grilled with the age-old "Good Cop-Bad Cop" tactic in an attempt to get a confession.[1555] The grilling ended at 6 AM without the desired confession.[1556]

So it would come to pass on the morning of September 21, 1934, two days after his arrest, Hauptmann stood before Judge McKinery in the Bronx County courthouse for his arraignment on extortion charges.[1557] Judge McKinery turned to H. Bennett Salomon, a Bronx attorney who was standing nearby, who quickly told the Court: *"Your Honor, in this case I have been tentatively retained. I do not desire to say anything now."*[1558] The Judge asked Hauptmann if he would consent to being held without bail while the matter was held over until Monday to which Hauptmann agreed and tonelessly replied:

[1553] Bornmann, L. J. Detective, N. J. State Police. New Jersey State Police Report. Search in New York City for a suspect in connection with the Lindbergh kidnaping case. September 8, 1934. New Jersey State Police Museum and Learning Center. (Note: The last dated entry on this report is for September 24th which I believe is the actual date the report was written).

[1554] Ibid.

[1555] Gardner, Lloyd C. June 2004. *The Case That Never Dies.* Rutgers University Press, pages 173-5. (Note: Lloyd describes the scenario perfectly.)

[1556] "Extradition Is Put Off." *The New York Times.* September 22, 1934.

[1557] Kelly, W. P. Det. Sgt., N. J. State Police. New Jersey State Police Report. Investigation in New York City regarding the Lindbergh Case. September 22, 1934. New Jersey State Police Museum and Learning Center.

[1558] "Lindbergh Suspect Denied Bail; Faces Murder Charge in Jersey." *Brooklyn Daily Eagle.* September 22, 1934. New Jersey State Police Museum and Learning Center.

"Yes, anything."[1559] Since the hearing was extended to September 24th, upon the completion of the arraignment Hauptmann was removed to the Bronx County Jail on Arthur and Tremont Avenue.[1560] Not long after, Salomon, his new Attorney, arrived and attempted to see him. He told the Sheriff he was Hauptmann's Lawyer but was told to file a "notice of appearance," which he did, but upon his return was told that Hauptmann *"did not know him."*[1561] Salomon explained he understood that he did not because he had just recently been retained and gave the Sheriff a note to give to Hauptmann which read:

> *"Lieber Richard—Wir haben Herr Salomon als Lawyer genomen. Habe Vertraucn wie mlr. Anny."*
> (Dear Richard: We have named Mr. Salomon as lawyer. Have courage as we have. Anny.)[1562]

Oddly enough, once the message was given to Hauptmann the Sheriff claimed he still refused the meeting.[1563] The next day, in the afternoon of September 22nd, Anna was seen by Reporters at the District Attorney's office accompanied by Salomon who she said she had hired to defend her husband.[1564] Salomon then began to debunk certain myths as he told Reporters that Anna's trip to Germany had been paid for by the family savings, and that Hauptmann's Dodge

---

[1559] Ibid.

[1560] Kelly, W. P. Det. Sgt., N. J. State Police. <u>New Jersey State Police Report. Investigation in New York City regarding the Lindbergh Case</u>. September 22, 1934. New Jersey State Police Museum and Learning Center.

[1561] "Extradition Is Put Off." *The New York Times*. September 22, 1934.

[1562] "Kidnap Ladder Builds Up Case Against Hauptmann." *The Philadelphia Inquirer*. September 22, 1934. New Jersey State Police Museum and Learning Center.

[1563] "Extradition Is Put Off." *The New York Times*. September 22, 1934.

[1564] Ibid.

was not stolen and had been legitimately purchased in 1931.[1565] He then announced to Reporters his intention to file a writ of habeas corpus to force authorities to show cause why bail could not be fixed.[1566] Unknown to Salomon, by the time Anna walked out of Foley's office, he was no longer her husband's Attorney. During Hauptmann's trial in Flemington, Salomon solved the mystery as to why he had been fired: He claimed Hauptmann did not want him because he was a Jew.[1567]

Salomon was wrong.

While Anna Hauptmann's account is somewhat different, especially with the dates being at odds with themselves, it needs to be outlined so the truth of this matter can rise to the top. According to her, on the early morning of the 21st she was coming out of the Bronx Courthouse and discovered Harry Whitney waiting for her. He was the husband of her cousin's daughter; they had known each other for quite some time and were on friendly terms. Whitney claimed, having seen a picture of Richard in the paper, he sought her out to offer his assistance telling her she needed a lawyer and suggested his friend James Fawcett.[1568] She claimed that he spoke with an associate of Fawcett's, Bernard Miesels, the "next day" and, with Whitney's recommendation, told them it would be "satisfactory" for the men to "look after her husband's interests."[1569] This seems to line up with the "historical" account of the situation we've all learned. However, she also claimed that on the 21st, another man, who was from Salomon's office, turned up at her house after she returned from the Bronx

---

[1565] Ibid.
[1566] Ibid.
[1567] Newspaper Clipping. Untitled. Paper Unknown. (1935?). New Jersey State Police Museum and Learning Center.
[1568] Hauptmann, Anna. Manuscript. Story of Anna Hauptmann. Page 43. September 1935. New Jersey State Police Museum and Learning Center.
[1569] Ibid.

Court House, advising her to hire him as her husband's attorney.[1570] She's writes it was the "next day" she met Salomon at her home and they went together to an appointment she had with District Attorney Foley.[1571] However, Anna said they stopped at a restaurant, and then upon leaving stopped again at an ice-cream parlor, with Salomon telling her to let Foley "wait."[1572] Anna was in a near state of panic, feeling that she should not do such a thing, and she insisted she be brought to the Court House immediately so she could keep her appointment.[1573] Her feelings toward Foley reflected here should not be taken lightly. He had a considerable amount of influence over her as she was convinced Foley was actually on "her side" and would try to "help." This sentiment persisted as late as October 29[th,] and was reflected in her Flemington Jail House conversation with her husband where she told him:

> *"Mr. Fawcett is honest and true, and it is safe for you to tell him anything you want. So is Mr. Foley."*[1574]

What was the reason for this? Anna had been treated terribly while at Greenwich Station by Police who were engaging in all kinds of torturous psychological tricks along with the generally rough treatment she received from them. One example was to purposely put her in a position to see her husband but refuse to allow her to speak with him by grabbing her and pulling her away from his

[1570] Ibid.
[1571] Ibid. page 44.
[1572] Ibid.
[1573] Ibid.
[1574] Smith, A. L. Lieutenant, New Jersey State Police. New Jersey State Police Report. <u>Guard Detail Flemington Jail</u>. October 29, 1932. New Jersey State Police Museum and Learning Center.

sight as she attempted to do so.[1575] Another was pretending that Hauptmann had just confessed and had implicated her by saying:

> *"Your husband in there just told us you know all about the money, and that you should tell us."*[1576]

When she told them it wasn't true, their response was to say she was calling her husband a "liar." Anna's response: *"No indeed, but somebody else is."*[1577] Another tactic was to put her in a room then tell her to "read the paper" which was all about Hauptmann's arrest and other things about him she claimed were not true. Yet another instance occurred when she was sitting in the hallway and she saw her husband as he was struggling to walk, seemingly ready to drop – then once she attempted to speak to him one of the Detectives *"pushed her against the wall and said to shut up."*[1578]

When she next saw her husband it was at the Bronx Courthouse cuffed to a Detective and she immediately asked him *"did they beat you?"*[1579] She claimed he looked at her but did not say a word being afraid to speak. But things changed after his transfer from the Greenwich Street Station over to the Bronx Jail. Anna was granted permission to arrange to see and speak to her husband.[1580] Richard was also treated much better, being properly fed, allowed the proper sleep, and being treated normally by the Guards who he did not

---

[1575] Hauptmann, Anna. Manuscript. <u>Story of Anna Hauptmann</u>. Page 39. September 1935. New Jersey State Police Museum and Learning Center.

[1576] Ibid. page 40.

[1577] Ibid.

[1578] Ibid. page 42.

[1579] Ibid.

[1580] Ibid.

fear and who spoke freely with him.[1581] It's quite obvious that the change in treatment was being credited to Foley. In fact, soon Anna could visit him every day, and if he wanted to see Manfred, Foley had him brought down to a room outside the cell in the 161st Street Station.[1582]

So Anna and Salomon finally arrived at Foley's office on September 22; she would claim that she left him outside. She would also claim that his advice to her before entering was not to tell him she was solicited, rather, that she read about him in the newspaper – and seeing he was a good attorney wanted him as a result.[1583] However, Anna's trust in Foley, together with her inability to lie, led her to fully disclose to him the truth concerning how she came to be represented by Salomon when Foley asked.[1584] His immediate reaction was to tell her:

> *"That's no way to get a lawyer. This man certainly cannot be any help to you. You know if a man is a good lawyer, he does not chase to your house and ask for a job, and this man would be no good to you."*[1585]

From that point forward Anna refused to speak with Salomon and his repeated attempts to speak with her were shunned. In the meantime, she met with Whitney again, who would bring her to Fawcett's

---

[1581] Stockburger, H. Trooper, New Jersey State Police. New Jersey State Police Report. <u>Report on Conversation between Mr. and Mrs. Hauptmann in the presence of Attorney Fawcett at the Flemington Jail at about 3:30 PM. October 20. 1934</u>. October 20, 1934. New Jersey State Police Museum and Learning Center.

[1582] Hauptmann, Anna. Manuscript. <u>Story of Anna Hauptmann</u>. Page 46. September 1935. New Jersey State Police Museum and Learning Center.

[1583] Ibid. page 45.

[1584] Ibid.

[1585] Ibid.

office which would be the beginning of his representation of her husband.[1586] This represents a double irony. One being that while she accepted Foley's argument concerning why Salomon should be dropped, the exact same methods were used for her to hire Fawcett. The second, that Fawcett, it seemed, was acceptable to Foley.

Unknown to Mrs. Hauptmann at the time (and probably until she died), Richard's first lawyer actually was a very good attorney. In fact, he had previously represented Lottie Coll, Vincent (Mad Dog) Coll's wife in 1933.[1587] Additionally, he was onetime colleagues with both Clarence Darrow and Sam Leibowitz.[1588] He would also establish "The Committee for the Defense of First Offenders" which was the "*forerunner of The Legal Aid Society*."[1589] One of Salomon's most notable cases came in 1938. Here he had the impossible task of defending Mrs. Patrica Ryan, who murdered her husband, a police officer, then confessed to Investigators that she had made up her mind to kill him in advance of shooting him three times.[1590] Salomon was able to prove to the Jury that Mrs. Ryan was the victim of (what we would call today) domestic violence telling the Jury to either "*give her liberty or give her death*" in his summation – the jury returned in just four hours of deliberation to find her "*not guilty*."[1591]

Mrs. Hauptmann wasn't the only one Foley spoke to about Salomon. Assistant Director Hugh Clegg heard Foley complaining that he was

[1586] Ibid.
[1587] "Mrs. Coll, Calm and Defiant in Jail, Displays Jekyll-Hyde Personality." *Brooklyn Daily Eagle*. June 28, 1933. Brooklyn Public Library.
[1588] "Bar Groups Pay Tribute to Salomon." *New York Post*. February 2, 1961. Fultonhistory.com.
[1589] Ibid.
[1590] "Mrs. Ryan Accused of Murder Intent." *The New York Times*. March 4, 1938.
[1591] "Mrs. Ryan Freed By Jury; Out 4 Hours." *The Evening News*. March 22, 1938. Fultonhistory.com

a "bad actor" and had attempted to get himself involved by defending Hauptmann.[1592] So how did Foley come to think so badly of H. Bennett Salomon? Well it seems that in 1933, Foley was investigating fraudulent voter registrations that appeared to involve supporters of Mayor Patrick O'Brien, stemming from his win in the special election following the resignation of Mayor James "Jimmy" Walker. Efforts were made to find a neutral investigator and Salomon was appointed "Special Deputy Attorney General" to investigate any fraud involving illegal voting registration in the Bronx.[1593] Salomon's conclusion was that Foley himself was an illegal registrant, and that the whole matter was instigated by Former Acting Mayor Joseph McKee (who lost the election), and in fact, Salomon determined the widespread illegal registration was sponsored by McKee's faction.[1594]

Might this be why Foley wanted no part in facing H. Bennett Salomon in Court?

Richard Hauptman

The night prior to his arrest, Hauptmann had been out late and had little sleep.[1595] After his arrest, Hauptmann was brought to the Greenwich Street Station in Manhattan, where he was immediately photographed, fingerprinted, and booked *"on a shotgun charge for the*

[1592] Hoover, John Edgar, Director, Division of Investigation (FBI). <u>Memorandum For Mr. Tamm</u>. September 22, 1934. National Archives at College Park Maryland.

[1593] "False Registry Laid to Foley In Fraud Probe." *Brooklyn Daily Eagle*. November 6, 1933. Brooklyn Public Library.

[1594] Ibid.

[1595] Hauptmann, Richard. Autobiography: Unedited & Uncorrected (Translated). <u>The Story of My Life</u>. Page 201. May 4, 1935. New Jersey State Police Museum and Learning Center Archives.

purpose of avoiding publicity."[1596] He was interrogated, and soon he was asked to give handwriting samples; Hauptmann complied.[1597] An interruption occurred once Joseph Perrone arrived. Perrone claimed he was met at his hack stand at Mosholu Parkway & Jerome Avenue by Det. Clune and Corp. Leon at 8 PM.[1598] From there Perrone said he returned his cab to the garage then accompanied the Officers to the station.[1599] According to Officer McNamara, police set up a line-up in Captain Bennett's office on the second floor that consisted of himself, Detective Coake, and Hauptmann at about 11:00 PM.[1600] [1601] Given this bogus lineup, and also considering that in the summer of 1934 Schwarzkopf had deemed Perrone *"unreliable"* and that he *"could not see how Perrone could identify a man he had seen for only a few seconds two years ago,"* it's easy to see why no reasonable

---

[1596] Sisk, T. H. Special Agent, Division of Investigation (FBI), <u>Letter from T. H. Sisk to Director, Division of Investigation</u>. September 20, 1934. National Archives at College Park Maryland.

[1597] Creamer, Philip G. Detective – New York. <u>Shield 795 – Bureau of Criminal Information</u>. Statement. November 22, 1934. Made to New Jersey Assistant Attorney General Robert Peacock. New Jersey State Police Museum and Learning Center Archives. (Note: the copies of these exact dictations, from "Spring 3100" Magazine, are not at the NJSP Archives.)

[1598] Perrone, Joseph. Statement. May 22, 1937. New Jersey State Police Museum and Learning Center Archives.

[1599] Ibid.

[1600] McNamara, John A. Patrolman, New York City Police. Statement. November 21, 1934. New Jersey State Police Museum and Learning Center Archives.

[1601] Note: Most Authors use the September 19th and 20th transcriptions to guess at the time. However, while these pages are numbered, they clearly weren't all transcribed at the same time and therefore can be out of chronological order. As a result, I have included versions from the two men actually there at the time to allow the Reader to draw their own conclusions.

conclusion was drawn from it.[1602] Yet history turns a blind eye to this. So after Perrone made the (dubious) identification, Hauptmann continued to write until finally sometime after midnight when he could hardly keep his eyes open.[1603] Each time, as he began to fall asleep, he was "*poked*" in the "*ribs*" and told to continue to write.[1604] As the night progressed he refused to write but would receive a "*couple of knocks*" again in the "*ribs*."[1605]

Handwriting

Nine sheets of these handwriting samples were driven over to handwriting expert Albert D. Osborn by Special Agent Turrou and Sergeant Ritchie around midnight; however, Osborn requested additional samples.[1606] Hauptmann wrote out more samples and Special Agent Turrou and Sergeant Zapolsky returned to Osborn's

---

[1602] Sisk, T. H. Special Agent, Division of Investigation. Memorandum for the Director. Unknown subjects. <u>Kidnapping and murder of Charles A. Lindbergh, Jr</u>. June 23, 1934. National Archives at College Park Maryland.

[1603] Hauptmann, Richard. Autobiography: Unedited & Uncorrected (Translated). <u>The Story of My Life</u>. Page 201. May 4, 1935. New Jersey State Police Museum and Learning Center Archives.

[1604] Hauptmann, Bruno Richard. Testimony. The State of New Jersey vs. Bruno Richard Hauptmann, <u>Hunterdon County Court of Oyer and Terminer</u>, page 2529, 1935. New Jersey State Law Library.

[1605] Ibid.

[1606] Ritchie, Thomas J. Sergeant, New Jersey State Police. New Jersey State Police Report. <u>Report of handwriting specimens taken from Richard Hauptmann and delivered by the undersigned to Albert Osborne, Junior for examination and comparison with handwriting on the Lindbergh ransom notes</u>. September 22, 1934. New Jersey State Police Museum and Learning Center Archives.

at 2:30 AM with these specimens.[1607] And according to Sgt. Ritchie, he was again detailed to Osborn's by Col. Schwarzkopf, this time accompanied by Lt. Finn and they delivered an additional fourteen samples.[1608] At 4:00 AM Osborn called Schwarzkopf with his findings, when Schwarzkopf hung up the first thing he said was "*it doesn't look so good*" and he added that Osborn was "*convinced*" Hauptmann "*did not write the ransom notes.*"[1609] He went on to say that Osborn Sr. was coming over that morning to review his findings, and when told he could have more samples, said that Osborn "*doesn't think that would change his opinion.*"[1610] Later, however, after both of these experts were advised of the ransom money discovery made in Hauptmann's garage, within an hour Osborn Sr. called over to advise they had "*positively decided*" that Hauptmann had written the ransom notes.[1611]

The Police must have felt pretty good as the evidence against Hauptmann continued to pile up. The interrogations continued

---

[1607] Sisk, T. H. Special Agent, Division of Investigation (FBI). Memorandum. Memorandum For Assistant Special Agent In Charge R. Whitley. Re: Bruno Richard Hauptmann, with aliases; Kidnaping and Murder of Charles A. Lindbergh, Jr. November 28, 1934. New Jersey State Police Museum and Learning Center Archives.

[1608] Ritchie, Thomas J. Sergeant, New Jersey State Police. New Jersey State Police Report. Report of handwriting specimens taken from Richard Hauptmann and delivered by the undersigned to Albert Osborne, Junior for examination and comparison with handwriting on the Lindbergh ransom notes. September 22, 1934. New Jersey State Police Museum and Learning Center Archives.

[1609] Sisk, T. H. Special Agent, Division of Investigation (FBI). Memorandum. Memorandum For Assistant Special Agent In Charge R. Whitley. Re: Bruno Richard Hauptmann, with aliases; Kidnaping and Murder of Charles A. Lindbergh, Jr. November 28, 1934. New Jersey State Police Museum and Learning Center Archives.

[1610] Ibid.
[1611] Ibid.

on September 20th running throughout the day and early evening hours until being interrupted for a second line-up. As previously mentioned, this time John Condon showed up at 5:30 PM and was expected to identify Hauptmann (who was positioned among the 13 cops in the line-up) as the mysterious Cemetery John who he had met in both Bronx cemeteries.[1612] At the conclusion of this long drawn out process:

> Inspector Lyons: *"But you cannot identify him?"*
> Dr. Condon: *"No, I have to be very careful. The man's life is in Jeopardy."*[1613]

Hauptmann saw Condon shake his head several times as he left the room – Condon could not (or would not) identify him.[1614]

The Beating

It was after this event Hauptmann was severely beaten.[1615] According to Hauptmann he was placed in a room and handcuffed to a chair. About 12 plainclothes policemen entered the room, showed Hauptmann a hammer (that he said was his), then told him they were going to beat him with it.[1616] Then the lights went out and they

---

[1612] Duane, J. J. Detective, MOD. Transcription. <u>Line Up Conducted in Office of Second Deputy Police Commissioner, 156 Greenwich Street, N.Y.C. – 5:30 p.m. September 20, 1934</u>. September 21, 1934. New Jersey State Police Museum and Learning Center Archives.

[1613] Ibid.

[1614] Hauptmann, Richard. Autobiography: Unedited & Uncorrected (Translated). <u>The Story of My Life</u>. Page 202. May 4, 1935. New Jersey State Police Museum and Learning Center Archives.

[1615] Ibid.

[1616] Dexter, Thurston H., M.D. F.A.C.P. <u>Report of Oral and Physical Examination of Bruno Richard Hauptmann</u>. September 25, 1934. New Jersey State Police Museum and Learning Center Archives.

indeed struck Hauptmann on the shoulders, back of the head, and right arm with the hammer, also kicked him in the legs and stomach, and twisted his wrists and ankles, all the while yelling out threats of *"we'll break your ribs," "I'll break your arms," "we'll knock your brains out"* etc.[1617] On September 25th, Dr. Thurston H. Dexter conducted an examination of Hauptmann and made this conclusion:

> *"I conclude from this examination that he had been subjected recently to a severe beating, all or mostly with blunt instruments. The injuries resulting from this are general and include the head, back, chest, abdomen, and thighs."*[1618]

Yet, in one of the oddest situations I have ever come across while researching this case, there are two pieces of evidence which appear to dispute Hauptmann's claims of being viciously attacked.... The first is a NYPD Memo claiming the existence of an entrance in the blotter dated September 20, 1934 at 10:35 PM signed by Police Surgeons John J. Loughlin, and John H. Garlock:

> *"Examined one, Richard Hauptmann this time and date, and find no evidence of marks of injury. This examination was made while the prisoner was completely stripped of his clothing. Heart negative, pulse 90 & regular, reflexes normal, gait normal."*[1619]

However, the blotter entry isn't the only documentation of this visit. In fact, there is a separate report written by Garlock to his

---

[1617] Ibid.

[1618] Ibid.

[1619] John A. Harriell, Captain - 2nd Precinct, New York Police Department. Memorandum To Lt. Finn. <u>Transcript of Blotter Entry And Examination of one Richard Hauptmann</u>. December 28, 1934. New Jersey State Police Museum and Learning Center Archives.

supervisor Chief Surgeon Thomas McGoldrick which claimed that on September 20th at 9:30 PM he examined Hauptmann specifically to "*determine the presence or absence of marks of injury*" at the request from the Telegraph Bureau.[1620] Garlock wrote that although he found Hauptmann to be pale and suffering from lack of sleep, his complete examination "*failed to reveal any evidence to suggest recent injury of any sort*" and mentioned the entry being made in the police blotter.[1621] These sources must be properly considered. One explanation is that Hauptmann was lying. The other is that Police, getting ready to thump Hauptmann, decided to call in for a specific documented review they could point to in order to neutralize any later claim. Finally, and most obvious, would be these sources were lies. In Flemington, Wilentz fought hard to keep out questions concerning a beating.[1622] In fact, even after Hauptmann's execution, New Jersey Assistant Attorney General Robert Peacock asserted "*no one ever attempted to force him to talk, nor did anyone ever use force on him.*"[1623]

However, Special Agent Sisk completely backed up Hauptmann's claim as reflected in an FBI Memo:

> "*Mr. Clegg asked that I tell the Director confidentially that Sisk had just informed him that while Hauptmann was being held by the police in Greenwich [sic] Street,*

[1620] Garlock, John H. Police Surgeon, New York Police Department. New York Police Department Report. <u>Bruno Hauptmann</u>. September 22, 1934. New Jersey State Police Museum and Learning Center Archives.

[1621] Ibid.

[1622] Hauptamnn, Bruno Richard. Testimony. The State of New Jersey vs. Bruno Richard Hauptmann, <u>Hunterdon County Court of Oyer and Terminer</u>, page 2520-5, 1935. New Jersey State Law Library.

[1623] Peacock, Robert. *Guilty As Hell – At Last, The Truth About The Hauptmann Case.* Manuscript: Unpublished and Undated (1935?). Page 124. New Jersey State Police Museum and Learning Center Archives.

they gave this fellow a real going over and punched him in the back and twisted his arms and legs and "gave him hell." Mr. Clegg stated this was about the second or third night they had him in custody; that the city police and the New Jersey police are the ones who actually did the work; that agents were present but, under Sisk's orders, did not touch him. Mr. Clegg stated that after the indictment is returned, he felt the Division should know all about the situation before it pops."[1624]

Now we can completely eliminate the explanation that Hauptmann was lying about this attack. With this is mind, when did it occur? According to Lt. Finn, *"various persons were questioning him"* and at *"about ten-thirty District Attorney Foley of the Bronx accompanied by Breslin, came down here."*[1625] A conference ensued, and at its conclusion Police were *"directed to take the prisoner to the Bronx County District Attorney's Office."*[1626] As a result of this information, if the time is correct, it seems highly unlikely police had time to conduct this assault between the time of his examination and the arrival of the Bronx DA. Additionally, Hauptmann would later claim that once Foley examined him at Greenwich Street Station, he saw his condition, *"and sent me to the Bronx prison."*[1627]

[1624] Tamm. E. A. Division of Investigation (FBI). <u>Memorandum For The Director</u>. September 24, 1934. National Archives at College Park Maryland.

[1625] Finn, James Lieut. New York Police Department. Statement. Made to New Jersey Assistant Attorney General Robert Peacock. Page 9. November 22, 1934. New Jersey State Police Museum and Learning Center Archives.

[1626] Ibid.

[1627] Hauptmann, Richard. Autobiography: Unedited & Uncorrected (Translated). <u>The Story of My Life</u>. Page 202. May 4, 1935. New Jersey State Police Museum and Learning Center Archives.

Closet

On September 25th at exactly 11:55AM, Hauptmann sat in front of a group of investigators led by DA Foley and was questioned about the closet molding. It's important to note that during this questioning, Foley outlined exactly what I have established above. That is, by emphasizing how great Hauptmann had been treated since he took control of him:

> Foley: *And all the time you have been in my hands you have been well treated?*
> Hauptmann: *Yes.*
>
> Q: *You have had visits from your wife?*
> A: *Yes.*
>
> Q: *You have cigarettes here that I have given you?*
> A: *Yes.*
>
> Q: *Your child has been brought in to see you?*
> A: *Yes.*[1628]

I find this to be of particular importance. While Hauptmann obviously didn't want to harm himself, he did have motivation to assist Foley. After all it's clear that, in his mind, he had been rescued by this man from future beatings:

[1628] Hauptmann, Bruno Richard. Statement. Made to District Attorney Foley, Inspector Bruckman, Captain Appel, Detective Gilmartin, Main Office Manhattan, Lieut. Arthur T. Keaten, New Jersey State Police, Captain J. J. Lamb, Assistant District Attorney Delagi, Charles F. Brodie, County Detective Hanley, T. H. Sisk, Special Agent, Department of Justice. September 25, 1934 at 11:55 A. M. New Jersey State Police Museum and Learning Center Archives.

Q: *I have helped you in every way possible?*
A: *Yes.*

Q: *Is all that true?*
A: *Yes.*[1629]

In front of Hauptmann was the actual closet molding piece which had been removed from the home and brought over to Foley's office by Inspector Bruckman. However, it's during this interview that BOTH the writing on this trim AND the writing on the back of the door were discussed. Since Bornmann claimed the door was brought over later in the PM there are three options to consider as to why it was being discussed: Bornmann could be mistaken about the timing of its delivery, Hauptmann could be looking at a picture of it, or Hauptmann simply brought up the door on his own. But because we have Hauptmann discussing multiple items, it's important to try to understand which of these he was actually talking about. Clearly, he was looking at the molding trim here:

Q: *Hauptmann, I want to ask you some questions about this board you know it is from your closet in your own house, don't you?*
A: *It must be.*

Q: *It is the same kind of wood – your handwriting is on it?*
A: *Yes, all over it.*

Q: *What did you write on that board, read it to the stenographer.*
A: *I can't read it any more.*

Q: *Who rubbed it out? Can you read the address on it?*

[1629] Ibid.

A: *2974. I can't make out the first. I read the number down below, 37154.*

Q: *What else can you read on that board that you wrote yourself?*
A: *I can't read – that is "a", "t", "u" and a "r". Another one I can't make out.*

Q: *That's Dr. Condon's address isn't it?*
A: *I don't know.*

Q: *Why did you write it on the board?*
A: *I must have read it in the paper about the story. I was a little bit interested and keep a little bit record of it, and maybe I was just on the closet, and was reading the paper and put it down the address.*

Q: *How did you come to put the telephone number there?*
A: *I can't give you any explanation about the telephone number.*[1630]

It's during this part of the statement where he seemed to be admitting that he did write the address. However, it is not clear whether or not he acknowledged the phone number. There appears to have been a weak attempt to erase some of this. Part of the "9" in "2974" was faded, some of *"Decatur"* mainly the letters *"De"* were faded, but the entire word *"Sedgwick"* was almost completely smeared away. The writing least affected was the *"3–7154."* To continue:

Q: *Your only explanation for writing Dr. Condon's address on this board, and telephone number, is that*

[1630] Ibid.

you were probably reading the paper in the closet and you marked it down, is that correct?

A: It is possible that a shelf or two shelfs in the closet and after a while I put new papers always on the closet, and we just got the paper where this case was in, and I followed the story of course, and I put the address on there.

Q: That's why you marked it on the door?
A: That's the only explanation I can give.[1631]

While Foley combines both the address and phone number in his question, Hauptmann is only replying specifically about the address. As Foley begins to wind up the interview, he asks Hauptmann if he has anything he'd like to add which was when, seemingly out of nowhere, this occurs:

A: No. About them two numbers I am sure it was 500 or $1,000 bills.

Q: When you say those two numbers, you don't refer to anything on this board – when you talk of the two numbers you don't mean anything on this board but other number written on the door?
A: On the door.

Q: But not on this piece?
A: I can't remember where I put it.

Q: And you say that they refer to bills of high denomination?
A: Yes.

[1631] Ibid.

Q: *Is there anything else you wanted to add?*
A: *No.*

Q: *Do you remember the day that you wrote this memorandum on the board?*
A: *No.*

Q: *You remember that you did write it?*
A: *I must write it, the figures that's my writing.*

Q: *The writing is yours too, isn't it?*
A: *I hardly can read it.*

Q: *From what you see of it, it is your writing, isn't it —it is your figures and your writing?*
A: *I really can't remember when I put it on.*

Q: *Regardless of when you put it on, it is your figures and your writing, isn't it?*
A: *The writing I can't make out so very clearly, I don't know.*

Q: *Do you know who rubbed it or tried to rub it out?*
A: *No.*[1632]

So what we see here is a rather confusing exchange that bounces between the writing on the door and the writing on the trim. However, in the end Hauptmann seemed to be backing off his original acknowledgement of the address by saying he didn't know because he could hardly read it. Hauptmann was quickly reinterviewed at 12:21 PM. I've always believed this was when the actual door was brought over; however, as I mention above, I cannot prove this either way:

[1632] Ibid.

Q: *Do you remember the date that you marked Dr. Condon's telephone number on the board in your house?*
A: *Absolutely not.*

Q: *You can't fix the time?*
A: *No, sir, impossible.*

Q: *Do you remember the time that you marked the numbers of the bills?*
A: *No.*

Q: *Which did you mark first, the telephone or the bills?*
A: *I can't remember that.*

Q: *Did you get the bills after you marked the number on the sash – when I say the number I mean the telephone number and the address?*
A: *I guess I marked the bills first, them two bills.*

Q: *Do you know when you got them?*
A: *I got them in 32 – early 32. I know it was the first two thousand dollars I got, I can't give any more, it was early 32.*

Q: *Was it before or after your wife went away that you got those bills?*
A: *Before.*

Q: *Long before?*
A: *Quite a while.*

Q: *Can you fix the time at all?*

A: *I only can remember this is the first money I got from Isidor. It was two big bills.*

Q: *Can't you remember when you got them?*
A: *It must be around March.*

Q: *In the early March, middle of March, or the end of March?*
A: *I can't fix any certain date on that.*

Q: *What month did you write Dr. Condon's phone number and address in?*
A: *It must be after.*

Q: *It was after the kidnapping, wasn't it?*
A: *Yes.*

Q: *Was it before the ransom was paid?*
A: *No, I guess it was after.*

Q: *What makes you think so?*
A: *After that whole paper was full of Dr. Condon.*[1633]

Two observations can be made from this: First is the line of questioning by adding the phone number to the question, and next, that this could somehow mean Hauptmann was admitting to it. While he is answering the question, he is still clearly explaining the address as coming from the papers. This is why it's important to look at everything from beginning to end and not jump on something we want to believe or ignore something we do not. Next, can the statement itself be trusted?

[1633] Hauptmann, Bruno Richard. Statement. Made to District Attorney Foley, Lieut. Keaten, County Detective Hanley, Captain Appel, Captain Lamb, T. H. Sisk. September 25, 1934 at 12:21 P. M. New Jersey State Police Museum and Learning Center Archives.

As we can see, during both statements Hauptmann made above, Special Agent Sisk was present. However, Sisk was giving additional information in his account concerning what Hauptmann said about the serial numbers on the back of the door:

> *Hauptmann admitted that he had written the serial numbers and stated in explanation "Those numbers represent the highest and the lowest from the serial numbers". Without any further questions being asked him he continued on, "That was the $40,000 I got from Fisch. I had $2,000. in the closet. I think they were $1,000. bills". Mr. Foley then pointed out to Hauptmann that the figure $500." was on the door, and Hauptmann then replied "I guess one of them was a $500. bill".*[1634]

The next day Hauptmann was again interviewed. Foley again slipped in this question:

> Q: *Hauptmann, yesterday I showed you a piece of wood from your house with Condon's address and phone number on it, is that correct?*
> A: *Yes.*
>
> Q: *You admitted that you wrote that on the board?*
> A: *Yes.*[1635]

[1634] Sisk, T. H. Special Agent, DOI (FBI). Memorandum For File. <u>Bruno Richard Hauptmann with aliases. Unknown Subjects. Kidnaping and Murder of Charles A. Lindbergh, Jr.</u> September 25, 1934. Author's Possession (Thanks to Amy35).

[1635] Hauptmann, Bruno Richard. Statement. Made to District Attorney Foley, Inspector Bruckman, County Detective Hanley, Captain Lamb, Lieut. Keaten, Joseph Lanagan, Ass't Attorney General. September 26, 1934 at 11:45 A. M. New Jersey State Police Museum and Learning Center Archives.

Not to beat a dead horse, but while Hauptmann is answering "yes" to this question, we can go back through these statements to see he never admitted to writing the phone number, and the only place one can point to in order to say he had is when Foley lumps that in with his questions which concerned the address.

Hauptmann would again face specific questioning that concerned this subject during his extradition hearing in the Bronx County Supreme Court on October 15th. Here Attorney General Wilentz, representing the demanding State (New Jersey), posed the following questions concerning the closet molding:

> Q: *So that when you looked at Exhibit A, which was presented by [to] you by the District Attorney of Bronx County, and you looked at the handwriting thereon, you said that was your handwriting, isn't that so?*
> A: *I said that is my lumber I could not make out the handwriting.*
>
> Q: *You said the number on there is your handwriting?*
> A: *Yes.*
>
> Q: *What about the "Decatur"?*
> A: *I could not make out whether that is my handwriting and numbers.*
>
> Q: *The numbers are in your handwriting, are they not?*
> A: *They are.*
>
> Q: *But the other writing, you are not sure of?*

A: *I could not make out.*[1636]

One can see how confusing and indefinite this all is. While at first he seemed to concede where he said the "number" (singular) was in his handwriting, during the very next question he said he could not say if the writing and numbers were his. Since the first set of numbers was the address, and the second set the phone numbers, could it be he was moving down the trim in order to answer the question further? Then to go back to say the numbers were in his handwriting – did he mean all numbers, and if so, why did he just answer he could not tell? Later during this questioning Wilentz revisited Foley's questions. He selected the statement of the 26th, while completely ignoring those contradictions included in his earliest statement on the 25th. Wilentz repeated those questions and answers, then asked Hauptmann if he remembered them to which Hauptmann replied "yes."[1637]

The next visit to this subject is reflected in the documentation about what occurred in the Flemington Jail after his extradition to New Jersey. Here any and all conversations were secretly written down by Troopers assigned to eavesdrop on him. In the following conversation, there were many present and it appeared Hauptmann spoke freely. It was during this friendly sit down visit with Condon (same as previously mentioned) where this exchange was written:

Condon: *Oh you did and how did you come to write my phone number on a board in your closet?*

[1636] Hauptmann, Bruno Richard. Testimony. The People State of New York ex rel. Bruno Richard Hauptmann, v. John Hanley, Sheriff of Bronx County. Supreme Court, Bronx County, Special Term Part I. page 68. October 15, 1934. New Jersey State Police Museum and Learning Center Archives.

[1637] Ibid. Page 99.

> Hauptmann: *That's what I always do. I was following the case like everybody and wrote the number on the board.*

> Condon: *I also write things on the wall or on mirrors to have it handy.*[1638]

This exchange makes no sense. Remembering Hauptmann's explanation to Foley for the address was that if he wrote it he must have read about it in the newspaper. The phone number he said he had no explanation for. Why? Because that number was not in the papers. So his answer is the one he gave Foley for the address but knowing the phone number was not in the paper he did not use it, only saying he had "no explanation." This could be because he did not write it there OR that he got it from some other place he did not want to mention. As an aside, the oddest thing of all was Condon's denial that Hauptmann had written it there:

> *"But to this day I cannot bring myself to accept the written telephone number and address in the kidnaper's closet, despite the fact that he, himself, admitted that he wrote them there."*[1639]

Condon didn't seem to like the idea of either of these things being written there. Why not? Next we have the testimony in Flemington to refer to. Under cross examination Hauptmann was once again shown the closet molding now marked exhibit "S–204":

[1638] Stockburger, H. Trooper, New Jersey State Police. New Jersey State Police Report. Conversation between Doctor John F. Condon and Bruno Richard Hauptmann at the Hunterdon County Jail in Flemington, N. J., on October 24, 1934 at about 1:00 P. M. in the presence of Colonel Schwarzkopf, Attorney Wilentz and Prosecutor Hauck. October 24, 1934. New Jersey State Police Museum and Learning Center Archives.

[1639] Condon, John F. (1936). *Jafsie Tells All!* Jonathan Lee. P205.

Q: *That is your handwriting on there, isn't it?*
A: *No.*

Q: *What?*
A: *No, sir.*

Q: *That is not your handwriting?*
A: *(Shaking his head)*

Q: *You take a look at that. You have seen it many times before. I will take the paper off for you so it will be easier (counsel removed the cellophane wrapper on the board). Take your time about it now. First, tell me, are the numbers your handwriting?*
A: *The numbers look familiar upwards. I can't remember for putting it on.*

Q: *Just keep looking at those numbers and tell me whether or not they are in your handwriting and that you wrote them, the numbers?*
A: *I can't remember putting them on.*

Q: *Did you remember better when you were talking to District Attorney Foley?*
A: *At that time I was quite excited.*

Q: *Were you excited when you got before a Supreme Court Justice in the State of New York in your extradition proceedings?*
A: *I say yes.*[1640]

[1640] Hauptmann, Bruno Richard. Testimony. The State of New Jersey vs. Bruno Richard Hauptmann, <u>Hunterdon County Court of Oyer and Terminer</u>, pages 2658-60, 1935. New Jersey State Law Library.

Here we can see Hauptmann answering as we would expect him to answer, and he seemed to be denying everything about this writing. After all, accepting some writing while denying some other writing wouldn't work in his favor. In an attempt to steer and develop Hauptmann back to where he wanted him to be, we see Wilentz asked this question:

> Q: *Now, Mr. Hauptmann, what you mean then is this, that you have got a habit of writing down telephone numbers and addresses of things that are interesting; isn't that right?*
> A: *Yes.*[1641]

In once again establishing this "habit," Wilentz now pressed for Hauptmann's past partial acceptance of some of the writing:

> Q: *You know that part of it, part of the numbers are in your handwriting; you know that don't you?*
> A: *It looks like it.*

> Q: *Yes. Well you know it is; you have said so many times, in the Bronx.*
> A: *I don't say it is.*

> Q: *Well, didn't you say in the Bronx many times that you wrote the numbers on?*
> A: *I said it looks like.*[1642]

Wilentz would later use Hauptmann's respect for Foley to try to finally score a victory in this exchange:

> Q: *Mr. Foley treated you well didn't he?*

[1641] Ibid. Page 2671.
[1642] Ibid. Page 2672.

A: *Yes.*

Q: *He is a very delightful man, isn't he?*
A: *Yes.*

Q: *A very fine man?*
A: *Yes.*[1643]

We can see that as the questioning continued, an attempt was made by the AG to bulldoze over Hauptmann until he got the answer he was looking for. Also, we see another potential issue as it related to Hauptmann's questionings, both here and previously:

Q: *Did you tell the truth about this Board in the Supreme Court of New York?*
A: *I—*

Q: *Why do you hesitate?*
A: *I am not.*

Q: *Well, then, why don't you answer? Either you did or you didn't.*
A: *You have to give me a chance.*

Q: *I will give you all day, but you ought to know whether you told the truth in court.*
A: *No, I have to trans— I am thinking in German and I have to translate it in American language, and it needs quite a bit of time; so excuse me.*[1644]

As the questioning moved along about this issue, we can finally see Hauptmann's weak explanation concerning his Bronx testimony.

[1643] Ibid. Pages 2675-6.
[1644] Ibid. Pages 2676-7.

However, it did bear out once reviewing it because he was answering "yes" to things he never actually said at the time. Now, whether it was true, partially true, or false is up to the researcher to decide:

> A: *When I saw Mr. Foley for the first time speak about this particular board here I never said Yes and I never said No, because I never could make out and I never could remember ever putting it out, and when it came up in the court room I only simple said Yes, without thinking of it.*[1645]

In reality this was all Wilentz really needed. This was because only those of us who have studied these exchanges from beginning to end would understand what Hauptmann is "trying" to say.

To consider Hauptmann's final word on the writing on this trim, here is what he wrote about it in his autobiography where he once again reminded us of his habit for writing things down on the walls in his kitchen and so …

> *….I thought when they showed the piece of trimming that when reading about the Lindbergh case in the newspaper, I had written down this address, as I did so many other things.*[1646]

Back of the Closet Door

In revisiting the issue of the numbers on the back of the closet door it is to be remembered that, at the time of their discovery,

[1645] Ibid. Page 2678.
[1646] Hauptmann, Richard. <u>The Story of My Life</u>. Autobiography: Unedited & Uncorrected (Translated). May 4, 1935, page 205. New Jersey State Police Museum and Learning Center Archives.

Police believed they were serial numbers of ransom bills. However, it was quickly discovered that these serial numbers did not appear on the lists which recorded those of the ransom money.[1647] Agent Sisk suggested that since a $5.00 serial was found among the list as "B–49349272–A" and a $10.00 serial was also found among the list as "A–77967162–A" that it was possible Hauptmann was recording ransom bill serials but that he simply "*left blank the first four digits.*"[1648] This theory did not take root, and unable to make sense of these notations, it seems the Police lost interest in them. What were they, and when did Hauptmann write this notation?

Foley

As seen earlier in this chapter, Hauptmann told Foley during his interrogation these serial numbers represented "*two bills*" that were either "*500 or $1,000 bills.*" Next, he claimed this was the "*first*" money he received from Fisch which he received in early 1932 "*around March.*"

Sisk

Also seen earlier, Agent Sisk, who was there during Foley's questioning, remembered what Hauptmann said somewhat differently. According to his version, Hauptmann said this was the $2,000 dollars he received from Fisch which he kept in that closet. Once the "$500" notation was pointed out, Hauptmann responded

---

[1647] Hoover, John Edgar. Director, DOI (FBI). Memorandum. <u>Memorandum For Mr. Tamm</u>. September 25, 1934. New Jersey State Police Museum and Learning Center Archives.

[1648] Sisk, T. H. Special Agent, DOI (FBI). Memorandum For File. <u>Bruno Richard Hauptmann with aliases. Unknown Subjects. Kidnaping and Murder of Charles A. Lindbergh, Jr</u>. September 25, 1934. Author's Possession (Thanks to Amy35).

that he guessed one of them was a $500 dollar bill. Hauptmann also claimed, according to Sisk, that these serials represented the highest to the lowest of all the money Fisch had given him which seemed to be the impetus for Sisk's theory above. Also attributable to Sisk was something Assistant Director Clegg told Hoover, namely that "*Hauptmann stated he wrote this in 1928.*"[1649] However, this revelation prompted someone to remind him that he said he hadn't even met Fisch until 1932.[1650] Now, regardless of whether or not Hauptmann had made such a suggestion, the police response was still a valid one concerning *when* Hauptmann actually met Isador. If, as he told Foley, he wrote these serials there in March AND they came from Fisch – it proves he knew him earlier than the summer of 1932.

Wilentz

While on the stand in Flemington, Hauptmann remained consistent concerning his uncertainty about the denominations; however, his memory now changed about exactly when these numbers were written there:

> Q: *What were the size of those bills, $500 and $1,000 weren't they?*
> A: *It was a thousand, I guess.*
>
> Q: *Thousand dollar bills?*
> A: *Thousand dollar bills.*

[1649] Hoover, John Edgar. Director, DOI (FBI). Memorandum. <u>Memorandum For Mr. Tamm</u>. September 25, 1934. New Jersey State Police Museum and Learning Center Archives. (Note: This is yet another and different Memo from any previous footnote).
[1650] Ibid.

Q: How many thousand dollar bills did you have?
A: I can't remember now. When I put it on, it was summer of '32.

Q: Yes, sure, summer time '32; after April the 2nd, 1932?
A: No; summer time '33; I wish to correct.

Q: Oh, I see.
A: I got $2,000 I should put in the stock market and I didn't put it in the stock market, I brought it to the bank, and I kept it home for a few days.

Q: Two one thousand dollar bills?
A: Yes.

Q: Tell me, where do you get those one thousand dollar bills?
A: That is Mr. Fisch brought it in my house, to put in the margin.

Q: Oh. Mr. Fisch brought it?
A: Yes.[1651]

Clearly this testimony was either suggesting he was now sliding back the date in order to support his position as to when he met Fisch OR he had legitimately been mistaken at the time of his questioning in the Bronx. So if he was willing to lie here, he was willing to support one thing while harming another. If, for example, he knew Fisch earlier, this appeared to put Hauptmann in the mix; however, it would destroy any notion about this crime being perpetrated by a

---

[1651] Hauptmann, Bruno Richard. Testimony. The State of New Jersey vs. Bruno Richard Hauptmann, <u>Hunterdon County Court of Oyer and Terminer</u>, pages 2682, 1935. New Jersey State Law Library.

Lone-Wolf. It's an "all or nothing" tactic – and one the Prosecution certainly enjoyed seeing.

Governor Harold Hoffman

It was sometime after Hoffman took a personal interest in this case that he heard a Reporter had written "Condon's Phone Number" in Hauptmann's closet. In fact, Hauptmann himself told the Governor that he suspected a Police Officer or a Reporter of writing both the address and telephone number there.[1652] The issue was also brought to his attention early on by his Public Relations & Press Secretary, William Conklin, who was obviously hearing about it through his contact with Reporters:

> *I am told – and the source is good – that Henry Paynter, of The Post, told two or three persons that he (Paynter) wrote Condon's phone number on the door panel.*
>
> *This is one of those things which would require more than overnight sheeking* [sic]. *This guy has exhibited considerable bitterness in stories relating to the present inquiry.*[1653]

However, as this "rumor" made its rounds, it was coming to the Governor at about that time that *"Paynter's handwriting"* did not *"check."*[1654] This seemed like a very strange comment; Hoffman

---

[1652] Hoffman, Harold Giles. *The Crime - The Case - The Challenge (What Was Wrong with the Lindbergh Case?)*, Original Manuscript: Unedited & Uncorrected, circa 1937. Page 21. New Jersey State Police Museum and Learning Center Archives.

[1653] Conklin, William. <u>Memo to Gov</u>: Undated (1936?). New Jersey State Police Museum and Learning Center Archives.

[1654] Ibid. (see handwritten note at bottom in Hoffman's handwriting).

assumed if Paynter had written it there, that he would use his own style of handwriting. But of course, using his own handwriting would have defeated the purpose. The better question might be why would Paynter have written it there at all? However, it wouldn't be much longer before Gov. Hoffman was rethinking his position on the idea someone may have written *"Dr. Condon's phone number on Hauptmann's closet wall."*[1655] As the Governor became swamped with correspondence between 1936 through 1938, among the things he received were an article and pictured diagram of the writing on the trim from Edward Oehler. In this article, Oehler alleged that someone entered Hauptmann's closet and noticed Condon's address written there. From here, Oehler asserted, *"Mr. X."* used the numbers already written there – "2974" – to mimic/copy when writing Condon's telephone number below that address. The set of "297" were written *"all steady and to the right"* as exemplified by the diagram. The "4" in that sequence was also written with a steady hand but with the top half ending to the left and without the hand ever leaving the wall.

Now in creating the phone number by looking at the numbers in this address, this left only the "3" and the "1" to be blindly written:

> *"He started the numbers above, a location making a successful copy possible. This number 3 was written carelessly and with too much pressure, 25 degrees out of position and 30% too small and with very poor penmanship. Next number 7 was to be copied, and at once Mr. X realized the pressure of the pen, changed the position 25 degrees and increased its size 30%, with good penmanship. Number 1 received more speed, a smaller but genuine American one. Number*

[1655] Winchell, Walter. "Broadway Gossip." *Salt Lake Telegram*. December 12, 1936. Utah Digital Newspapers (digitalnewspapers.org)

> *5 received speed, written 40% smaller and 10 degrees out of position, poor penmanship. Mr. X knowing the danger of his job, with a nervous hand rushed no 4 changed his pen 10 degrees for proper position to correspond with upper numbers, increased the size 40% over number 5…".*[1656]

His diagram also clearly showed that the "4" in the phone number was written in the opposite direction of the "4" in the address and that the writer's hand left the wall when making it. While I am not a big fan of handwriting analysis, this diagram is a convincing piece of evidence to support Oehler's position when looking at both numbers as they appeared on that trim. It clearly demonstrates to me that, at the very least, these numbers were written at different times. The analysis of pen pressure, pen lifts, letter formations, size, speed, and steadiness shows the science behind it, yet, there is also a degree of guess-work involved when "identifying" a writer. This is usually why both the Prosecution and the Defense can find Handwriting Experts to testify against each other's position in court.

The other supporting fact is that someone smeared this writing. The State's own handwriting expert, John Tyrrell, noted that "*an attempt had been made to erase the penciling*" and finding it "*of unusual interest,*" he wanted an "*infra-red*" picture taken of it which he believed could reveal something further.[1657] This unusual request was squashed by Schwarzkopf who explained that the Attorney General was not considering it since "*Hauptmann himself admitted*

[1656] Oehler, Ed. Article "*History of the Closet Numbers!*" Undated. New Jersey State Police Museum and Learning Center Archives.

[1657] Tyrrell, John F. <u>Letter from John F. Tyrrell to Co. H. Norman Schwarzkopf, Jr.</u> November 24, 1934. New Jersey State Police Museum and Learning Center Archives.

this writing."[1658] In looking at this "smear" it shows that it started at the "9" coming over the "Dec" then down over almost all of "Sedgwick" but barely touching on "3–7154." What was it all about? Was this Hauptmann attempting to erase these notations but doing a poor job of it? Or was it someone who screwed up "Sedgwick" simply trying to eliminate an obvious forgery?

Regardless of whether or not one accepts Oehler's position, it is unusual in that it claimed Hauptmann actually wrote the Condon address. While this is not helpful to him, it is an interesting possibility once considered. Hauptmann did not have a telephone in his house, and any pay phone he would use had the phone book available for Condon's number to be looked up.[1659] So while there might be a need for Hauptman to have Condon's address handy, there was no such need for that phone number. It was sometime during this period Hauptmann's Lawyer Lloyd Fisher told Hoffman, point blank, that:

> "*...the telephone number of Dr. Condon had been written upon the panel by a newspaper man, and he gave me the name of the reporter who had told him personally that he had written the number upon the door.*"[1660]

[1658] Schwarzkopf, H. Norman. Letter from H. Norman Schwarzkopf to Mr. John F. Tyrrell. December 7, 1934. New Jersey State Police Museum and Learning Center Archives.

[1659] Hoffman, Harold Giles. *The Crime - The Case - The Challenge (What Was Wrong with the Lindbergh Case?)*, Original Manuscript: Unedited & Uncorrected, circa 1937. Page 149. New Jersey State Police Museum and Learning Center Archives.

[1660] Hoffman, Harold G. Letter from Governor Harold G. Hoffman to Mr. Ralph S. Heuser. October 24, 1938. New Jersey State Police Museum and Learning Center Archives.

This revelation is important in more ways than one. First, it appears to back up Oehler's theory that only the Condon Phone number had been written there by the Reporter, and more importantly, that a Reporter <u>admitted</u> to Lloyd Fisher that he had been the one to write it there.

So who was this Reporter? Tom Cassidy? Henry Paynter? Some other person?

The Ken Article

In the 1938 April edition of Ken Magazine, an article entitled "*Off the Hauptmann Record*" created quite a stir.[1661] The article claimed that in February 1936, a "New York Editor" sat with Reporters John Randolph and Bruce Henry at the Roney Plaza Hotel in Miami Beach, Florida. During this conversation the "Editor" claimed to know "*the name of the newspaper reporter who wrote 'Jafsie' Condon's telephone number in Hauptmann's closet.*"[1662] Once the talk ended, both men raced to beat the other to get the story. Suspecting a hoax, the "Editor" was contacted for verification. However:

> "*He admits everything he said is true, but he claims he thought it was off the record stuff. Says he'll deny it if we print the story … and you know what his word would mean against that of a reporter and a press agent.*"[1663]

And so neither man was able to get the story, and it wasn't until this magazine article that anyone would know anything about it. The

---

[1661] "Off the Hauptmann Record." *Ken.* Reprinted (April 1938). New Jersey State Police Museum and Learning Center Archives.

[1662] Ibid.

[1663] Ibid.

reaction to this story was negative. For example, Walter Winchell wrote that it put "*some of us who covered the Hauptmann trial in stitches.*"[1664] Most simply wanted to know whether it was true. Leon Ho-age quickly penned a letter that asked this very question of Governor Hoffman after reading it. Hoffman quickly replied:

> "*I have known for some time that the Dr. Condon telephone number was written by a newspaper reporter and I know the name of the reporter.*"[1665]

In an attempt to get the "Editor's" name who was mentioned in this article, Bill Conklin wrote to George Clarke, Managing Editor for the New York Daily Mirror, to see if he knew. Clarke said he believed the "Editor" to be "Walter Howey" who was in Florida and at the Roney Plaza at that time.[1666] Also imparted to Conklin by Clarke, interestingly enough, was that although the name of the Reporter was "*Henry Painter*" [sic], his handwriting did not match because it had been "investigated" by having his old expense accounts from the Mirror files reviewed by a handwriting expert who made a comparison. Clarke also felt it was not "*beyond the realm of possibility that one of the servants of the people wrote the number.*"[1667] But would it compare if the Reporter wrote in a disguise and/or attempted to write like Hauptmann? Regardless, based upon what Lloyd Fisher told him, Hoffman was certain Paynter wrote that number:

[1664] Winchell, Walter. "Walter Takes Rap at Reformer Clan." *Salt Lake Telegram.* April 15, 1938. Utah Digital Newspapers (digitalnewspapers.org)

[1665] Hoffman, Harold G. Letter from Governor Harold G. Hoffman to Mr. Leon Hoage. April 27, 1938. New Jersey State Police Museum and Learning Center Archives.

[1666] Conklin, William S. Memorandum from William S. Conklin to Governor Hoffman. May 17, 1938. New Jersey State Police Museum and Learning Center Archives.

[1667] Ibid.

> *"I know the name of the newspaper reporter – so does Lloyd Fisher, to whom the reporter admitted, after Hauptmann's conviction, that he had written Dr. Condon's telephone number inside the closet in order to "make a good story."*[1668]

Hoffman would go on to explain that he did *"not mention this incident or give the name of the reporter"* expecting that facing a loss of his job, he *"would undoubtedly deny that he had ever written the telephone number in imitation of Hauptmann's handwriting."*[1669] Lloyd Fisher would once again back up this important claim about Paynter's confession to him. During an interview in 1951, he told George Hawke that:

> *"Henry Painter [sic] wrote and found Condon's phone number and address in Hauptmann's closet as a joke. Working as a reporter at the time, he never realized the consequences. It was a publicity stunt."*[1670]

In further support of Fisher's claim, as if everything above wasn't enough, found among Fred Pope's trial documents and correspondence was this note:

[1668] Hoffman, Harold. *There Is More To Be Told*. Original Manuscript: Unedited & Uncorrected, circa 1938. Page 4. New Jersey State Police Museum and Learning Center Archives.

[1669] Ibid.

[1670] Hawke, George G. *Trial By Fury: The Hauptmann Trial*. Princeton University Senior Thesis. (1951) Page 118. New Jersey State Police Museum and Learning Center Archives. (Note: citing an interview he conducted with Lloyd Fisher on January 28, 1951.)

"Arthur Reeve & Hank Paynter would like to see you at 111 Main St. immediately after the close of session. Arthur sez it's very important."[1671]

[1671] Postal Telegraph – Cable Company. <u>Press Telegram</u>. Handwritten & Unsigned. Undated. Rob O'Keefe Collection.

10

Isador Fisch

Was Isador Fisch involved in this crime, and if so, did he possess ransom money? There are several issues to be reviewed along these lines to discover what the truth behind this mysterious figure might be. History records that Fisch died both sick and penniless. Was Fisch "destitute" and sleeping on park benches? Or was he the guy who paid for private lessons at the Bronx Dancing School so that he could learn how to Tango?[1672] According to Hauptmann:

> *"Fisch always said that you should make believe to be very poor, then one would have no trouble. Also, one would never have to loan anyone money."*[1673]

[1672] Haussling, E. A., Sgt. Det., New Jersey State Police. New Jersey State Police Report. <u>Continued investigation re: Isidor Fisch</u>. November 17, 1934. New Jersey State Police Museum and Learning Center Archives. (Note: according to this report, he became so good he sometimes acted as an instructor. Although the report does not state which school he attended, I found the school's card among Fisch's belongings at the NJSP Archives).

[1673] Hauptmann, Richard. Autobiography: Unedited & Uncorrected (Translated). <u>The Story of My Life</u>. Page 179. May 4, 1935. New Jersey State Police Museum and Learning Center Archives.

A review of the police reports shows that Fisch portrayed himself in whatever way was necessary to capitalize financially from any given situation. One fact that is indisputable was that he was suffering from Tuberculosis. Police interviewed one of his doctors, August Spiegel, who told them he saw him four times in the summer of 1931 when he paid $5 in cash per visit.[1674] When next he saw Fisch, it was on November 4, 1933, and he was in very bad shape with TB in his right lung and suffering from a high fever. This caused Dr. Spiegel to advise against any trip to Germany and instead recommended he go to the hospital. When asked if he had the money to do so Fisch said he did have the funds but he declined to go.[1675] Spiegel further claimed that Fisch appeared to be of *"ordinary circumstances"* financially then offered up to police his personal observation that Fisch, being both very erratic and nervous, would be the type to commit *"a crime of this sort."*[1676]

Henry Breckinridge

One of the blockbusters Lloyd Gardner revealed in his book was that on September 28, 1934, Breckinridge gave a statement explaining two separate encounters which occurred during the ransom negotiations with a frail Jewish man he suspected was Isidor Fisch.[1677] It was the strong resemblance to all of the newspaper photos he had seen which led him to this position.[1678] It was *"just*

[1674] Ruggiero, F. J. Det., New Jersey State Police. New Jersey State Police Report. Lindbergh Investigation in N.Y. City, from Sept. 21, 1934 and including Sept. 25, 1934. New Jersey State Police Museum and Learning Center Archives.

[1675] Ibid.

[1676] Ibid.

[1677] Gardner, Lloyd C. June 2004. *The Case That Never Dies*. Rutgers University Press. Page 408.

[1678] Breckinridge, Henry. Memorandum. September 28, 1934. New Jersey State Police Museum and Learning Center Archives.

about the time" Breckinridge received the *"kidnap letter"* that this man came to his office. According to Breckinridge:

> *"He told me that I must deal with "us." He engaged in a long mysterious conversation all around the point but never coming to it. With a peculiar glint in his eyes he stated that I must realize that the needs of science must be served and that human life was of no consequence in comparison with the importance of science."*[1679]

Breckinridge was worried at the time that if this man had anything to do with the crime, *"the child would be killed or had been killed."*[1680]

> *"The man so aroused the suspicion of the young ladies in my office that Miss Rajdl searched his coat pockets when he was in my office and discovered a number of soiled handkerchiefs."*[1681]

Shortly after this man's last visit, Condon became intermediary, and Breckinridge never saw him again.[1682]

The Fisch Story

We have all heard about the story over the years that Fisch gave Hauptmann a box to keep, the implication being that it was Fisch who gave Hauptmann the ransom money which led to both his arrest and demise. Dubbed "The Fisch Story" by just about everyone, this was indicative of the fact there weren't many people who actually bought it. It was my friend Lloyd Gardner who told me that during

---

[1679] Ibid.

[1680] Ibid.

[1681] Ibid.

[1682] Ibid.

his interview with Sam Chiarvalli in 2001, it was brought out that even the Defense team didn't believe it.[1683] But is there anything at all which can be pointed to so that the assertion Fisch had been in possession of ransom money can be backed up?

One of the best sources of information concerning this matter is Hauptmann's own Ledger.[1684] This source is sometimes challenged as "fraudulent," apparently based on Special Agent Genau's report where he wrote that *"the entries can neither be substantiated nor proven to be fictitious."*[1685] With this in mind, the first step is to determine whether or not this account book is reliable. After all, it clearly reflects a fur and stock trading partnership with Fisch. According to Special Agent Frank:

> *"As all of Hauptmann's other records were found to be quite accurate and as, at the time of his arrest on September 19, 1934, 400 Hudson Seal skins were found in his possession, which amount agrees with his records, it is my opinion that Hauptmann's account book does record his investment in fur trading with Fisch."*[1686]

[1683] Author's conversation with Lloyd Gardner, September 2003.

[1684] National No. 814, Exhibit S-258. New Jersey State Police Museum and Learning Center Archives.

[1685] Genau, J. A. Special Agent, United States Bureau of Investigation (FBI). USBOI Report. <u>Kidnaping And Murder Of Charles A. Lindbergh, Jr.</u> Page 39. October 8, 1934. New Jersey State Police Museum and Learning Center Archives.

[1686] Frank, William E. Special Agent, United States Treasury Department. Internal Revenue Service Special Report. <u>Financial Activities of Bruno Richard Hauptmann and his wife, Anna Hauptmann, nee Schoeffler, 1279 East 222nd Street, Bronx, New York City.</u> January 8, 1935. Page 15. New Jersey State Police Museum and Learning Center Archives.

Having established this source as legitimate, Agent Frank pointed out the ledger indicated that Hauptmann invested $9,262.50 in the fur trading account by paying in *"net cash."* However, Frank also noted there were no corresponding withdrawals from any of Hauptmann's *"bank or brokerage accounts."* While he still believed these transactions occurred, he implied this amount of cash represented either ransom money or laundered proceeds of ransom money and that Hauptmann "should be made" to explain where it came from.[1687] As to Fisch's involvement in stocks, on pages 50 and 51 of the ledger it shows the purchase and sale of five different stocks. To Agent Frank, these figures...

> *"...indicate quite clearly that Fisch was interested in stock trading with Hauptmann and that Hauptmann took the trouble to list separately their joint interest, for in connection with four of the five stocks entered on pages 50 and 51, the brokerage transcripts show the purchase of 100 or 200 share lots, while Hauptmann's account book lists a 50 or 100 share lot purchase in his own records on pages 6, 7, 8, and 9, and a similar 50 or 100 share lot purchase on pages 50 and 51, which apparently was the record of Fisch's holdings."*[1688]

At the bottom of page 50, we see the following notation:

> *"Isidor Fisch put over to Conto*
> *Of Isidor and Richard <u>2103.00</u>*
> *July 10, 1933 to 20% Basis."*

According to Agent Frank, this notation meant:

[1687] Ibid.
[1688] Ibid. Page 18.

> "...that on that date they changed their method
> of operating and instead of listing their holdings
> separately, they continued to purchase and sell stocks
> but listed the transactions together on pages 100 to 103
> of the account book, with Fisch having a 20% interest
> in the transactions. This interpretation of the notation
> appears quite obvious, for the brokerage accounts show
> that from August 1932, when Hauptmann resumed
> trading, up to July 10, 1933 he had put exactly
> $10,103.10 into the account. If Fisch's investment of
> $2,103.00 is compared to Hauptmann's investment it
> will be seen that the ratio is exactly 20%."[1689]

A "double line" was drawn on both pages 102 and 103 by
Hauptmann.[1690] A notation under the double line on page 102
indicates the date of "*October 21, 1933.*" Frank believed this also
designated a "*change in the account*" at that point. He explained this
change occurred because:

> "Fisch, contemplating a visit to Germany (he
> purchased passage on November 15, 1933) desired to
> withdraw from the account. Actually, on November
> 14, 1933 Hauptmann drew a check on the account for
> $2,057.00 and a notation on page 73 of the account
> indicates that Fisch received $2,000 from the stock
> account on that date. Further, on pages 102 and 103
> Hauptmann made the notation "Am 21.10.1933 put
> in Stock 12,000$ in furs 5500$." The $5,500 exactly
> represents Hauptmann's half interest in 2,000 Hudson
> Seals skins as set forth on pages 76 and 77 of the account

[1689]   Ibid. Page 19.
[1690]   See Exhibit S-267.

*book and the $12,000 represents approximately his
interest in the stock account...".*[1691]

Why is this important? Because Frank pointed to this to show that
Hauptmann personally invested *"approximately $17,500"* in both
furs and the stock market during this time and that amount was
"also reflected on page 72 where he specifically shows that amount." This
fact, Frank asserted, *"disproves"* Hauptmann's position that *"all of the
cash deposited in the brokerage accounts came from Fisch."*[1692] So while
that is terribly damaging to Hauptmann, Frank's next observation
created the exact opposite situation. On page 73 there is a notation
"Isador account." The figure of:

> *"17,000 with a 5 superimposed on the 7, thus
> making the amount 15,000 – (17000 less the $2000
> withdrawal on November 14, 1933). This notation
> appears to indicate that somewhere or other Fisch had
> a $15,000 credit coming to him. Without any definite
> information available it is impossible to say what the
> $15000 figure represented; however, the record on
> page 76 of Hauptmann's account book indicated that
> Fisch on November 3, 1933 had a $12,050 interest
> in the joint fur trading account with Hauptmann. It
> might be that the $15,000 entry on page 73 is intended
> to represent Fisch's interest in the furs, or it might
> represent the $14,600 in ransom money found by the
> police in Hauptmann's garage and which he claims*

[1691] Frank, William E. Special Agent, United States Treasury Department.
Internal Revenue Service Special Report. <u>Financial Activities of Bruno
Richard Hauptmann and his wife, Anna Hauptmann, nee Schoeffler,
1279 East 222nd Street, Bronx, New York City</u>. January 8, 1935. Page 19.
New Jersey State Police Museum and Learning Center Archives.
[1692] Ibid.

Fisch left with him for safekeeping when he sailed for Germany."[1693]

Although Frank was speculating here, he went on to write that this $15,000 notated on page 73 "*does not appear in an identifiable form in any of Hauptmann's accounts...*".[1694]

Alexander Singer

Alexander Singer was interviewed by Special Agent Turrou at the Steiner, Rouse & Co. brokerage house concerning Hauptmann, and it was developed that he and Hauptmann had become quite "friendly," with Hauptmann on many occasions consulting or seeking his advice concerning stocks.[1695] On one occasion Singer asked Hauptmann for a loan to purchase a specific stock because he didn't have sufficient funds at the time but Hauptmann's response was:

> "...*after some consideration, told him he could not advance him any money without the consent of his partner, who at that time, which was about six months ago, was in Germany; that Hauptmann further explained that he had an investment of over $10,000 together with his partner in the fur business and also in the purchase of stock, and that any outlay of money for any purpose must be with the consent of both and regretted that he could not comply with Mr. Singer's request.*"[1696]

[1693] Ibid. Page 20.

[1694] Ibid.

[1695] Turrou, L. G. Special Agent, Division of Investigation (FBI). Memorandum For The File. Re: Bruno Richard Hauptmann with alias, Unknown Subjects, Kidnaping and Murder of Charles A. Lindbergh Jr. October 3, 1934. New Jersey State Police Museum and Learning Center Archives.

[1696] Ibid.

White Sulphur Springs

Something I discovered among Criminologist Robert Hicks's material was this interesting handwritten observation tucked among the pages of his copies of the trial transcripts:

> *"Bills found in Albany, Troy and Utica indicated that the testimony noted later but which was excluded and not heard to the effect that Fisch had large amounts of gold notes and that one of the Lindberg* [sic] *notes was about to be shown as coming from Fisch would, had it not been excluded, have proved another original source for Lindberg* [sic] *ransom bills."*[1697]

Hicks had attended the trial practically the entire time.[1698] Was this an observation made while in the courtroom? Was it something he learned from the State side of the case due to his previous working relationship with Prosecutor Hauck? Or did he come by this information during his stint working for the Hoffman investigation? Regardless, he certainly was in a position to know this, and it's quite a unique piece of information. In checking the trial transcripts it can be seen these bills were brought up during Special Agent Seery's cross examination:

> [**Q**]: *Well, now, is it a fact or is it not a fact that ransom bills did show up in Albany, Utica, Troy, and near Chicago?*

[1697] Hicks, Robert Waverly. Handwritten Trial Notes. Undated. New Jersey State Police Museum and Learning Center Archives. (Note: These notes written on his copies of the trial transcripts.)

[1698] Hicks, Robt. W., Criminologist. <u>Letter from Lt. Robert Hicks to Honorable Harold G. Hoffman.</u> January 2, 1936. New Jersey State Police Museum and Learning Center Archives.

[A]: *That is correct.*[1699]

Seery testified that these ransom bills were $5 denominations with the Albany bill turning up on April 28, 1934, the Utica bill turning up on May 25, 1934, and the Troy bill turning up on May 10, 1934.[1700] Reilly was able to point out that these bills originated a considerable distance from New York City but nothing more. There was also another $5 ransom note recovered which originated in Elmira, New York, and that bill was traced back to a March 26th deposit at a local bank in this city.[1701]

But what would be the nexus between Fisch and these four very specific bills? We know for a fact that Fisch spent the "Jewish Holidays" in September 1933 in White Sulphur Springs, New York.[1702] We also know that he spent "*3 weeks*" there spending "*$12 per week*" in board.[1703] And so, at the very least, Fisch spent $36 dollars on this occasion. We also know that more often than not $5 bills were "floaters" which meant because of the amount, they could stay in circulation much longer than the bigger bills. Yet, why this cluster of bills surfacing within a month of each other if that was the case? One possibility would be that Fisch spent these four $5s at the same place, and that whoever he passed them to did not spend them right away but then did so at or nearly at the same time. Something

[1699] Seery, William F. Testimony. The State of New Jersey vs. Bruno Richard Hauptmann, <u>Hunterdon County Court of Oyer and Terminer</u>, page 1543, 1935. New Jersey State Law Library.

[1700] Ibid. Page 1544.

[1701] Horn, William Cpl. New Jersey State Police. New Jersey State Police Report. <u>Report of investigation, concerning a recovered $5.00 bill, which is part of the Lindbergh Ransom Money</u>. April 3, 1934. New Jersey State Police Museum and Learning Center Archives.

[1702] Haussling, E. A., Sgt. Det., New Jersey State Police. New Jersey State Police Report. <u>Continued investigation re: Isidor Fisch</u>. November 10, 1934. New Jersey State Police Museum and Learning Center Archives.

[1703] Ibid.

else to consider was a similar situation which occurred in August of 1934 when three more $5 ransom bills would turn up north of NYC... The first traced to Albany on the 6th, the next traced to Danbury, Connecticut on the 7th, and the last traced to Old Forge, New York on the 17th.[1704]

There had been 2000 $5s packed among the ransom money turned over at Saint Raymond's Cemetery, and the FBI had concluded in August of 1934 that *all* were in circulation.[1705] Only 115 had been recovered by October 18, 1934.[1706] Does this fact bolster the significance of these finds or make them irrelevant? A final discovery originating in Utica came on September 29, 1934. However, this was a $20 gold certificate. While $5s were accepted as "floaters," the gold notes, once passed, did not remain in circulation but were sent to the Federal Reserve. The best explanation for this that I've found came from LKC researcher Rab Purdy:

> *"I don't think anyone really feared arrest for having gold notes. But I do think it is human nature not to want to get "stuck" with something. I think that there*

[1704] Recapitulation Of Ransom Money. Unsigned. Undated (May 1935). Page 13. New Jersey State Police Museum and Learning Center Archives. (Note: Other sources trace the Old Forge $5 to August 13th but no attempt was made to search for its source beyond the bank.)

[1705] Seery, W. F. USBOI (FBI). USBOI Report. Unknown Subjects. Kidnaping and Murder of Charles A. Lindbergh Jr. August 28, 1934. National Archives at College Park Maryland. (Note: The FBI had changed its name from USBOI to DOI by this time but the heading on this particular report still says "United States Bureau of Investigation")

[1706] Seery, W. F. USBOI (FBI). USBOI Report. Bruno Richard Hauptmann, with alias. Kidnaping and Murder of Charles A. Lindbergh Jr. October 18, 1934. National Archives at College Park Maryland. (Note: The FBI had changed its name from USBOI to DOI by this time but the heading on this particular report still says "United States Bureau of Investigation")

were probably two broad sections: people who wanted gold notes and hoarded them and people who wanted nothing to do with them in case they ended up losing out."[1707]

Police attempted to trace the passer of this $20 ransom bill, finding it could only have originated from one of four sources. Three deposits made on the date of September 12th: an $80 deposit from a man in Yorkville (suburb of Utica), a $20 deposit from a Utica Insurance Company, and a $20 deposit from Schulte Cigar Store in Utica. The final possible source was a $40 deposit made by Planters Tea Company also of Utica made on September 20th.[1708] Since it seems unreasonable that this bill "floated" it's way to Utica from NYC due to its circulation, this means either Hauptmann drove up there to pass it or someone else was spending ransom money in that area. Oddly, I've found no follow up to this investigation so unless something new turns up we'll never know from which deposit this bill originated.

George Steinweg

The question of whether Fisch had possessed ransom money has it's "historical" origins in Sidney B. Whipple's book The Lindbergh Crime. In it he recorded that George Steinweg recalled:

[1707] Purdy, Robert. Internet Work. *Who Helped Hauptmann (Turchiarelli)*. March 5, 2006. lindberghkidnap.proboards.com.

[1708] Horn, William F., Cpl. New Jersey State Police. New Jersey State Police Report. Report of investigation concerning a recovered $20.00 gold certificate (U. S. Currency), which is part of the Lindbergh Ransom money. October 1, 1934. New Jersey State Police Museum and Learning Center Archives.

* That "*on or about November 14, 1933*" while Fisch was there to pay for his passage to Germany, he was "*surprised*" to see all the money Fisch had on him.

* That Fisch payed for his passage to Germany with "*gold certificates.*"

* That "*bank officials*" had discovered checking the certificates over that it was "*part of the Lindbergh ransom money.*"[1709]

Obviously, for anyone interested in this case, these points need to be sorted out and examined, considering all available information. The story begins on August 18, 1934, when Isador Fisch, along with Henry Uhlig, went to the Steinweg Steamship Agency and reserved two round trip tickets to Germany by handing over a $100 cash deposit.[1710] On November 14, 1933, Fisch returned alone to buy Reich Mark checks and pay for the remainder of this trip which totaled over $1000.[1711]

During the Flemington trial, the idea that Fisch spent so much money there presented somewhat of a problem for the Prosecution. However, during Hauptmann's testimony, we can see Wilentz was able to smoothly navigate this issue by getting Hauptmann to testify to the following:

[1709] Whipple, Sidney B. March 1935. *The Lindbergh Crime*. Blue Ribbon Books. Page 190.

[1710] Haussling, E. A., Sgt. Det., New Jersey State Police. New Jersey State Police Report. Continued investigation re: Isidor Fisch. November 10, 1934. New Jersey State Police Museum and Learning Center Archives. (Note: Adriatic Exchange Company).

[1711] Steinweg, George. Testimony. The State of New Jersey vs. Bruno Richard Hauptmann, Hunterdon County Court of Oyer and Terminer, page 3625, 1935. New Jersey State Law Library.

Q: *Now, that went on from that time on, then, to the 13th of November, and Isidor Fisch came to you and said, "I want to go to Germany." Isn't that right?*
A: *Yes.*

Q: *"And I need some money—"*
A: *Yes.*

Q: *And you said, "No, let's wait with the skins. Maybe the market will be better."*
A: *Yes.*

Q: *"Shall we sell some skins?"*
A: *Yes.*

Q: *And you said, "No, let's wait with the skins. Maybe the market will be better."*
A: *That is what I said.*

Q: *"I will give you $2,000 in cash?"*
A: *I took $2,000 I guess.*

Q: *From your account?*
A: *Yes.*

Q: *Your money?*
A: *Yes.*

Q: *Not Fisch's money?*
A: *Well, really, he was interested with $2,500 still in them $12,000, I didn't mention, but I wrote him in January or February about them thousand shares, I sold them for him, I got to sell them.*

Q: *Did you give him $2,000 of your money from your account, your money in November, 1933?*
A: *Yes, yes.*

Q: *Not his money?*
A: *No.*

Q: *No. Well, why do you then say, well, two thousand you had of his and all that sort?*
A: *You still got an interest from him, 2,500.*

Q: *But the 2,000 was yours?*
A: *Yes.*

Q: *So, what the bank account shows, are your moneys going to Fisch, isn't that right?*
A: *Them $2,000, yes.*[1712]

And so, once Wilentz was given the opportunity to re-direct George Steinweg on the stand in Flemington, he swooped in by using Hauptmann's testimony to show the money Fisch was spending on November 14th actually came from Hauptmann:

Q: *And on November the 14th, 1933, don't you know that Hauptmann gave him $2,000 for that very purpose?*
A: *I don't know.*

Q: *The very same day?*

[1712] Hauptmann, Bruno Richard. Testimony. The State of New Jersey vs. Bruno Richard Hauptmann, <u>Hunterdon County Court of Oyer and Terminer</u>, pages 2848-9, 1935. New Jersey State Law Library.

A: *Well, I don't know. How should I know that?*[1713]

This was a crushing blow to the Defense in more ways than one. First it implied the money originated from Hauptmann, and next, if the money Fisch used really was Lindbergh Ransom, then the State just proved that it actually came from Hauptmann and not Fisch! Unfortunately, the problem was that it misrepresented the facts; it was not true.

Where ever a source exists that has Hauptmann saying he gave $2,000 to Fisch for his trip to Germany, it is taken to mean he believed he was paying for the costs of the actual trip itself. In fact, Hauptmann even wrote to Isador's brother Pinkus explaining that he lent him the money for *"traveling expenses to Germany."*[1714] But was this a problem in translation? Perhaps a lie designed to recoup the 2K by saying it wasn't business related? Or was it true? From the very beginning, in addition to stocks, Hauptmann informed police his partnership was about furs:

> Q: *Did you have any property belonging to him at that time?*
>
> A: *No. I should have property but I guess he was a liar to me. I gave him money for furs before and he said "when you come back you get more" speculating on furs.*

[1713] Steinweg, George. Testimony. The State of New Jersey vs. Bruno Richard Hauptmann, <u>Hunterdon County Court of Oyer and Terminer</u>, page 3629, 1935. New Jersey State Law Library.

[1714] Hauptmann, Richard. <u>Letter from Richard Hauptmann to Pinkus Fisch</u>. (Translated). May 4, 1934. New Jersey State Police Museum and Learning Center Archives.

Q: *You were speculating on furs with Fish [sic] at that time before Christmas?*

A: *Yes.*[1715]

Fisch's trip, Hauptmann explained, was motivated by the fact he "*wanted to return to his brother in Germany at Christmas time, because he wanted to make an arrangement for importing and exporting furs.*"[1716] Furthermore, Hauptmann made this claim about the trip:

> "*When Fisch left for Germany he said to me if we are willing to sell some of the furs because he needed $2,000.00. He said to me he was probably going to buy some furs in Germany and bring them over here, but I said to him it is no use to sell furs when we just bought them, let it lay in the storage house, so he was making me to take out $2000.00 from my stock account. That was what I did. That was our last transaction.*"[1717]

As to the time Fisch made this transaction on November 14th, author Anthony Scaduto quoted a report taken by a private investigator in his book *Scapegoat* that was given to him by Grace McGrady (who asked that the PI's name be kept out of it) which said "*on November 14 at 11 A. M., Fisch again came to the agency...*".[1718] This report is

[1715] Hauptmann, Bruno Richard. Interrogation. Conducted by Inspector John A. Lyons "and others." September 19(?), 1934 at 9:13 P. M. New Jersey State Police Museum and Learning Center Archives

[1716] Hauptmann, Richard. Autobiography: Unedited & Uncorrected (Translated). <u>The Story of My Life</u>. Page 185. May 4, 1935. New Jersey State Police Museum and Learning Center Archives.

[1717] Hauptmann, Bruno Richard. Statement. December 6, 1934. New Jersey State Police Museum and Learning Center Archives.

[1718] Scaduto, Anthony. 1976. *Scapegoat: The Lonesome Death of Bruno Richard Hauptmann*. G. P. Putnam's Son, page 458.

a legitimate source since it was taken by private investigator Henry Kress. Kress worked for the former NYPD detective William Martin whose agency had been among those hired originally by James Fawcett. Kress and Grace's husband, Associated Press Reporter Pat McGrady, had been especially close and he was the source for several of McGrady's articles concerning this crime. However, this isn't the only source for this information. Chief of Burlington County Detectives Ellis Parker also personally interviewed Steinweg who told him:

> "Fisch was here in the morning, first, he came and made a deposit, I don't remember anything but on the 14th of November, in the morning Fisch was here and brought about $1,000."[1719]

Detective William S. Mustoe, of the Monmouth County Prosecutor's Office, along with Private Investigator Leo Meade, also interviewed Steinweg who again claimed that Fisch had made his final payments to the Steamship Agency on "the morning of November 14, 1933." [1720]

This is vital information. We know for a fact that Hauptmann withdrew $2057 from his stock account in the form of a check on

[1719] Steinweg, George. Statement. By Ellis H. Parker. Stenographer – Anna E. Bading. October 25, 1935. New Jersey State Police Museum and Learning Center Archives.

[1720] Mustoe, William S. Detective, Monmouth County Prosecutor's Office, and Leo Meade, Private Investigator, Meade Detective Bureau. Report. George Steinweg, Steamship Agency, 226 East 86th St., New York, N.Y. February 19, 1936. New Jersey State Police Museum and Learning Center Archives.

579

November 14, 1933.[1721] But why is the timing of Fisch's return to that office so important? Because according to Hauptmann:

> *"I gladly agreed and so I drew a check for $2000. from my stock account. He did not want to have anything to do with the check, so I changed it myself at the Yorkville National Bank and gave it to him in cash. I exchanged the check five or ten minutes before 3 o'clock. I believe that the day was the 14th of November 1933. I considered it a peculiarity of his that he wanted the money in cash, because he had each time given me all money to purchase stock in cash. It was my opinion therefore, that he had no confidence in checks."[1722]*

The Mustoe and Meade report included this information which backed up this claim:

> *"After giving testimony at Flemington, Mr. Steinweg checked up and learned that the $2,000 which Hauptmann turned over to Fisch was given to Fisch on the afternoon of November 14, 1933, and, therefore, the money thus derived from the cashing of this check*

[1721] Genau, J. A. Special Agent, United States Bureau of Investigation (FBI). USBOI Report. <u>Kidnaping And Murder Of Charles A. Lindbergh, Jr.</u> Page 13. October 8, 1934. New Jersey State Police Museum and Learning Center Archives.

[1722] Hauptmann, Richard. Autobiography: Unedited & Uncorrected (Translated). <u>The Story of My Life</u>. Page 185-6. May 4, 1935. New Jersey State Police Museum and Learning Center Archives.

could not have been the same money that he, Fisch,
paid into the steamship agency...".[1723]

Kress's report, quoted by Scaduto, also backed this claim up by
stating the following:

> *"The police claim that on November 14, 1933,*
> *Hauptmann gave Fisch $2,000 which Fisch then used*
> *to buy tickets and marks. But Fisch paid for all this at*
> *11 A. M. but Hauptmann did not take out the money*
> *which he gave to Fisch until a few minutes before 3*
> *P. M. that day. Therefore Fisch must have paid with*
> *his own money and not with that he received from*
> *Hauptmann...".*[1724]

In a letter which advised Governor Hoffman of the developments
surrounding this situation, Ellis Parker wrote the following:

> *"Mr. Steinweg states that this transaction with Fisch*
> *occurred around the noon hour and the testimony shows*
> *that Hauptmann went to the Steiner and Rausch* [sic]
> *stock market and got $2,000. just before they closed,*
> *around 3 o'clock and this money was given to Fisch by*
> *Hauptmann. So the money used by Fisch to purchase*

[1723] Mustoe, William S. Detective, Monmouth County Prosecutor's Office,
and Leo Meade, Private Investigator, Meade Detective Bureau. Report.
George Steinweg, Steamship Agency, 226 East 86th St., New York, N.Y.
February 19, 1936. New Jersey State Police Museum and Learning
Center Archives.

[1724] Scaduto, Anthony. 1976. *Scapegoat: The Lonesome Death of Bruno Richard
Hauptmann.* G. P. Putnam's Son, page 458.

*the tickets and travelers checks, couldn't have been the
money that Hauptmann gave him.*"[1725]

Moreover, once Fisch had paid for the marks and the balance of his
tickets which totaled around $1,000, Steinweg testified that he had
a lot more in his wallet besides that amount:

Q: *Now, did he exhibit to you any money in addition
to the thousand dollars that he spent with you?*

A: *He had quite some money in his wallet that he
took out.*

Q: *Did you see his wallet?*

A: *Yes.*

Q: *Describe to the jury the condition of the wallet in
so far as money was concerned, after he was finished
paying you over a thousand dollars.*

A: *He had quite considerable more money in his
wallet, because I asked him to buy more checks; but
Mr. Fisch said that his friends would send more money
afterwards if he needed it.*[1726]

During his interview with Mustoe and Meade Steinweg made a
similar comment, saying that he explained to Fisch that if he bought

[1725] Parker, Ellis H. Chief of Detectives, Burlington County Prosecutor's
Office. Letter from Ellis H. Parker to His Excellency, Harold G.
Hoffman. December 5, 1935. New Jersey State Police Museum and
Learning Center Archives.

[1726] Steinweg, George. Testimony. The State of New Jersey vs. Bruno Richard
Hauptmann, Hunterdon County Court of Oyer and Terminer, page
3625-6, 1935. New Jersey State Law Library.

more and didn't use them, they could be redeemed at the purchase price, but that Fisch replied he "*had more money here, and if he needed more reichmarks friends of his in the United States would purchase them here and send them to him.*"[1727]

Gold Certificates

While on the stand, Reilly never asked Steinweg whether or not Fisch had given him Gold Certificates in payment for his trip. However, just as in the Kress report, Steinweg claimed Fisch paid with many of the bills being the "*gold seal type.*"[1728] The counter clerk, Otto Kuhn, who was the actual salesman for the Reich Marks, had originally told the police he could not recall "*the kind of money*" Fisch gave him.[1729] Despite this, Steinweg was certain of the type used in payment:

> "*He distinctly recalls seeing these bills and, because of his Wife's birthday was only a few days off, he exchanged ten of the gold seal certificates out of the cash drawer for $100.00 of his own money and put the*

[1727] Mustoe, William S. Detective, Monmouth County Prosecutor's Office, and Leo Meade, Private Investigator, Meade Detective Bureau. Report. George Steinweg, Steamship Agency, 226 East 86th St., New York, N.Y. February 19, 1936. New Jersey State Police Museum and Learning Center Archives.

[1728] Ibid.

[1729] Leon, Samuel J. Cpl. NJSP. New Jersey State Police Report. The picking up of Otto Kun, the selling clerk at the Adriatic Exchange, 226 East 86th Street, New York City, at which place Isidor Fisch exchanged American money for German Reich marks, before sailing for Germany. September 28, 1934. New Jersey State Police Museum and Learning Center Archives.

gold seal certificates in his pocket, intending to present them to his wife on her birthday."[1730]

Later though, Steinweg felt his wife might run into a problem if taking them to a bank and decided it was best to abandon this idea; he put the gold certificates back into his business and "*in due course they were deposited in his bank.*"[1731] However, Steinweg did tell Ellis Parker that:

> "*...recently I spoke to the man in the bank and said, "Did you have trouble too? Did you ever get any of the Lindbergh money?" He said "Yes, they were here, but we couldn't check that up, nothing that you could trace that.*"[1732]

Importantly though, Steinweg would later tell the Mustoe and Meade that he "*never heard anything further*" from either the bank or the authorities about this money to "*definitely know that they were ransom notes.*"[1733]

[1730] Mustoe, William S. Detective, Monmouth County Prosecutor's Office, and Leo Meade, Private Investigator, Meade Detective Bureau. Report. George Steinweg, Steamship Agency, 226 East 86th St., New York, N.Y. February 19, 1936. New Jersey State Police Museum and Learning Center Archives.

[1731] Ibid.

[1732] Steinweg, George. Statement. By Ellis H. Parker. Stenographer – Anna E. Bading. October 25, 1935. New Jersey State Police Museum and Learning Center Archives.

[1733] Mustoe, William S. Detective, Monmouth County Prosecutor's Office, and Leo Meade, Private Investigator, Meade Detective Bureau. Report. George Steinweg, Steamship Agency, 226 East 86th St., New York, N.Y. February 19, 1936. New Jersey State Police Museum and Learning Center Archives.

Louis Gartner

Louis Gartner, a friend and associate of Steinweg, used to stop by his agency often. Since Gartner was planning a trip to Europe, he stopped by and said: *"If you have any gold, I will take it and take it over with me and I get more for it."*[1734] On November 14th he happened to stop by and was in luck because Steinweg had taken in so many gold notes before noon that day.[1735] Gartner then bought some of the gold certificates. He...

> *"...exchanged $100.00 for $100.00 worth of them. Later, on this same day, Gardner [sic] decided he wanted some more of the gold certificates and, having no further available cash in his pocket, issued his check in the amount of $150.00 payable to the Adriatic Exchange, and took another $150.00 worth of the gold certificates."*[1736]

To further demonstrate this point, Steinweg had handed over to Parker the canceled check from Manufacturers Trust Company Bank for $150.00 written to him from Louis Gartner dated November 14, 1933.[1737] Gartner would eventually turn in $100 of these gold certificates *"in the last part of March, 1934"* at the *"Federal Reserve*

[1734] Steinweg, George. Statement. By Ellis H. Parker. Stenographer – Anna E. Bading. October 25, 1935. New Jersey State Police Museum and Learning Center Archives.

[1735] Ibid.

[1736] Mustoe, William S. Detective, Monmouth County Prosecutor's Office, and Leo Meade, Private Investigator, Meade Detective Bureau. Report. George Steinweg, Steamship Agency, 226 East 86th St., New York, N.Y. February 19, 1936. New Jersey State Police Museum and Learning Center Archives.

[1737] Copy in Author's possession.

Bank on Nassau Street" in exchange.[1738] During the summer of 1934, Gartner traveled to Hungary taking some of the gold certificates he had left with him. *"Thinking that he might benefit by the increased value of gold"* he deposited $100 of this money in *"Winer Bank – Verein"* in Budapest.[1739] Gartner told Parker that: *"I didn't dream it was this* [Lindbergh] *money, at the time."*[1740]

After Hauptmann's arrest, sometime in *"October or November,"* 1934, *"income tax"* men showed up to look over Gartner's books when suddenly one of the men said:

> *"You have a bank account under the name of Faulkner."*
> *"I* [Gartner] *said, "You are crazy," "Under the name of Faulkner?" He said, "Yes, you write down the name of Faulkner"* and I wrote down the name of Faulkner *and a few other names. Faulkner I remember."*[1741]

Gartner recalled to Parker that all of the gold bills he passed in Budapest were *"$10"*s and that all of them *"I had secured from Mr. Steinweg."*[1742] None of this was a joke. In fact, on October 1st, Treasury Agent Frank met with both Frank Wilson and Elmer Irey to share his files on the Steinweg Steamship Agency (Adriatic

---

[1738] Gartner, Louis. Statement. By Ellis H. Parker. Stenographer – Anna E. Bading. November 29, 1935. New Jersey State Police Museum and Learning Center Archives.

[1739] Mustoe, William S. Detective, Monmouth County Prosecutor's Office, and Leo Meade, Private Investigator, Meade Detective Bureau. Report. George Steinweg, Steamship Agency, 226 East 86th St., New York, N.Y. February 19, 1936. New Jersey State Police Museum and Learning Center Archives.

[1740] Gartner, Louis. Statement. By Ellis H. Parker. Stenographer – Anna E. Bading. November 29, 1935. New Jersey State Police Museum and Learning Center Archives.

[1741] Ibid.

[1742] Ibid.

Exchange) and Louis Gartner with them. Wilson advised Frank to make an intrusive exam and to specifically search for handwriting that looked like the J. J. Faulkner signature.[1743] Then, on October 5th, Wilson held a conference in Trenton with Colonel Schwarzkopf and Lt. Keaten where they specifically *"discussed the possibility of Louis Gartner having handled some of the Lindbergh ransom money."*[1744] Wilson informed Lt. Keaten that he had secured samples of Gartner's handwriting that were given to Dr. Souder for comparison. Dr. Souder had written back that he *"found some similarity in the writings"* and requested additional samples for comparison.[1745]

> *"When the desired samples are secured, they will be submitted to Dr. Sauder,* [sic] *and you* [Keaten] *will be promptly informed if it appears that the writing of any person associated with Gartner corresponds with the Faulkner slip."*[1746]

Wilson had secured copies of Gartner's tax returns for the previous three years. These are the observations found in his notes:

> *"The tax returns of Louis Gartner for 1931—1932 and 1933 bear his signature and it is not like the Faulkner or other writings in which we are interested. The body of the return was filled in by a bookkeeper or some other person than Gartner and the figures are a little bit like the figures in the Faulkner $2980 deposit*

[1743] Wilson, Frank John. Handwritten Notes. <u>1934</u>. Entry for "Oct. 1." American Heritage Center. University of Wyoming.

[1744] Wilson, Frank J. Special Agent in Charge, Internal Revenue Service, Intelligence Unit. <u>Letter from Frank J. Wilson to Lieutenant A. T. Keaton.</u> October 15, 1934. New Jersey State Police Museum and Learning Center Archives.

[1745] Ibid.

[1746] Ibid.

slip. Attention is invited to the fact that these figures are similar as follows: on 1931 return the figure 0 is small as on the slip, five made as by an accountant; and in a few instances there is an upward stroke at end of a word, also the letter n is made with sharp point viz n. The same similarities are apparent on the returns for 1932 and 1933."[1747]

However, one of the points made by Ludovic Kennedy in his book about this subject was that there was *"no notification of receipt of this money at the federal bank"* and therefore, the claim it was Lindbergh Ransom should be *"treated with caution."*[1748] Two questions must be asked concerning this observation..., the first being whether or not it's true, and the next being, if this was true, why Wilson, Frank, McQuillan, and Irey believed it possible Gartner had handled ransom money. The Treasury Department was well aware of when and where the ransom bills had turned up during this time. So if they did not turn up in connection with Gartner at the bank, why continue to use their time and resources to investigate him?

Ignoring the money spent later in Europe, Gartner said he turned in $100 of these gold certificates in 1934 sometime in "March" at the Federal Reserve Bank on Nassau Street. His reason for remembering this date was that it *"was the last day that the gold certificates were called in."*[1749] However, since the Presidential Proclamation was made

[1747] Wilson, Frank. Handwritten Notes. Untitled. Undated. New Jersey State Police Museum and Learning Center Archives.

[1748] Kennedy, Ludovic. 1985. *The Airman And The Carpenter*. Paperback. Viking Penguin Inc. Page 154.

[1749] Gartner, Louis. Statement. By Ellis H. Parker. Stenographer – Anna E. Bading. November 29, 1935. New Jersey State Police Museum and Learning Center Archives.

on January 17th, it is probable he made this deposit sooner.[1750] Despite that possibility, in searching through the documentation that I have (and I have a lot) what I find supports Kennedy's reasoning behind his "disclaimer." To clarify, while there is reference to Ransom Money being found there during this time, it was traced as coming to the Federal Reserve from other banks. So if Gartner made the deposit to the Federal Reserve Bank directly during anytime near the proclamation – it was either missed, or he cannot be the source for that money.

John Wilkens

Next, in attempting to trace Steinweg's gold certificates which he had placed back into his business and said "*in due course they were deposited in his bank,*" I find a ransom money deposit showing Steinweg as a potential source. Steinweg specifically told Ellis Parker to check up on his deposits "*in the Yorkville National Bank from the 14th to 20th, and the Corn Exchange National Bank.*"[1751] On January 5, 1934, a $10 Gold Certificate found to be a Lindbergh Ransom Note was discovered at the Federal Reserve.[1752] Police investigation revealed this bill was deposited in a $500 bundle which came from

[1750] Horn, William F. Cpl. New Jersey State Police. New Jersey State Police Report. Report of investigation concerning a $10.00 Gold Certificate which is part of the recovered Lindbergh Ransom Money. January 22, 1934. New Jersey State Police Museum and Learning Center Archives.

[1751] Steinweg, George. Statement. By Ellis H. Parker. Stenographer – Anna E. Bading. October 25, 1935. New Jersey State Police Museum and Learning Center Archives.

[1752] Recapitulation of Ransom Money. Unsigned. Undated (May 1935). New Jersey State Police Museum and Learning Center Archives.

the Corn Exchange Bank on December 27, 1933.[1753] Upon visiting the Corn Exchange Bank, it was determined that Assistant Teller William Heinke strapped the bundle in question. Heinke believed this bill must have been *"received by any of the five tellers, on December 26th or December 27th, 1933, from what individual depositor, he nor* [sic] *any of the other tellers could tell…"*[1754] However, suspicion was directed toward someone named John H. Wilkens due to the fact he had *"deposited a considerable number of gold certificates in the past."*[1755] Lt. Finn stated that while *"no definite information could be learned"* he pursued this lead and a *"complete list of each cash deposit was obtained so that a check in an effort to learn the identity of the source of this bill"* could be made.[1756] However, the only list of deposits pertaining to this investigation that I've found belonged to Wilkens. In fact, Police only investigated Wilkens in connection to this bill because almost immediately they found him a favorable subject when it was learned he had a deformity on his index finger of his left hand.[1757] The lead then became red hot as police learned the bank was also where Condon had an account and that Wilkens had previously worked as a bar tender at the Bronx Park River

---

[1753] Finn, James J., M.O.S., New York City Police Department. 18th Division Report. Cooperation accorded by Banks re: Lindbergh Ransom Money. January 23, 1934. New Jersey State Police Museum and Learning Center Archives.

[1754] Ibid.

[1755] Ibid.

[1756] Ibid.

[1757] Horn, William F., Cpl. New Jersey State Police. New Jersey State Police Report. Report of investigation concerning one John H. Wilkins, 591 East 233rd Street, New York City, re Lindbergh Case. January 10, 1934. New Jersey State Police Museum and Learning Center Archives. (Note: Based on John Condon's account of "Cemetery John's" hand).

Inn which was located near Woodlawn Cemetery.[1758] Furthermore, once his handwriting was shown to Captain Oliver, he believed it *"somewhat resembled that of the Ransom notes"* which prompted investigators to send off copies to Lt. Snook for comparison.[1759] It was at this point in the files that this investigation seemed to end. I have two sources subsequent to that time, the first of which is a reference in a post-Hauptmann arrest FBI "Recap" claiming *"no information was developed at this bank indicating the previous holders of this bill."*[1760] This is important due to the fact that Agent Manning accompanied both Leon and Horn during the numerous investigations which surrounded Wilkens and would naturally be the source for any information concerning this bill. The second source is the "Recapitulation of Ransom Money" document which simply notes the bill was received *"Prior to 12/27/1933."*[1761] And so it appears the Wilkens investigation died and was merely a distraction. Could this be the reason, then, that once Steinweg spoke to his bank, they agreed money had been discovered but it was nothing they could trace? Did police revisit this particular matter to discover its source as the Adriatic Exchange? Could this have been the reason Wilson, Frank, McQuillan, and Irey believed it possible Gartner had handled ransom money?

[1758] Leon, Samuel J. Cpl. New Jersey State Police. New Jersey State Police Report. <u>Investigation of one John H. Wilkens, formerly connected with the Bronx Park River Inn, 591 East 233rd Street, Bronx, N.Y., which is right next to the Woodlawn Cemetery, re Lindbergh Case</u>. January 16, 1934. New Jersey State Police Museum and Learning Center Archives.

[1759] Ibid.

[1760] FBI Ransom Money Recap. Untitled. Unsigned. Undated (September 1934). New Jersey State Police Museum and Learning Center Archives.

[1761] <u>Recapitulation of Ransom Money</u>. Unsigned. Undated (May 1935). New Jersey State Police Museum and Learning Center Archives.

Ellis Parker

During Ellis Parker's investigation into this matter in 1935, he was convinced Fisch had passed Lindbergh Ransom Money to Steinweg on November 14, 1933, and equally sure some of it was traced to Gartner as a result. In his letter to Governor Hoffman he wrote:

> "*Mr. Gartner went over to Germany and spent about $100. of this money in $10. Bills in Budapest. This proves that the money Fisch gave to Steinweg, was the Lindbergh money without a question of doubt, as one of the investigators were sent over there to check on that money and when they traced it back to Steinweg and discovered it was Fisch who passed it, the investigation stopped right there. Also, you will notice in Gartner's statement that a couple of Government men interviewed him and made him sign the name of "J.J. Faulkner".*[1762]

Not long after this letter was written Parker was talking to the press. He was quoted in several newspapers as saying that Fisch had paid for his trip to Germany with Lindbergh Ransom Money. He also told reporters that he "*received confirmation from detectives in Europe that Isadore Fisch, Bronx furrier, spent part of the Lindbergh ransom money in Germany.*"[1763] While there is no doubt Parker had a network of contacts all over the world with whom he communicated, I have no documentation concerning this specific information or the identities of these European Detectives from whom he secured it. However, Parker never strayed from this assertion. A couple of months later he

---

[1762] Parker, Ellis H. Burlington County Chief of Detectives. <u>Letter from Ellis H. Parker to His Excellency, Harold G. Hoffman</u>. December 5, 1935. New Jersey State Police Museum and Learning Center Archives.

[1763] "Fisch Used Lindy Cash in Europe." *Carroll Daily Herald*. December 12, 1935.

wrote that "*Fisch undoubtedly was one of the extortionists, as there was money traced to him long before Hauptmann ever spent any of his.*"[1764] Parker wrote further:

> "*Fisch spent over one thousand dollars of the Lindbergh money with the steamship company when he bought tickets for himself and Henry Uhlig to go to Germany. Had the steamship company had been notified Fisch would have been arrested before he got out of this country. This was neglect on someones part.*"[1765]

Edward Sohr

Like Alexander Singer, Edward Sohr was another person who speculated on the stock market at Steiner, Rouse & Company claiming he was there every day. Sohr also encountered Fisch there and had the opportunity to interact with him on some occasions. One of those times which stood out in his mind was an encounter in the bathroom. Sohr's account of this was as follows:

> "*He was very much excited and talked to himself. I can only remember half of what he said. He said "what a dumb fool I am, now I have money and can not do anything with it. I would prefer to threw [sic] the whole thing (package) in the toilet. Well. I am leaving (the country) anyway." He said some more, but I could not understand it clearly.*"[1766]

[1764] Parker, Ellis H. Chief of County Detectives. <u>Letter from Ellis Parker to Mrs. Grace K. Mall</u>. February 10, 1936. Andy Sahol Collection.

[1765] Ibid. (Note: "notified" meaning they did not have ransom money lists to check the bills against)

[1766] Sohr, Edward. Typed Statement. January 6, 1936. New Jersey State Police Museum and Learning Center Archives.

Upon leaving the bathroom, Sohr joined him on the trading floor. Curious, he asked Fisch if he also lost money in stocks, "*but he laughed and said 'no'*" then reacted to this question by getting "*excited and red in the face.*"[1767] Sohr noticed that Fisch had a "*small package*" under his arm and a "*longish pocketbook in his coat pocket.*" Later, he heard Fisch speaking to himself again saying "*anyhow, he does not know what I am talking about*" and Sohr immediately thought to himself "*this man must be half crazy.*"[1768] A month after Sohr provided this information to Authorities, Detective Mustoe and PI Meade interviewed him finding that "*he repeated practically verbatim*" what was contained in his statement.[1769] During and after this interview these men attempted to verify his statements and concluded that "*it appears he has been and is acting in good faith and is sincere in his statements he had made…*" and that he went "*to a lawyer assigned to the German Consulate*" with his story and even "*forwarded it to the prosecuting authorities at Flemington…*"[1770] However, the investigators did not feel too much emphasis could be given to his account because:

> "*The occurrence was at a time when all stocks were going down so that when, from his position in the lavatory, Sohr heard this other man raving about money he presumed that the other man must have also suffered losses in speculations.*"[1771]

[1767] Ibid.

[1768] Ibid.

[1769] Mustoe, William S. Detective, Monmouth County Prosecutor's Office, and Leo Meade, Private Investigator, Meade Detective Bureau. Report. Affidavit of Edward Sohr, 328 East 90th St., New York, N. Y. February 19, 1936. New Jersey State Police Museum and Learning Center Archives.

[1770] Ibid.

[1771] Ibid.

Additionally, concerning his account of noticing the wallet inside Fisch's coat pocket the investigators did not find this unusual due to the fact most "*foreigners*" typically carried these types of wallets.[1772]

Emil Schwarz

Emil Schwarz claimed in either March or April of 1933 that while walking down East 86th Street he was approached by a man introducing himself as "*John Fish.*" This man had been standing in front of Kreutzer Hall and asked if he'd be interested in buying "*hot money.*"[1773] "Fish" continued that he had about $50,000 worth which could be obtained at about half of the "*regular value.*" Schwarz claimed he asked this man why he approached a total stranger who he never saw before to make such a transaction but that "Fish" answered that he "*knew he had a stationery store and therefore could dispose of the money in an easy way.*"[1774] "Fish" had also said to Schwarz: "*Ich bin auch ein Deutscher.*"[1775] Schwarz asked if the money was "*counterfeit*" but was told:

> "*it was good money but stolen and the owner had been recently released from jail and therefore could not spend the money himself.*"[1776]

Schwarz claimed he was given a "*Bronx*" phone number to call that had an "*extension*" but that he did not pay any attention to this offer.[1777] It is interesting to note that Kreutzer Hall would

---

[1772] Ibid.

[1773] Schwarz, Emil. Affidavit. County of New York. May 4, 1936. New Jersey State Police Museum and Learning Center Archives.

[1774] Ibid.

[1775] Ibid. (Meaning: "*I am German too.*")

[1776] Ibid.

[1777] Ibid.

begin hosting Nazi sympathizer groups right around this time. In fact, after being denied access to Liederkranz Hall because of the objections of Jewish members, these groups moved their weekly meetings over to Kreutzer Hall on May 6, 1933.[1778] However, since their move happened sometime after this encounter, and since Schwarz was Jewish too, it seemed no effort was made to avoid this area at the time of this event. Besides, if Schwarz was inventing this story, it would make no sense to place the event in an area where it could not have happened. Another issue that struck me was Fisch introducing himself as *"John."* However, Schwarz wasn't the only person to ever say Fisch did this. Henry Kress had located a Mrs. and Mr. Curt Schwarz (no relation to Emil) who had taken the trip to Germany on the Manhattan the same time as Fisch, and they claimed that Fisch was known as *"John"* too and he was entered into her husband's address book as *"John Fisch."*[1779] Mrs. Schwarz said that during the trip Fisch appeared to be both *"sick"* and *"nervous"* and that once they landed *"he could scarcely get down the gangplank; he sort of wobbled down it and had to be helped."*[1780] Mrs. Schwarz claimed it wasn't *"until after the voyage"* that they learned *"from the passenger list that his name was Isidor."*[1781]

Philip Wohrman

Wohrman claimed that he was walking near Lincoln Hospital in the Bronx sometime between April 1932 and July 1932 when he was approached by a man whom he *"later from newspaper photographs*

[1778] "Local Nazis Ridicule German Jewish Soldiers, Resent May 10th Protest." *Jewish Telegraphic Agency.* May 9, 1933. www.jta.org

[1779] McGrady, Pat. "Woman Claims Fisch Was Known As "John"." *Ogdensburg Journal.* January 21, 1935. nyshistoricnewspapers.org

[1780] Ibid.

[1781] "Knew Fisch as 'John'." *New York Times.* January 22, 1935.

recognized as Isadore [sic] *Fisch.*"[1782] This man told Wohrman he was a stranger to New York and had just arrived from California and was looking for the address of a *"contractor who he thought was in the neighborhood."* Then *"a moment later another man joined them"* who Wohrman believed was *"well acquainted with the man I identify as Fisch."*[1783] This man was *"stocky"* about 5'4" with a *"light"* complexion and he suggested that Wohrman go with them to locate this contractor. Once Wohrman hesitated…

> *"Fisch pulled out of his pocket a ten dollar bill and asked me to change it and keep five for myself. I told him I did not have any money with me to change the bill. He then asked me if I knew a good bank where he could deposit the money he had with him. He opened his coat and in both inside pockets this man had bundles of money."*[1784]

Wohrman saw both "red letters" and "Gold Certificate" on the money, and Fisch told him his brother had died and he had received *"$80,000"* and wanted to know if Wohrman *"had a bank account."* Wohrman told him he did, but that he had no money in it, and it was at that point *"both the men then seemed to lose interest in me."* It was Wohrman's belief that these men were feeling him out to see if he *"could buy some of the money the man Fisch had in his pocket paying five dollars for every ten dollar note."*[1785]

[1782] Wohrman, Philip. Affidavit. County of New York. December 28, 1935. New Jersey State Police Museum and Learning Center Archives.
[1783] Ibid.
[1784] Ibid.
[1785] Ibid.

Oscar Bruckman

Bruckman had formerly worked for Fisch at his pie baking business on Downing Street as a driver/salesman for about a year.[1786] During his testimony in Flemington Bruckman detailed an encounter he had with Fisch in May of 1933 which caused Wilentz to object. In rebuttal to this objection, Reilly explained the Defense position to Judge Trenchard and the sparring continued:

[**Reilly**]: *I think it is competent. It is offered for the purpose of showing the sudden affluence of Fisch and his wealth and his display of certain gold-back bills that he had in May, 1933.*

[**Wilentz**]: *Now, if your Honor please, that I object to.*

[**Reilly**]: *Your objection forces me to tell the Court what I am offering this witness for.*

[**Wilentz**]: *I know but I object—that is just why I object to this man taking from the mouth of a dead man and bringing it into this court words which it is impossible to meet and which he knows it is impossible to meet, a conversation. It is not material. It is not competent, if your Honor please.*

[**Reilly**]: *I say it is material and it is competent to show— and we have charged here in the defense repeatedly— that this money was in the possession of Fisch and the box that he gave to Hauptmann, Hauptmann has testified he left with him, and it contained money*

[1786] Bruckman, Oscar John. Testimony. The State of New Jersey vs. Bruno Richard Hauptmann, <u>Hunterdon County Court of Oyer and Terminer</u>, page 3718. 1935. New Jersey State Law Library.

which afterwards people have demonstrated here contained notes that had been registered as part of the Lindbergh money.

Now it is unfortunate that Mr. Fisch died, but still it is part of our case, we contend, to show that Fisch was going around New York after the ransom money had been paid by Dr. Condon, exhibiting gold bills to different people and trying to exchange them with different people, and that he left part of them with Mr. Hauptmann.[1787]

The State's objection was ultimately sustained. After recess, there was a confusing exchange where the Judge interrupted the questioning to tell Bruckman to answer Reilly's question concerning what Fisch exhibited to him. Bruckman answered that "*he pulled a roll of bills out of his pocket and gave me a five-dollar bill.*" Bruckmann continued that "*I don't know whether they were gold notes or not. That I don't know. I didn't swear that I saw gold notes.*"[1788] This response once again drew an objection from Wilentz; it was sustained, and the Court was ordered to "*strike out the answer of the witness.*"[1789]

Prior to the trial, Bruckman met Reilly in the ante room of the court house in Flemington and he remembered Reilly as being "*very abrupt and didn't seem to have much time to talk to me.*"[1790] According to Bruckman the exchange went as follows:

"He said to me, "How much money did Fisch have?" and I said that I didn't know. I told him I saw he had

---

[1787] Ibid. Pages 3719-20.
[1788] Ibid. Pages 3723-4.
[1789] Ibid. Page 3725.
[1790] Bruckman, Oscar. Affidavit. County of New York. January 8, 1936. New Jersey State Police Museum and Learning Center Archives.

a bulge in his pocket from which he took the $5.00 which he paid me. He said to me, "Didn't you see a great big bundle of money, and I said "No," and he said "didn't you see a bundle like this" and he indicated with his hands about six inches, "and didn't you see a lot of gold backs in the roll?" and I told him I didn't see that, and he then said "Couldn't you say you saw a big bundle of money like this, and couldn't you say there was gold back bills in it?" "Can't you use your imagination?" "Can't you say that the bulge you saw in his pocket, you actually saw in his hands, and that there was some gold bills in it"? and I said, "No, I can't say that." He never let me tell the rest of my story. He seemed anxious to get away from me and I really never had a chance to tell him all I knew."[1791]

So what exactly was the story? When looking over the affidavit there are actually three separate events. The first occurred when Bruckman still worked for the Pie Baking Company...

"...Fisch called me aside and handed me a .32 snub nosed revolver, blue steel, and told me to meet him the next morning in front of the Franklin Savings Bank, 42nd Street and 8th Avenue. He said he had some people to meet and a lot of money to get. He wanted me to go with him because he had some considerable money to get. I have [sic] him back the gun and told him I would be glad to meet him, but I wouldn't carry the gun. I went the next morning at about eight-thirty to the Bank he had named and waited there for about two hours, but Fisch didn't show up. I went back to the Knickerbocker Pie Company and went back to work.

[1791] Ibid.

About five o'clock that night, I saw Fisch and he said to me that the deal had been completed and that he didn't need me. He gave me a couple of dollars and told me to forget it."[1792]

After the pie company went bankrupt, Bruckman began driving a taxi. Bruckman claimed that *"in the fall of 1933"* which was *"about a year after I stopped working"* with the pie company he encountered Fisch near his hack stand on Columbus Circle.[1793] (It should be noted that there is a problem with specific timing of this because the Knickerbocker Pie Company started to fail in May of 1931.[1794] In fact, on June 22, 1931, The City of New York posted a Marshal's Sale Notice on the front door of the establishment for the tables, chairs, racks, motors, ovens, and other pie baking equipment to be sold on June 25th.[1795] And so, if his encounter was in 1933, it was more like two years after he left the pie company. Or, it could be that he was completely a year ahead of himself. I'll leave that for the reader to decide). Fisch asked Bruckman several casual questions then asked for a ride to Radio City but suddenly asked him to pull over before they got there.[1796] Once pulled over he asked Bruckman to get into the backseat so they could talk. Here is some of the account:

[1792] Ibid.

[1793] Ibid.

[1794] O'Donnell, F. X. Special Agent, Division of Investigation (FBI). Memorandum For File. <u>Re: Bruno Richard Hauptmann, Charles Lindbergh, Jr. – Victim, Kidnaping – Extortion. (Isador Fisch – Accomplice)</u>. September 27, 1934. New Jersey State Police Museum and Learning Center Archives.

[1795] Joffe, Julius. Marshal, City of New York. "Marshal's Sale" Notice. Writ of Execution. <u>Pancrust Plate Company, Inc. vs. Knicerbacker Pie Baking Co., Inc</u>. June 22, 1931. New Jersey State Police Museum and Learning Center Archives.

[1796] Bruckman, Oscar. Affidavit. County of New York. January 8, 1936. New Jersey State Police Museum and Learning Center Archives.

"He then said to me "You don't have to drive a cab if you don't want to. I know a better proposition then that for you." He said "You know my racket, you know that I sell stocks. I sold some stocks and I got some hot money like I got out of the Pie Company, and I can't pass it in New York." He said "I'll buy a small car and you drive me out of town, and I think I can get rid of the money, and you can make more money then you can driving a hack." After we talked for a while he said "How much do I owe you?" and I told him thirty-five cents, and he reached in his pocket, and as though he was taking a bill from a roll, he pulled out a five dollar bill and said to me "Just keep the change." He told me he would see me the next night at my hack stand. He asked me what time I started working and how long I worked. I told him, and I also told him I would take the job of driving him, and it was arranged that he would see me the next night. I waited at my stand the next evening but he never appeared."[1797]

The final story was that Fisch's pie company associate, Charles Schleser, appeared only *"a week or ten days later"* with the exact same proposition except that he was attempting to sell *"machinery."* Once again Bruckman agreed to drive; however, just like Fisch before him, Schleser was a no-show.[1798]

Gustave Lukatis

After Hauptmann's arrest, Gus Lukatis walked into the William A. Martin Detective Agency on 7 E. 42nd Street. Lukatis had known

---

[1797] Ibid.
[1798] Ibid.

Martin for over 25 years.[1799] There he volunteered information to PI Henry Kress concerning an attempt to sell him "*hot-money*," believing it was important to the Defense.[1800] According to Lukatis, sometime in May 1932 while walking in the Yorkville section of the city, he was approached by a man named "Fritz" who he had worked with several years earlier on a job at Briarcliff Lodge, in Briarcliff Manor, New York.[1801] The men engaged in conversation which amounted to nothing more than small talk. About three days later Lukatis again ran into Fritz, and this time Fritz asked him if he or anyone else would be interested in buying "*hot-money*." When asked the price, Fritz told him "*75¢ on the dollar*" which Lukatis declared was too high. Fritz arranged a meeting anyway for two days later when he would bring Lukatis to the people who had the money.[1802] Lukatis kept the appointment and...

> "*...we then went to a house located at either 323 or 325 East 84th Street, New York City. On our walk to this house he told me that there was $50,000 of "hot money" to be sold. Upon our arrival I met two men, one of whom was introduced to me under the name of "Izzy".*"[1803]

Once it was established through Fritz that he knew Lukatis well enough to do business, Izzy again said the price was 75¢ on the

---

[1799] Albrecht, A. H. Det. Sgt. New Jersey State Police. New Jersey State Police Report. <u>Investigation of Gustive Lukatis with reference to report that this subject may be called by defense as an alibi witness</u>. January 5, 1935. New Jersey State Police Museum and Learning Center Archives.

[1800] McGrady, Pat. "Says Fisch Wanted To Sell Ransom." *Ogdensburg Journal.* January 16, 1936. nyshistoricnewspapers.org

[1801] Lukatis, Gustave. Affidavit. County of New York. June 14, 1935. New Jersey State Police Museum and Learning Center Archives.

[1802] Ibid.

[1803] Ibid.

dollar.[1804] Lukatis stated that this man "Izzy" looked very much like Isador Fisch from the pictures he had seen of him in the paper. He asked if the money was "counterfeit" and was told "no," then he inquired if anyone had been "killed" connected to this money and was given the same answer.[1805] Lukatis still claimed the price was too high then left with Fritz. While walking together after leaving this place toward *Third Avenue and 86th Street*...

> "*...he* [Fritz] *asked if I wanted any cigars. I replied that I did and he handed me a $5 bill, with which I purchased cigars for myself and cigarettes for him at the Schulte Cigar Store at the southwest corner of 86th Street and Third Avenue. When I returned from the store with the cigars and cigarettes he informed me that the $5 bill I had just changed was one of the bills which was a part of the "hot money.""*[1806]

"Fritz" was described as about 30 years of age with blond hair, standing about 5 feet 7-1/2 inches, weighing about 170 to 180 pounds with a fair complexion, no mustache, and clean shaven. "Izzy" was described as about 30 years of age, dark hair and complexion, standing about 5 feet 5-1/2 inches, weighing about 125 pounds with "*large protruding ears*" and "*decided Hebraic features.*" A third man who was present but did not engage Lukatis in conversation was described as 6 feet tall, about 30 years of age, "*powerfully built,*" weighing about 210 pounds with dark hair and complexion.[1807]

[1804] Ibid.

[1805] Albrecht, A. H. Det. Sgt. New Jersey State Police. New Jersey State Police Report. <u>Investigation of Gustive Lukatis with reference to report that this subject may be called by defense as an alibi witness</u>. January 5, 1935. New Jersey State Police Museum and Learning Center Archives.

[1806] Lukatis, Gustave. Affadivit. County of New York. June 14, 1935. New Jersey State Police Museum and Learning Center Archives.

[1807] Ibid.

Police learned about this potential witness for the Defense and were immediately detailed to investigate by Lt. Keaten on January 2, 1935.[1808] Police located and interviewed Lukatis who was fully cooperative and spoke freely. In fact, he revealed to them he went back to the 84th rooming house with two men (who he refused to identify) for the purpose of "*hi-jacking*" the "*hot money*" but once they arrived discovered the sellers were no longer there.[1809] In winding up the conversation with police, Lukatis shared that he had not been subpoenaed by the Defense and did not expect to be called. Det. Sgt. Albrecht concluded the following:

> "*The subject is a willing talker but not convincing. He no doubt gave his information to Investigator Martin for reason of friendship and believing that he would be paid for same.*"[1810]

However, despite their position, the police did not stop investigating Lukatis's claims. Both Albrecht and Sgt. Grafenecker of the New York City police visited both addresses mentioned by Lukatis a couple of days later. While at the 325 address, they spoke with Mrs. Julia Kern who informed them that Detective Henry Kress had been there to see her multiple times and had canvassed the entire block.

[1808] Haussling, E. A. Det. Sgt., New Jersey State Police. New Jersey State Police Report. <u>Information received from Willaim A. Martin, 7 E. 42nd St., N.Y. C., relative to Gus Lukatis, 778 Trinity Avenue, Bronx, N.Y.</u> January 2, 1935. New Jersey State Police Museum and Learning Center Archives

[1809] Albrecht, A. H. Det. Sgt. New Jersey State Police. New Jersey State Police Report. <u>Investigation of Gustive Lukatis with reference to report that this subject may be called by defense as an alibi witness.</u> January 5, 1935. New Jersey State Police Museum and Learning Center Archives.

[1810] Ibid.

"Kress had shown Mrs. Kern pictures of Isidor Fishe [sic] and she denied having had a roomer in 1932 who even resembled Fishe [sic]. Her records do not show the name of Fishe [sic] nor Hauptmann. Mrs. Kern stated that she has other roomers in the house whom were with her in 1932 and none of them had stated that there had been a tenant who resembled Fishe [sic] or Hauptmann."[1811]

The cops then asked Mrs. Kern about any "Jewish roomers" she may have had living there at the time and she said she had two Jewish roomers about August, 1932. She had evicted them because she *"learned they were gamblers and had taken money from the men they had invited into their room."*[1812] One of the men she knew as "William Block" who was about 27 years old, 5'7" tall, and the other she only knew as "Goldstein" who was about 40 years old, 5'6" tall, 150lbs., with black hair and medium complexion.[1813] On January 18, 1935, police showed Mrs. Kern their own picture of Isidor Fisch but she, as she had with Kress, did not identify it. Police were able to uncover an arrest record dated October 15, 1932, for "non-support" concerning "Max Goldstein" listed as 36 years of age who had been born in Romania. The Officers proceeded to the Parole Commission

[1811] Albrecht, A. H. Det. Sgt. New Jersey State Police. New Jersey State Police Report. <u>Addition information with reference to Gustive Lukatis, re: report dated January 5, 1935</u>. January 7, 1935. New Jersey State Police Museum and Learning Center Archives.

[1812] Ibid.

[1813] Meade, Joseph Det. New Jersey State Police. New Jersey State Police Report. <u>Further investigation of the information furnished by Gustave Lukatus of 788 Trinity Avenue, Bronx, and who is believed to be a defense witness. Previous investigation having been conducted by Det. Sgt. Albrecht and Det. Sgt. Wm. Grafenecker of the New York City Police</u>. January 18, 1935. New Jersey State Police Museum and Learning Center Archives.

in search of his address and mug-shot. These records were turned over and Detective Meade made this observation in his report:

> *"Attached to the Parold* [sic] *Officer's report is a photo of Goldstein and in comparing the photo with that of Isidor Fisch there is a very striking resemblance."*[1814]

This seemed to show the police now <u>did</u> believe Lukatis but that his account had mistaken Goldstein for Fisch. Goldstein's Parole Officer, Mr. Koch, quickly set up an interview for police with him for January 21st. During this meeting, Goldstein admitted that he and William Block had rented a room from Mrs. Kern and *"held regular card games"* in order to make a living.[1815]

> *"The other players would be men that they had met or would meet in the various speak-easies in Yorkville. Goldstein could not recall anyone by the name of Gustave Lukatus* [sic] *having visited them at this address. He stated that William Block was more familiar with the men that came there."*[1816]

The next day Detective Meade interviewed William Block. He also admitted to police that he and Goldstein...

> *"...ran card games in this room and had many men visitors, some of which were strangers to both of them. Block said that he does not recall Gustave Lukatus* [sic]

[1814] Ibid.

[1815] Meade, Joseph Det. New Jersey State Police. New Jersey State Police Report. <u>Further investigation of the information furnished by Gustave Lukatus of 788 Trinity Avenue, Bronx, who is believed to be a defense witness.</u> January 21, 1935. New Jersey State Police Museum and Learning Center Archives.

[1816] Ibid.

> *by name, but that if he seen him or a photo of him, he*
> *would surely recall whether or not Lukatus [sic] had*
> *been at their furnished room. Block further stated that*
> *when he and Goldstein were at 325 East 84ᵗʰ Street,*
> *an Isidor Fisch did not live there."*[1817]

And here, having been satisfied that Fisch did not "live" at this room, is where the police investigation ended. Their obvious belief was that Lukatis's story was a case of mistaken identity. But how does this explain that no one at the rooming house, including Mrs. Kern, saw the similarity when shown the photo of Fisch? Or that there's no alarm or care on the part of police concerning the "hot-money" regardless of whether it was or was not connected to the Lindbergh case? And why must Fisch "live" in this room for this event to have occurred?

Kress, however, was convinced his investigation revealed Lukatis was correct:

> *"Lukatis's information dovetails into several other tips*
> *and testimony I have secured," Kress said. "I think that*
> *if it is all handled properly we can arrive at the real*
> *solution to the Lindbergh Kidnaping [sic] and murder*
> *before the time the Hauptmann trial is scheduled to*
> *come to an end."*[1818]

[1817] Meade, Joseph Det. New Jersey State Police. New Jersey State Police Report. <u>Further investigation of the information furnished by Gustave Lukatus of 788 Trinity Avenue, Bronx, who is believed to be a defense witness</u>. January 22, 1935. New Jersey State Police Museum and Learning Center Archives.

[1818] McGrady, Pat. "Says Fisch Wanted To Sell Ransom." *Ogdensburg Journal*. January 16, 1935. nyshistoricnewspapers.org

Despite this, Lukatis was never called as a witness for the Defense. The explanation for this, I believe, will be revealed in the coming pages.

Gustave Lukatis (hiding face from reporters)
(Courtesy NJSP Museum)

Arthur Trost

Arthur Trost was a painter by trade and knew Isidor Fisch personally since "*July or August 1931*" and "*frequently met him at a billiard parlor*" on the corner of "*86th street and Third Avenue*" during this time.[1819] Trost claimed Fisch had told him he lived with "*two other men on East 84th street.*"[1820] He asserted that Fisch was a man who was:

[1819] Trost, Arthur H. Affadivit. County of New York. June 19, 1935. New Jersey State Police Museum and Learning Center Archives.
[1820] Ibid.

> "...*forever borrowing small sums from his acquaintances. He borrowed some money from me and never paid it back.*"[1821]

Trost also claimed he knew a man "*Fritz*," a painter like himself, since "*March or April 1931*" who he described as being between...

> "*28 and 30 years of age, about 5 feet 6 inches in height, weighing about 140 pounds, of medium build, blond hair, and complexion, clean shaven, blue eyes, and prominent Roman nose.*"[1822]

In the summer of 1932, Trost met "Fritz" at a restaurant at which time Fritz asked him if he "*wished to buy some "hot money" for 50¢ on the dollar from a friend of his.*"[1823] Once Trost agreed to meet the friend, Fritz brought him to the billiard parlor on the corner of "*86th street and Third Avenue*" then introduced him to "*Isidor Fisch.*"[1824] Trost told Fritz he "*was already acquainted*" with Fisch and that Fisch "*was already indebted to me for borrowed money*" and he therefore neither trusted nor believed him. Trost was certain the introduction made by "Fritz" to Fisch was for the purpose of selling him the "hot money."[1825] Trost had seen photographs of Fisch in the newspaper and he identified them as the man he knew as Isador Fisch. Once again, PI Kress investigated this information, and it was through this investigation that he learned Trost and Lukatis had

---

[1821] McGrady, Pat. "Says Fisch Offered To Sell Ransom." *Ogdensburg Journal.* February 4, 1935. nyshistoricnewspapers.org

[1822] Trost, Arthur H. Affadivit. County of New York. June 19, 1935. New Jersey State Police Museum and Learning Center Archives.

[1823] Ibid.

[1824] Ibid.

[1825] Ibid.

never met.[1826] Concluding this information was legitimate, Kress brought Trost to meet with Ed Reilly. Reilly flatly refused him then accused Trost of being *"a stool pigeon for the State of New Jersey."*[1827] No doubt Reilly was a little gun shy after learning that Charles Schleser, who had been privy to some of the Defense strategy by feigning interest in being their witness, was actually a mole for Wilentz and the State Prosecutors.[1828] According to Lloyd Fisher, Schleser was actually on the State's *"payroll"* during the trial and was *"paid through a dummy."*[1829] We see that not only was this unethical, it was the cause for other Witnesses to be dismissed that may have actually been beneficial to Hauptmann and his Defense.

Despite this rejection, Trost continued to wrack his brain in an attempt to remember "Fritz's" last name. He recalled the man *"had gone to Europe in 1932, 1933, and 1934"* traveling *"in style"* when before 1932 he did not seem to have any money.[1830] Kress also continued to investigate and was never ready to let go of an angle he was sure would break the case.

Richard Hauptmann

Had Hauptmann met "Fritz?" During his questioning by Detective Ellis Parker, he was asked about meeting "Fritz":

[1826] McGrady, Pat. "Says Fisch Offered To Sell Ransom." *Ogdensburg Journal.* February 4, 1935. nyshistoricnewspapers.org

[1827] Ibid.

[1828] Gardner, Lloyd C. (2004). *The Case That Never Dies.* Rutgers University Press. Pages 262-5. (Referenced Statements in Author's possession).

[1829] Fisher, Lloyd. Typed Notes. *Hauptmann's Case.* (1935?). New Jersey State Police Museum and Learning Center Archives.

[1830] McGrady, Pat. "Says Fisch Offered To Sell Ransom." *Ogdensburg Journal.* February 4, 1935. nyshistoricnewspapers.org

"How did we first meet? I think the regular bathing place and when I came out he was sitting with another fellow and spoke German together. This fellow and Isadore [sic] spoke German together and we started talking together for quite a while and then I said to him, "I will take you to the Subway Station…". [1831]

However, Hauptmann could not remember his name. Hauptmann could not recall if this was in the beginning of March or possibly April but did recall that no one "bathed" and everyone there had on "overcoats."[1832] He gave his description as "*he spoke German, but with the Austrian accent*" which caused him to conclude he was "*Austrian.*" Hauptmann also added that this man was about "*two years younger*" than he was, a "*little bit smaller and stout build,*" with "*blonde*" hair, "*sideboards*" and a "*mark*" on the left side from his chin.[1833] The next time Hauptmann saw Fisch he was alone, and he never saw this other man that accompanied him previously again.[1834]

Fritz Karge(r)

By late 1935, Kress had been teamed up with Fred Shanbacker, a reporter who at one time worked for the New York Evening Post.

[1831] Hauptmann, Bruno Richard. Statement. By Ellis H. Parker. Stenographer – Anna E. Bading. June 5, 1935. New Jersey State Police Museum and Learning Center Archives.

[1832] Hauptmann, Richard. Autobiography: Unedited & Uncorrected (Translated). The Story of My Life. Page 173. May 4, 1935. New Jersey State Police Museum and Learning Center Archives.

[1833] Hauptmann, Bruno Richard. Statement. By Ellis H. Parker. Stenographer – Anna E. Bading. June 5, 1935. New Jersey State Police Museum and Learning Center Archives.

[1834] Hauptmann, Richard. Autobiography: Unedited & Uncorrected (Translated). The Story of My Life. Page 177. May 4, 1935. New Jersey State Police Museum and Learning Center Archives.

During his time with the paper he fearlessly investigated the famous disappearance of Rothstein associate Dr. Charles Brancati.[1835] Keeping in close touch with Trost, Detective Kress continued to develop information leading to the identity of the mysterious "Fritz." Trost, it had been learned, had been in touch with "Fritz" as late as 1934, which was how he knew this man had been traveling back and forth to Europe.[1836] More information was learned from Trost that proved quite fruitful. It seems that "Fritz" had had been keeping company with a young woman who Trost encountered with him on several occasions. On October of 1932:

> *"During that month the Hamburg American line offices in Hamburg reported that a girl named Fraulein Ilse Witthoeft had sailed on one of its ships, the Albert Ballin, as a stowaway. Trost said that several days after the sailing of this boat for Germany he received a telephone call from the New York offices of the line stating that his wife was a stowaway. He explained that there was a mistake, for his wife was sitting with him. Later, the line notified him that the woman's name was Ilse Witthoeft and that she had given the captain of the ship Trost's name. The line wanted Trost to pay for her passage."*[1837]

Trost recognized the name of "Ilse Witthoeft" as Fritz's "*sweetheart*."[1838] Apparently Fritz had jilted her when he left for Europe so she followed

---

[1835] Shankbacker, Fred. <u>Western Union from Fred Shanbacker to Ellis Parker, Chief Detective Burlington County</u>. December 26, 1935. Andy Sahol Collection.

[1836] Shanbacker, Fred. <u>Letter from Fred Shanbacker to Ellis H. Parker Esq</u>. March 11, 1936. Andy Sahol Collection.

[1837] Shanbacker, Fred. <u>Letter from Fred Shanbacker to Ellis H. Parker</u>. March 2, 1936. Andy Sahol Collection.

[1838] Ibid.

him as a stowaway on the ship.[1839] Kress immediately began an arduous investigation by *"obtaining the names of everyone sailing"* on that ship *"whose first name was Fritz"* and by process of elimination determined the man's last name was *"Karger."*[1840]

> *"Trost, Kress says, identified the name of this purported stowaway as that of the girl who danced attendance on Karger. Trost said Karger made at least several trips to Germany during the ensuing years, always seemed to be plentifully supplied with money, and never appeared to have steady employment."*[1841]

As a result of this information, Kress searched for anyone by that name who might have been living in the New York area and he discovered a man by the name of *"Fritz Karge"* currently living in Chelsea, Massachusetts. Kress and Shanbacker loaded up Trost then drove up in an attempt to get Trost to identify the man.[1842] Upon seeing this man:

> *"Trost emphatically denied that the man we pointed to him was the Fritz Karge with whom he talked in 1934 several days before Karge sailed for Germany. Equally emphatic is Trost that Fritz Karge is the right name of the man with whom he talked."*[1843]

1839 Shanbacker, Fred. <u>Letter from Fred Shanbacker to Ellis H. Parker, Chief Burlington County Detectives</u>. January 26, 1936. Andy Sahol Collection.

1840 Shanbacker, Fred. <u>Letter from Fred Shanbacker to Ellis H. Parker</u>. March 2, 1936. Andy Sahol Collection.

1841 Ibid.

1842 Ibid.

1843 Ibid.

Unknown to the men, after learning Fritz's last name, Ellis Parker had already investigated this man and ruled him out.[1844] Parker wrote further:

> "*The Fritz Karge that Trost says he knows his right name, and that he saw with Isidor Fisch, is the man we want to locate. I have written a letter to the German Counsel General's office in New York City, and asked them to check on the Hamburgh* [sic] *Line, and others to try and find if any Fritz Karge or Karges went over from this Country to Germany in 1932, and to furnish me with the addresses that he had in this Country, and all other information possible. As soon as I receive a reply I will immediately forward it to you, as I think this would be a most important discovery. If Trost is correct this man would know how Fisch came in possession of that money, and might be in a position to assist us, and no doubt would if we could locate him.*"[1845]

I have never found a follow up to this communication. Of course it was only a couple of weeks later that Parker turned Paul Wendel over to the Mercer County Detective Kirkham. It was here where the beginning of the end was created for the best Detective this country has even known – and with him perhaps the solution to this mystery. The last known communication that I have found tells the tale:

> "*It's been sometime since we corresponded, and many things have happened. The reason I haven't contacted you is because I didn't want you in any way, to become*

[1844] Parker, Ellis H. Chief of County Detectives. <u>Letter from Ellis H. Parker, Chief of County Detectives to Mr. Fred Shanbacker</u>. March 12, 1936. Andy Sahol Collection.

[1845] Ibid.

embarrassed by anything that was going on, and I know that all my lines have been tapped. I would like to have a talk to you and Henry sometime later, perhaps after a month or so."[1846]

Unfortunately, that talk never occurred.

Isidor Fisch
(Courtesy NSJP Museum)

Isidor Fish
January 1933 Bronx, NY
(Courtesy NJSP Museum)

[1846] Parker, Ellis H. Chief of County Detectives. <u>Letter from Ellis H. Parker, Chief of County Detectives to Mr. Fred Shanbacker</u>. September 19, 1936. Andy Sahol Collection.

Printed in the United States
By Bookmasters